BEYOND
ART FUNDAMENTALS

A GUIDE TO EMOTION, MOOD, AND STORYTELLING FOR ARTISTS

3dtotal Publishing

3dtotalPublishing

Correspondence: publishing@3dtotal.com
Website: store.3dtotal.com

*Beyond Art Fundamentals: A Guide to
Emotion, Mood, and Storytelling for Artists.*
© 2016, 3dtotal Publishing. All rights reserved.
No part of this book can be reproduced in any
form or by any means, without the prior written
consent of the publisher. All artwork, unless
stated otherwise, is copyright © 2016 3dtotal
Publishing or the featured artists. All artwork
that is not copyright of 3dtotal Publishing or
the featured artists is marked accordingly.

Every effort has been made to ensure the credits
and contact information listed are present
and correct. In the case of any errors that have
occurred, the publisher respectfully directs readers
to the **store.3dtotal.com/pages/information** for
any updated information and/or corrections.

First published in the United Kingdom, 2016,
by 3dtotal Publishing.
3dtotal.com Ltd, 29 Foregate Street,
Worcester, WR1 1DS, United Kingdom.

Reprinted in 2024 by 3dtotal Publishing.

Soft cover ISBN: 978-1-912843-64-0
Printed and bound in China
by C&C Offset Printing Co., Ltd

Visit **store.3dtotal.com** for a
complete list of available book titles.

Editor: Marisa Lewis
Proofreader: Melanie Smith
Lead designer: Imogen Williams
Designer: Aryan Pishneshin
Cover designer: Matthew Lewis
Managing editor: Simon Morse

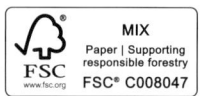

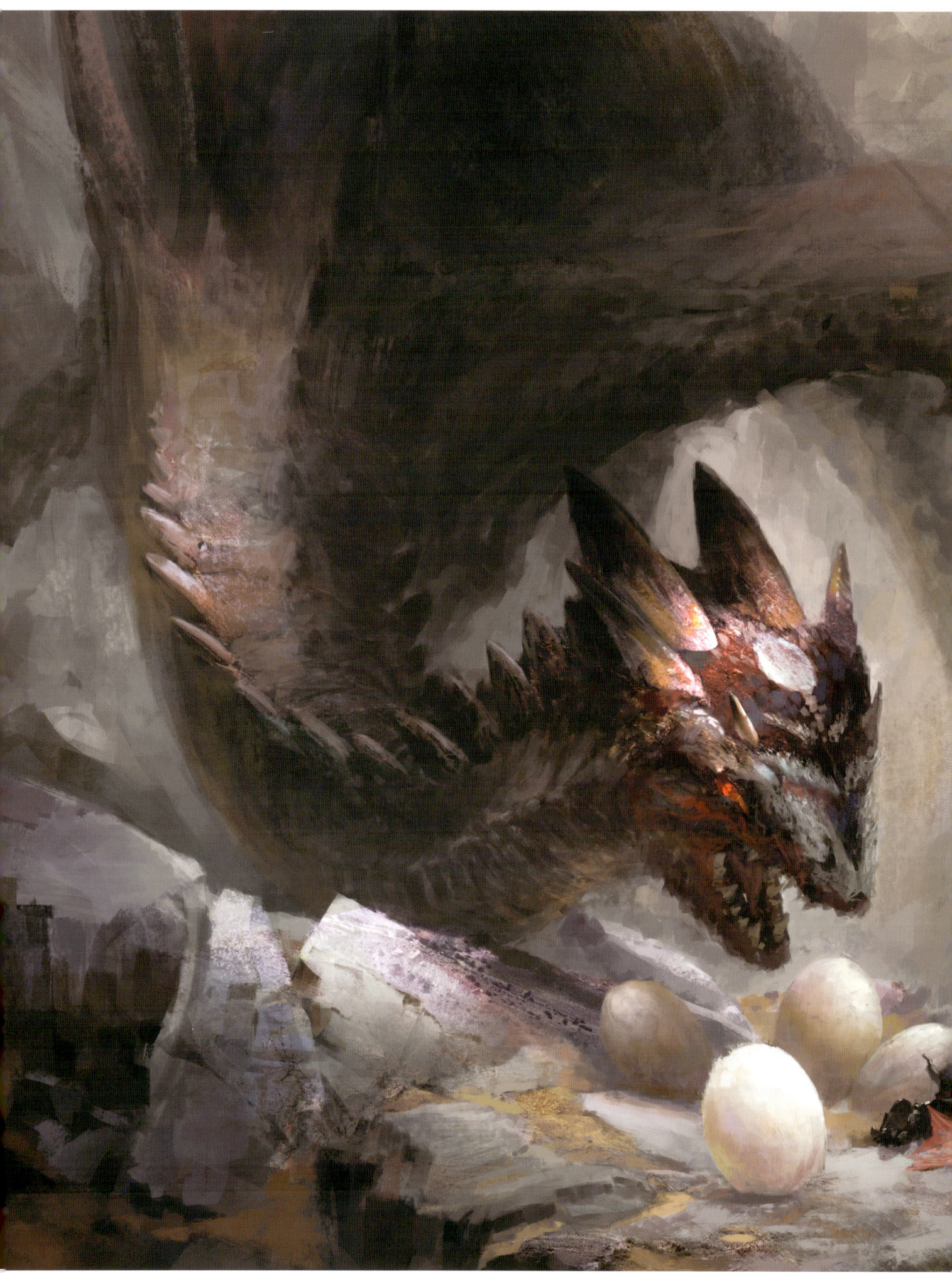

Contents

Introduction

Think about your favorite images. Why do you find them so memorable and resonant? Why do you keep coming back to them? It's probably because they depict something that excites your imagination or elicits your sympathy. Beyond the pure technical fundamentals, such as lighting and perspective, they possess something deeper that invites you to look closer, and rewards you for doing so. Every artist wants to make images that people remember, that stick in the viewer's mind after they've looked away, that encourage them to come back and look again.

What better way to pull your viewer into an image than with a story – something that invites their wonder, empathy, or curiosity? What better way to make your work memorable than by evoking a mood or feeling? Knowing the fundamental theories for creating an image is one thing, but how do you bring those principles of color, value, and composition together to make something that will excite, amuse, or intrigue the viewer? The latter is a crucial question, no matter what genre, style, or medium you work in.

How does an artist strike a balance between making work that shows technical know-how, and making work that says something more? Why do fundamental concepts like color and composition matter to a narrative image, and how can they be used to support and tell a story? It is often those few moments of extra research and reflection that push a good image to become a *great* image; a few extra touches and thoughtful observations that can make a solid but generic image into an interesting, individual one with your personal stamp on it.

Over the following chapters, this book travels through a wide range of moods, emotions and atmospheres, showing how they are interpreted by different artists. There are many ways to convey a narrative, whether it's through a detailed scene, the nuances of a character design, or

with subtle environmental cues, and this book takes a deeper look at some of those exciting possibilities. We will learn how artists create ideas for images, how they add twists that are personal or unexpected, and how they make illustrations and concepts with a variety of techniques, tools, and media. Each artist has their own unique approach and workflow, and their own perspectives that inform their stories and subject matter.

We hope the valuable insights offered by this book's many talented artists will inspire and motivate you to take your images that extra step further.

Marisa Lewis
Editor, 3dtotal Publishing

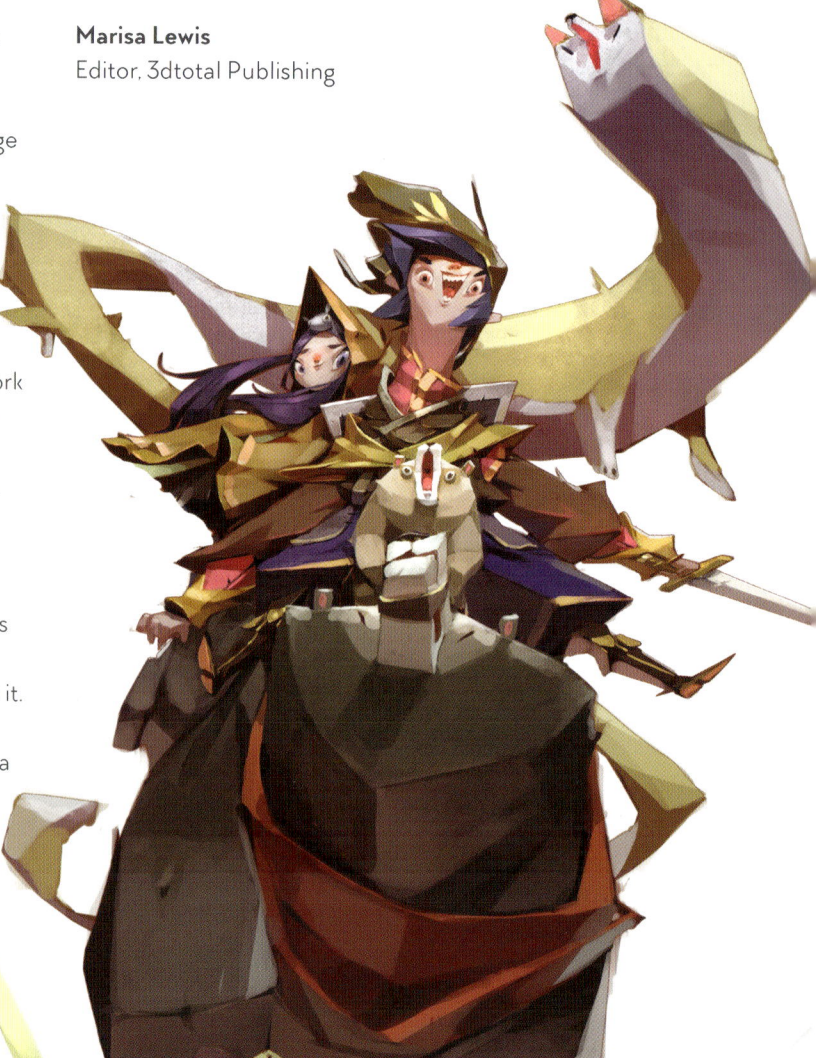

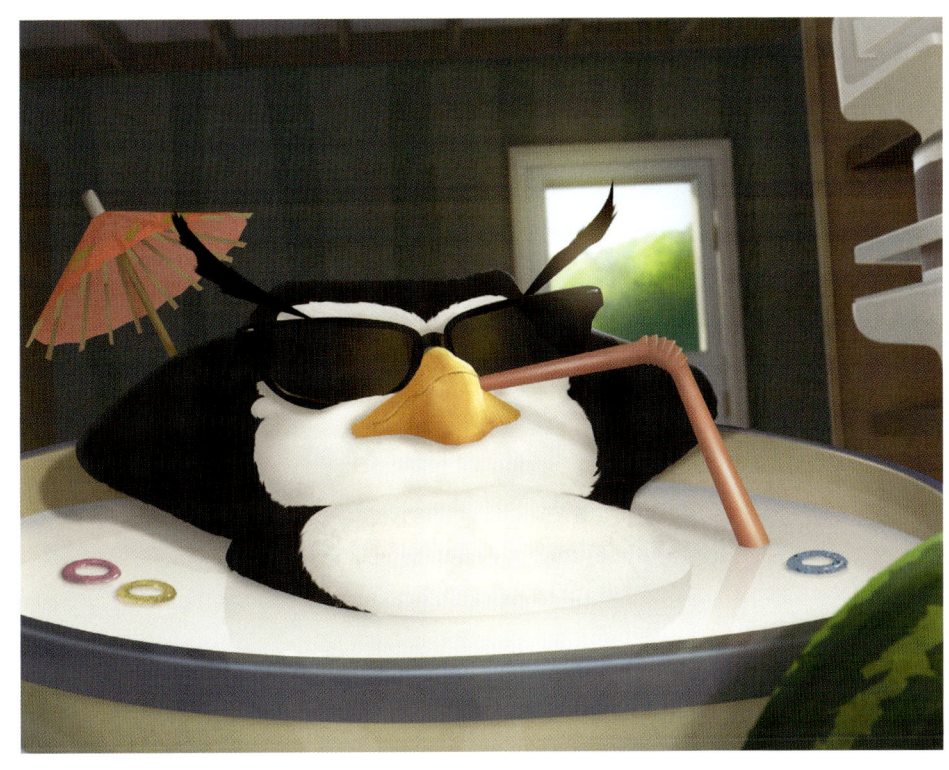
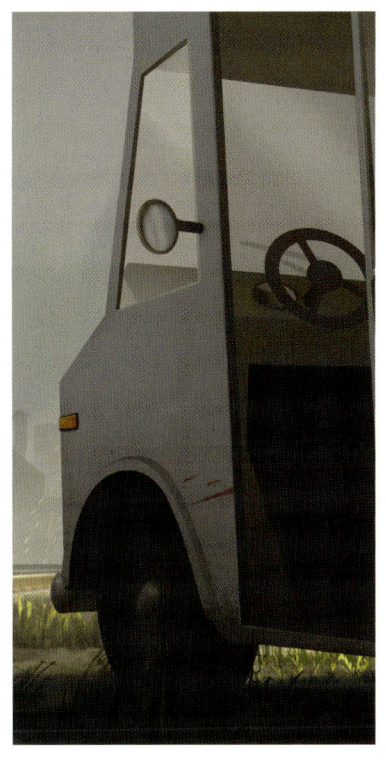
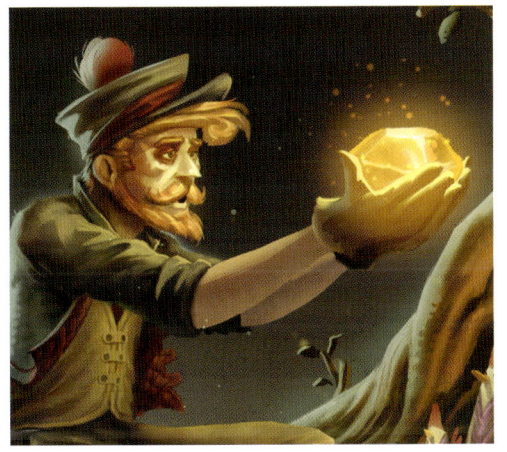
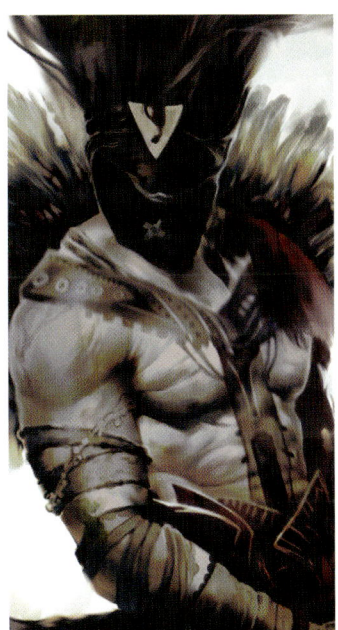
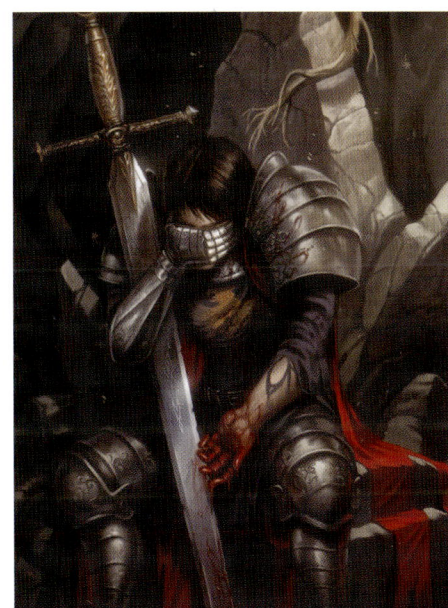
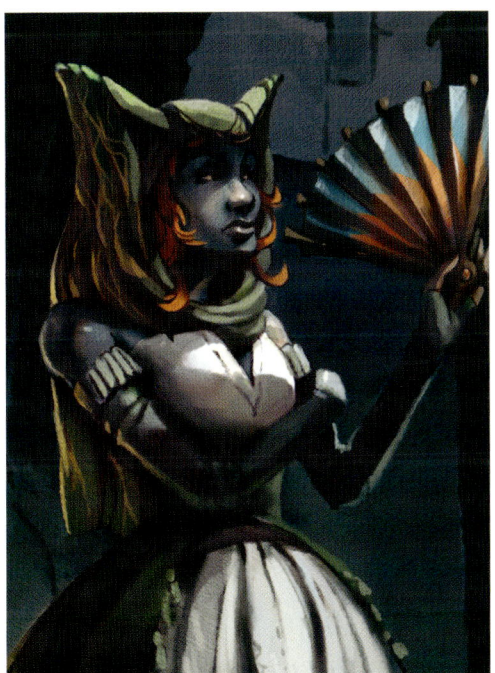
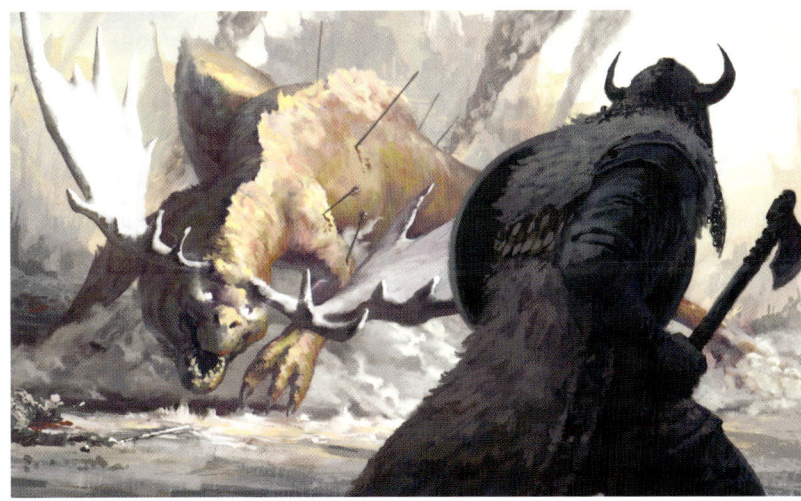

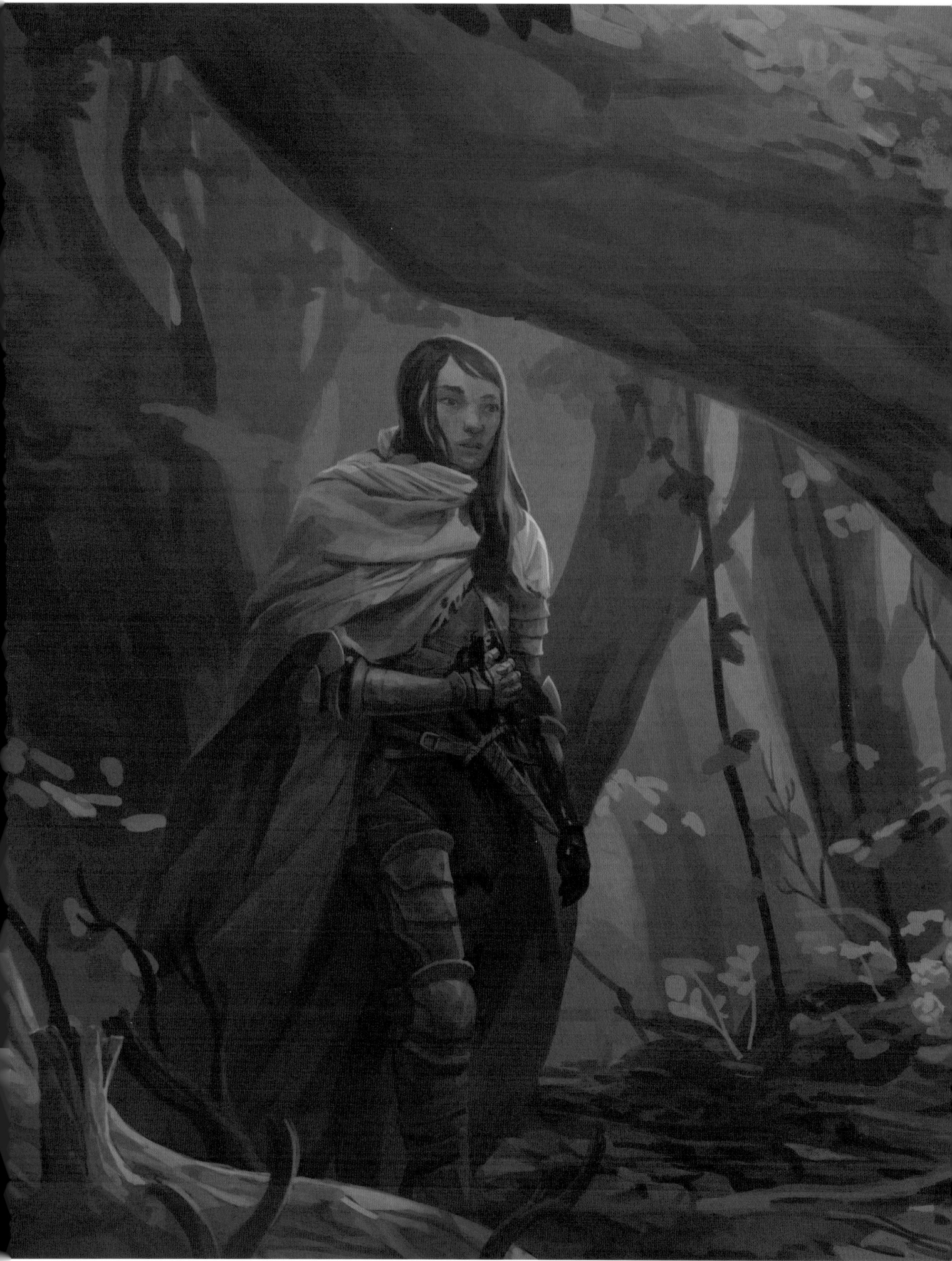

Emotions

In this main section of *Beyond Art Fundamentals*, you'll see how a range of artists interpret and illustrate eighteen different emotions and moods, from the angry, lonely, and fearful to the brave, adventurous, and cheerful. Whatever style, genre, or tools you're working with, we're sure you'll enjoy the thoughtful and inspiring guidance these artists have to offer.

Ahmed Rawi | www.rawi.artstation.com

Adventure

In this chapter I will illustrate the theme of "adventure." In my image, I want to show a weary adventurer on the verge of completing his quest to uncover the mysteries that lie hidden in a distant cave.

In general, I'm fascinated by the idea of mythical creatures, giving them extra teeth, elongated horns, tentacles, and various other forms of intimidation well suited to creatures of darkness. So my creative process for this will be to incorporate those same elements, but this time for creating an environment with ominous "teeth." This environment needs to be huge and convey appropriate distance; in addition, landscape elements such as grass and trees need to be added. However, as the nature of monsters is dark and foreboding, I need to think of a way of balancing that idea with the theme I'm aiming for: "adventure" and a sense of wanderlust.

In the following steps I will showcase my standard process of searching, thinking, and painting, explaining some of my artistic techniques and of course having fun along the way!

>01 Research, research, research!

I cannot convey how important preliminary research is to materializing an idea. As a concept artist I am always researching ideas and references even when I do not have a project, and that method has proven quite useful for future projects. I start looking at references before drawing a single line, gathering lots of material relating to the idea in general. For this scene, I search for a multitude of mountains, related textures, and specific landscapes that will conjure up ideas of travel and adventure. I consider the research stage to be a kind of a warm-up exercise for the brain; it will broaden my imagination and refresh my visual memory.

>02 Sketches and thumbnails

Carrying out research and some initial sketches helps me to visualize my idea and the story behind the picture. Usually, although I work digitally, I try to give my scenes a kind of traditional look, with rough touches and loose drawing.

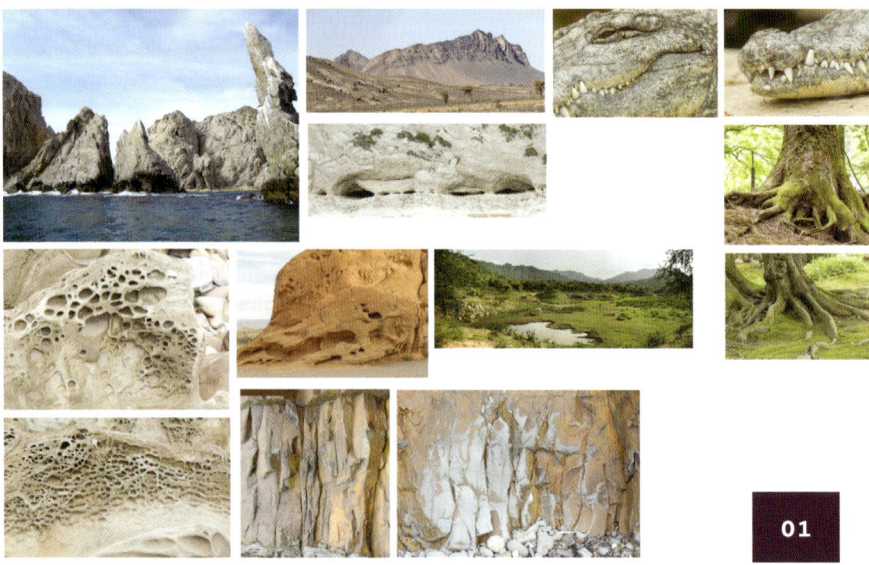

01

// A selection of reference images from www.textures.com

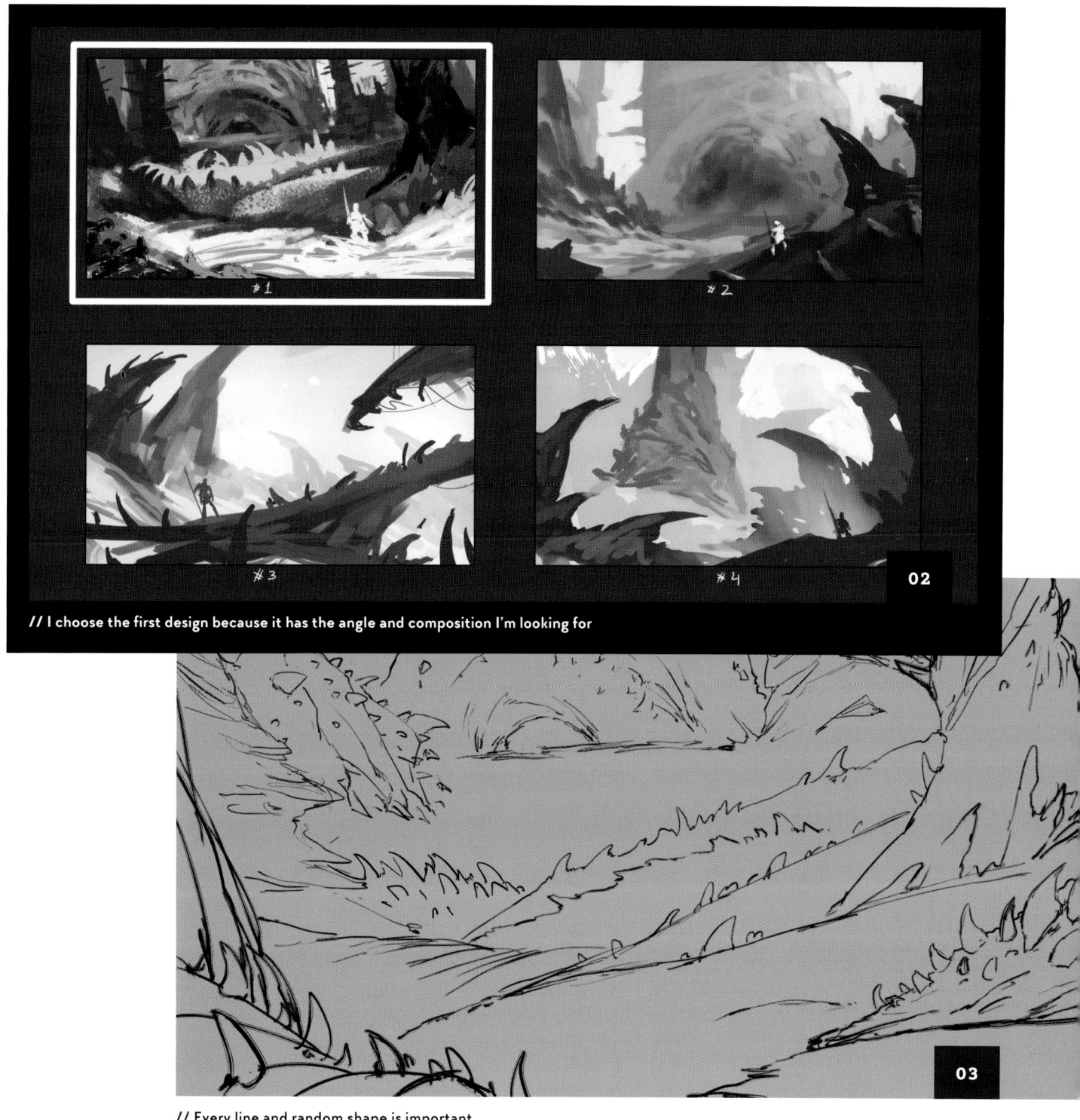

// I choose the first design because it has the angle and composition I'm looking for

// Every line and random shape is important

Even for rough sketching, I always start with a large canvas in Adobe Photoshop, between 5,000 and 7,000 pixels in size. It's easier for me to work clearly if I have sufficient space for all my ideas, without the need to create additional canvases; at the end I can see all my sketches in one place. Large canvases also allow scope for printing in the future, if needed.

When working on a landscape scene, I usually create four thumbnails (around 2,000 pixels each) with a fifty percent gray background. I then use rough brushes with dark and light tones of gray to sketch. I don't really focus on details; the most important thing

here is the composition and lighting, figuring out the shapes of the "teeth" and the depth of the scene.

>03 Line work

I draw rough line work on top of the selected thumbnail, which is really helpful for figuring out the proportions of the environment and how I want to shape it. This stage allows me to add more details and describe the composition in a clearer way, and also to plan my shading for the next step. Working digitally, I usually use a rough brush for sketching, because it gives me the feel of a pencil and makes the sketch look more traditional.

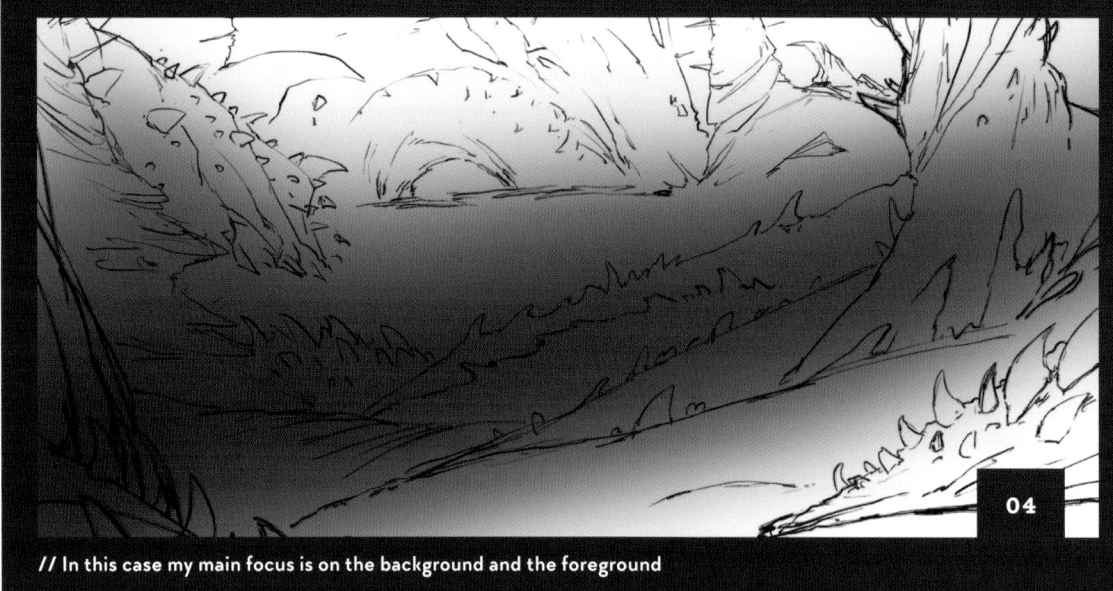

// In this case my main focus is on the background and the foreground

04

05

// Planning the sketch in grayscale

>04 Anatomy of values

I don't always use this stage, but with this kind of complicated layout I really recommend starting with a rough lighting study. I want to highlight the background and foreground in this image, because I want to place a character in the foreground and imply that he's heading towards a target somewhere in the background, telling a bit of a story. I darken the values in the middle ground so that I can use this for reference as I progress with the painting.

>05 Grayscale underpainting

Now I start sketching the basic details in grayscale values. Steps 03 and 04 really help me to start the shading

with more confidence, knowing exactly what to shade according to the shapes and flow of the elements. I establish the background and foreground as highlighted areas, as I planned in step 04, and keep the middle ground darker. I use ten to ninety percent of the grayscale value range – never fully black or white – to give the painting a good variation of gray values for the next step.

>06 Coloring

I now start to add color to the image. For the color palette, I pick warm colors for the foreground and middle ground, and a cool color for the background. This color composition helps me to create more depth and strengthen the image's contrast.

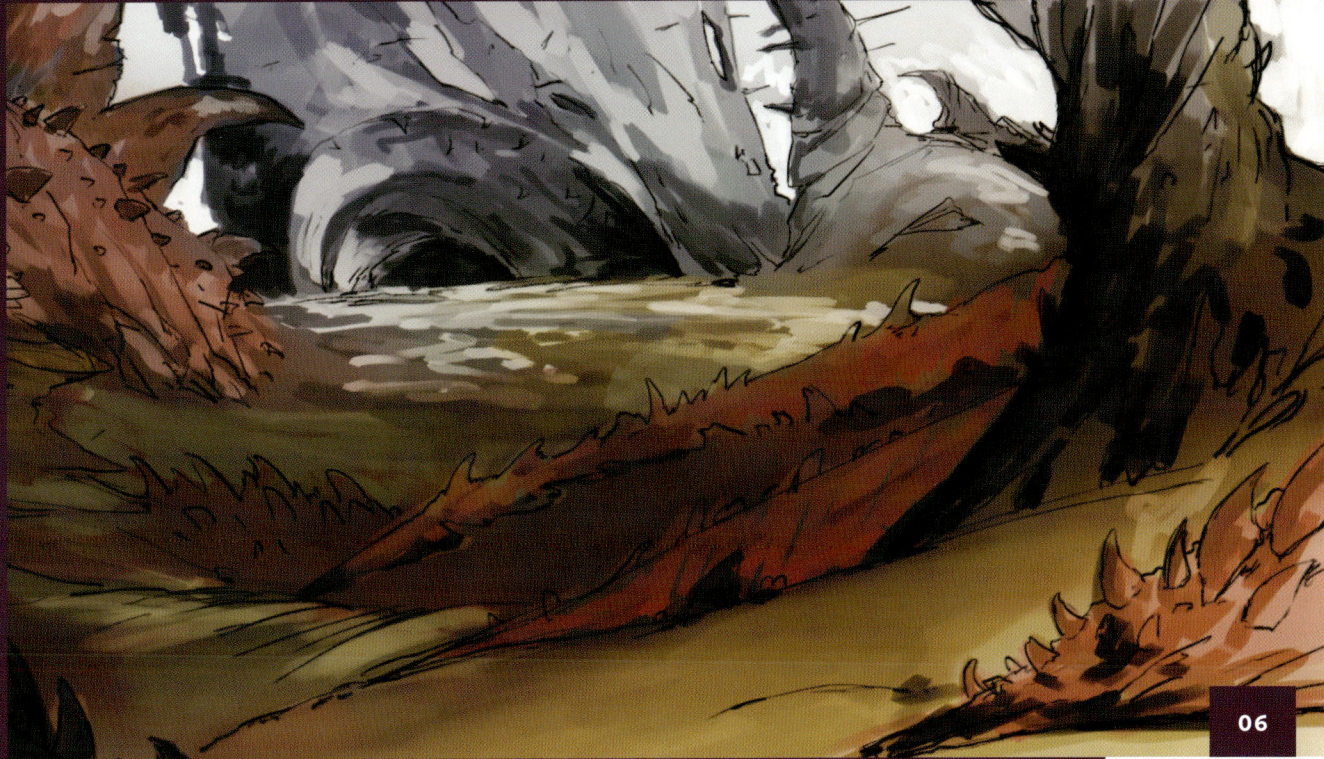

// Adding colors

My method for adding color is to create a new layer on top of the grayscale image in Photoshop, with the blending mode set to Overlay. Overlay mode is one of my favorite blending modes, working perfectly on top of a grayscale image while retaining the values underneath. I select a smooth brush because it gives me more control, and use it to blend the colors between the areas. There are no details at this stage, I'm just filling in color.

>07 Composition test #1

Spontaneity is fun, but an environment scene needs some rules. Because I've worked on many scenes before, I have a good sense of composition – but that doesn't mean it's perfect! So before adding any extra details, the first thing I do is to test the "golden ratio," a mathematical formula often found in nature and used by artists throughout history to create aesthetically pleasing compositions. As you can see in image 07, the white curve flows perfectly with the elements starting from the right tree, to the left parts ending with the arch of the cave in the background.

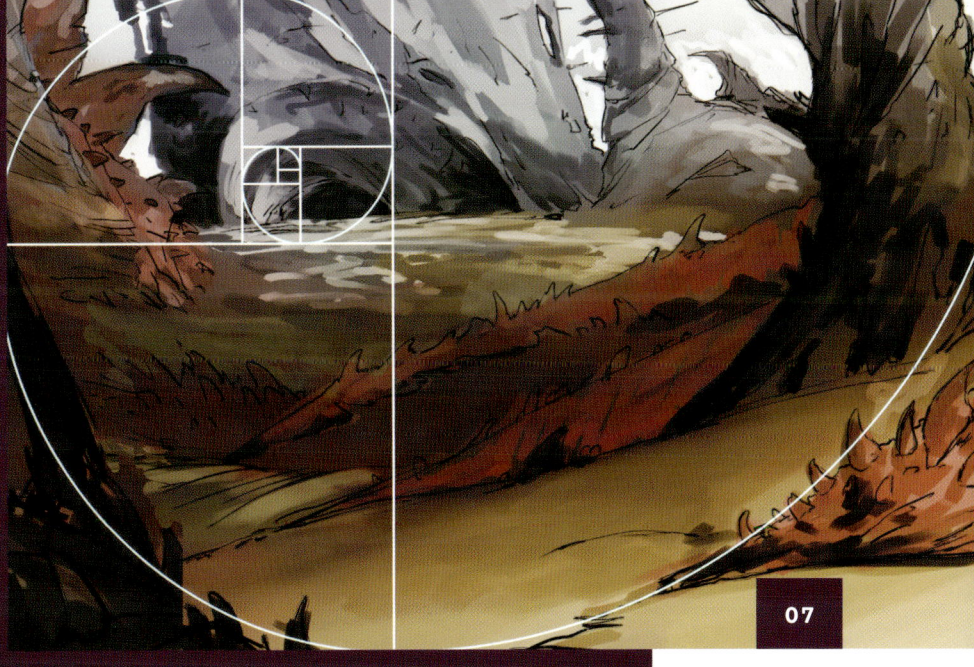

// Testing the golden ratio

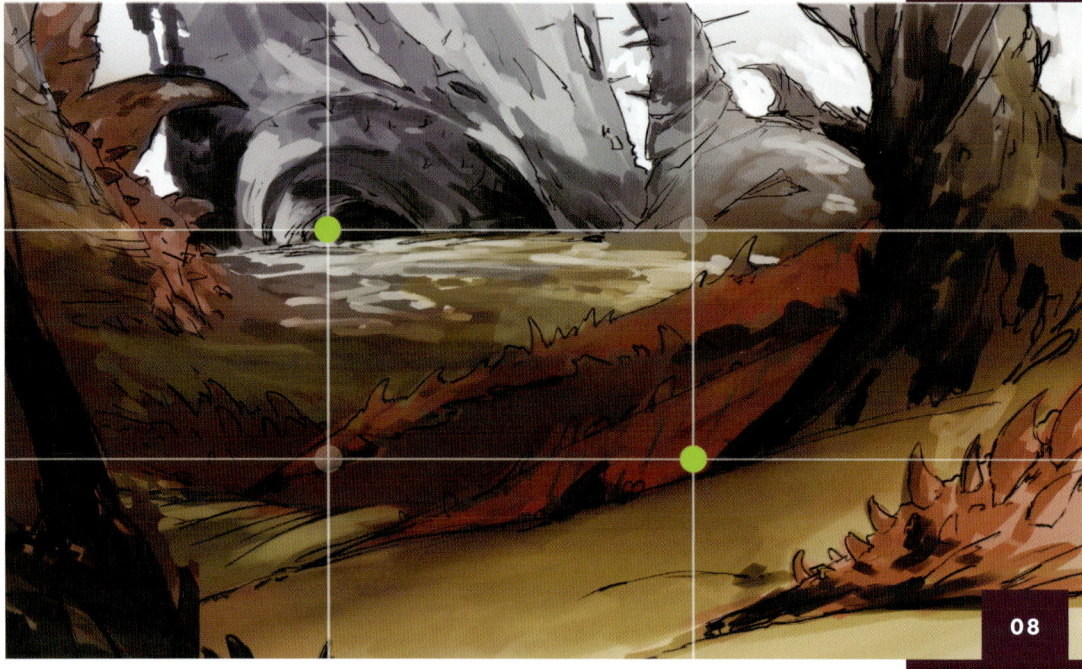

08

// Testing the rule of thirds

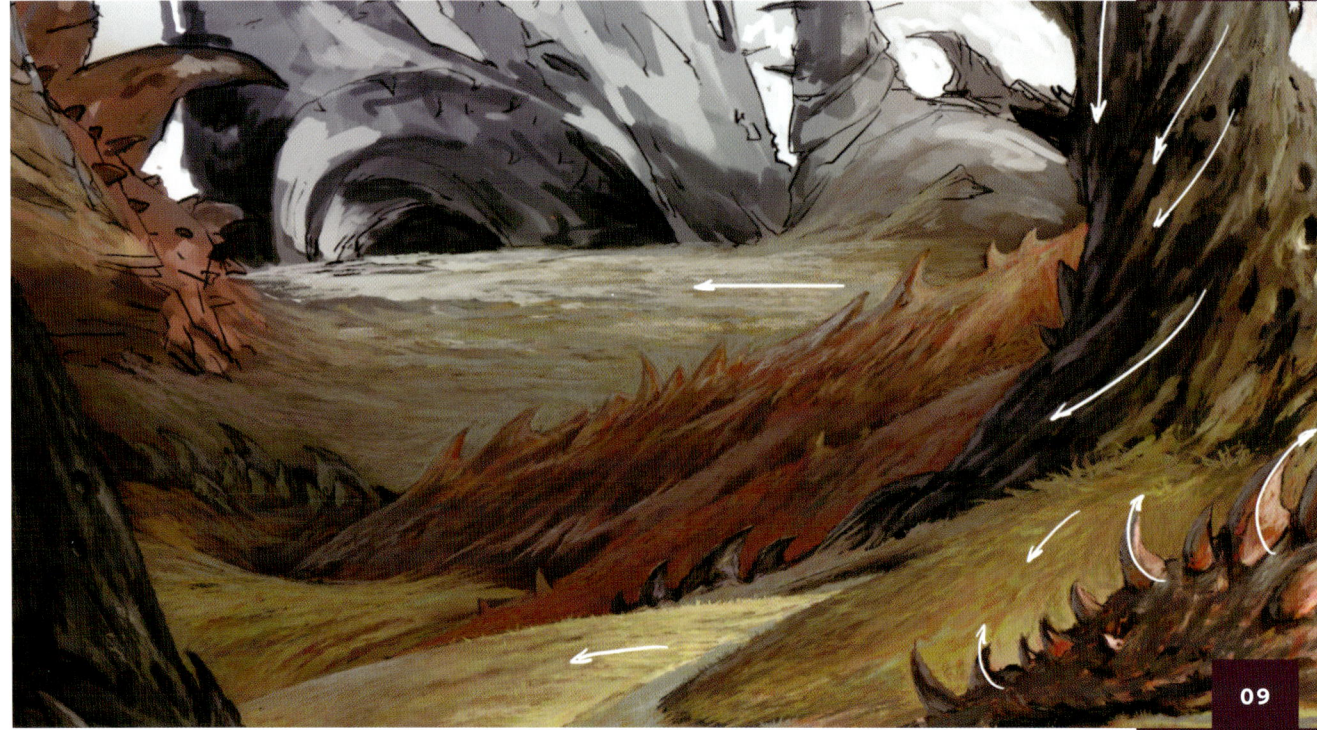

09

// It's very important to paint objects that suit the flow of the image

>08 Composition test #2

The rule of thirds is also one of the most important tests that I have to do to guide my eyes. Like the golden ratio, it helps me to place objects with a flow that feels natural and balanced. I try to find the best place to position the character according to his target in the distance, placing these focal points where the lines intersect. In image 08, the bottom-right green spot is the character, and the top-left green spot is his distance.

>09 Into the details

Now I can begin painting details. I start working on the foreground. As I already have a color base, I pick my colors from the background and tweak the brightness values from the color palette for shading.

"Everything will look flat if I use the same brush. Because the foreground is painted in a bit of a textured, 'noisy' way, I want to make the background look further away by using a smoother brush"

In Photoshop I use Color Dynamics in the brush settings to give me more variations during coloring; I add a small amount of Hue Jitter and Saturation, so that wherever I paint, I'll have more tones to pick from for the next brushstroke.

The white arrows in image 09 show how I paint the environment's flow to describe its form, making it look more real and not just flat. On the edge of every dark area, I always add a rim light that comes from the ambient light, even on non-reflective materials.

>10 The background
Everything will look flat if I use the same brush. Because the foreground is painted in a bit of a textured, "noisy" way, I want to make the background look further away by using a smoother brush. This time I use cool colors as the base, and I'm very careful to create a smooth transition between the highlights and shadows in the background area, adding some fog and weather elements in the middle ground to lessen the contrast and detail levels.

>11 Polishing
After taking a ten-minute break to rest my eyes, I come back to my landscape and find that there is a bit too much contrast in terms of detail. I decide to improve the balance between the foreground and the background by using a smooth brush to polish the foreground without decreasing the details there. I also change some of the "teeth" from red to a more creamy white, which balances out the image more.

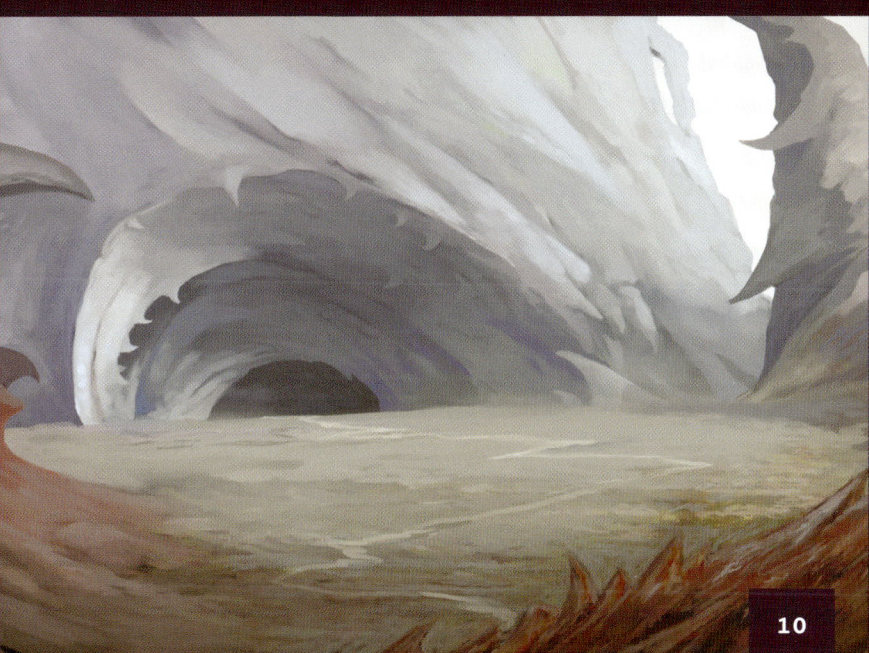

10

// Lessening the contrast and detail in the distant background to give a sense of depth

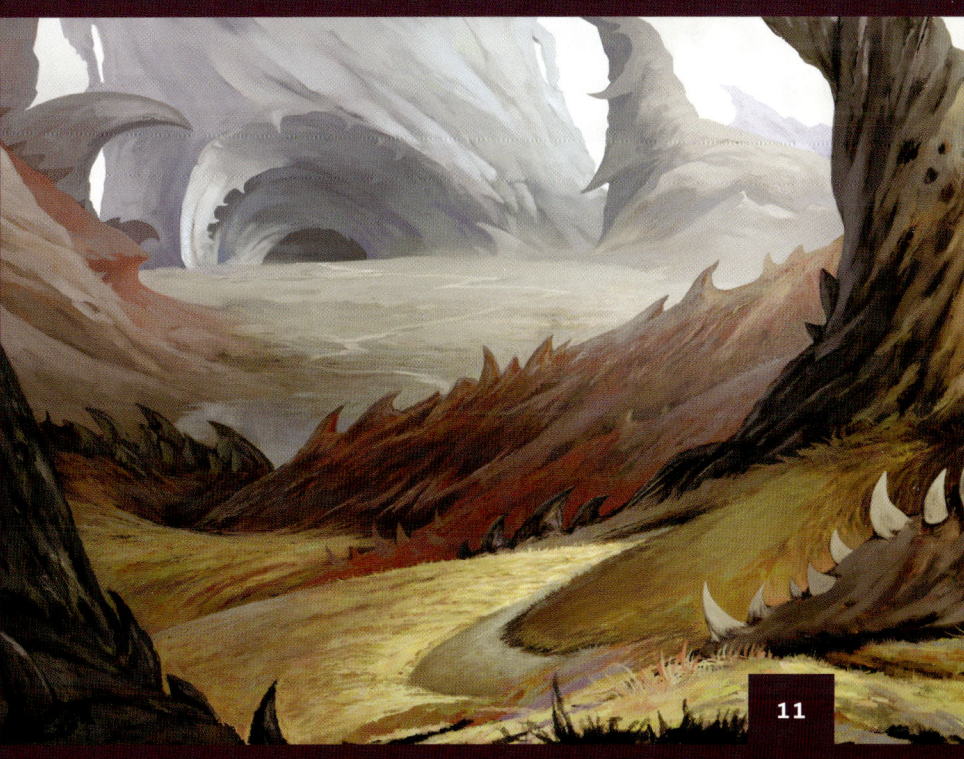

11

// Checking closely for errors and mistakes

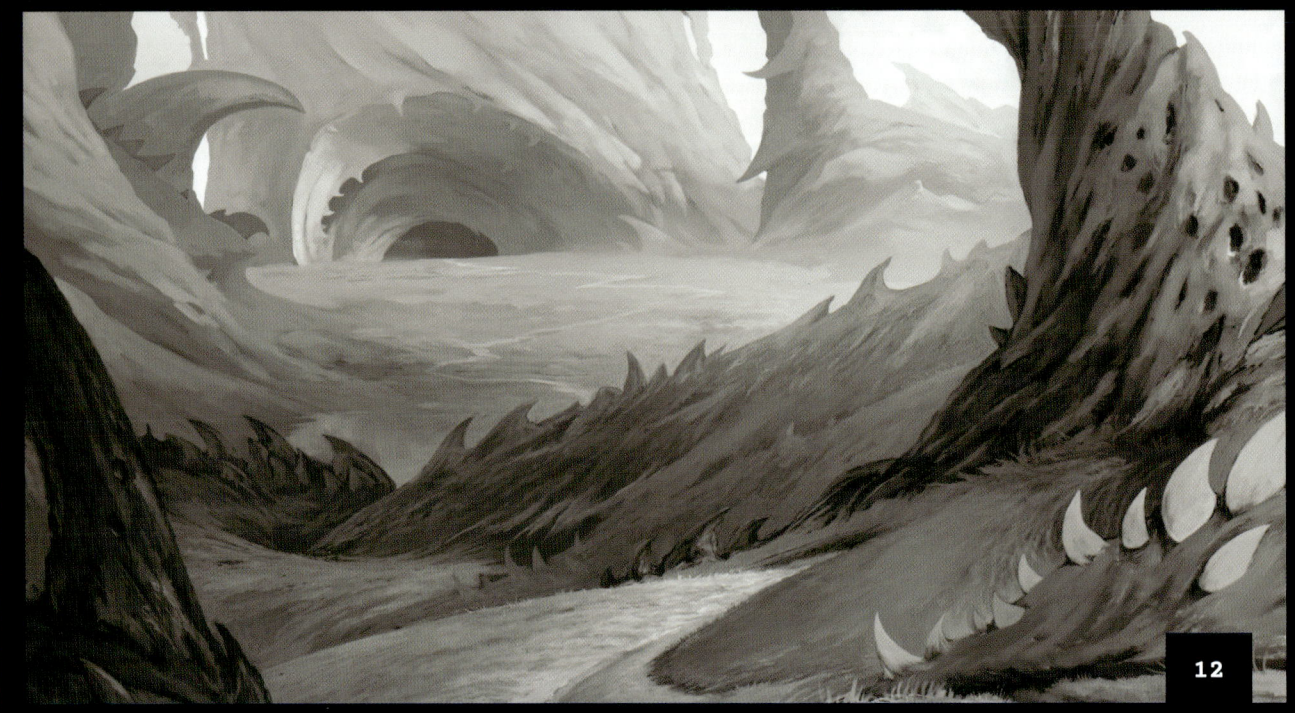

// Grayscale helps me to check if the image's depth is correct and pleasing to the eye

12

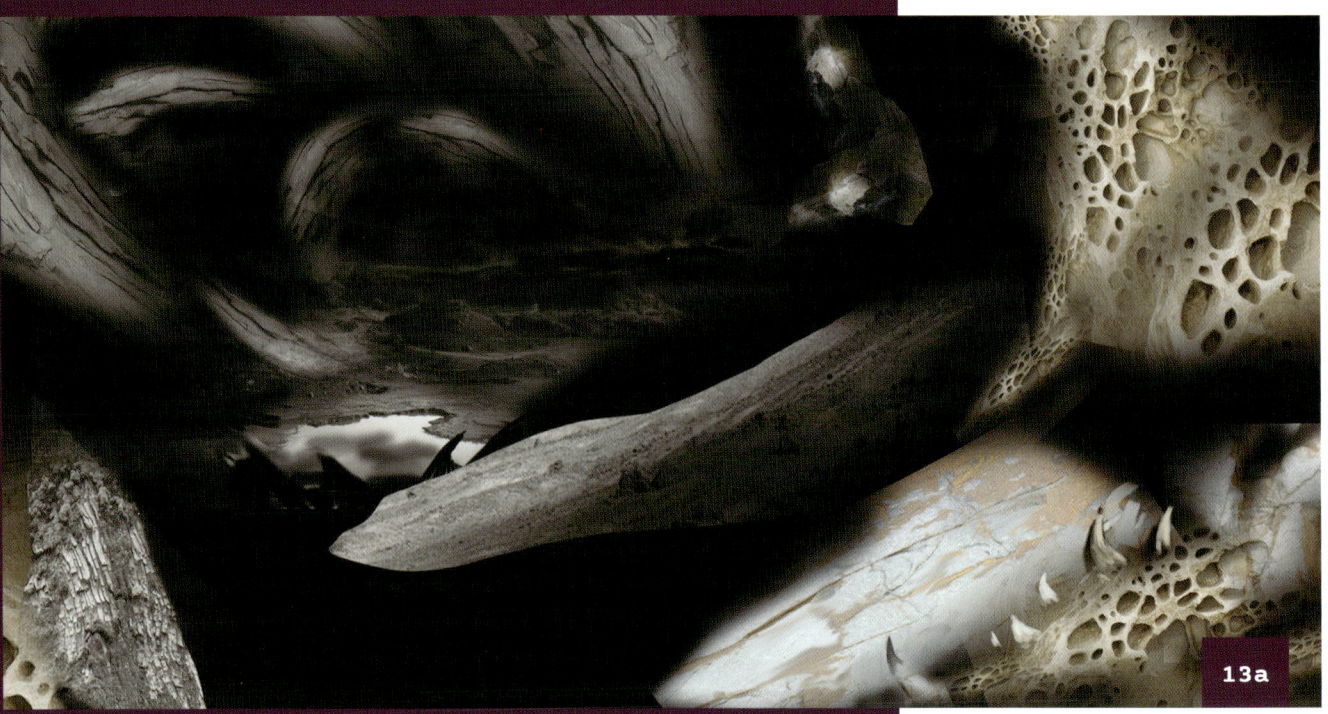

// Textures add detail and interest to the scene

13a

12 Adjusting the hue and saturation
Since my landscape contains many tones and variations, I create a Hue/Saturation adjustment layer in Photoshop and set the saturation to –100. This fully desaturates the image, which helps me to check that objects are separated correctly and that I've achieved good depth between the image's elements. I keep this adjustment layer on top of all the layers, where I can turn it on and off when needed.

This stage shows me that I'm on the right track, according to my plans in step 04, so I'm happy with the scene's progress!

If you are working traditionally, you can try squinting, which will help you to see the values more clearly. Refer back to the value study in step 04.

>13 Adding textures
Now I return to the importance of research and references. I already

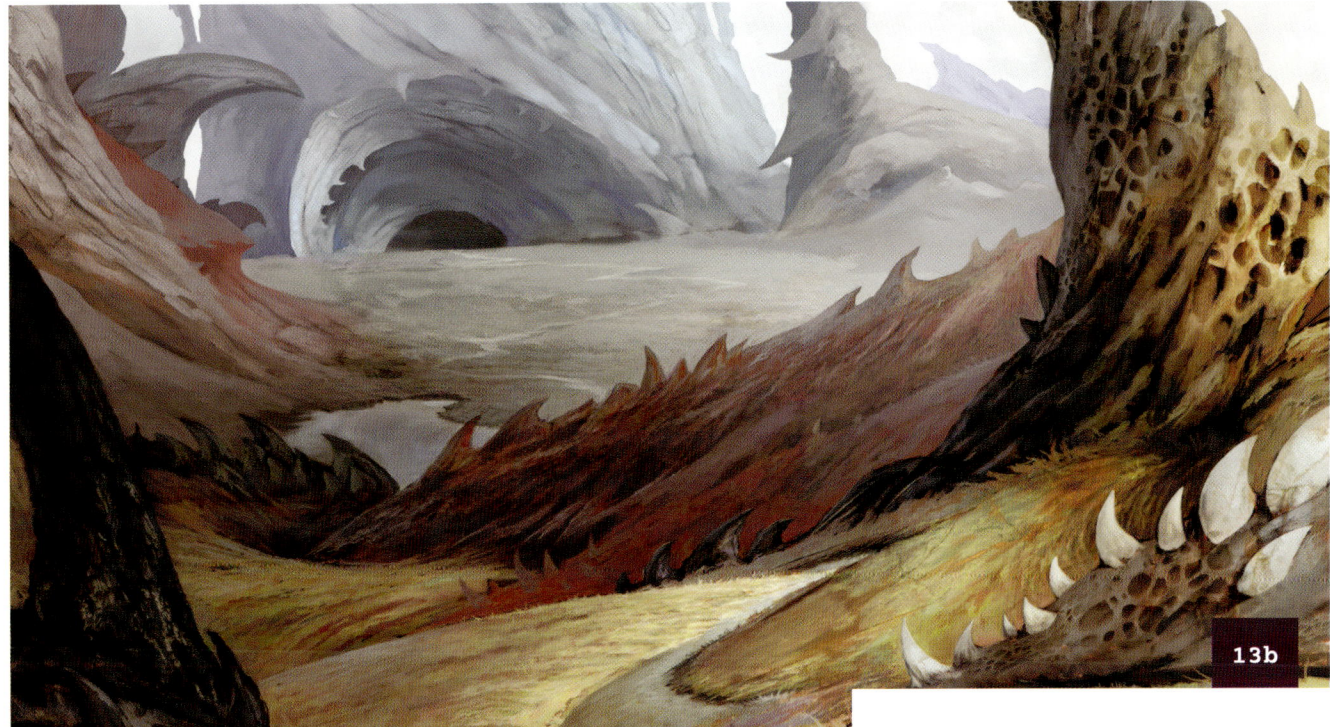

13b

// The image with the textures applied

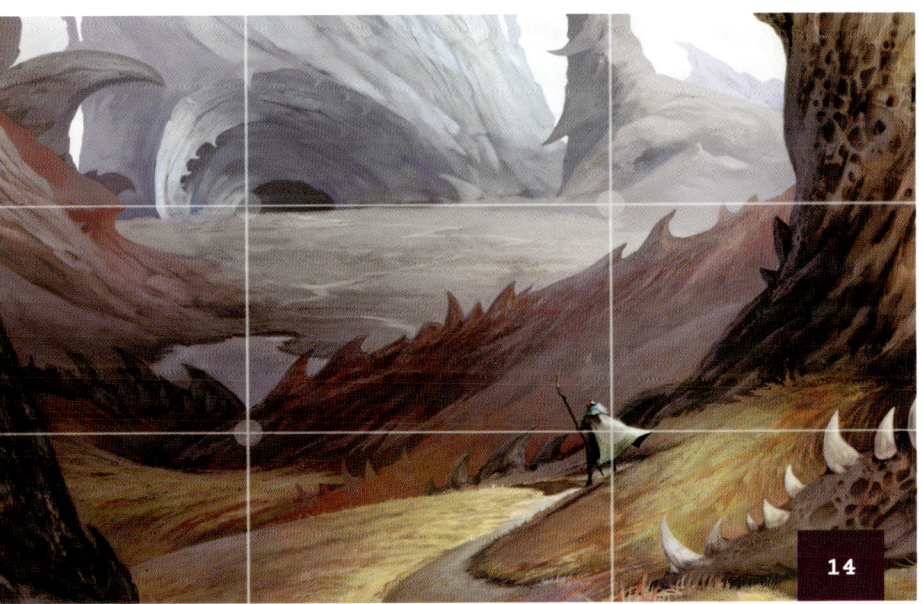

14

// Adding human scale to the scene, setting the story

used them as an inspiration, but now it's time to use them again as a support touch for the brush work in Photoshop. Textures give more life to a scene, and increase the sharpness of the details in a more believable way than I have done so far.

I use a perforated rock texture from **www. textures.com** for this stage (image 13a). I tend to desaturate texture images, sometimes to a full grayscale look,

depending on where I want to use them I change the layer mode to Overlay or Soft Light, then scale, rotate, and stretch until the texture fits as I want (image 13b). A dry brush or sponge with paint would be a good way to make a speckled texture traditionally.

>14 Say hello to my little friend

I always try to add an element that shows how big my scene is – usually a

human! In step 08, I checked the image against the rule of thirds to decide where to guide the viewer's eye. Now I place my hero in that bottom-right spot, with a pose and wind effect that adds some drama; it's as if he's standing there after a long journey and looking at his goal wearily but eagerly, as it is finally within his reach. I don't add too many details because I want him to be simple, but I use different colors to suggest that he is from another world and has a mission here to complete.

>15 The final touches

I'm really enjoying working on this piece. Every new touch, texture, or reference can teach me something. After taking a break, I add some tweaks here and there such as some extra details and shading. My usual final touches are using Brightness/ Contrast. Color Balance, and Curves in Photoshop to increase the contrast and fix color values; I use all of these effects on separate adjustment layers so I can control them as I like. I add some glowing effects and also add some sun rays from the right side, focusing on the character to make for an extra dramatic mood. You can see the final image on the next page, which is all set up to suggest the idea of adventure.

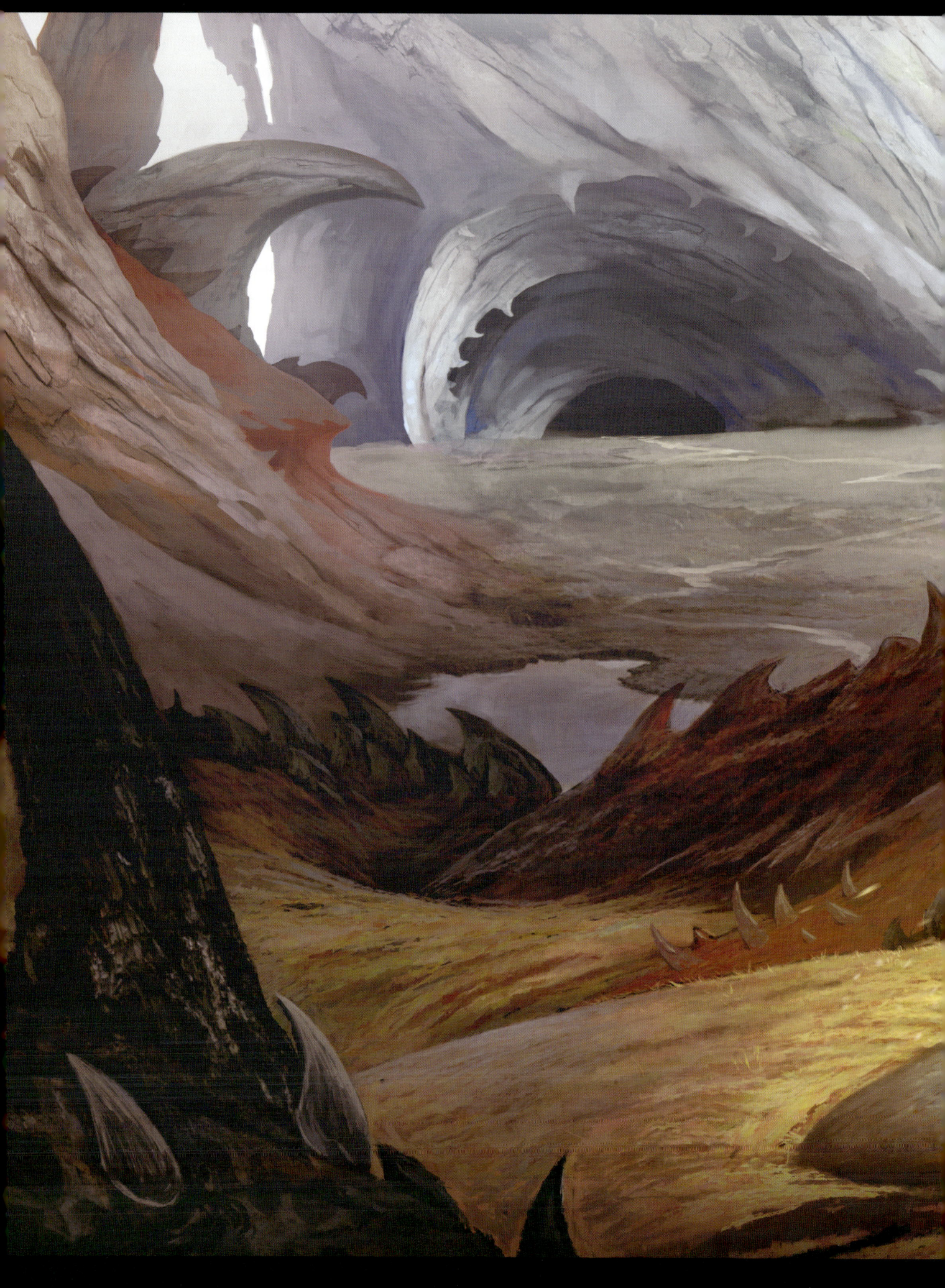

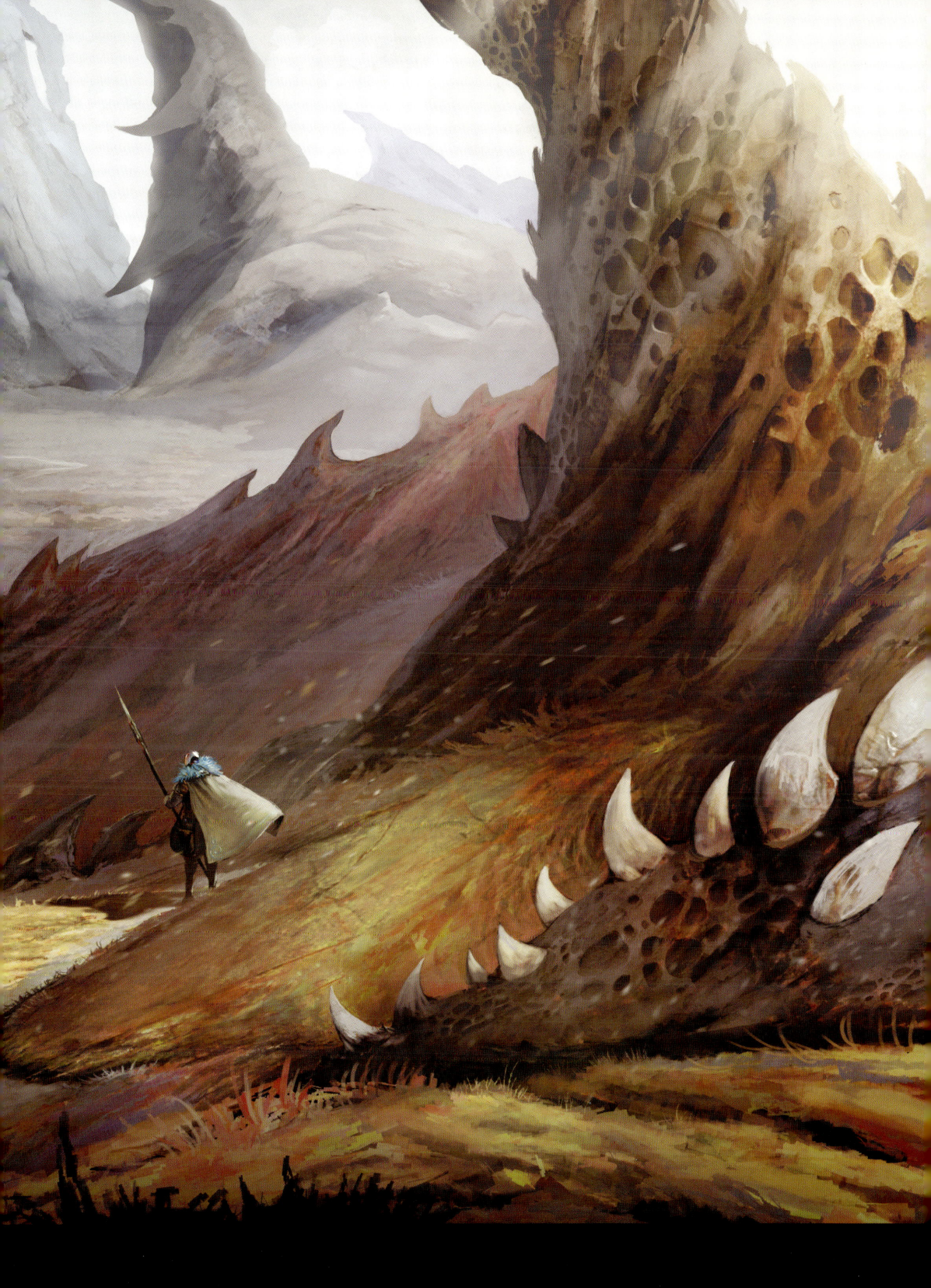

Ky Tran | www.kytranart.com

anger

When I was prompted to create a piece based on "anger," I thought of angry parents, and what could be angrier than angry dragon parents? Jokes aside, when I work with an open-ended theme like this, I like to work as freely as possible. Line drawings are helpful when faced with more specific prompts but can sometimes limit your creativity. Paint strokes, however, can be interpreted in many ways and inspire ideas, much like looking at clouds. I like to jump straight into color when it's a viable option for the project. This approach often takes me to designs, and compositions I wouldn't reach otherwise.

Thinking of anger and related themes like aggression, inhospitable environments, predatory animals, reds, spikes, fire, and so on, automatically pushes my ideas in that direction. Doing some image searches on related topics can really help get you in the right mindset. I'd like to preface that I don't have a very systematic workflow. It's an iterative process for me and I don't put anything down expecting it to remain unchanged. This tutorial will be a loose guide to my techniques, mistakes and all.

>01 Visual brainstorming

I begin by sketching multiple ideas on one divided canvas (image 01a). If you are working digitally, you can put black bars in a top layer to divide your canvas, and then paint underneath them; if you are working traditionally, try using masking tape in a similar way. Being able to jump between sketches helps me to generate more ideas, and faster. It's important that each idea is different, as this will force me to be more creative.

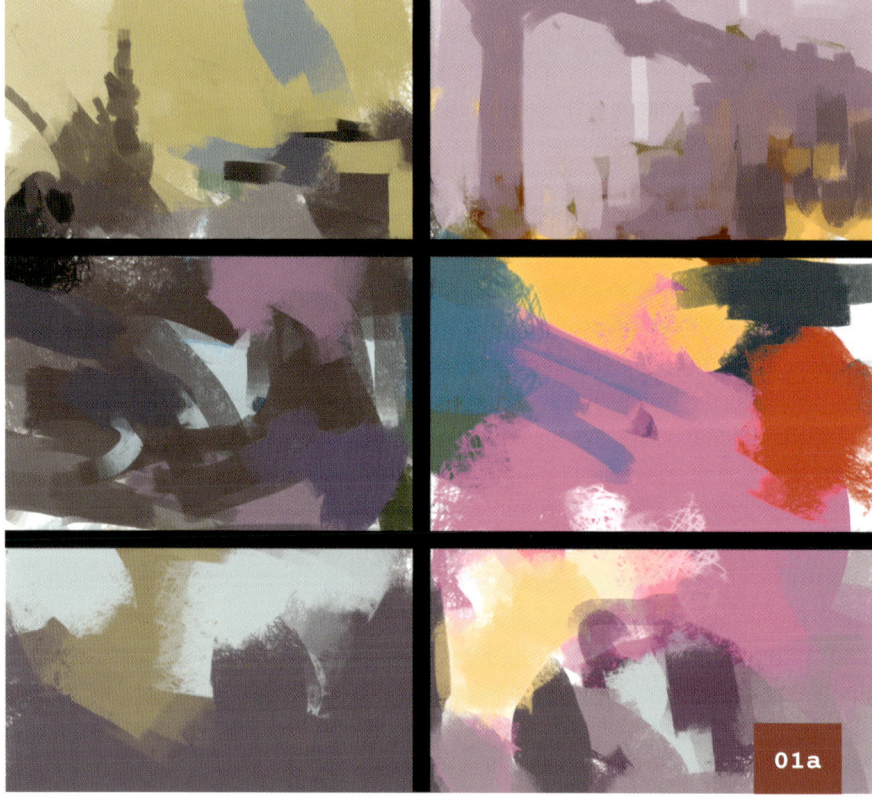

01a

// **Brainstorming with brushstrokes on the canvas**

"Not every sketch has to turn into a fully formed idea, but the opportunistic nature of this sketching process allows me to think visually from ground zero"

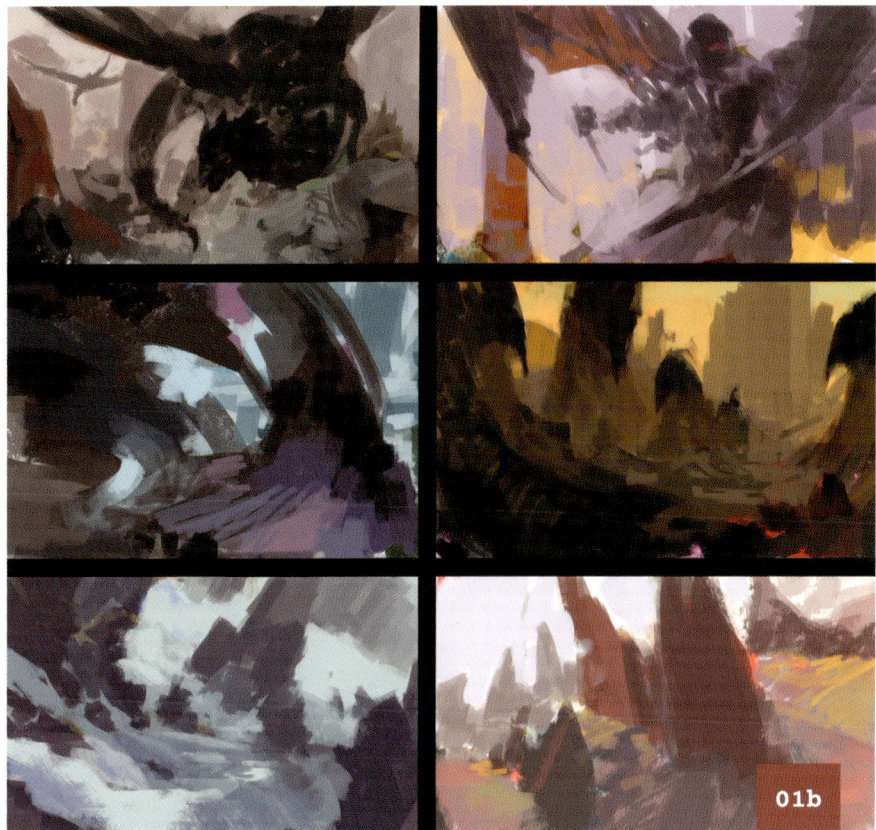

// More examples of rough brushstroke concepts

When sketching, I think about what visual cues convey anger, wrath, aggression, and danger. At this point I want to establish mood and interesting shapes as soon as possible (image 01b). I stay loose and don't worry about the details. Not every sketch has to turn into a fully formed idea, but the opportunistic nature of this sketching process allows me to think visually from ground zero. Once I begin to favor a sketch over the others, I develop it until I've settled on the idea. Things will be messy before they are pretty, but stick through it and invest in a satisfying starting point.

>02 Moving forward with an idea

At this point I figure out exactly what is going on in this illustration. What's making this dragon so mad? How can I make her really look like a force to be reckoned with? Lighting, textures, and secondary details can come into play later, but blocking in the main shapes will give a sense of where to take the painting. I want to make sure my dragon has the general shape and form of a dragon, yet still work to draw the eye around the composition. I think about what motifs I can push to convey to the viewer that this is a rage-filled moment. I want to make the dragon big and overbearing, so I position her high in the composition, as if the viewer would see her head and then look up to see a massive powerful body.

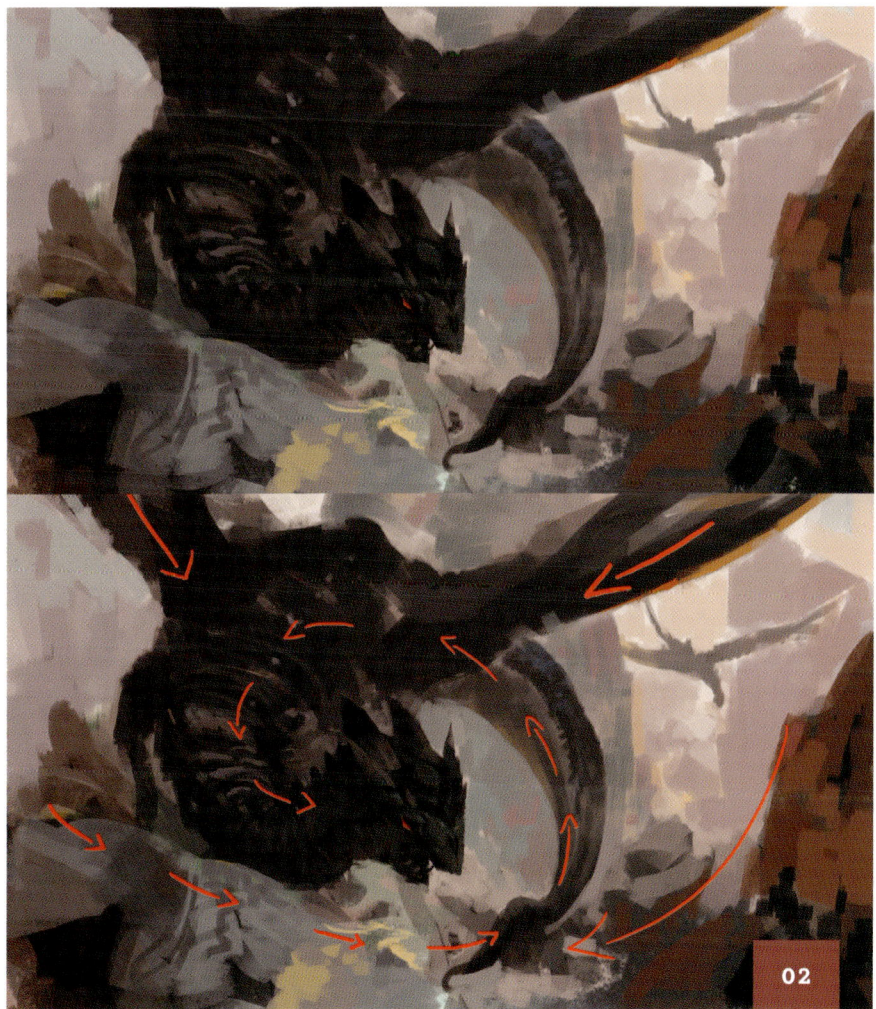

// Beginning to elaborate on my idea

>03 Developing the focal point

I decide that the illustration will be about a mother dragon who is enraged at an intruder meddling with her eggs. Because the illustration is about the mother dragon's reaction, I want her head to be the focal point. From this point on, all artistic decisions will be made to enhance the focal point and draw the eye there first. Dramatic lighting, high contrast, saturation, and detail density are some ways to draw the eye to your focal point.

Dramatic lighting presents a good opportunity to add high saturation. As the light only illuminates part of her horns, it creates an area of midtones between the light and dark. In real life this often causes a natural increase in saturation at the midtone area. In a painting this effect can be exaggerated to punch up your colors.

>04 Establishing colors

I further push the saturation and brightness of Mother Dragon's head. This sets up the value structure for the rest of the painting. It lets me know how bright I'm allowed to make other areas without losing the visual focus on her head.

A warm light will match with the earthy tones of the painting for better color harmony. If you are working digitally, setting your brush to Color Dodge is a quick way to push the lighting further. If your light is warm, Color Dodge with a warm color like yellow, orange, or pink. If you want a cool light, use blues and cyans. Be careful not to overdo Color Dodge, as it can get out of hand quickly.

After brightening her head, I indicate some light also hitting her neck to help show off her form but also to move the viewer's eye around the piece and create visual interest. It's about striking a balance between saying to the viewer "Hey! Look here!" and "Look at these other interesting areas you can feast your eyes on!"

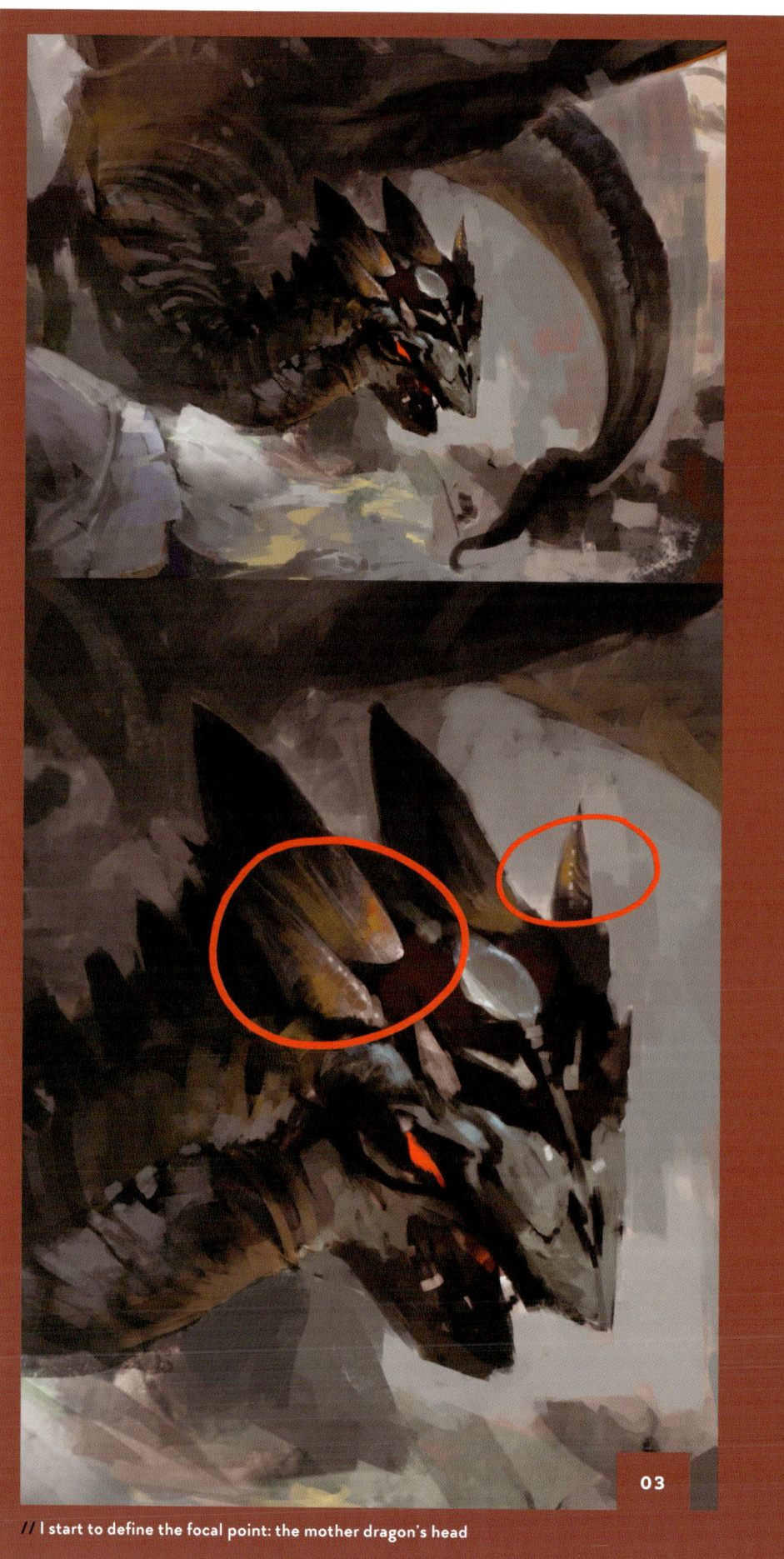

03

// I start to define the focal point: the mother dragon's head

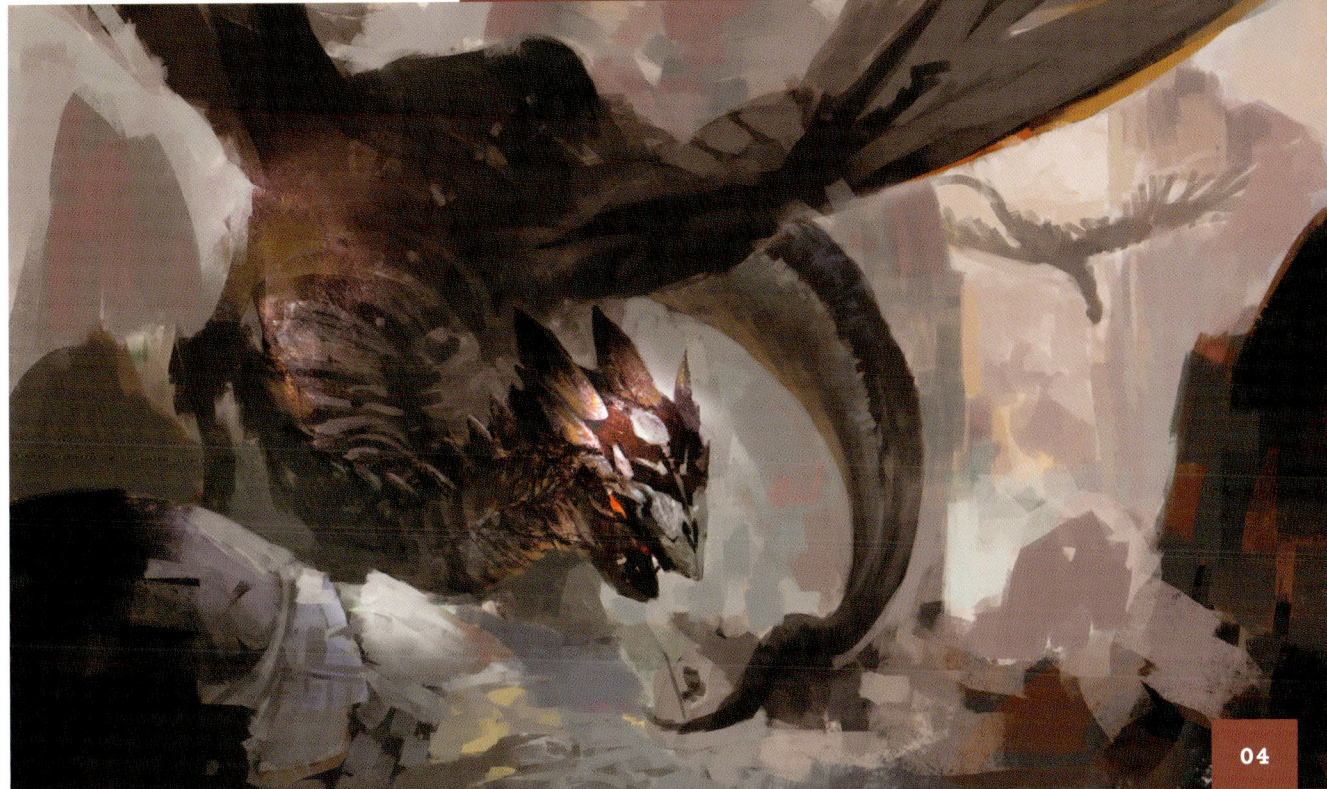

04

// I begin to work out how brightly I want to light Mother Dragon's head

>05 First details

There's no right or wrong order to work in, but I find that once the main subject is well established, the rest of the composition can easily be built around it. In this case, I perform a quick online search for bats, lizards, and birds, as well as dragons, to see how other artists have approached dragon design and anatomy. Natural weapons like spikes, teeth, and claws make her feel more aggressive.

Here I can also begin to design the environment to enhance the flow of the composition. There is a lot of personal touch that can go into shapes. Solutions that are visually comfortable to look at are generally easy to come up with, but it's the time spent looking for unconventional solutions and shapes that can really set your work apart. I like to use strong exaggerated shapes as well as a variety of large and small shapes. Too many small shapes can create busyness, while only having large ones can be boring to look at.

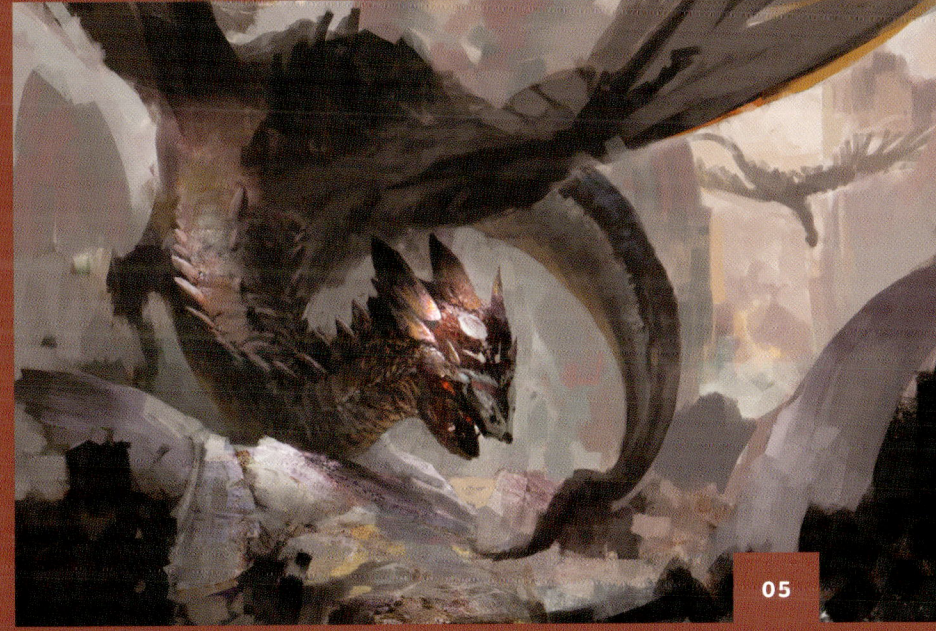

05

// Resolving the design of the main subject first will make the rest of the image easier

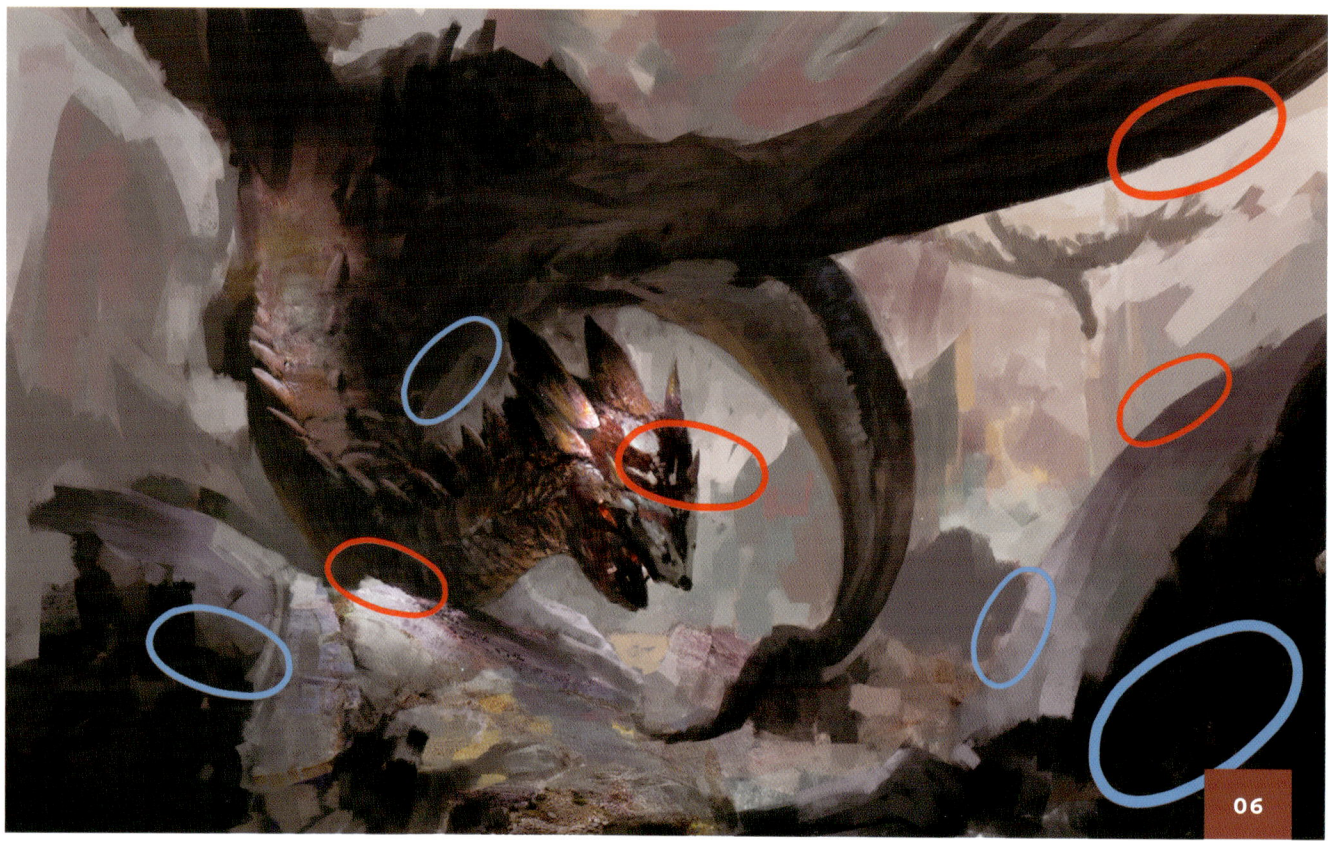

// Areas circled in blue are soft edges; areas in red are hard edges

>06 Using light to control edges

Light can be used to emphasize parts of the environment to create visual interest. I add and remove contrast to areas by adding and removing light. You are the artist and you can justify putting light anywhere so long as lighting fundamentals are followed. In this image, I consider whether perhaps there is fog only allowing the light through in certain areas, or if maybe rocks are casting shadows from above. You have full control. Being purposeful with your lighting and shapes will make your work more cohesive and engaging.

Hard edges have high contrast and command a lot of attention. Soft edges draw less attention. I try to use a variety of edges with varying intensity to move the eye around the piece, however I keep the majority of the hard edges near the focal point of the illustration.

>07 Reassessing composition

After looking at the same painting for enough hours, your sense of good art begins to drop off fast! One way to combat

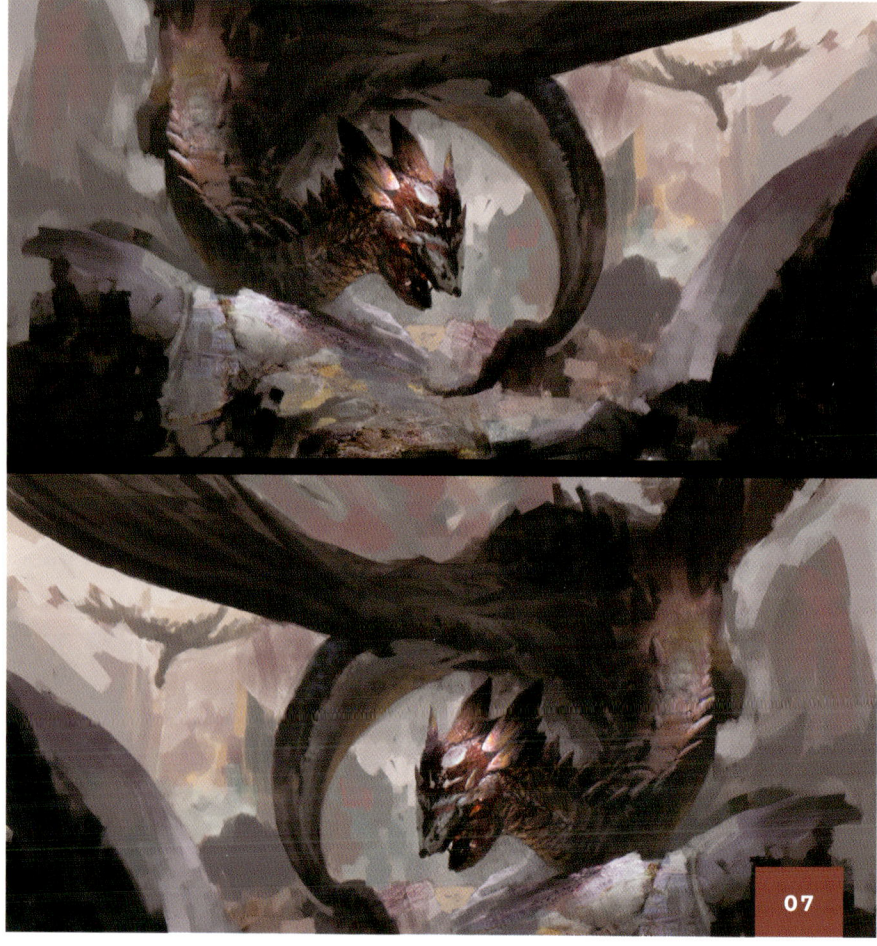

// It's easy to become lost in an illustration, so stop to re-evaluate

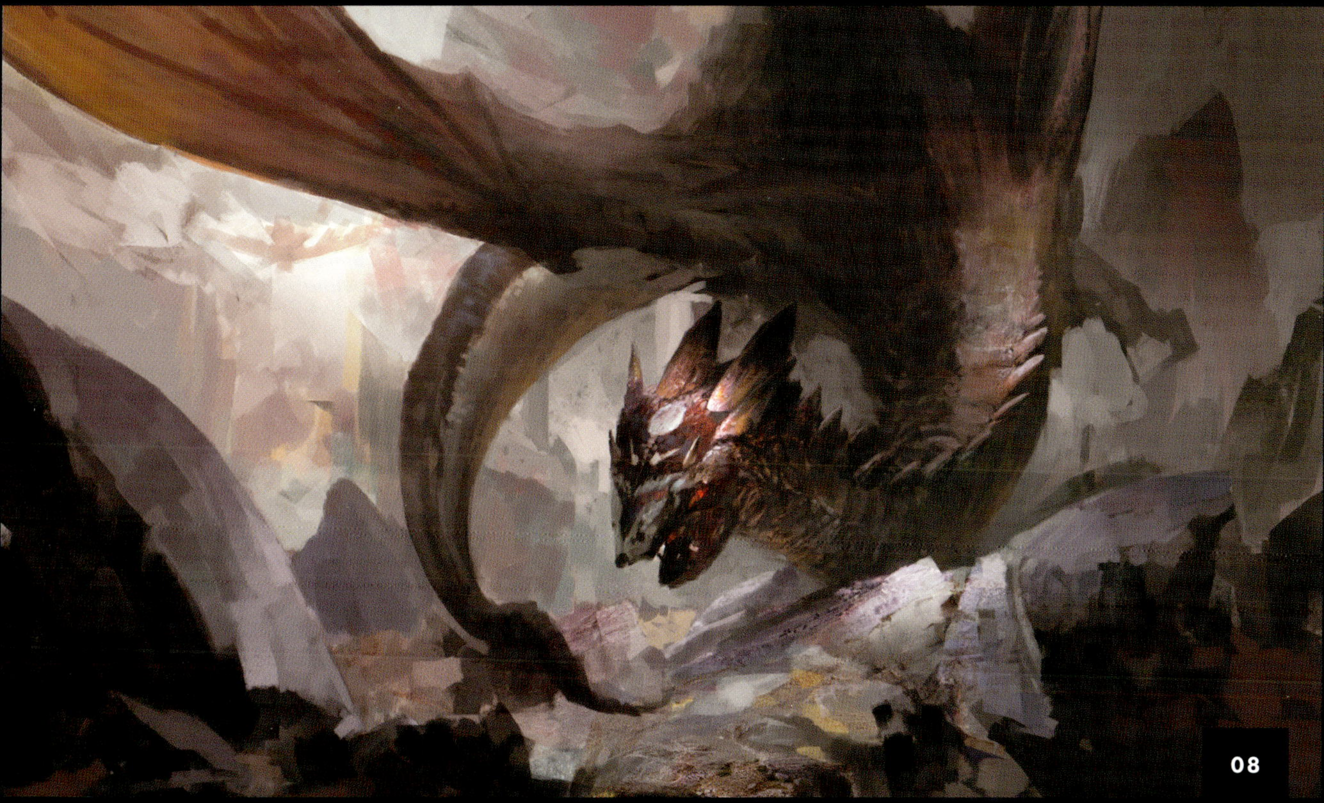

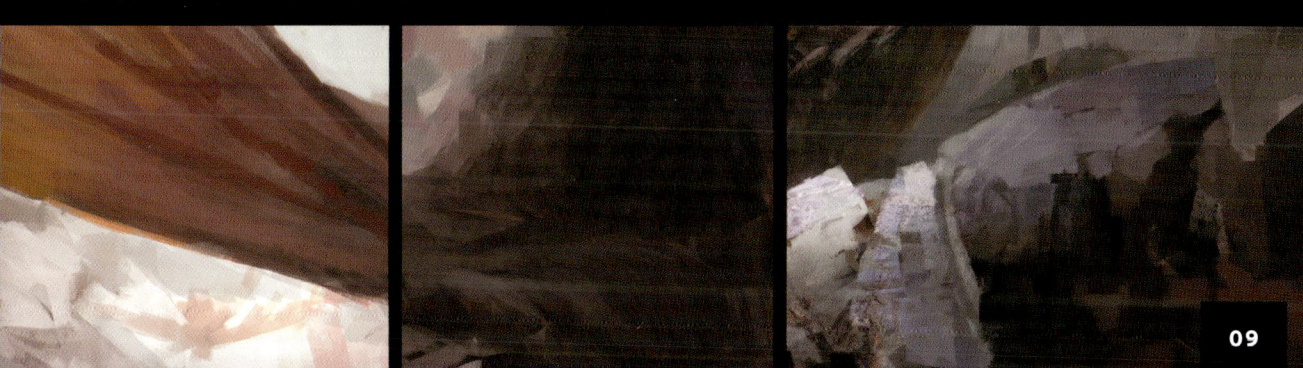

08

// Making big changes can be nerve-wracking

09

// Brushstroke details on the dragon's wing and muscle, and on the rocks

this is to flip the canvas from time to time. This will allow you to see something new and catch fundamental mistakes. If your composition is not balanced, it will look awkward after being flipped. Taking a break and coming back to the painting is great for getting a much-needed fresh look at your work in progress.

>08 Making necessary changes

After a fresh look at my flipped painting, I decide to darken the (new) right side to reduce contrast, as I feel it's drawing too much attention away from Mother Dragon's head. I brighten the (new) left side to bring some attention to Father Dragon in the background, and also

because it gives me a chance to shine light through the mother's wings. This creates an effect called "subsurface scattering," which occurs when light interacts with semi-transparent mediums. For example, murky water tends to take on strong greens or yellows when hit with light, and skin tends to takes on warm colors due to blood vessels under the surface. In this image, the light passing through blood vessels in the dragon's wings will result in saturated reds.

>09 Beginning to render

Once a strong value scheme has been established and the parts are working together, it's time to start figuring out the

details and rendering the loose areas. For my personal style, I like to keep my brushstrokes loose and expressive. I try to make the nature of the stroke reminiscent of the subject. For rocks, I like rough, blocky strokes. For the wings and indication of muscles, I use larger, swooping strokes for a more organic feel.

Brushstrokes can be very expressive and every artist should find their own vision for mark-making. My goal is not to capture every detail as accurately as possible; I think of painting as representing a subject with marks. To do so, I consider what the essence of the subject is and try to capture that.

>10 Separating secondary forms

There are so many parts to a painting that it can be hard to handle them all at once. This is why I start with rough, simple forms, then break them into smaller secondary forms. The rough forms work as placeholders while I assess the illustration as a whole. Once I have a strong vision, further defining forms is the beginning of the beautifying stage. In image 10 you can see how a large form is detailed with a smaller secondary form.

>11 Exploring other avenues

If there is a part of your painting that you have been dissatisfied with throughout your process, that is a telltale sign that you need to find a better solution. In this step, I reduce the tail, which seemed too big and awkwardly positioned. It can be painful to repaint parts that you have spent a lot of time on, but your overall momentum will improve after taking care of the nagging issues. I also try opening up the left side of the image to reduce clutter, but later decide against this change.

>12 Finalizing story elements

I feel comfortable adding the eggs and a character later in my process because they are not central focal points. Eggs are relatively simple to paint, and the egg thief is so small that it is hard to

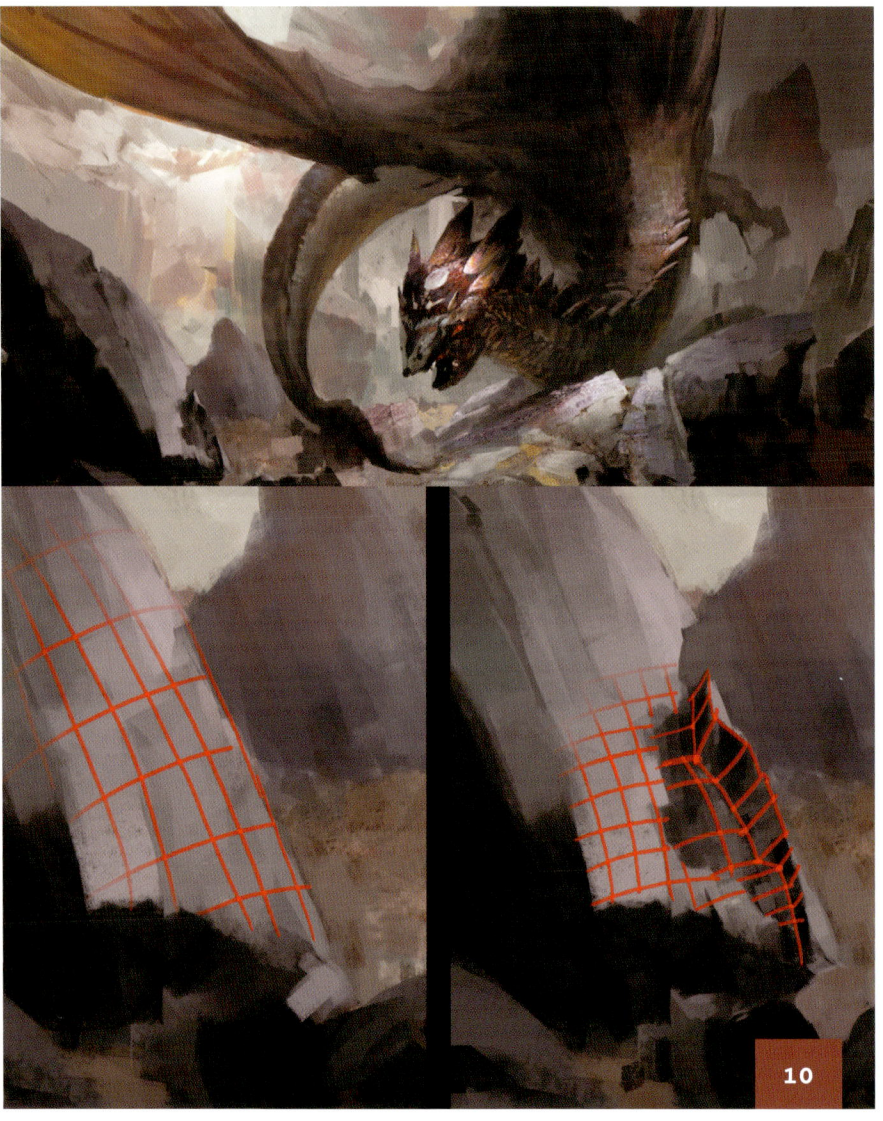

// **Always work from broad to detailed**

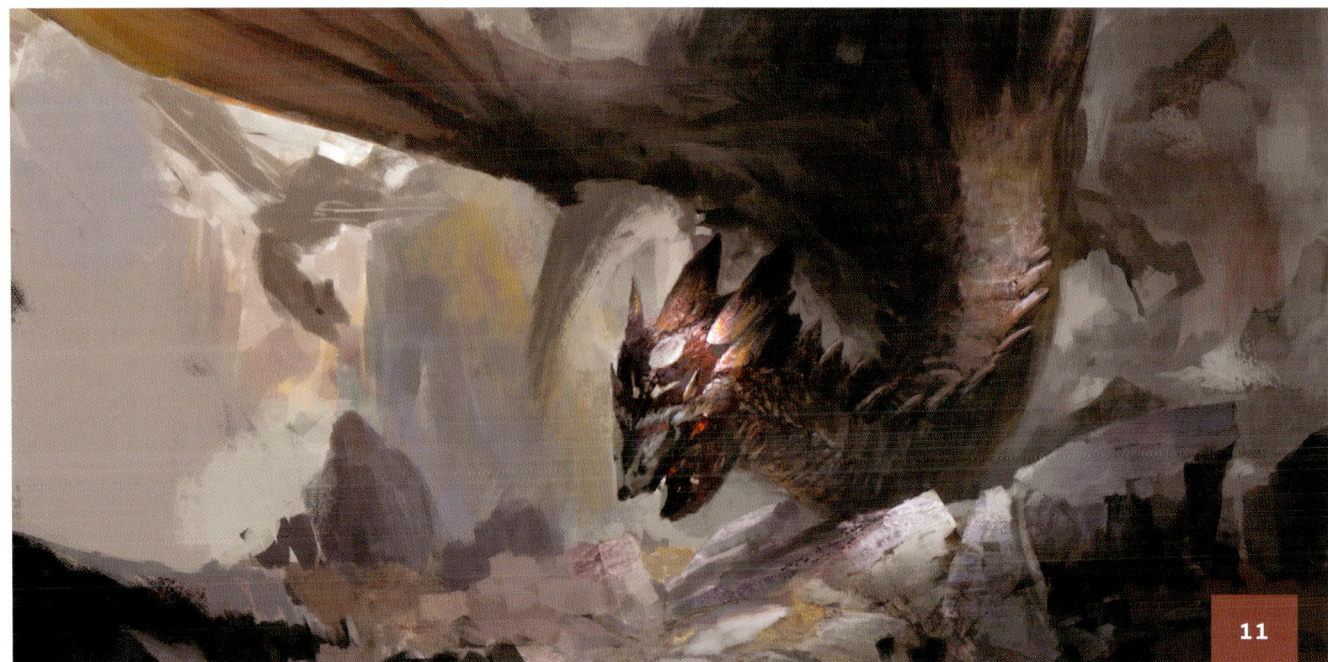

// **Even if a piece is working, you can always make it better!**

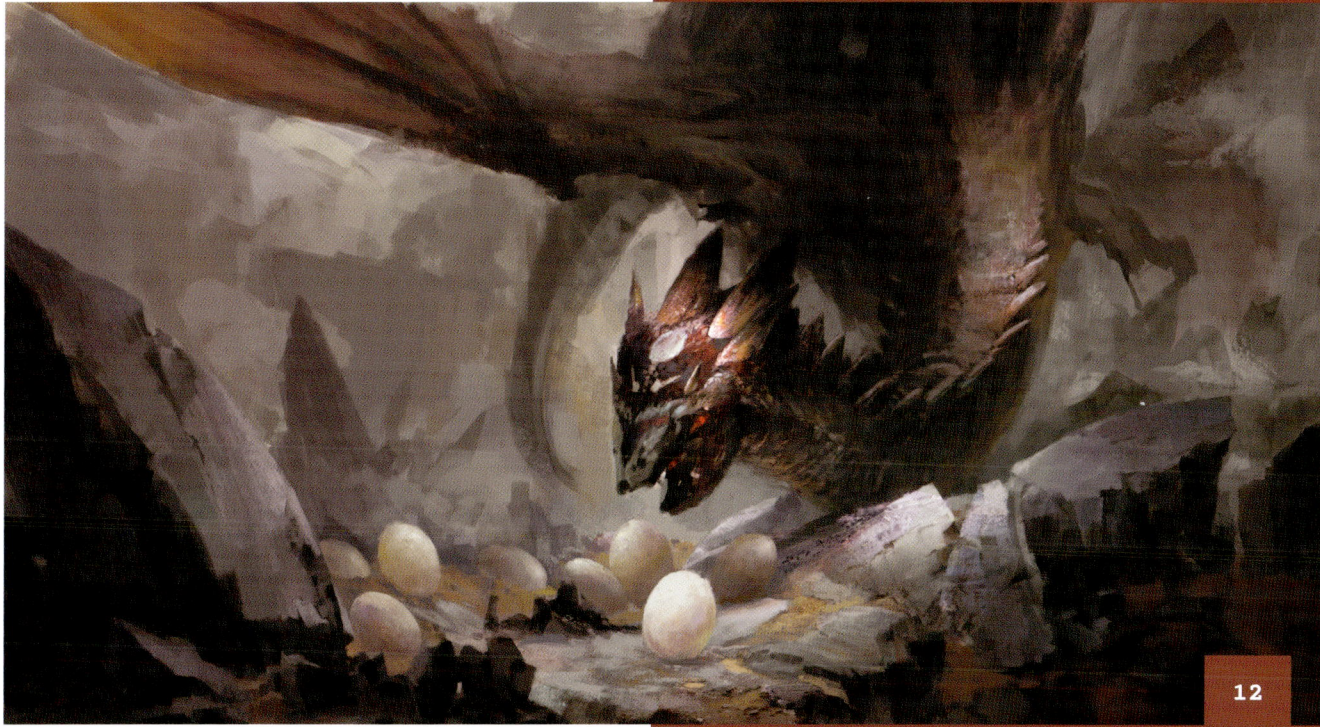

// I add the dragon eggs and start to block in a foreground character

mess up once there is a solid lighting scheme already established. At this stage, I decide that the pink background is not giving off the inhospitable vibe that I want. Instead, a foggy gorge full of sharp, jagged rocks gives off more of the dangerous mystique I'm looking for, which will help convey the sense of anger needed in the painting.

>13 Final details and atmosphere
An over-rendered illustration can look lifeless and lose personality. Final details such as hair and scale textures and cracks in rocks are therefore added selectively to give the illusion of a very detailed image, when in fact it's mostly loose.

Adding atmosphere is always my final step before I call it quits. It brings the whole piece together and deepens the sense of space. Elements can easily be pushed back by adding fog or dust, and particles can be added to indicate wind. This final step ties everything into a cohesive scene.

>14 Painting complete
You can see the final painting on the next page. Remember, too much detail can draw unwanted attention to unimportant parts of an illustration, so make sure you keep in mind the structure of the image as you render.

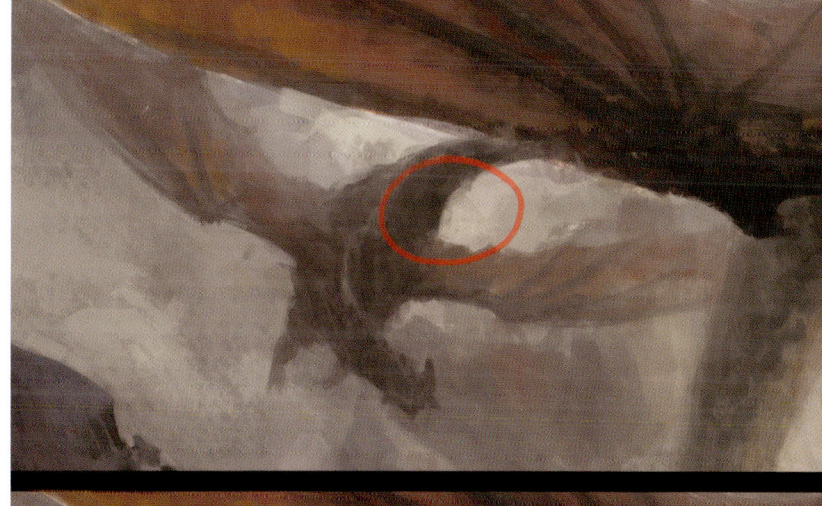

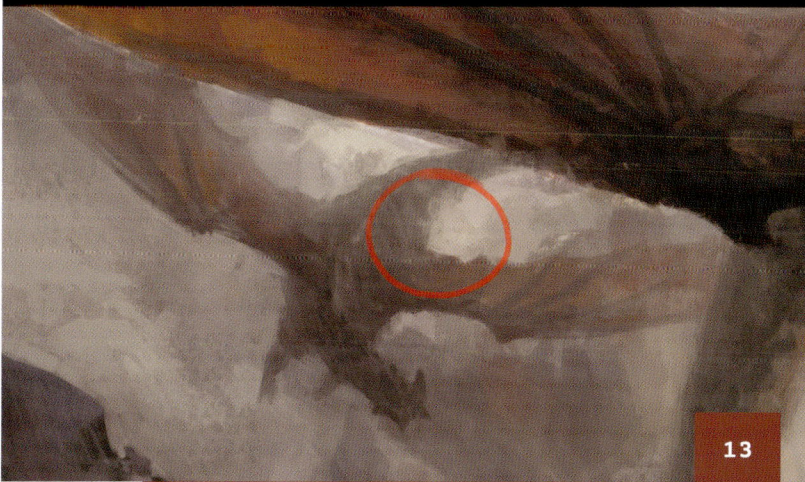

// Adding fog to push back elements of the image and create atmosphere

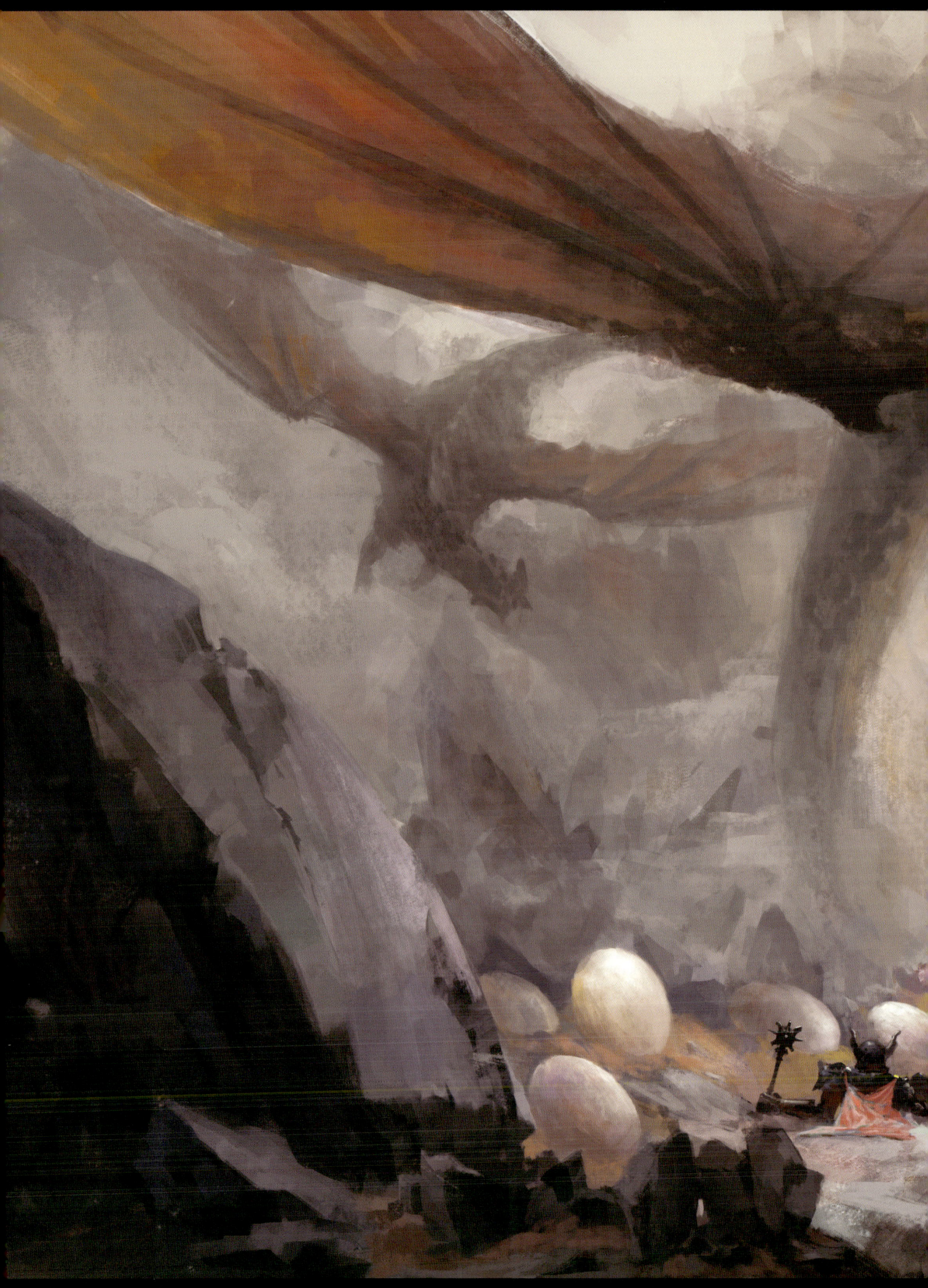

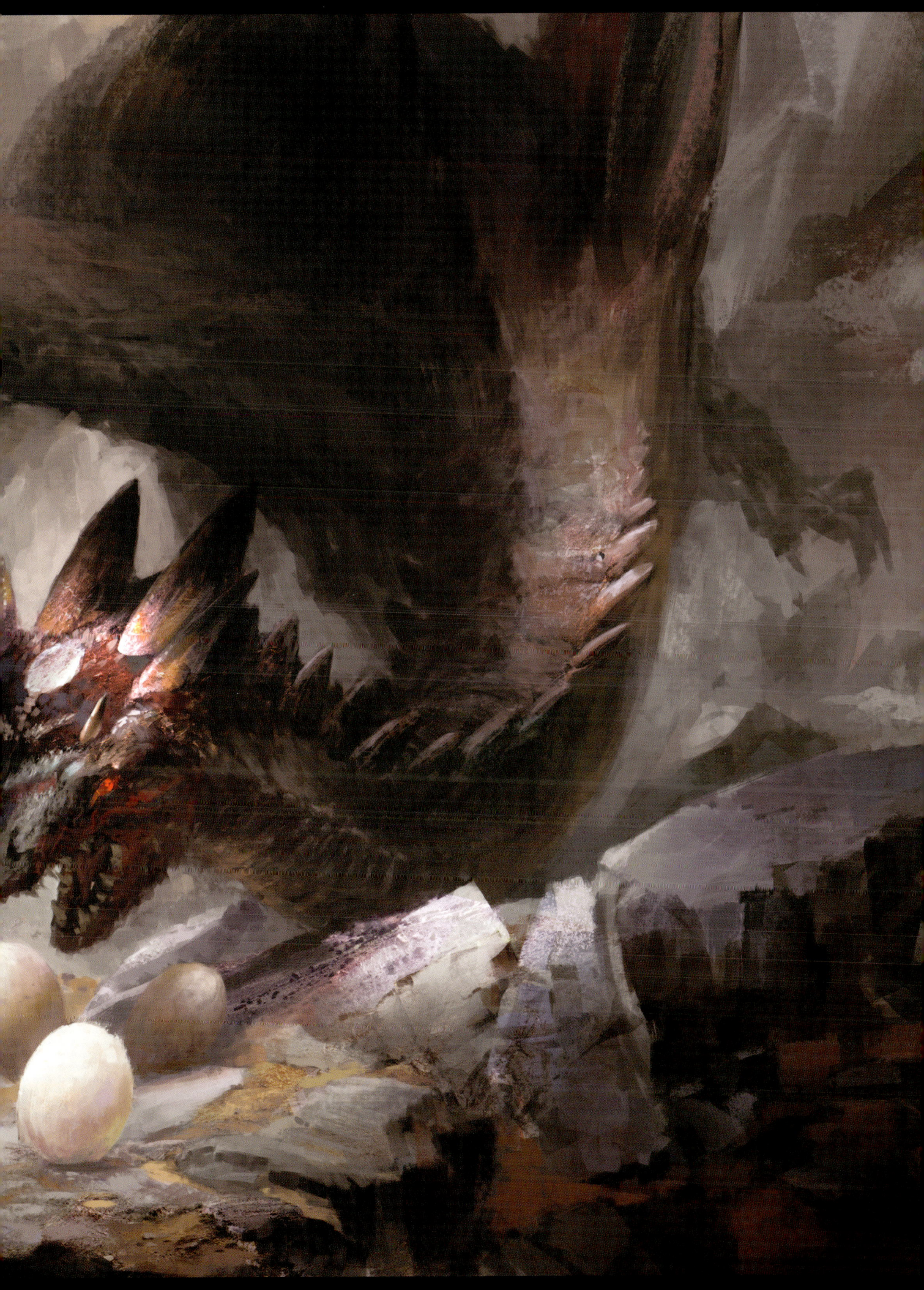

Scott Murphy | www.murphyillustration.com

awe

In this tutorial I will discuss the many thoughts and processes I go through to help infuse a sense of emotion and narrative into an illustration. For this image I want to give a feeling of awe and grandeur to a dark character and setting.

I often gravitate towards dark imagery and subject matter in my work, so for this particular painting I choose to depict the goddess Mictecacihuatl, Queen of Mictlan (the underworld from Aztec mythology). I do not wish to create an accurate "historical" representation of the goddess, nor do I want to create a world that is an exact depiction of Aztec culture. Instead I want to use the legends and historical references to inform my own version of this setting and character. I often like to use mythological beings as the subjects of my artwork because they tend to have a rich history with plenty of interesting information to use as a basis for generating my own ideas.

Choosing a character and theme is fairly easy, but the real challenge here is how to take the image beyond a figure or environment study, and incorporate more of an implied story and a sense of drama. Sometimes emotion can

be achieved through a mere look or interaction between characters. I want to show Mictecacihuatl standing tall on an ornate balcony in a large underground hall with carved pillars that evoke Aztec relief sculpture. She is surrounded by her subjects, the souls of the underworld Mictlan, who crowd around their keeper in a frenzy. She presents a large owl. In Aztec mythology, owls often served as messengers and companions to the

gods of the underworld. The goddess emerges from her domain in order to preside over her subjects. This is the one moment of the day that they eagerly await: their one moment of joy, but also agony, to see their master standing before them in all her glory.

>01 Thoughts on paper
As with all of my projects, the first step is to get down as many ideas

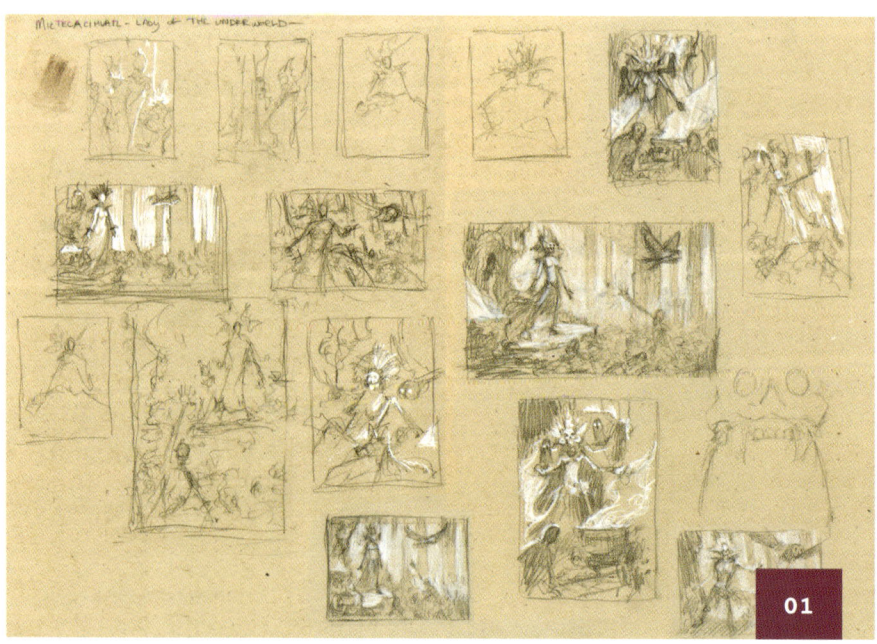

// Thumbnails can be very loose; the important part is getting down the ideas in your head

on paper as possible. The resulting thumbnails represent tiny potential versions of the image. I like to draw them on toned paper so I can use both a dark pencil and white charcoal or ink to indicate light sources and depth. These sketches are always very rough and can be almost abstract at times.

I like to think about composition and the different viewpoints I can show my scene from, almost like having a movie camera in my mind and traveling around a scene trying to find the most interesting still shot to recreate. For this illustration, I consider which angle and composition will help to showcase the goddess and the surrounding crowd and set the mood accurately. Finding the right vantage point can help with the emotion or story you are trying to portray.

>02 Evolving ideas

Once I have enough quick ideas sketched out, I pick some of my favorite thumbnails and start to add gray tones and highlights to develop the scene further. In this step I think about how I want my image to be lit. The lighting within an image can have a big effect on the ambience. To get across the sense

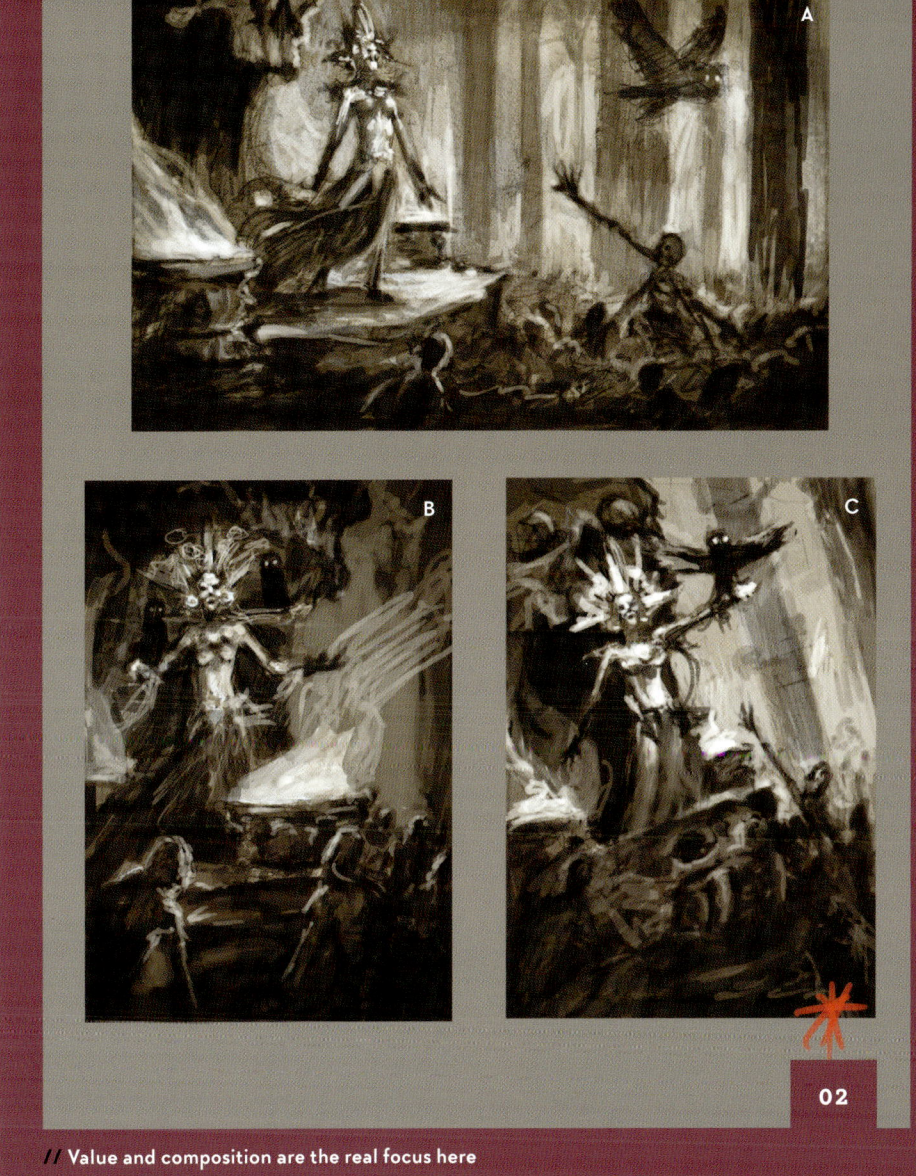

02

// **Value and composition are the real focus here**

of awe that I want my painting to have, I choose to make the goddess brighter than the rest of the image, as she's both the focus of the image and the focus of the tormented souls around her. I decide to go with option C in image 02 as my final design; I like the vertical format and slightly lower angle to help give her a sense of grandour. A low angle often helps to portray a more majestic character, and I think adds to the "awe" factor. It will also make the viewer feel as if they are among the crowd below her, looking up.

>03 Character design

After I have decided on my thumbnail idea, I want to make sure I figure out what my Mictecacihuatl will look like. Here I sketch a more detailed portrait of her, focusing on costume design and a little on expression. Though this sketch does not quite capture the feel I want for the final, it is fine for this portion of my process. This step will help save time when I am working on the larger final sketch, since I won't have to think about her design as much and can just focus on how she fits into the final composition.

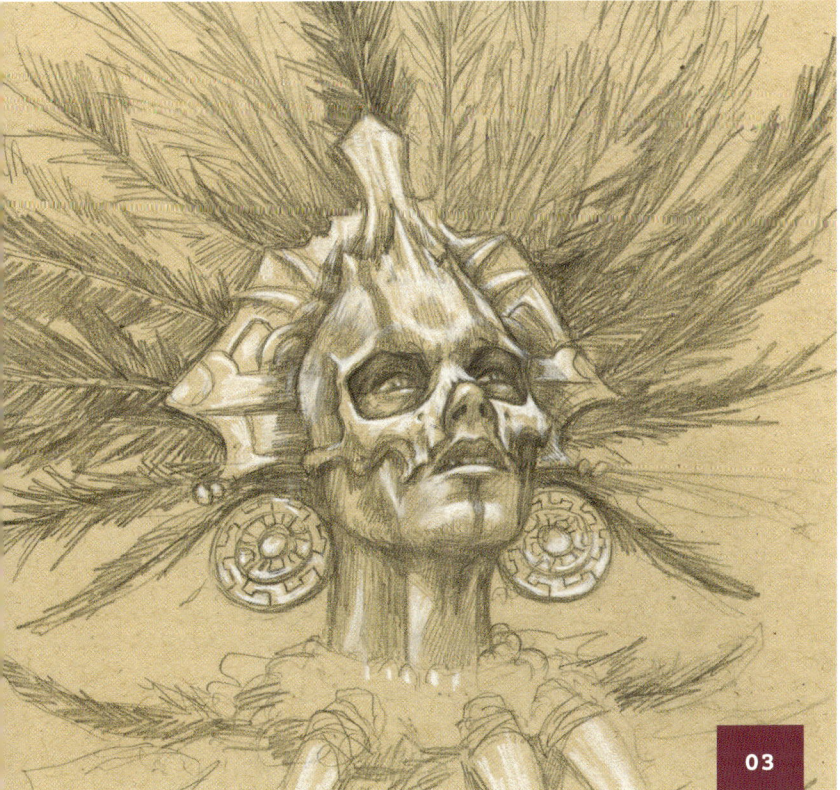

03

// **Pencil and white charcoal on toned paper can be great for preliminary studies**

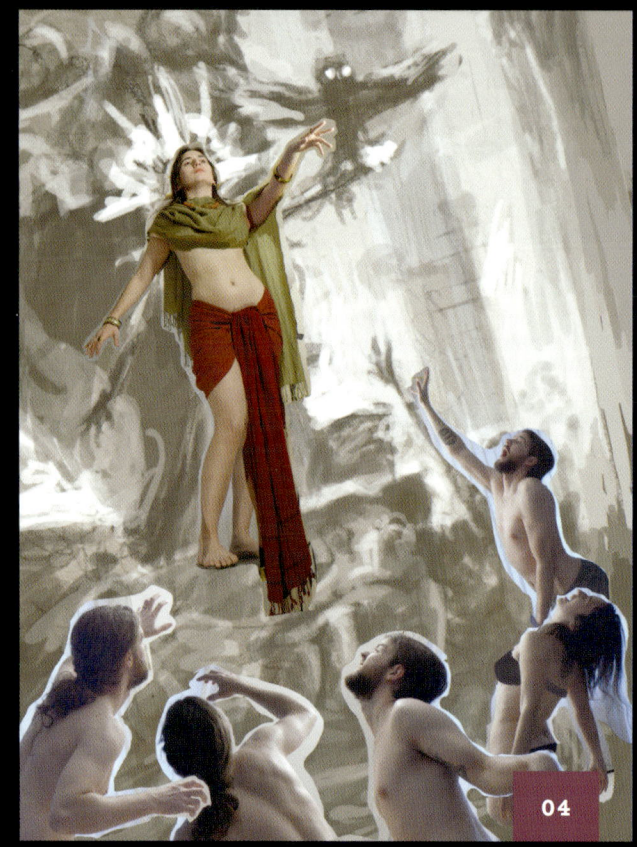

// This is my photo layout with reference images laid on top of the thumbnail (and edited for modesty!)

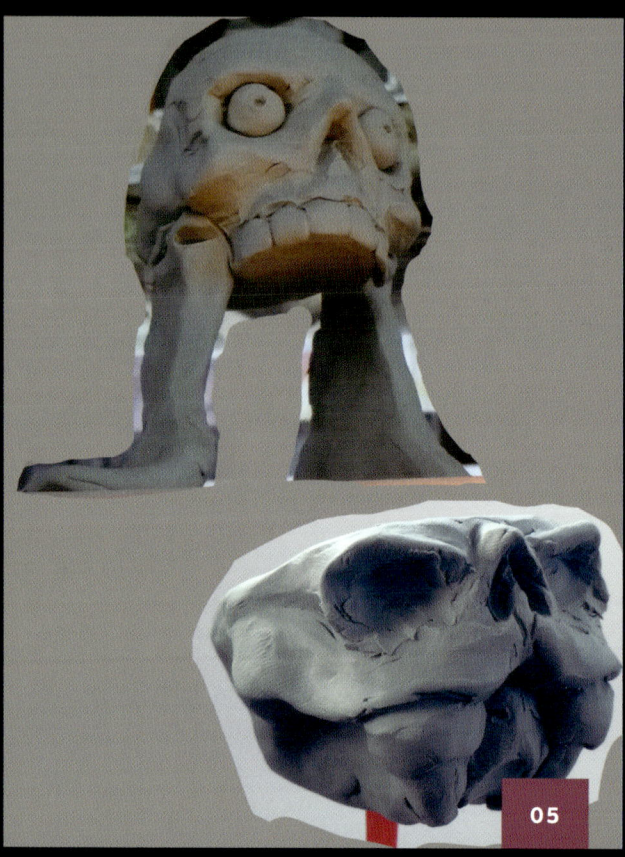

// Maquettes can be more or less detailed – as long as you have a basic form, they will be a big help in determining lighting

>04 Inspiration and references

Often when conceptualizing a new painting. I take some time to look back through my books and the internet at many classic works that provide me with additional inspiration. In this case, I look at images such as Herbert James Draper's *Tristan and Isolde*, Adolf Hiremy–Hirschl's *Souls on the Banks of the Acheron*, and John William Waterhouse's *Circe Offering the Cup to Ulysses*. The old masters and Golden Age illustrators provide such a great resource for composition, colors, and character interactions that can help ignite your imagination and bring new light to a current project.

Now I have my basic preliminary sketches and idea figured out, it's time for me to start gathering some photo reference. For this project I am able to set up a model with some basic costuming to closely relate to my character designs. I will often have the model wear less so that I

have more basic anatomy to go from. It's easier to make up jewelry and costume elements than accurate anatomy. It's important to pay attention to how I'm lighting the model, as well as shooting various poses to make sure I catch the figure's best gesture, as these will contribute to the emotion of the painting.

>05 Maquettes

Another great way to help figure out elements in a painting, in this

case sculptures and architectural elements, is to build a maquette. I often build these small models out of clay based on my preliminary sketches. They are very helpful for maintaining consistent lighting within a reference, and I can take photos from various angles to match up with my thumbnail sketch. Going the extra distance to make maquettes helps to flesh out the environment and gives that extra sense of realism.

// PRO TIP

The benefits of taking photo reference

Taking photo reference is an important step for many artists. Do you want to draw nice clothing folds? Do you want accurate and interesting lighting? The easiest and best way to get photos that will closely match your concept is to take your own. Nowadays it's easy to take good photos, even with just your smartphone, so there's really no excuse! Using photo reference is also good practice, like a figure drawing class. It will make drawing from imagination a lot easier too; for example, when you've drawn from a lot of photos of hands, you will find them becoming easier and easier to draw!

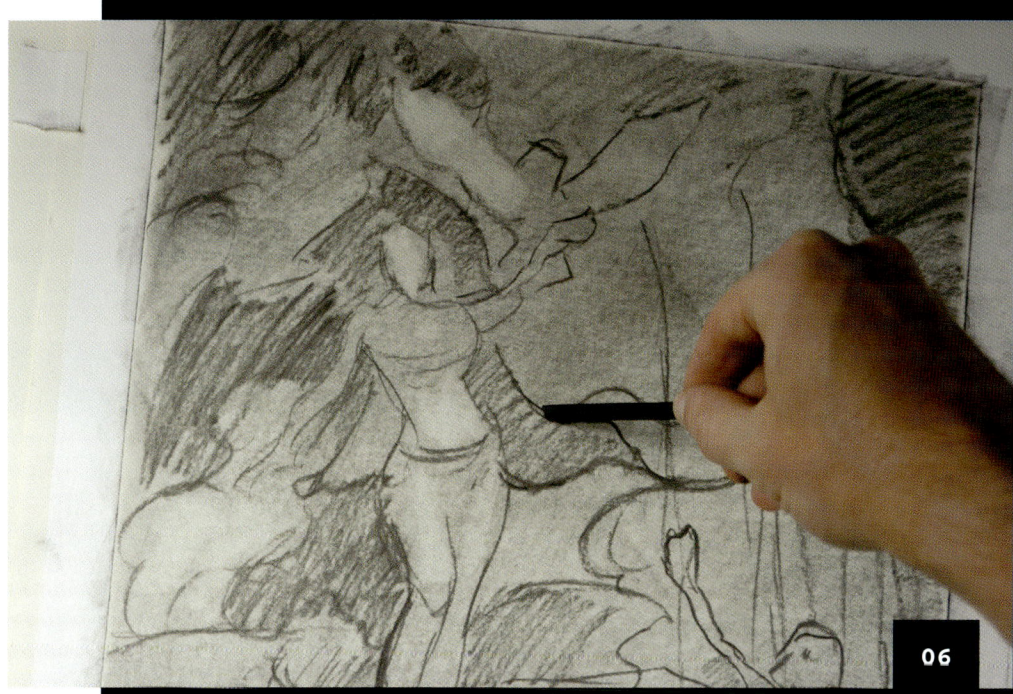

06

// Work from general shapes and tones at first, then start to refine once the main elements are in the right place

>06 Beginning the final sketch

Now that I have put in the extra legwork to make sure I have all of my reference, I'm ready to start the refined sketch. I typically like to use vine charcoal on a middle gray charcoal ground for my sketches. With this surface I can draw in dark lines and tones, as well as pull out lighter highlights with a kneaded eraser. My preference for charcoal arose because I find that with pencil one can often become caught up in fine details too quickly. The loose quality of the vine charcoal allows me to be more spontaneous and free with my lines, as any mistakes can quickly be wiped away with a hand or eraser. This helps me to focus on the gesture of my characters and the overall composition and ambience before becoming too focused on details.

>07 Let it flow

I think a lot about the flow of my picture in this early stage of the drawing. I want to make sure that all of my angles, implied and actual, benefit the composition overall. The direction of everything in your composition can greatly improve the mood of a piece. I try to get the viewer's eye to move all around my image to take in the implied narrative. The best way to do this is by utilizing angles that will lead the view first to the focal point, in this case the goddess, then down to the tormented people below, and then back around up to her again.

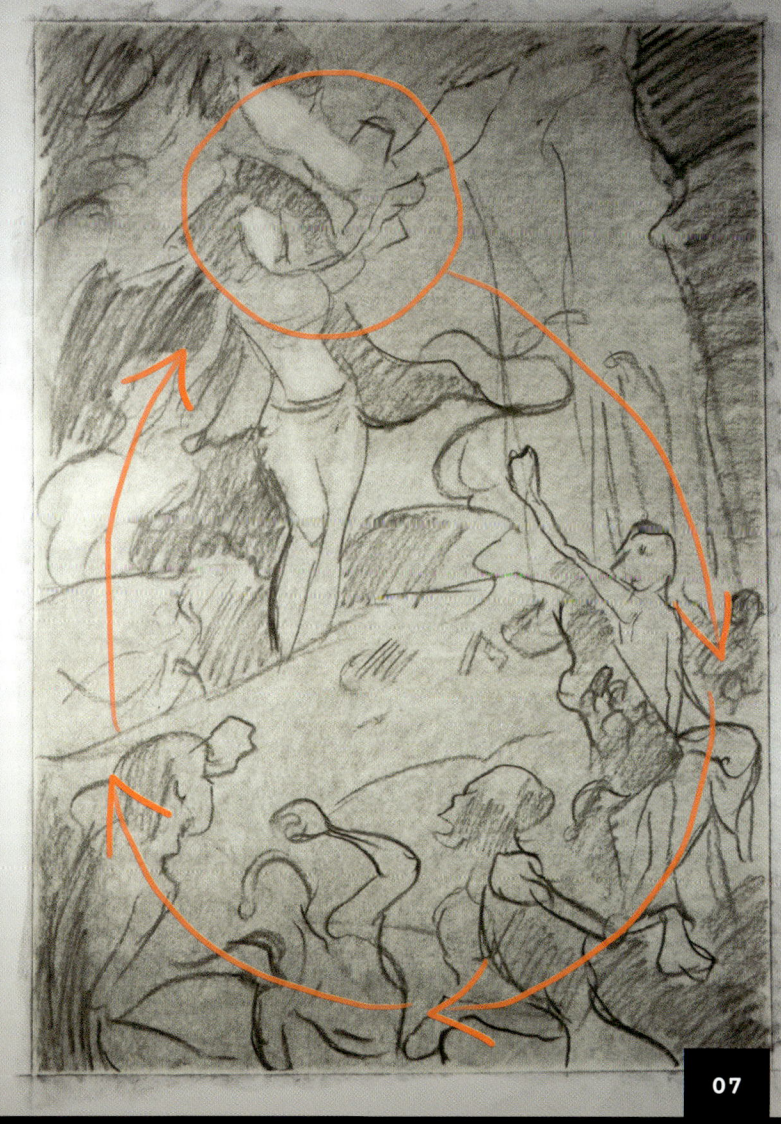

07

// Showing how I'd like the viewer's eye to travel around the composition

>08 Wrapping up the charcoal

Once I have my composition worked out, with all of my characters and environment elements where I want them, I begin to add details with a charcoal pencil and fine-point eraser stick. In this step I start to think about costuming details, architectural designs, and expressions. Many of these details help to give the scene more narrative and a sense of reality. I also try to make sure that my character interactions work well together. At this point, the sense of awe and infatuation should start to come through.

Before I move on to painting I want to be sure that my drawing captures the feel I had initially conceived when I started my thumbnails. Fixing any problems or pushing ideas further is much easier at the drawing stage than once you begin painting. I want the demeanor and expressions of my crowd at the bottom to be a cross between awe, fear, and starstruck frenzy; I need to make sure my goddess is still the focus of the image with a commanding yet graceful pose.

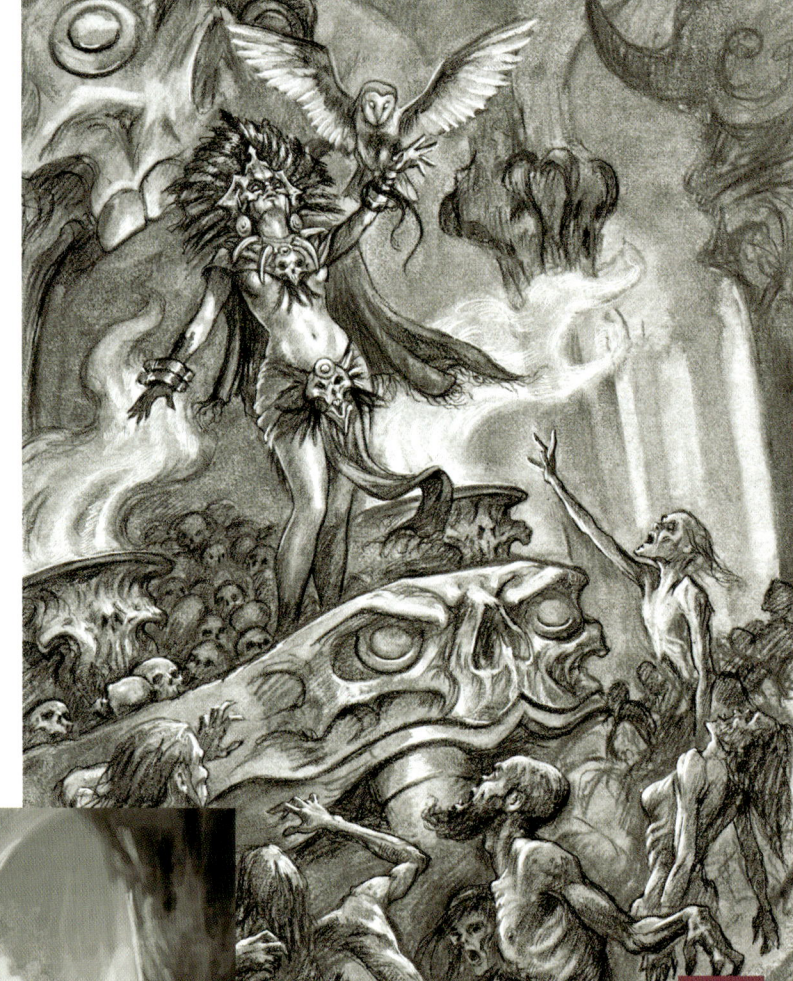

// The finished pre-digital charcoal drawing

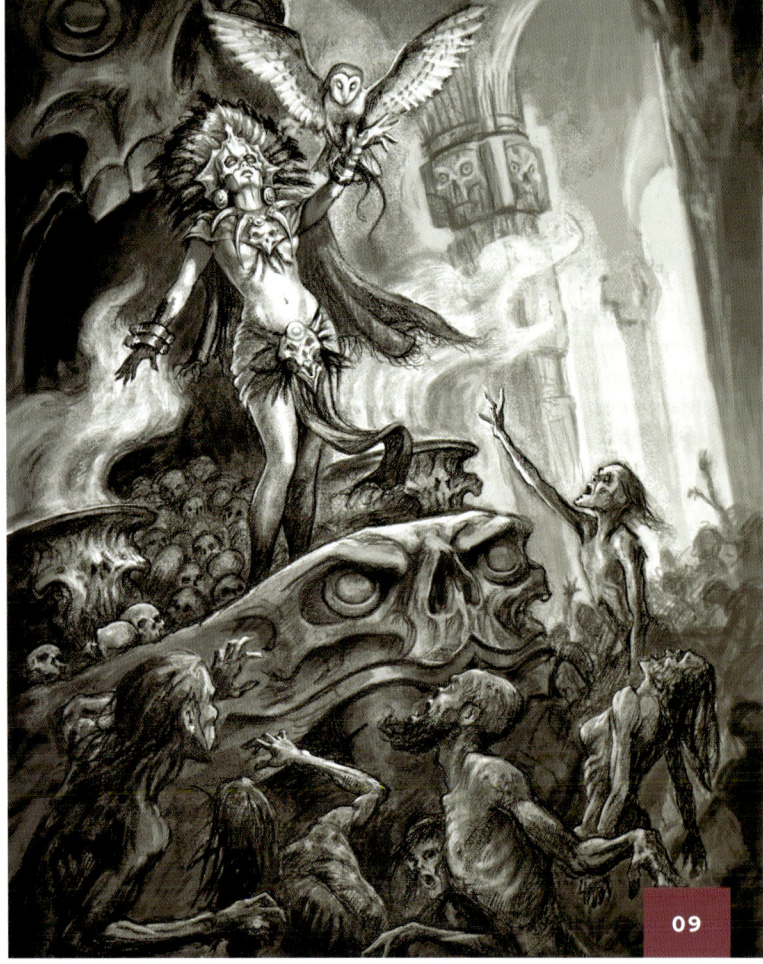

// The complete drawing after digital edits

>09 Taking a step back

At this stage it can be useful to take a step back and make some further tweaks. When my charcoal drawing is at a point where I can no longer add fine details to it or erase out lighter areas without ripping the paper, I like to spray the drawing with fixative and make a scan. I open the file in Adobe Photoshop to continue to push the drawing further. I find that working digitally at this stage makes it much easier to darken some areas, add additional details, add brighter highlights, and even modify the scale of some parts. For example, I have changed the sizes of some figures in the foreground so that they are not quite so uniform. This adds interest and dimension to the composition and helps break up the repetition along the bottom of the image. You can manually make the same sort of adjustments if you are continuing to work traditionally at this stage.

>10 Color options

Since the color of an image can very easily affect the mood, I want to make sure I know what I'm doing before getting into the final painting. This is when I create a series of color roughs – I choose to do this in Photoshop through a series of color and adjustment layers over my finished sketch file. I create very loose approximations of final color options when I make these studies. I look at color relationships such as complementary colors, warm versus cool hues, and saturated versus unsaturated colors. I want to make sure that the overall palette achieves the desired atmosphere that will help to capture the emotion I want. In this case, I opt for choice B in image 10, because I feel that the warm tones on and around the goddess help to give her an aura of awe, especially juxtaposed against the various cool blues, grays, and purples of the surroundings.

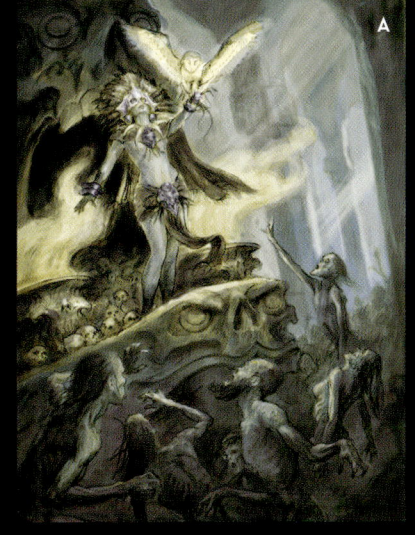
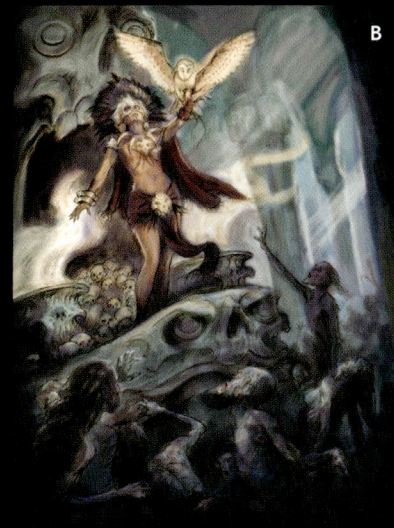
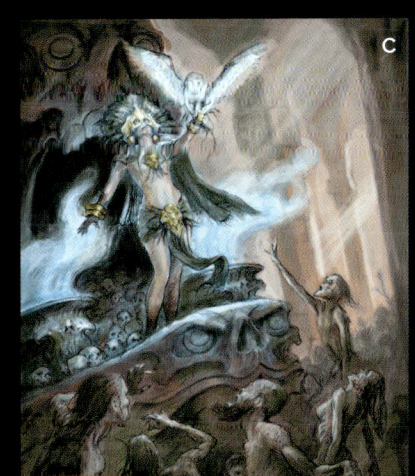
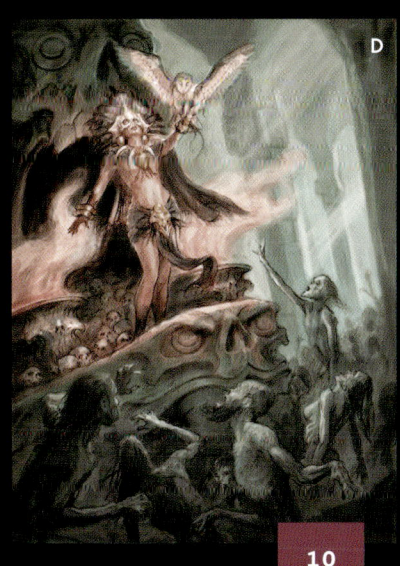

10

// My rough color studies

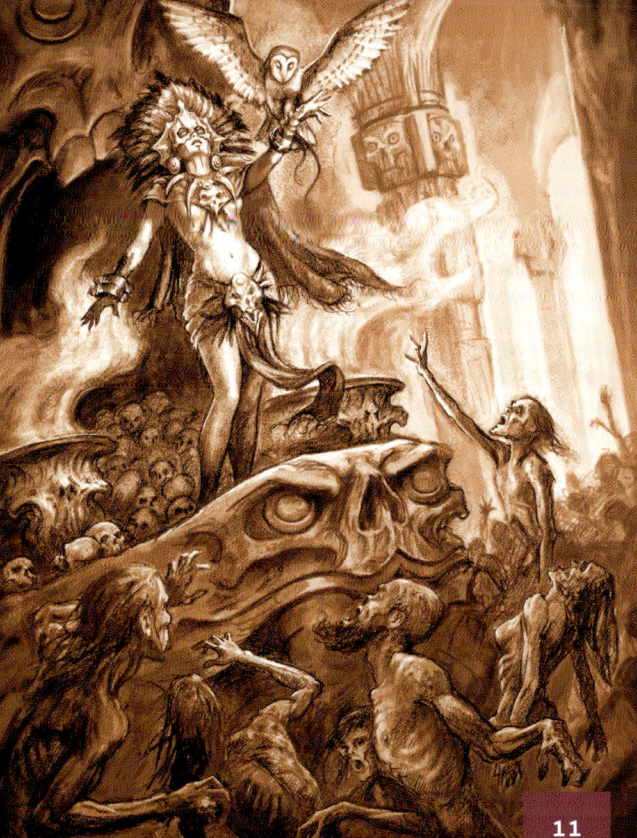

11

// The drawing colorized, ready to print and paint over

>11 Printing the drawing

I now need to transfer my drawing to the painting surface. To save time in the process, I make a large printout of my sketch, rather than redrawing the whole image onto the new surface. First I tone the image in Photoshop using Colorize. I like to select an overall color that will work as a base layer, a complementary color to those which I will be applying on top, just like doing a tonal underpainting.

>12 Mounting to my painting surface

Once I print this image out, I mount the print to Masonite using acrylic matte medium. The print should be on good-quality, acid-free drawing paper, and printed using pigment-based ink and not dye, otherwise the ink will run all over the place. I use an Epson Stylus Photo R1900 printer to make my prints. Since the printer can only handle a 13-inch width, and my painting is wider than that, I print the full image in sections and combine them on the board.

Once printed, I coat both sides of the print with water so that the paper can expand. I then coat my Masonite panel with acrylic matte medium, as well as the back side of the paper. I place the paper carefully onto my Masonite using an ink roller, making sure I line up my separate sheets, and slowly roll out from the center, sealing the paper to the surface of the board. Lastly I coat the surface with an additional three coats of matte medium, allowing it to dry between each coat.

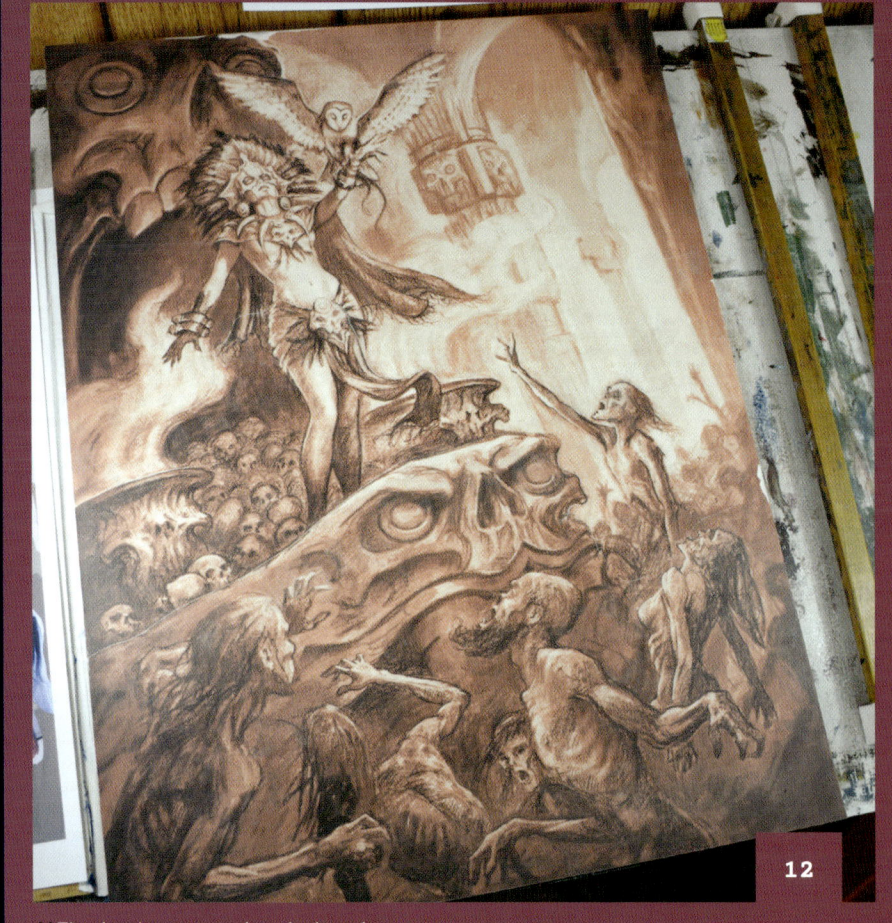

12

// The drawing mounted to the board

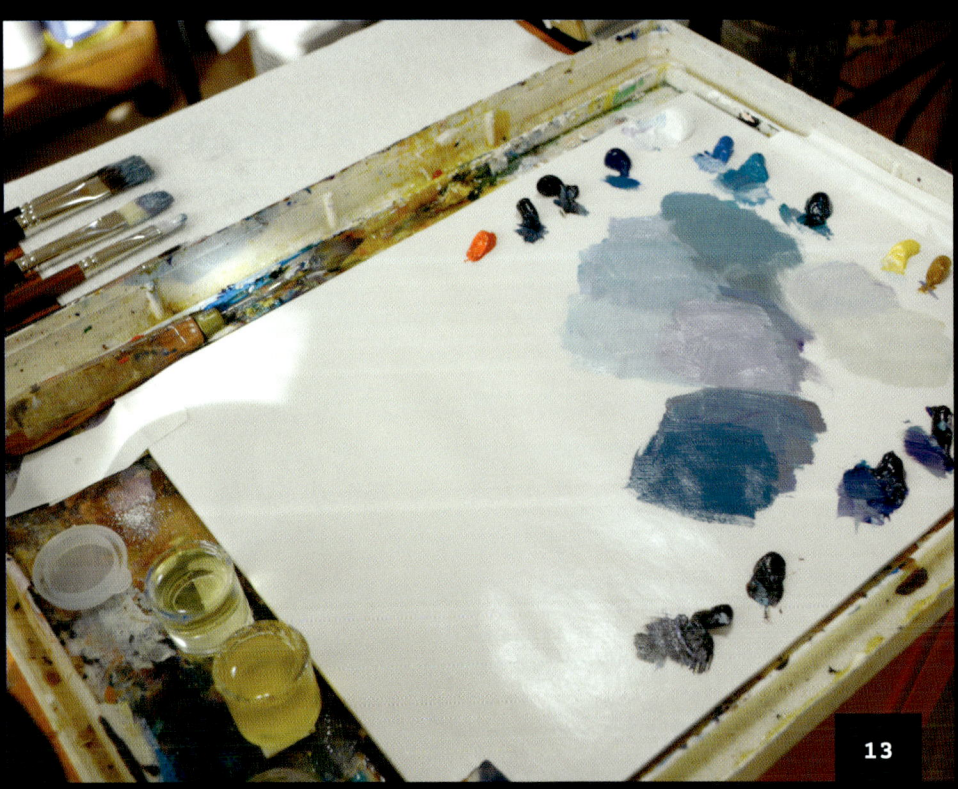

13

"Since the mood of this painting calls for various cool and dark tones, I've selected a range of pigments that will help me to achieve a similar result to my color rough"

// My palette box with pigments, and jars for M. Graham & Co Walnut Alkyd Medium and Gamblin Solvent-Free Fluid

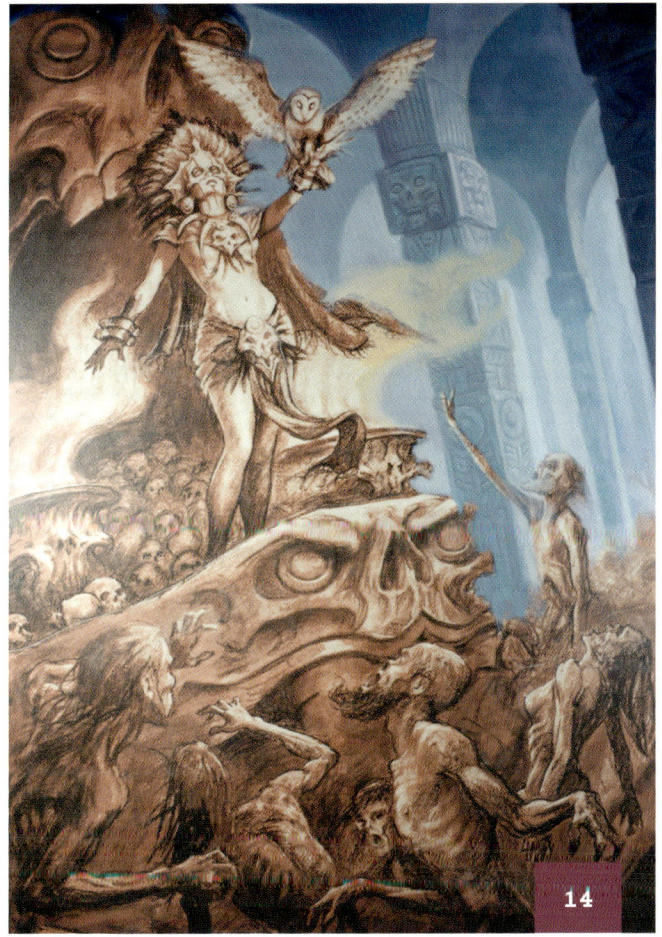

14

// The atmosphere of the chamber starts to take shape

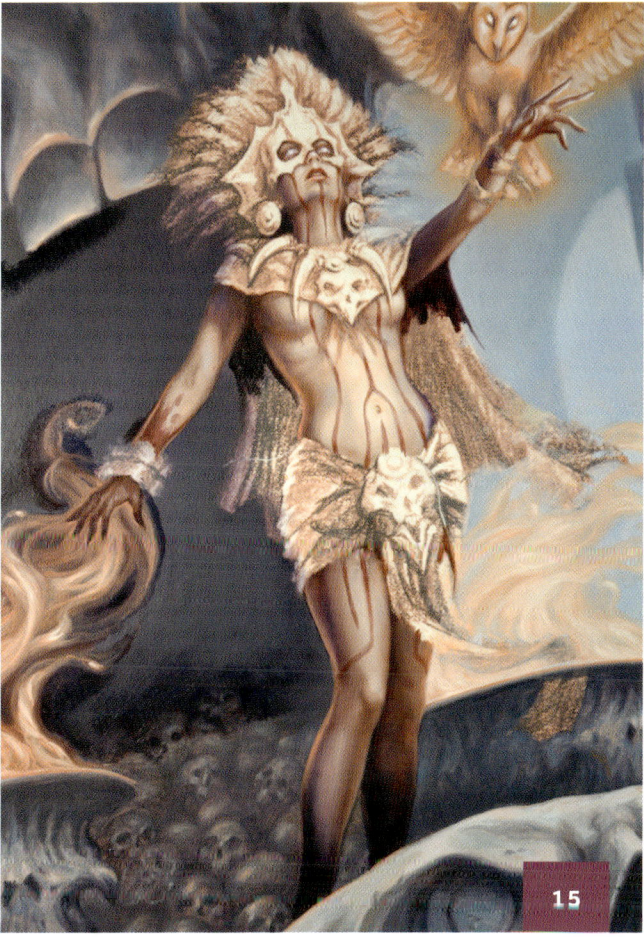

15

// Her skin tones painted from my pre-mixed group of colors

>13 Palette

Now it's time to start painting! First I need to select which pigments I will need on my palette to correspond with my color study. For this painting I choose titanium white, ultramarine blue, Payne's gray, sepia, Prussian blue, turquoise, Naples yellow, yellow ocher, burnt sienna, scarlet lake, alizarin crimson, Mars violet, ultramarine violet, dioxazine purple, raw umber, and burnt umber. Since the mood of this painting calls for various cool and dark tones, I have selected a range of pigments that will help me to achieve a similar result to my color rough.

>14 Starting with the background

I start this painting in the same way as most of my paintings: background first. I usually begin with the elements in the distance, in this case the far columns and vaulted ceiling of the goddess' underworld hall. Painting parts of the scene that are further in the distance allows me to more easily overlap objects

// PRO TIP
Glazing

If you are painting with oils, a good technique for adding hints of color, pumping up the saturation of a magic spell, darkening a shadow, or adding a glow (such as the shafts of light) is called "glazing." Glazing is a method that involves using colors that are made very thin by adding a lot of painting medium to them so that they become transparent. This thin layer of paint can be added on top of a section you have already painted, like a Photoshop layer, but you have to be a hundred percent sure that the section is dry first or else you will risk smearing. If you add these thin layers slowly, allowing each application to dry first, you can achieve very luminous results.

in the foreground and create smooth transitions. That way I don't have to worry so much about accidentally painting over something I have spent a long time working on. As I work, I pay close attention to my colors and values, using my sketch and color study as guides.

>15 Color grouping

Just as I work in groups from background to foreground, I also often work on

specific sections that contain a certain group of colors one at a time, for example the goddess' skin. I mix up a batch of colors that relate to all of her skin tones and paint those sections from start to finish in one sitting. This way I can avoid trying to match exact color mixtures again after part of the section has dried, helping me to save time and avoid problems later.

>16 Solidifying and expanding upon

As I work through completing the painting, section by section, I constantly improve upon and modify minor details that were only suggested in my preliminary sketch and color rough. Paying close attention to my reference photos as well as using my imagination keeps the process fun. I constantly check to make sure that my colors and details add to the mood I want to evoke. In the case of "awe" I make sure that Mictecacihuatl is standing strong and is highlighted enough to make her pop. I also make sure that the tormented souls have appropriate expressions, especially the one who is reaching up. I want him to stand out enough and have just the right desperate yearning on his face to strongly visually tie the crowd in with goddess.

>17 Finishing up

Once I have filled in all my sections for the painting, I often have a few last touches before calling it finished. Usually this stage involves glazing thin layers of color to darken or enrich areas, as well as adding small final details and highlights. This is when I add some shafts of light into the background to give that area some extra interest. These beams of light also make everything look a little more majestic. The finishing touches are always my favorite part, because this is the stage when a painting really comes to life!

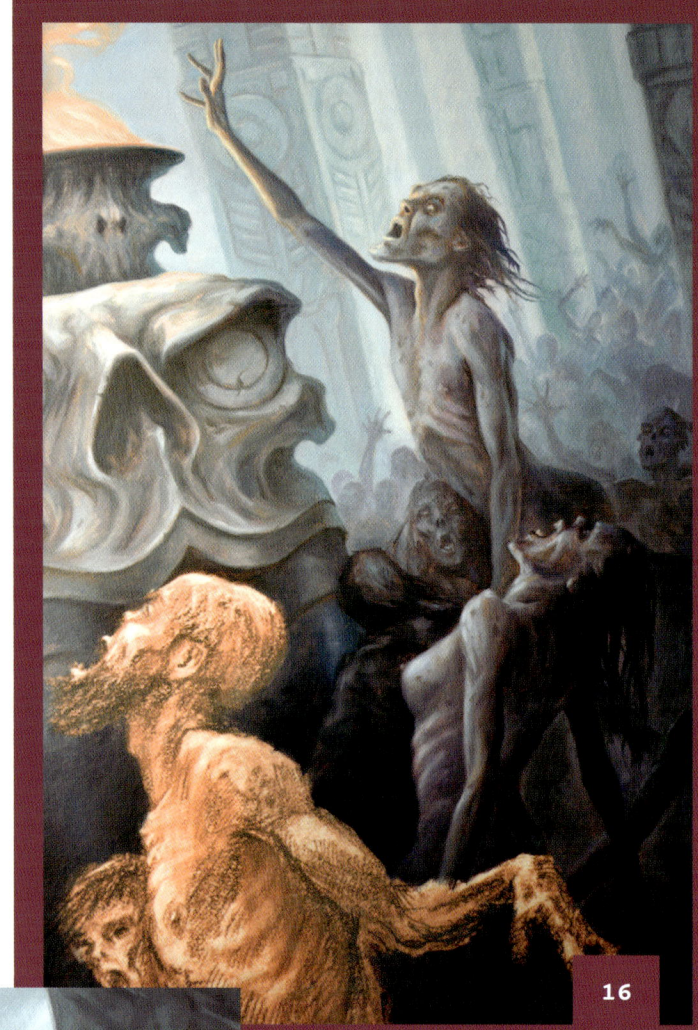

16

// I defined the distant figures more and included a few new faces

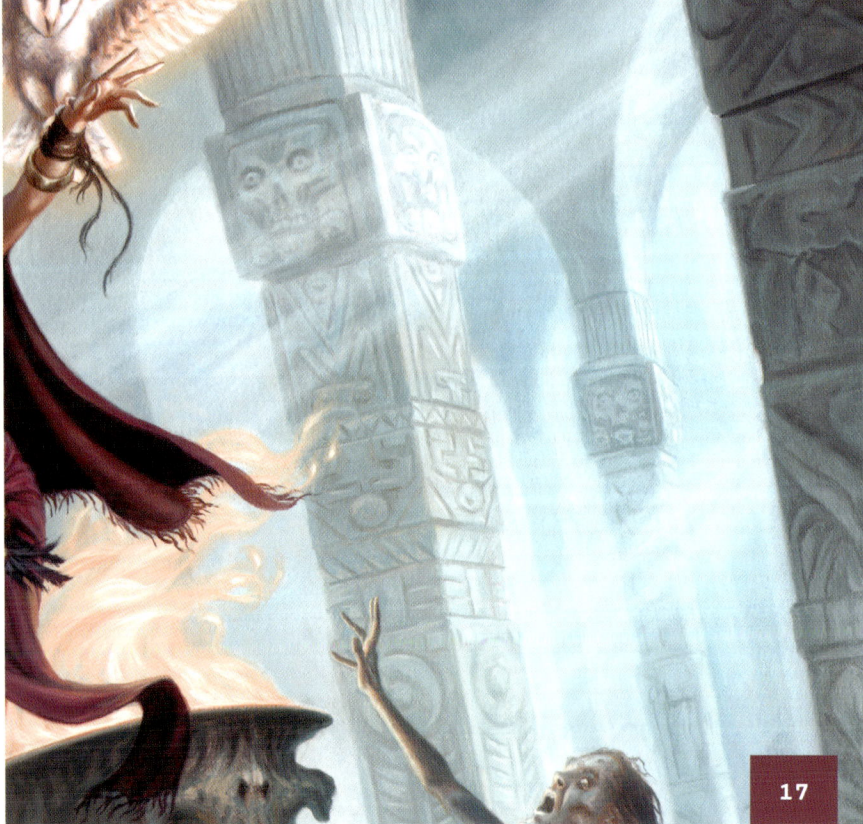

17

// A detail of the light beams that I add as one of the final touches

>18 Final digital tweaks

After coating the finished painting with spray retouch varnish, I like to scan the image into the computer for the last step. Sometimes scanning or photographing a painting doesn't capture the colors or feel of the painting accurately, so I often open the file in Photoshop and use slight color adjustments to get the image as close to the final painting as possible. If there are some areas that I feel can be pushed darker or made lighter, I make those minor adjustments now. I want the digital image to look as good as possible, since this is the file that will be used for printing, my website, social media, and so on.

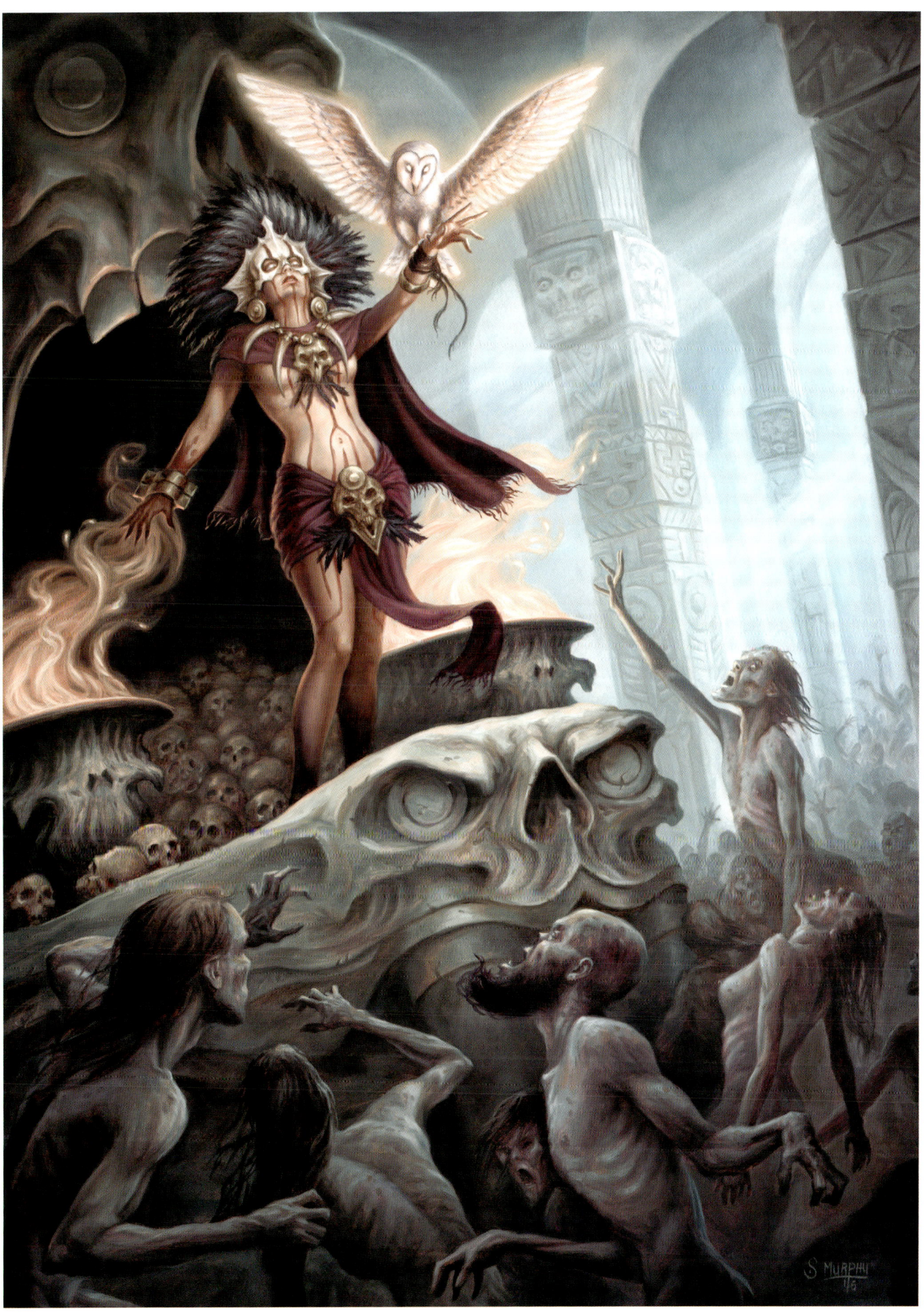

Ørjan Ruttenborg Svendsen | www.svendsenart.com

Courage

The theme for this tutorial is "courage" and I will produce a fantasy illustration for this. You could come up with a thousand different ways to portray this particular theme but, being a Norwegian myself, my mind instantly jumps to Vikings in an epic battle scene, fighting a presumably undefeatable monster. The Vikings believed that everything was fated and planned out by the gods, so whether or not you would be successful in battle was already decided before it started. They also believed that the only way into Valhalla, the hall of the gods and their representation of "heaven," was to be fearless in the face of death and die a glorious death in battle.

I remember when I was in school how much I hated all the work they made us do before even starting a painting. But now, as I become more experienced as an illustrator, I find that I spend more and more of my production time in the planning and early stages of a painting than I do on the rendering itself. In this tutorial I will try to show you why, and cover every step I take when making a full production painting. I will show you the decisions and struggles I face, how I solve them, and help you to understand how you can improve your own process and decision making. I will be using Adobe Photoshop, but you can still follow my workflow if you are using traditional medium.

When I plan out my paintings, I like to ask myself these questions: "What?", "Who?", "Where?", and "Why?" You can of course tailor this process to your own needs, but these basic questions never fail to give that one-line pitch you need before you start. In this case it becomes: "A Viking returns to his village as it is being attacked by a fearsome beast and comes to its defense!"

>01 Inspiration and reference

So I've decided what I want to paint. However, just pulling an epic scene out of nowhere can be hard, and that white canvas can be intimidating.

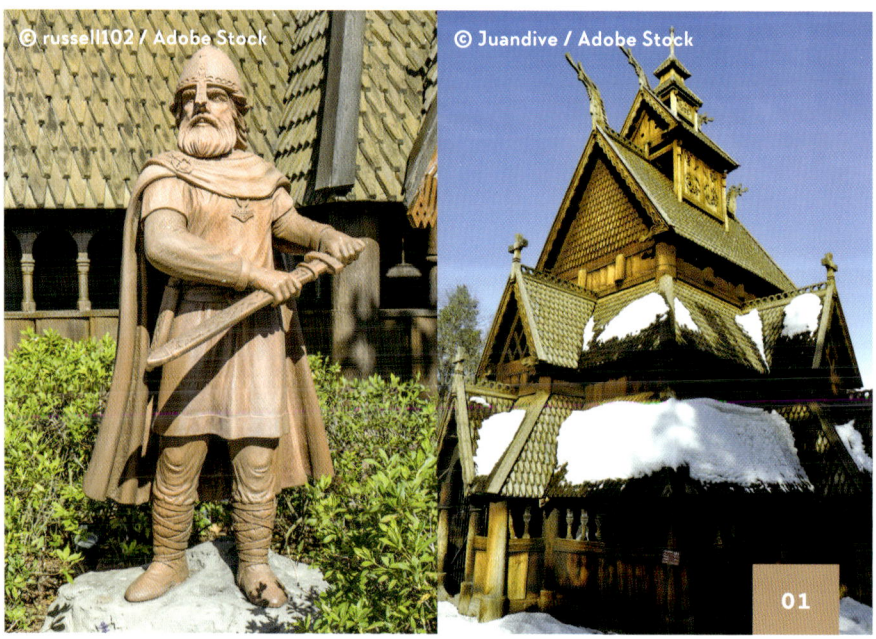

© russell102 / Adobe Stock

© Juandive / Adobe Stock

01

// **Inspiration and reference**

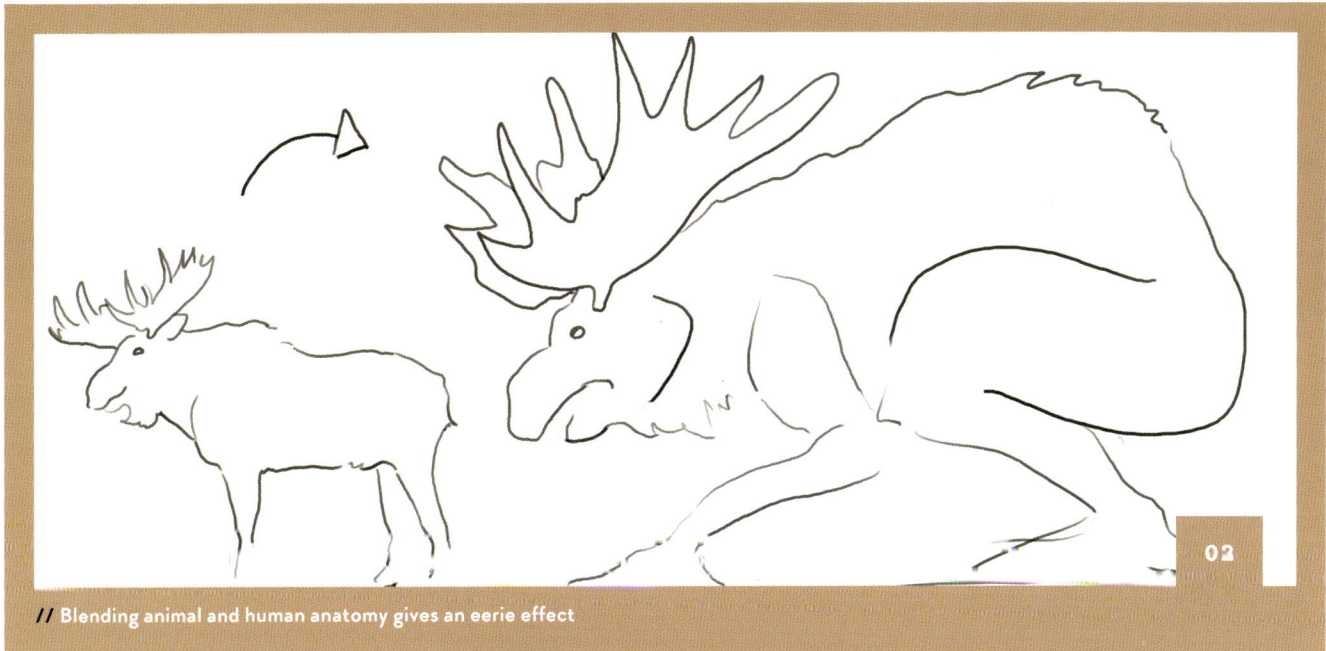

// **Blending animal and human anatomy gives an eerie effect**

scaring you to procrastinate time and again. When I need to get in the mood to make art, I scour the internet for pictures and artwork that match my selected theme until something pops into my head. Movies, music, and games are also great sources of inspiration, and having something appropriate running in the background is a great way to keep myself in the mood.

Whenever I'm dealing with something historical, it's mandatory to research it. Apparel, architecture, and nature are the most visually important, and we should not forget the cultural cues we can use in our storytelling either. When looking for reference, I try to find historical and factual ones. Looking at other people's artwork can be inspirational, but I don't want to base my own designs on that. Even though I'm making fantasy art, I always try look at reality, and find the most original point of reference to avoid being derivative.

>02 The ten percent rule

In the first step I talked about limiting myself to reality, so now I must try to take the shackles off. After all, I *am* producing fantasy art, and restricting myself to the rules of the real world and the facts of history just won't do! Some people might be satisfied depicting "what is" or "what was," but if I have a choice in the matter, I will always spice it up. Keep

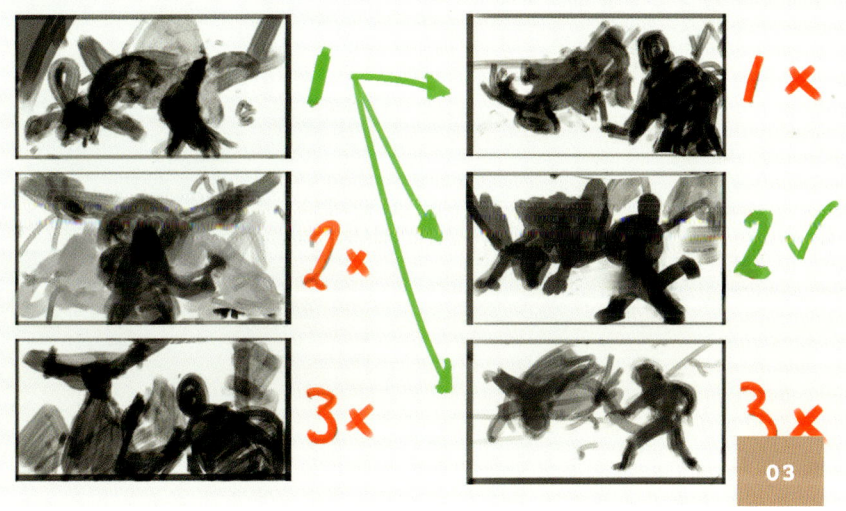

// **Three initial thumbnails, then three more variations of the "best" one**

in mind, though, that if you make it too unrealistic, people will lose their point of reference, so a good basic rule of fantasy is to change ten percent while keeping ninety percent true to reality.

When designing all fictional elements, I start the factual to ground the fantasy in reality. I have chosen to base my design on a moose, an animal common to the Norse woods. These are about the size and shape of a horse, with large antlers and a broader back. The really defining feature are the antlers so I have decided to emphasize these and make them the biggest recognizable element. The head will also be moose-like, but I will greatly enlarge its size and give it a more human-like crawling

body. Mixing animal anatomy with human always produces something creepy and mystical in my experience!

>03 Thumbnails and composition

Thumbnailing, in my opinion, is the most important step of the process. Sometimes you might be set on a certain composition in your mind, but I urge you to take the time to make some thumbnails anyway. You might just surprise yourself. Create at least three, but it wouldn't be unwise to double that, then show them to a trusted art friend. Whether you agree with their choices or not, you might gain valuable tips or insights you had not thought of, or hadn't previously noticed, that can help you optimize your final composition.

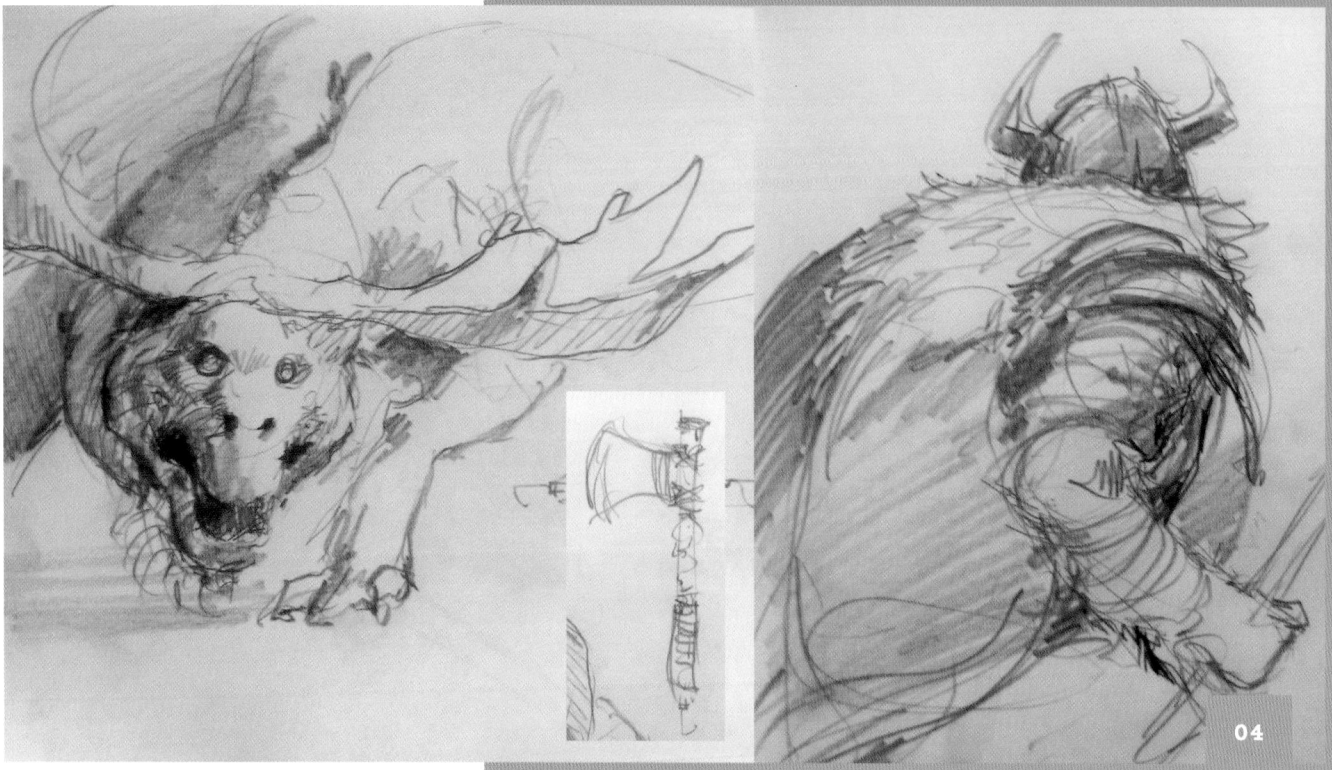

// **Having fun sketching out individual parts of the composition**

>04 Doodles and sketching
Before I start refining my thumbnail, I like to sketch out parts of the painting that I feel will become important, or concept ideas I have for the characters and environment. These sketches are loose and fast, but can be very useful to have around when you start putting hours into the rendering. Usually, the more you detail something, the harder it is to keep the life and vigor of the sketch, so having these concepts up on the wall next to you while working can help remind you of what you initially wanted to achieve.

>05 Refining the thumbnail
Now I've chosen my thumbnail and produced some sketches, the hardest part of the process is complete, considering a bad composition will almost never result in a good painting. Positioning the viewer behind the warrior increases the sense of bravery and danger, placing the audience in the scene and helping them to associate with the image more.

Now it's time to marry the composition and sketches together, aiming to produce some interesting shapes and planes. It's important

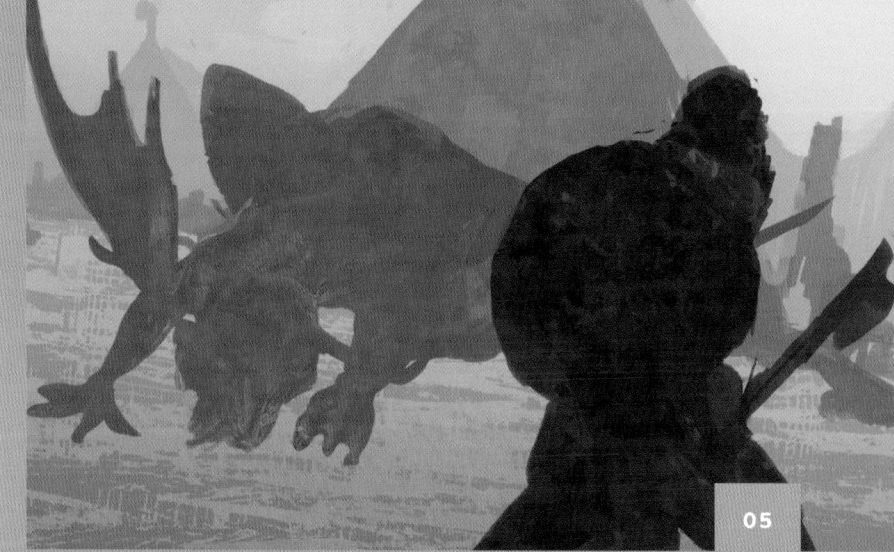

// At this point I tighten up the thumbnail and divide the planes into layers

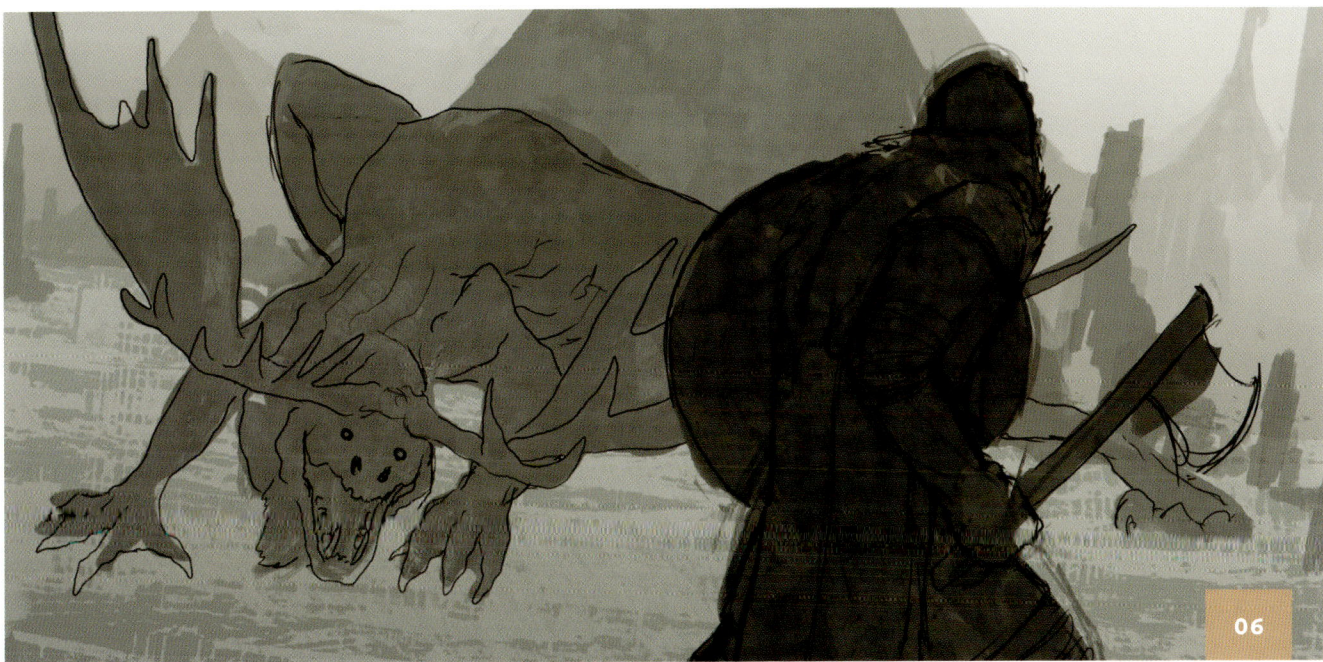

// I roughly define the content within the shapes

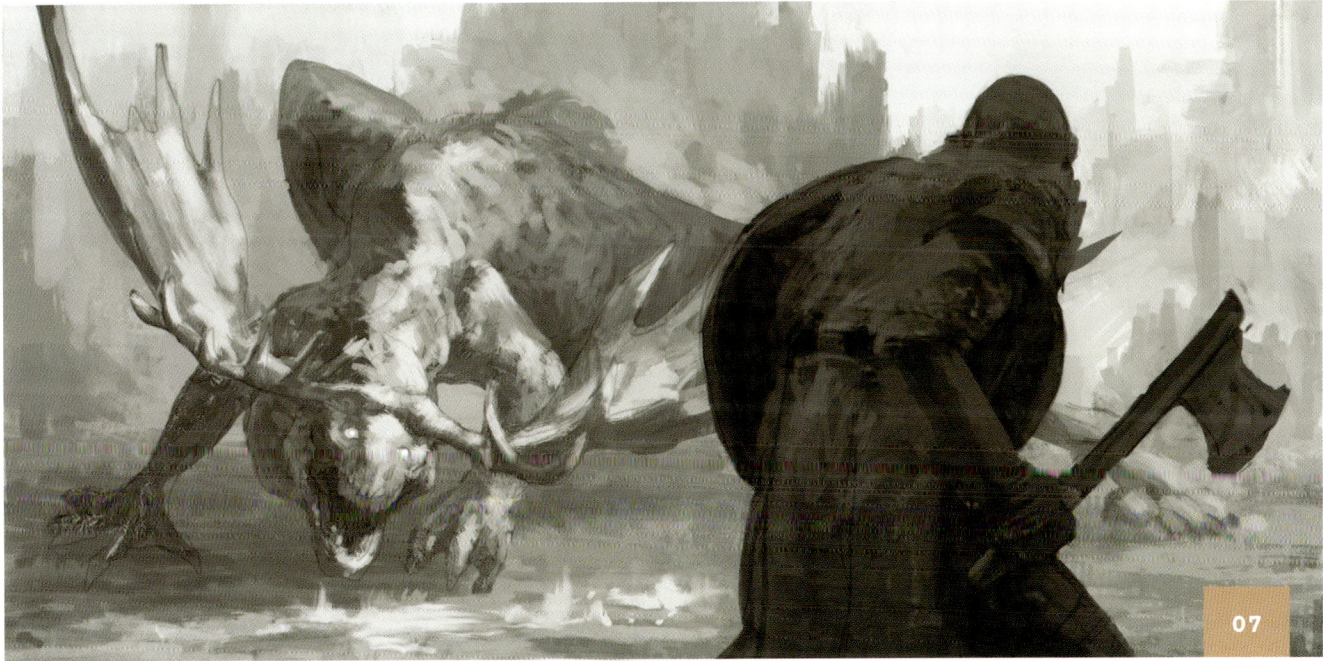

// I like to start painting in grayscale

that the tones of these planes are clear, with distinct foreground, middle ground, and background areas to create depth and distance. I try to add some texture to it sooner rather than later (rather than adding solid blocks of color), as it helps to me to get into a more "designer" mindset.

>06 The final sketch

When all the elements fit well together, I use the work from step 04 to create a fast sketch on top of my shapes. Some artists

carry out a detailed line drawing and some might just go straight into painting, but I like to define the most important parts before I start hacking away at the image. It takes a little more time, but in my experience it always ends up better in the end. Do what fits your workflow best.

>07 Values

Some people go straight to color, but I always start in grayscale, as it's easier to get the values down accurately. I

make sure I don't take the painting too far at this stage, as I find it very hard to achieve good colors by just colorizing a "finished" black-and-white painting. I always keep a small version of my painting on a second screen to check the shapes appear correct (if you are working traditionally you can simply step back and take a look at it from a distance); achieving the right shapes and values is the most important task at this point!

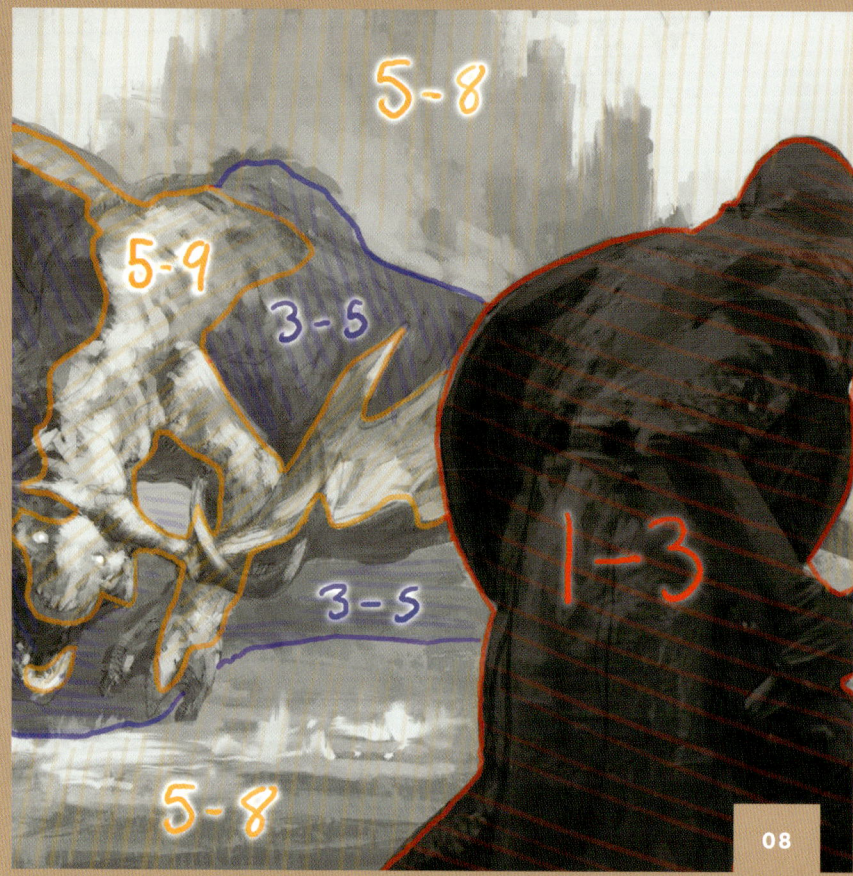

// **Know your values and keep it consistent**

>08 Starting with the mid-range

When creating values, I always build them up from the mid-range, and try to separate what is in light and what is in shadow. I never start with totally white and totally black. Imagine if white is 10, and black is 0; I make the light 7 and the dark 3, then use 5–10 to render in the light, and 1–3 to render in the dark. I don't use anything above 5 in the dark, or anything below 5 in the light. I learned this from digital painter Craig Mullins on the Sijun Forums.

>09 Choosing my palette

Picking colors has always been one of the hardest parts of painting for me. When you are painting digitally, you have all the colors in the world to choose from, and that can lead you totally astray. I advise you to find a color wheel, draw a triangle on it, and use only the hues contained in that triangle. This will give you two main colors that are close to each other, and one contrast color. Use these three colors first! You can always add more hues later, but keeping the base color scheme simple is the key to good balance. Research "gamut masking" if you'd like to learn more about the theory behind this, or see another example of it being used on pages 160–161.

>10 Laying down the base colors

I use gradient maps and color layers to lay down a basic hue based on my palette before I proceed. Make sure you don't mess up your values in this step, and keep your colors muted and transparent. I only want to get rid of the grays, like laying a wash over it, so I can start building up the painting on top of that.

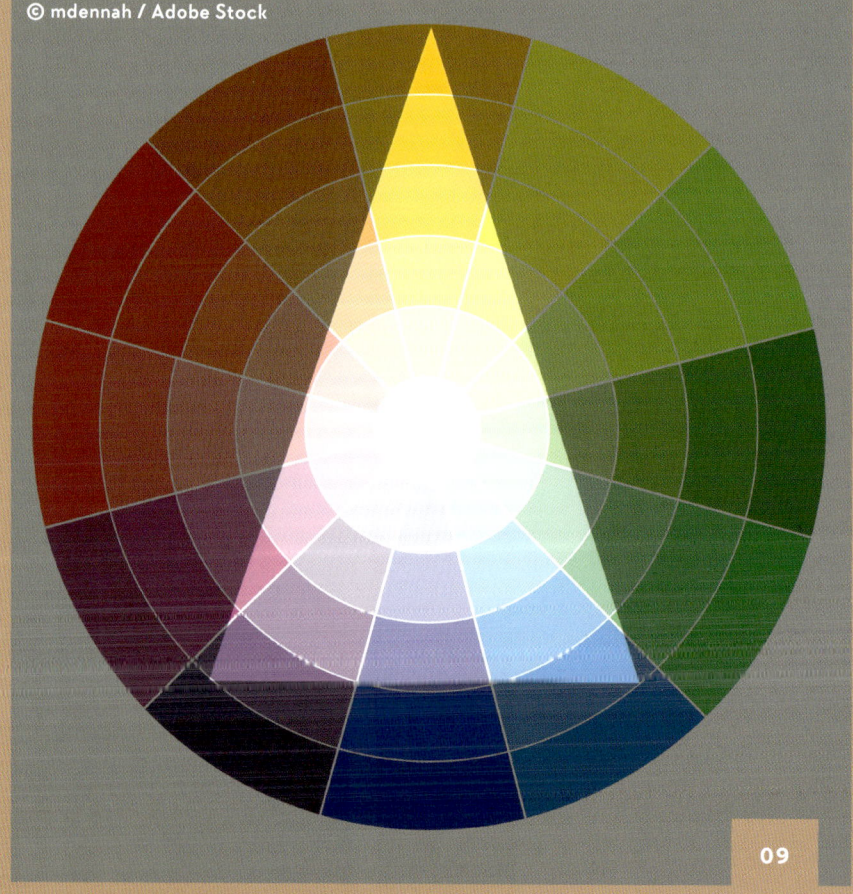

© mdennah / Adobe Stock

// **Choosing a palette**

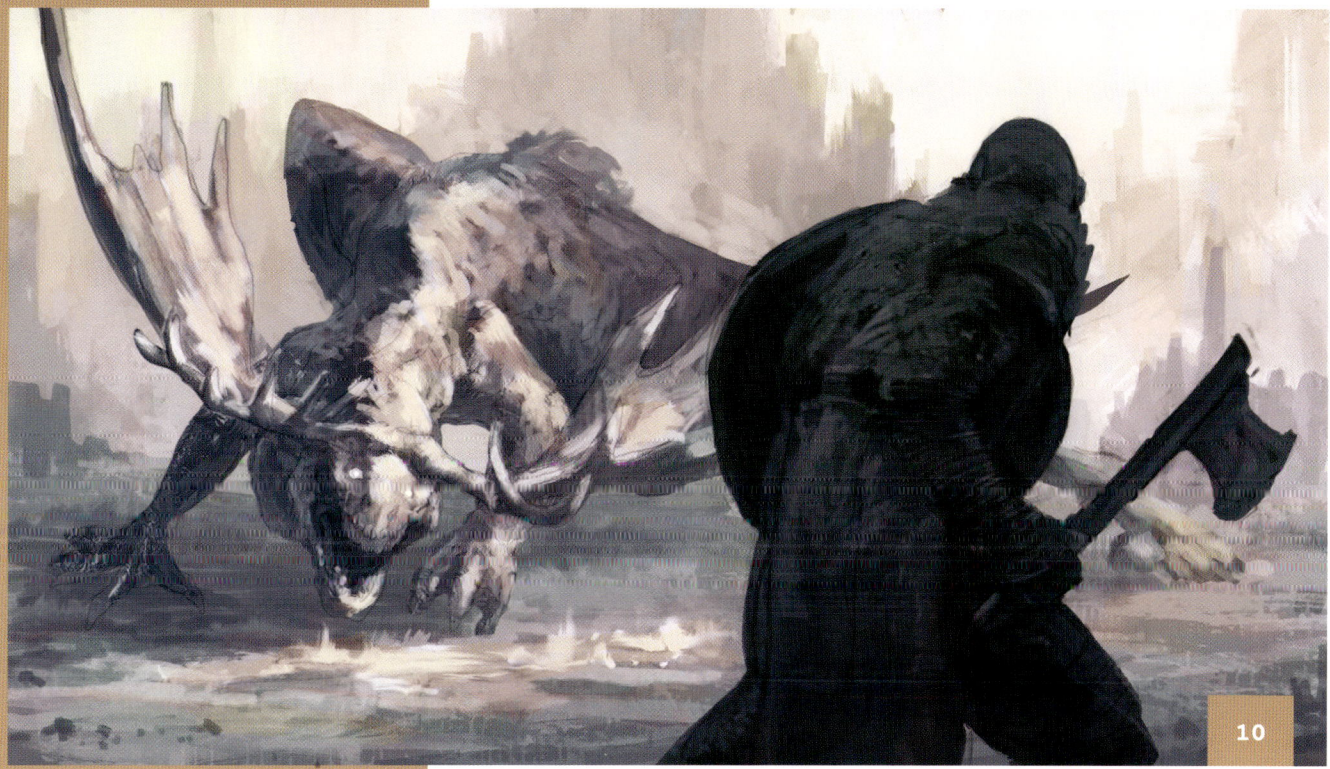

// I am only producing an underpainting at this point, so I avoid becoming too caught up in it

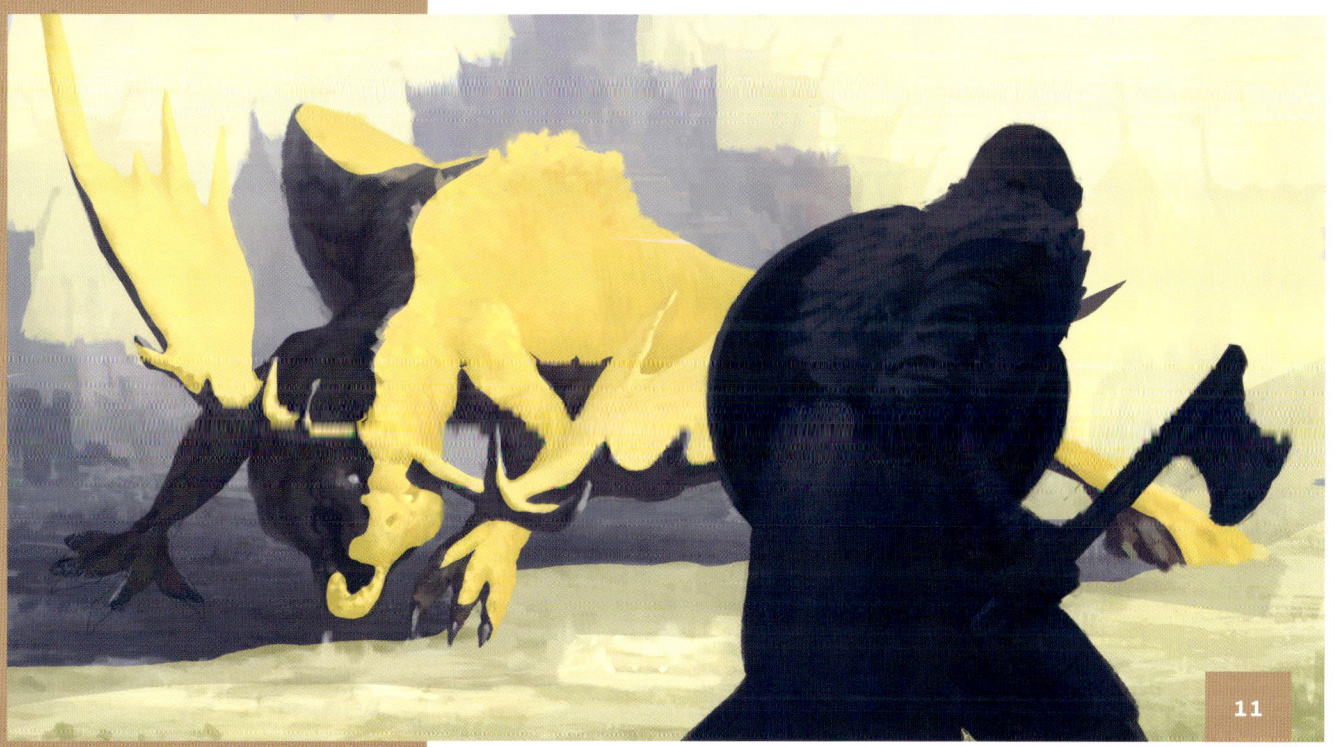

// Plan your colors to tell your story

>11 Shape the story with color and composition

Now it's time to take that palette and start smearing it across the painting. The important part here is to decide which color goes where, and that is where we must start considering the narrative

more. When I think about Vikings, I think of seas, snow, and mountains, so ideally I want to use the blues on the protagonist and his village, and let the contrasting color fall on the monster. I can do this by making blue the shadow color, and orange the sunlight color.

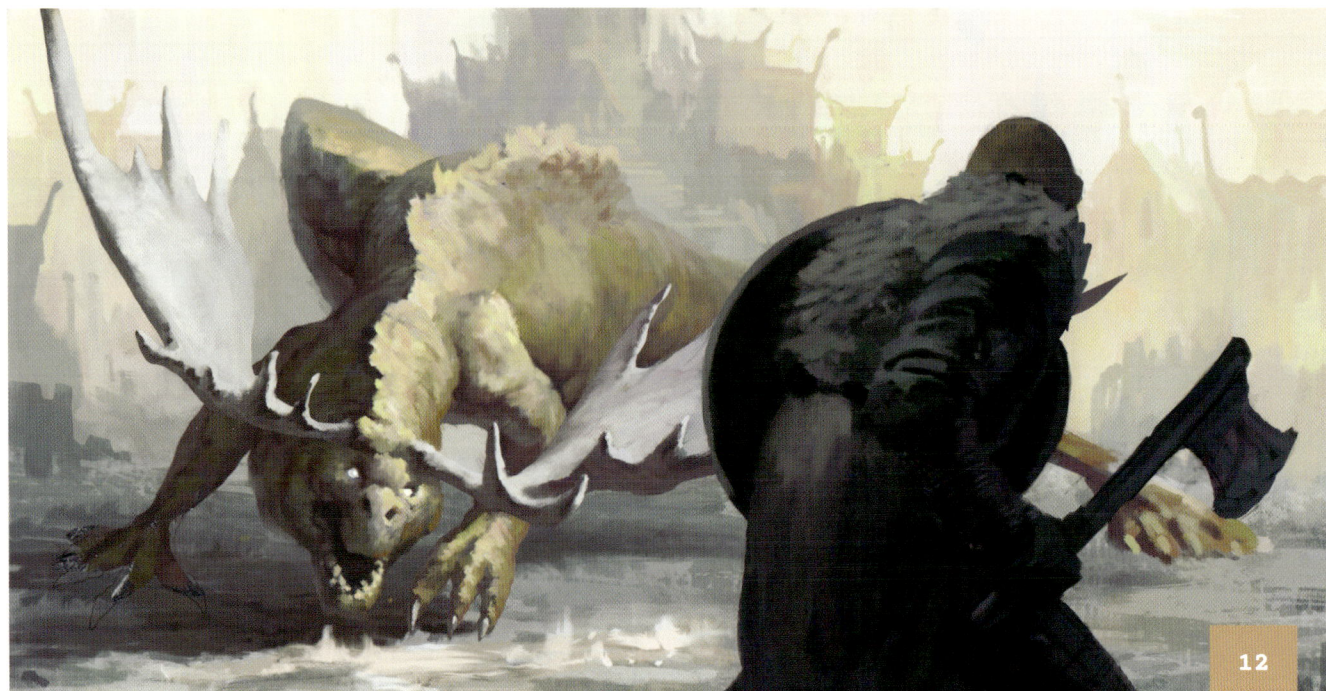

// **It's finally time to start rendering**

>12 Adding to the story

The monster has attacked his village, and I must show that the place is in peril. I want to do this by having the monster's color "take over" the village color in the form of sunlight and fire, while still keeping the shadow areas distinctly blue, symbolizing that is hasn't "fallen" just yet.

Also, in the Western world, we read and write from left to right, and therefore think of left as "home." This Viking is on his way home, but he is not there yet, so putting him to the right of the composition, while keeping the monster to the left, will help enforce the feeling that he is being kept from coming home.

>13 Keep the background subtle

I want all the focus to be on the impending fight between the Viking and the monster, so I don't want to give the background too much spotlight, but rather use it as a subtle tool to underline where the story is taking place. One of the most recognizable Norse architectural styles is the "dragon style," which can still be seen all over Norway. I decide to exaggerate these features in the buildings to make them even more

// PRO TIP

Color pick from your palette, not your painting

Whenever you mix two colors, the resulting color will be less pure, so unless you are working with solid brushes without pressure sensitivity, your strokes will never represent your selected color in its hundred percent opaque state. Considering this, you will find that continuously color picking from within your painting will desaturate your colors more and more, until you are left with bland representations of your actual palette. I like to organize my palette around what I'm painting, so I can just blend new colors if I need to and add them to it, while making sure that the saturation is still intact. It might seem like a hassle, but trust me, it really makes a difference!

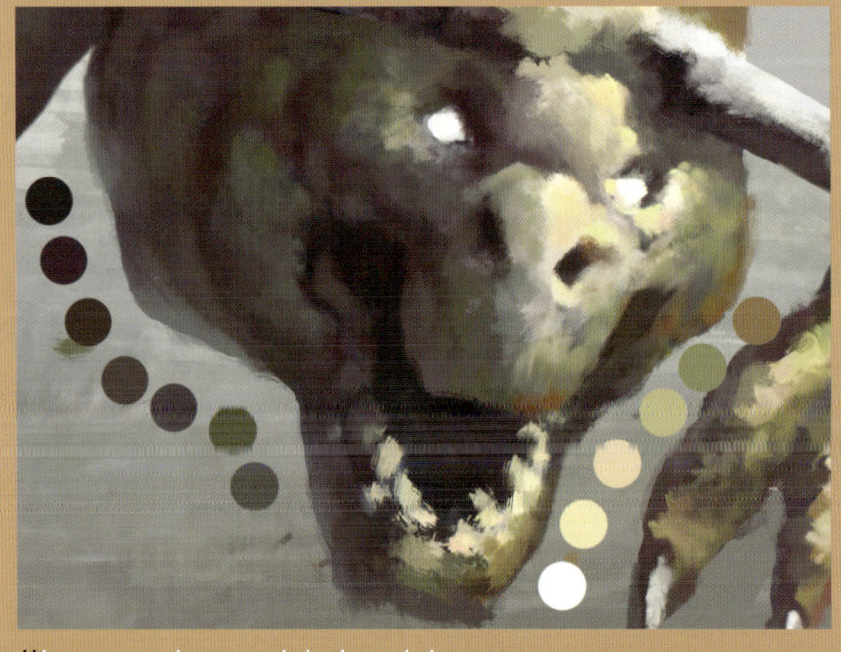

// **I arrange my palette around what I am painting**

recognizable. I use an impressionistic and loose style in order to prevent it from catching the eye too much.

"Make sure that all of your shapes read like they are supposed to, and that the storytelling elements of your illustration pop out"

>14 Add effects and story elements
When I reach the point where I am basically just rendering out, I start looking for things to add that can help to tell the story. I add smoke pillars and fire to bring some more chaos into the scene. There are also some small people in the background on the left, running towards the action.

I give the Viking hero a fur cloak, indicating that he's coming home from a trip of some sort, and also give him a horned helmet. Though the Vikings didn't actually wear these, they have become one of the most recognizable pieces of Viking attire, so it deserves a place in the fantasy universe. It gives him a more fearsome appearance, adding to the theme of courage.

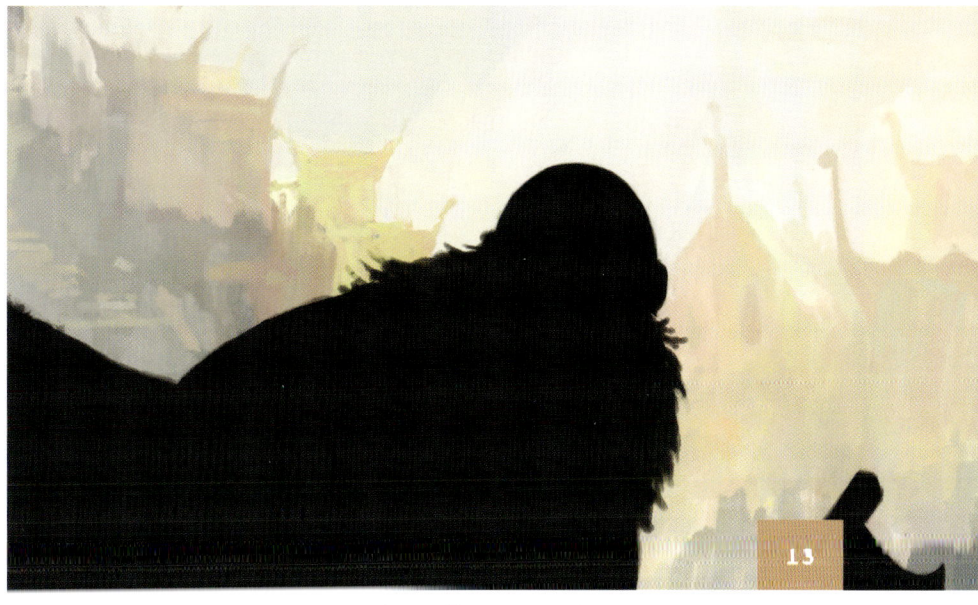

// A loose style prevents the background from taking too much focus away from the main points

>15 Finalizing the illustration
When I feel like my strokes aren't impacting the overall look of the painting any more, I put the stylus down, and let my illustration rest until the next day. Nothing spots mistakes like a pair of fresh eyes, and I want to make sure I don't overwork the painting.

When finalizing the image, you should make sure that all of your shapes read like they are supposed to, and that the storytelling elements of your illustration pop out. You might have to sacrifice some elements to achieve this, but it will always look better if you do. At this stage I would normally show the piece to a couple of trusted art friends, and unless they have some great last minute critiques for you, I would call it complete. The Viking warrior is successfully positioned and posed to convey courage in the face of battle, with color, composition, and details adding to the narrative.

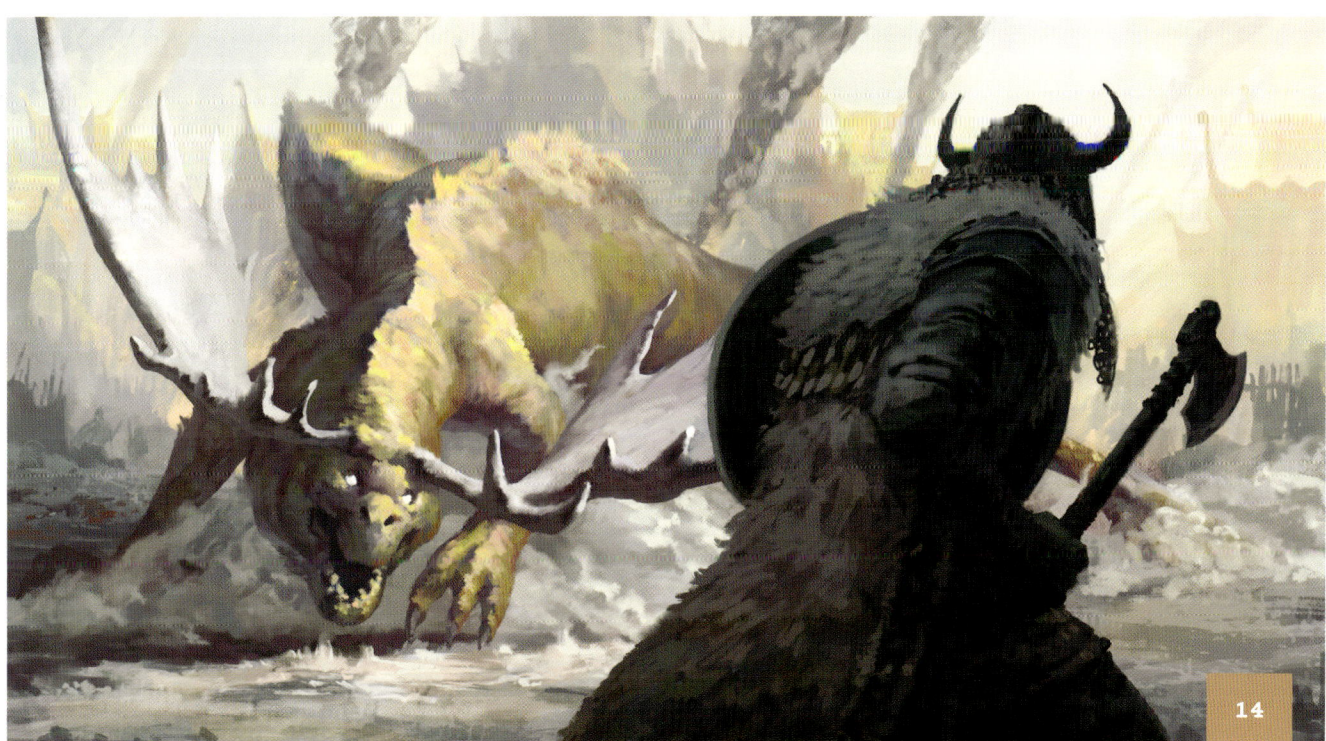

// Details help to tell the story

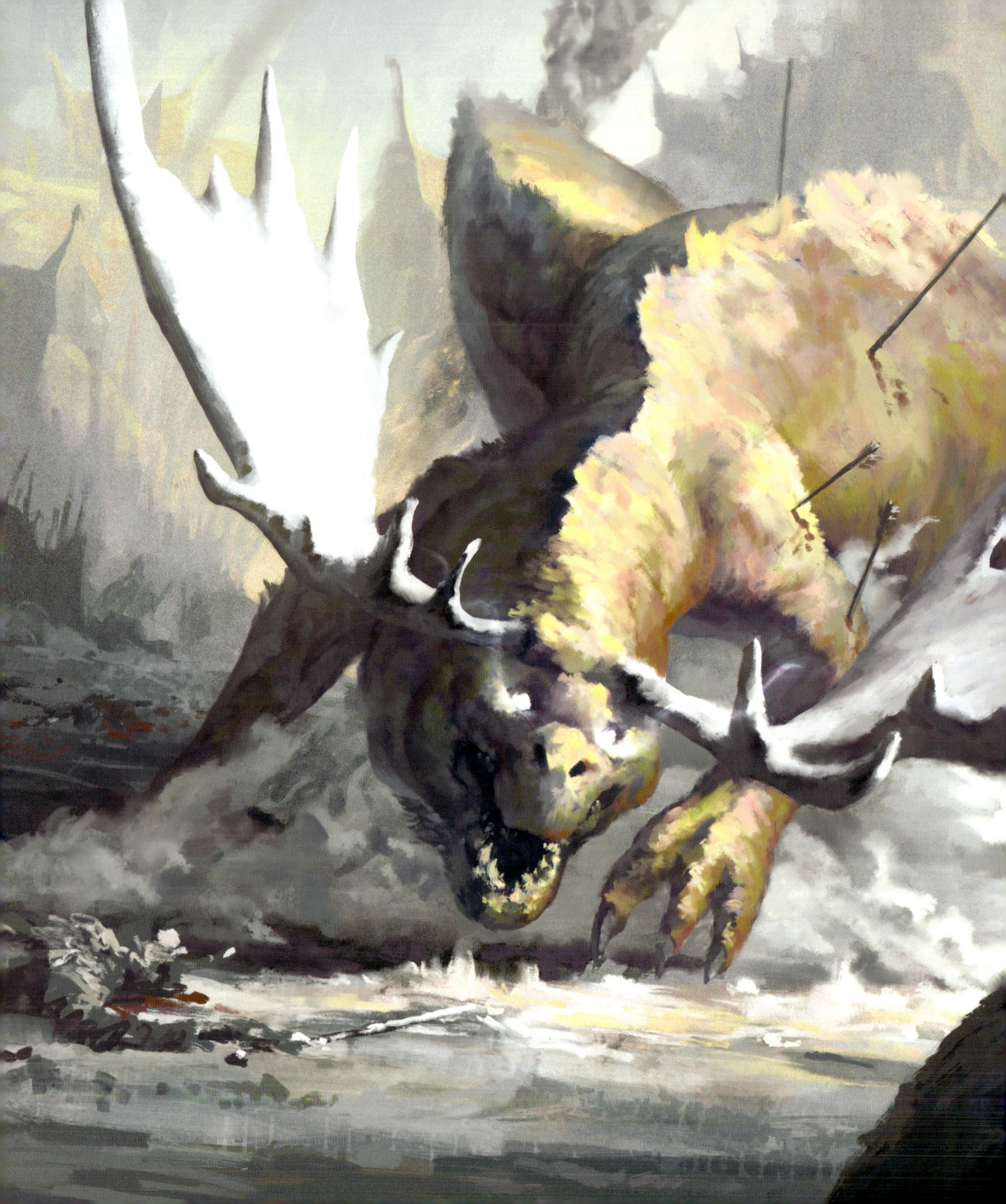

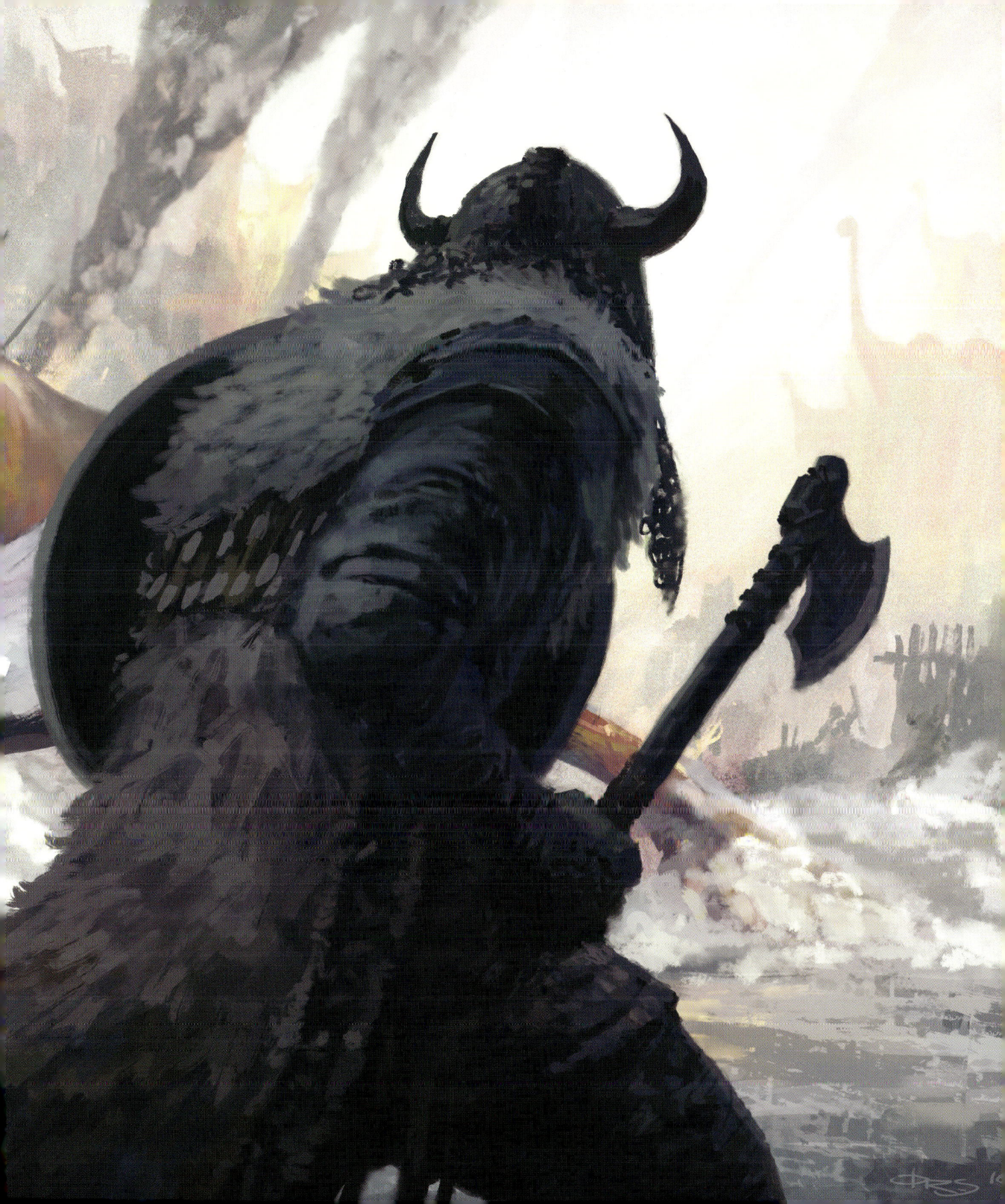

Damien Mammoliti | www.boneandbrush.com

Despair

In this tutorial I will cover the basics of illustrating the concept of "despair" as an emotion. In particular, I will focus on despair as the evocation of the lack of hope, to feel lost and helpless.

Depicting this emotion can be tough, as there are many varying degrees of hopelessness and loss. To refrain from using any real-world (or current-day) topics, I will focus on something edging more towards fantasy, using the idea of hopelessness and despair to fuel my thought process.

I will begin the tutorial by discussing the basics of setting up thumbnails to quickly sketch out ideas I may have. From there, I will delve more into evoking emotion through body language, lighting, and even color. Producing a full illustration in any media can be daunting and sometimes confusing, but I'll narrow down the complications for painting by focusing on taking early steps to make ideas clear and concise.

Despair can be a powerful emotion to evoke in your art, but don't lose hope. It won't be too hard!

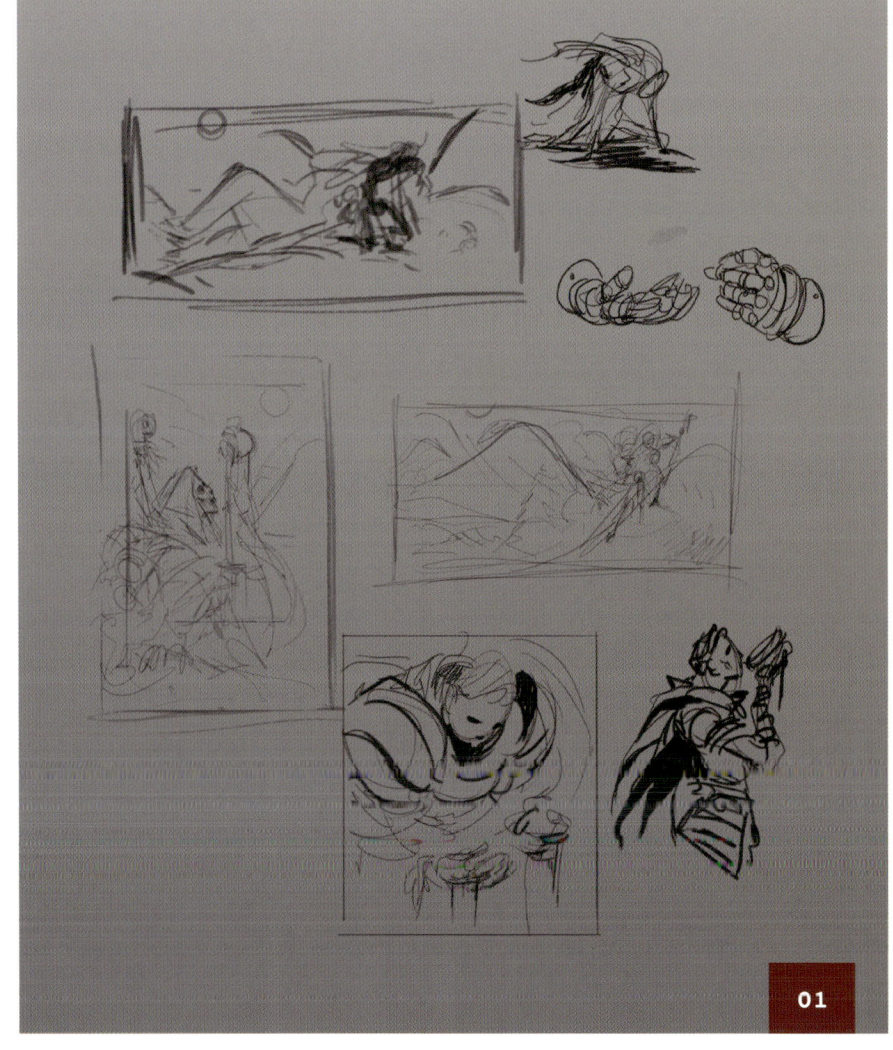

01

// *Jotting down sketches in a sketchbook for some wild ideas*

50

>01 Clarifying ideas

Sometimes ideas can come on the spur of the moment: you find yourself with a flash of an image in mind and quickly grab your tablet or paper to jot it down before it disappears. Sometimes you find that you have an idea, but you're not quite sure how to start thinking it through. Typically, when this happens, the best thing you can do is ask yourself what it is that you hope to accomplish in your painting. In this painting, I know I want to work with a figure, isolated, and hopeless. So I begin to scribble some ideas on a blank page.

>02 Sketches to thumbnails

Once I've scribbled some loose ideas, I want to try and take them to a thumbnail phase. Doing this, I can quickly create some sketches with values, and work in some thoughts about what type of figure and composition I'm looking for. The first thumbnail is a man alone in the desert desperate for water. The second is a despairing knight, having lost something. The third is a more direct representation of the emotion. Pondering through these concepts, I narrow down my ideas and move on to my references.

>03 Reference images

Once I know that I will press forward with my despairing knight idea, I go into my folders to find references of places I've visited and photographed, hoping to find some images of gnarled trees and dry grass. Luckily, I have plenty to hand, as I often journey out into the wild to find these sorts of references – they are great to have when you are an illustrator. Don't fear using references to fuel your inspiration and guide your hand. You are not the only one!

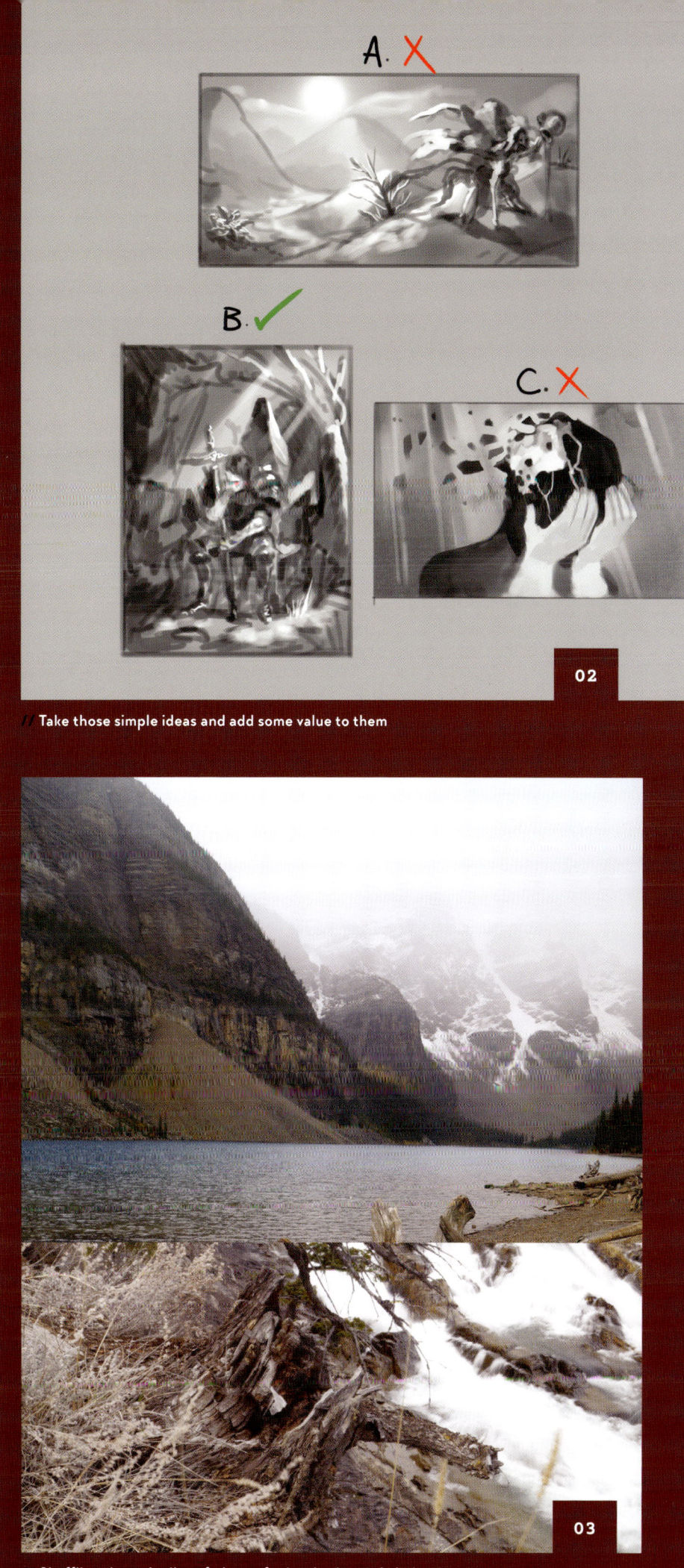

02

// Take those simple ideas and add some value to them

03

// Shuffling through piles of photos for inspiration and clarity

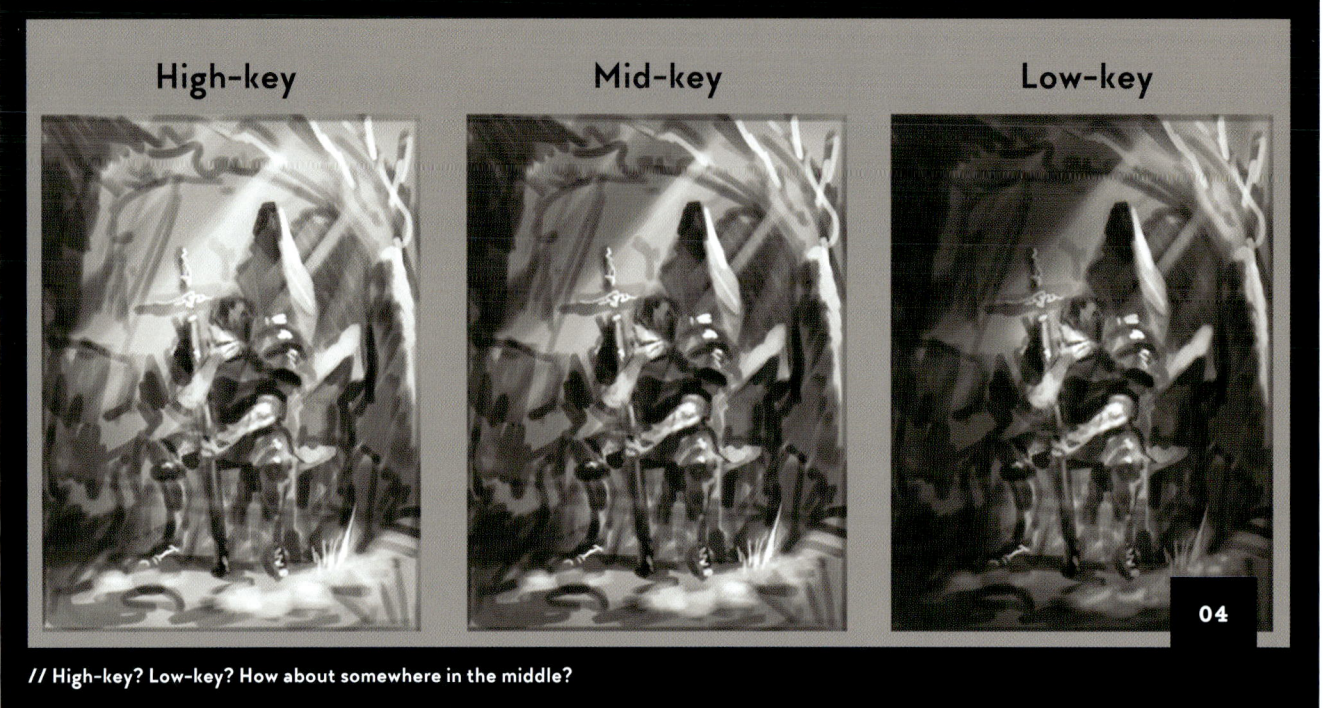

High-key   Mid-key   Low-key

04

// High-key? Low-key? How about somewhere in the middle?

>04 Keys and values

Taking my thumbnail, I want to carry out a bit of adjustment to try to find the perfect balance of light and dark before moving into my actual painting. Doing this gives me further clarity on what I hope to depict, and here I test different "keys." In photography and film, with 0% being brightest and 100% being darkest, "high-key lighting" uses values closer to pure white, so up to 10% and 30% brightness, with very little use of values darker than 70%. The opposite is true for "low-key lighting," which uses darks up to 100% (though rarely), and sparingly adds light back into a figure. For this image, I will go

// PRO TIP

Use real life
Use your own experience when depicting emotions. When was the last time you experienced despair? How did it make you feel? If you could personify and create a character based on that emotion, how would it look? Asking yourself these questions can help you to create a narrative for illustration.

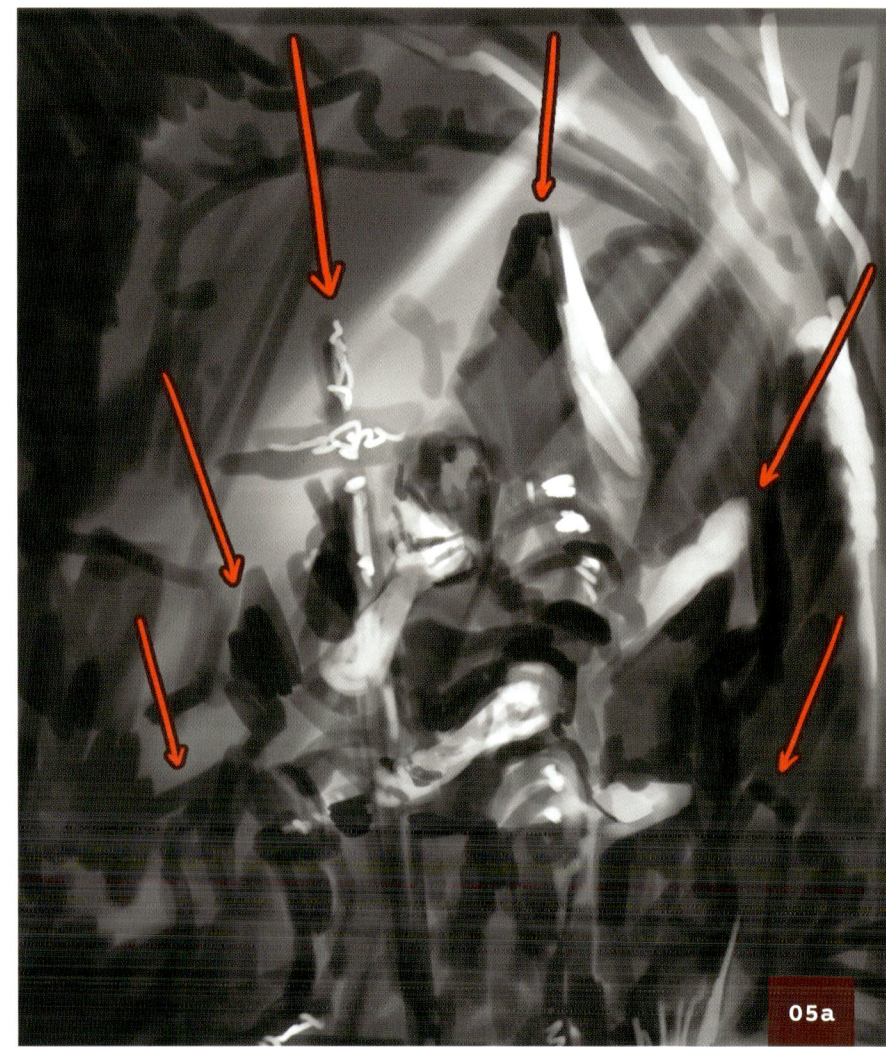

05a

// Creating directional emphasis in the composition

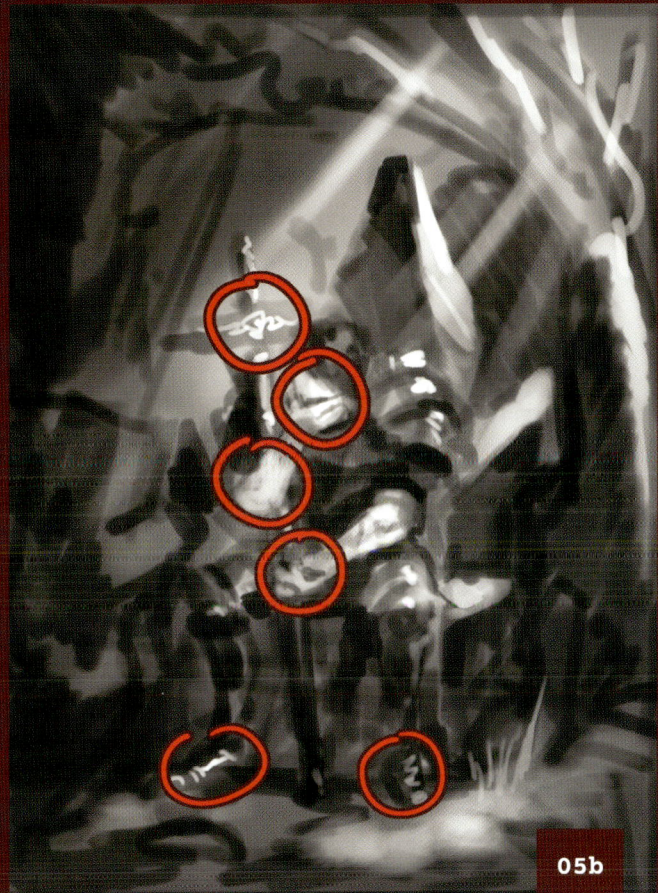

05b

// These are some areas for the viewer's eyes to rest

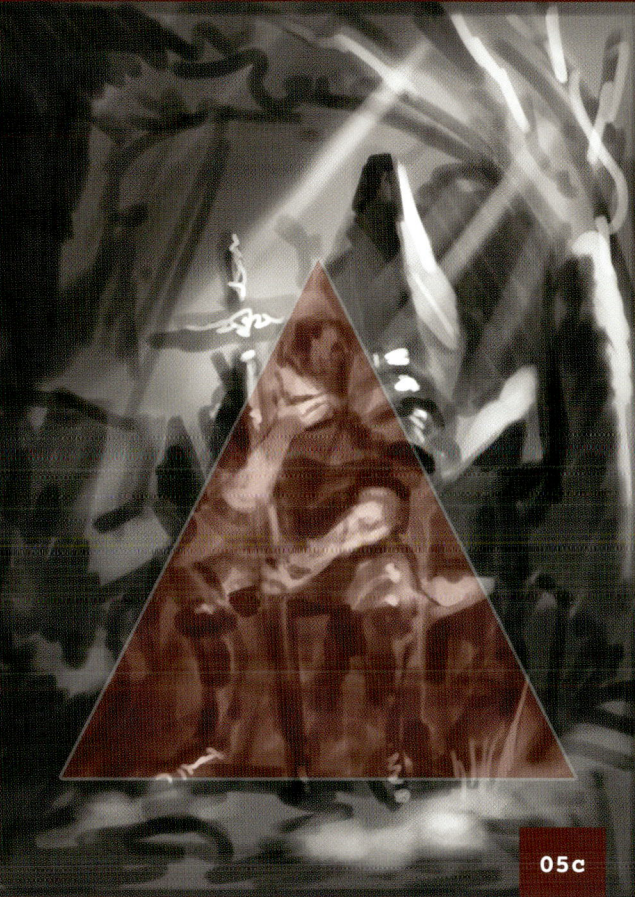

05c

// The whole image should still have a clear focal point

somewhere down the middle, as high-key lighting is
very bright but low-key lighting can be too shadowy.

>05 Compositional notes

Composition is one of those fundamentals that, when executed
correctly or incorrectly, can do a lot to affect the readability
of your work. In Images 05a and 05b my thumbnail shows
signs of directional stressing, and plenty of places to rest
the eye. It's important that the viewer has moments to look
through your image, using intersecting parts (like the cross
on the handle, or the feet resting firmly on the ground), so
the eyes wander with ease through the whole illustration.
The best compositions have things to look at throughout
the image, while also having a clear focus (image 05c).

>06 Sketching it out

Now that I have a great base to work with, I can finally start
producing my painting. I like to start with a general sketch
– one that offers a bit of a grayscale value to it, so I have a
good idea of where the key points and colors will be once
I get into them. I'm not interested in creating a sketch that
has every detail exactly as I want it, as everything incorrect
will be corrected once the painting process has begun.

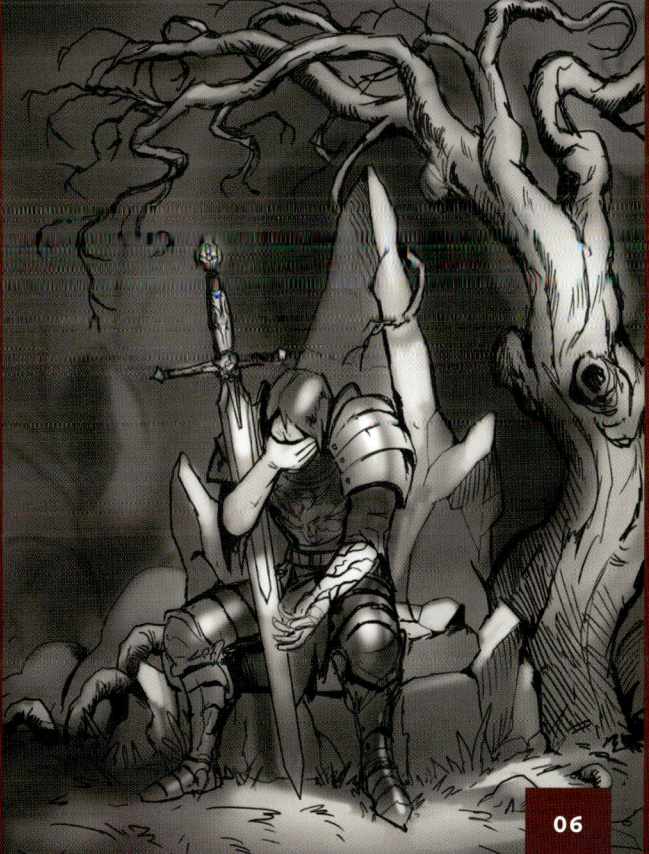

06

// Finally, the drawing begins!

// PRO TIP

Color harmony

When plotting out ideas for colors, I often like to test different ideas using some typical color combinations; complementary, analogous, and achromatic combinations being some of my favorites. Complementary means what it sounds like: opposites on the color wheel match well together and will often create a great contrast for paintings. Analogous colors are colors that sit next to one another on the color wheel; these types of combinations will offer balance. Achromatic is the lack of saturation on those colors you've chosen, which can be used to make a more emotional scene. This image will have a slightly desaturated complementary palette to help reflect the feeling of despair.

Complementary
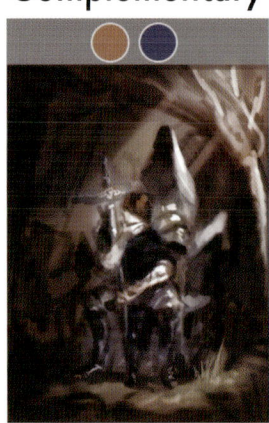

Analogous
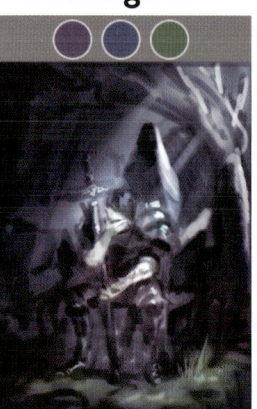

Achromatic
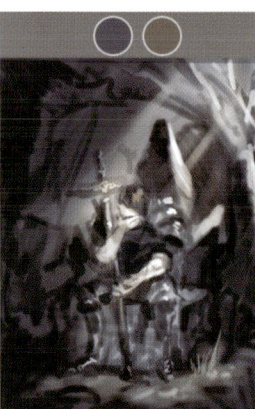

// Complementary, analogous, achromatic – what does it mean?

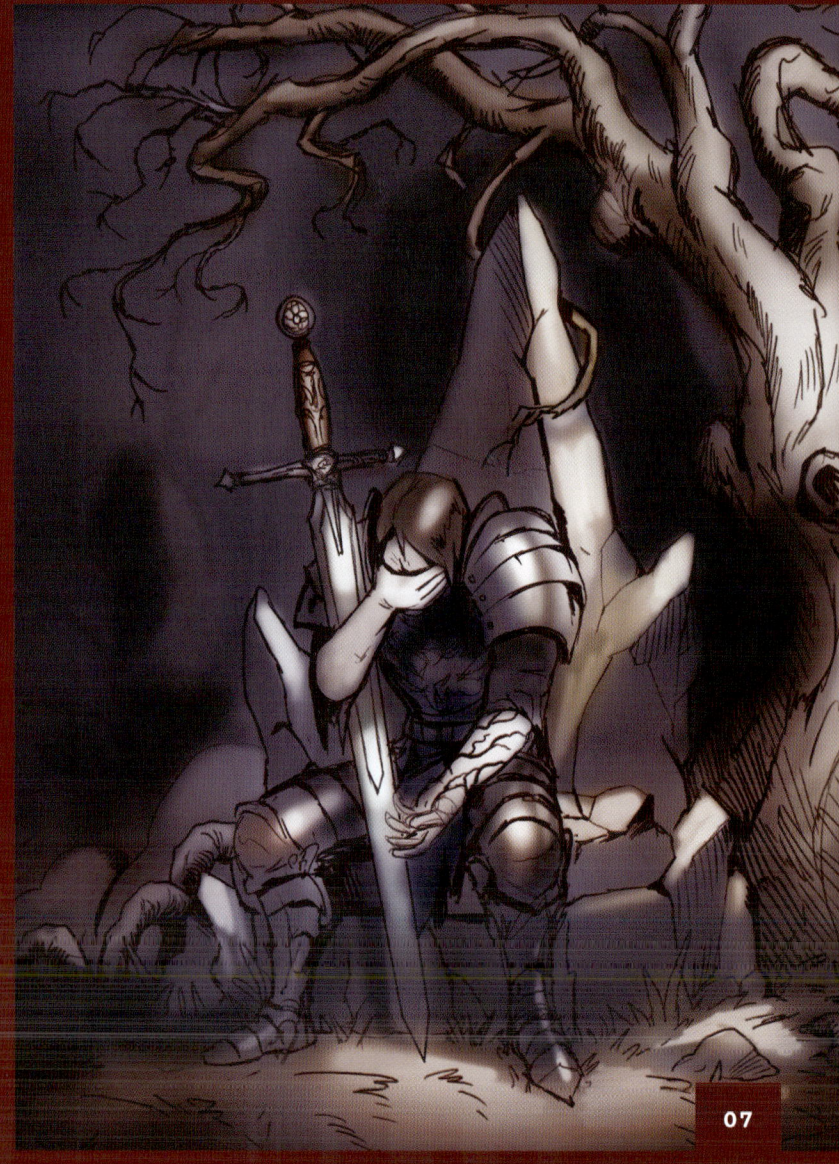

>07 Color roughing the sketch

Now that I have my basic values, I can add in some basic colors. The goal here is not to achieve every variation of blue or orange I may use in the illustration, because in the process of painting, the blend of some of these base colors will work wonders to create a palette for me to choose from. For now, my approach is simply to add in some colors until the whole image feels balanced and at the right saturation.

07

// Choose your colors, but don't worry about choosing them precisely yet

>08 Light it up

Now that I have the basic idea of what colors the light and shadows are, I can emphasize those ideas by adjusting the lighting from the base sketch I made before. Knowing that I want to create a sort of "spotlight" on the character, I add in some basic light rays and general shadows, giving a bit more clarity and guidance to how the character will be lit for the final piece. I keep in mind the layering of objects (see next step), to understand what will be lit and what will not.

>09 Layering

When I think about the depth and structure of an image, I look for the foreground, middle ground, and background. I know the character will be in the foreground, and yet just behind him is the tree, along with the rocks and roots. I pay attention to these as I know they need to be visually separated and further back from the knight; I don't want them to compete for attention and make the image appear flat. The background, hidden far behind, keeps things in perspective.

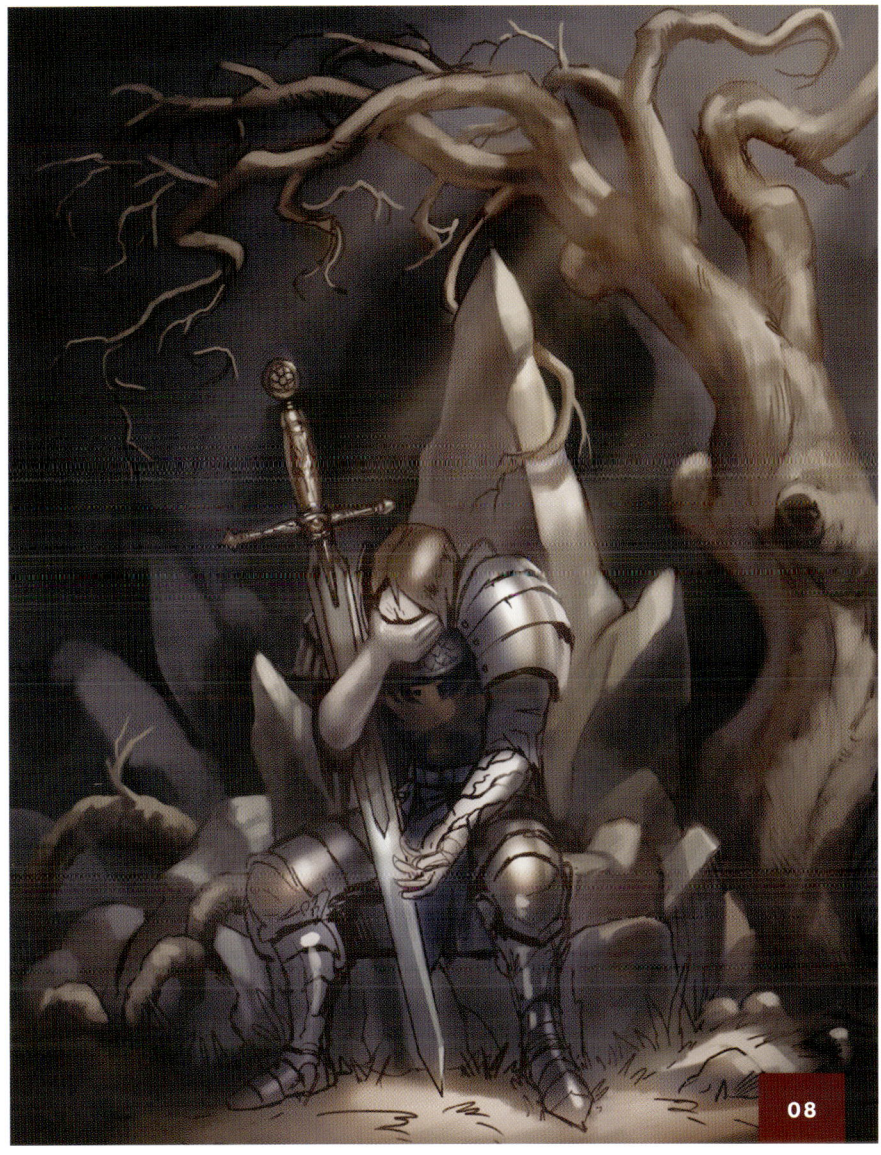

// Putting the greater values over the color rough

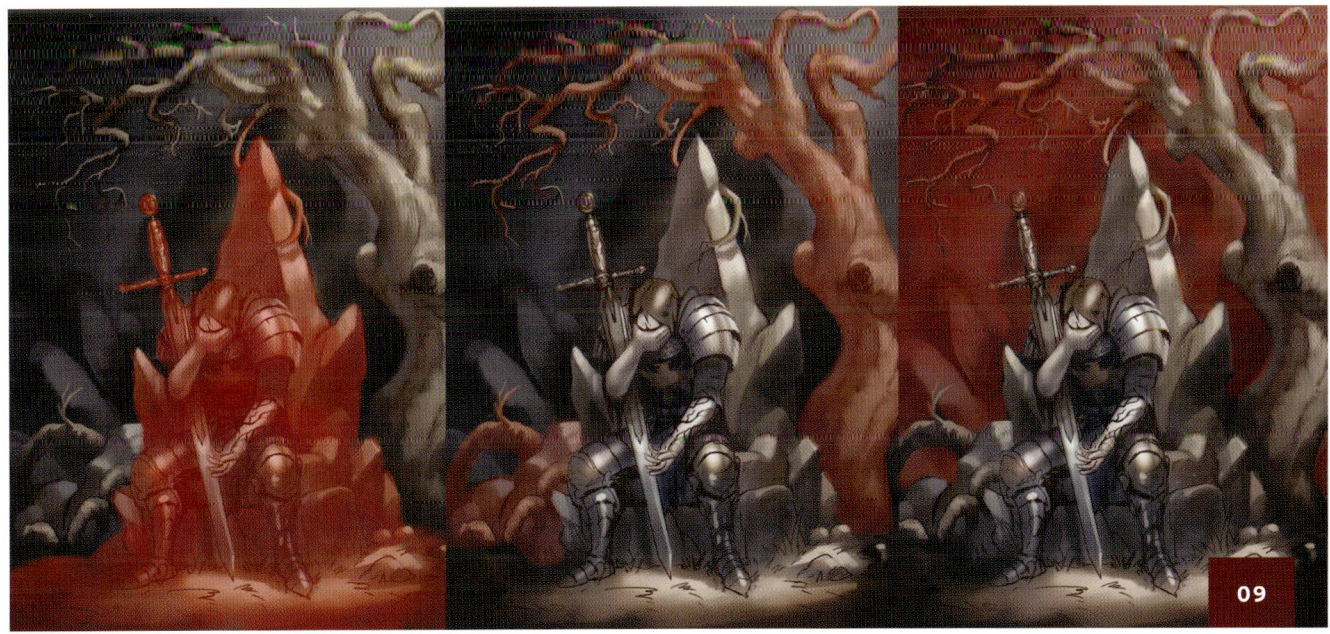

// Layer your objects and figures to give your image breathing room and perspective

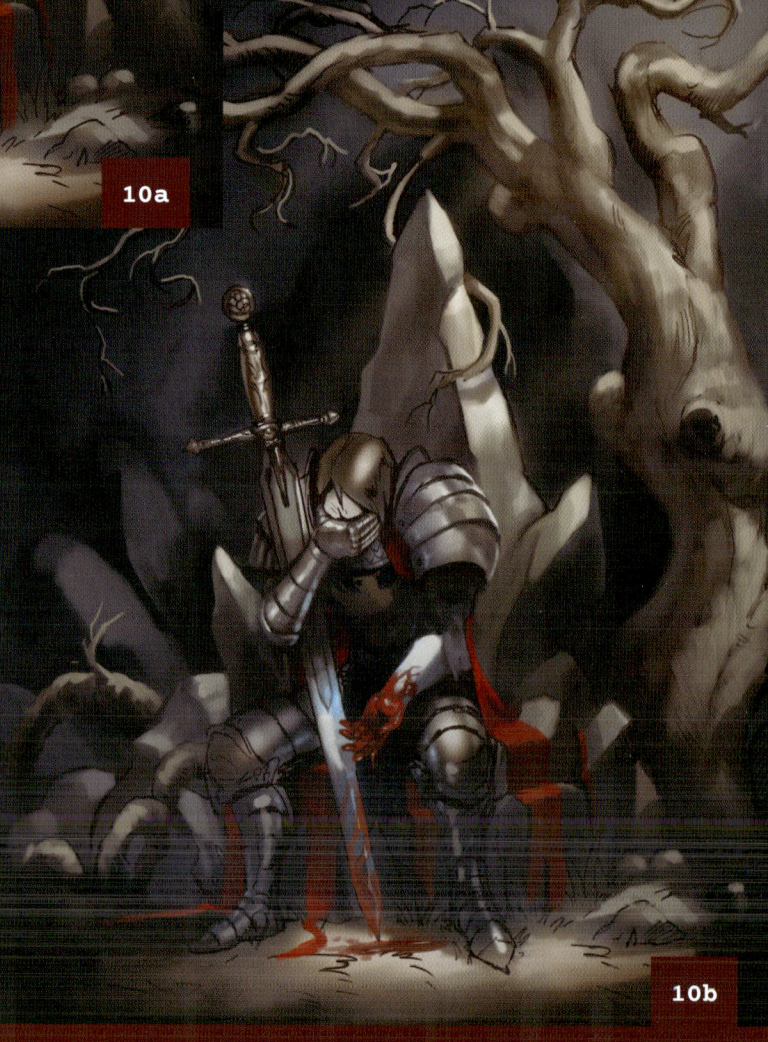

10a

// I reconsider the story behind the knight's arm

10b

// It's not too late to rethink your narrative before diving into your rendering

>10 Changing my mind

Going into this image, I had the idea of a knight, possibly with his arm blackened and veined, as if corrupted by a poison or curse. However, when thinking through the sketch phase, it became apparent to me that the idea may not be so easily portrayed to the audience. So, going further into it, I had a few more ideas to play with. Maybe the knight took the wrong poison and was slowly turning undead? Or maybe, more strikingly, he killed his first enemy, and was despairing over the loss of his innocence? Thinking about the narrative behind your illustration is important for even the smallest details and is key to developing a good, readable image (images 10a and 10b).

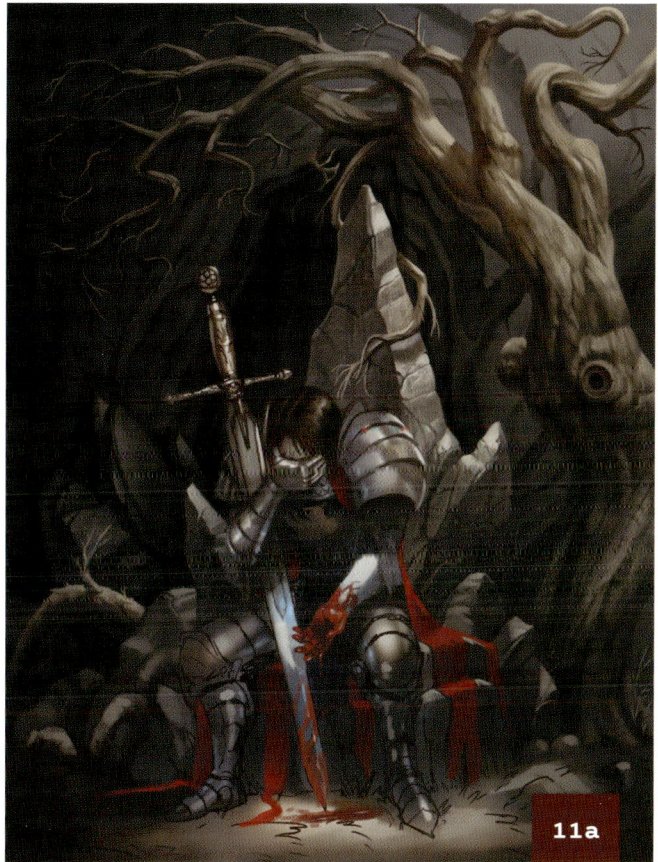

// The painting so far

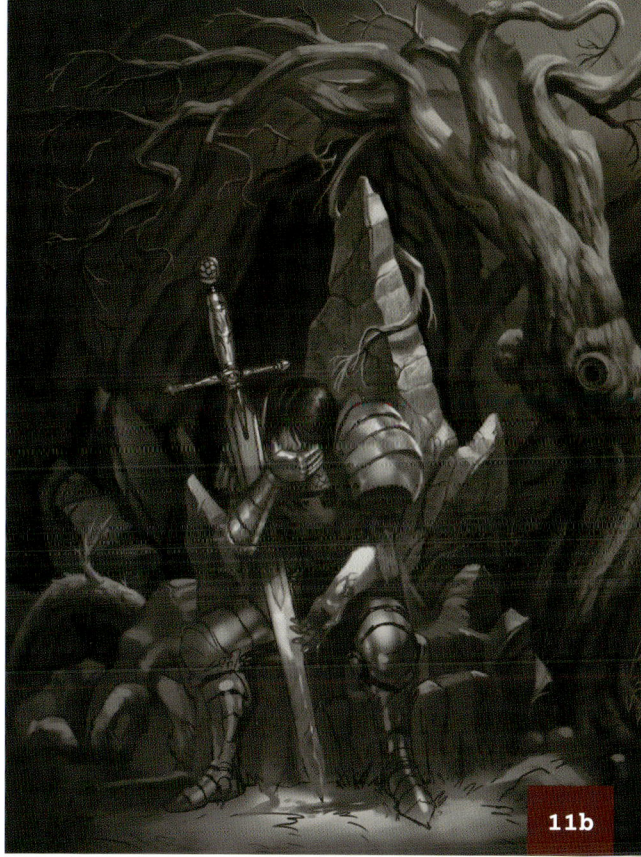

// Checking the painting's values

>11 Checking my values

Inevitably, when you are rendering in color, you may come across some difficulty in separating values without destroying your saturation. If you are working in Adobe Photoshop, one trick that helps is to constantly check your values by desaturating your image using the Hue/Saturation menu. Problem areas (such as the tree's shadow against the dark background) may become apparent when doing this, and it can help you to render those areas more clearly (images 11a and 11b). In image 11c you can see the separation of color and value by taking the same part of the image and desaturating it next to its colored equivalent.

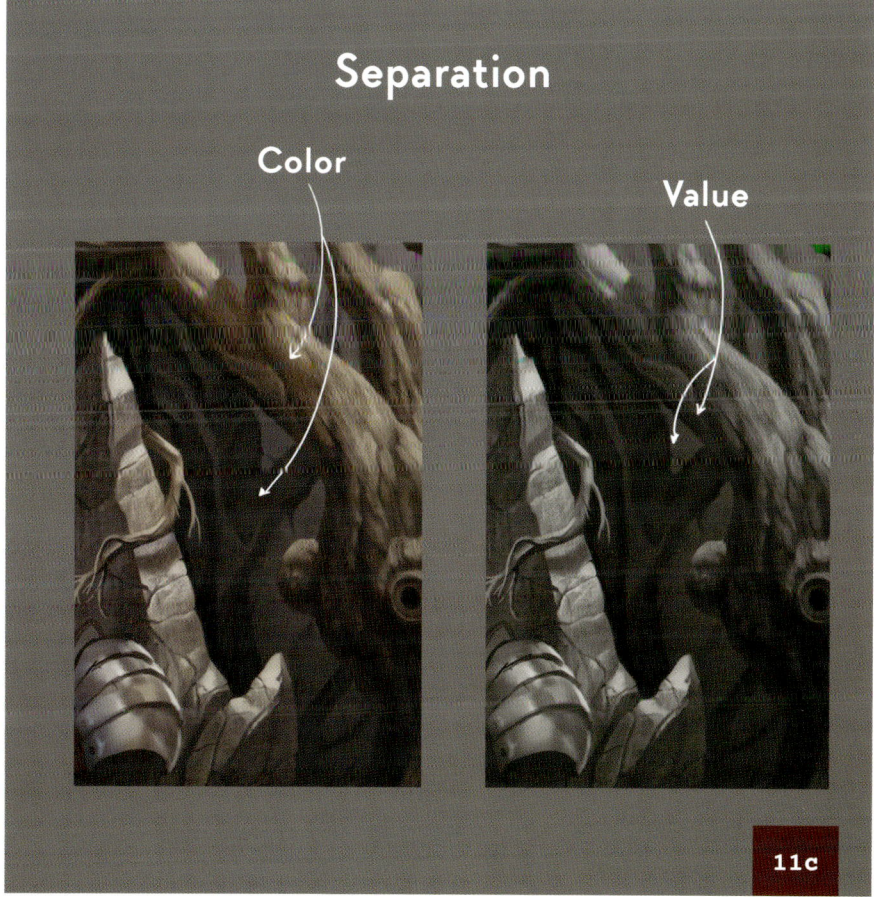

// A trick that may help with rendering headaches

Step 01
Base values and layers

Step 02
Adding lines and detail

Step 03
Final shadow and detail

`12`

// Taking the right steps can save you from problems when painting armor

>12 Painting armor

The one important thing to remember when painting something reflective or shiny, like armor, is to not underestimate the alteration of values that can happen in something as simple as a leg. Often I find it best to start with the values and color layers before even approaching detail. In doing this, the foundation of the values will remain strong when finalizing the pieces of armor. Often the cast shadows and the brightest of highlights are the last things to add.

>13 Putting things to rest

Once I am happy with the general rendering of the image (armor, trees, grass, and rocks), the last (and often the most fun) step of the process is to add some special effects and lighting boosts to help the image pop and come to life. Sometimes when rendering for so long, you may muddy the colors and values – no one is perfect! This final step helps to bring some color back to where it may have been lost, or effects that can help the foreground or background pop when it may have been lost previously. For example, I add the beam of light and floating dust motes to tie the image together and add atmosphere.

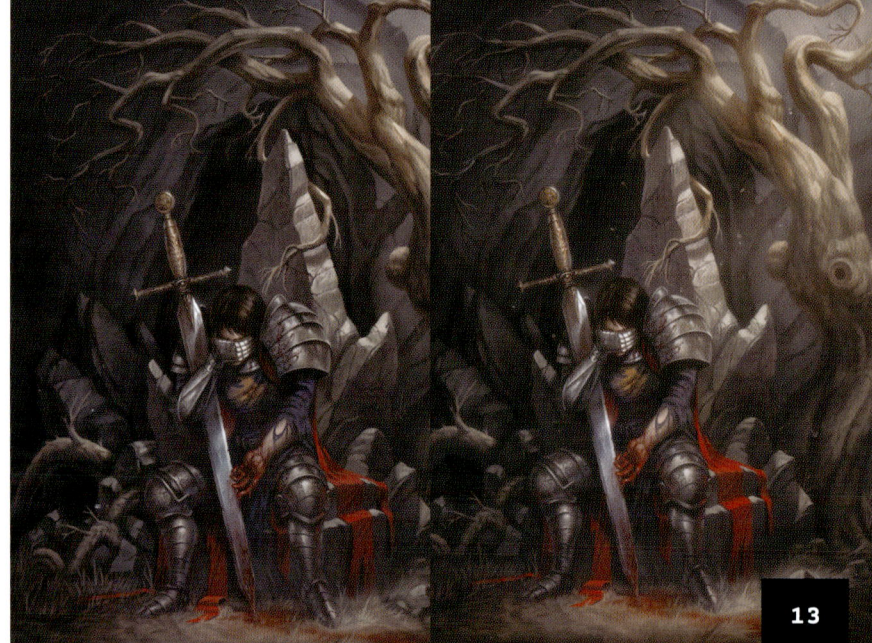

`13`

// Small details can add the biggest effects

>14 Conclusion

Now that I've worked out some of the kinks, and smoothed out the lighting and particle effects, my image is complete. The knight despairs over the loss of his innocence: a young man, shaken and vulnerable under the discerning warm glow of light. With an insight into how to evoke despair, as well as how to ladder your steps when painting, you should have a clear running start on your next project.

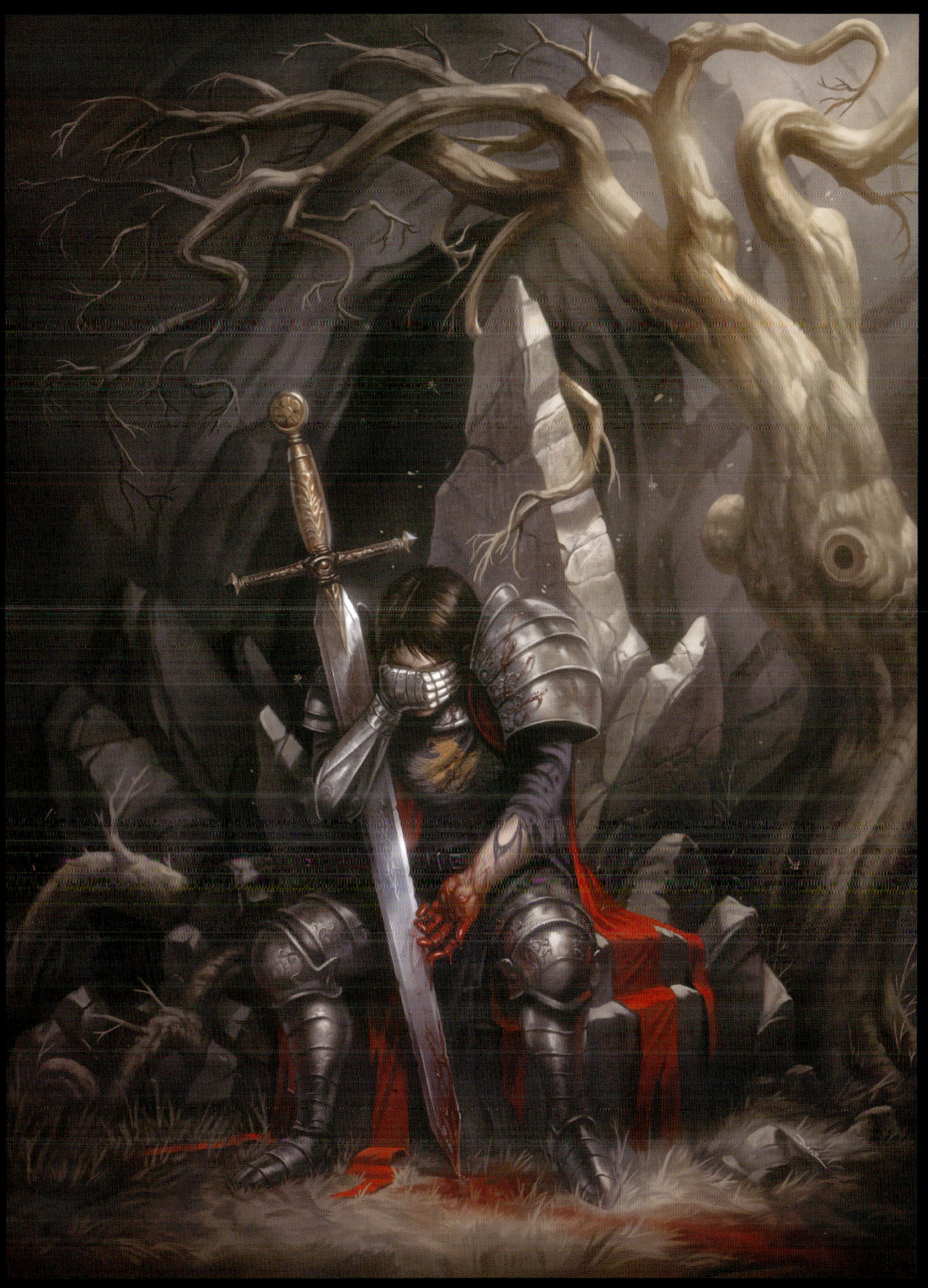

Sebastian Kowoll | www.skalienart.com

Empathy

In this chapter I will show you how I approach a painting when I only have a vague idea of what I want to depict. The theme is "empathy" and it's pretty much what motivates most of my personal work. I will share with you my motivation, struggles, and solutions for crafting an image that's sincere. I'm going to stress and go over this goal of sincerity a lot, because the only way to make your art stand out is to make it say what only you can say.

Personally, I try to paint scenes where there are animals coexisting with humans, which works well in the context of empathy, as one being respects the feelings of another and has compassion for them. Art serves as a window for what I hope our own relationship with the environment could be. There is plenty of violence in the world so having art as our "Zen" space can be, at the very least, therapeutic.

>01 Doodling
There are two ways for me to start a painting: I either know where I'm going from the start, or I have to struggle through a river of "could be" ideas that

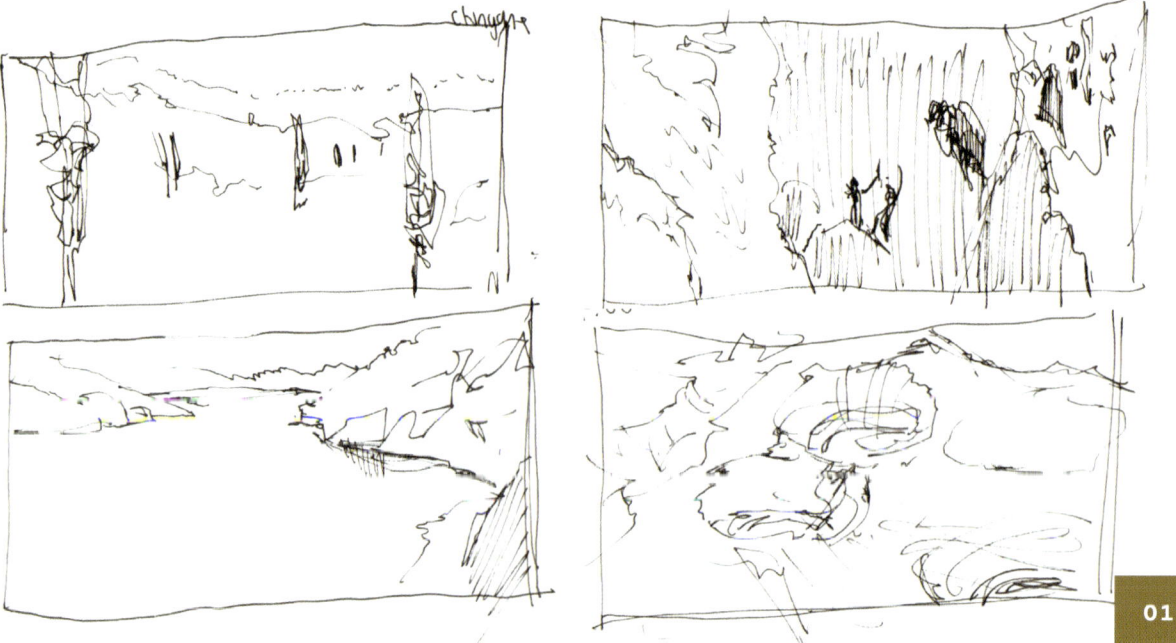

// **Super rough, general scribbles whose purpose is to get the ball rolling**

01

lead absolutely nowhere. This painting is the latter, so this first step is just about doodling around until I can start closing in on a possible concept for a decent painting. I don't care if the sketches look bad at this stage – I only need them to allow me to see a hint of the road ahead for the image. After some quick attempts, I settle for an idea. That's all that matters for now.

>02 Catharsis

Sometimes I can sketch for a very long time and still not find a theme that resonates with me. Hence the absolute importance of this step: keeping up with the world. While I'm sketching, news is announced that one of the most iconic, natural places in my country is threatened by the possibility of oil drilling. I think it would be a perfect setting, or at least a perfect reference, for the painting that I'm about to start. I know it's a cliché, but allowing art to be an outlet through which to express your

feelings will make an illustration feel that much more sincere. In image 02 you can see that I carry on developing rough sketches to reflect my ideas.

In a perfect world, I would collect all the reference I might need in this step and then proceed with the painting without having to look for any extra information. But that never happens! However, this step still exists as a major part of the process. I collect images that will guide my major decisions and the general direction of the painting: light, materials, water, mood, and other artists' works. There is no need to worry about references that will only guide minor, very specific parts of the image for the moment.

> "Allowing art to be an outlet through which to express your feelings will make an illustration feel that much more sincere"

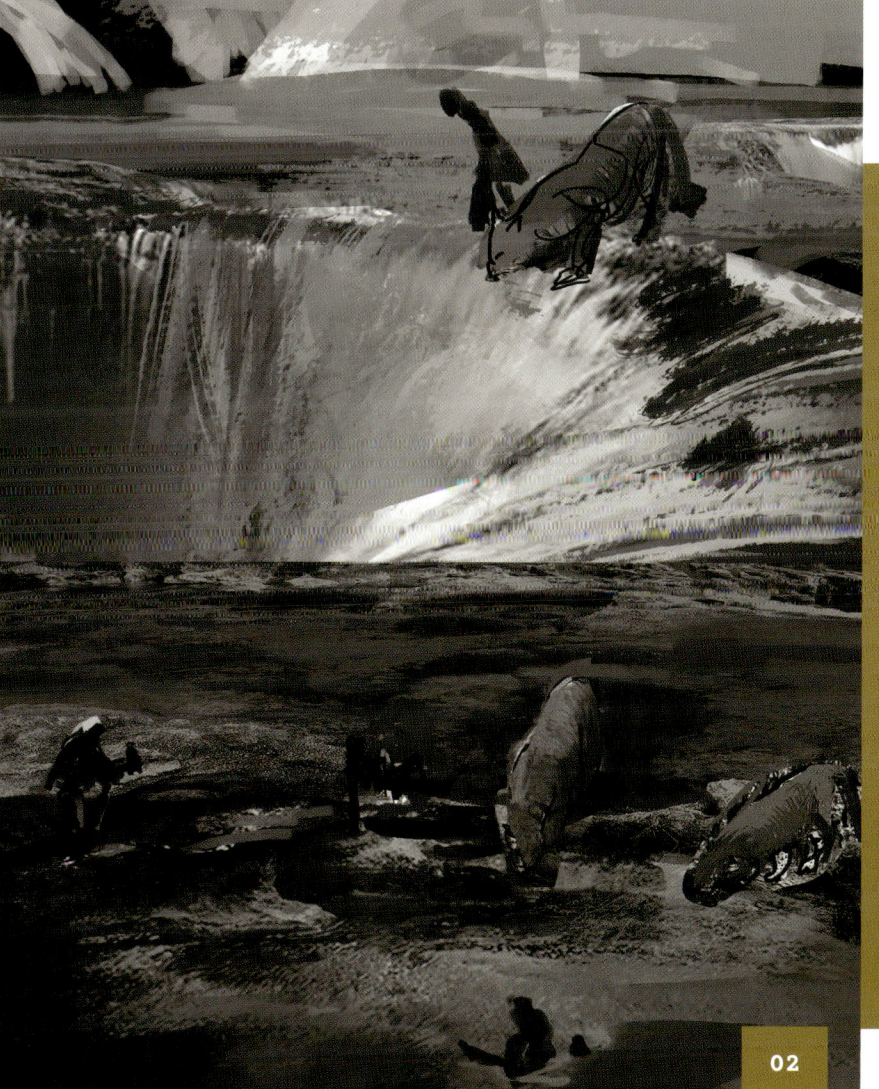

// Rough sketches exploring compositions for a simple idea: the things and needs we share with other species

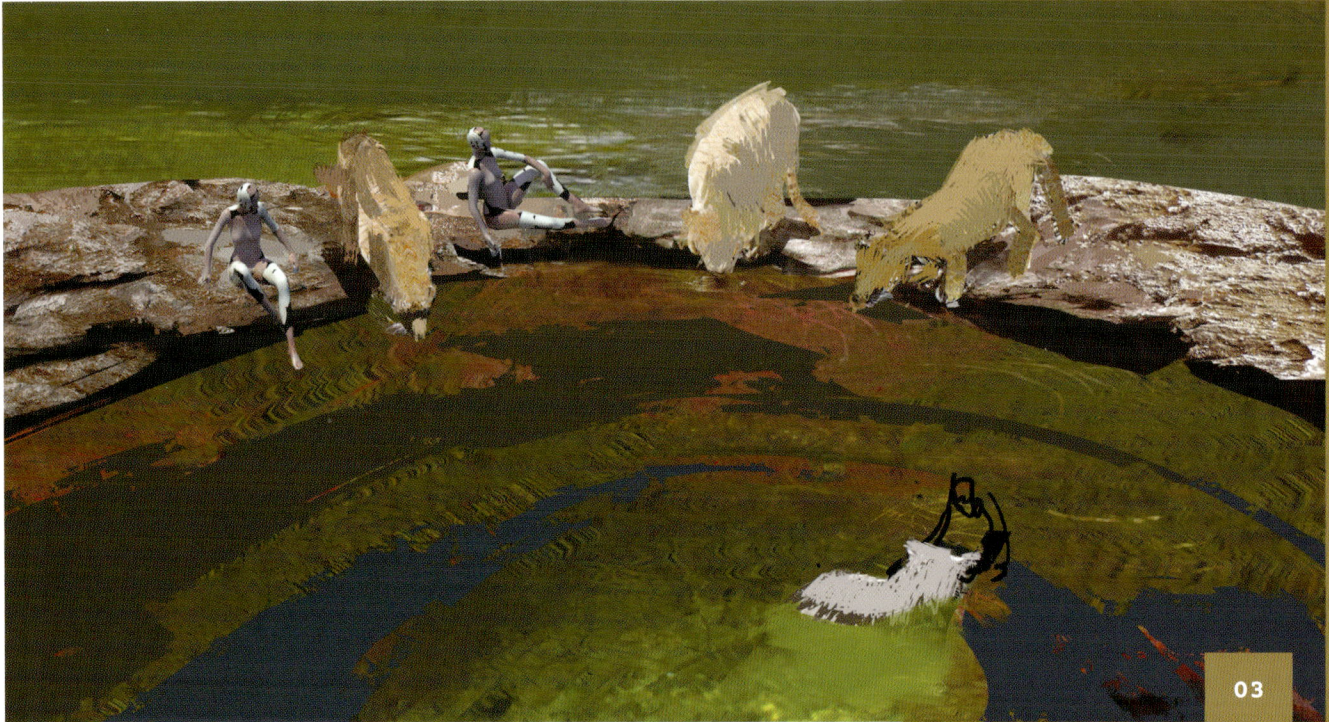

03

// The road begins! Laying down the basic elements of the painting

>03 Block in

Now I lay down the major shapes and values in their place, defining my approach to the painting. As I am working digitally, I use 3D software called DAZ Studio (**www.daz3d.com**) to pose some characters in order to give me an idea of what I want each of them to be doing, and spend some time designing the riverbed shapes.

I know I want the area to look like a place from my country called Caño Cristales, so I start laying down some basic colors to get me on the right path. I add a rocky texture to the main shape, which I paint over a bit.

>04 Taking photos

I now have poses of the 3D characters, but I need more reference images. I ask my girlfriend for her help with this part and take many many photos (she's the female model for most of my artwork). She has a perfect outfit that could serve as a simple starting point for a costume. I know that I want to have a black panther cub there somewhere, so her little dog serves as reference as well. You've got to work with what you have and get all the help you can.

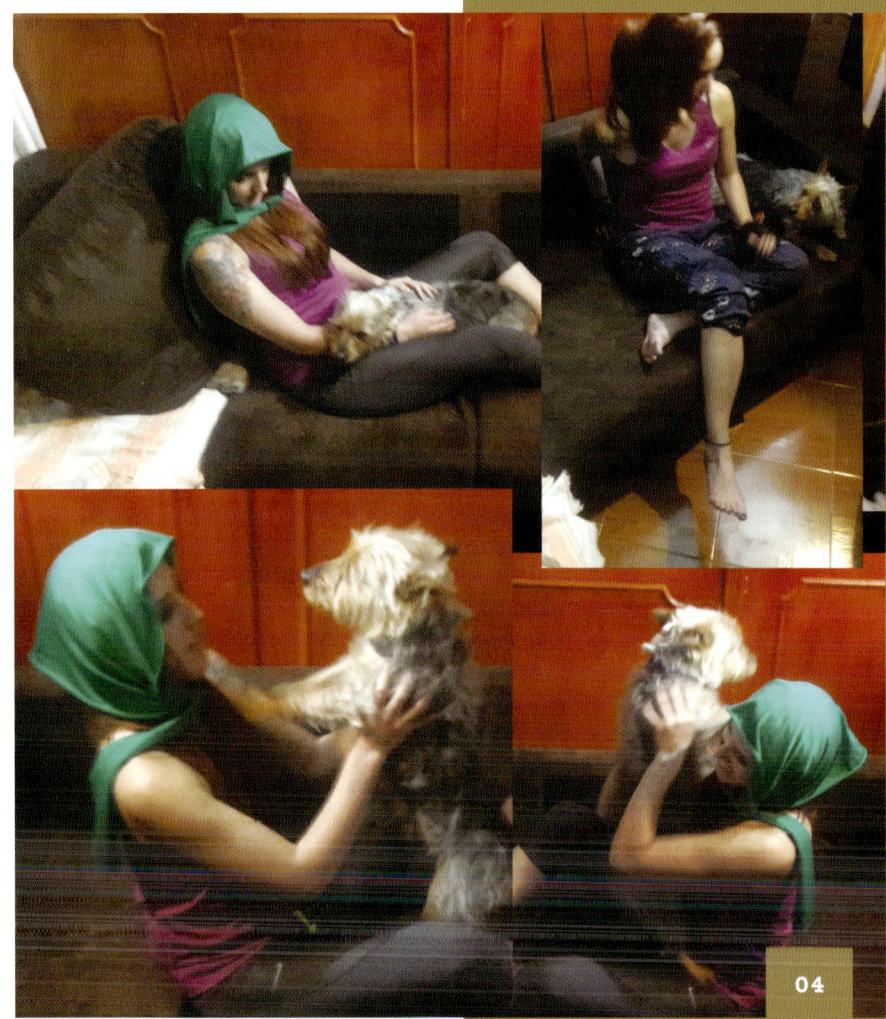

04

// If you need to take pictures, go and take them – they are lifesavers!

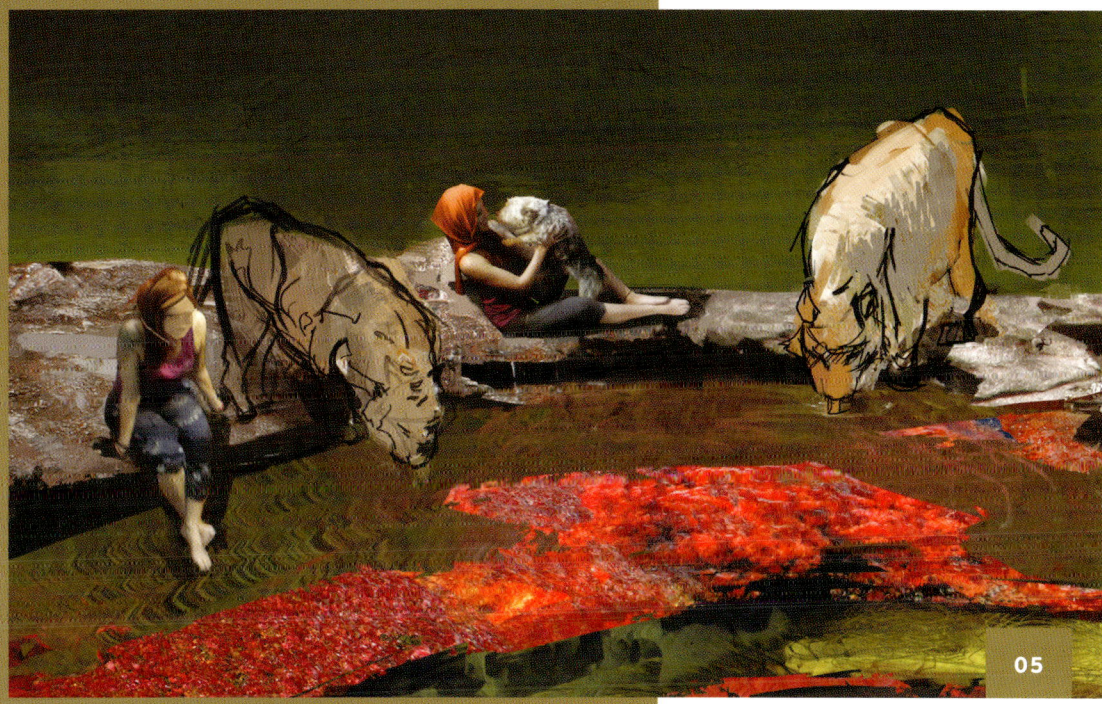

// Defining the characters and giving the flowers texture

05

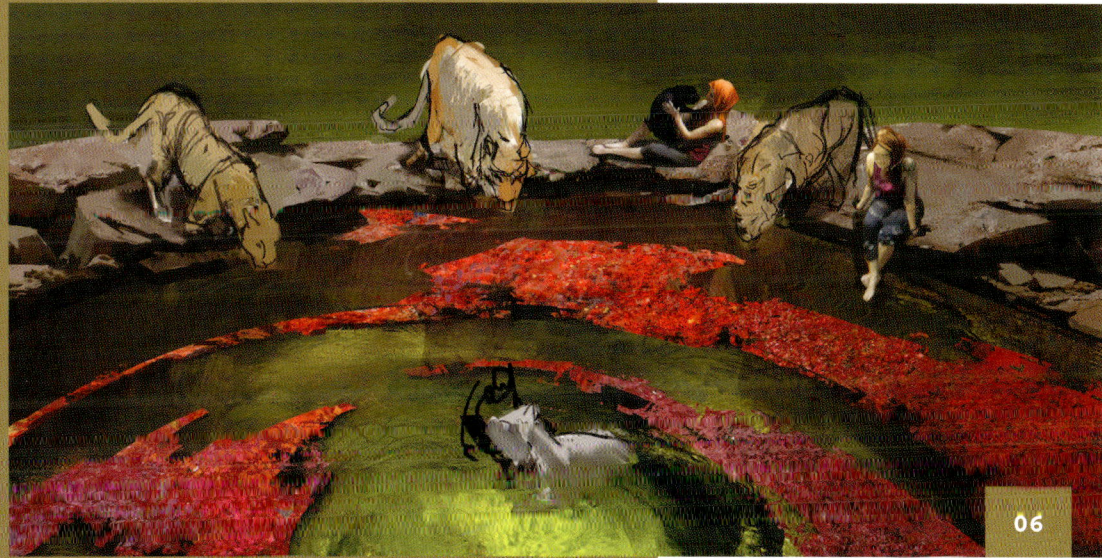

// I shuffle things and re-evaluate decisions until I'm happy

06

>05 Baby steps

I now have a very crude layout of all the characters in place. I sketch in the big cats around the scene, after carrying out some studies that enable me to stylize and paint them the way I want to. They are very rough at this stage, but I'll polish them later on. I use some of the photos I've taken to create more defined characters sitting on the rocks and give the flowers more texture. I also start to add more color variation to the green parts of the water – the dynamic between those hues with the reds from the flowers is going to be vital for the image. I use smudge brushes by John Silva (**www.twitch.tv/johnsilvaart**).

>06 Is this going somewhere?

I flip the image to get a fresh look at it; if you are working with traditional medium, you can use a mirror for this. I re-evaluate the composition: if the image is about a peaceful moment, why not emphasize that with a balanced, harmonious layout? This is the reason I choose to move the character in the river to the center. Now he's the main focal point, with the rest of the characters creating lines and pointing at him. I've had an unjustified fear of centering things since I started studying composition, but sometimes an image calls for it, so don't be afraid of it! I start to iron out the rocks a bit more and introduce a white tiger cub to push the river's colors even more.

>07 Exploring possible stories

My first loose sketch of the main character doesn't cut it, not only aesthetically, but narratively. With every single painting, there is a moment of self-doubt where it seems like there is no light at the end of the tunnel. Remember though that there is no "painting" without "pain." What does his action, his pose, currently have to do with anything? How can I properly sell a peaceful, loving message if the main character is just randomly there? This step is about figuring out what he is doing: is that tiger cub his? A friend, or a mere pet? I want to portray a friendship there, so I settle for a hugging pose. At this point it doesn't have to be perfect; I only need

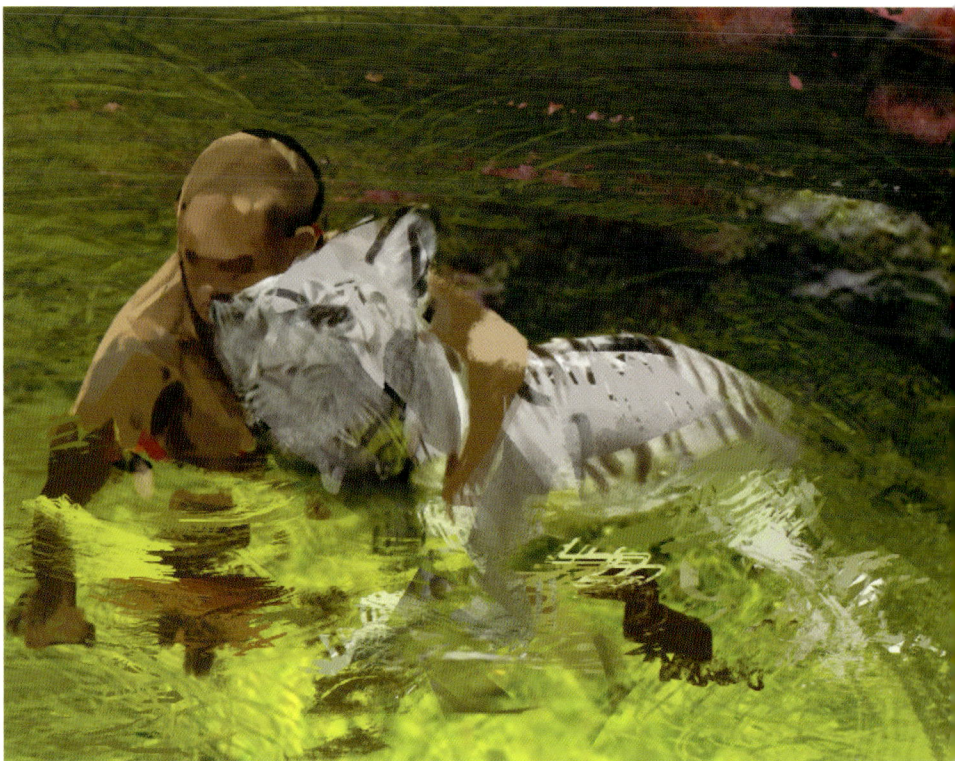

// Try different possibilities until the right choice clicks with you

to convey the idea. Once I feel that the action works with the rest of the painting, I can proceed to bring it to a finish.

>08 Building up the painting

I jump around different parts of the painting, adding more to the background so it's less simple, fixing and balancing the colors, and adding underwater flowerbeds carefully designed to serve as pointers for the characters. I work loosely and use a lot of a smudge and mixer brushes to control the edges and keep them from

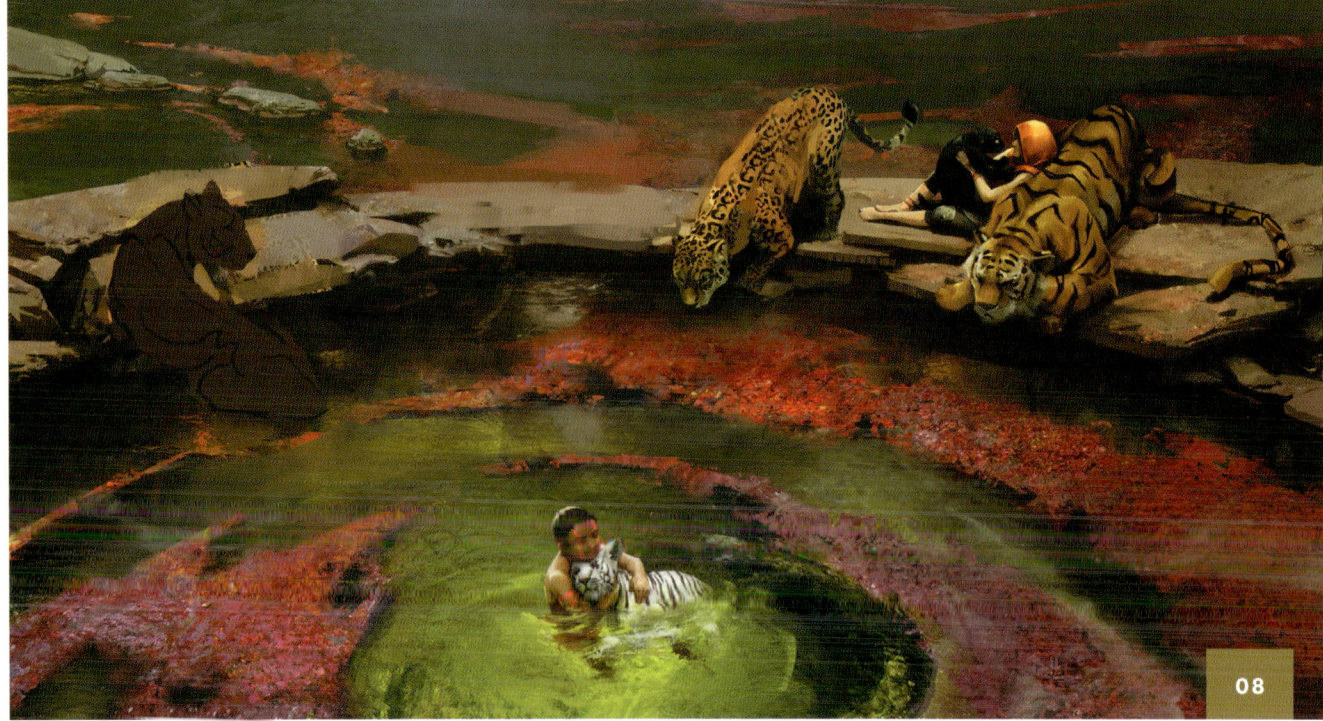

// Changing elements and sketching in a new tiger. Don't be afraid to make changes if you are convinced they matter!

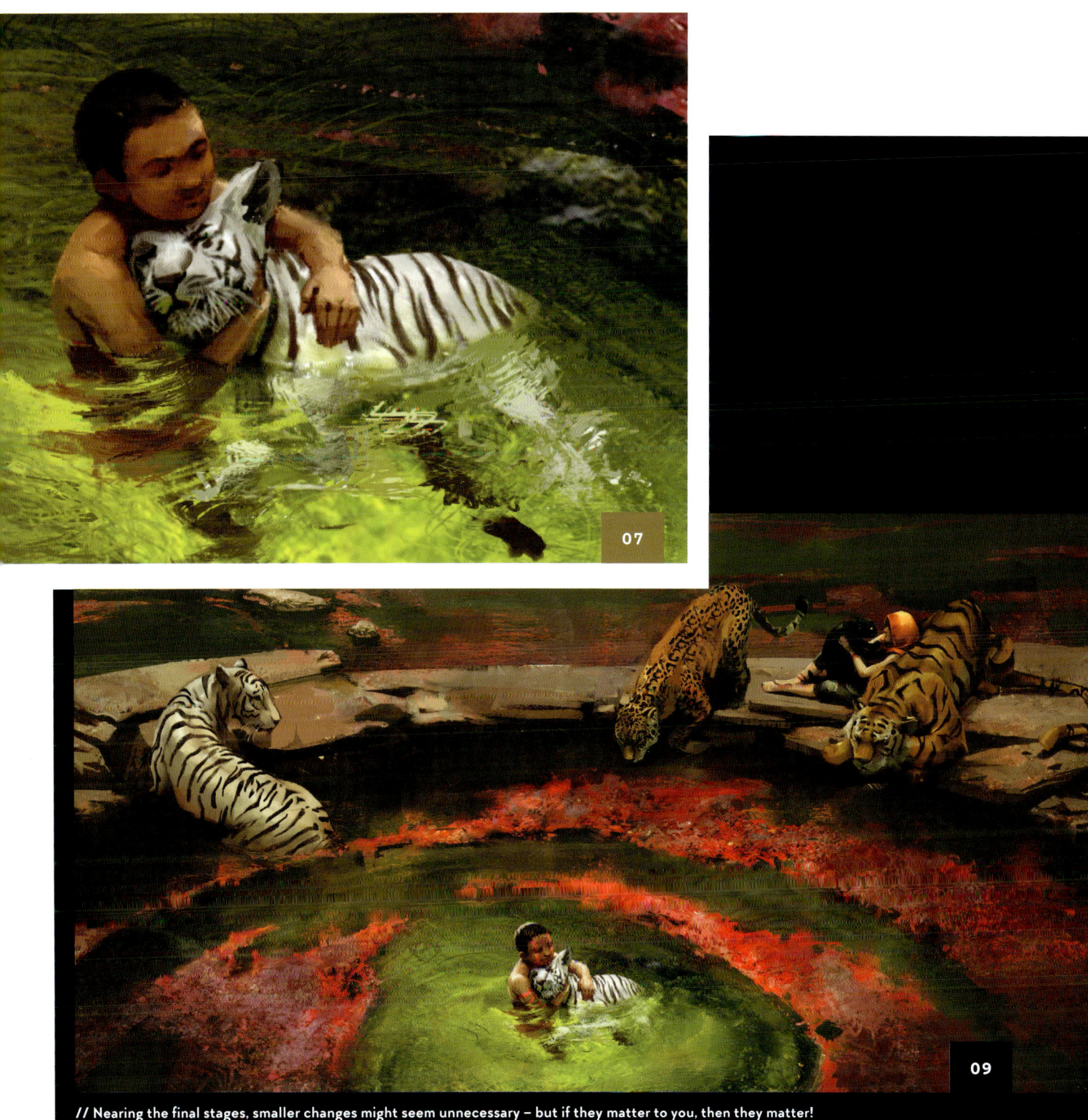

// Nearing the final stages, smaller changes might seem unnecessary – but if they matter to you, then they matter!

drawing too much attention away from the focal areas. I also adjust the main character's arm – it has to be simple but feel right – and decide to remove the second character on the rocks.

Up until this point, I have felt something is not correct with the size of the tigers.

Zooming out of the image and looking for specific references allows me to judge their size compared to a human's, and I choose to make them bigger. All of a sudden they feel right! I paint over one of the tigers, turning it into a jaguar to add more variety. I also move the big cats around and give them

different poses to make the composition more natural and less symmetrical.

>09 Tidying up

Changes in this step might not seem too evident, but they're critical for the ongoing process. A simple statement is a better statement, so I try to better group my values, and tone down some bright areas that don't require such brightness. The mindset here is to lock and limit the values to the places where I want attention. Having the white tiger in the water as the brightest value in that area will lock focus on him, instead of drawing it to the distracting bright area that was below him. I use a mixer brush on the rocks to soften the texture noise, as again, I don't want that area asking for more attention than it needs. The left-hand tiger was initially orange, but I change it to white for variety.

>10 Styling

This is one of my favorite stages: styling shapes. I spend my time working on the shapes' edges, adding and removing strokes with both an eraser and a smudge tool. I draw inspiration from some old master paintings by Winslow Homer, which I study carefully before attempting to replicate, and adapt their solutions in my painting. Knowing our own flaws is important; I tend to overwork elements that don't need that much detail. Consulting Homer's paintings helps me aim toward simplification, value grouping, edge control, and shape design, but most importantly guides me in how to suggest and control detail.

I keep trying to find better ways to say what I want visually: summarizing, cleaning, and balancing. At this point I'm comfortable with the shapes in the image, and can afford to play a bit with color (subtly, of course, because I don't want to mess up what I've built so far). I play with adjustment layers and masks in Photoshop to create little hue changes throughout the image. Nothing drastic, again: little changes that, hopefully, go a long way in selling a joyful scene. I also make the boy a bit smaller, as he seemed slightly off before

>11 What's the story?

Now the details come forth! I add some saddles and equipment for the jaguar and white tiger, and shoes on the rocks for the boy in the river. I want to strengthen the idea that they are

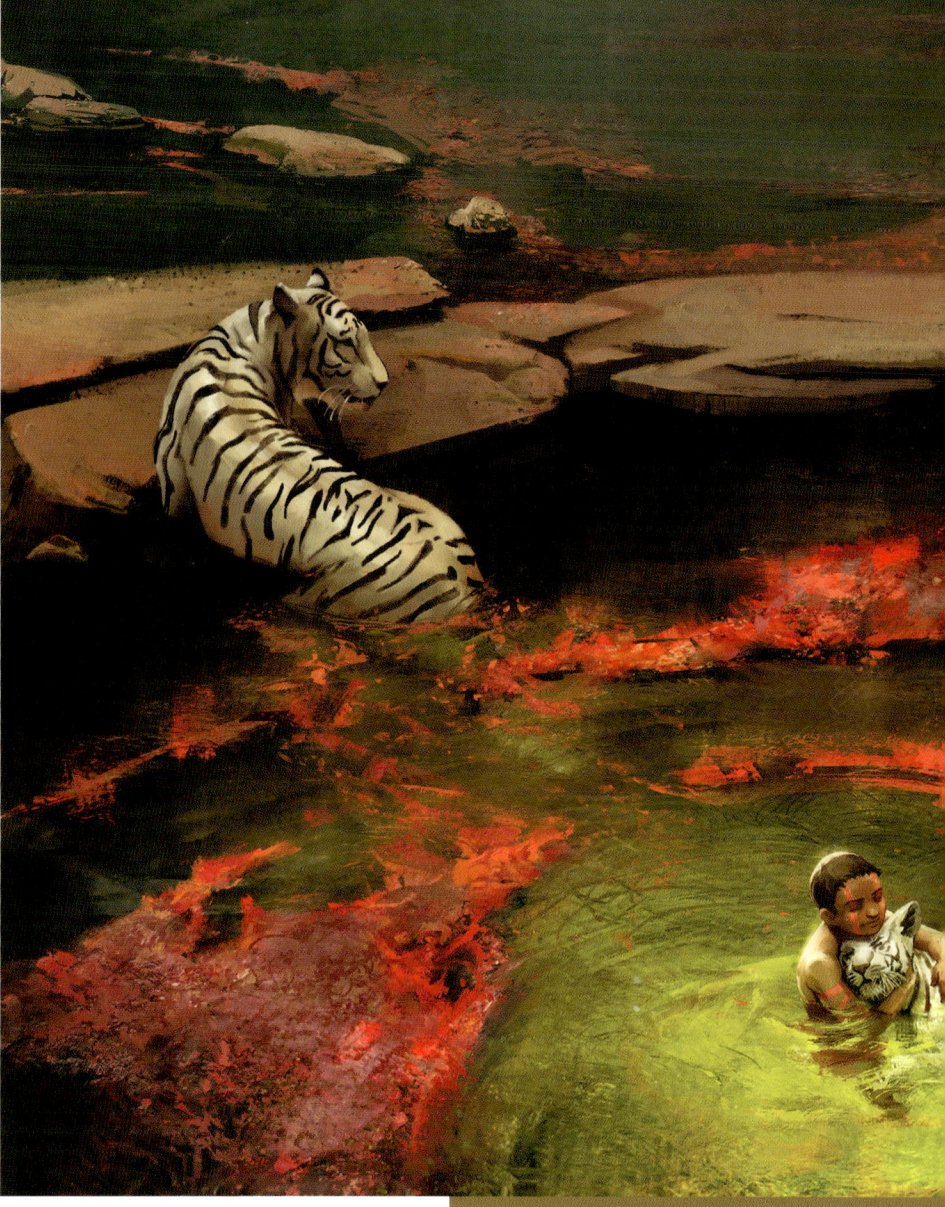

// **Making further adjustments to tidy up the scene**

all traveling together and that this is simply a leisure stop. While painting, I ask myself questions about the scene: who are these people? Why are they all together? Are they friends? I don't expect to find answers, because I think there is more fun in just adding some visual clues for the viewer and letting each person build their own narrative.

>12 Final illustration

I now add some final touches such as pumping up the color, sharpening the focal points, and adding a noise layer on top. You can see my final painting by turning the page. Remember, use all the techniques at your disposal to create amazing images, but above all, create sincere images – creations that only you could have produced; keep your art honest.

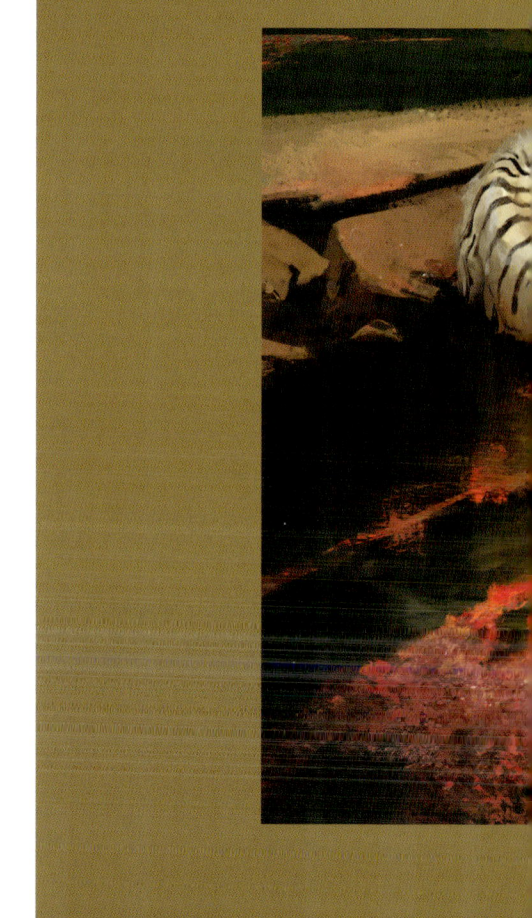

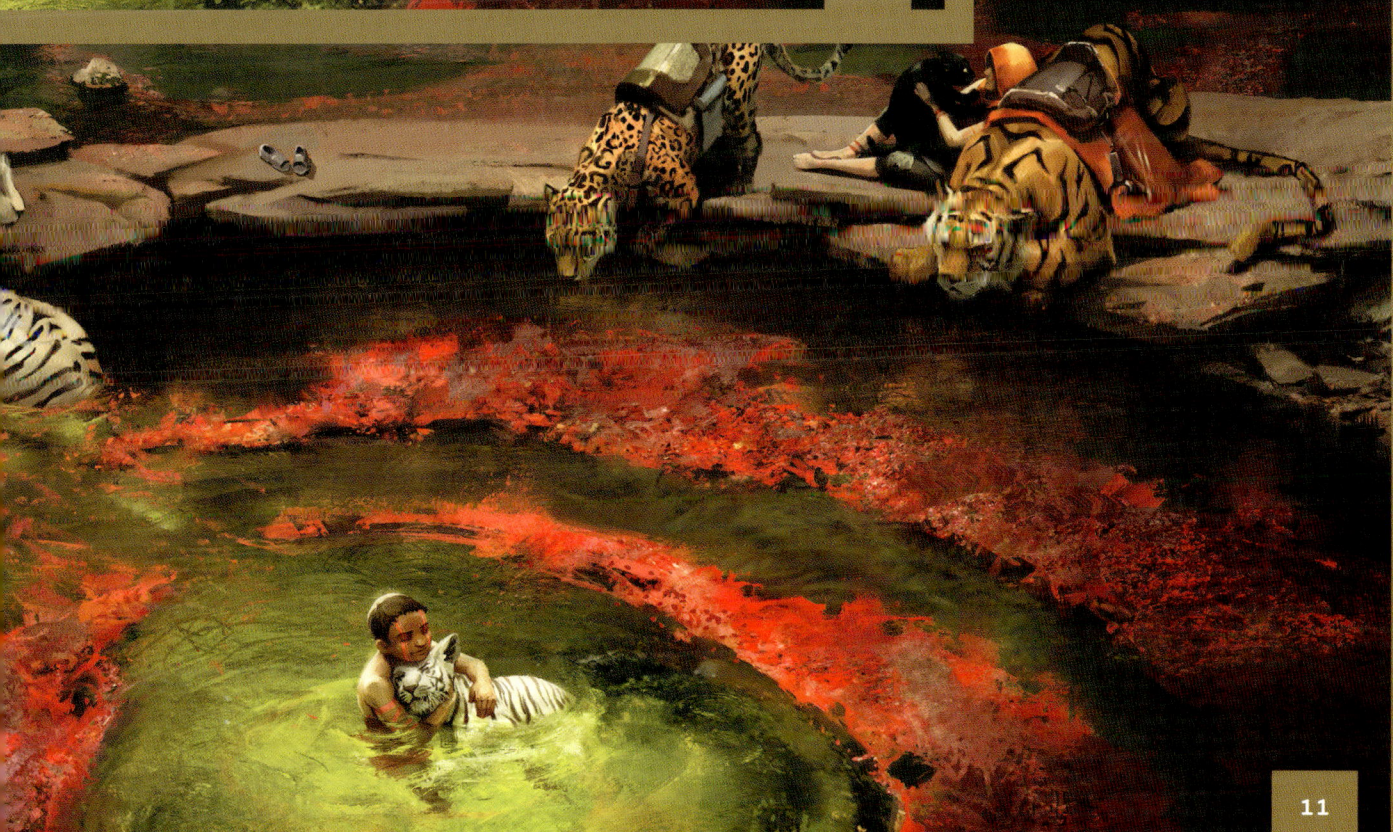

> "I keep trying to find better ways to say what I want visually: summarizing, cleaning, and balancing"

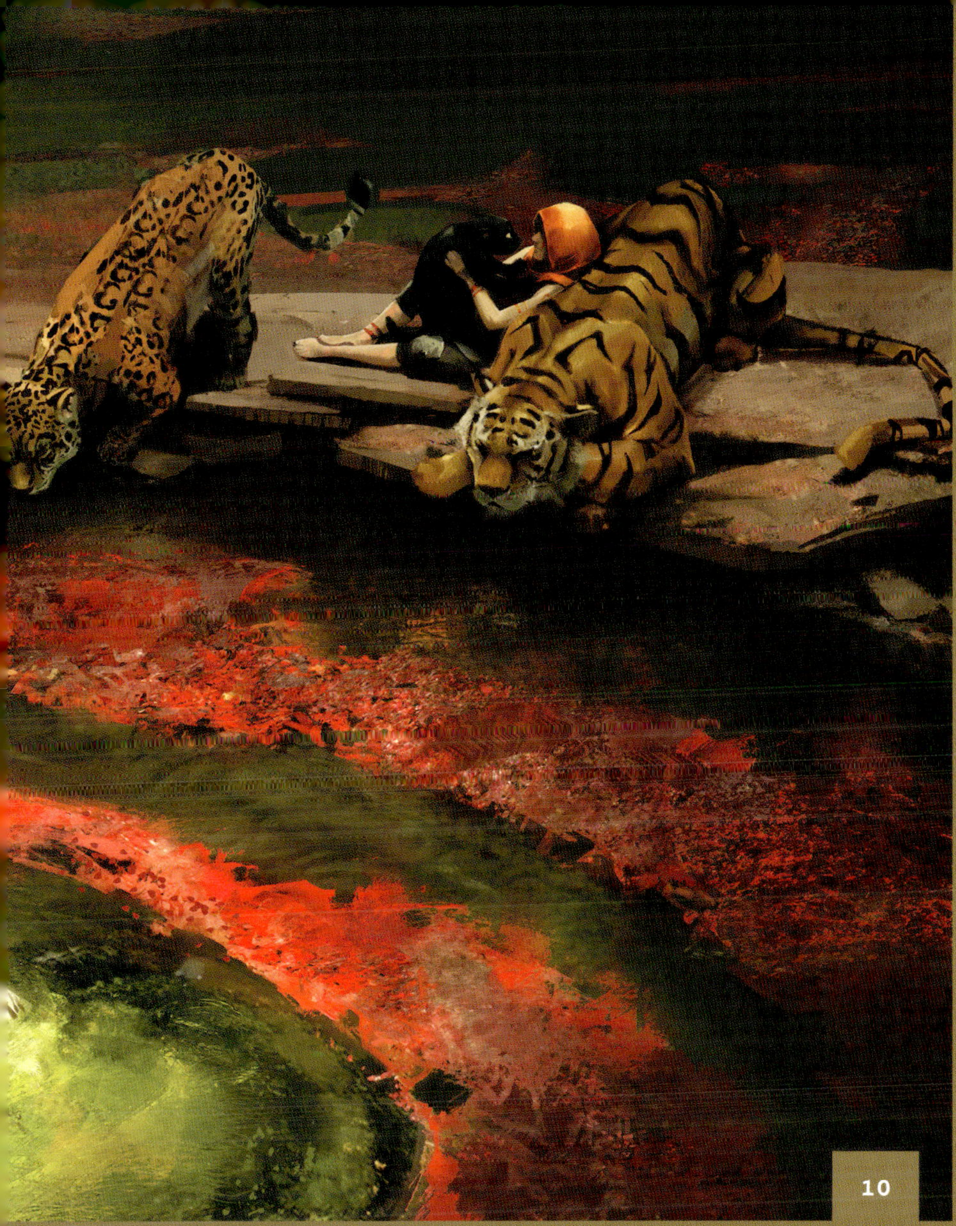

10

11

// Suggest a story and leave room for viewers to interpret it

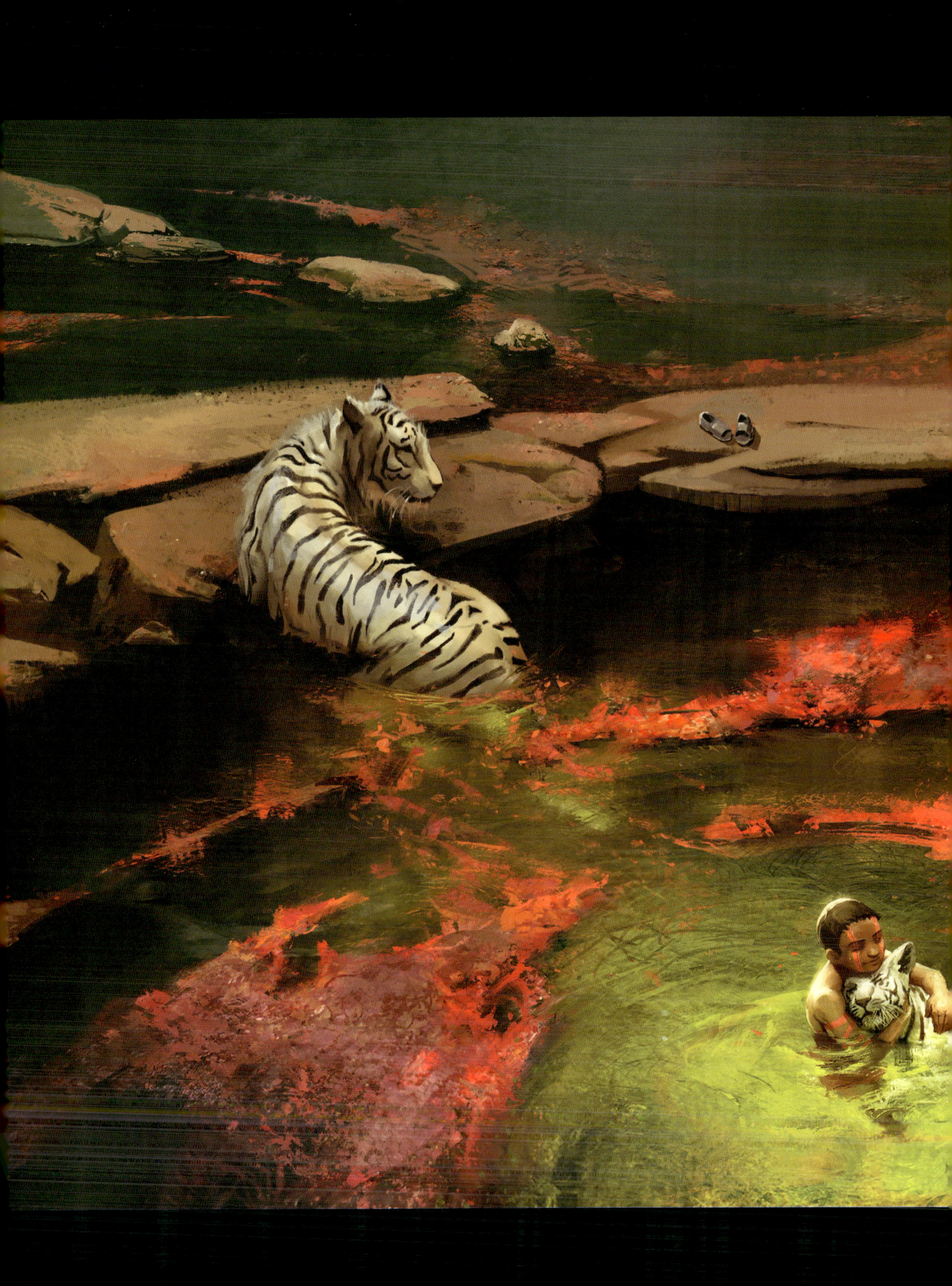

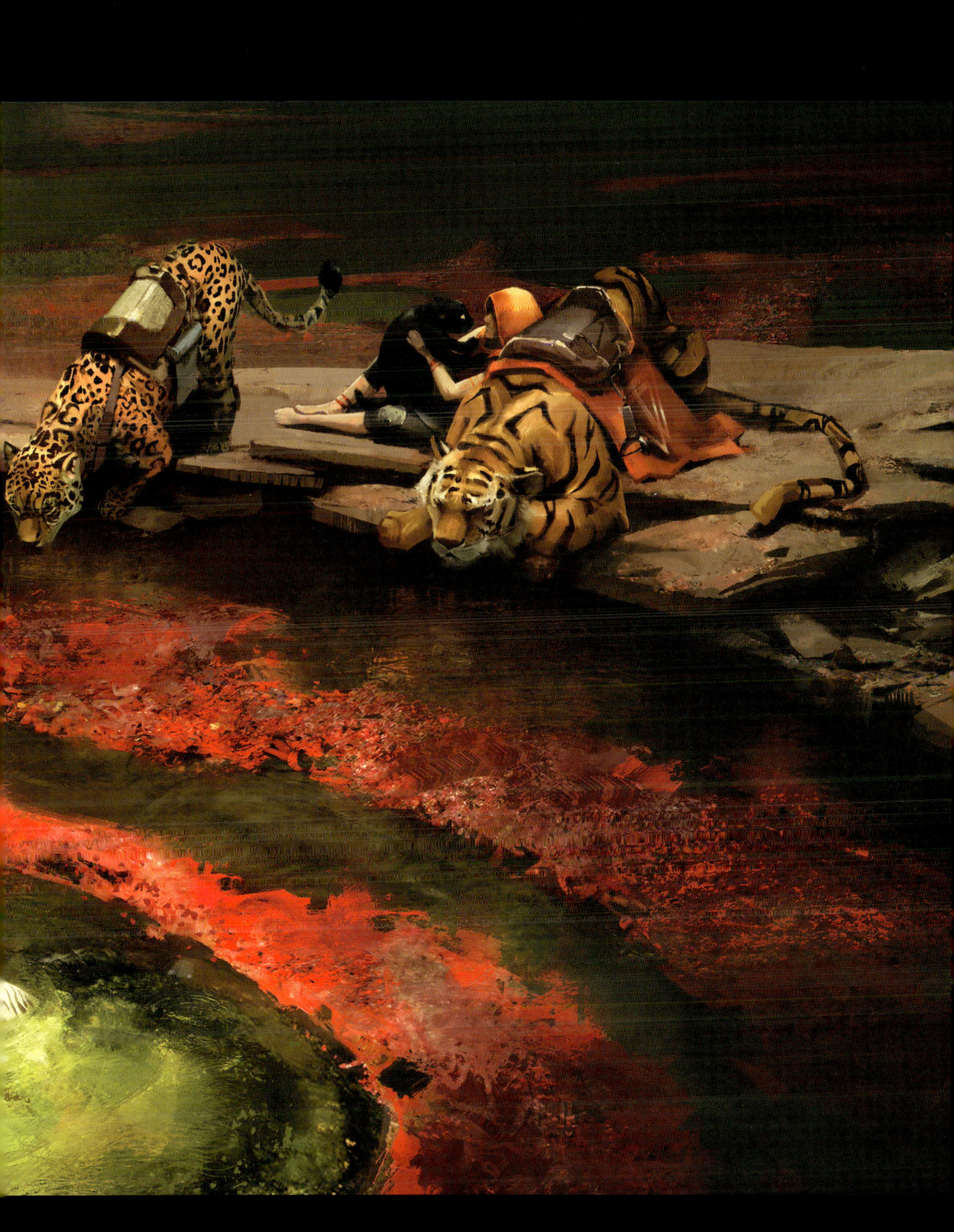

Maria Poliakova | www.artstation.com/artist/tubikraski

Envy

In this chapter you will see my process for creating a character based on the theme of "envy." I will cover the most important stages of my work from the very beginning of the process. My main objective is to portray the theme of envy – a kind of jealousy or unhealthy desire – and create a spectacular pose, suitable mood, and beautiful color palette.

>01 Free lines

Before starting, I usually do little warm-up exercises for my hands. I take my sketchbook and draw free-flowing lines based around one specific theme. During this exercise I am very relaxed, and my thinking process occurs as follows: "The theme is 'envy'... I like to paint portraits of women ... probably a character who looks like an evil queen ... a queen in a majestic pose, with her hair fluttering ... with a heavy decoration on her head ..." This exercise is like meditation, during which I often got good ideas, and at the same time prepare myself for drawing.

>02 Sketches

After I have finished drawing my flowing lines, I choose the most favorable ones and continue to refine them, using them as a base for my sketch.

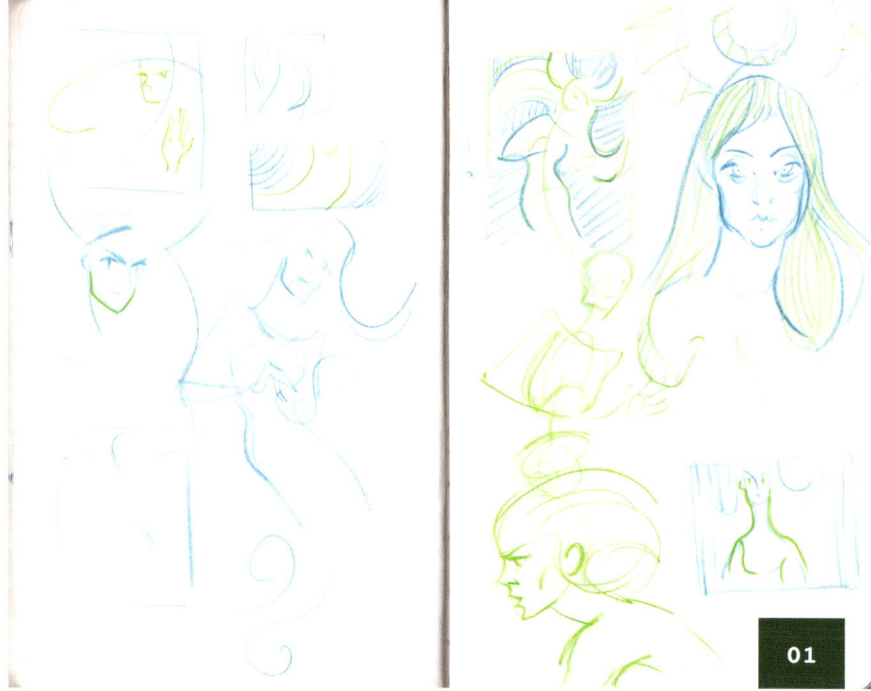

// Simple lines can just be an exercise for hands, and can also help to generate ideas

Sometimes I do this on paper, sometimes directly in Adobe Photoshop. In this instance, I use my sketchbook.

I decide that this will be a waist-length portrait, an image of an arrogant, somewhat evil woman with flowing hair. On her head there are horns or a crown. In her hands she holds something that represents envy. I often work out the details during the painting process if I cannot come up with specific concepts at the very beginning. The main things I do during this step are work out the composition and arrange the geometric forms. These should complement each other; the smaller details are not so important at this stage.

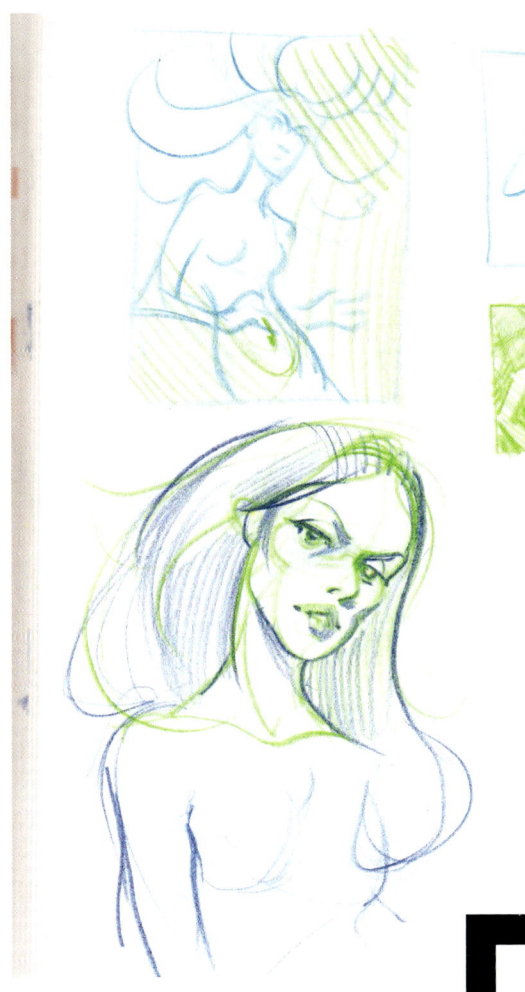

// Small thumbnails before starting work in Photoshop

>03 Color sketch

In this step I test out some color options, which I do in Photoshop because it allows me to change colors quickly and efficiently. This is an important stage of my work, and I approach it in a similar way as the previous sketch; without details, just the basic color strokes, and zoomed out so I can see everything at once. I do it quickly, using different tools to achieve a range of effects. I'm just experimenting, maybe creating color combinations that are too bright, which will be toned down by shadows and midtones in the later stages of painting.

"The main things I do during this step are work out the composition and arrange the geometric forms. These should complement each other; the smaller details are not so important at this stage"

02

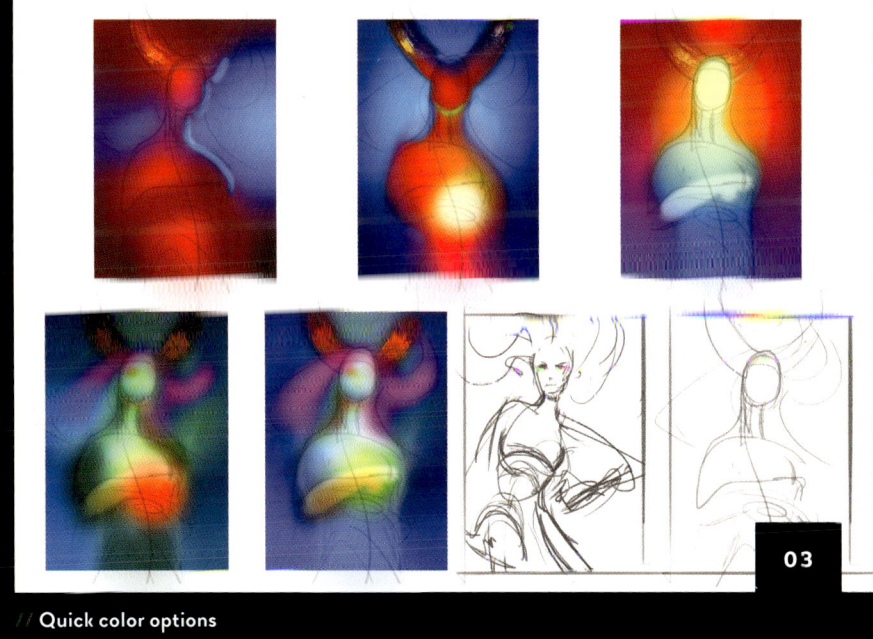

03

// Quick color options

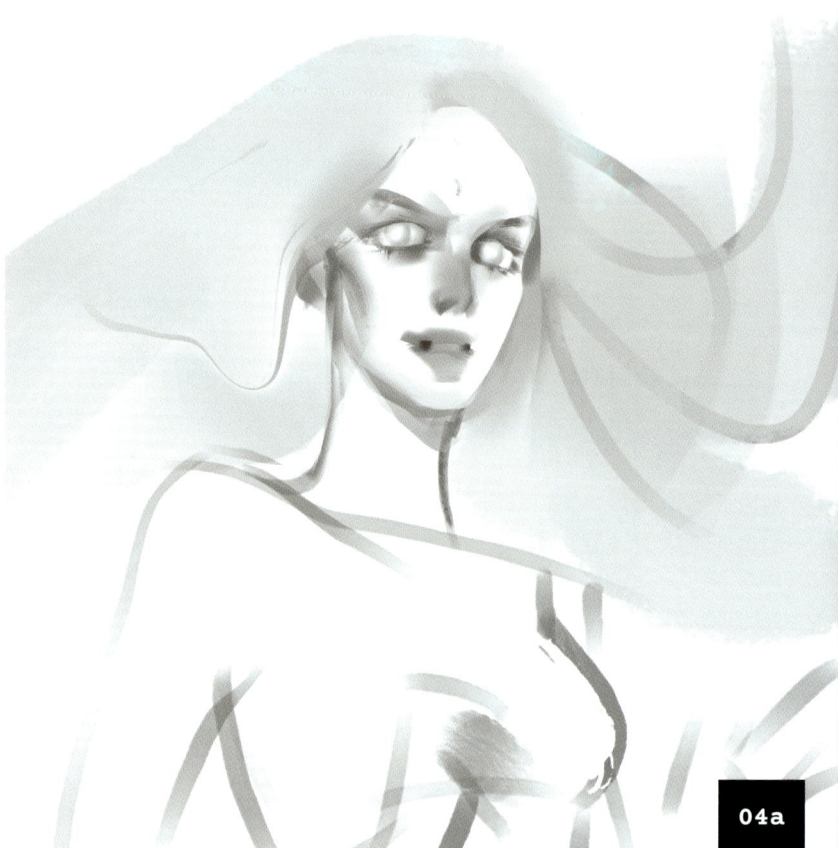

"Multiple views allow me to see my work constantly from a distance and with grayscale values, so that I don't lose my sense of form and lighting"

04a

// The rough silhouette and slightly detailed face before adding color

>04 Merging the sketch and color

Now I combine my chosen color rough with a sketch, creating the base for my painting. After my quick sketches, I make a more detailed outline of the face and the basic shape of the body (image 04a). I choose a favorite color sketch – a heavily green palette to suit the theme of "envy" – and place it under the line art by setting the line art's blending mode to Multiply in Photoshop (image 04b). This creates the colored base for the rest of my painting. If you are working with traditional medium, you can add your selected color scheme as an underpainting to your sketch.

It can help to view the image in grayscale every now and then (or create a value study to refer back to) and also zoom out or take a step back from the image regularly. These multiple views allow me to see my work constantly from a distance and with grayscale values, so that I don't lose my sense of form and lighting.

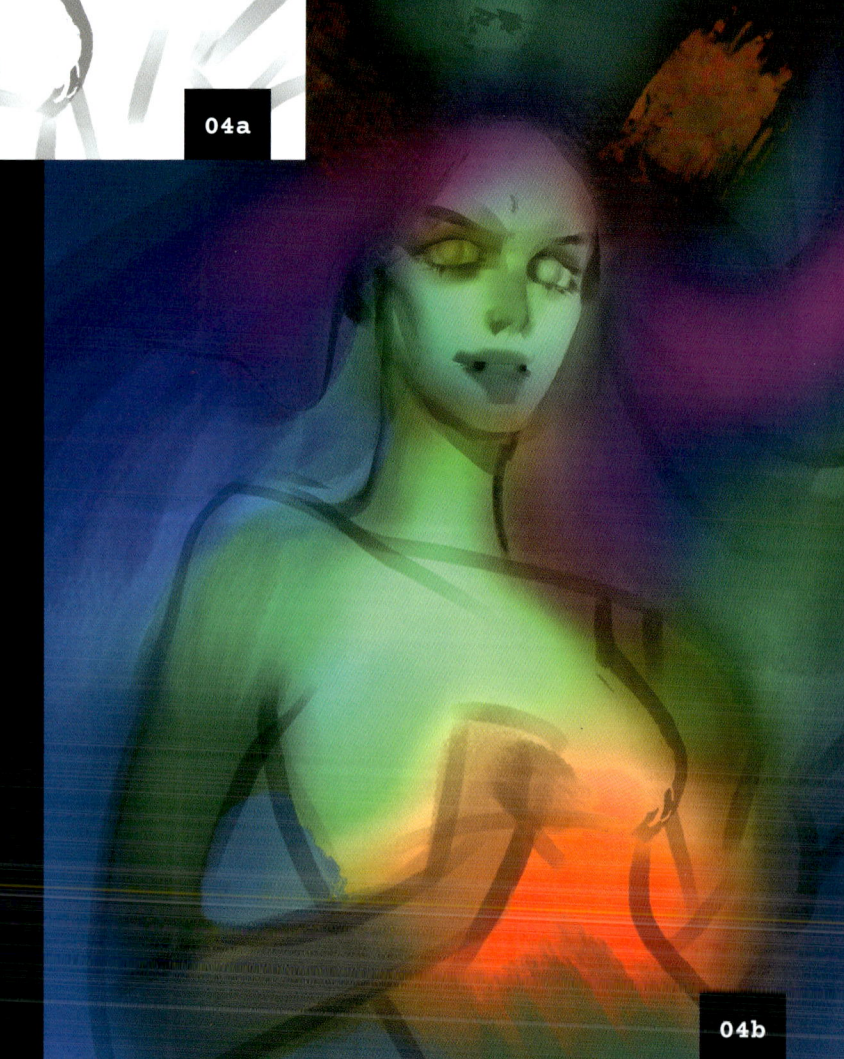

04b

// The line art and colored sketch merged together

>05 Adding details

Now that my underpainting is ready, I can begin to add details. Using a simple textured brush, I sketch a decoration on the character's head, draw her face and neck roughly, and change her hair color. I often use textured brushes to start with because they allow me to create simple forms with a few details and add atmosphere and dynamism to the piece. For example, I make the decorations on the head with a brush in Hard Light mode (an effect which acts as if you are directing a very bright spotlight on the painting area), which adds contrast and color to the piece.

>06 Sketching the face and hair

Now I start to draw her face and correct its perspective. I decide that her eyes will be yellow and not have pupils, because I want her to look sinister, but not terrible; I want her to seem aloof, with a cold stare. I also sketch out the volume and shape of her hair; the blue will contrast with her warm eyes and help them stand out, drawing the viewer into the image. I also work on the positions of her hands. I'm still seeking out the final expression and pose, and this is why lots of changes are applied to the face.

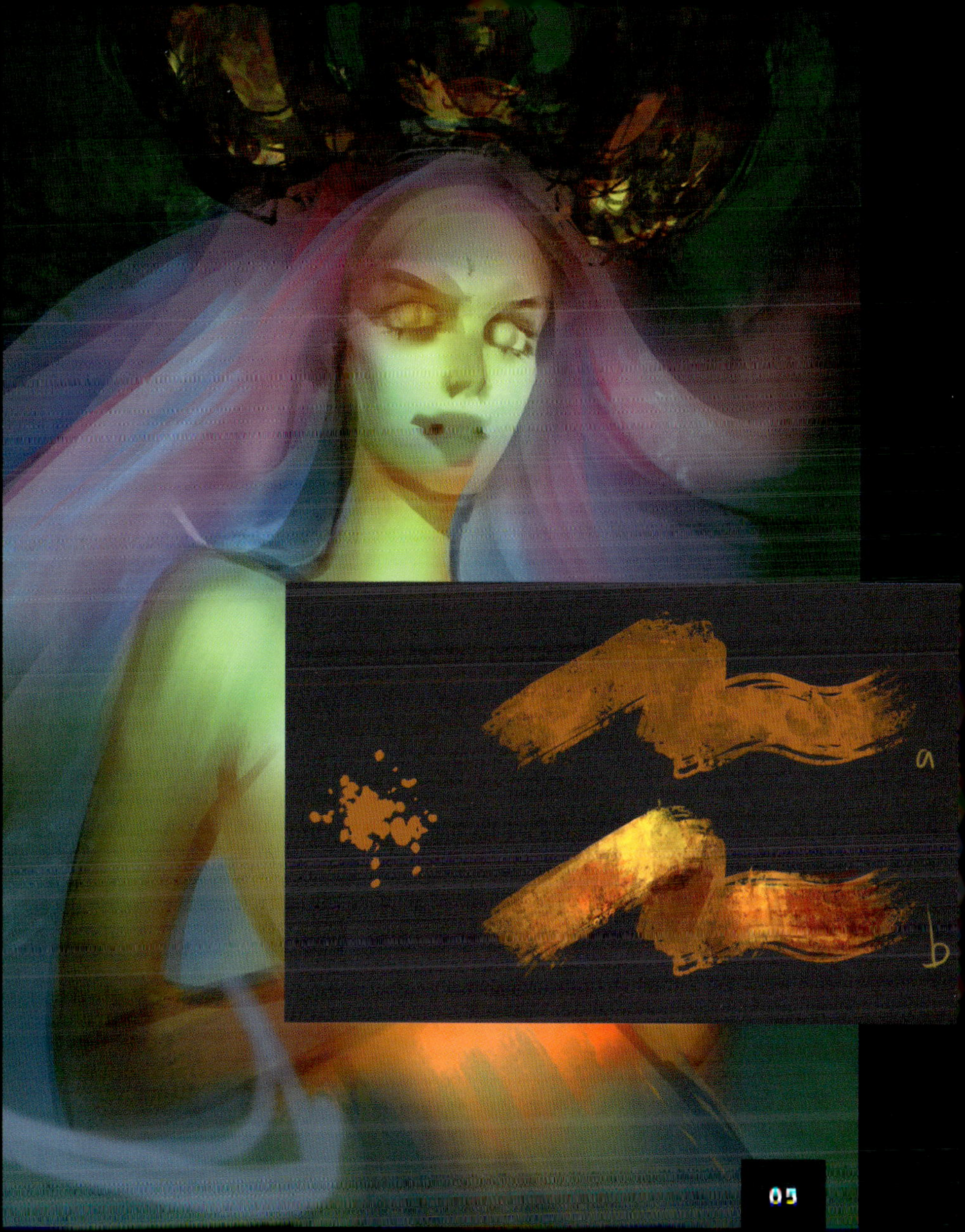

// I keep working using textured brushes

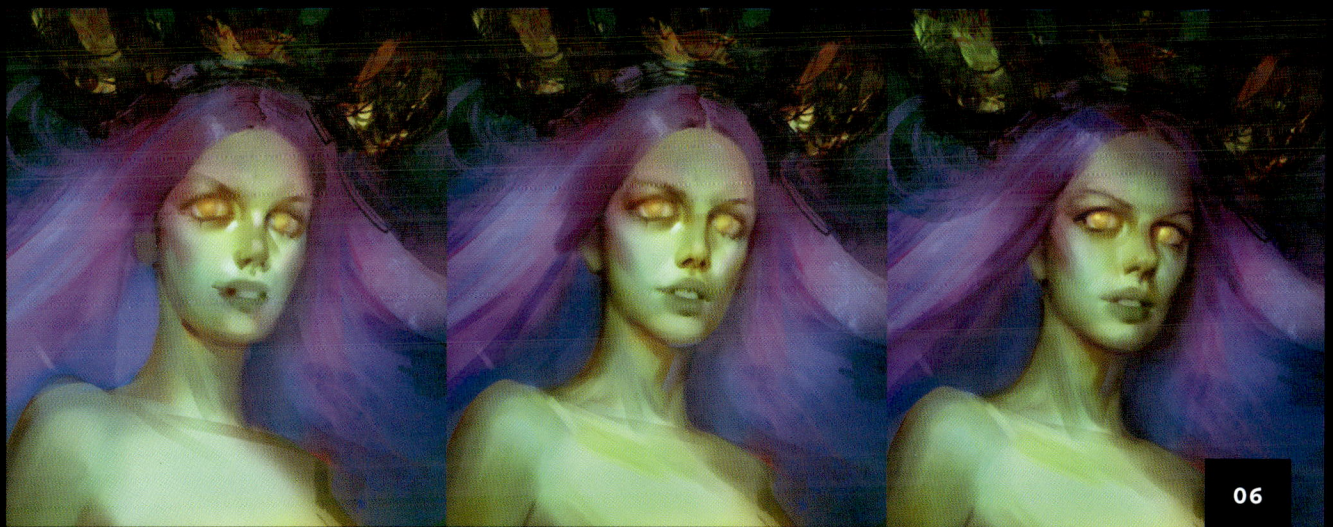

// I'm in search of the right face. I draw until I find my favorite variation

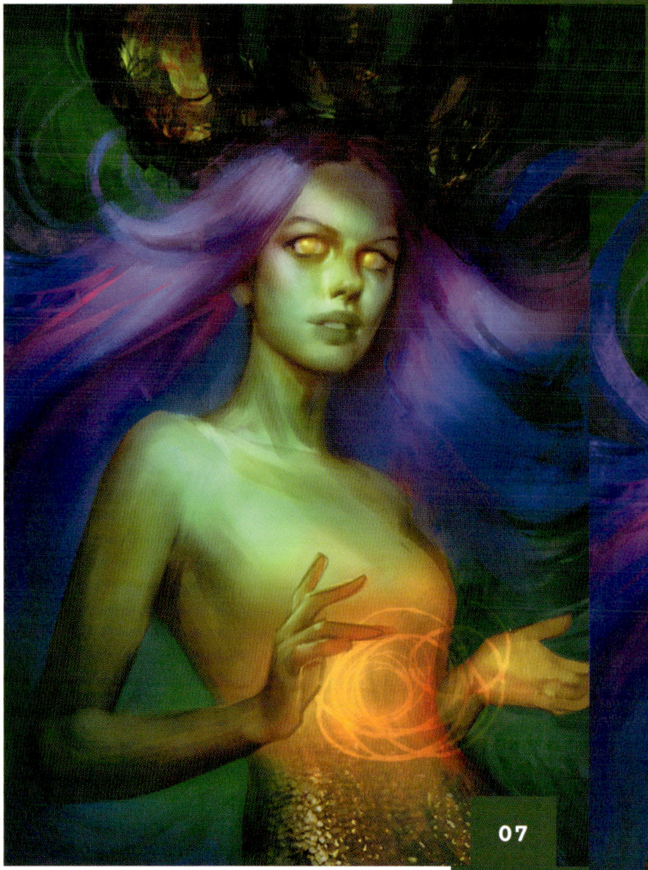

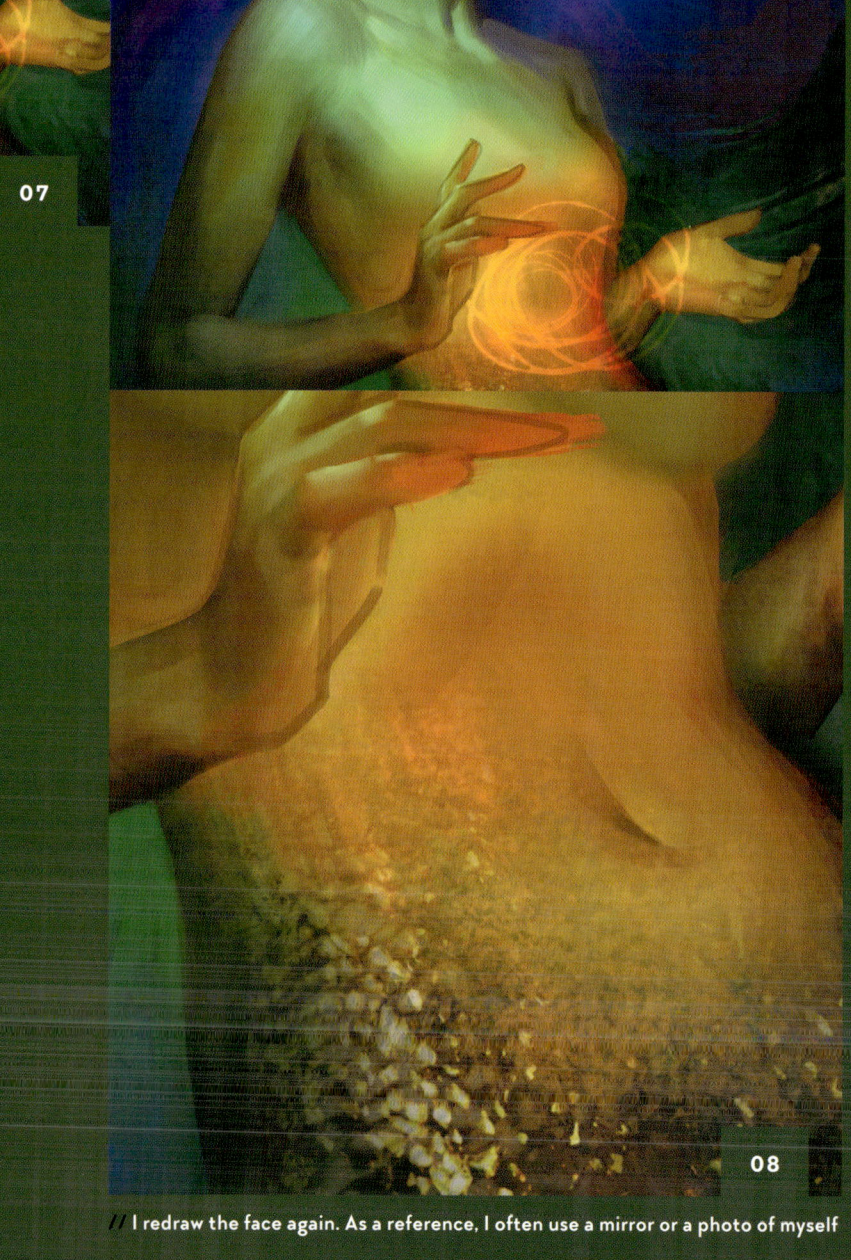

// I improve the lighting on her face and use shadows to emphasize general volumes

>07 Overcoming obstacles

It often happens that I work on one piece for a long time and can't finish it properly. A lot of time is spent on it and the result is not enough! I find myself in this situation now, working on the face for a long time but not liking the result. When this happens, I force myself to work on another part of the picture.

I therefore focus on lighting next, and decide that a cold green light will fall on the character's face. With the help of Soft Light and Multiply modes in Photoshop, I darken the image's corners, so that the main contrast is focused on the face and the viewer's eyes are drawn there as a result. I also start to paint her hands, with glowing particles, and add some scale textures to her hips.

>08 Face and anatomy

I begin to see more clearly what the finished piece should look like. It will be a portrait of a snake-girl or a mermaid, with cold, greenish skin. Maybe she

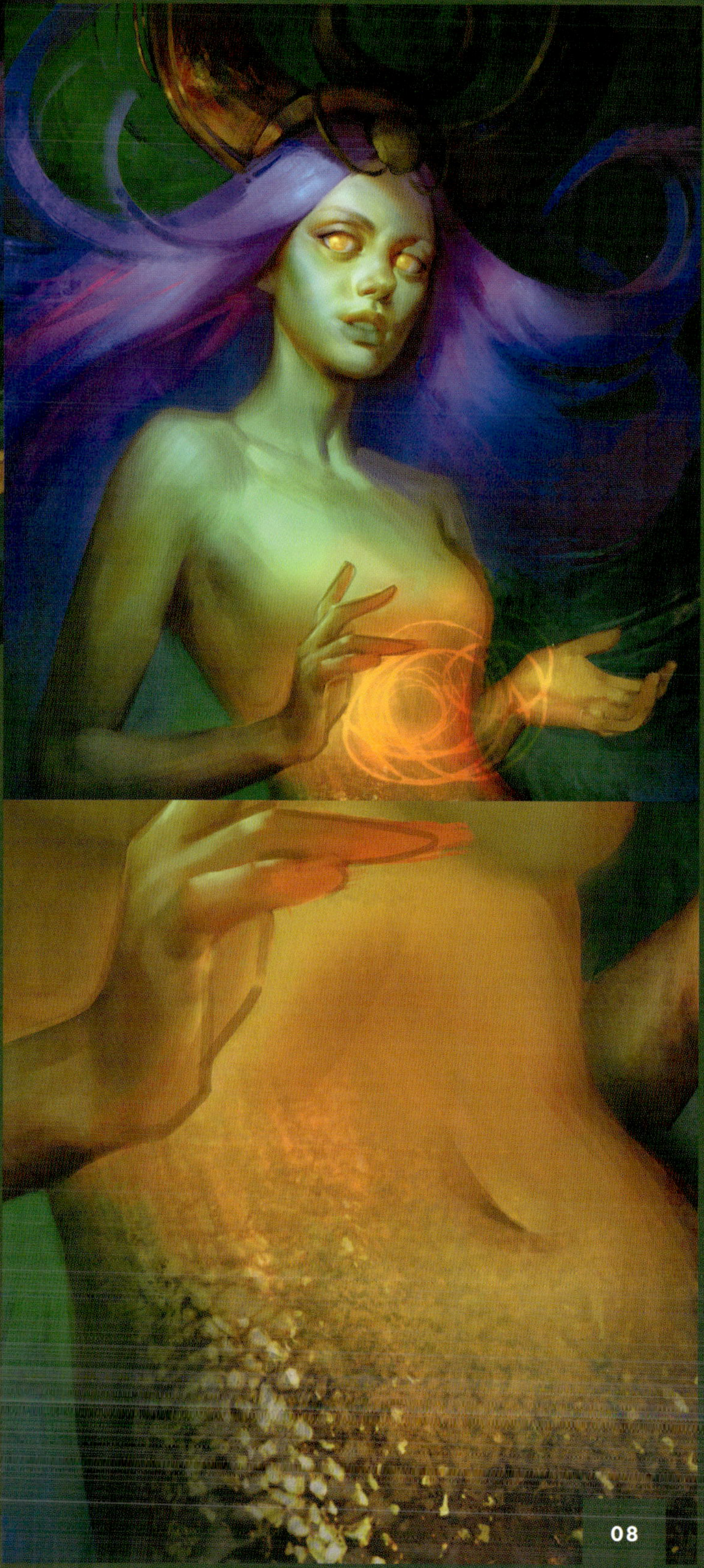

// I redraw the face again. As a reference, I often use a mirror or a photo of myself

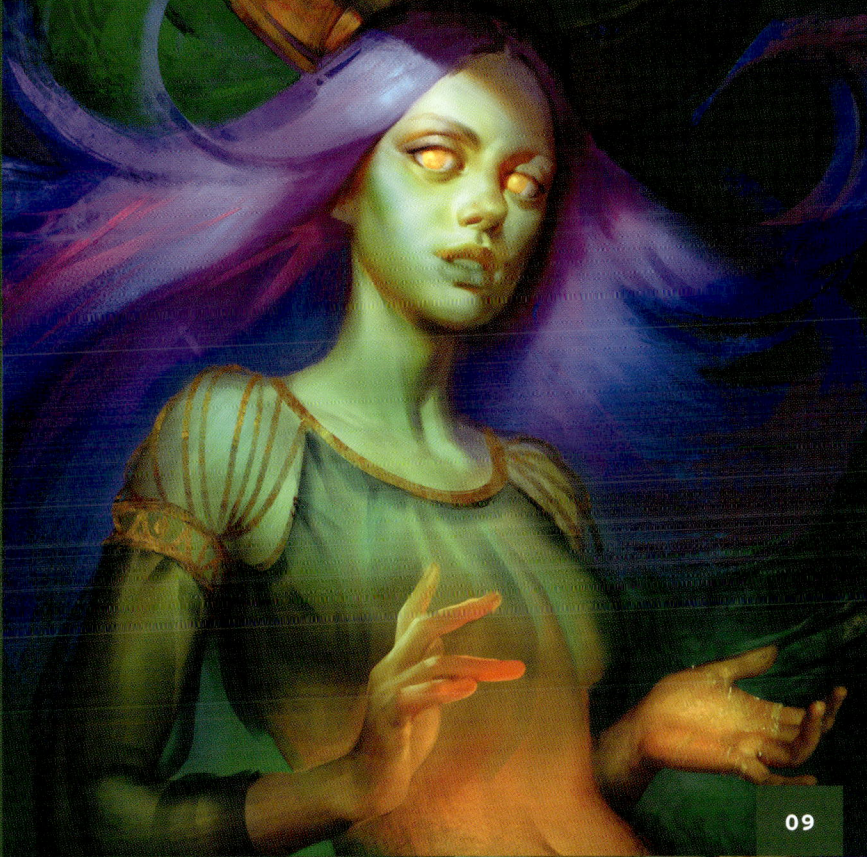

09

in Photoshop: first I use Levels, and then I use Selective Color to correct any color changes made by Levels. I also sketch a transparent fabric decorated with gold patterns at this stage. I want the blouse to flutter, creating an ethereal effect and adding to the mystery of the illustration

>10 The snake

Thinking on the theme of "envy," I come up with the idea of a "hot" yellow-orange snake in the girl's hands. Envy is a strong, sizzling, toxic feeling, and the warm-colored snake creates a strong contrast against the character's cold, green skin. The yellow snake also complements the girl's yellow eyes and scaly body.

// Here I use a soft brush to convey the soft, smooth, transparent nature of the fabric

can only live in the dark, and this is why her eyes are nearly blind. Perhaps, long ago, she was an ordinary human girl, but now she is cursed. Thinking about this makes me want to repaint her face and make it softer. Introducing a narrative aspect to your painting will help you think more carefully about your decisions, and increase the audience's engagement with the image.

Now that I've decided what the face will look like, I also render the body, although not too much because there will be clothes on top of it. I adjust the place where her neck and chest join, and render her shoulders and belly.

>09 Contrast and fashion design

Often, after long hours of drawing, the picture becomes a bit dull and the contrast is lost. So as I progress towards the final stages of work, I bring some contrast back into the painting. To do this I use two functions

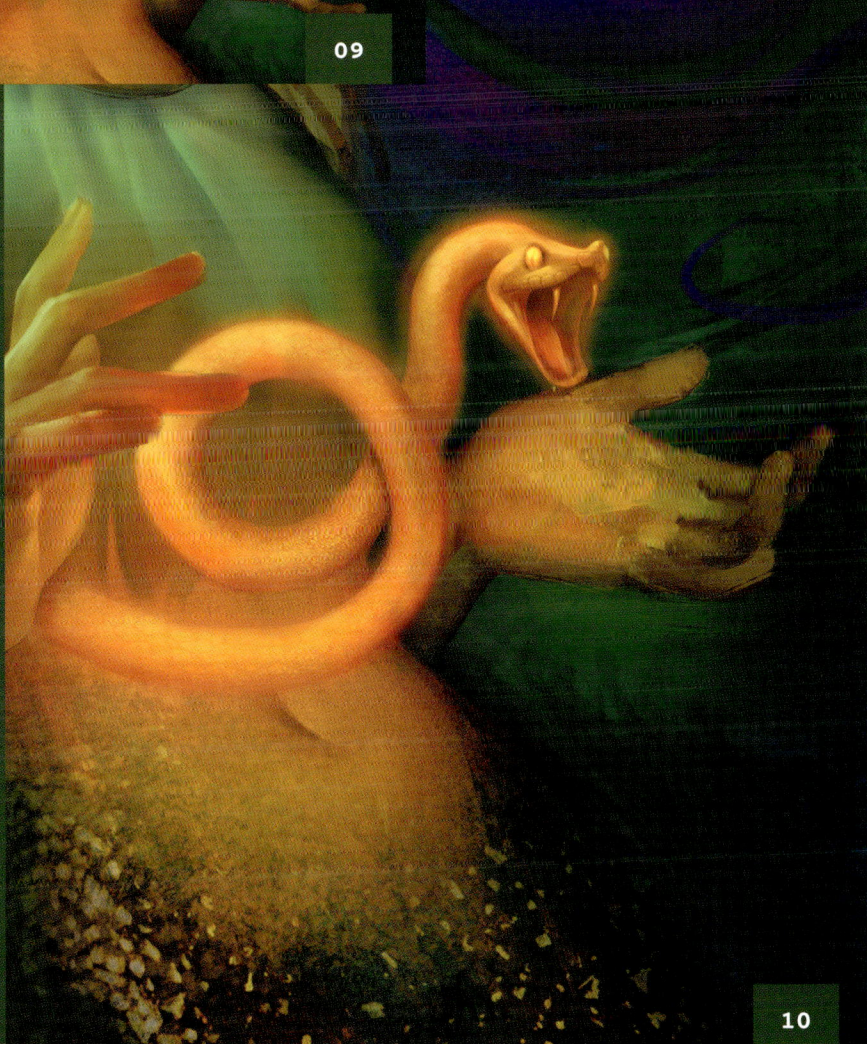

10

// The yellow snake ties the image and theme together

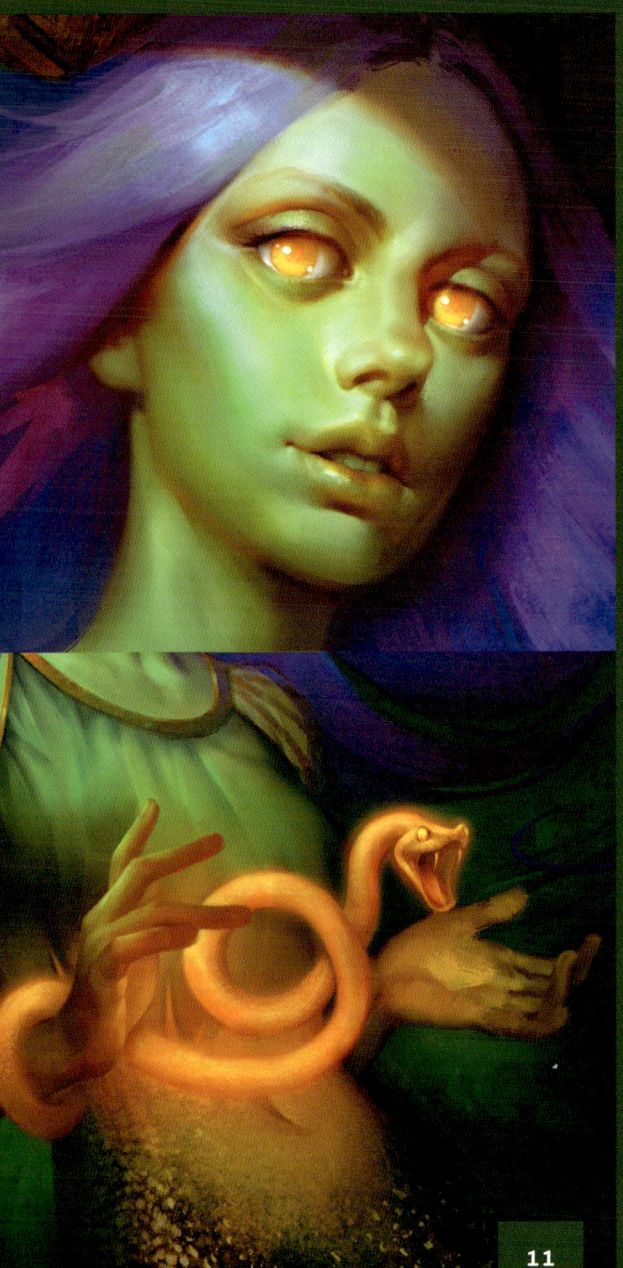

12

// Refining the colors and rendering

11

// Reviewing the character's face and hands

>11 The face and hands

A character's hands and face are important focal points, so I return to them in this step. In my opinion, when you draw a character, the most important things that you need to draw are their hands and face. Depending on the focus I want to create, I remove rough brushstrokes in some areas; in other areas, on the contrary, I add even more brushstrokes. I also add more texture to the skin.

>12 Final refinements

All the major work has been carried out already, so I just have to finish off the details – the hair, decoration on the head, and different particle effects – to create a sense of movement in the picture. Details should be drawn in, but not everywhere, to keep the image looking fresh.

>13 Finishing effects

In the final step, I extend the warm glow from the snake to reach up to her hair and face more, enhancing the impact of the symbol of envy in the illustration. I also extend the snake itself to increase the curves and flow of the composition. I add to the headdress to heighten the feeling of power.

Photoshop offers some useful effects for finishing an image, such as the Unsharp Mask filter, or a Noise filter with a quantity of around 2.5. My advice at this stage is to play around with different effects to see what enhances your image and helps it to stand out.

Now, finally, I can relax. It's necessary to have a rest after hard work, so that my next day will be even more productive.

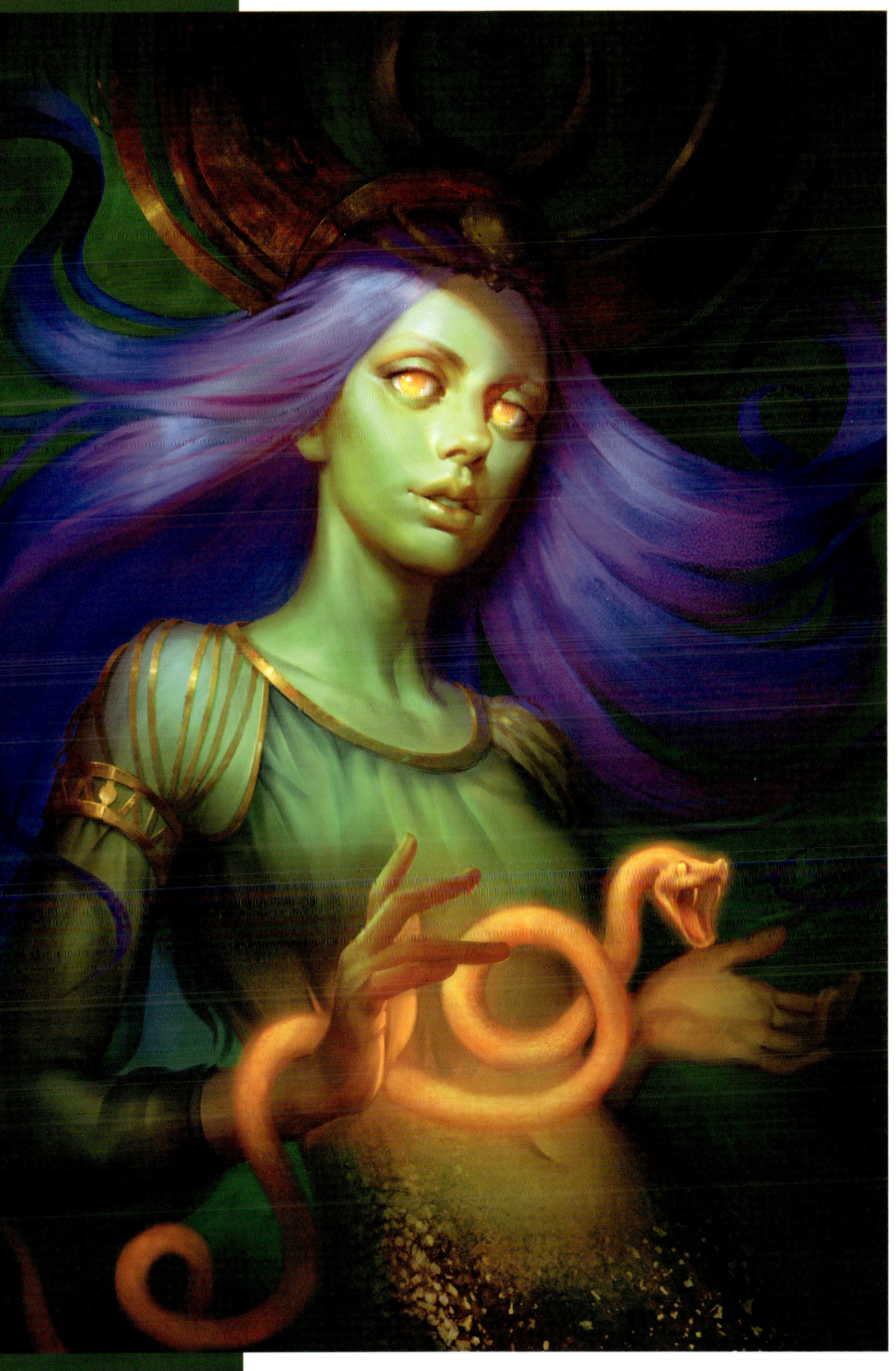

Damien Mammoliti | www.boneandbrush.com

Fear

What strikes *fear* in your heart?

For this tutorial, I will focus on implementing and portraying the striking emotion of fear. In illustration, such a powerful emotion is great to work with as it brings a lot of potential for unique symbolism and subject matters. As it's such a human emotion, we can use that to our benefit when choosing what subject matter to

paint. I will focus on finding those small details to help evoke powerful emotions through tactile imagery.

To start off, I'll work my ideas from imagination and inspiration through personal experience, which will help to fuel the subject matter for the painting. I will be using Photoshop so from there I'll delve into the details of producing quick concept thumbnails,

sketches, color roughs, and lighting, to create a complete digital illustration. By the end, I will have a striking illustration that evokes the most primal of all human emotions: fear.

>01 Ideas and inspiration
Starting off, I find myself asking what I want to portray, knowing fear well. From experience, I know that my own fears are clear to me: fear of drowning, fear of the unknown, and, more specifically, fear of the *dark* unknown. So, heading into this image, I know that I want to work with water and to depict a human (either by portrait or body part) being dragged into those dark and unknown depths. A quick search of my own photo library yields some great imagery of dark water debris that I know I'll use going forward.

>02 Gathering reference
Looking through my photo library, taken on multiple trips out to nearby lakes, I know I have some reference on hand that will give me an idea of how objects and debris look through murky waters. Going into the idea phase, it is important to gather references that help you envision your idea, more than references you would use to copy and replicate

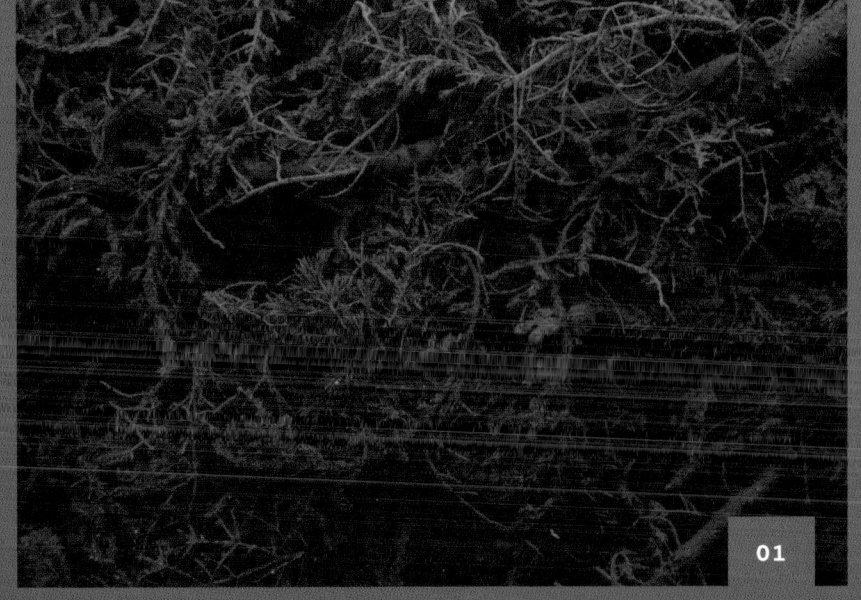

// **A personal photo taken of some sunken foliage in a lake**

01

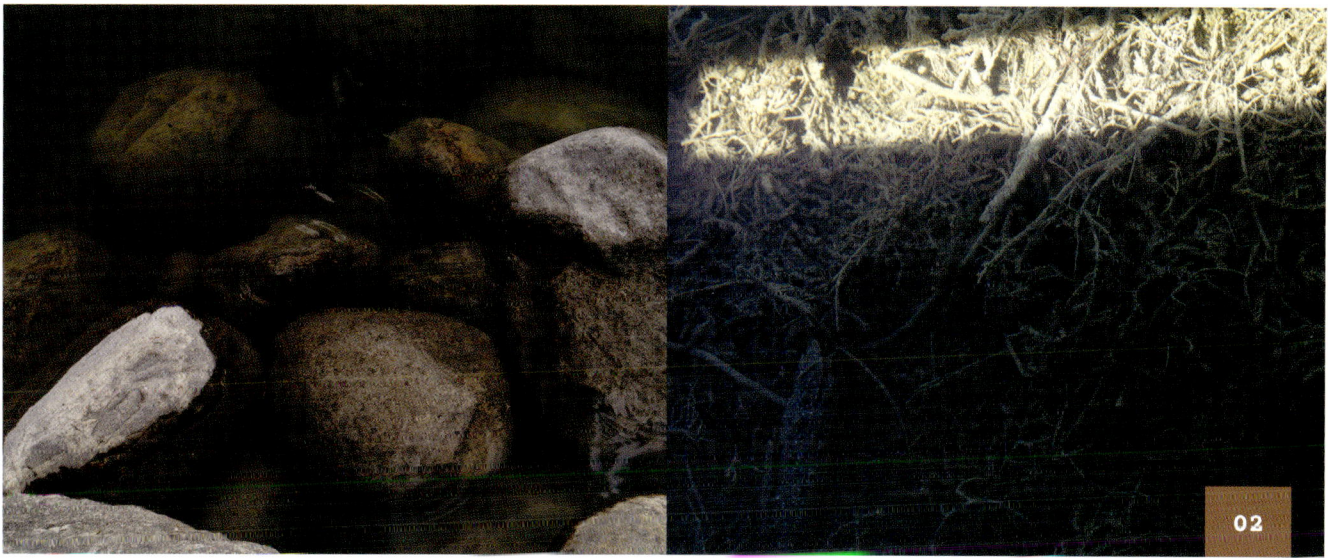

// More personal photos taken of dark water, with debris and lighting variance

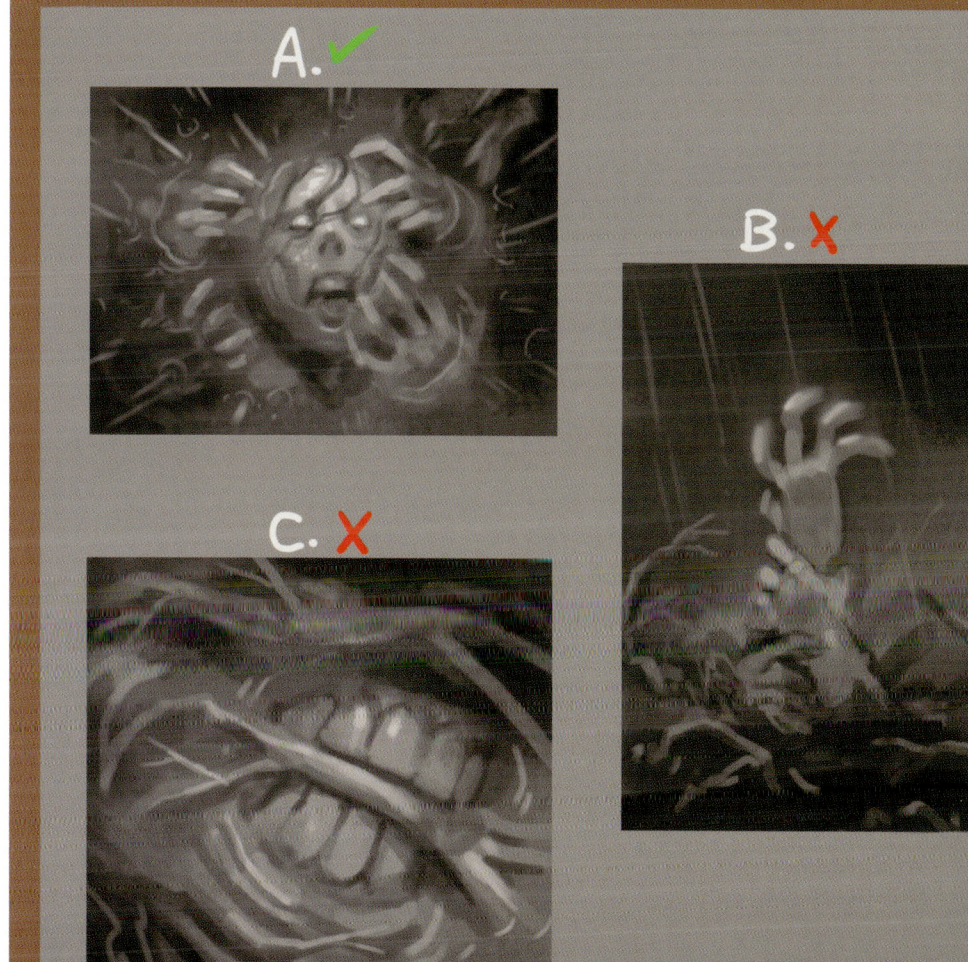

// A small collection of concepts jotted down into thumbnails to pinpoint my ideas

into your painting. What you need to look for the most is reference you can use alongside your painting process, to make your thoughts clear about how you want to depict things such as lighting, shadows, or special effects.

>03 Thumbnails and ideas
Getting into the painting process, it's best to start off with a small number of value thumbnails to help clarify my ideas without spending a whole lot of time doing so. The great thing about working on thumbnails is the effort saved from struggling with a sketch at a higher resolution. Using smaller sketches to look at ideas from afar will be of great benefit to me going into the actual image production phase. It also helps me to try out some quick ideas – even if I may not end up using them at all, I didn't spend much time on them anyway!

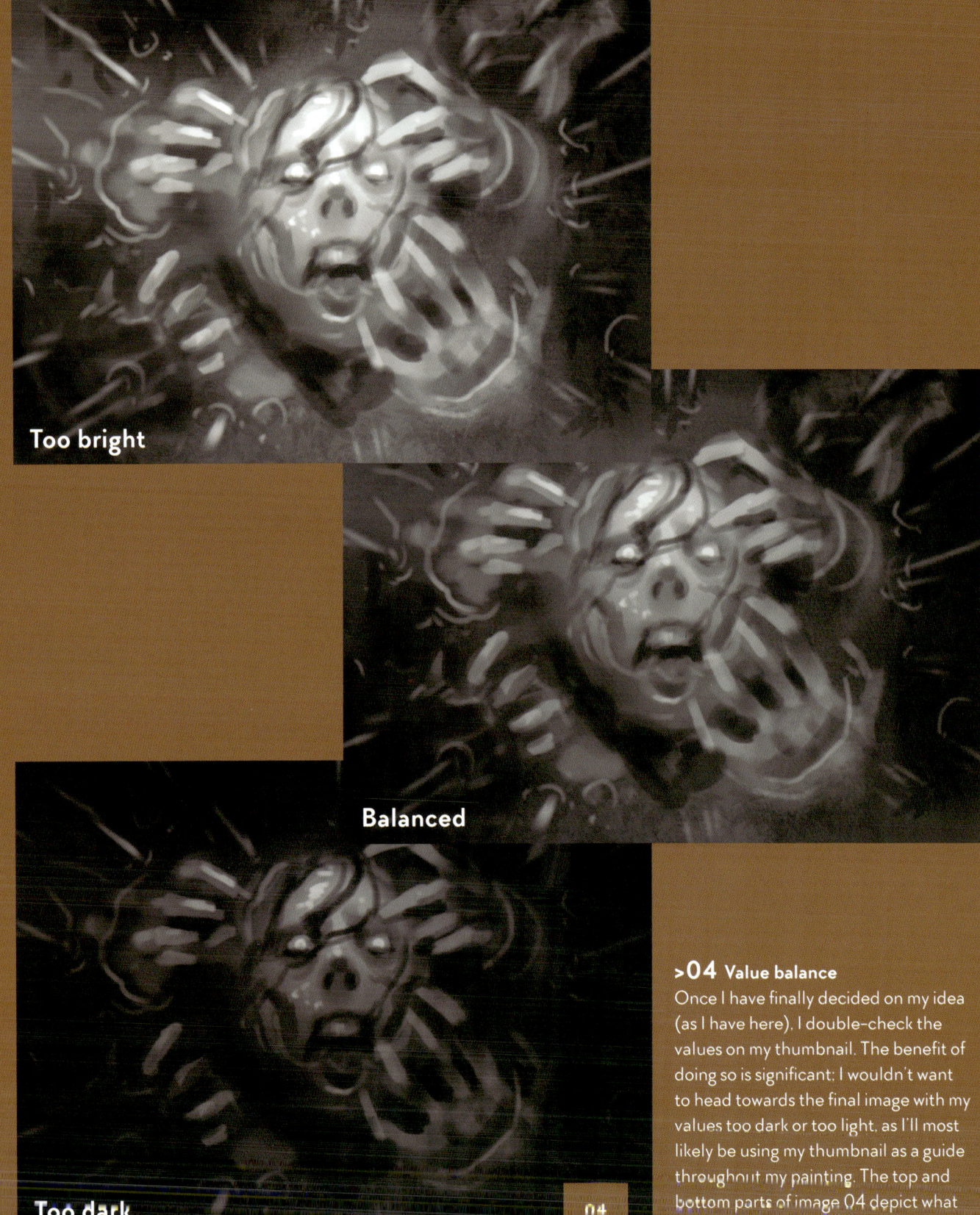

Too bright

Balanced

Too dark

04

// Before beginning with color, I need to check my values

>04 Value balance

Once I have finally decided on my idea (as I have here), I double-check the values on my thumbnail. The benefit of doing so is significant; I wouldn't want to head towards the final image with my values too dark or too light, as I'll most likely be using my thumbnail as a guide throughout my painting. The top and bottom parts of image 04 depict what the thumbnail looks like when the values are too bright or too dark, respectively. The one thing to look for is balance; I make sure the brightest highlights are as easily spotted as the darkest darks, as in the middle thumbnail in image 04.

>05 Composition

Composition helps me to define and convey my image with the help of directional lines and shapes. I use diagonal lines to draw the attention of the viewer (rain drops), a circle to frame the portrait (the ring of hands grabbing onto it), and a triangle (for the emotion of the face), which is a harder-edged shape to help convey the fear apparent there. Each of the fingers points toward the face, as do each of the rain drops. It's very evident where the focus needs to be when looking at the thumbnail's composition.

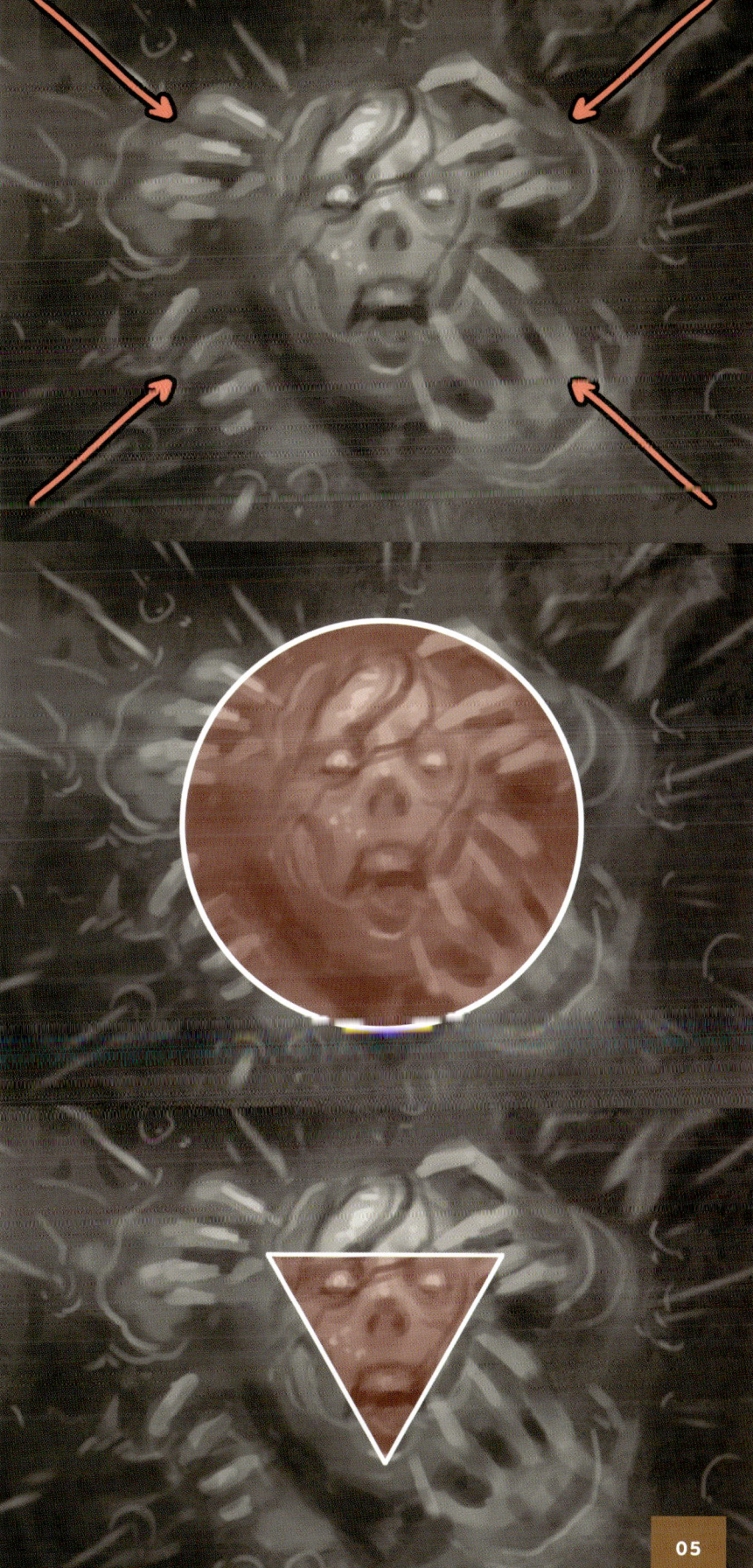

05

// Use simple shapes to create focus in your image

// PRO TIP

Fear is everywhere

From your favorite horror movie to real-life events, fear is an emotion we all experience one way or another. Use your knowledge of famous events or media to help fuel your ideas when creating your own paintings. Perhaps you were inspired by a recent event in your life, or a recent book you've read. Whenever you are inspired, jot down your ideas, even if you plan to come back to them later.

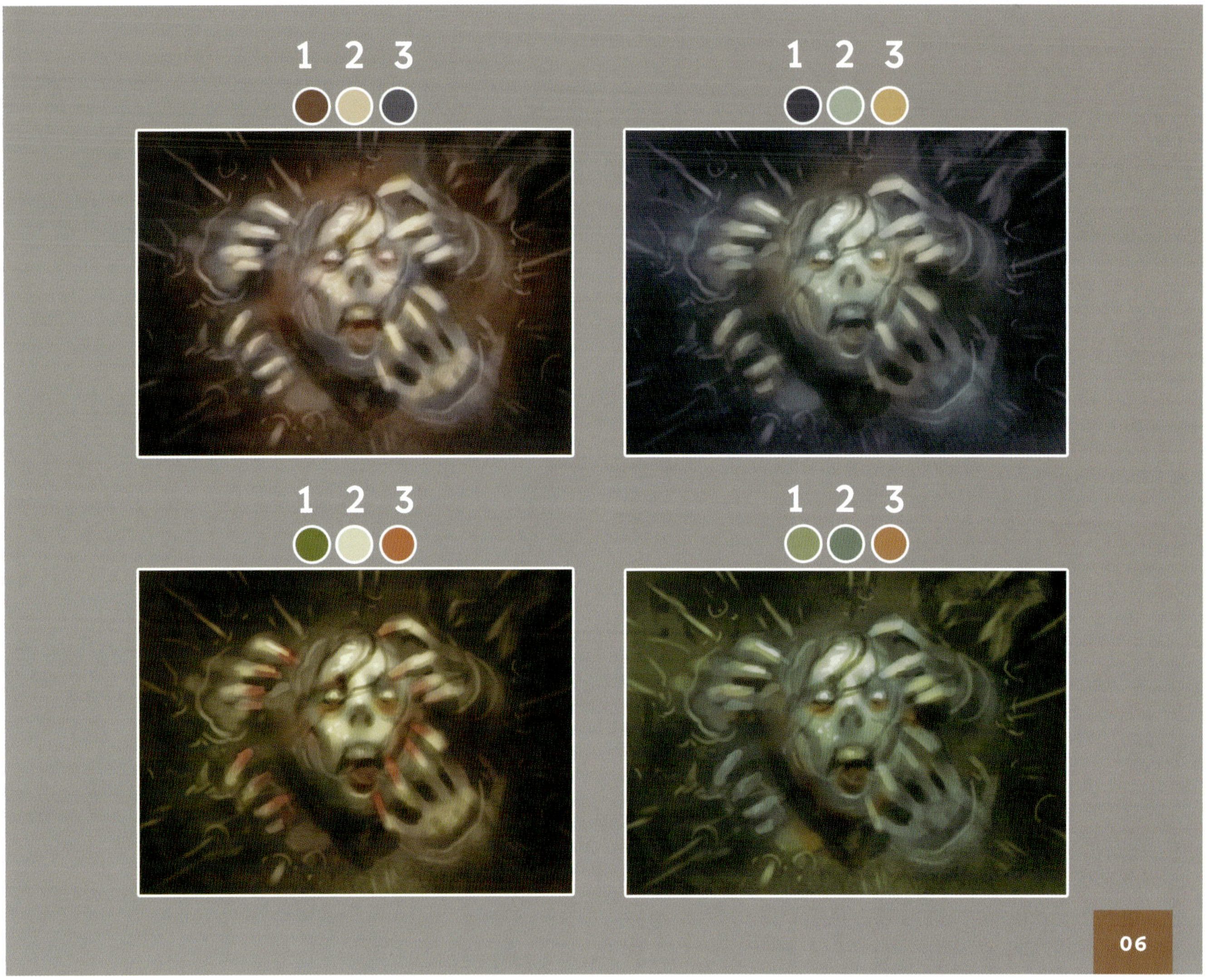

1 2 3

1 2 3

1 2 3

1 2 3

06

// Testing different three-tiered systems of colors

"Now that I have a clear idea of the direction I want to go in for my final image, I can move towards the rendering"

>06 Color-boarding and mood

Once I am happy with my thumbnail, it's time to touch on color. The main point here is to evoke a powerful emotion of fear. In the chart above, you can see four rough ideas I try, manipulating a three-tiered system of colors to achieve this. The first color is the overwhelming color dominating the thumbnail. The second colors are used for lighting on the hands and face. The third colors are used as accents, only placed in key areas (like eyes, fingertips, and mouth) to help home in our focus to the portrait. I decide on a palette with a blue-green main color.

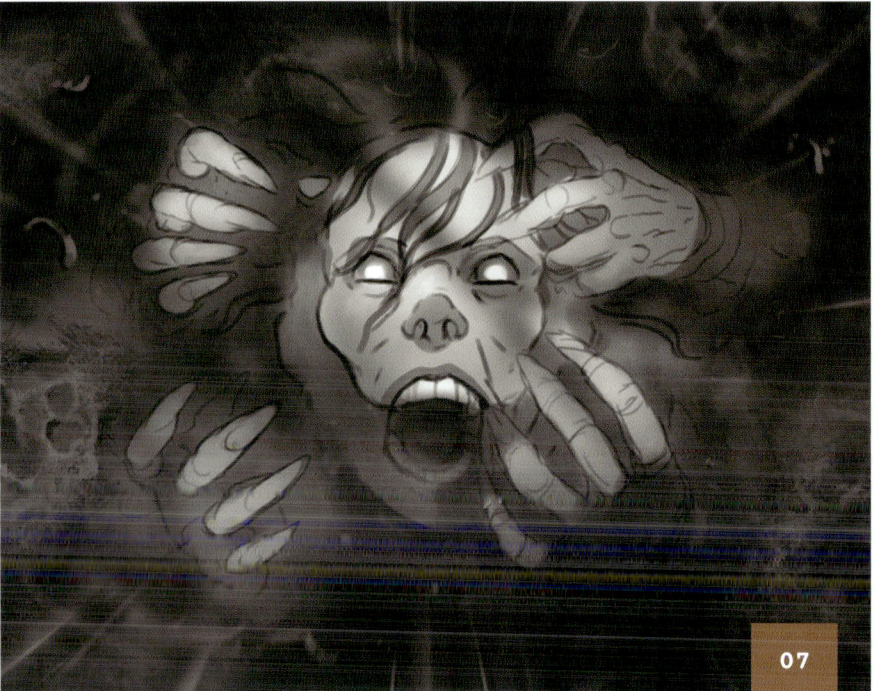

07

// Using the thumbnail to produce a sketch

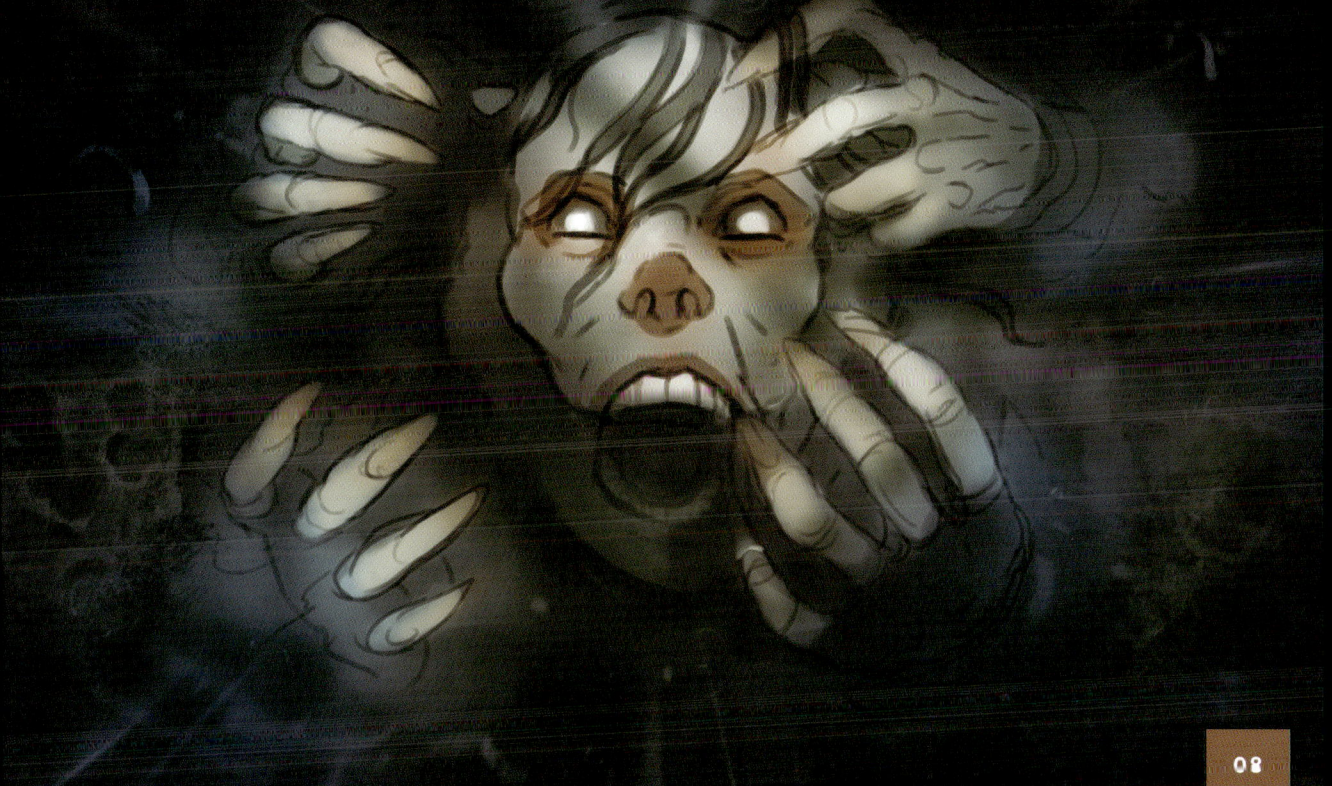

// Putting in the basics for my three-tiered color scheme

>07 Sketching

Now that I have a clear idea of the direction I want to go in for my final image, I can move towards the rendering stage and use my thumbnail as a base for the sketch. I don't worry about stretching my thumbnail too far and pixelating it when blowing it up for the final image size (which should be around 6,000 pixels wide at 300 dpi for great quality), as I will be drawing over it anyway. I therefore use this stage as a base to start sketching my idea with a little more clarity.

>08 Color rough and preparation

Now that I have a good start to my values and sketch, I can proceed to setting up the colors. I start to add in colors chosen from the color rough in step 06. As I am using Photoshop, I use an Overlay layer to do this. Now I have a solid foundation with which to begin my rendering.

// PRO TIP

Inspiration and reference gathering

Some websites work wonders for gaining inspiration and reference. From Pinterest to textures.com, you can find loads of inspirational material and references for textures to use in your own creations. Create an easily accessible folder that has anything you may need to help fuel your fire when working on a painting!

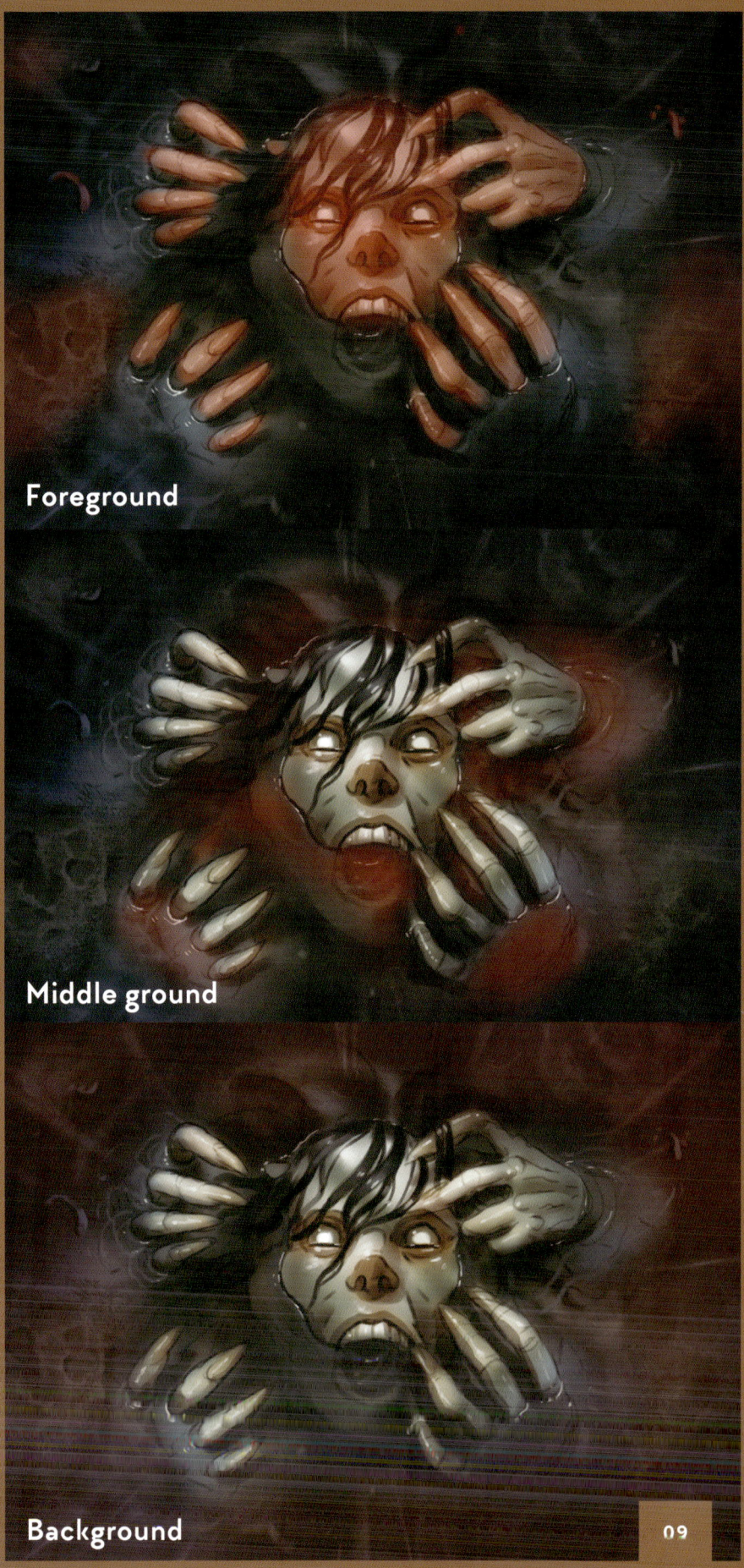

Foreground

Middle ground

Background

09

>09 Separating forms

It's important to consider the different elements of your painting carefully so that you detail each one appropriately. In image 09 you can see how I separate different parts of my painting (highlighted in red in each image). In the foreground, I have the face and hands as the most legible part of my image. From there, I have the middle ground, where there will be water effects such as ripples and droplets, and perhaps some leaves left floating on the water. Behind all of that, I have the background, which shows the murky water and whatever happens to be floating beneath. Separating the forms like this gives me a greater understanding of how I'll layer my subjects.

>10 Lighting and presentation

Before I start painting in details, it's best to spend some time finalizing and mulling over where I want the light source to be. For this image, I know I want a light source evenly spaced from the top, as if a flashlight is shining down on the face when a passer-by happens to wander upon it. From that, I know where my highlights, shadows, and cast shadows need to be placed, as seen in the before and after images (images 10a and 10b). With this knowledge, it's time to start painting.

// Foreground, middle ground, and background; setting up the focus areas of your painting

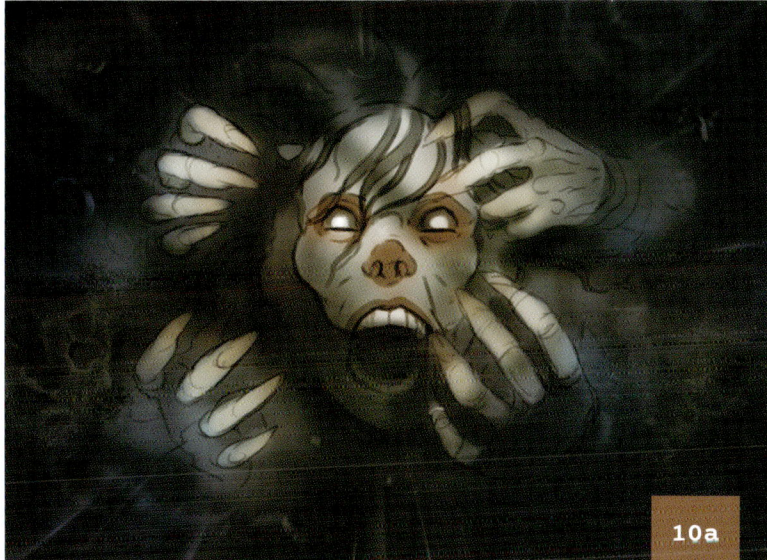

// The image before I add the light details

>11 Emotional detail

Fear is a very interesting emotion to depict; using some basic ideas, we can easily evoke those emotions in the viewer. Uncomfortable feelings like hair laying on an open eye, or water filling into the mouth, demonstrate what types of sensations can be played with in an image like this. Here, I can evoke empathy by disrupting useful sensations (such as tasting or breathing) or placing things where they are most unwanted. This helps the viewer gain empathy towards the subject matter, heightening their experience of the emotion.

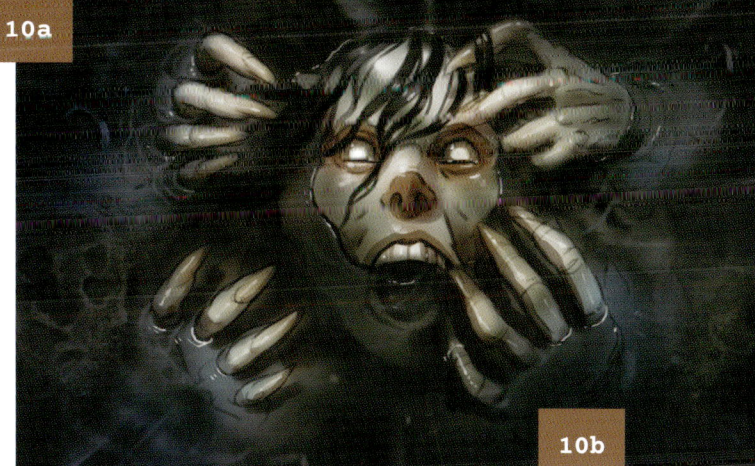

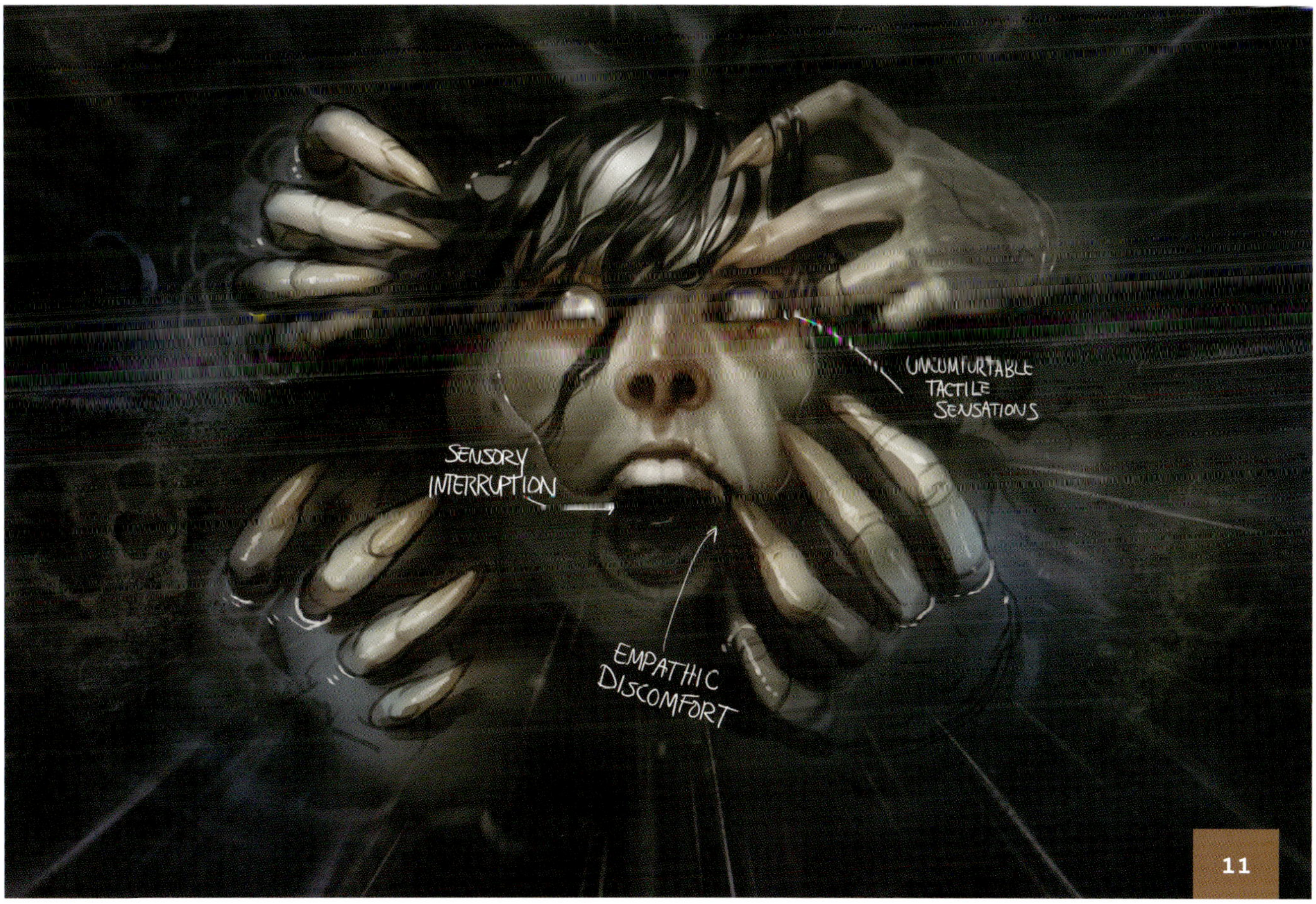

// Setting up lighting before working towards rendering

// Using some small details to help convey big emotion

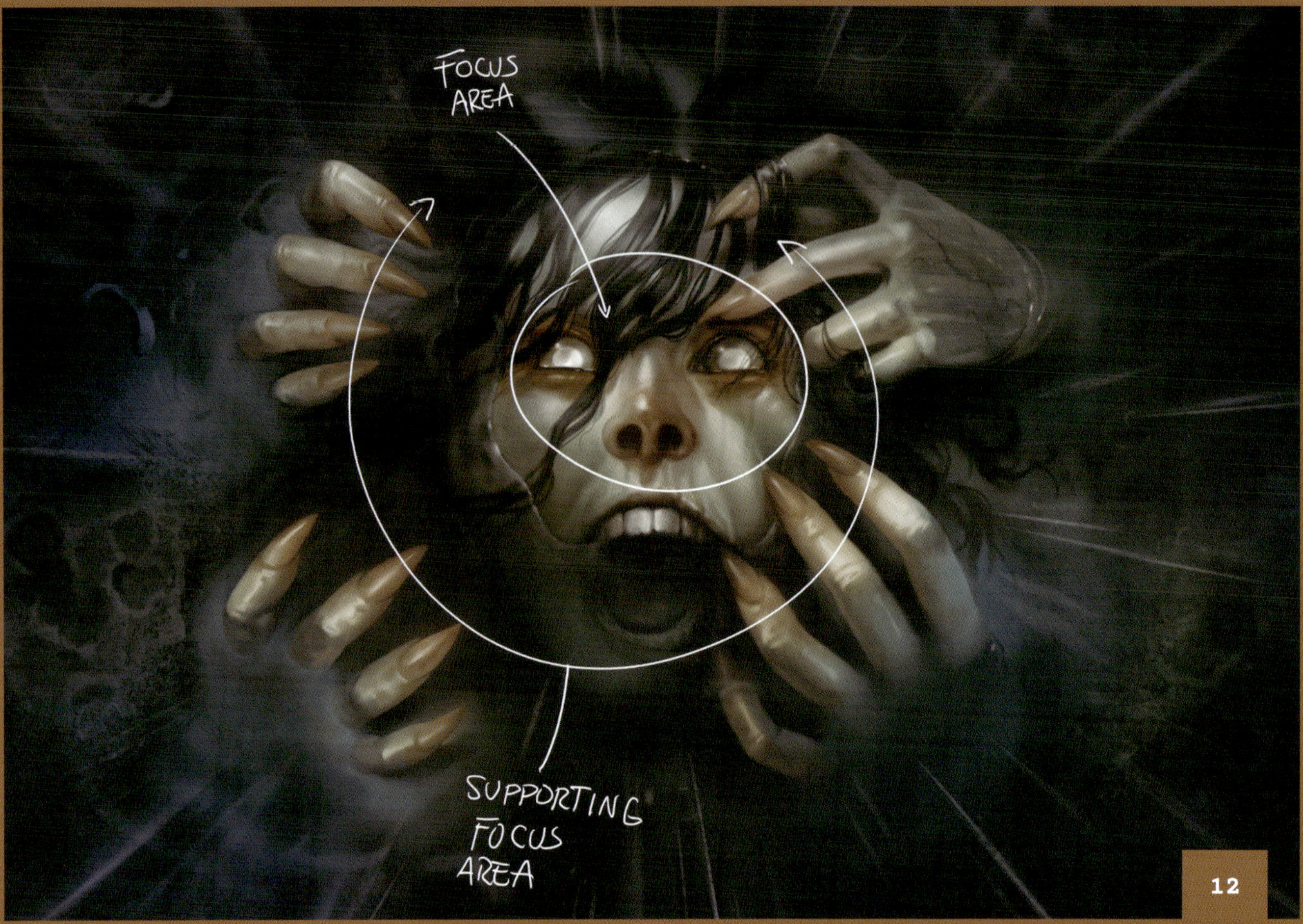

FOCUS
AREA

SUPPORTING
FOCUS
AREA

12

// Color saturation and contrast helps put focus where it needs to be

>12 Color emphasis

As I render, I keep an eye on how the colors blend and contrast. The biggest contrast in this image comes from the blue waters and orange focal points in the face and hands. This contrast helps to draw the viewer into the image exactly as I want, and blending those lightly saturated oranges into the pale flesh keeps the foreground elements described in step 09 in front of the middle ground and background.

>13 Water effects

Moving away from the foreground, I now work on the middle ground of water effects painted on top of the objects lying below the water. I can use the water effects to help accentuate the foreground elements further. Waiting to do this until after I've worked on the face and hands is best, because I will know how strong the water effects should be in order to keep them far enough in the background to not compete with the foreground.

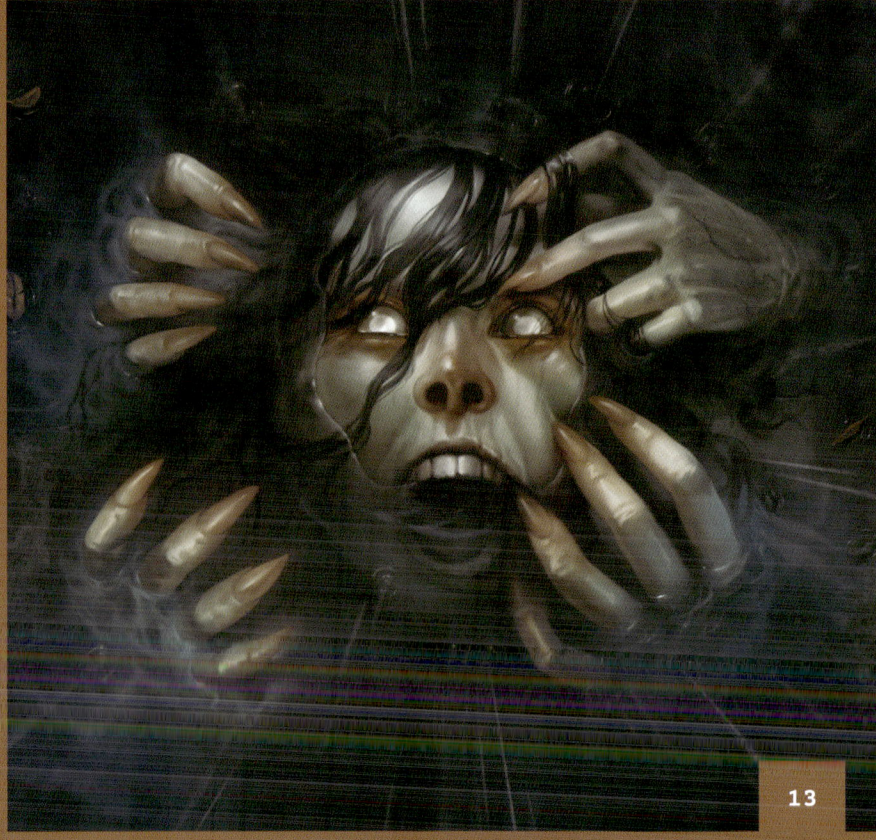

13

// Rendering water effects in the middle ground

>14 Adjustments and touch-ups

Nearing the final stage of rendering, it's time to take a step back and check on the overall color balance and lighting. For now, the rendering seems a bit flat, so I use a Curves adjustment layer to check my colors and bring back some of the swamp-water hue. I also add an Overlay layer with some yellow to add a natural light across the face (images 14a and 14b).

>15 Final image

After working out my lighting adjustments and colors, the image is now complete with a few more rendering touch-ups! At last, I have an image that depicts fear in its raw and horrible glory. It's time for you to go out and evoke fear in your audience by making your own terrifying creation. Just remember: the more raw the evocation, the more terrifying the image will be to the viewer. Keep your ideas simple but powerful, and your audience will read your message with greater success.

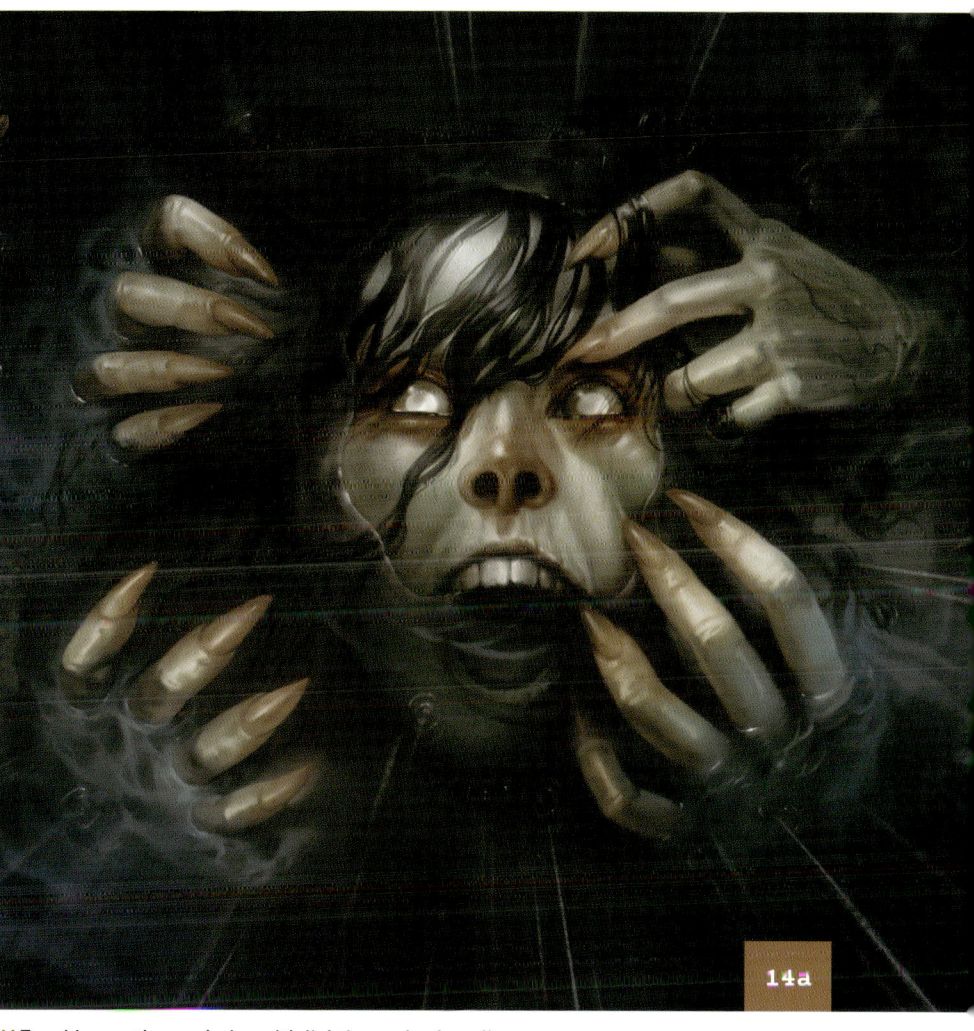

// Touching up the rendering with lighting and color adjustments

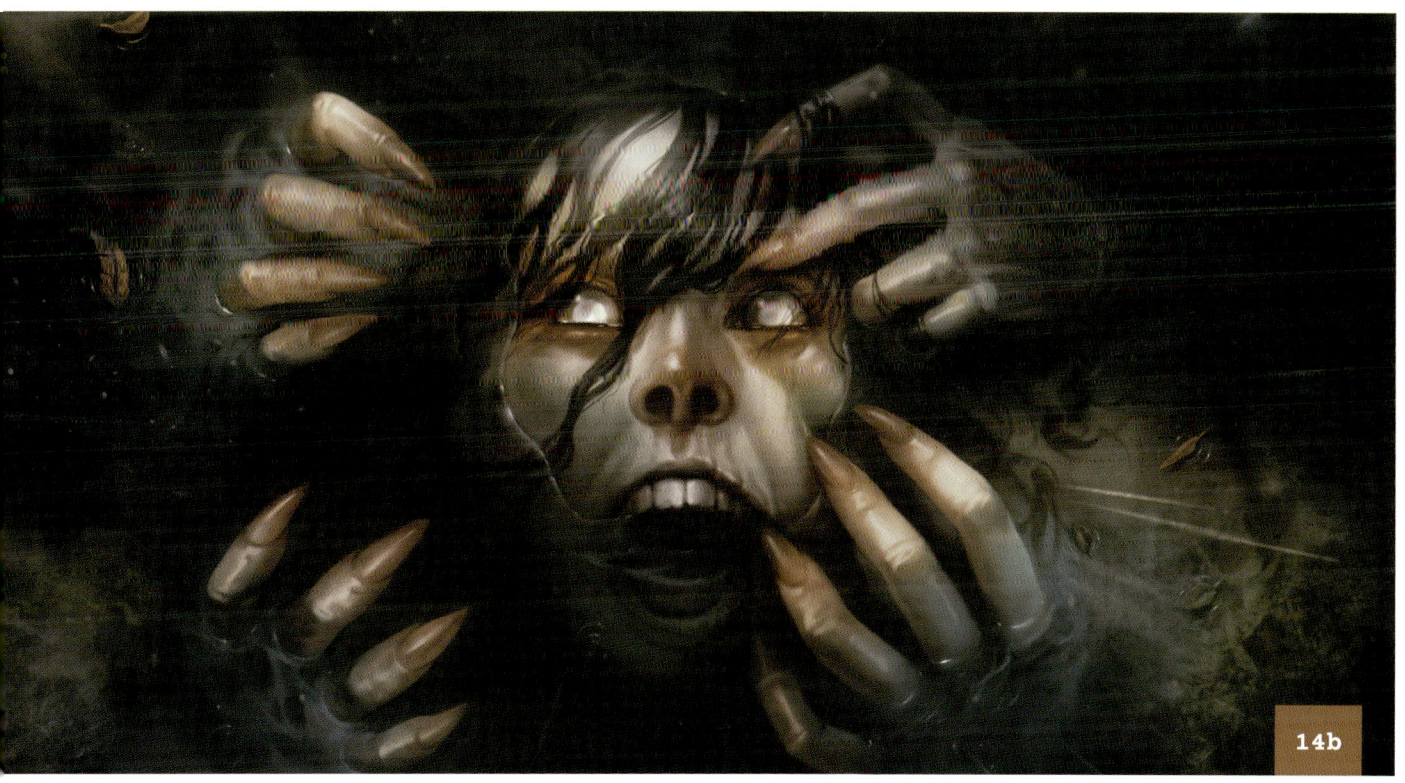

// Adding natural light across the face

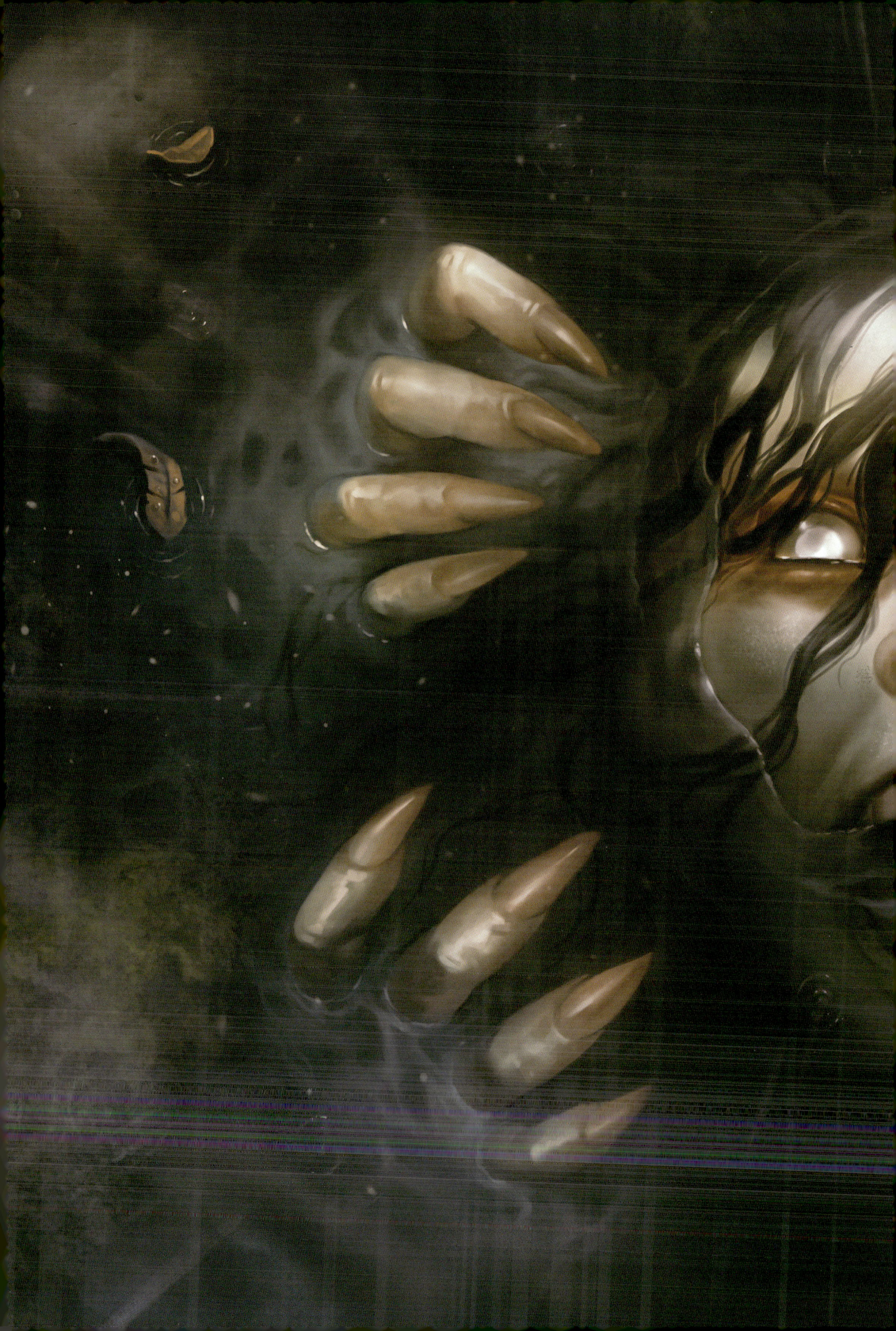

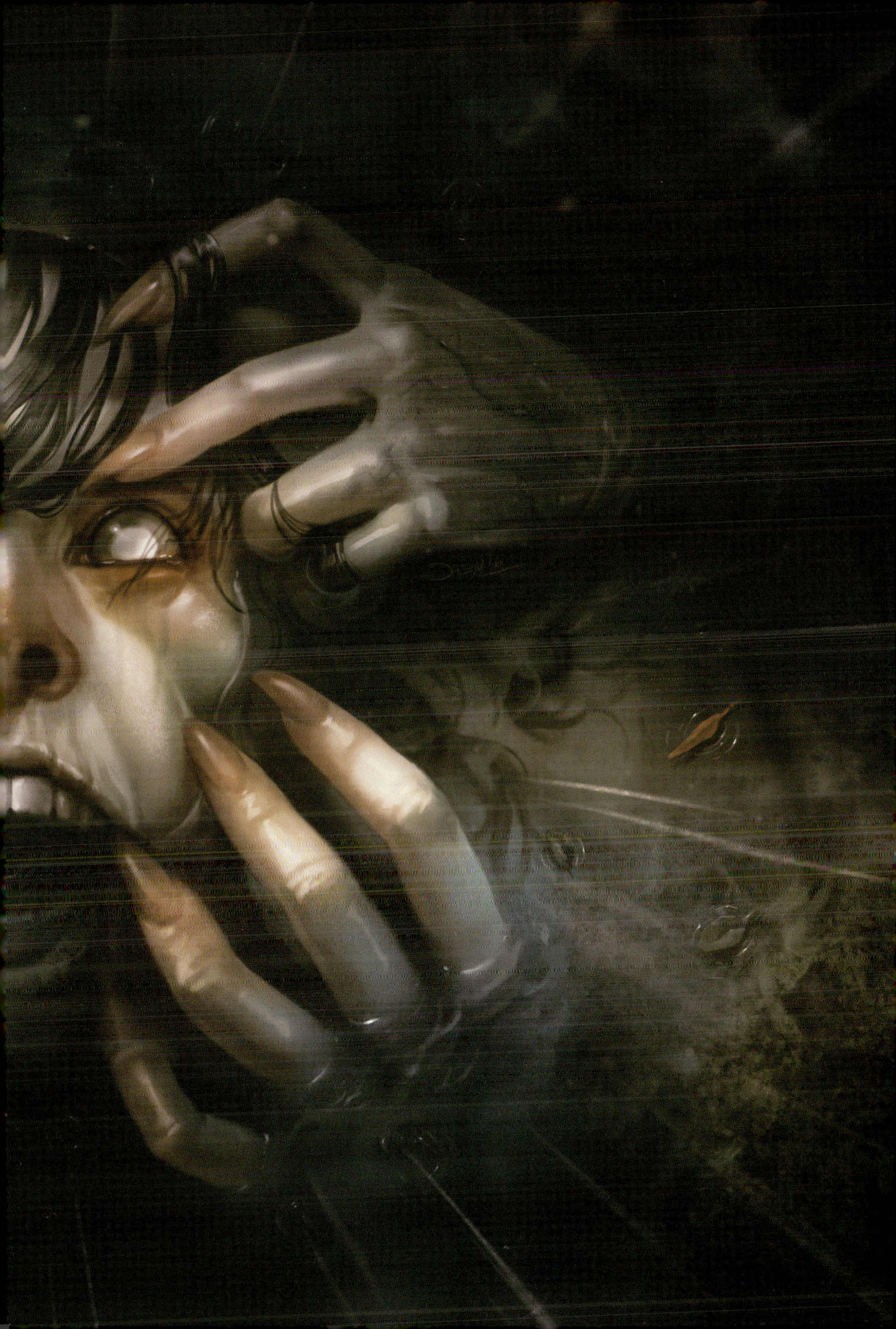

Zachary Montoya | www.zachmontoya.com

Hope

The theme of this illustration is "hope." With the help of the art director's suggestions, I have some initial images in my head that I need to get down on paper in thumbnail format. Based on the concept of stumbling upon a symbol of hope, I want to develop the idea of a wounded and travel-weary warrior trudging through a harsh landscape.

>01 Thumbnails

My thumbnails are really only legible to me, so they are almost entirely utilitarian.

I explore different environments and compositions to help refine my ideas. The thumbnail I keep coming back to is a sort of flowery oasis in alien-like, dark and twisted woods. The very first stages of an illustration involve me sketching down around twenty thumbnails, from which I then select one to go forward with.

>02 Sketching

As a general rule I like to get as much drawing and planning done as possible, so that the surprises that sprout up

throughout the process are generally good ones. I don't want the composition to change too much throughout the painting. I take the idea of the initial sketch – the knight walking away from the viewer – and flip it around so there is more character to see in the wounded knight.

I bring the sketch into Adobe Photoshop and increase the image size to the final dimensions and 300 dpi. Then I start to lay down the overall tones of the lighting throughout the piece.

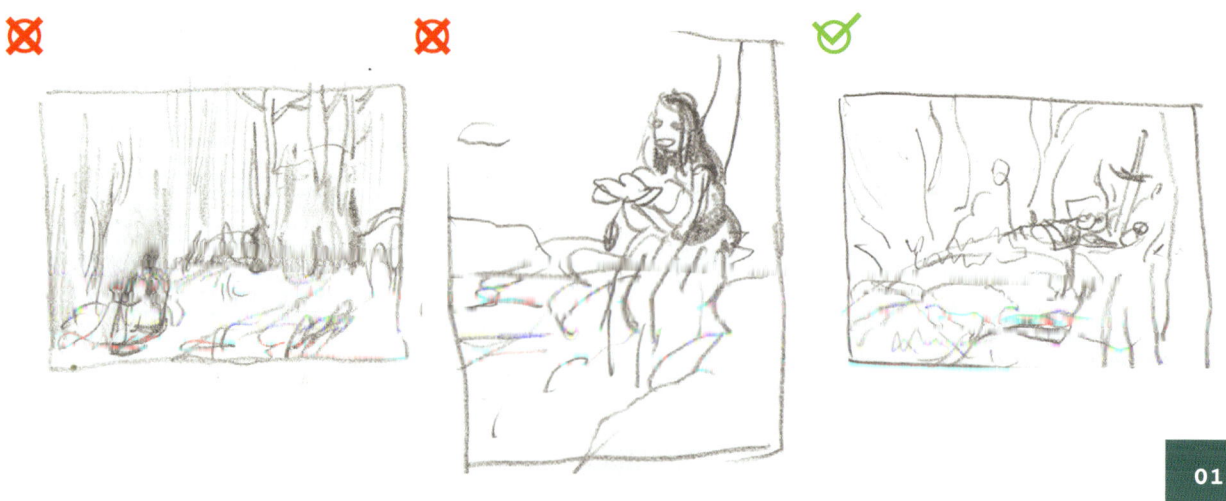

// Selecting an initial thumbnail

01

>03 Defining the scene

I always start out with broad strokes and ambiguous shapes, and essentially carve out and refine the painting step by step. Here I lay down the tones and become slightly more detailed with the drawing. I like to have more defined drawings outlining the focal points in the piece. Later on in the painting these will have the most amount of detail. I want the eye to be drawn to the knight and the sword. The whole composition takes place in a heavily wooded area, so there will be lots of "noise" in the background. This means that the focal points will need to have the most detail and contrast in order to stand out against the rest of the painting.

>04 Color palette

I already have a general color palette and mood in mind before I dive into the painting. I like the idea of using a dark, twisty forest as a cold, almost alien landscape. I have this dark greenish-blue in my head, and a warmer orange ground to contrast with the blue, along with various warm yellows sprinkled across the composition to tie it all together.

I'm not sure what colors the flowers should be, so I place a few pink ones down along with the yellow. If this were an oil painting, my aim here would be to fill up the entire canvas before I start getting down to the nitty-gritty details.

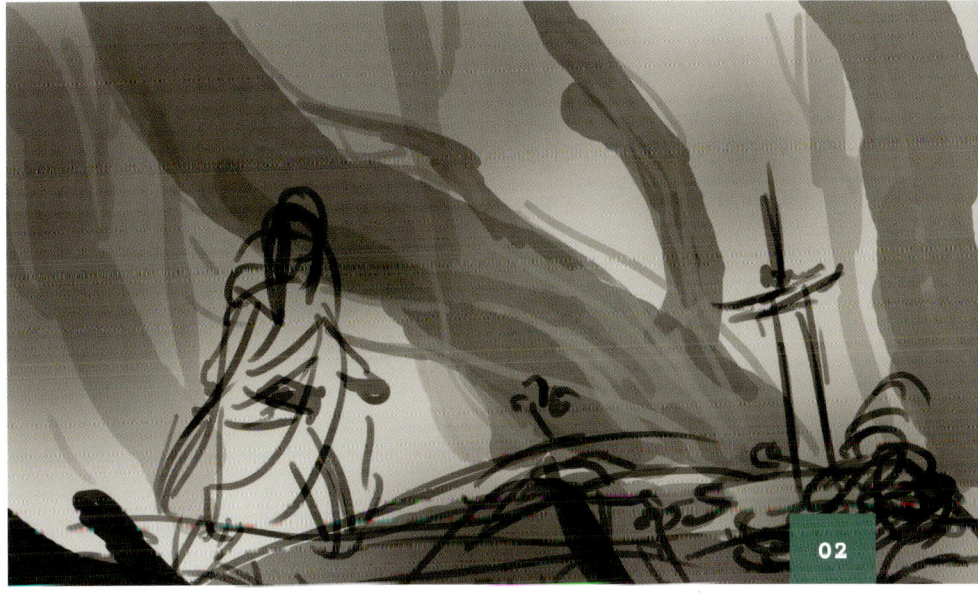

// **Developing the thumbnail concept**

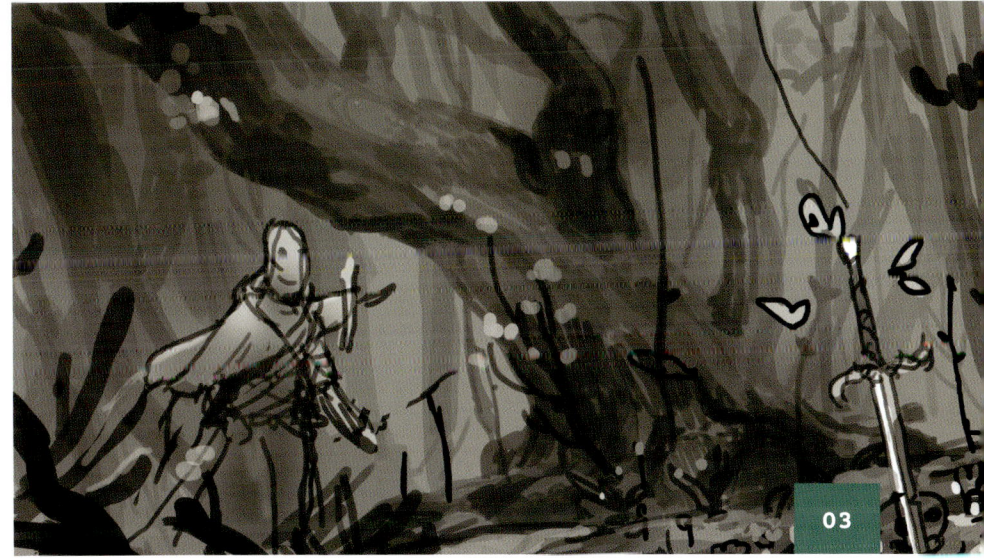

// **Building up the grayscale sketch in more detail**

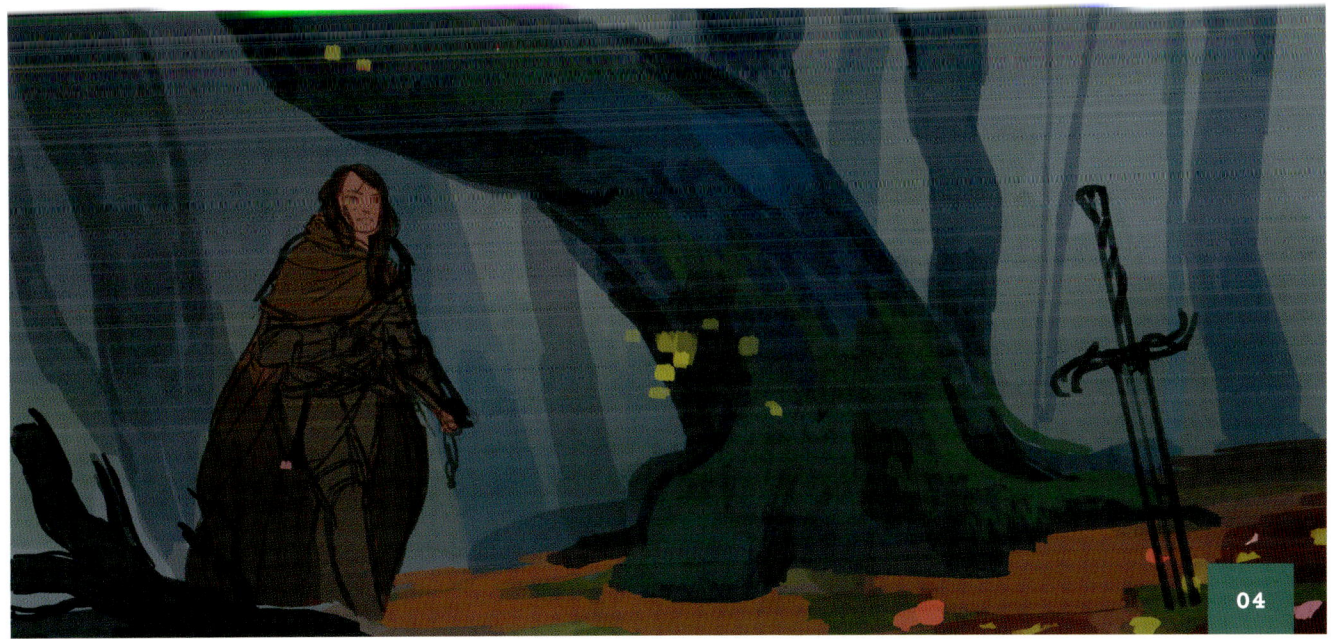

// **Establishing a color palette**

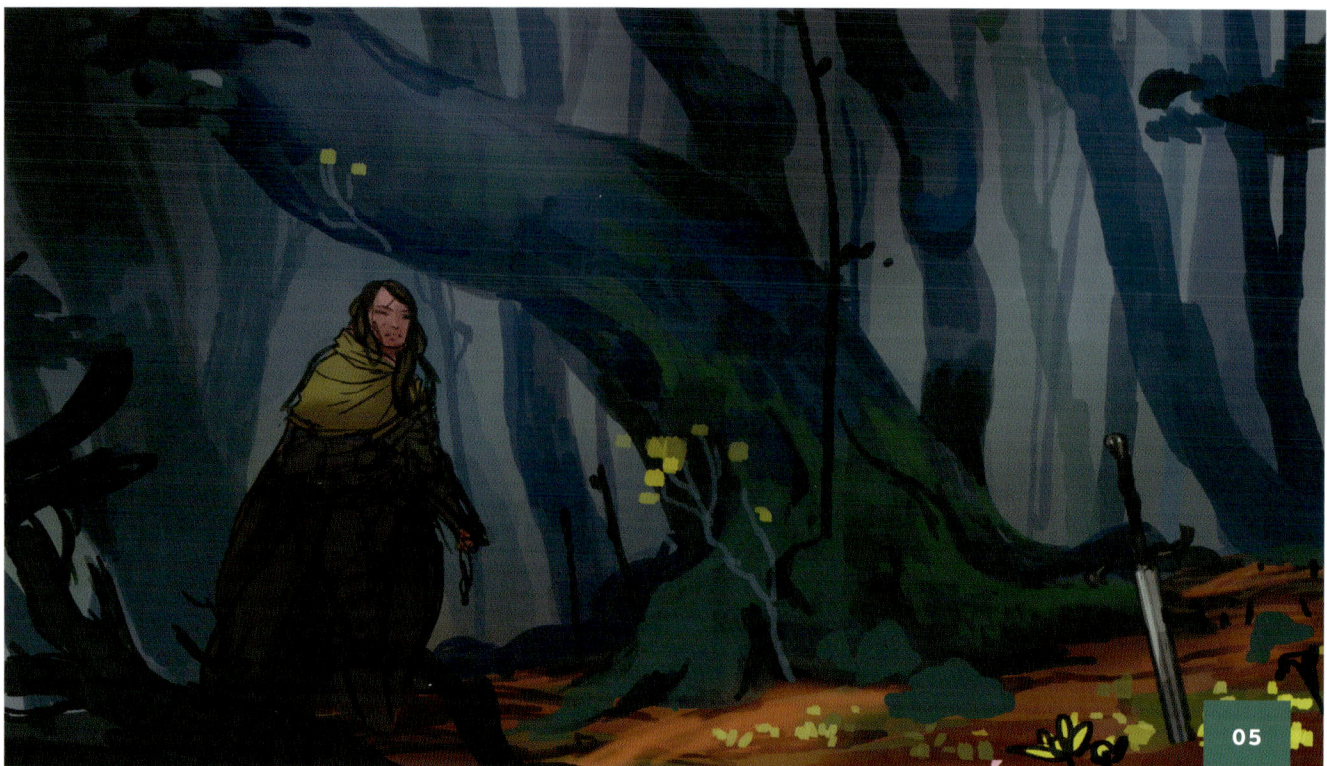

// **Adjusting the composition, color, and light**

>05 Starting to paint

There is a lot of pushing and pulling throughout my process: pieces are moved around slightly, and I go in and out of "drawing" on top of the broad paint strokes to flesh out some details, then back to adding broad strokes again. I decide to keep all of the flowers yellow, as adding more colors looks too noisy, which could detract from the main character and the sword.

I add brighter bright tones and darker dark tones to give a stronger sense of darkness to the woods, and rays of light to brighten the foreground and highlight the symbol of "hope" in the sword. To do this I use a soft feathered brush and lay down a Multiply layer in Photoshop for the dark tones, and either a Color Dodge or Screen layer for the bright tones. This is so that I don't have to fundamentally change the colors and can slowly add in the highlights and the dark tones. In oil painting, this would be the equivalent of "glazing."

>06 Underpainting and more color

I know the character will soon need to be fleshed out, but at this point I work on the details evenly overall. Before I

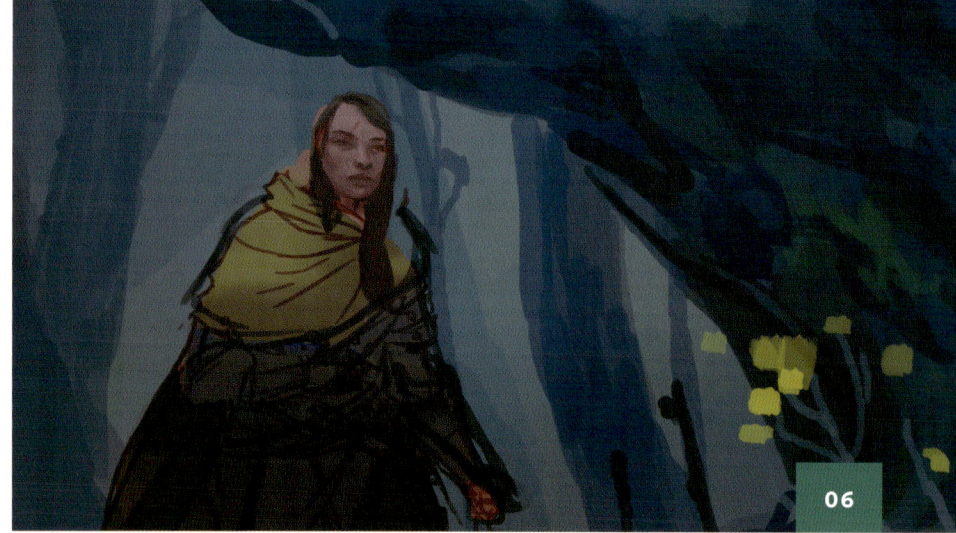

// **Establishing the character's face and layering up color and texture**

dive into anything too much, I make a start on rendering the face, then return to the background before I become too focused on a specific area. I like to use a textured brush and stay very loose with laying down brushstrokes, so as to add a layer of texture. This means that when I eventually start adding more details later, what will show through between the details will be an interesting textural underpainting.

When choosing colors, I feel that using a monochromatic scheme looks a bit stale, but it's also easy to make everything very muddy if you start out using too many colors at once. What I do here is lay down the monochromatic tones for an object, then start adding more colors one by one. For example, the tree is a monochromatic blue initially, but after enough detail is rendered, I go over parts with a green color to suggest the moss and leaves.

>07 Blending colors

Without making it look too stark, I lay down light strokes of a transparent green over the blue, and then blend the resulting colors together. I like having impressionistic brushstrokes akin to an oil painting, so I "blend" by setting down decisive hard strokes that transition between the two colors, instead of using something soft like a feathered brush.

>08 More painting and color

I add more texture and highlights on the trees and ground, as well as underpainting for the foliage and flowers in the foreground.

Objects in the very forefront of the foreground, like the leaves and logs, need to be high contrast by either being very light or very dark. This will help to convey more depth and keep the painting from becoming flat. The colors in the metal of the armor and sword are desaturated bluish grays so that they stand out from the more saturated blue and orange colors of the background and foreground, helping to add focus to the symbol of hope.

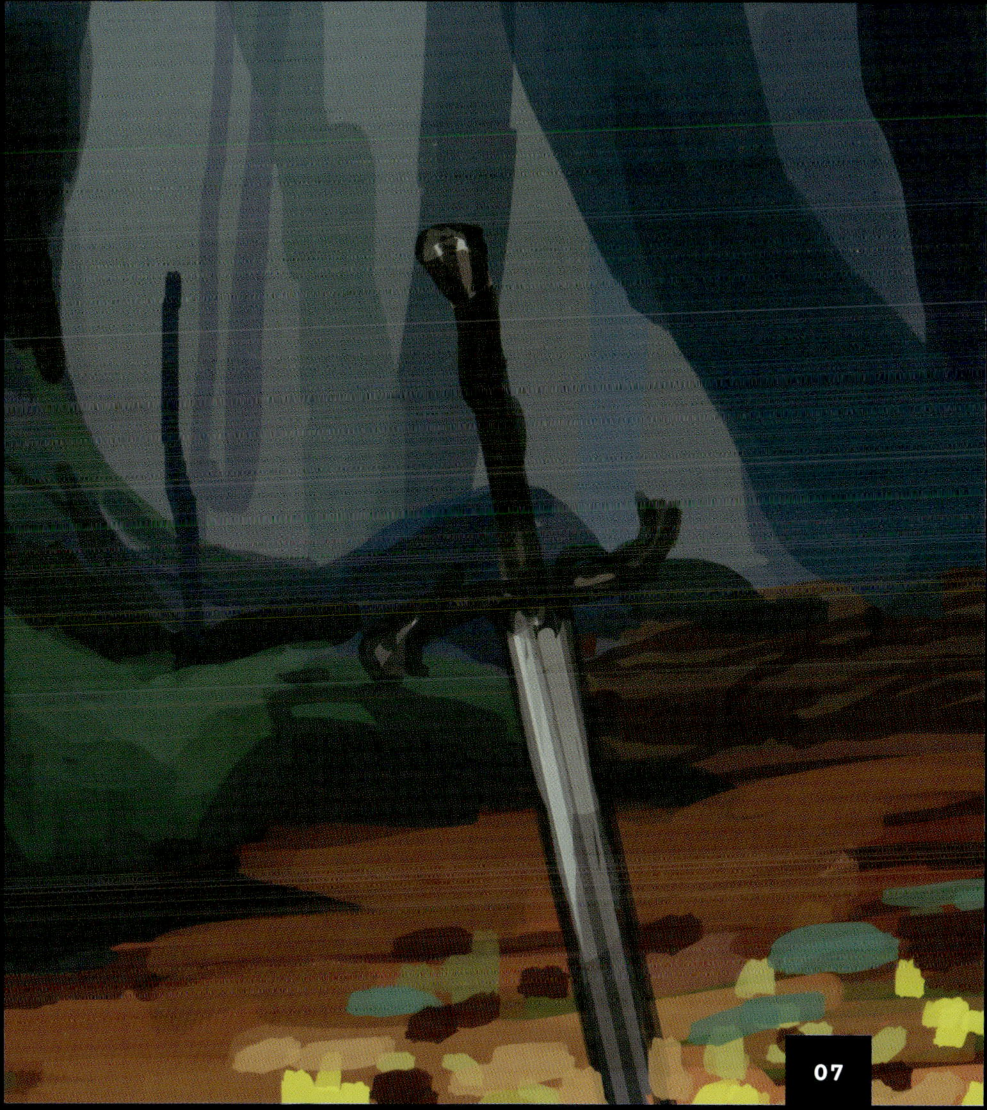

07

// **A close-up of how I blend colors and strokes**

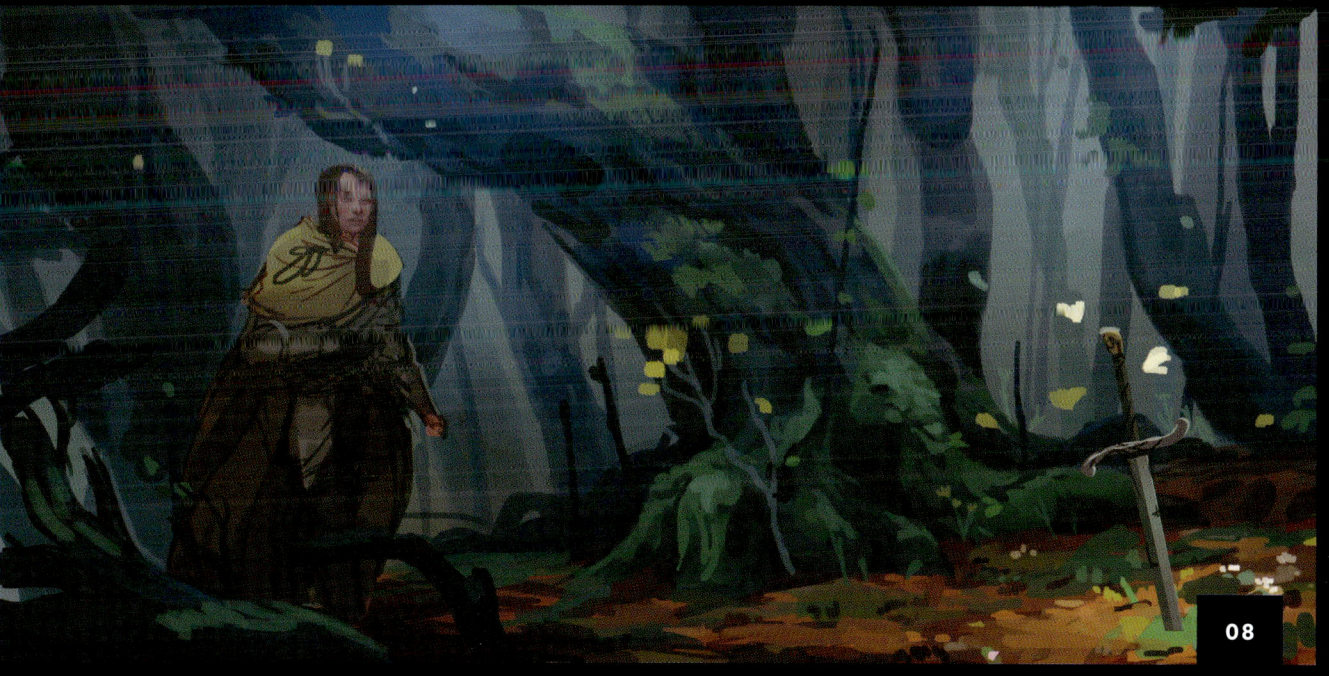

08

// **Gradually building up the whole scene**

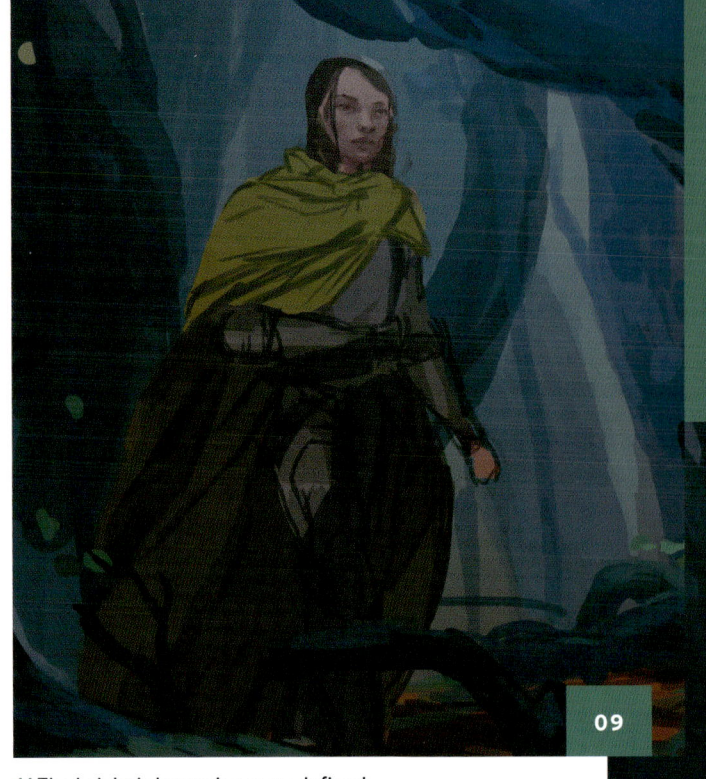

09

// The knight is becoming more defined

>09 Developing the knight

For the initial design and pose of the knight, I sketch in a loose idea of how I want the knight to be walking. In each iteration of the design, I pull in more reference for the hands, body, and armor, and make the line drawing more anatomically correct and defined. Even if you are familiar with anatomy, it can still be good to use references for different positions, for example.

>10 Clothing references

This is where I start pulling in reference for the cape and armor. Generally I like to use two or three different reference photos per object I'm referencing, but I try not to stick to them too closely. I want my style to come through, as if I'm relying on my imagination.

However, cloth is something I always adhere strongly to the reference for. It's almost impossible to find the exact reference you have in mind on the internet, so in the case of the cape, I take a bed sheet, drape it over my back, and take various reference shots of myself in the same pose as the knight. At this stage the sketch is still a bit loose.

>11 Refining the armor

Now I go over the loosely sketched armor with more refined line work. Typically, for organic objects like the figure or trees, I just start laying down paint freehand, and go from there. But when painting something hard like metal, it's good to ensure that the underpainting is hard-edged and precise. Now that the armor's line work is done, I lay the flat colors underneath.

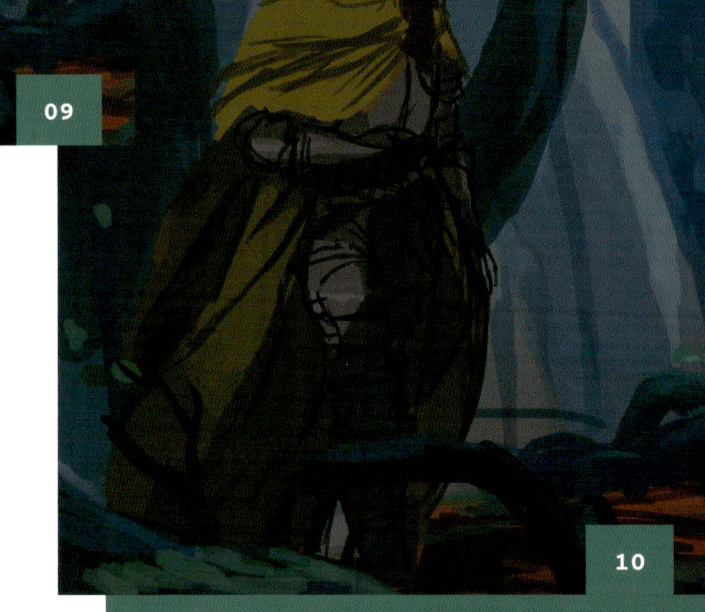

10

// A few references help with detailing the knight's costume

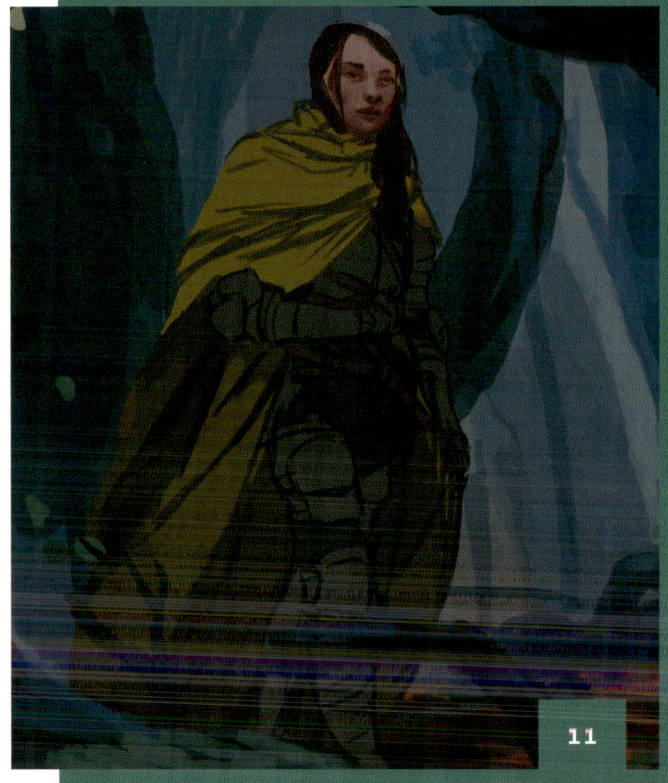

11

// The knight's armor is starting to come together

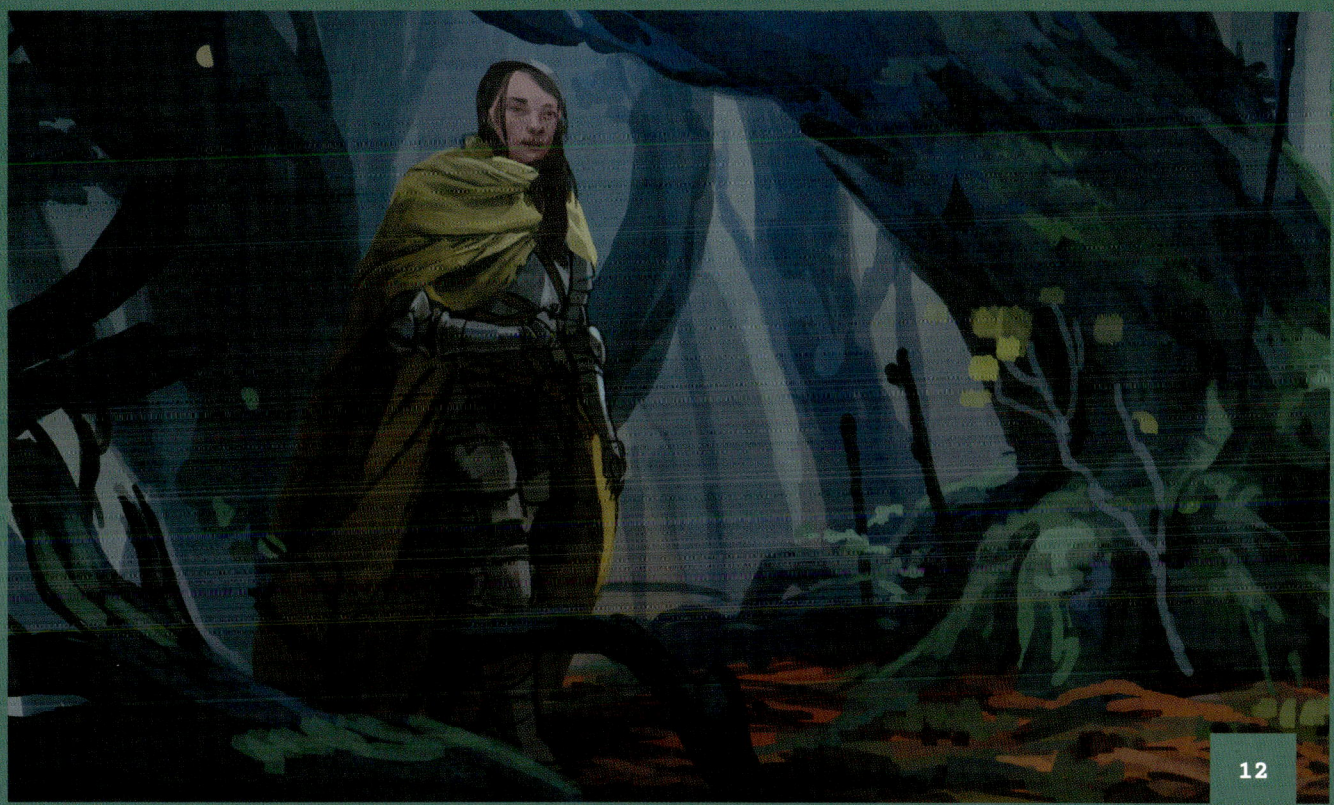

// Rendering more character detail

"Something that really helps me is to squint my eyes and look for large bodies of tone in the reference image, then lay them down as simple shapes on the painting"

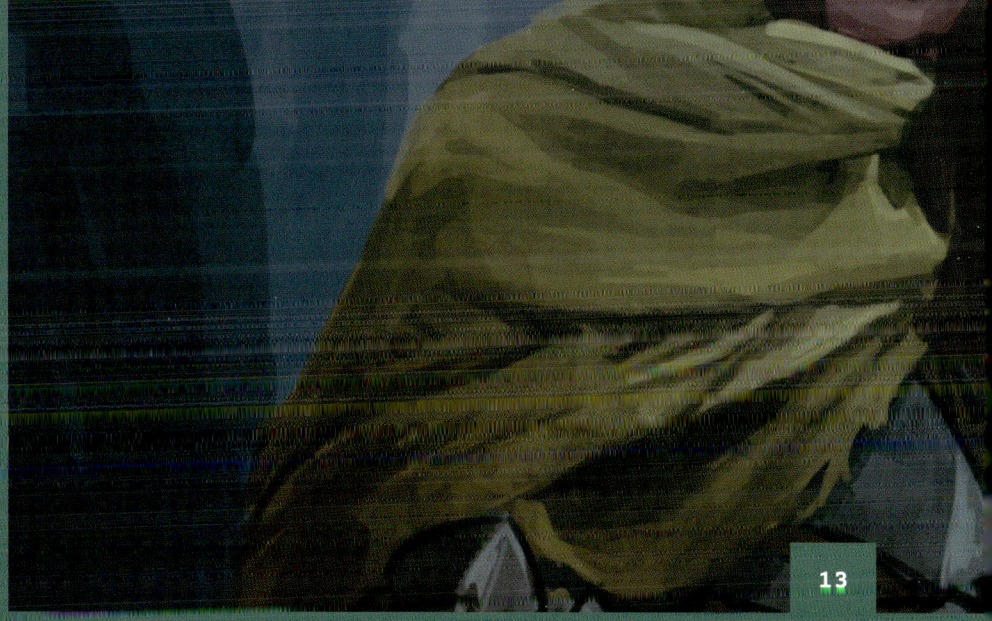

// Rendering more realistic folds in the cape

>12 Rendering with masks
I carry on building up detail on the character. The cape, armor, clothing, and leather are on separate flat layers. In order to render within the layers without going outside of the edges of the flat base colors, I mask the subsequent layers within the corresponding flats. You can scribble as much as you want outside of where the flat colors are, and they won't appear until you unmask them!

>13 Painting cloth
At this point in the process I start adding more tones to both the cape and the armor. Rendering cloth can be really tricky, as it is easy to make it look like mashed potatoes. Because the cloth material is so soft, it is easy to mistakenly believe that it doesn't create any hard edges. Something that really helps me is to squint my eyes and look for large bodies of tone in the reference image, then lay them down as simple shapes on the painting. This keeps me from over-rendering the cape, and when I zoom out and look at the painting at its final viewing size, ideally it will blend seamlessly together and appear to be the material of draping cloth.

>14 Painting armor

The knight's metal armor is supposed to be fairly worn from use, so it won't be as reflective as a more glossy, polished metal. The highlights on metal are generally starker than the local colors of the metal, and reflect the light of the environment it is in. In this case, I use a much brighter and slightly more saturated blue on the edges of the armor that are hitting the light.

To give the character visual depth within the painting, the tones will generally be darker the lower they are on her body, as they are further away from the light. This means that the brightest bright areas on her legs are going to be darker than the brightest bright areas on her left forearm. The same goes for the bottom of the cape, as it is further away from the ray of light.

>15 The sword

At this point the stressful part of the painting is over. I've already established all of the tones and colors, and now I just need to render and polish them. For the armor, I blend the colors using

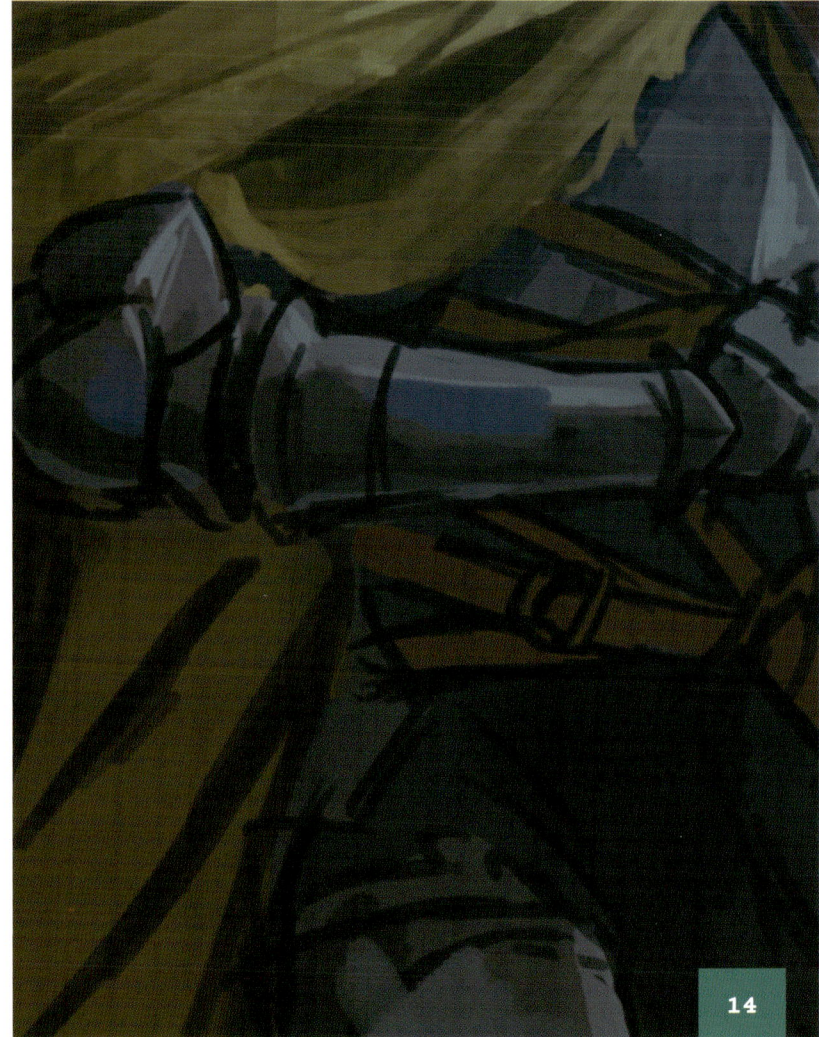

14

// I carefully consider how ambient light will affect armor highlights

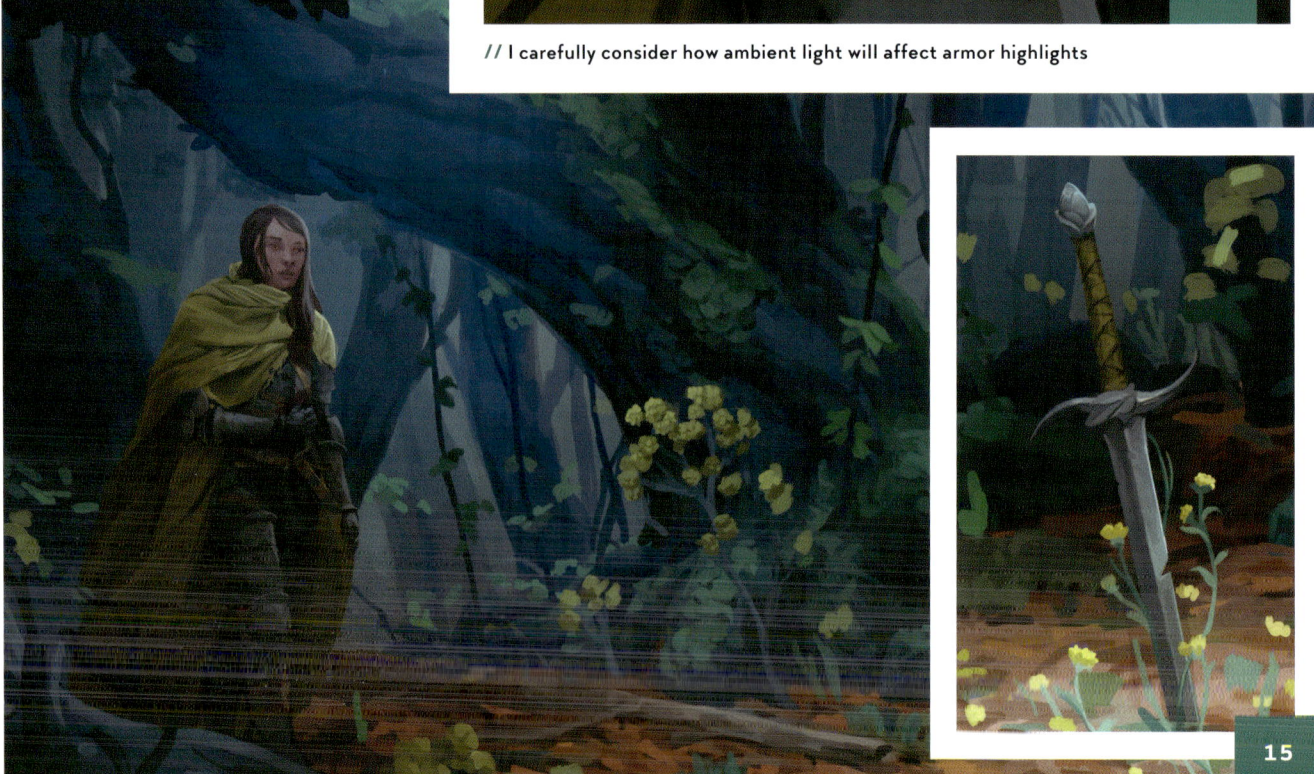

15

// Polishing the colors and developing the sword in the foreground

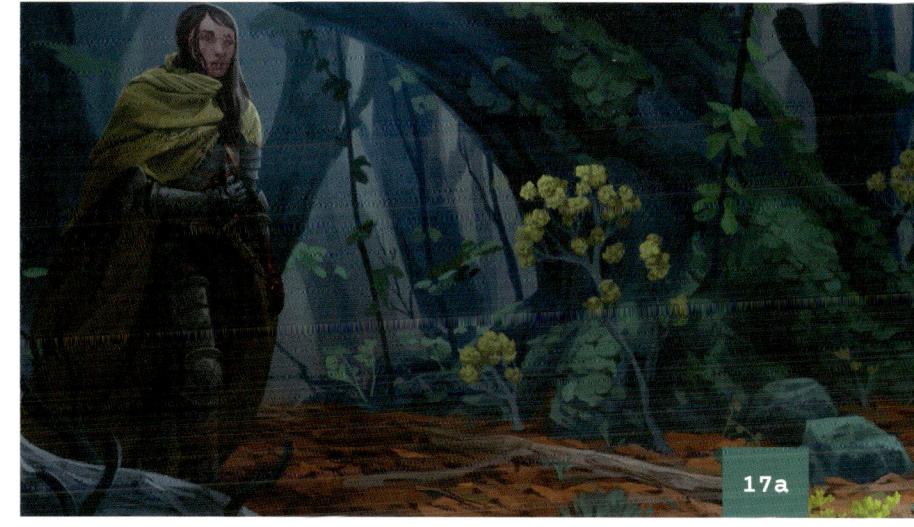

17a

// Finishing off the rendering and adding some last tweaks

16

// Adding subtle detail to the background trees

impressionistic brushstrokes. I start adding more details such as leaves and moss on the tree and underpainting for the flowers on the ground.

I also redesign the sword in the foreground. After repainting the sword in various styles many times, I discover a concept that I am happy with. As a symbol of hope, the top of the sword's hilt is a rose amidst sprouting flowers. To give the design even more of an edge, I give the hilt sharp pointy edges that resemble thorns, and leaves in the center. It is important to make the edges of the sword as precise as possible, and the thin highlights on the edges of it help to indicate its sharpness. This will help it to stand out from the impressionistic background as a focal point.

>16 Background painting
I add more definition to the trees in the background. I try to keep the colors interesting by adding some saturated blue highlights to the trees, making them look more painterly. It is important not to become more detailed in the background than in the foreground, and to keep in mind that the objects further back in the scene will become lighter in tone and more desaturated.

17b

// A scanned acrylic paint texture

>17 Final touches
The last stage involves finishing up all of the rendering in the details of the piece. I define the petals in the flowers, and the leaves on the ground and trees (image 17a). I resize the sword to a smaller scale that matches the knight's body. I add highlights throughout the image, particularly around the edges of the leaves and the knight's shoulders and hair, which I want to be starkly thin and bright so that it stands out against the dark background. I add the blood on the knight's armor by painting with a dark red color. I use a highlight to brighten the sword in the foreground, and darken areas in the background to provide more contrast.

Now that everything is rendered and edited, I finish it off with a texture layer. You can find free textures online, but I create this one myself (image 17b). I make three or four thin, even washes of

matte medium on some Rives BFK paper, then take watered-down acrylic paint and add a thin wash over all of that. The acrylic dries over the matte medium texture in a way that gives a very interesting, grainy, painterly texture. Ideally the tone of the acrylic should be something like thirty percent gray, so that the texture doesn't overpower the image when I bring it into Photoshop. I scan in the texture at 300 dpi and large dimensions, and add it into the image. I can simply drag the file into the Photoshop window and place it as a new layer. From there, I can edit it to get the desired effect; in this case, I set it as a Multiply layer.

>18 Illustration complete
Finally, after a lot of blood, sweat, and tears, the digital painting is complete. If you turn the page you will be able to see the weary warrior walking towards the bright hope of the sword standing out from the gloominess of the forest.

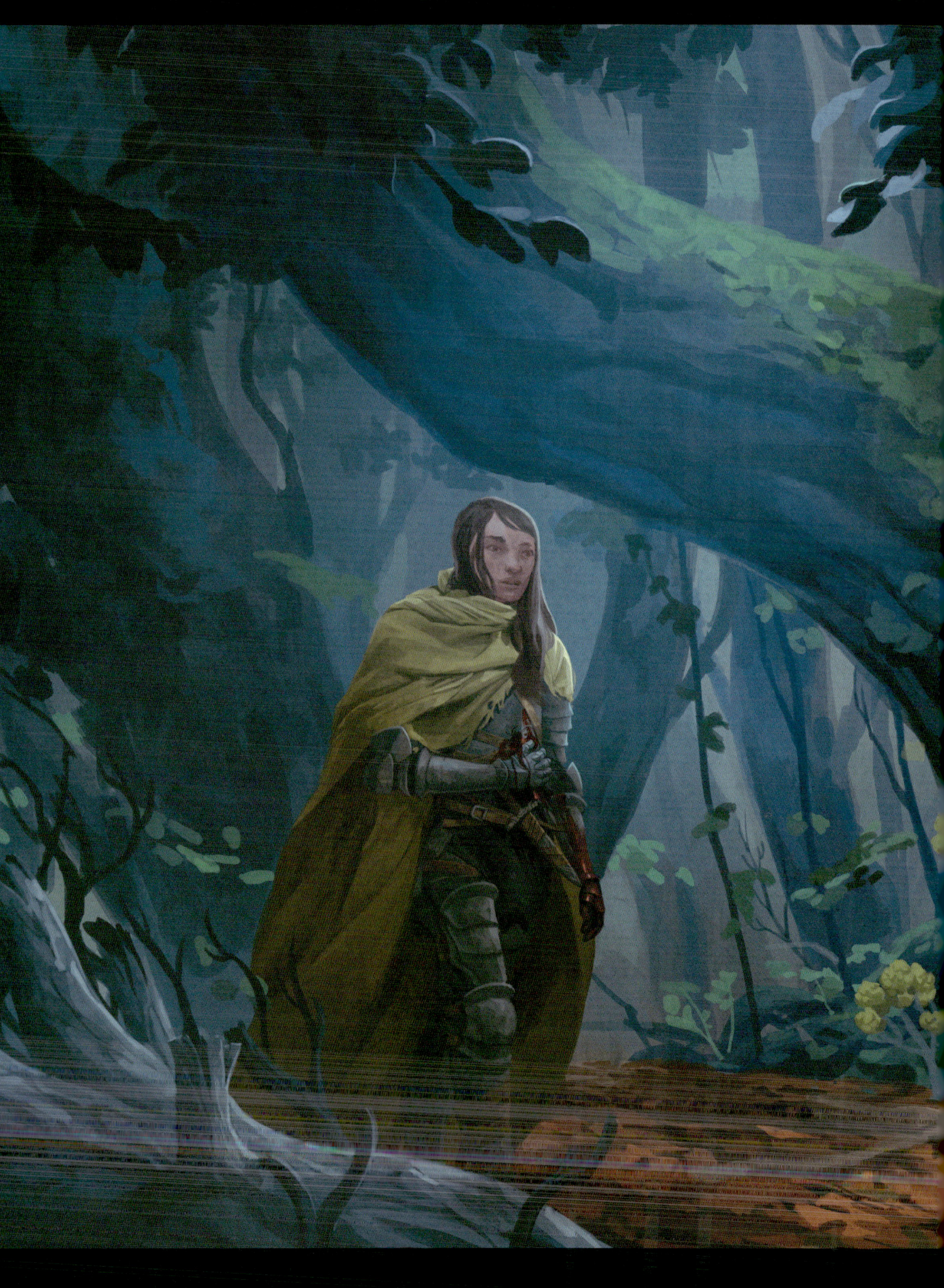

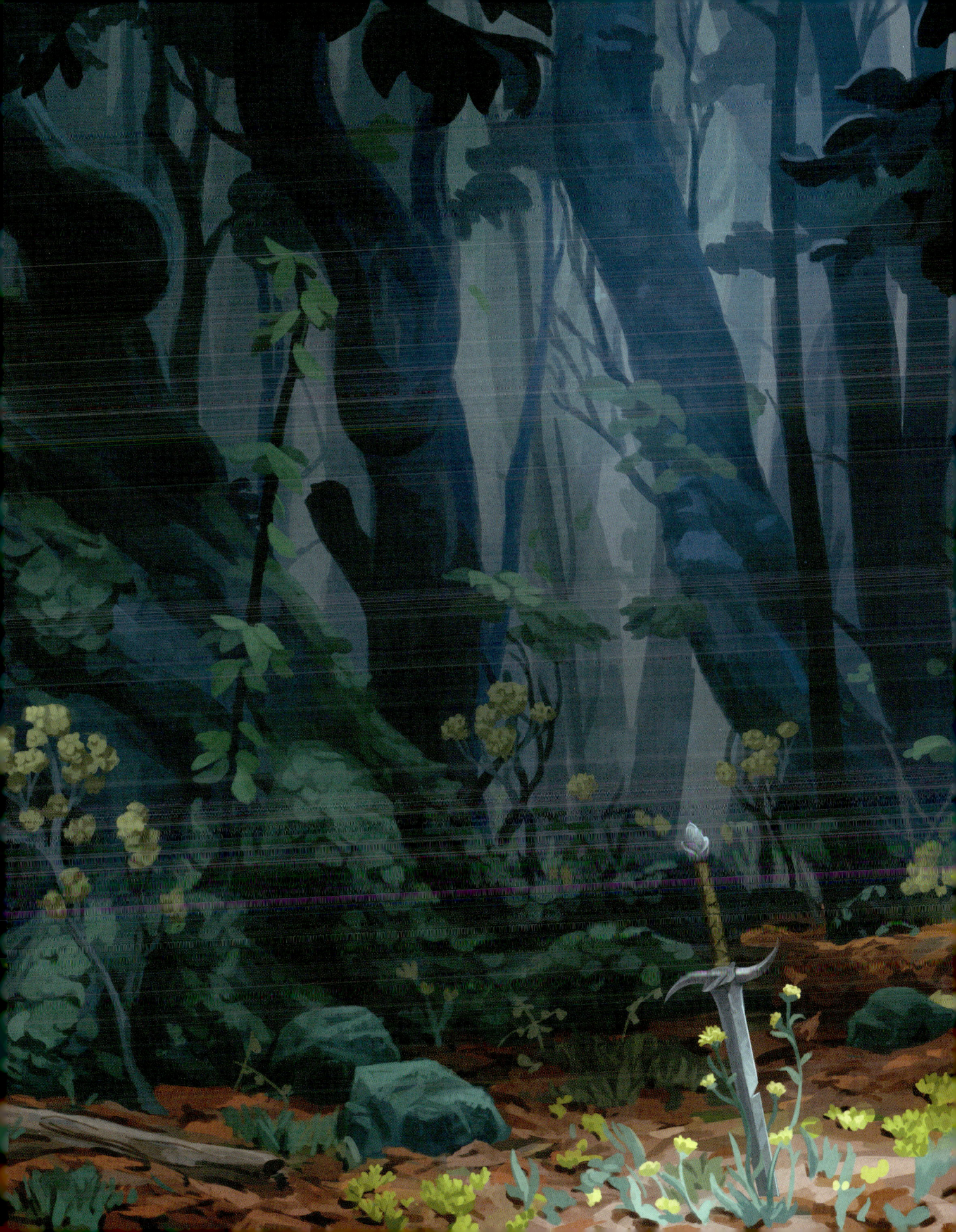

Andy Walsh | www.stayinwonderland.com

Horror

I'm thrilled to be illustrating the horror chapter in this book, as that's always been my favorite genre of entertainment. I know the challenge will be to stay away from obvious clichés while allowing room for some well-known horror cues.

When tasked with creating a piece where the brief is simply to illustrate "horror," there's an initial knee-jerk response of full moonlight and cold, blue colors. I decide that I want to at least avoid that and instead go for a fairly neutral gray-brown palette and use a foggy day setting rather than a moonlit night. I toy with the idea of creating a full daytime horror scene, which is possible, however I think it's better to meet somewhere in the middle so that I am producing something a little different but still imagining that there's an audience – they want horror and I've got to give it to them in a still image.

A decision I make early on is that I want to switch the style of the piece from my usual realistic approach to something stylized, so that I can use shape language and color to exaggerate reality here and there. I use 3D software to make a base before going into Photoshop, but you can still follow along if you don't use 3D.

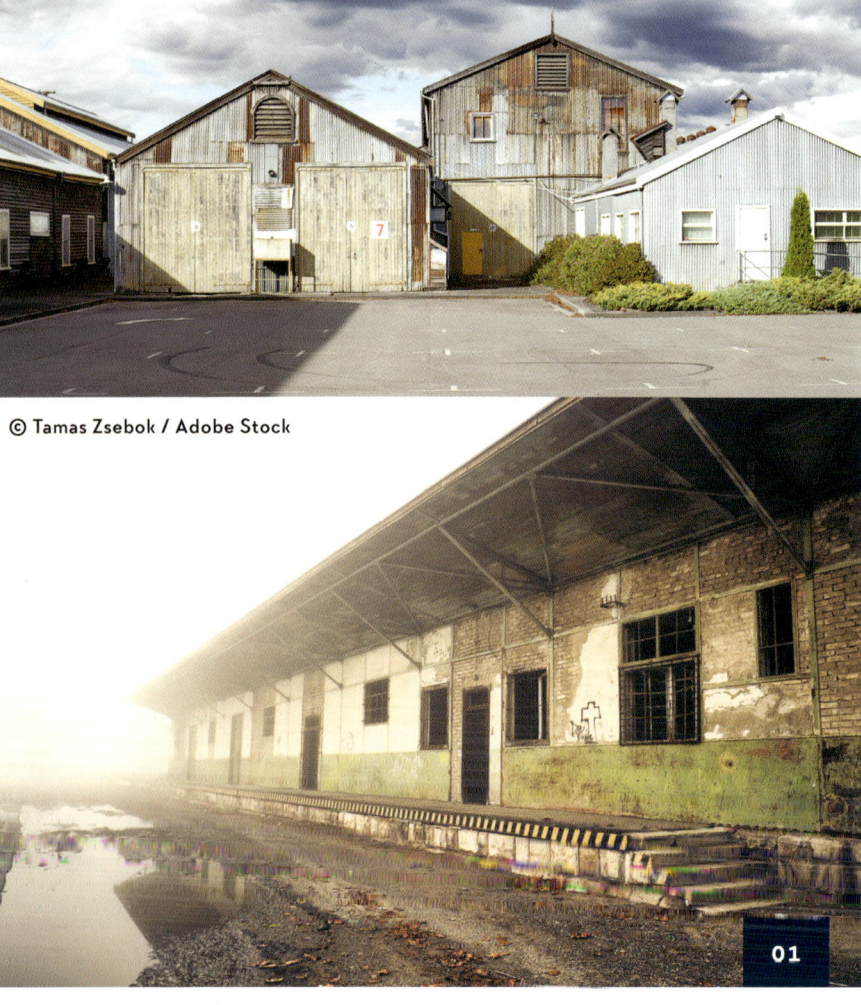

© Steve Lovegrove / Adobe Stock

© Tamas Zsebok / Adobe Stock

01

// Search for relevant reference material online, or take your own photographs

If you prefer, you can start working from step 05 if you're using a 2D medium, although I still cover some important research in the earlier steps, so I recommend you read them. You can also check out my Tranquility tutorial on page 164 for a 2D variant of this workflow.

After looking through my inspiration folders on my computer I decide that a good way to showcase the horror theme is to set it in a decaying, industrial environment. Let the terror commence!

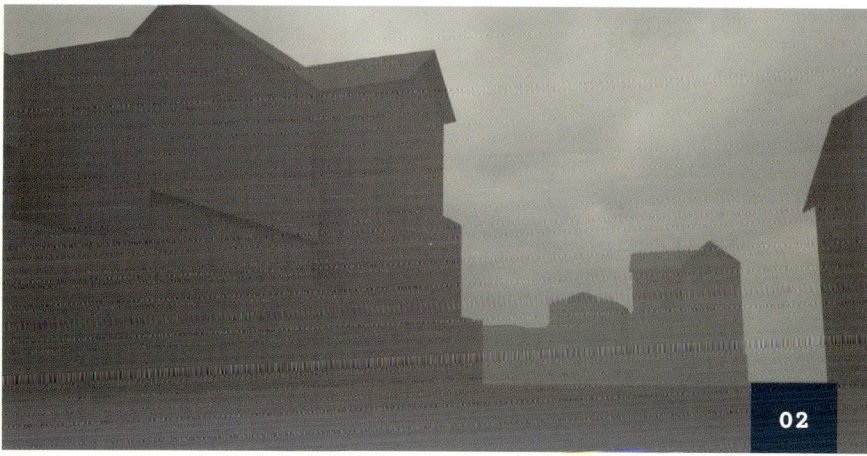

// The 3D block-in stage allows me to quickly set up basic shapes, lights, and camera angle

>01 Gathering reference

My first step is always reference-gathering. There's something fascinating about twentieth-century American architecture centered around industrial themes. There's so much character in the shapes and materials, combined with how well they age. I begin searching online for photos of old warehouses and try to think of a story. Perhaps there's an old abandoned warehouse in an industrial area where dark things are happening? Maybe someone is going there to investigate? The architecture itself sells a lot of the concept. I want to avoid having a character present, because that can be too obvious. I think it might be better to say it with just an environment and some kind of underlying narrative.

>02 Initial 3D block-in

To represent horror is to present a situation where there are unknowns, sort of a mystery. For me, horror is about representing questions with ambiguous answers; physical forms and locations with ambiguous edges and corners. So I want to combine fog and atmosphere with aged, abandoned architecture to give an unsettling vibe.

I use Autodesk's 3ds Max to block in the scene, using a single dome light with a cloudy sky image for lighting. I think about wooden materials while building these forms, as well as silhouettes that will read clearly and quickly convey the notion of "spooky and abandoned."

>03 Experimenting with composition

I try a few different moods using different images. The top-left design in image 03 is the first idea I arrive at, and I put it into Adobe Photoshop for a quick paint-over. I like the idea of having a vehicle in the scene, so I think a van might be interesting. While pondering the narrative aspect of the horror theme, I decide it would be great if the van is an ice-cream truck! It will contrast with the unhappy surroundings. However, the first render no longer feels intimate enough, as we're too far away. The second render (image 03, top right) is a little better, but I want more of the ground plane to be visible, which the third render achieves. Finally I arrive at the render in the bottom right.

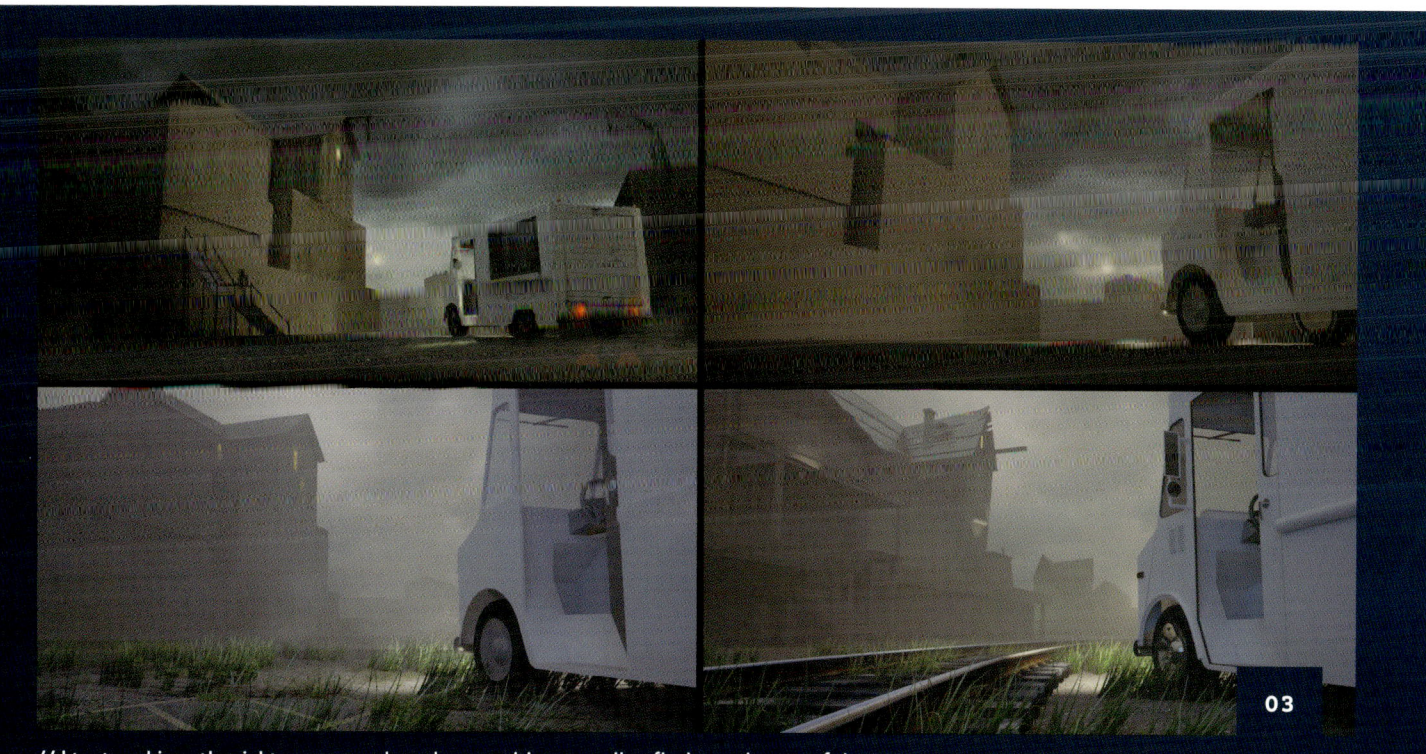

// I try to achieve the right camera angle and composition, as well as flesh out the rest of the scene

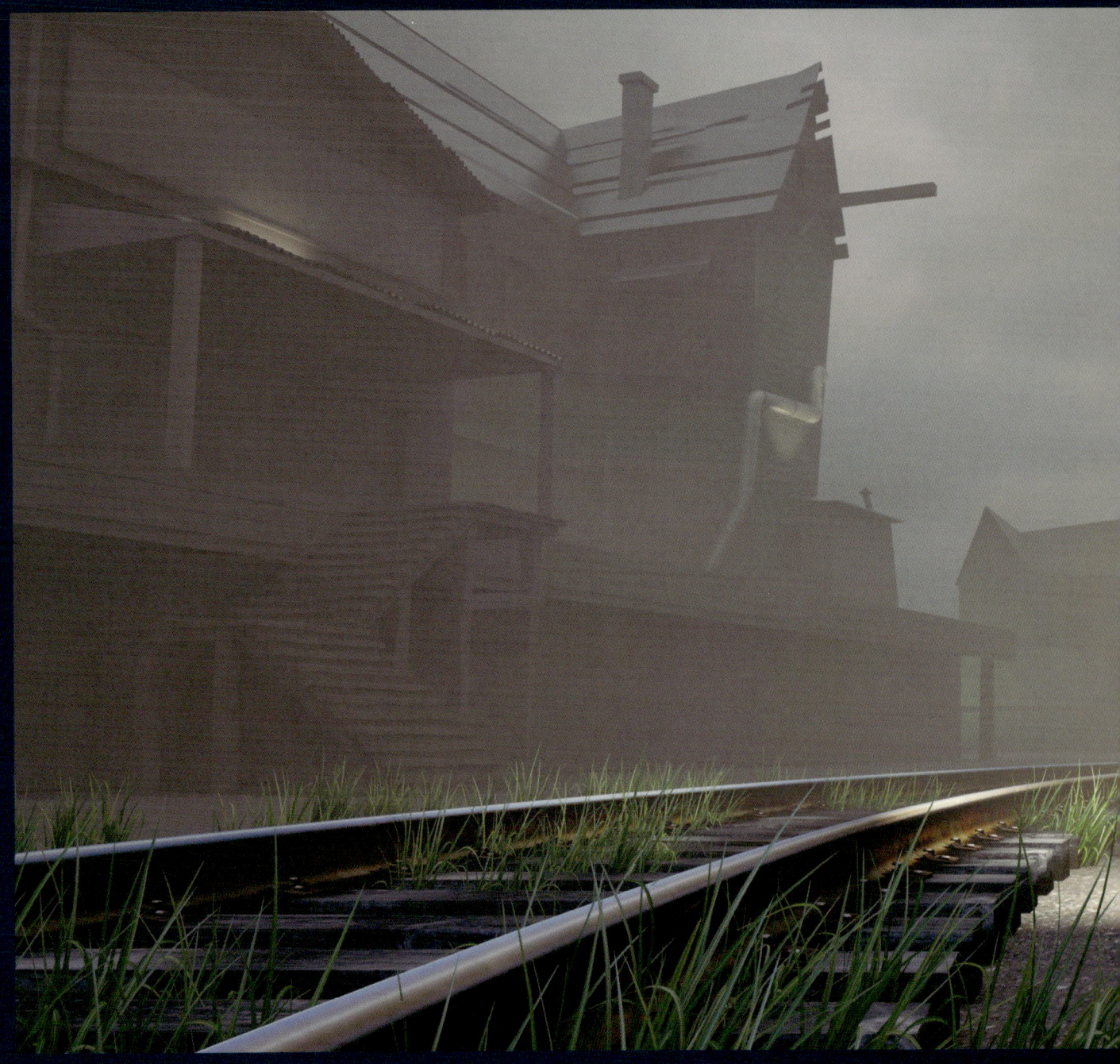

// Here I arrive at the final composition in 3D, which gives me enough confidence to know that it will work as a painting

>04 Final composition

In the previous step and leading up to this step I had begun with a scene that I was happy with (in the very first thumbnail), but something is telling me that it isn't enough. This is a key voice to listen to. I realize that I'd made this mistake before and the problem is not getting in close enough to where the heart of the scene is. I decide to edit the image's point of view so that the truck is up close and we can associate with it but then also feel the ominous looming of the abandoned building.

>05 Line art

For those of you who don't use 3D, you can rough in your composition using Photoshop or pencil instead, and then create a tighter line drawing to arrive at this stage.

To create the line art from my 3D scene, I render the scene out with just the dome light on. Then I use Photoshop's Find Edges filter to convert everything in the 3D render to lines. It's a very useful way to give you a line art basis for a painting.

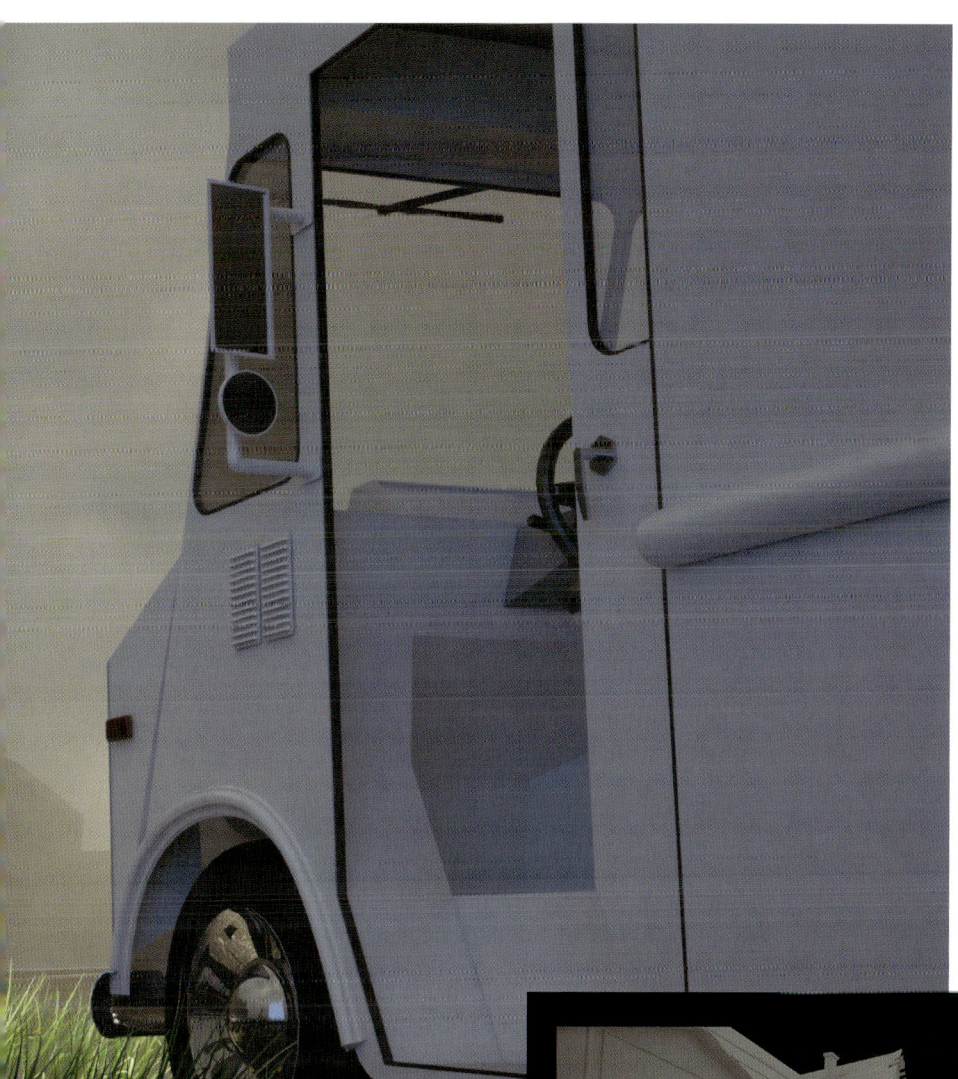

04

05

// PRO TIP

Creating narrative

I intend for the building to have some kind of light or activity going on at the top, as though someone is in there conducting strange experiments. I want a hanging body as the focal point, which would be hanging via a protruding beam, giving a strong silhouette. The truck will have its lights on to show signs of life. It's important that I don't just do "mystery" but actual horror, and that's where the useful clichés come in: hanging bodies, crows, blood, and an overall sense of threat.

"I had begun with a scene that I was happy with, but something is telling me that it isn't enough. This is a key voice to listen to"

// Here we reduce everything down to lines and get rid of the 3D render

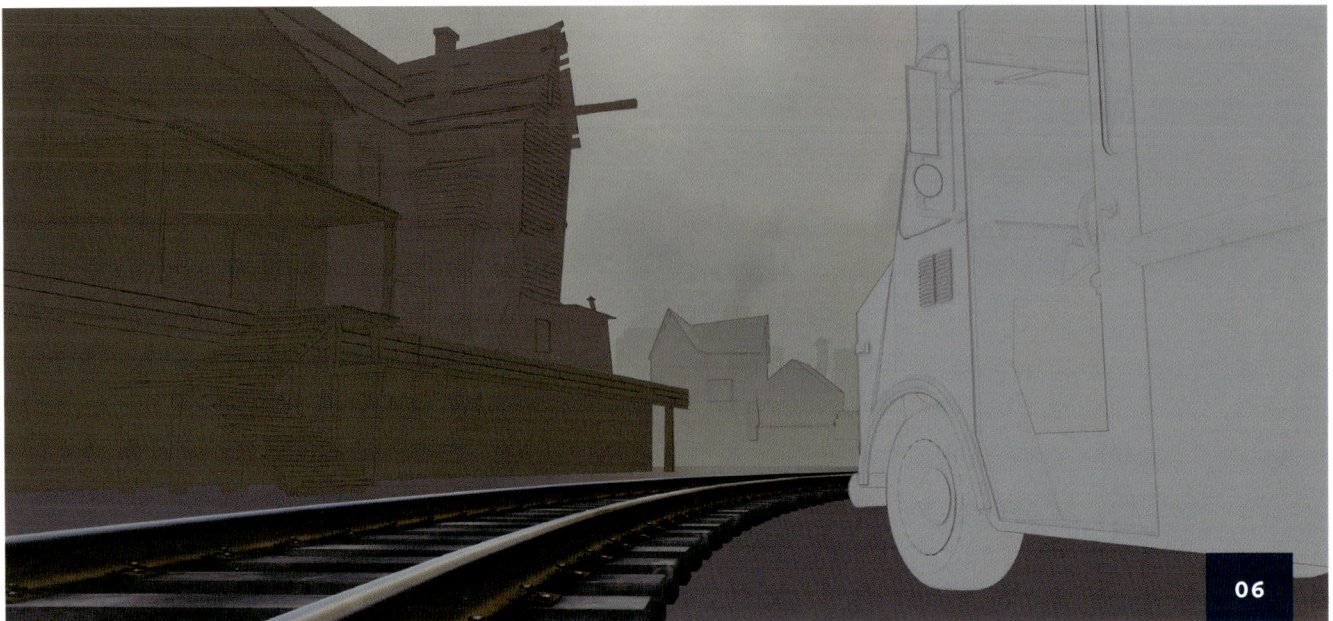

// Now we can start to paint under the line work

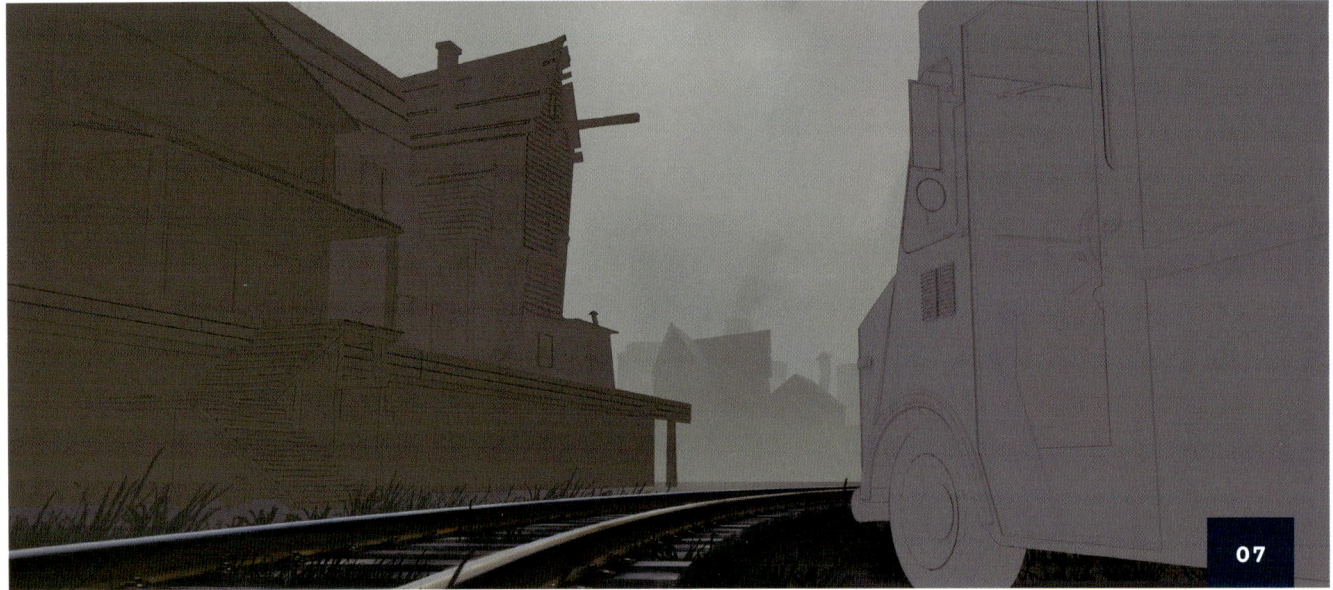

// Now that I have the basic shapes blocked out, I can start the painting process

>06 Initial values

My converted line drawing is now on its own layer at the very top of the document and set to Multiply. Now I can paint underneath it and match the overall value structure of the test render. I create a separate folder for each complete block of values and create a basic structure of values to build upon, but how you organize and apply your values is up to you. If you are working traditionally, it can help to do some separate value studies of your composition that you can refer back to as you paint.

>07 Start of the paint work

In this step I paint in the far buildings and begin work on the ground plane and grass. I try to use a neutral brown-gray palette. There's not much color in the ambient light at all, so everything will be kept roughly to its local color. My main consideration will be the atmosphere: the values will lighten and the saturation will diminish as they become farther away, and often within the space of one building because there's also a thick fog. I like how vague the distant buildings are, again playing on the theme of mystery.

"The values will lighten and the saturation will diminish as they become farther away, and often within the space of one building because there's also a thick fog"

>08 First lights added

It's worth mentioning that my workflow here is a little tight. I deliberately use lots of layers in Photoshop for maximum control – I'm not making a loose painting So rather than paint the light directly onto a single layered painting, I have a collection of lightening layers such as Exposure and Color Dodge which I apply using masks. This way I can achieve a consistent, clean addition of light which hits whatever is underneath it, and also allows for some warmer colors to break up the colds. Of course, your approach to adding lighting may differ. If you are working traditionally, make sure you are familiar with the fundamentals of lighting and have a lot of references available.

>09 Establishing a look

To achieve a consistent style (in a piece that is intended to have a particular style), I like to work on one area tightly, establish the look, and then use that as reference for other areas of the painting. Here I start on the stairs; you can see in image 09 that the wood is a little crooked. I have chosen to use an art style which is inspired by the styles of recent animated movies, but pushed a little further towards cartoon while retaining fairly realistic lighting. It's an interesting combination that, in this piece, allows for a certain amount of grit without putting the viewer in the safe and comfortable genre of "cartoon." It enables me to push the shape language and colors and to allow those to help sell the creepiness I want.

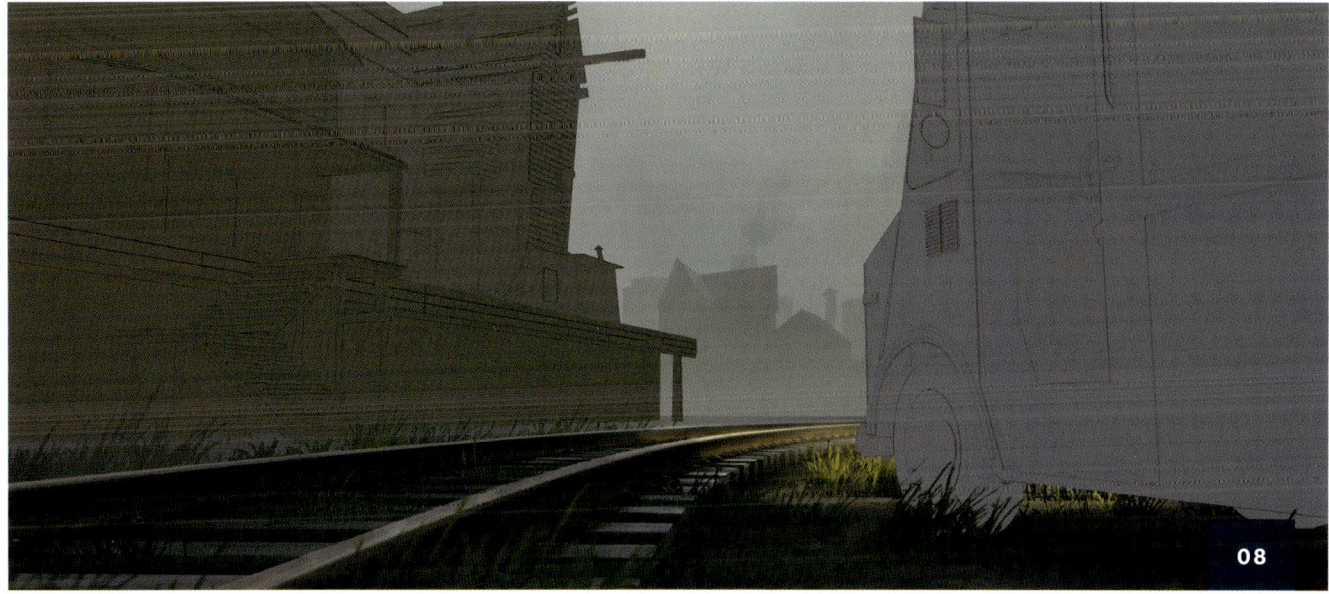

08

// It's time to add some light effects to the scene via the headlights

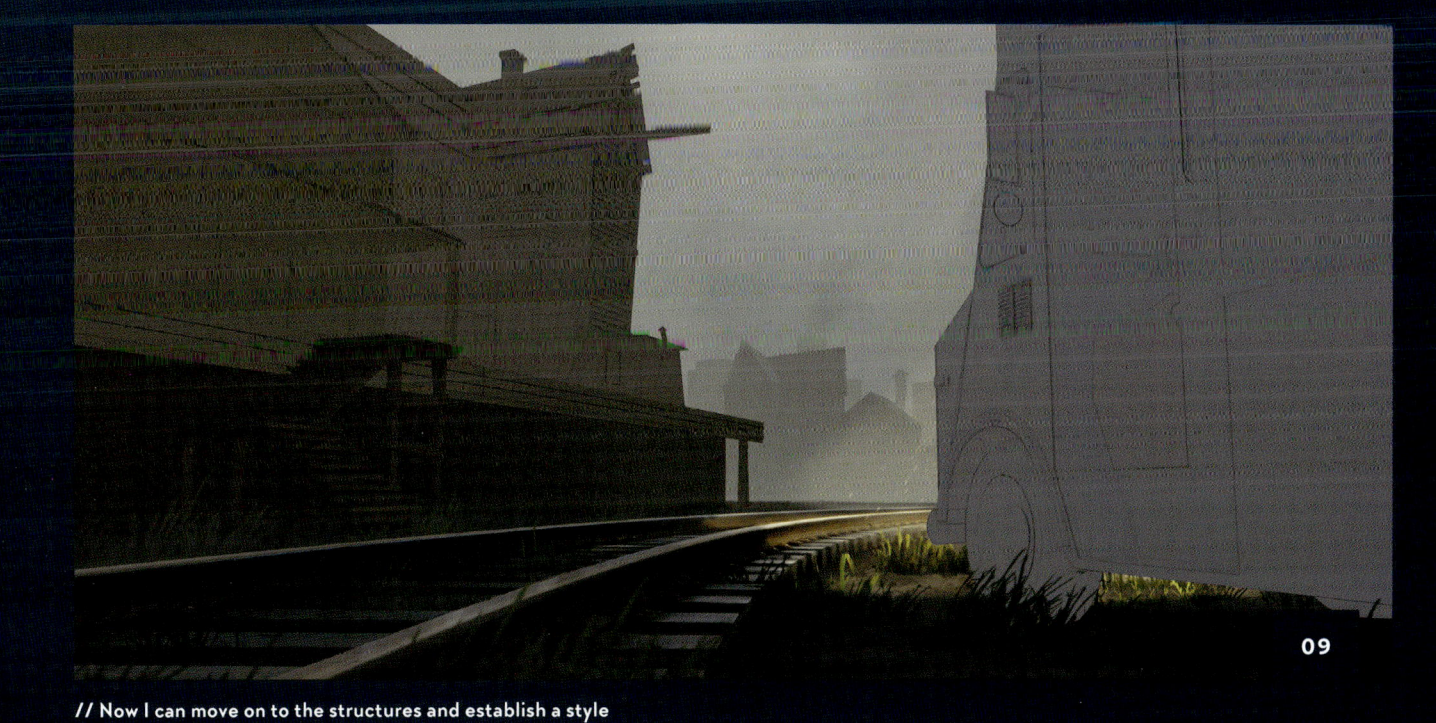

// Now I can move on to the structures and establish a style

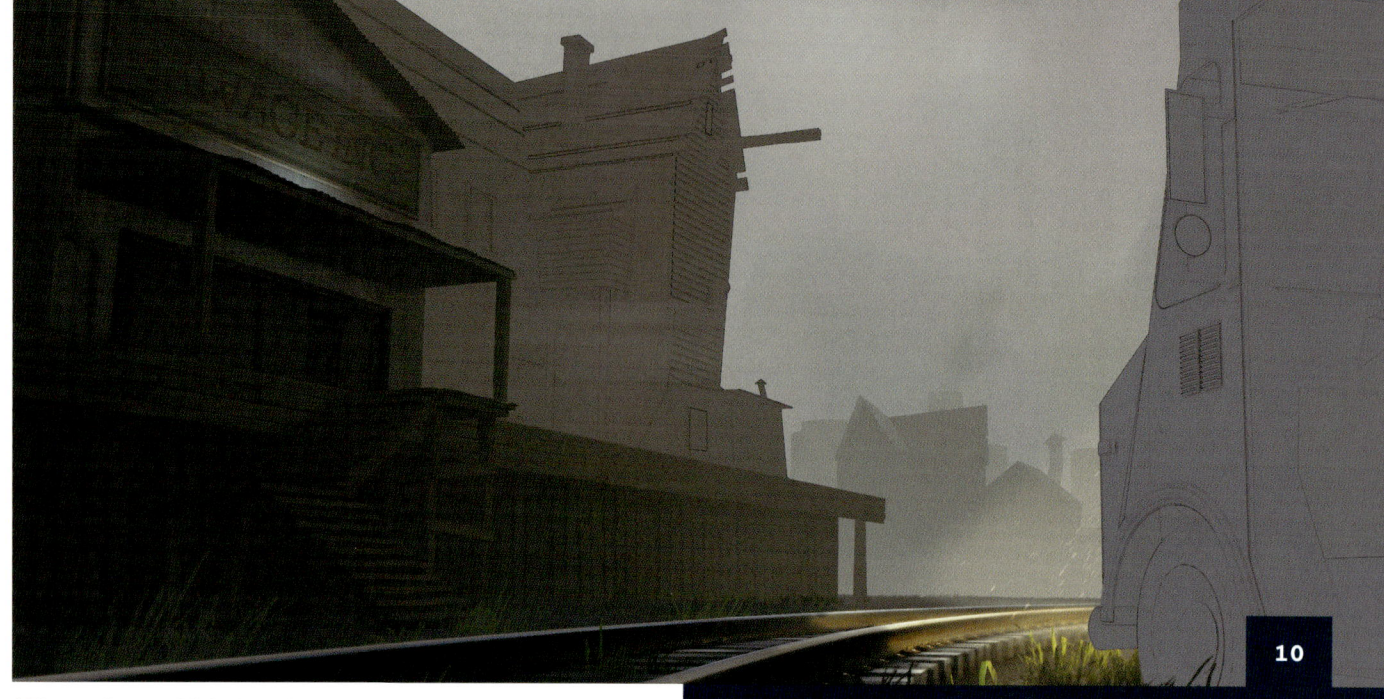

// By now I've established a style and can start to apply it to the buildings

>10 Architecture

I return to my photo references here to get a general idea for how this first building will look. It's a mixture of sheet metal and wood. I think the sign will be a key element in selling this building, as well as the light which illuminates it. Lighting something from beneath always looks spooky and I use the same method as in step 08 (with masked lightening layers), this time going for a cooler tone. I experiment with a few sign types before choosing the one you can see in image 10, as it's quite subtle. I also start to build up the fog here to better match the initial concept.

>11 Architecture, continued

With the previous structures in place I have an established workflow for painting the architecture, so I can now apply that to the main focal building. The wood has to be uneven, and so too does the actual geometry of the walls.

It's important to make sure that all the elements, with respect to their values, group visually together within their value group. So the values for all the buildings could be considered as one middle ground value group, and the truck and the background

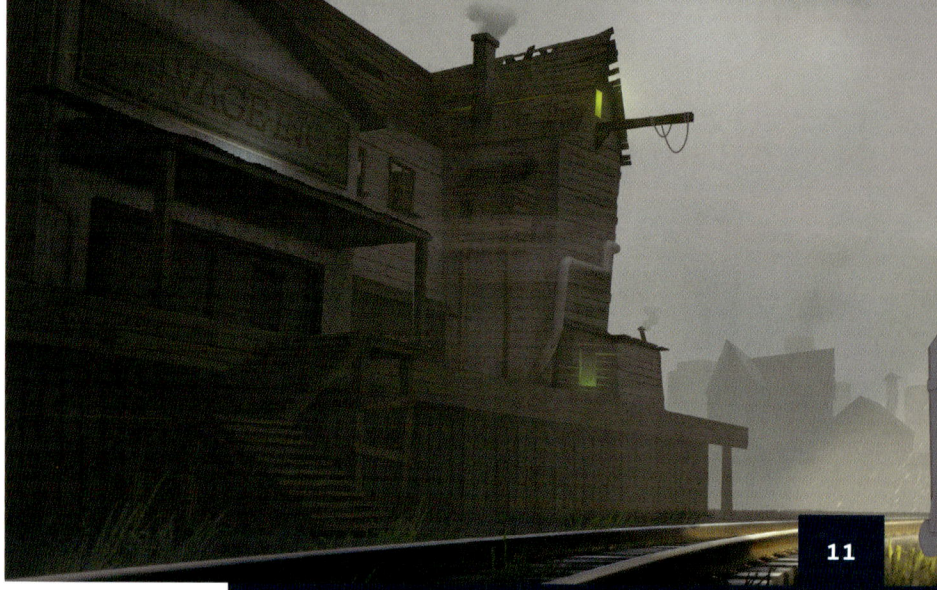

// The building is our main focal point so it's important that we get it right

// PRO TIP

Story comes a close second to composition

Story is the overall idea or concept of the piece. Sometimes you make art that's just pretty and you'll notice it doesn't get much attention. But throw in a little backstory or some elements that make us go deeper into the scene or character, and your audience will not just appreciate the piece but delight in it. As with composition, don't just settle for a guy standing on a mountain and call it a story. Really think about elements that make your audience curious as to what's going on and invite them in to explore. What's in the box? Who's around the corner? What story happened to get us to this scene?

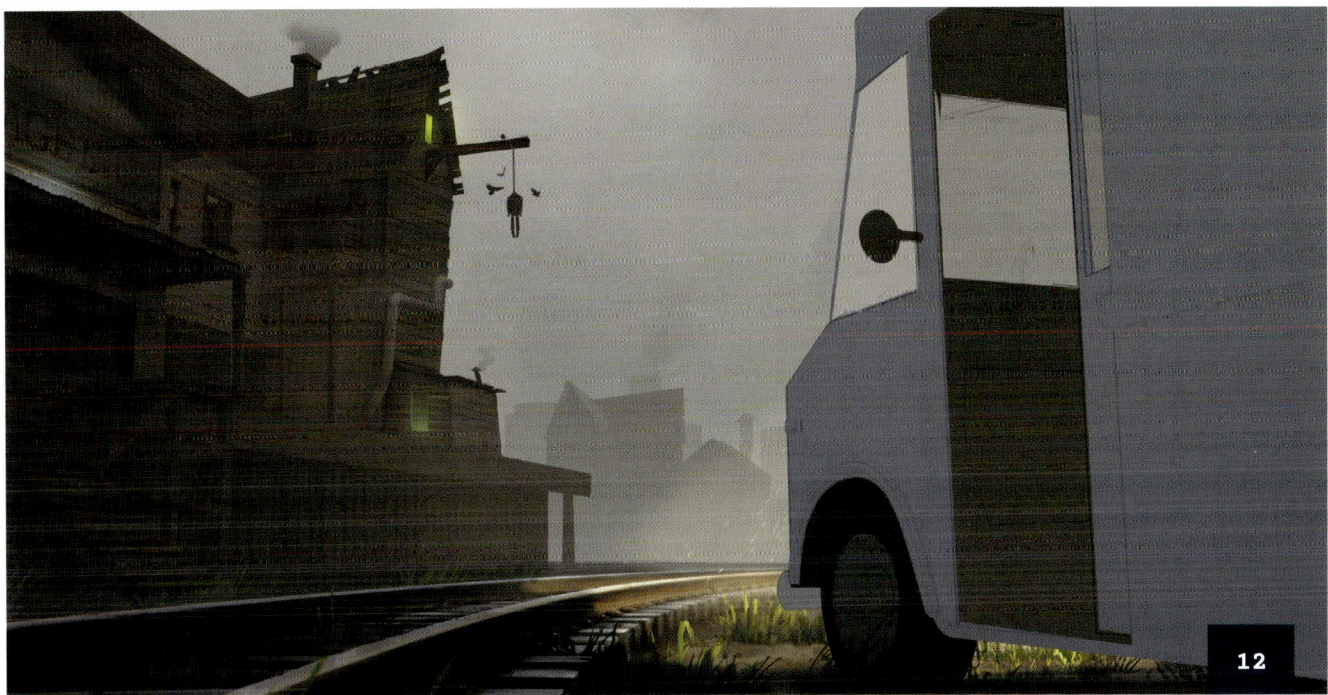

// Now I work on the ice-cream truck's basic structure

would be the other two. Within its own value group, no value should jump out and distract the eye or create visual noise. Here I add the eerie green light coming from within the building, plus a little smoke to imply activity.

>12 Foreground truck
I feel that the line work of the ice-cream truck is a little too complex for a stylized image, so I reduce the details and then add the basic color masses. I also add the silhouette of the hanging body. This will remove the ambiguity of the scene and push it towards horror. We don't want to go up to that room with the green light!

>13 Foreground truck, continued
I want the truck to have some story to it. The fact that it's an ice-cream truck is a good narrative element, but I want to take that further and give it some wear and tear as though it's been through a little adventure already, possibly leading up to this final encounter. It's these kinds of elements that really help with storytelling. So here I add a little dent over the wheel and some mud splashes.

>14 Finishing touches
I add the ice-cream menu on the side, which already brings out the story

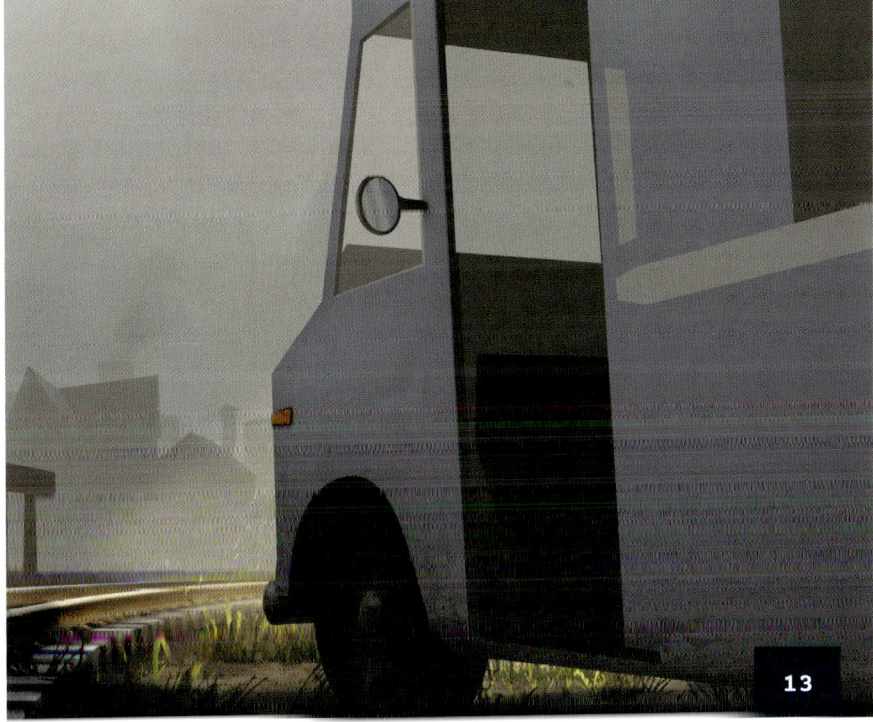

// The rendering of the truck must be treated with the same style as the rest of the piece

element of that component. Then of course I add a little blood smeared on it for extra horror goodness! It's around this stage that I experiment with placing a little hint of a person in the driver's seat, but every attempt looks forced and too obvious, so I decide to leave it up to the audience to decide where the driver went.

I also add a little value separation between the near building and the main building to create more of a silhouette there. Finally I shift the color palette towards green, as it's becoming a little warm and the scene needs to be slightly less friendly. Overall I'm pleased with the mood this piece conjures up, as well as the story lines that could unfold from it.

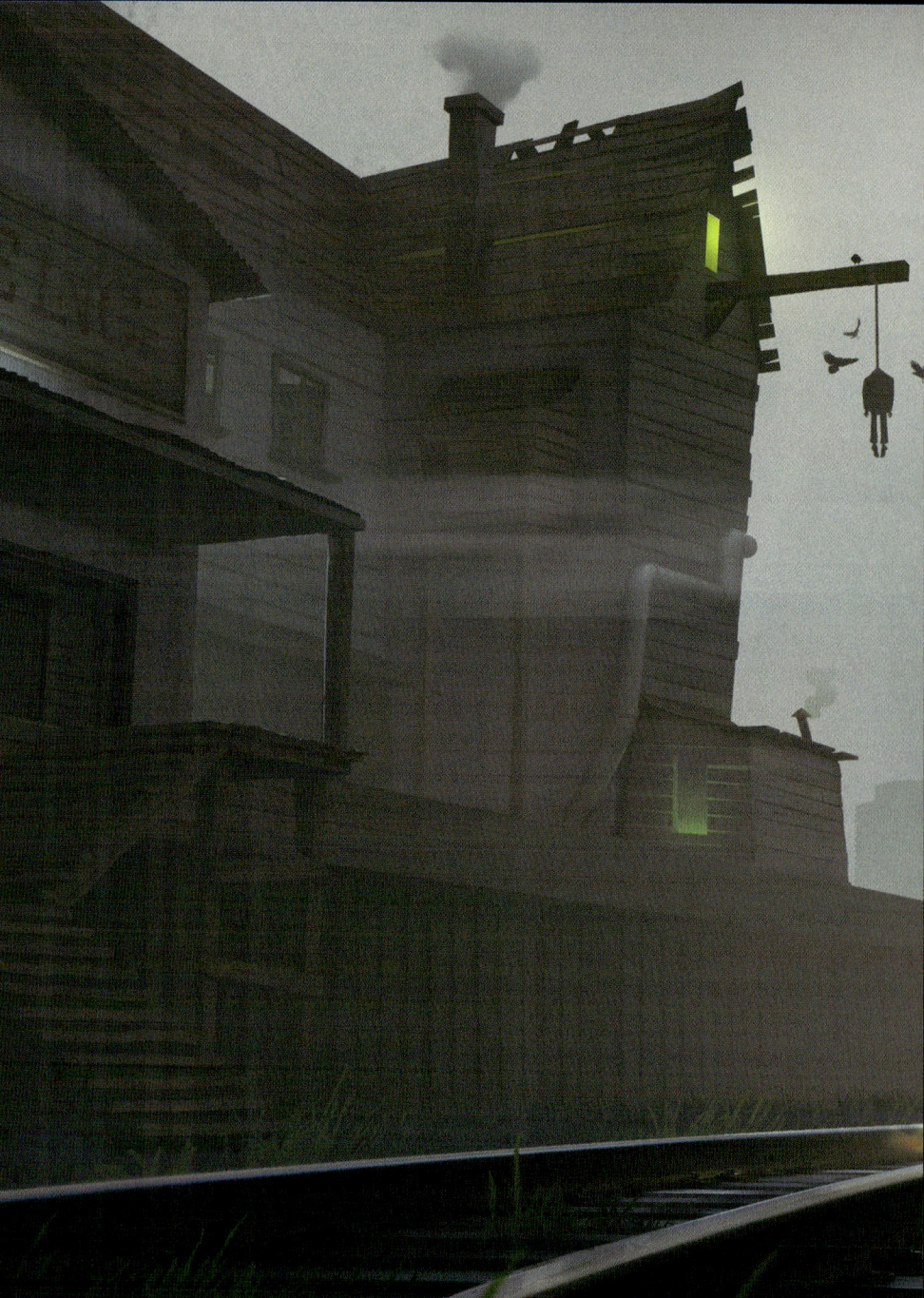

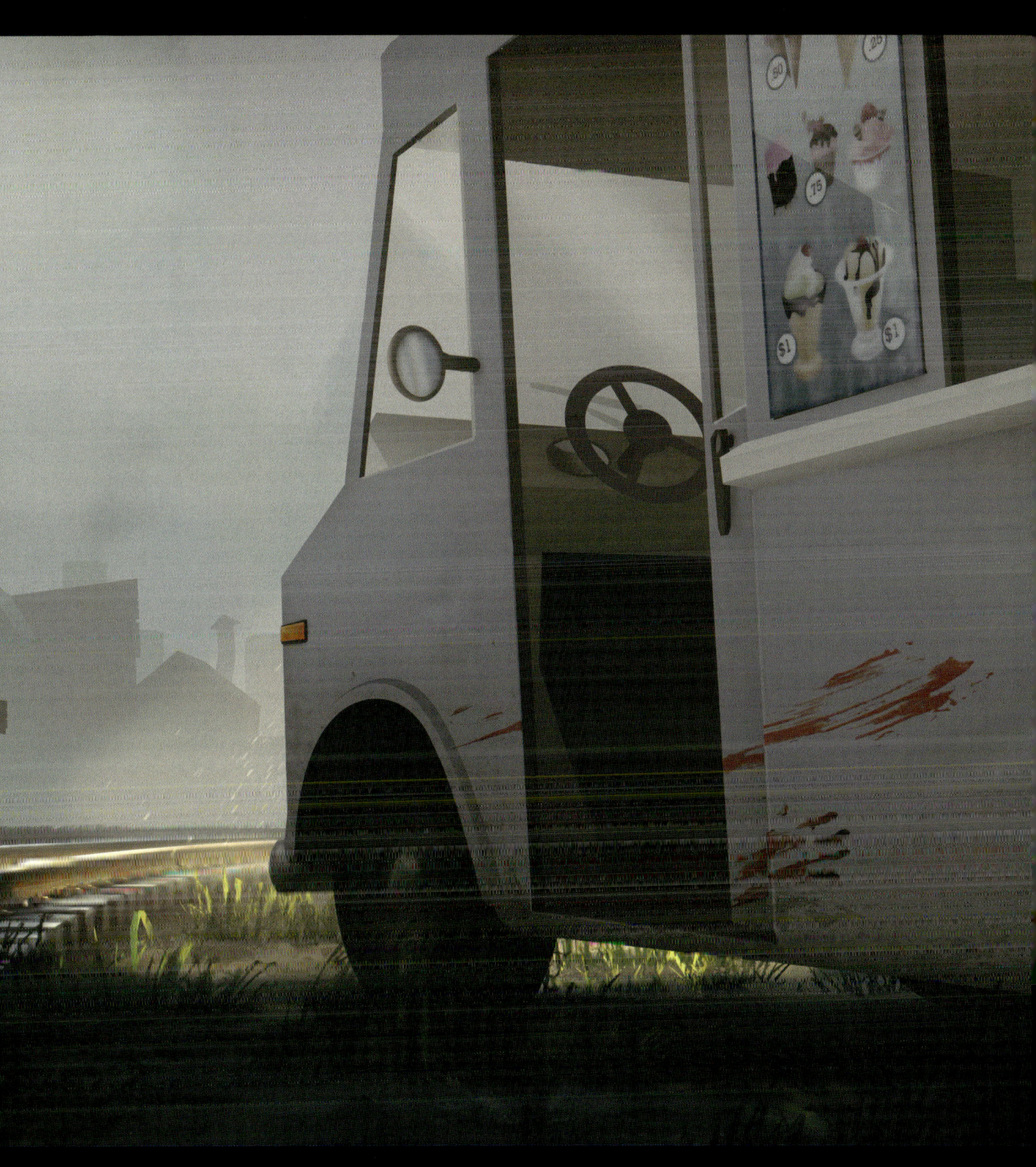

Juan Pablo Roldan | www.artstation.com/artist/roldan

Isolation

In this tutorial I will create an image based on the theme of "isolation." I will explain some methods that I use in my daily work that aim to give my images a realistic and cinematic look. I'm interested in adding some narrative content to the image. To achieve this, I'll show you how to tell a story through simple silhouettes, shapes, textures, atmosphere, light, and mood. The main goal here is for the audience to catch the narrative content of the image instantaneously, with no further explanation or reliance on too many elements; always keep in mind that "less is more." I will utilize just the right number of elements to build a simple idea and let the viewer complete the story with their own thoughts – that's even more interesting!

I will use basic fundamentals such as perspective, composition, values, depth of field, and lighting to help produce an image that not only looks great but transmits a clear idea of the story. By reading about my process you will learn new tips that you can apply to your own creative process.

The scene will take place on a rocky island where someone has survived alone for quite a long time. I want to add a ship to the scene that crashed a long time ago and couldn't fly again. The surviving crew members gradually died and now there is just one person remaining. He is trying to communicate with someone, or is maybe just using his last equipment to gather some food to survive. Let's begin!

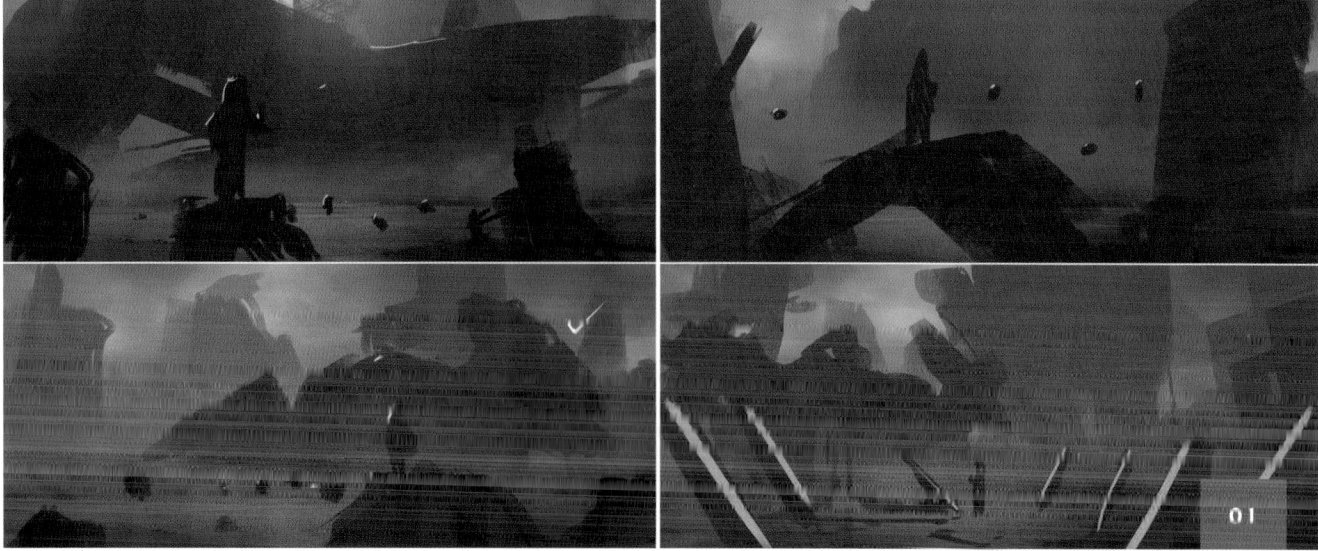

// I start with little explorations (thumbnails), just focusing on silhouettes and main compositional elements

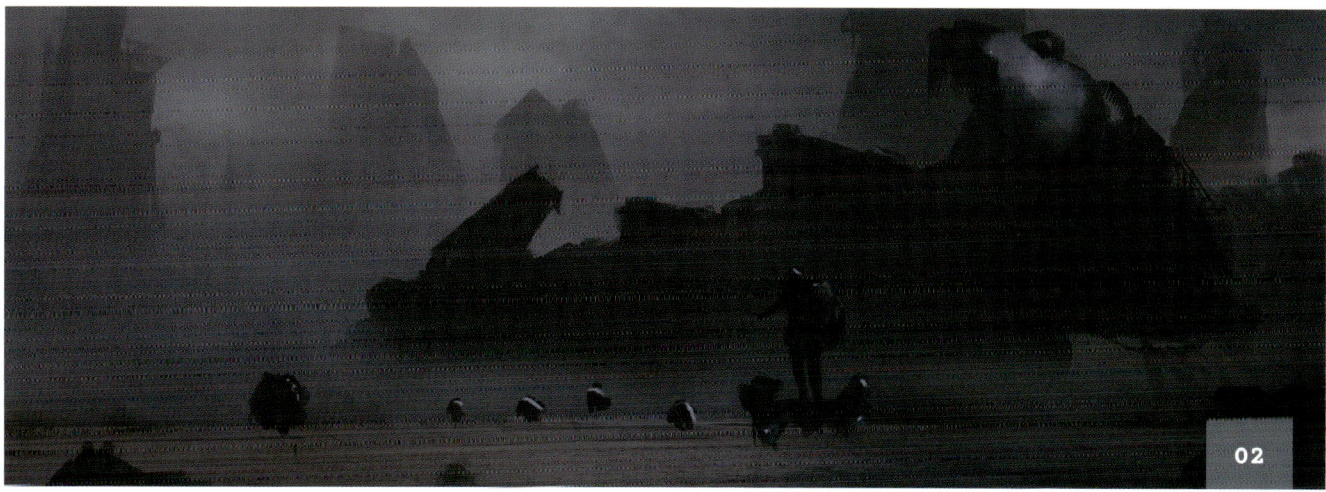

// **It's time to redefine the silhouettes and composition of the image**

>01 Exploration

Before I start any piece I spend time looking for inspiration. Since my theme for this image is "isolation," I seek references that reflect this general topic and write down my ideas. Sometimes, if I have enough time, I watch movies to get into the mood. For this image, I'm inspired by some of my favorite movies: *Alien*, *Prometheus*, and *The Road*. I like all genres of sci-fi, but I've always been inclined towards dark, horror, or survival sci-fi. I love the color palettes that are generally used there, the epic and lonely scenarios, the abandoned ships, and the feeling that there's always something that will come out of the darkness. I love the exploration and search for life on other planets, with creatures and environments full of mood and mystery, so these films really are a source of inspiration for me when I approach this type of topic.

Once I'm inspired, I create a new document in Adobe Photoshop and divide the canvas into four sections. In each cell I experiment with different silhouettes and angles until I find a composition that's good enough to tell the story. I focus on the basic planes – foreground, middle ground, and background – by setting the scene with simple shapes. I work with a big, rigid brush combined with sharp strokes that help me find interesting silhouettes more quickly.

>02 Silhouette

This step is all about the understanding of each element. For this, I work on defining the silhouettes even further

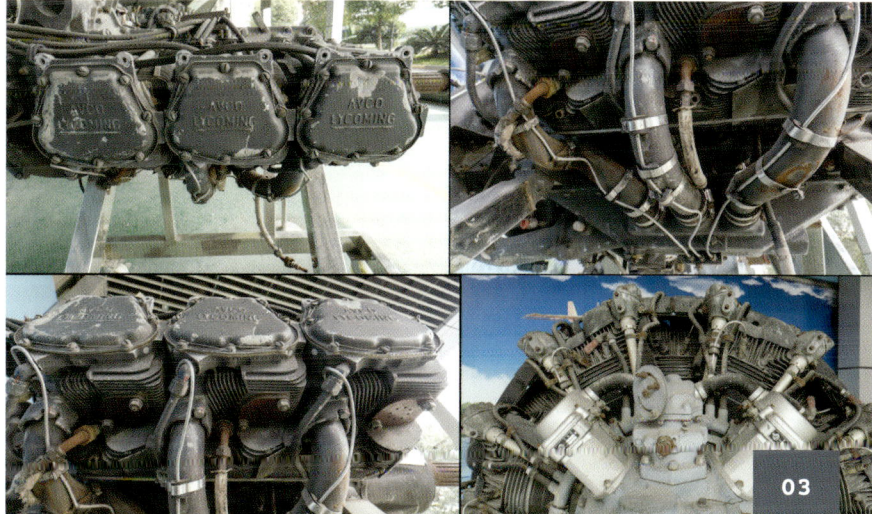

// **Some textures from www.photobash.org that I will use to get some color and shapes**

and refining the composition. Now the mountains, ship, and character are more clear to the eye. I also add some indications of light to decide the main direction of the lighting in the scene.

This is also a step in which to improve my initial idea by adding more elements. In this case, I add a moving platform as a transport for the character, from which he is controlling droid units that are searching for food. Remember, "less is more," so keep these first elements as simple as you can. Details will come later.

>03 Textures

After defining the composition and main shapes for the scene, it's now time to extract information from some interesting textures that I downloaded online from **www.photobash.org** for a very small fee (specifically the Aircraft Engine pack). Textures are useful because

they can help to make unexpected and attractive shapes. If they are well controlled, they'll bring a tight look to the whole scene, especially to the ship, droids, and main character here.

If you are working traditionally, you can use textures as reference. It's always good to have a large and diverse image bank for reference and textures. You can build one by taking your own pictures or downloading them. There are a number of websites that offer royalty-free images you can use. If it's a specialized topic you're working on, it's harder to find good images for free, but nowadays it's easy to buy packs of images for different topics. Some of them are really affordable and absolutely useful.

I have a dusty, dense, and polluted atmosphere in mind, so I want to keep the background mountains as silhouettes.

>04 Integration

First of all, I use some Photoshop tools such as Levels, Curves, and Hue/ Saturation to adjust the color and light of every texture I want to use and get a color palette that fits with what I want for the image. Having defined the silhouettes of the main elements, it's now easy to manipulate the textures. That's why it's so important to have the textures polished in advance. If you are working traditionally, you can still use these next few steps to think about how you will add shapes and designs to your image.

I place the texture layer just above the silhouette layer (the ship's silhouette, in this case) and create a clipping group. This stage is personally one of the more interesting stages of the process, because I design every element by taking advantage of the random shapes and colors that come with the textures. I experiment with the texture and then refine the design by painting over it.

It's important to keep it simple and not add too much detail. I just focus on the overall design of the ship, especially the front view that could eventually be one of the engines. I also add some touches of light to give a more three-dimensional look to the element.

>05 Characters

Once the ship design is defined and I've established the light direction, I continue the same process with the other elements. Now it's time to focus on the characters in the scene. In the same way as in the previous step, I look for the right application of texture inside the main character and droid silhouettes. It's important to match the accidental shapes I get with the silhouette in order to create an interesting result.

You can see in image 05 how I integrate the texture with the man's silhouette in order to create something that resembles a backpack. Later on it will be connected somehow to the platform, but at this moment that level of detail is not important.

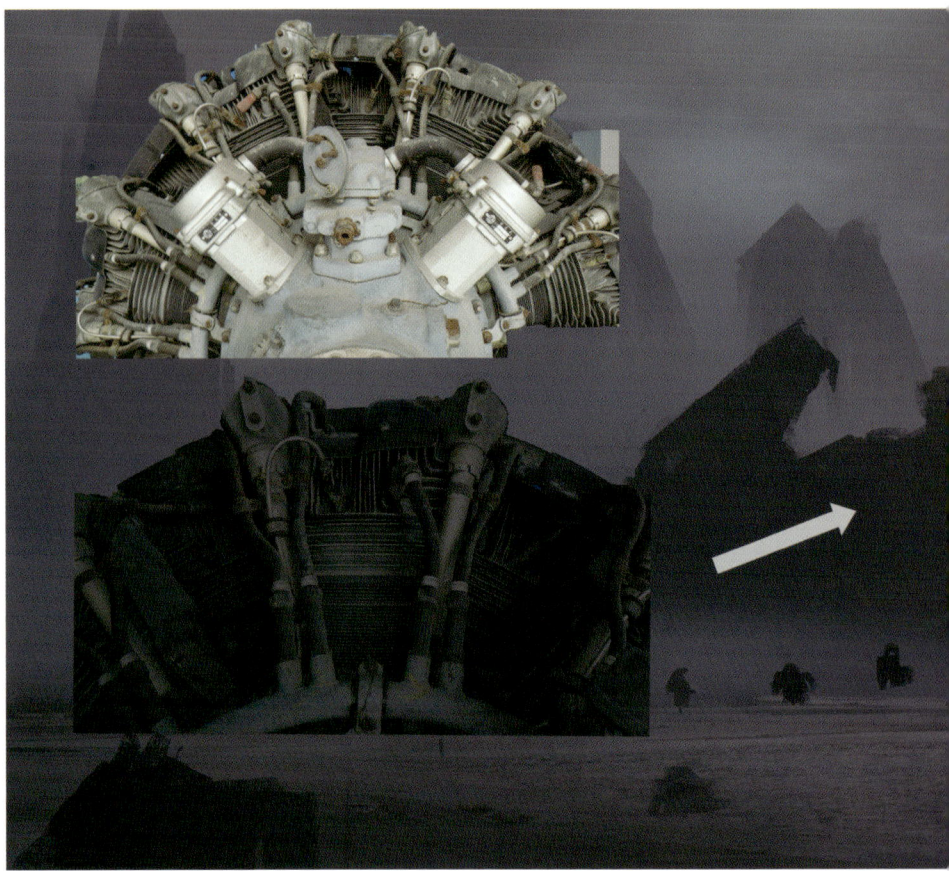

// Before applying textures, I adjust them to match the image and mood I want to achieve

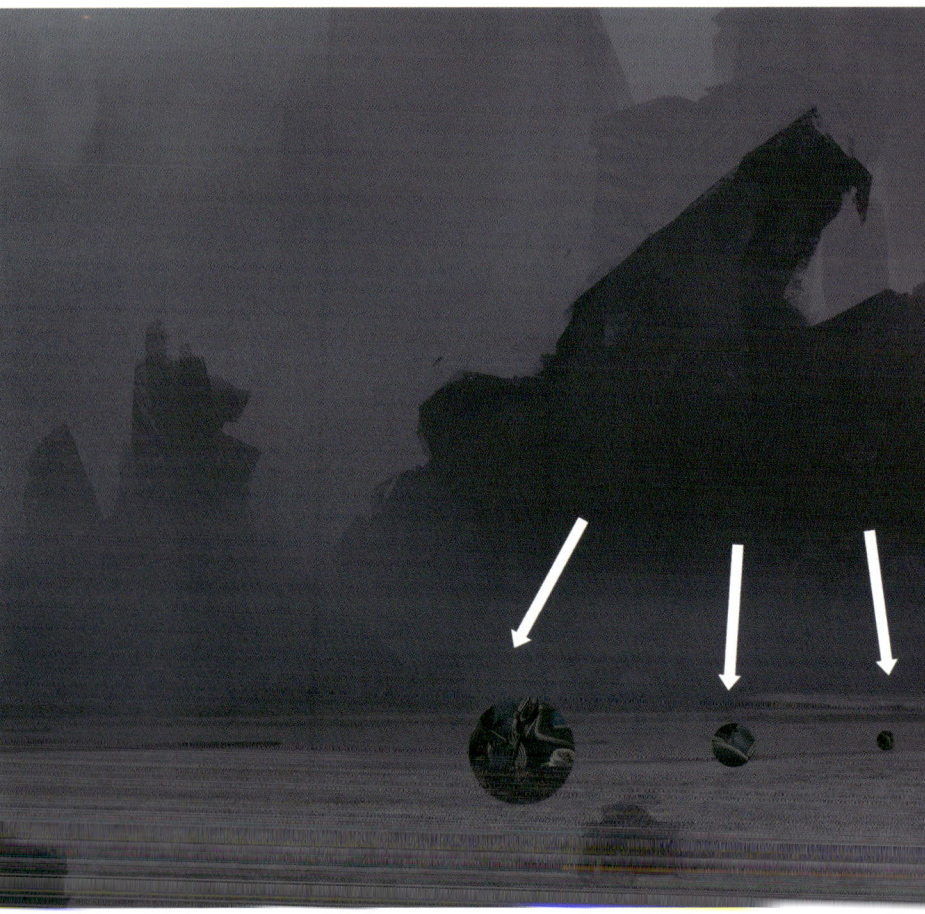

// Integrating more textures, this time into the silhouettes of the main character and the droids

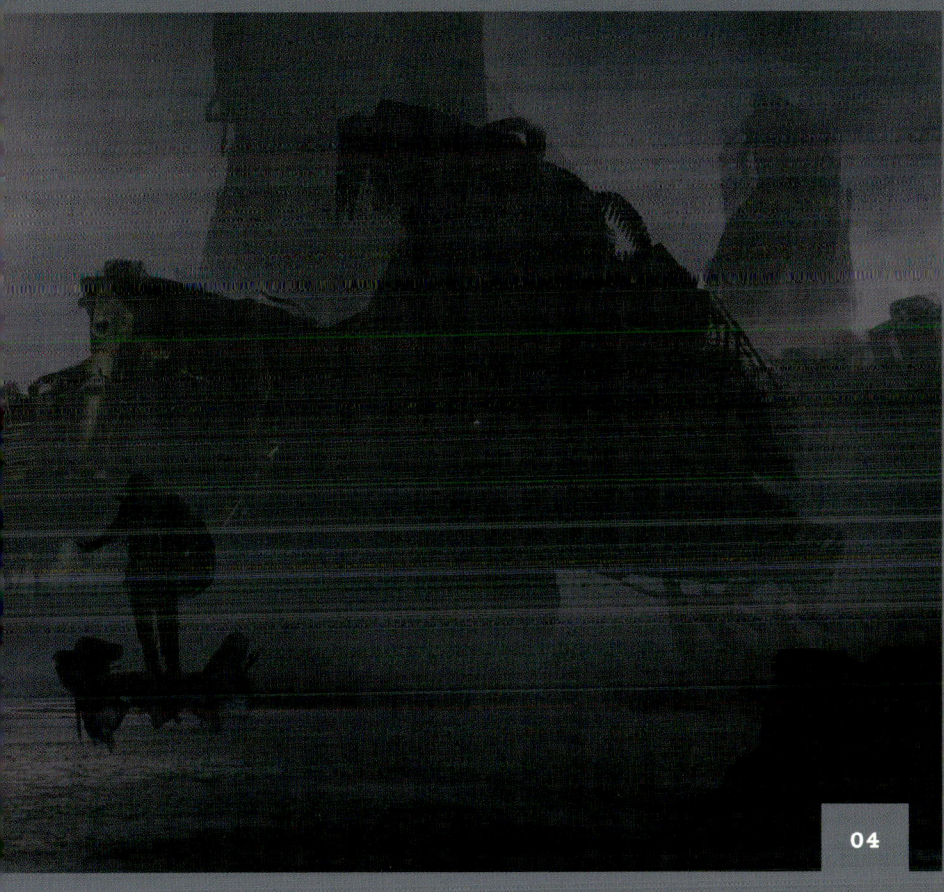

04

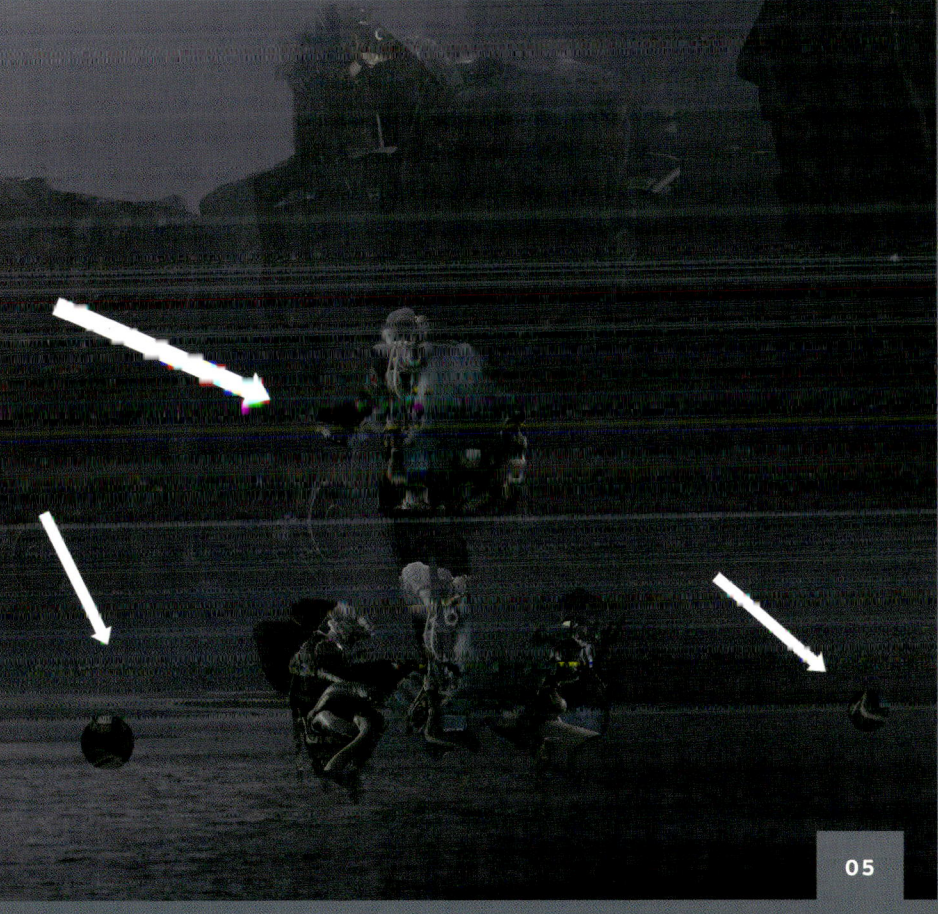

05

"This stage is personally one of the more interesting stages of the process, because I design every element by taking advantage of the random shapes and colors that come with the textures"

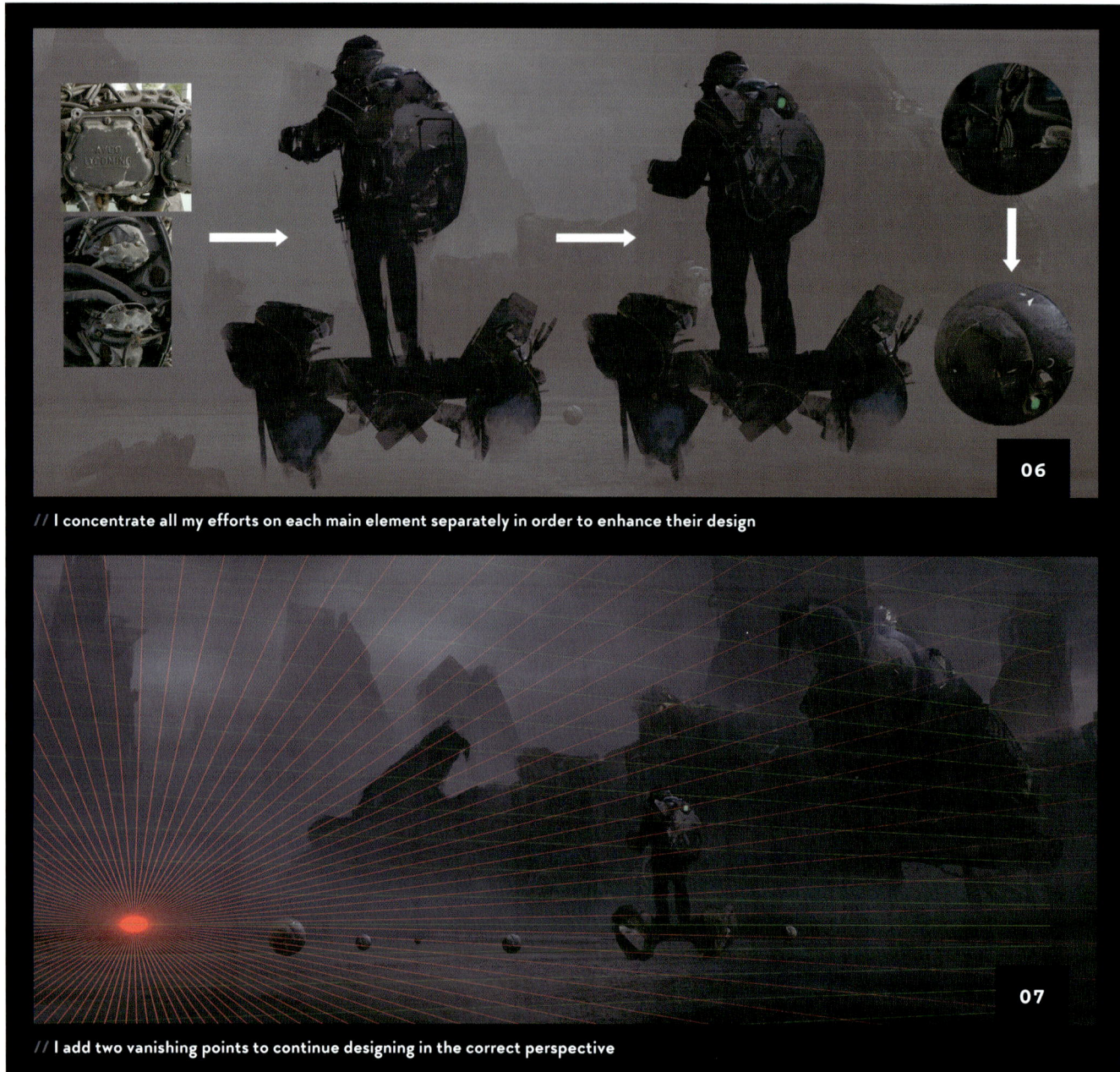

06

// I concentrate all my efforts on each main element separately in order to enhance their design

07

// I add two vanishing points to continue designing in the correct perspective

>06 Close up

By this stage, I have a clear idea of my image. Now it's time to focus on every main element independently to polish the design, add detail, and enhance each part. As you can see, no matter which element I want to polish, the process is still the same: I start adding texture to the element, and then paint over it to incorporate colors and shapes into a coherent and believable design.

During the process, I look for ways to unify the visual language of the overall piece and to find designs that fit the concepts I already have in mind. For

example, I use organic shapes like circles, not only in the character's bag but also in the droids, which match the organic appearance of the ship.

>07 Perspective

Before polishing the design of the main elements, I add two vanishing point guides to the scene that I need to follow while I'm painting and designing inside the silhouettes. These will help me to keep accurate perspective for the elements in the space. I prefer to distinguish the two vanishing points with different colors: red and green. The reason is simple: I need to visualize

the lines clearly in order to understand the direction of every point. As I'm using Photoshop, I also put these perspective guides into a layer group folder on top of the other layers, and change the opacity so that I can see them without hurting my eyes.

>08 Background

In order to address the background elements like the mountains, I start to polish their silhouettes to convey the initial idea of an isolated island with rocky mountains. It's quite important to define the geography of the image, as it can be used as a tool to transmit the mood I want to convey. In this image, for instance, I want to create a desolate place rather than a dangerous one. Therefore I avoid sharp mountains and keep them as simple silhouettes due to the dense atmosphere of the setting.

To create more depth, I add a metallic element that could resemble a part of the ship, which I place in the lower section of the composition. These ruined transports and the fact that they are a crashed piece of advanced technology makes the character seem more lonely

and unfortunate, enhancing the concept of abandonment and isolation.

>09 Depth

I add new elements and adjustments to the image that help me to reinforce the sense of depth. First I flip the image horizontally to change into a more flowing left-to-right reading order. Then I refine the ship's silhouette to provide a rhythm to the image, redefining the reading direction to draw the audience's attention to right side, which could be the direction the main character is heading towards.

I add some rocks to the foreground as a starting point for the rhythm of the image; the viewer's eyes will start there and follow the reading direction through the rest of the composition.

I keep the background simple, avoiding the temptation to add a lot of extra complexity to the silhouettes, as they are hidden by the mist. I want to produce curiosity in the audience about what's beyond there. The mist also adds to the feeling of isolation by creating a slightly ominous feeling of the unknown.

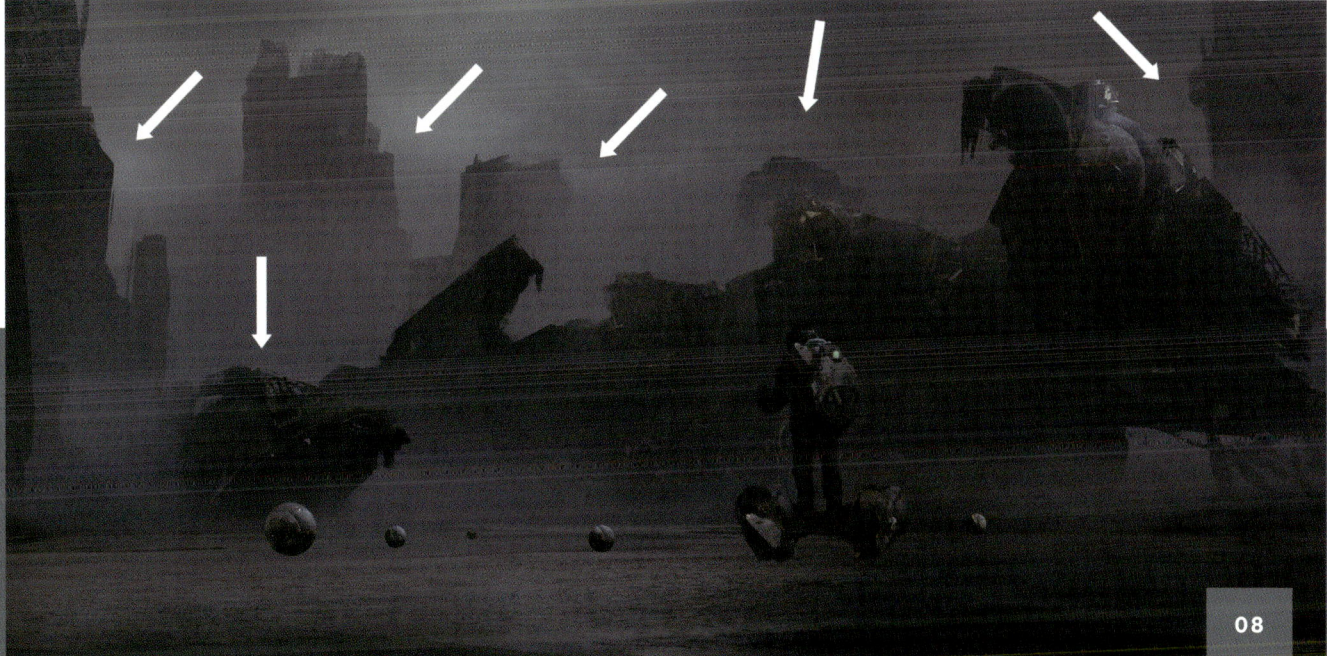

08

// It's time to take charge of the background silhouettes, enhancing and polishing the mountains

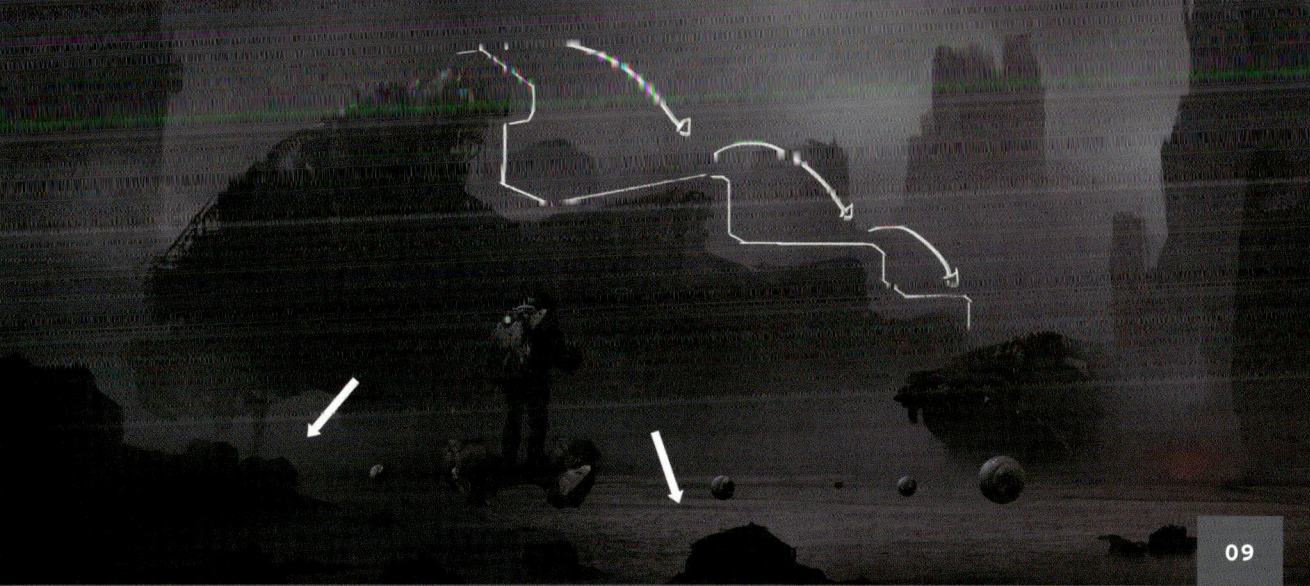

09

// Reinforcing the sense of depth in the overall scene

>10 Ship enhancement

Now I start adding detail to the ship. My main goal here is to give the feeling that the ship has been abandoned for a long time, using some ruins and debris textures that I gathered earlier. I apply the textures to the image using a Lighten layer in Photoshop. I find this method really useful to add detail and subtle light touches to the elements. I control the textures by painting over them in a new layer, polishing all the details even more, and integrating them to make them believable. To keep a clear focal point, it's important to control the textures that you use, adding detail just in the illuminated areas of the image. Similarly, if you are working traditionally, control the detail you add to your image so that you don't distract from the key areas.

>11 Character detail

With the ship almost complete, I enhance the character with some elements like the harpoon, which will help to reinforce the idea that he's trying to get some food, a hard task in this hostile environment; he really needs help from the droids. The other element that I detail is the platform. In order to keep the organic language I've previously used for all the elements, I give it a form that resembles a stingray, a shape that is easily recognizable. I also add a cable connecting the backpack to the platform, just to give an indication that they work together.

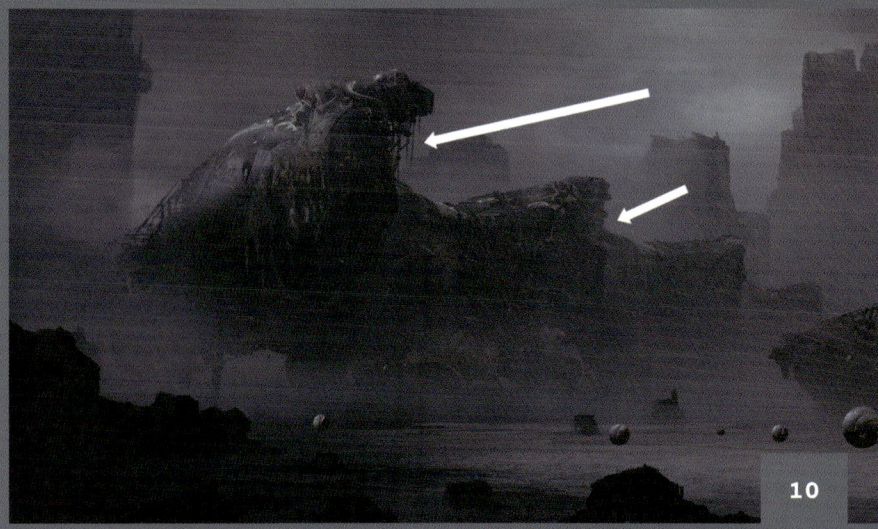

// I use some ruins and debris textures to detail the ship

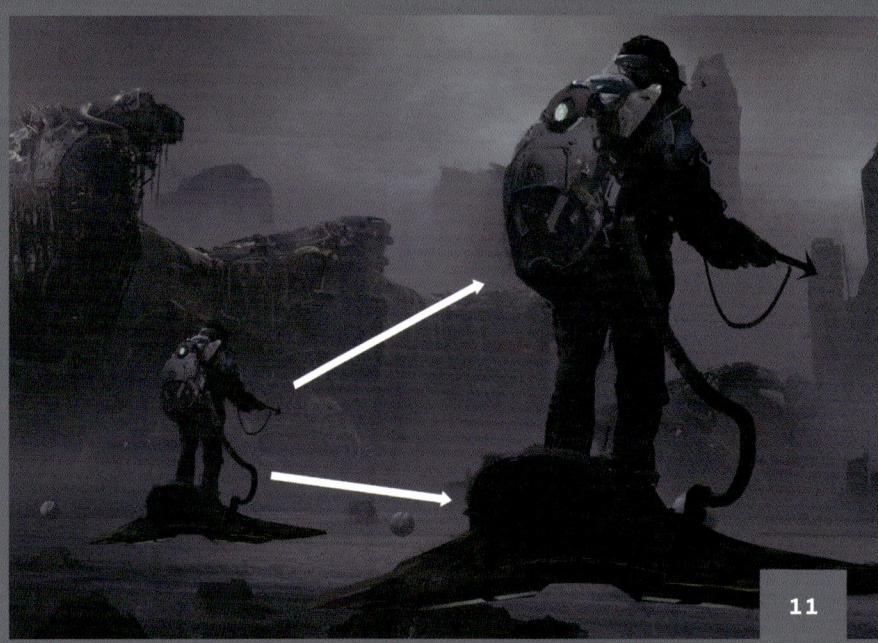

// Polishing other aspects of the character

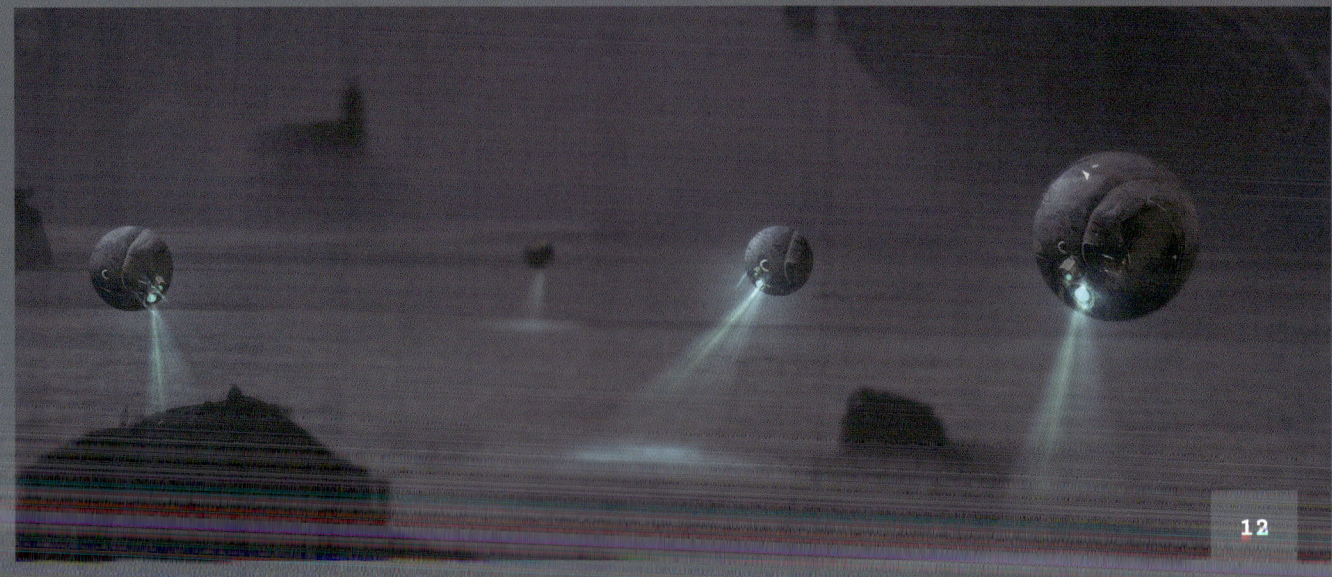

// Now I will work on the droids to reinforce the story. They're searching!

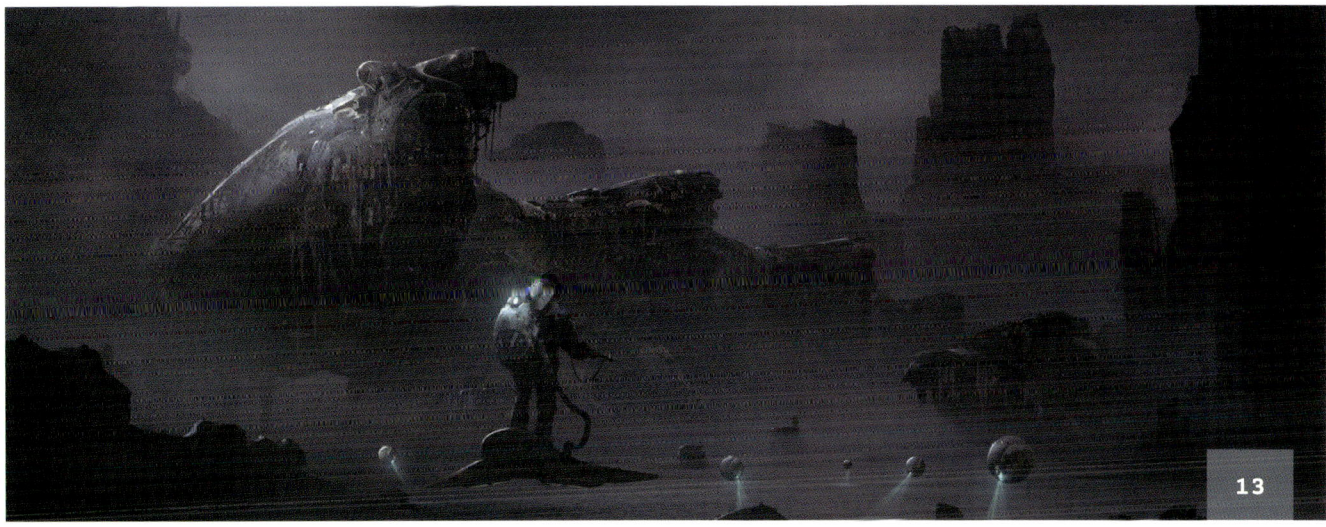

// Time to reinforce the lighting

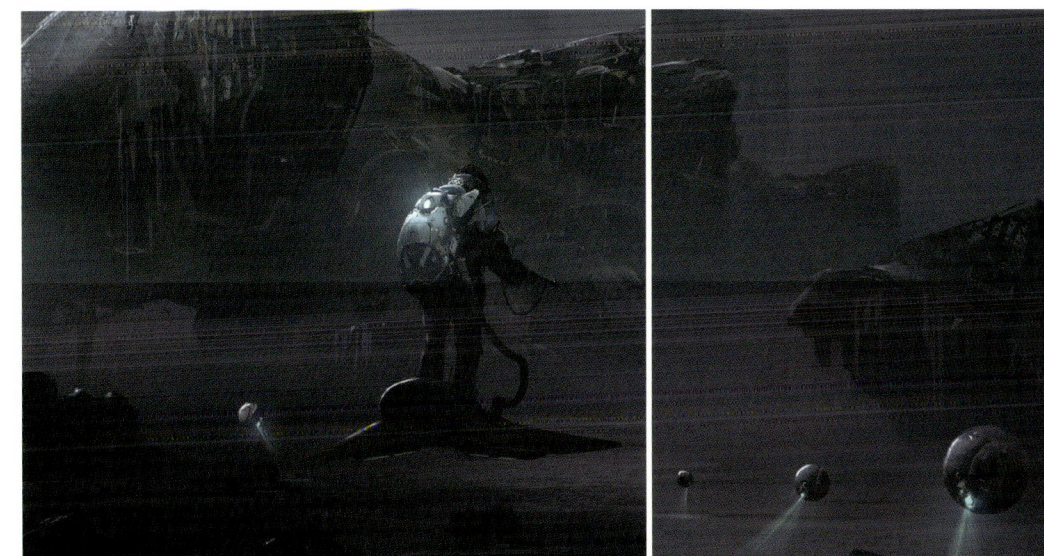

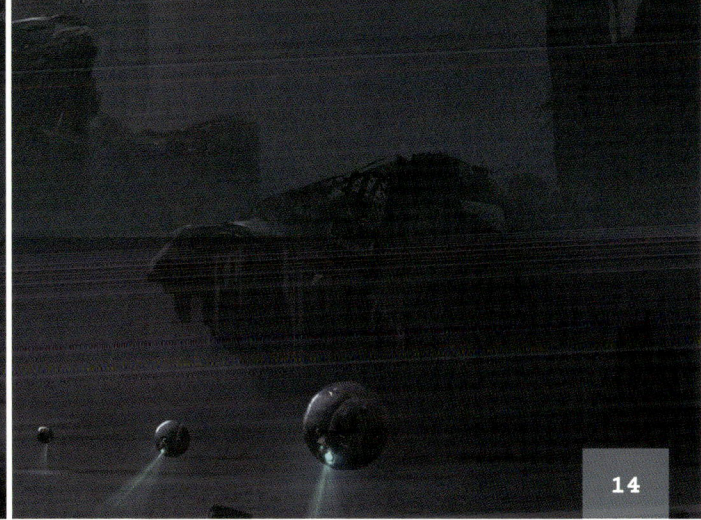

// This step is about balancing and smoothing out the colors in the image

>12 Droids

It's now time to bring those droids to life. Maybe they have been programmed to help my character to find his food using some kind of sensor or laser scanner to detect movement. I use a Color Dodge layer in Photoshop to simulate a light that comes from the droids. This helps the image not only because it looks interesting, but because the light adds rhythm, reinforces depth, supports the narrative content (the idea that they are searching for something), and finally because it helps to keep the viewer's sight on the focal areas. In addition, as the droids and main character are the only sources of artificial light in the scene, the sense of being isolated is enhanced further.

>13 Lighting

My illustration is almost ready. The next stage is to improve the clarity of the image through the lighting. For this I add some highlights on the main aspects of the composition and on some other elements around them. The important task here is to reinforce the focal point of the image: the main character and his droids.

Using Color Dodge in Photoshop again, I place some indications of light on the highest part of the ship, taking care not to exaggerate this and steal the attention that the main character and droids need. Then I add more highlights around the character and droids, always being careful with the light direction. My final touch for the

lighting stage is to add some reflections for the droid's lights on the water enhancing the realism of the image.

>14 Color filters

I'm getting closer to the final step, but first I'll need use color filters to give the image a cinematic look. As I am working digitally, I add two different color filters to the image: first a green one at 50% opacity, and then a deep blue one at 20% opacity. If you are using a traditional medium you could use a color wash.

I choose this palette because the dark green and blue tones convey a sense of mystery, loneliness, and desolation, and are widely used in the styles of sci-fi that I'm aiming for with my final image.

These filters not only add a realistic atmosphere, they also give a sense of uniformity and balance between all the colors that already exist in the image.

>15 Final adjustments

Now I carry out some final touches to improve the overall appearance of the scene. Digital tools can be useful for this: I apply a sharpen filter that enhances the details and eliminates the blurry spots. Next I use a lens correction tool combined with a chromatic aberration filter to give a realistic lens distortion effect to the image, creating a cinematic look. To tie in with this, I lastly apply a grain filter to simulate the "noise" that we might see on a movie screen.

>16 Image complete

In the final image below you can see that I have added some flying creatures in the distance to strengthen the scale and movement of the image, and also because, although the atmosphere feels dead and lonely, I want to show some life. The main character is now looking to survive, and I want to show that the place is not entirely dead – there are some creatures or animals that are surviving too.

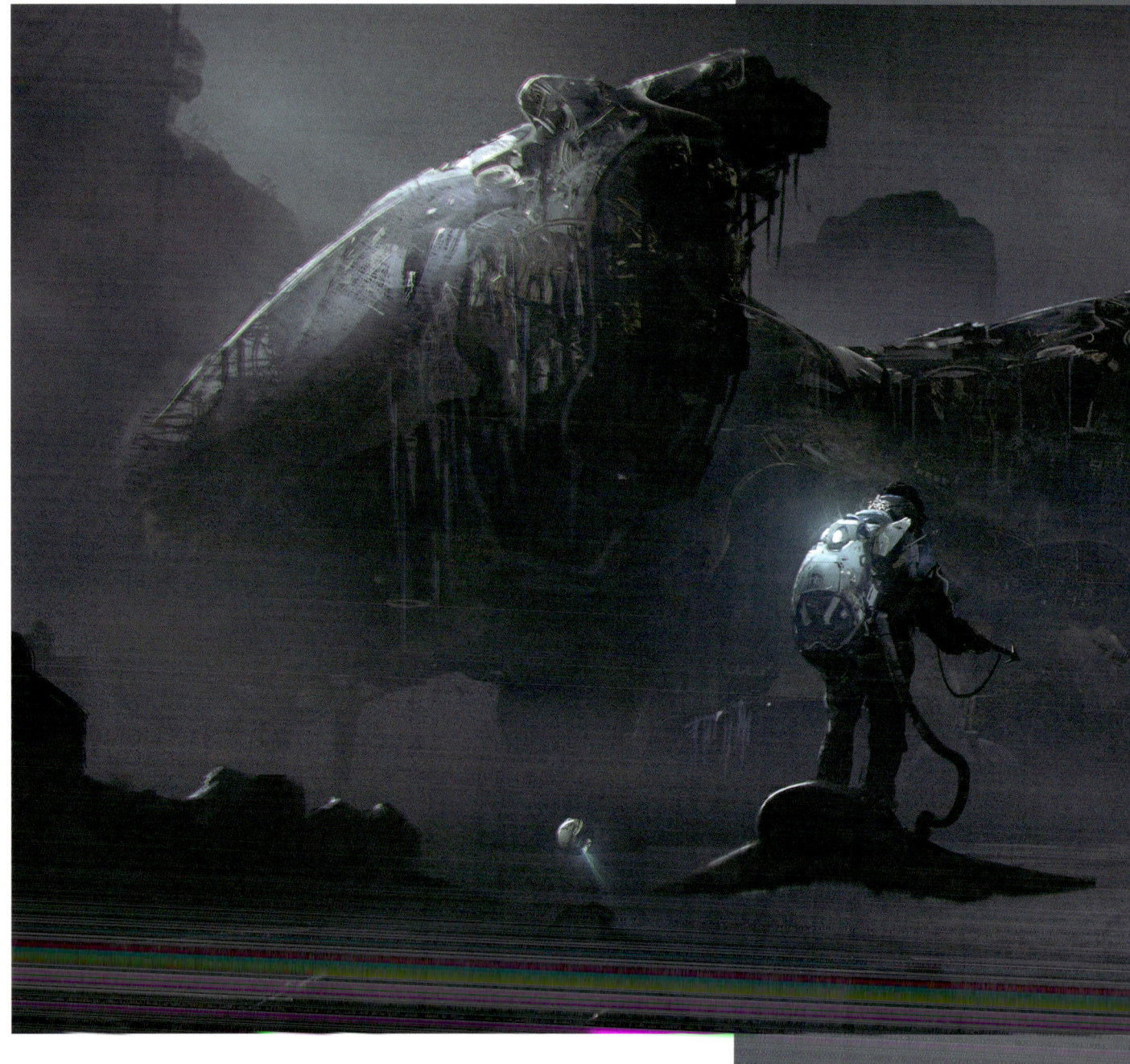

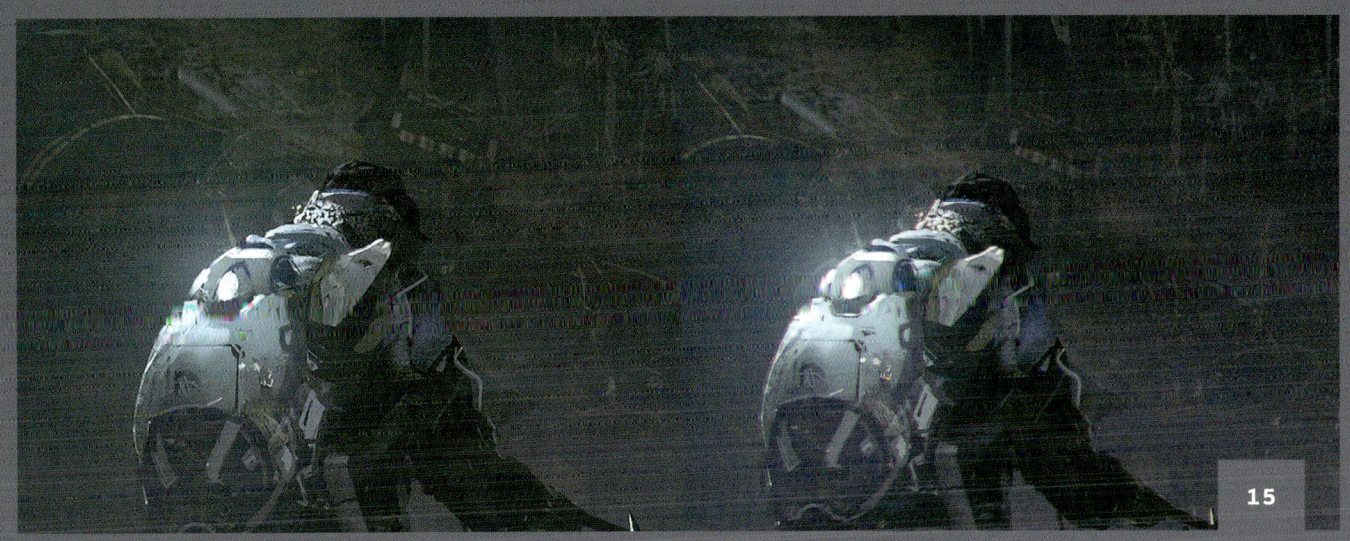

15

// Wrapping up the scene with some finishing touches

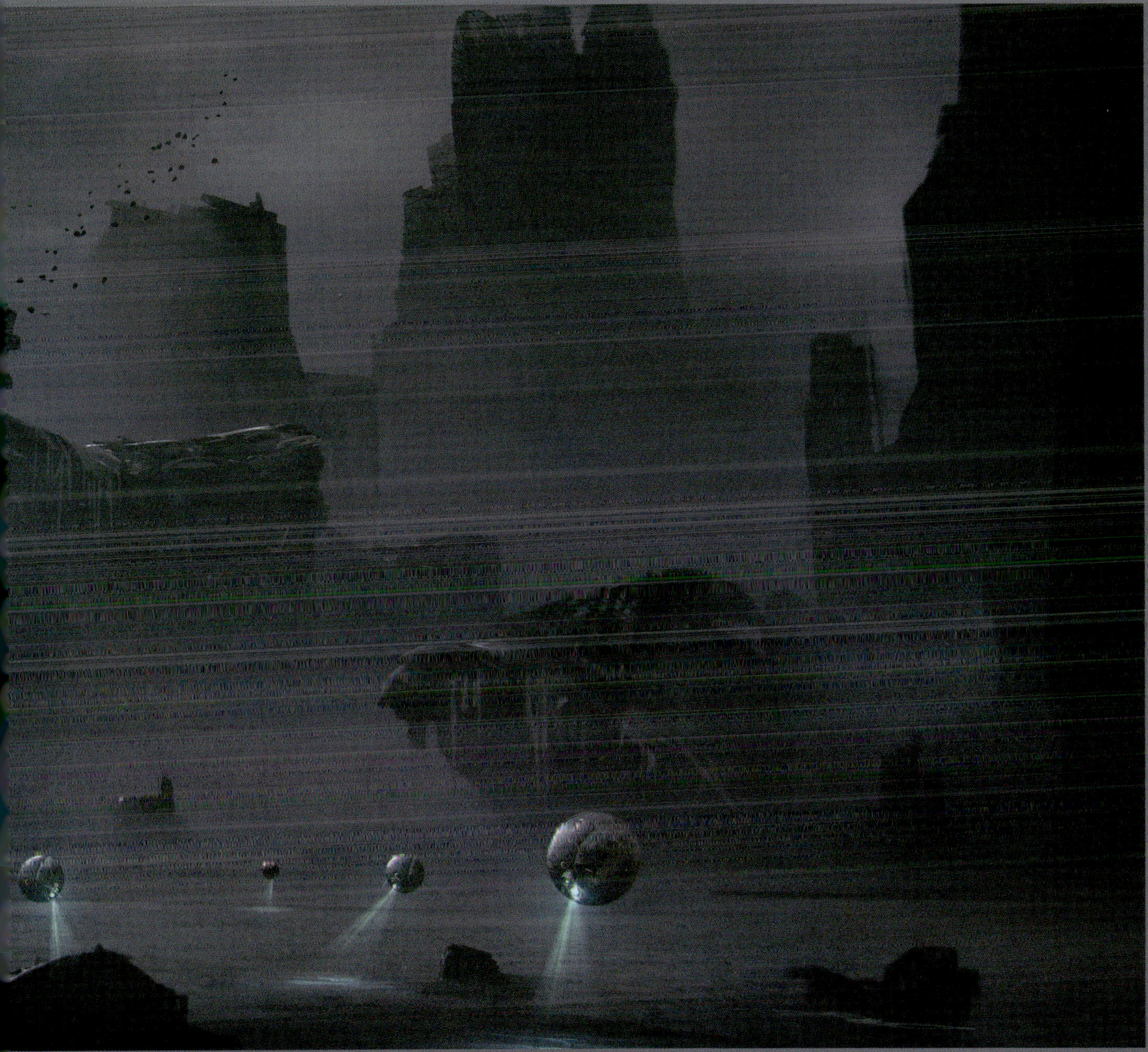

Tan Zhi Hui | www.artstation.com/artist/kudaman

Joy

In this tutorial I will demonstrate how I usually go about designing and illustrating characters. When I initially think of the theme of "joy," ideas that come to mind are: eating a lot, becoming filthy rich, traveling around, and spending time with my loved ones! But when I think about it again, eating a lot and becoming rich aren't really forms of happiness, so I decide to illustrate a scene incorporating myself and my loved ones on an adventure!

>01 Ideation and sketching

In this first step, I make a rough sketch of my initial idea (image 01a). I work in Adobe Photoshop, so I use a brush with pressure sensitivity that is the most similar to a pencil. I also darken the canvas so that it's not too plain and bright to work on. I want to illustrate a piece with multiple characters, and to show the interactions between them. The characters are based on myself and my girlfriend, the bears are my girlfriend's stuffed toys, and our pet dog will be in the background!

I personally prefer to use simple forms and shapes to express my designs, and I usually illustrate subjects in motion.

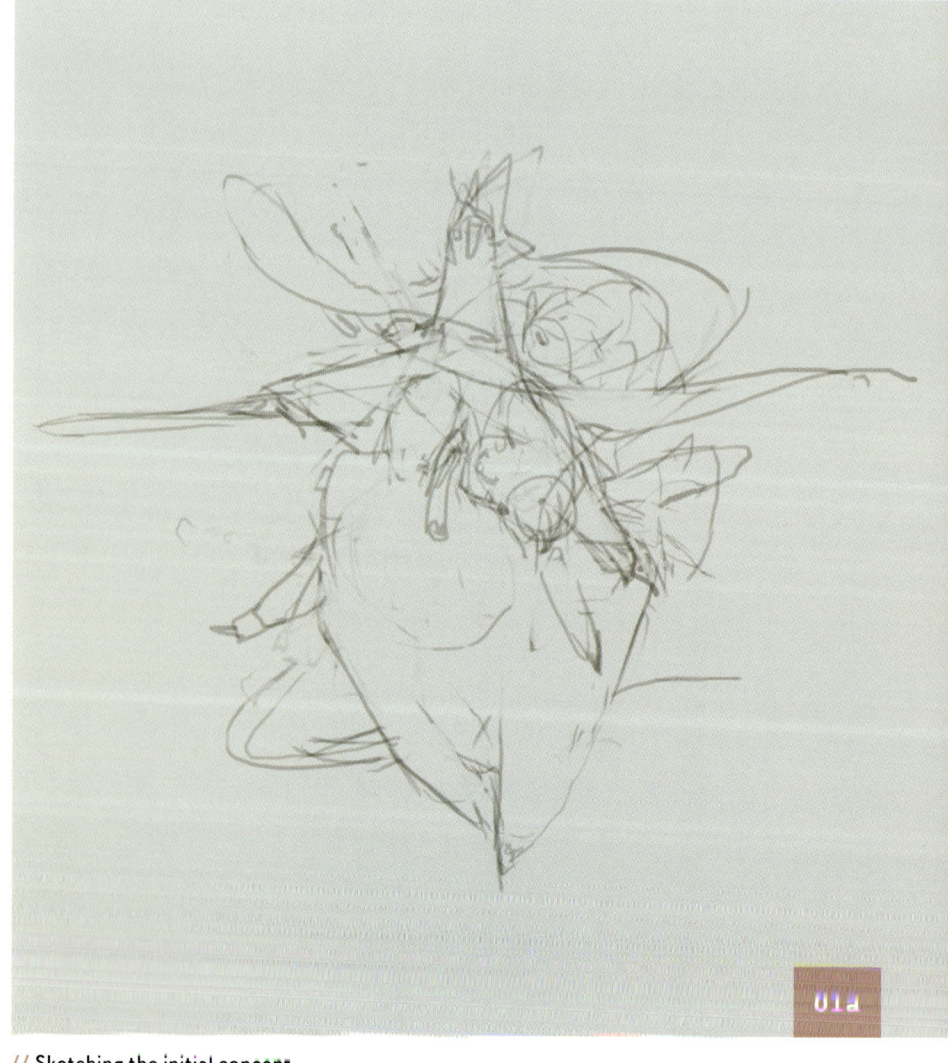

// Sketching the initial concept

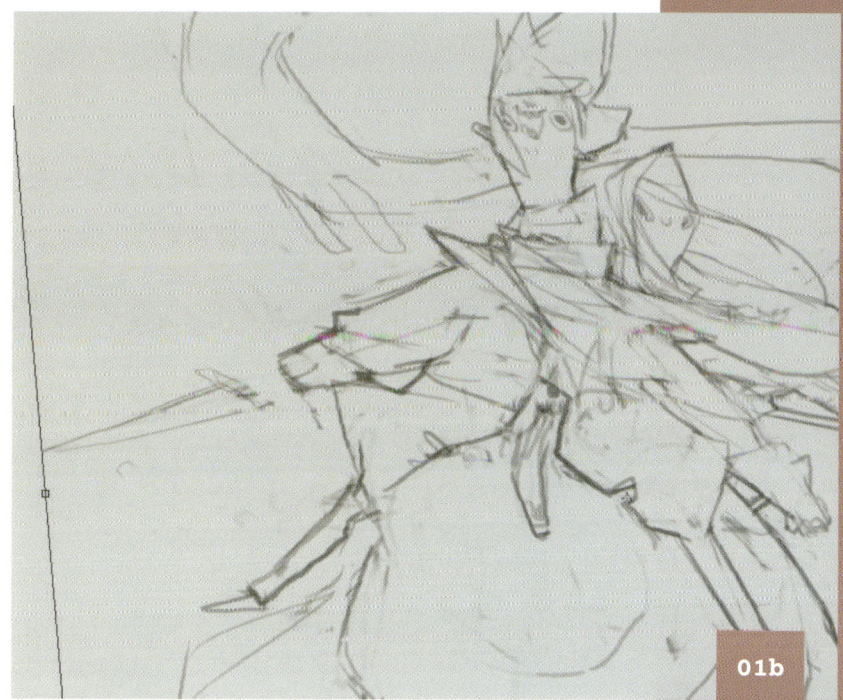

01b

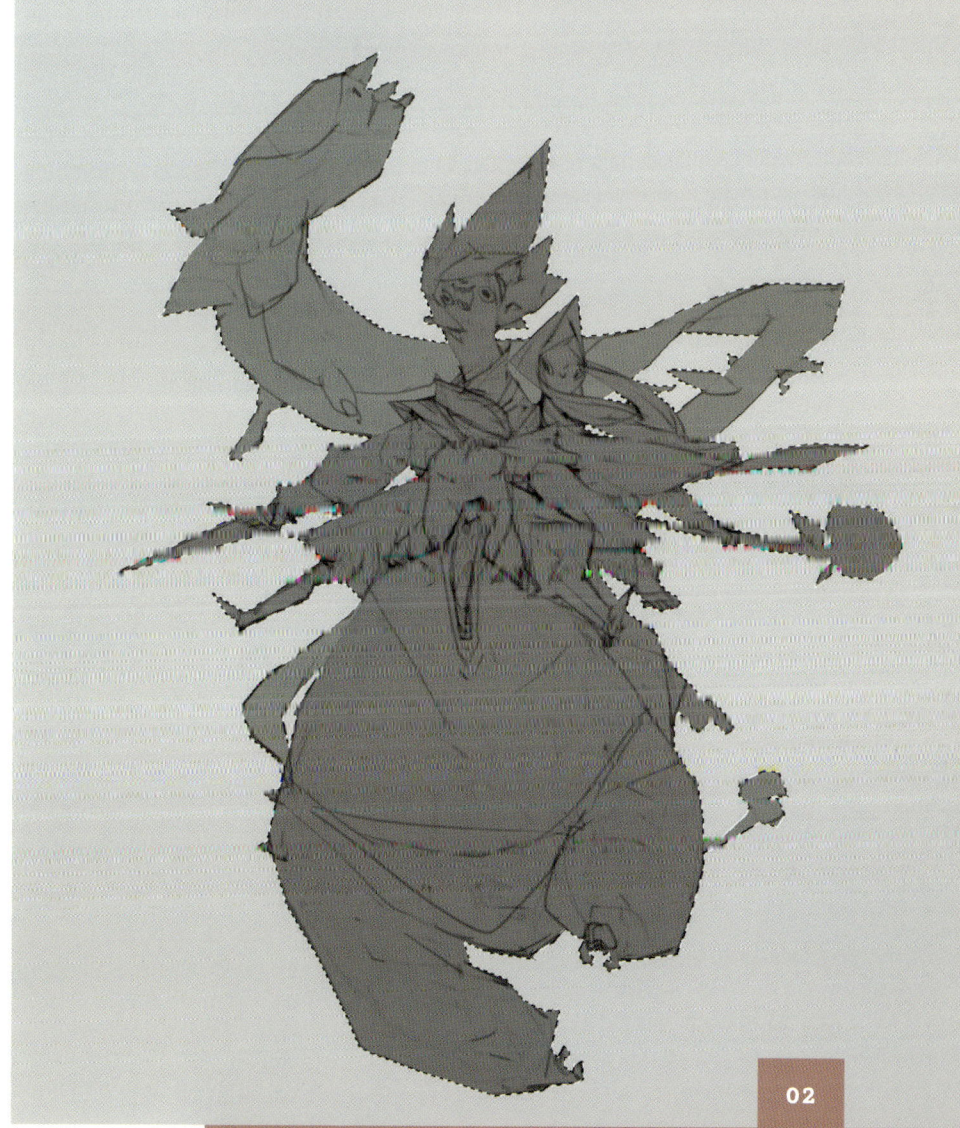

02

"I want to illustrate a piece with multiple characters, and to show the interactions between them"

// I tweak the sketch into my desired shape

I think that if someone is going to draw something in a very stylized manner, it's best to be as unique as possible, and not just adopt other people's styles. Create your own interesting characteristics with shape, silhouette, expression, and color palettes.

After blocking out the overall feel and design, I start to develop it with large simple shapes (image 01b). I also use Photoshop's Free Transform tool, or the Transform > Distort setting, to balance out the weight of the entire composition.

02 Defining the silhouette
Now I can go in and start defining more elements on the characters. To create a silhouette base for the areas I want to paint, I use the Polygonal Lasso tool to create a selection for the area I want to fill in with grayscale. This serves as a useful mask for me further along in the process, and can be used as a sort of underpainting.

// Blocking in a silhouette base

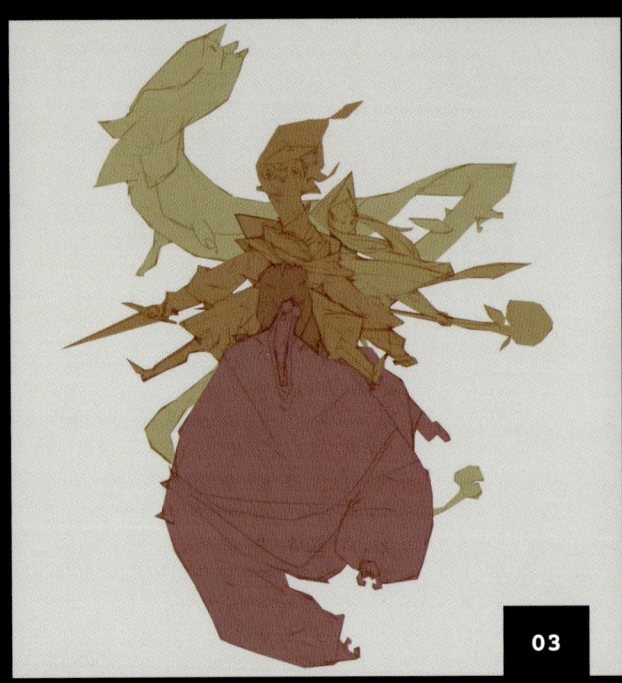

// I split the image's elements into sections with different values — **03**

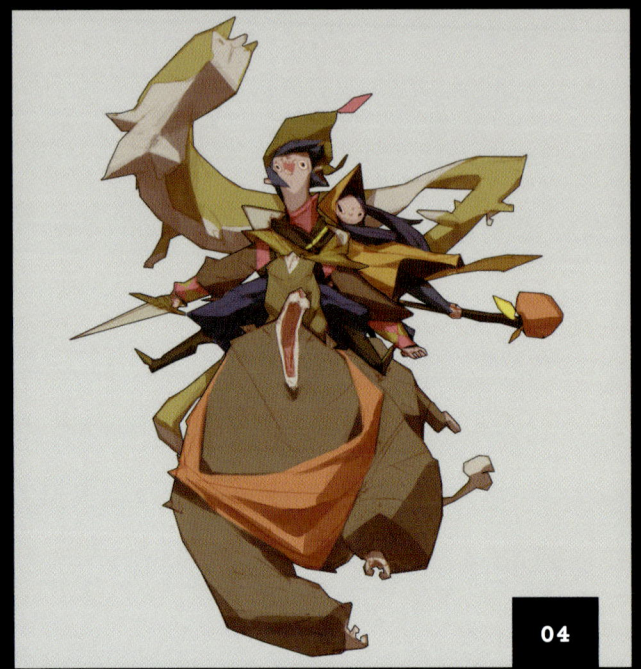

// Developing the color palette — **04**

>03 Separating large elements

It is useful to think of an image in layers, with a foreground, middle ground, and background. This will remind you to consider the depth when painting your characters. Here I separate the different elements and characters into their own layers and start to fill in colors to create depth. I use darker values for characters in the front, and lighter values for characters in the back, so that they seem farther away.

>04 Color exploration

In this step, I break down the different elements even further, adding more color within each character for their skin tone, outfit, weapons, and so on. I spend more time on this stage as it has a significant impact on the outcome of the final piece – these colors establish most of the finished image's vibe.

I'm going for a lively, fantasy style feel; since this piece doesn't have many limitations, I want to make something more fun and unusual. Using a variety of colors will add to the sense of vibrancy and joy

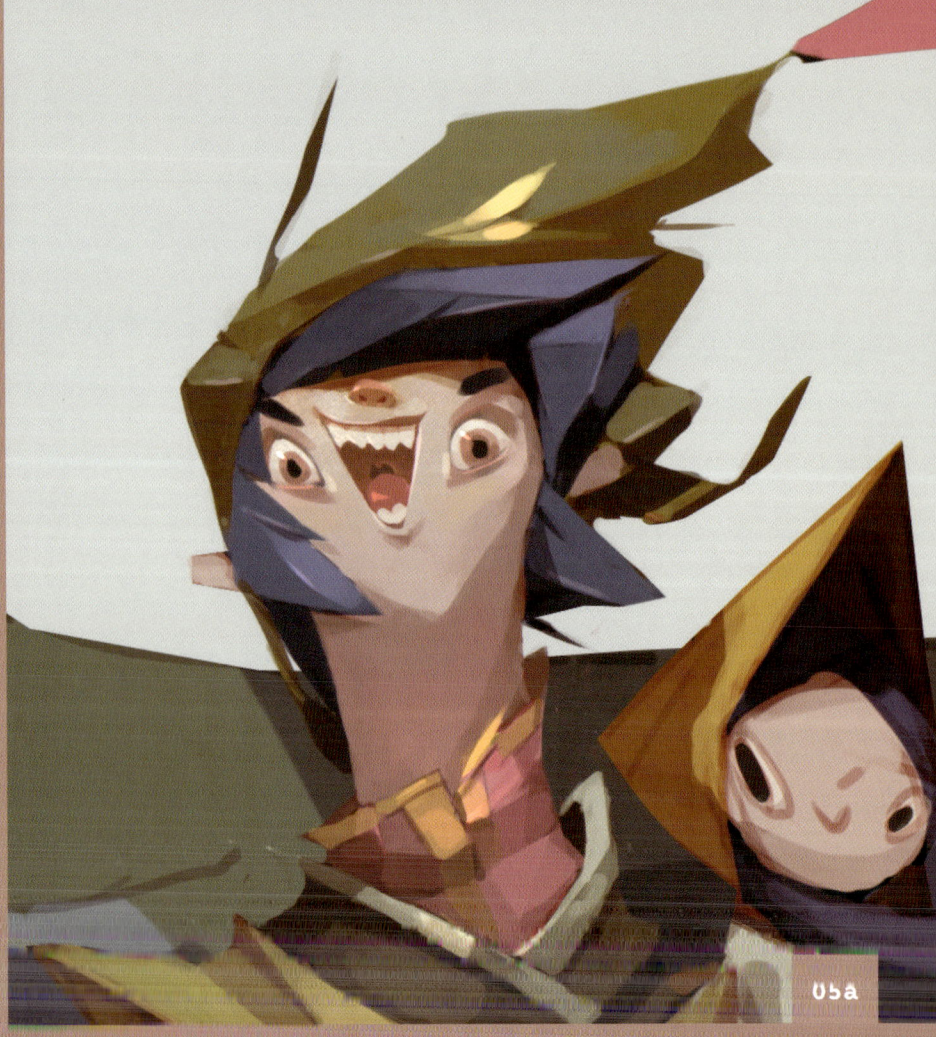

// Building up the main character — 05a

>05 Starting to render

Here I begin to render in the details of the characters, starting from the main character's face (image 05a). I prefer to start from the face because it's the part of the character that expresses the most emotion. Developing this early on will help establish the sentiment of the rest of the image. For the highlights on the upper part of the character, such as the hair, I add in a hint of blue to suggest that the lighting is affected by the color of the sky.

When rendering materials, I use lighting and blending to create different material qualities for the various fabrics, giving the designs a more layered feel so that the characters are distinct from each other rather than being flat (image 05b). I also add a yellow highlight on the hat, just to bring the viewer's attention back to the head area.

>06 Painting the female character

Once the main character is done, I follow the same process to paint the female character. The flow of the fabric on her costume will help create a sense

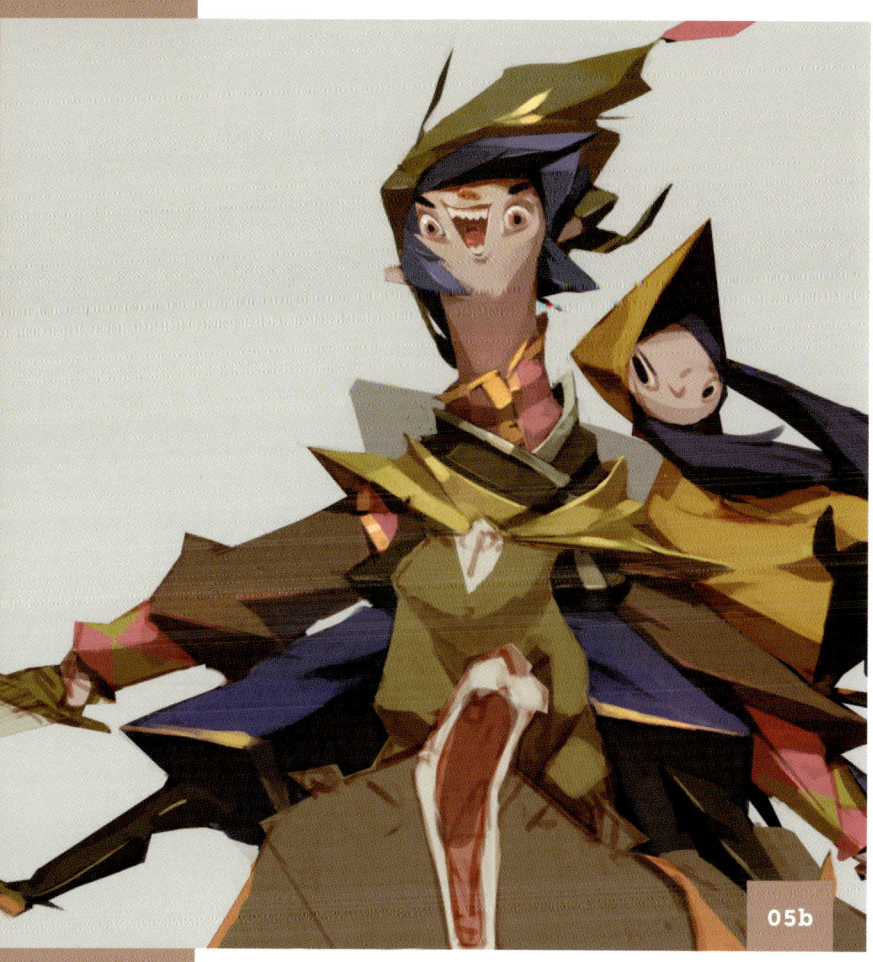

// Using light and blending to suggest different materials

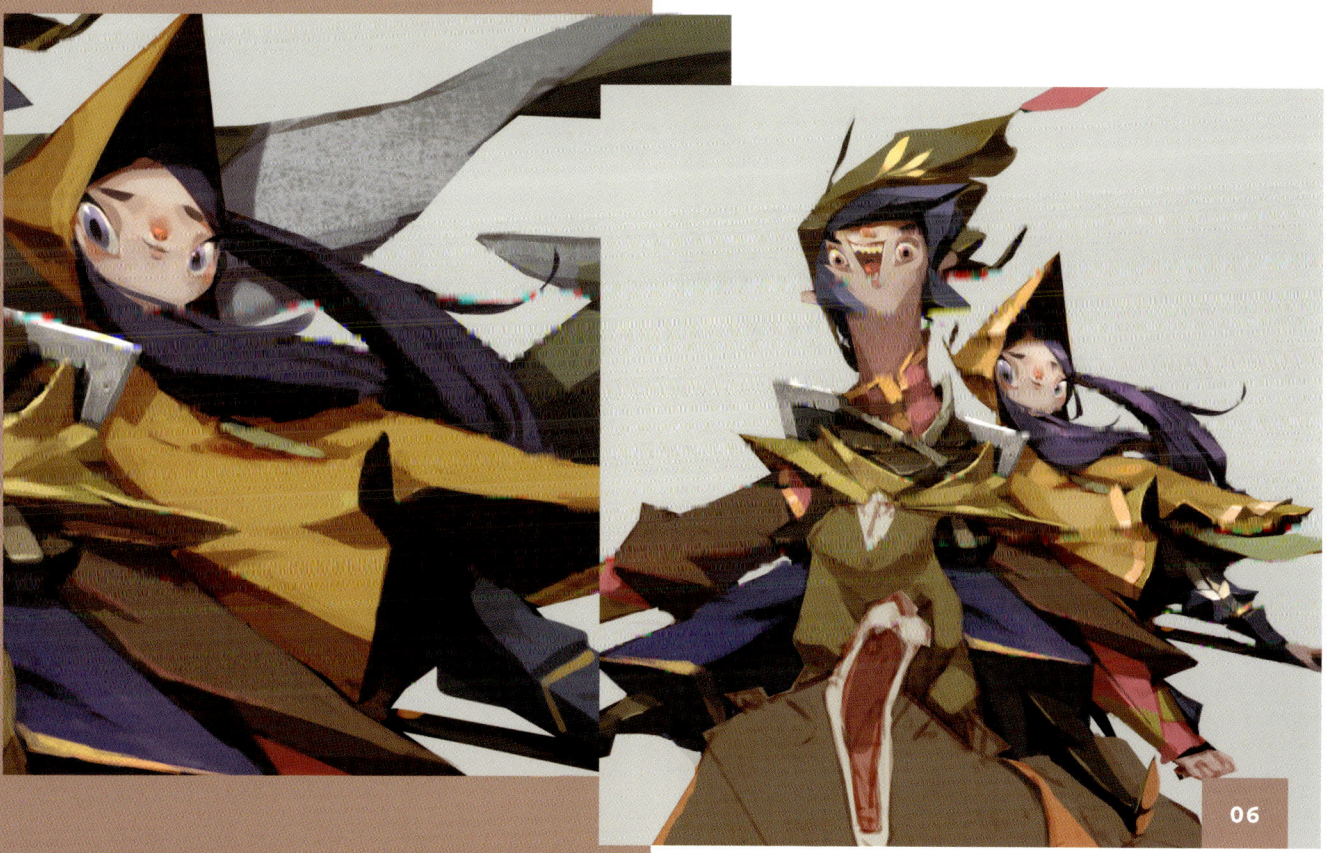

// Rendering the second character

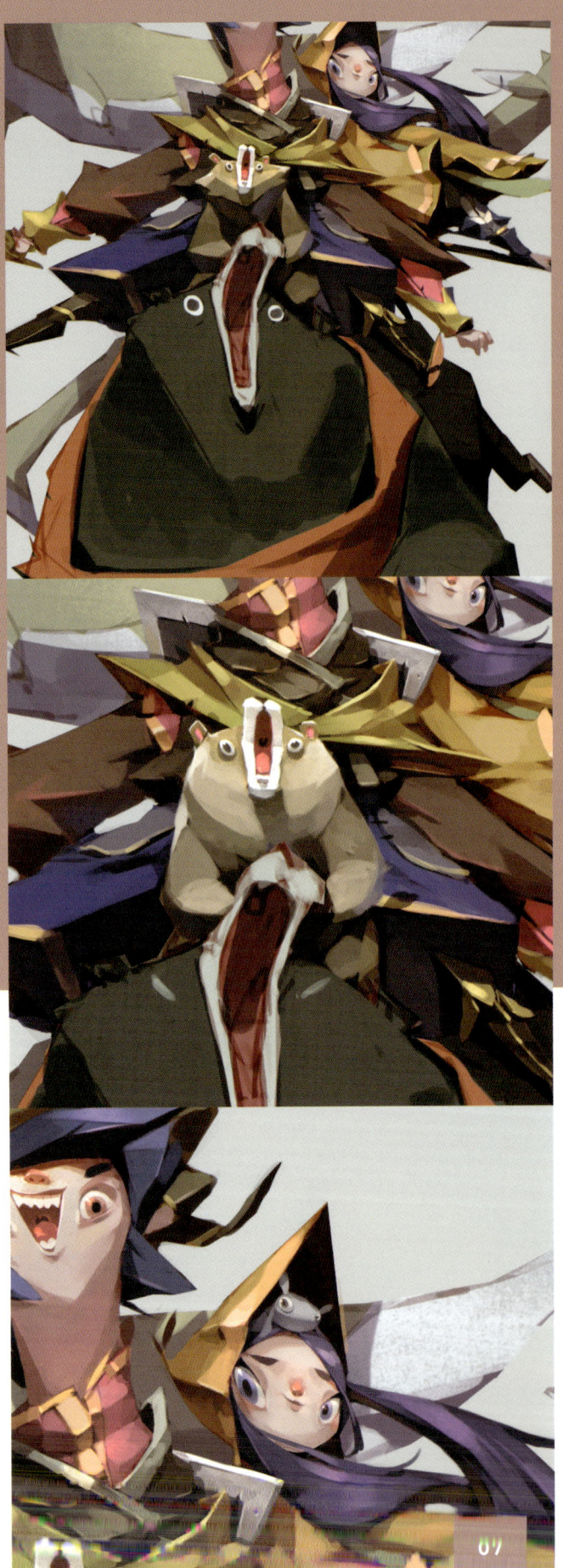

// Developing the bears and filling in spaces in the image

"Now I can start painting the bears, giving them different expressions from the human characters, just to make things more interesting"

of motion in the piece, adding to the feeling of joy. I make her facial features more feminine by enlarging the eyes more and painting in a smaller mouth. I also add further details to her outfit and start defining the structure of her arm more. So far, the colors that I've used are quite similar and coordinate among the characters. I choose to do this because otherwise it might make the painting look too complicated.

>07 The bears

Now I can start painting the bears, giving them different expressions from the human characters, just to make things more interesting. I realize that the smaller bear blends into the main character too much, so I decide to change the design of its head, enlarging the entire bear and adjusting its fur color to something more desaturated. I also realize that the space between the female character's head and her hood is too empty, so I add a small creature to fill in that space!

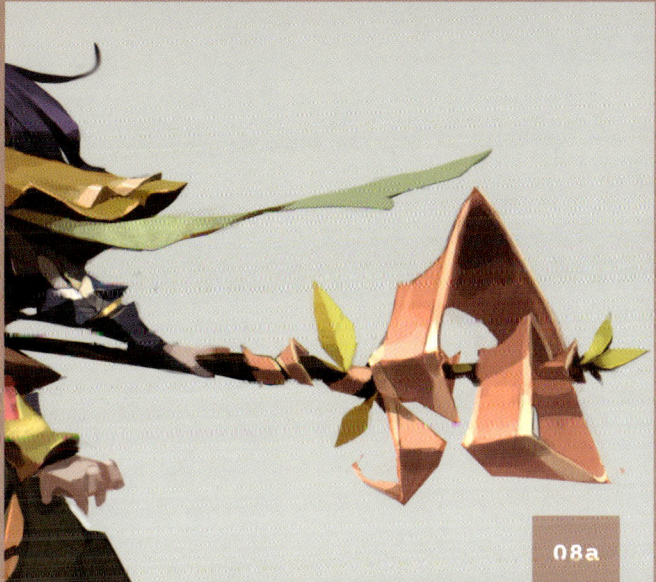

// I try to keep the weapons stylized

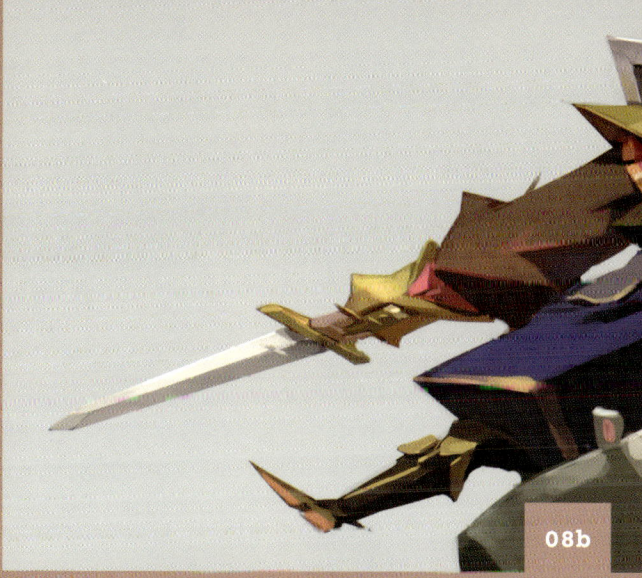

// Developing the sword

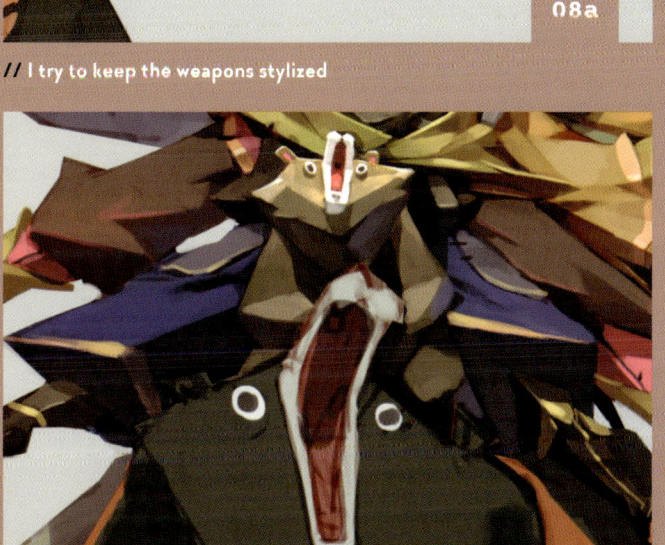

// Before I change the big bear's facial expression

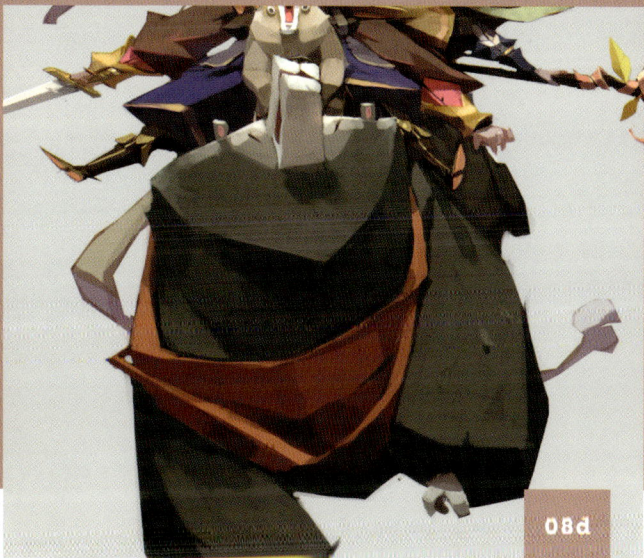

// The new facial expression and outfit

>08 Weapons and the big bear

At this stage I paint in the details of my adventurers' weapons, keeping them stylized (images 08a and 08b). I also change and finalize the big bear's facial features, because it looks to similar to the smaller bear (images 08c and 08d). For the bear's outfit, I choose a complementary red-orange, but keep the outfit simple so that it doesn't look too distracting. I also darken the girl slightly to add more depth between the characters (image 08e).

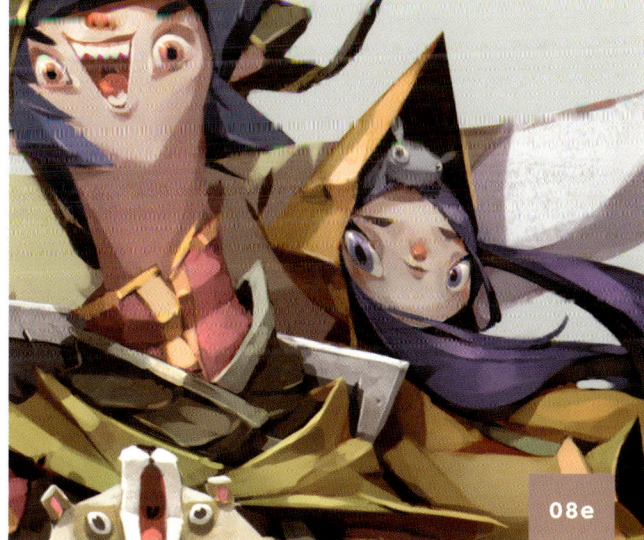

// Darkening the female to add depth

>09 Bringing everything together

Now I start painting in the dog-like companion in the background, based on our real dog. When that's done, I want to tie everything together with a very soft red outline around the entire silhouette of the painting, which will help to separate it from the gray background. To do this, I duplicate a flattened layer of all the characters, fill the entire shape with a red color, and apply a small amount of Gaussian Blur filter. When this layer is placed underneath the characters, the blur is just enough for the red to spill out and create a very soft outline.

>10 Final touches

At this point the fur on the dog still looks very plain, so I add a highlight tone over it. Finally, I paint in a simple background platform to help create a little more context, suggesting that they are outdoors, happily bouncing along on an adventure. Now the image is complete.

As you can see from my workflow, I move around my painting a lot because I don't plan out all the details completely; this allows me to have more room for exploration as I progress through the image. Every painting for me is a very fun experience because I feel as though that image has its own life, and every different painting has its own potential to be something unique. When I find the right feel and attitude through my explorations, that is a breakthrough for me.

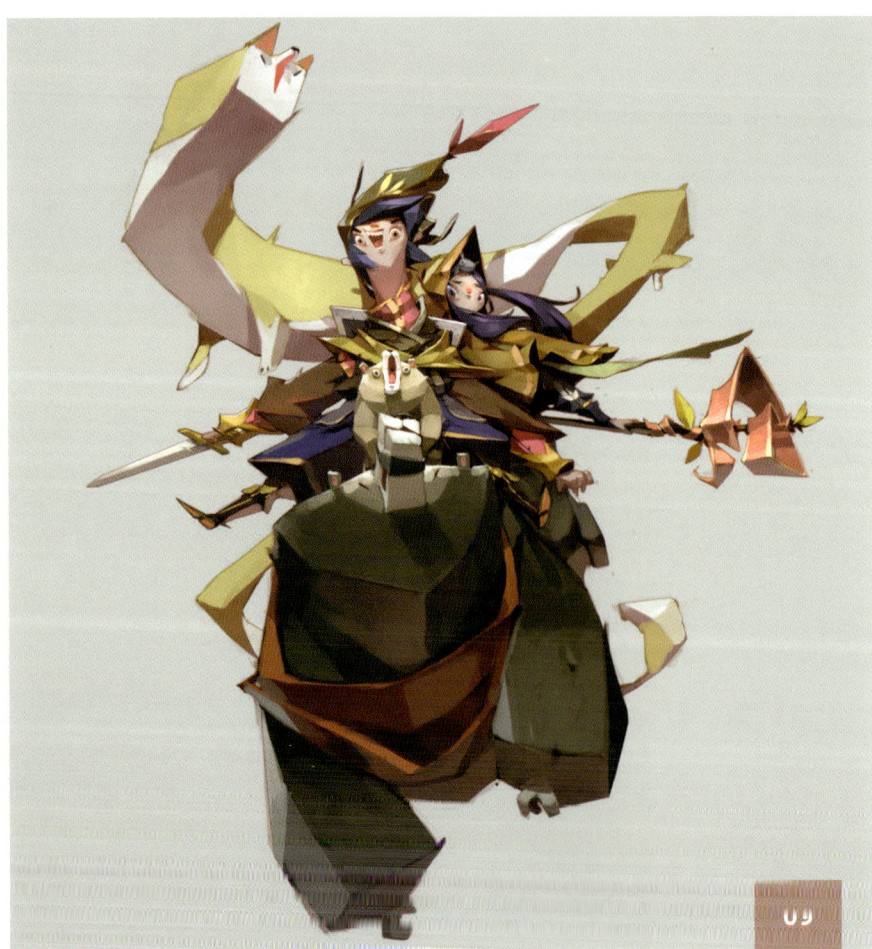

// A subtle blur effect unifies the whole scene

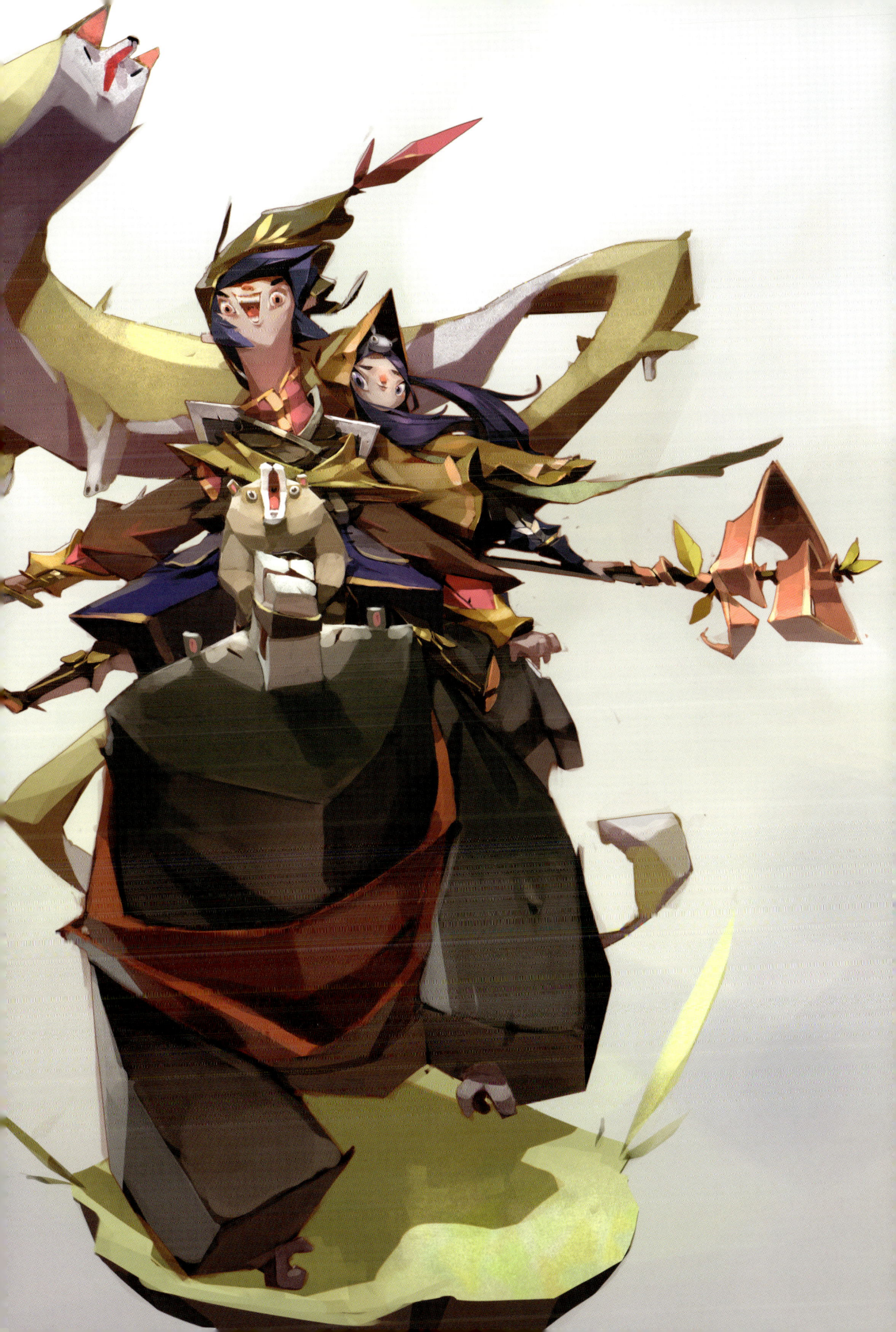

Eliza Ivanova | www.elizaivanova.com

Love

In this tutorial, inspired by the theme of "love," I want to tackle the concept of loving someone who isn't in your life any more, but the strings between you are still attached and the memory of them is still fresh. I want to create a simple, memorable image that captures this uneasy feeling while still executing it with elaborate details and design.

>01 Thumbnails

I have several ideas about the layout of the piece and am not one hundred percent sure which will work best. The quickest way to weed out the ones that won't work is to make a thumbnail pass of all my ideas. While some of the compositions in image 01 are interesting to look at, they don't quite capture the mood I'm going for. I combine elements of several thumbnails to come up with the layout of the final piece.

>02 Rough first pass

In this step, my goal is to outline the big shapes that dictate the overall design and placement of elements in the illustration. I am not concerned with the details or appeal of the drawing. I am only paying attention to the figures' position and the negative space around them.

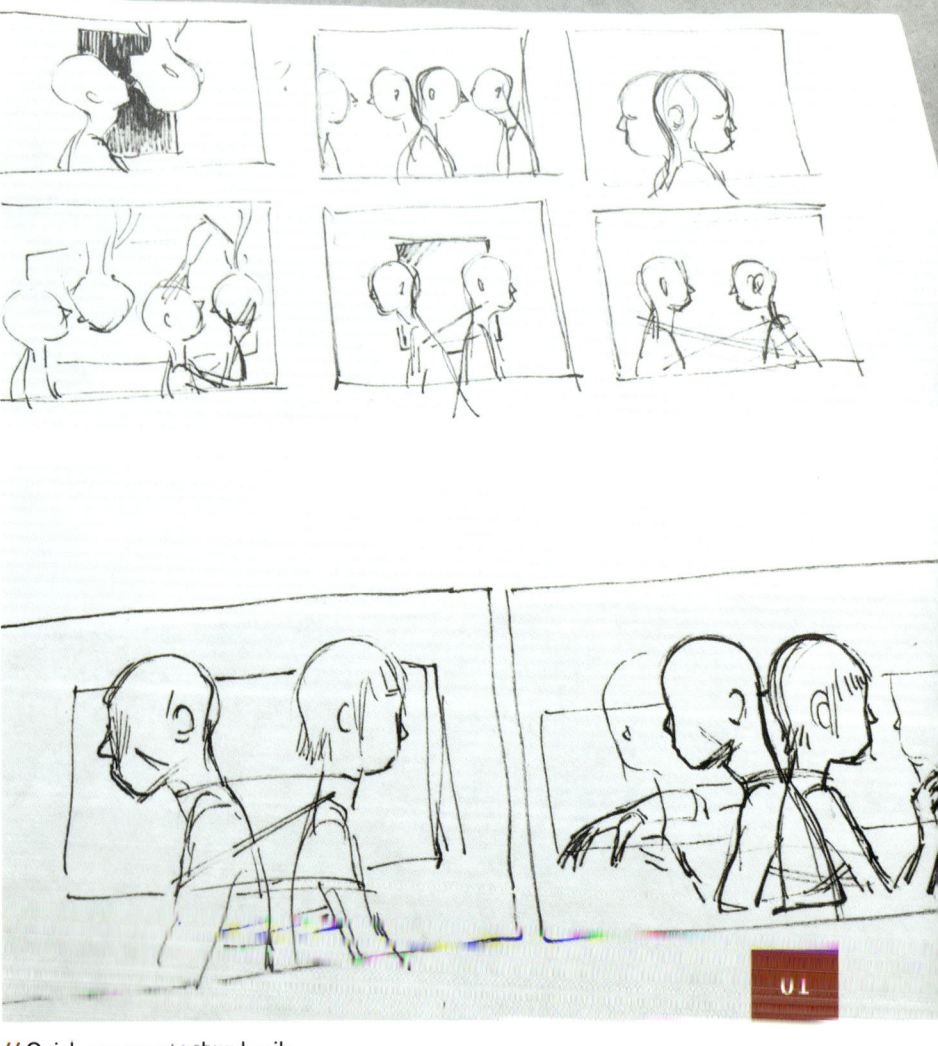

// Quick one-minute thumbnails

Sometimes this first pass takes a few redraws, and this image is no exception!

>03 Redrawing

As I rough in the initial silhouettes, I notice that the woman and man look way too similar, almost mirroring each other. Additionally, my idea behind this image is a "phantom kiss," so it has to look as if the two people are kissing each other, even though they are embracing other unknown people. In order for the kiss to work, I have to change the position of the woman's face, as if she is kissing the man.

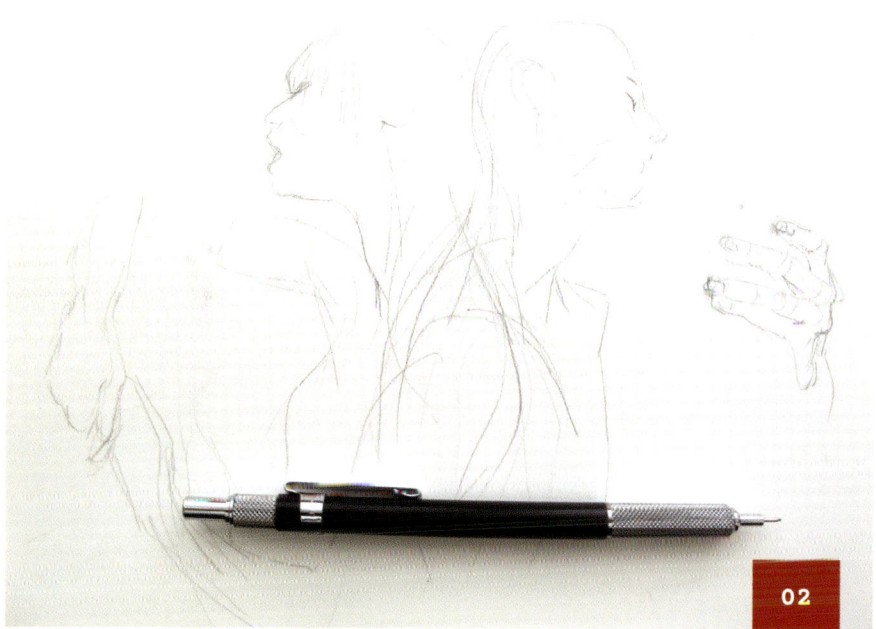

02

// Quickly sketching the general shapes

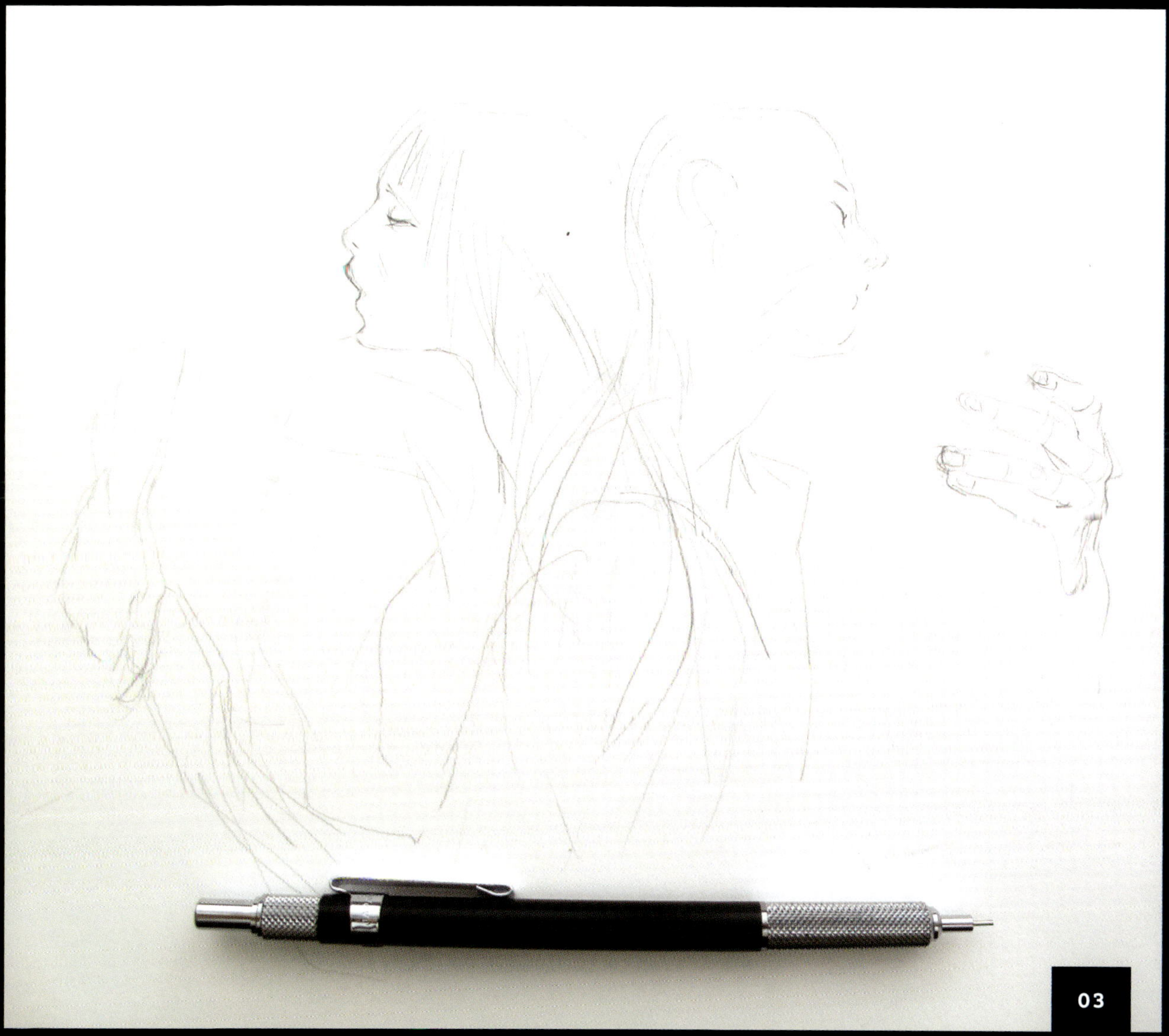

03

// Redrawing the woman's face

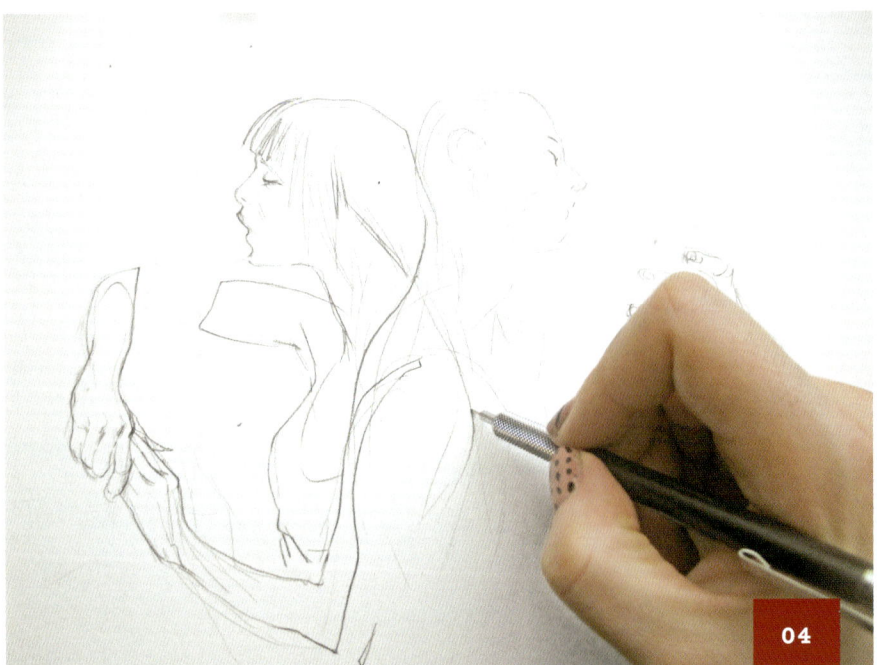

// **Adding some design elements to convey flow**

>04 Never too early for a design element

If you know my work, you are aware that I love adding design elements from the get-go to introduce flow and interest to my pieces early on. I do this because it's fun, but also because it forces me to think in an abstract way and not become too stiff once I go into "detail mode." In image 04 you can see how I loosely connect the two silhouettes while breaking up the arm structure.

The design elements give me the idea of breaking up the bodies of the two figures even more, further enforcing the concept of loss, breaking up, and being partially damaged. However, I want to add details to the hands and faces that aren't as stylized as the rest of the drawing. The purpose of this is to have contrast, which creates interest. If the sketch is too even overall, it will not be using the simplicity of the layout to its full potential.

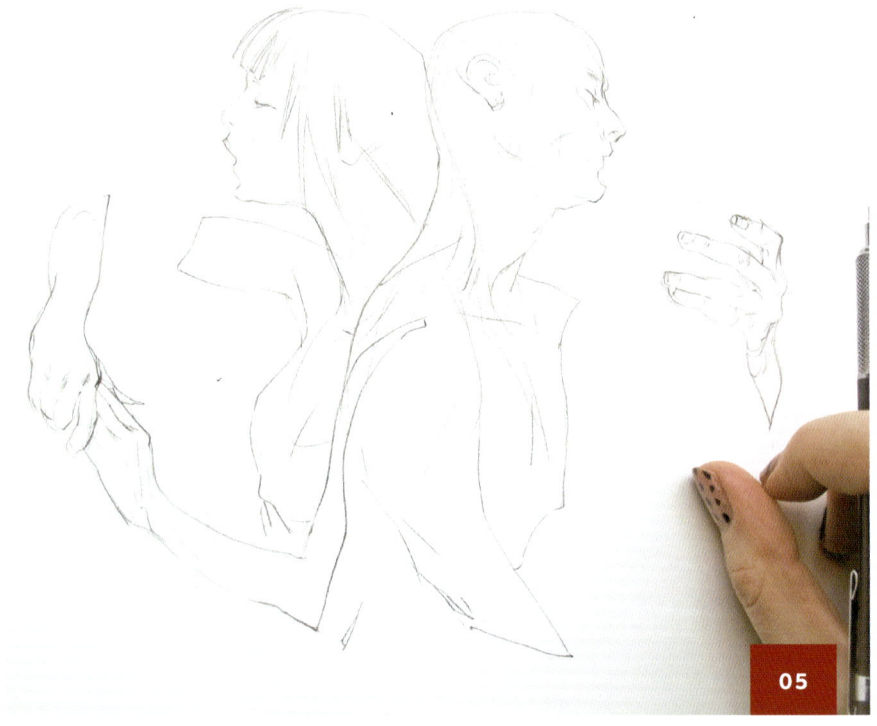

// **Evaluating the concept**

// PRO TIP

Trust your gut feeling

I used to be insecure about my approach towards fine art and illustration, and I ended up mimicking other artists' "styles" and trying to decipher them constantly. It took me quite some time to realize that I have an internal taste and design mechanism that only manifested itself when I was doodling aimlessly. One day I decided to fully embrace that gut feeling about my art and push it to see where it would take me. My "style," or my sensibility, isn't a forced decision to be different from other artists, but rather naturally comes out, sometimes without me realizing it.

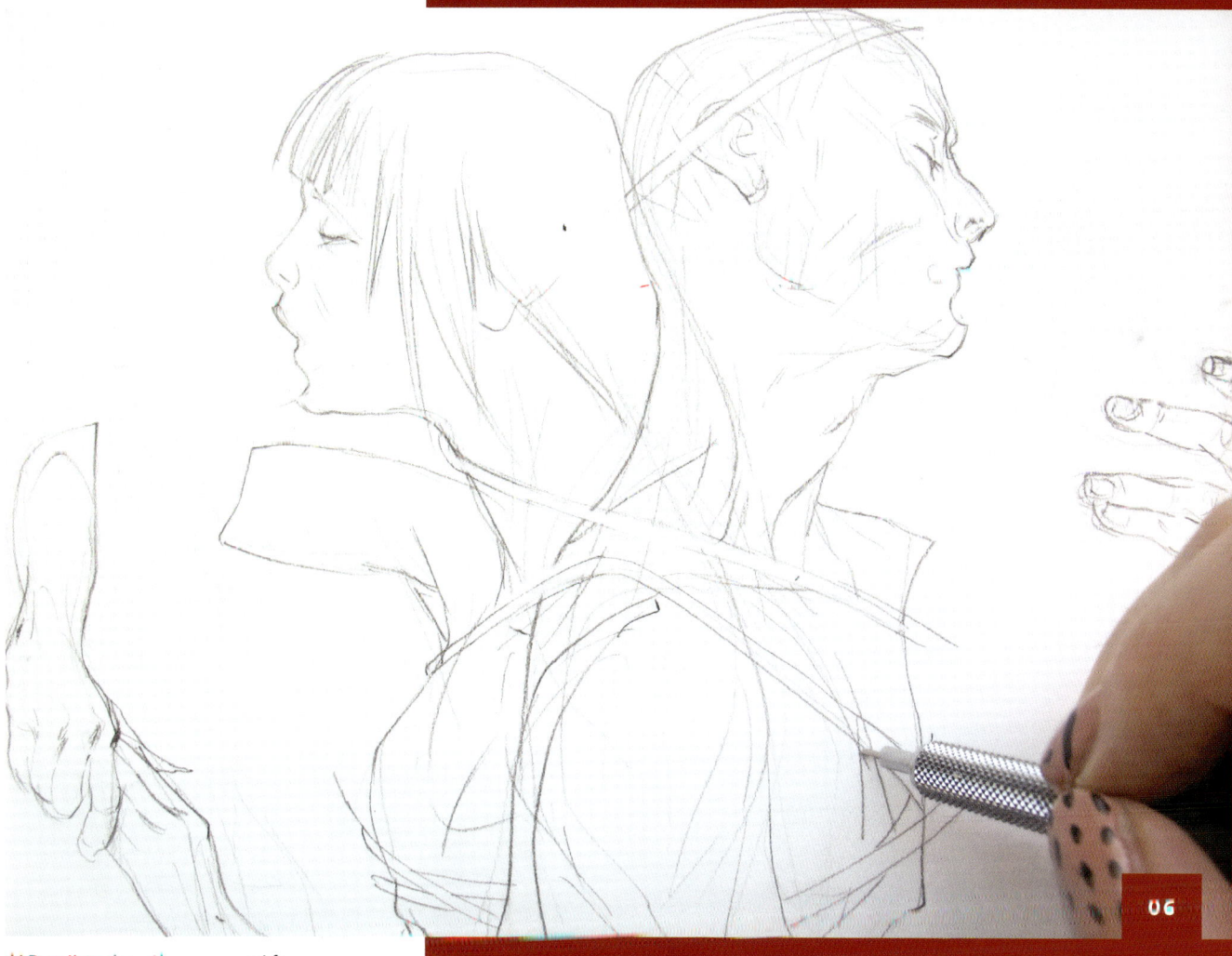

06

// Detail work on the ropes and faces

>05 Taking a step back

This piece is very conceptual and each element is there for a reason: to convey the idea I'm trying to illustrate. As I draw the piece, I feel like it lacks the element of a "bond" between the two, the kind of attachment that keeps your mind locked to the feelings of love and regret. I decide to add ropes that represent that bond, and will later shade and color them in a way that makes them appear ghost-like rather than literal

>06 Layering some details

I add the ropes I mentioned in the previous step and try to design them in a way that suggests they feel uncomfortable and tight. I also begin to add details to the faces of the man and woman, and start to refine their features. I sometimes add too many layers to my line work, but it helps me visualize the shading later on.

"I add design elements to my pieces because it's fun, but also because it forces me to think in an abstract way"

>07 Founding it in experience

I thought long and hard about whether I should draw a cisgender, non-binary, or androgynous couple before I even began sketching. As you can tell from the thumbnails, I kept the gender part rather ambiguous because I was struggling to decide how to tackle this piece. In the end, what pushed me to go down a more cisgender route is personal experience – my own memories of dealing with lost love and the pain of longing. However, the ghostly figures the two are kissing could be anybody, and the references for the two people were not cisgender couples.

>08 Initial blending

I always start the shading process with a quick pass with a tortillon (a rolled cylinder of paper, sometimes called a blending stump). It allows me to map out the topography of the figures and decide where the light sources are, as well as design the shaded shapes. If you are working digitally you could use a smudge tool in a similar way. For bigger drawings. I use my fingers for

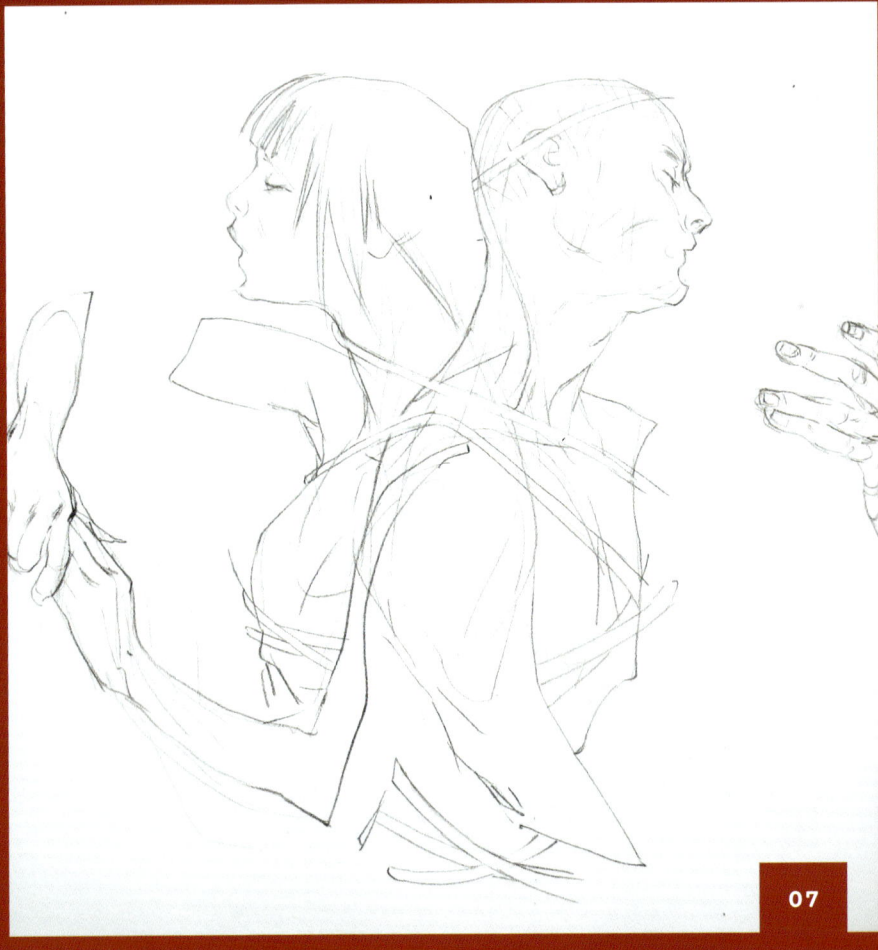

07

// It's important to consider all elements of an illustration carefully

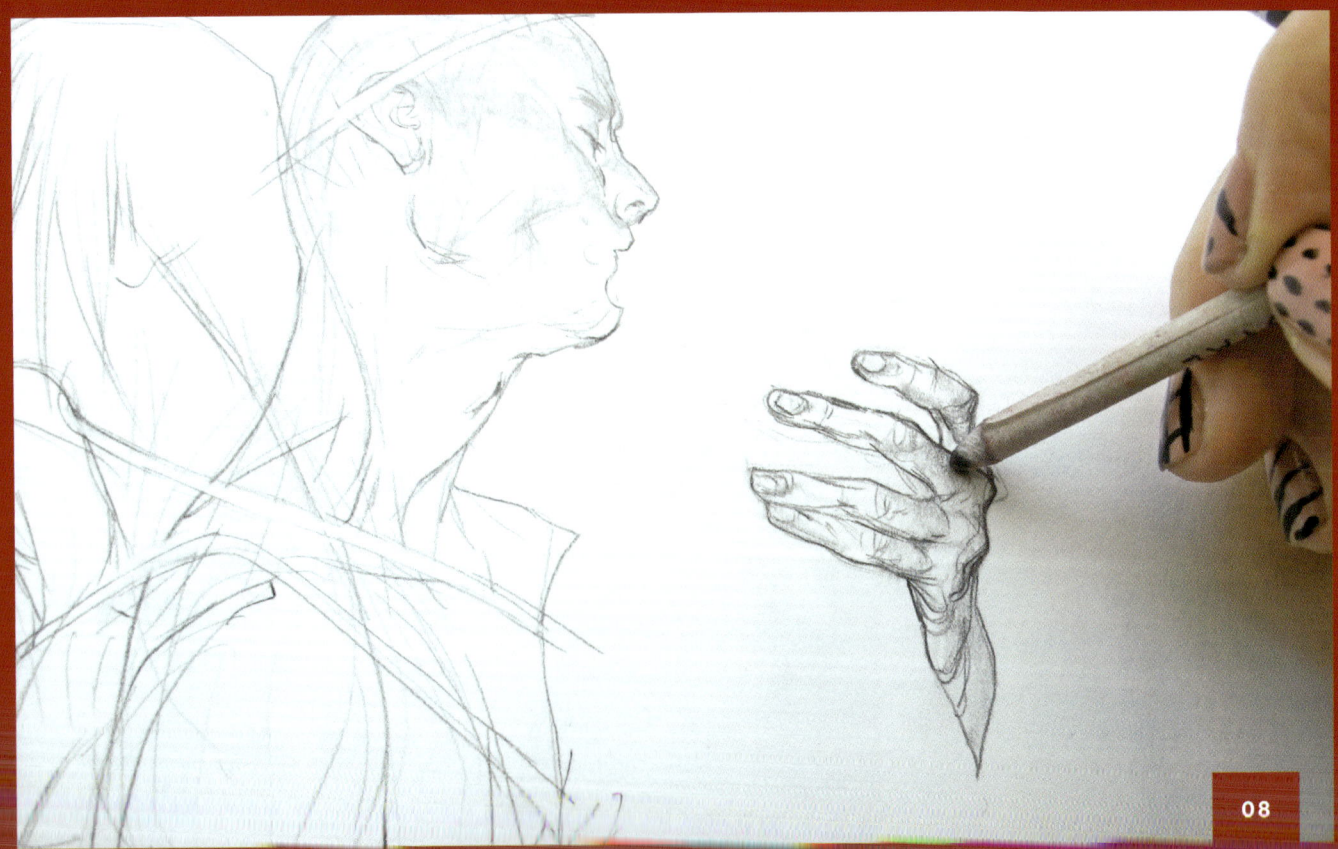

08

// Using a tortillon to add first pass shading

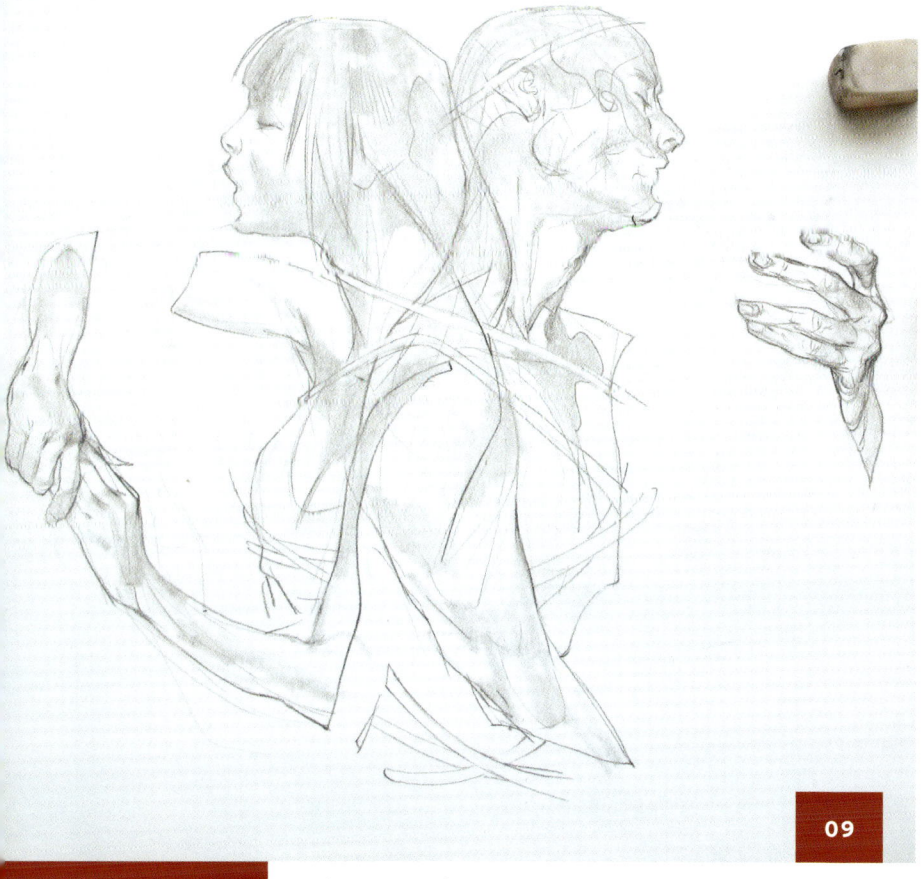

09

// A completed first shading pass

10

// Adding line work on top of shading

blending instead. This stage creates a basis for more detailed shading later.

>09 Roughed-in shading

I go back and forth between the tortillon and a graphite pencil or stick to add all the shading shapes and initial tones. I tend not to overload the sketch with dark values, in order to give myself room for further shading exploration. Reference is key in this step, because it gives me lighting and shading ideas that I wouldn't have necessarily come up with from my imagination. I don't, however, rely too much on reference; I get the information I need and filter it through my own aesthetic sense.

>10 Final layered details

My favorite part is working in some details on top of the shading. It's the step that allows me to be spontaneous while working on a smaller scale and push the design of the sketch to the next level. I decide where the focal point would be, if any, and also focus on areas that interest me the most while leaving other areas rougher for contrast.

In image 10 you can see the final sketch before I scan and digitally color it. I'm pleased with the clarity and the design, especially with how the negative space complements the silhouettes.

"Since there isn't much information on where the people are and what they're doing besides kissing someone, I take the opportunity to suggest a location using color and lighting"

>11 Blocking in color

I now add some color to finish up the image; I choose to do this digitally. After I complete the graphite sketch, I scan and clean it up in Adobe Photoshop. Then I block in the silhouettes with a single color on a separate layer, so I'll be able to quickly select and isolate the parts of the drawing I want to focus on. I keep that layer only for selection purposes, and I don't draw in it. If you are working traditionally, you could use watercolor as it's a translucent medium that you can layer over with pencil once it's dry.

>12 Developing a color palette

I now add more layers of color to the drawing. The colors in this case determine the setting of the sketch. Since there isn't much information on where the people are and what they're doing besides kissing someone, I take the opportunity to suggest a location using color and lighting. I want to show both people under artificial lighting, in either a club or at a party, which is why I use multicolored light sources.

>13 Final piece

Here I add a simple background to contain the silhouettes and unify the piece. I layer in some spots of color and a tonal blur as a substitute for a smear I would do if the piece was colored by hand. Now the illustration is complete! I hope seeing the thought processes behind each step of this image will help you to consider your decisions carefully when creating your own pieces.

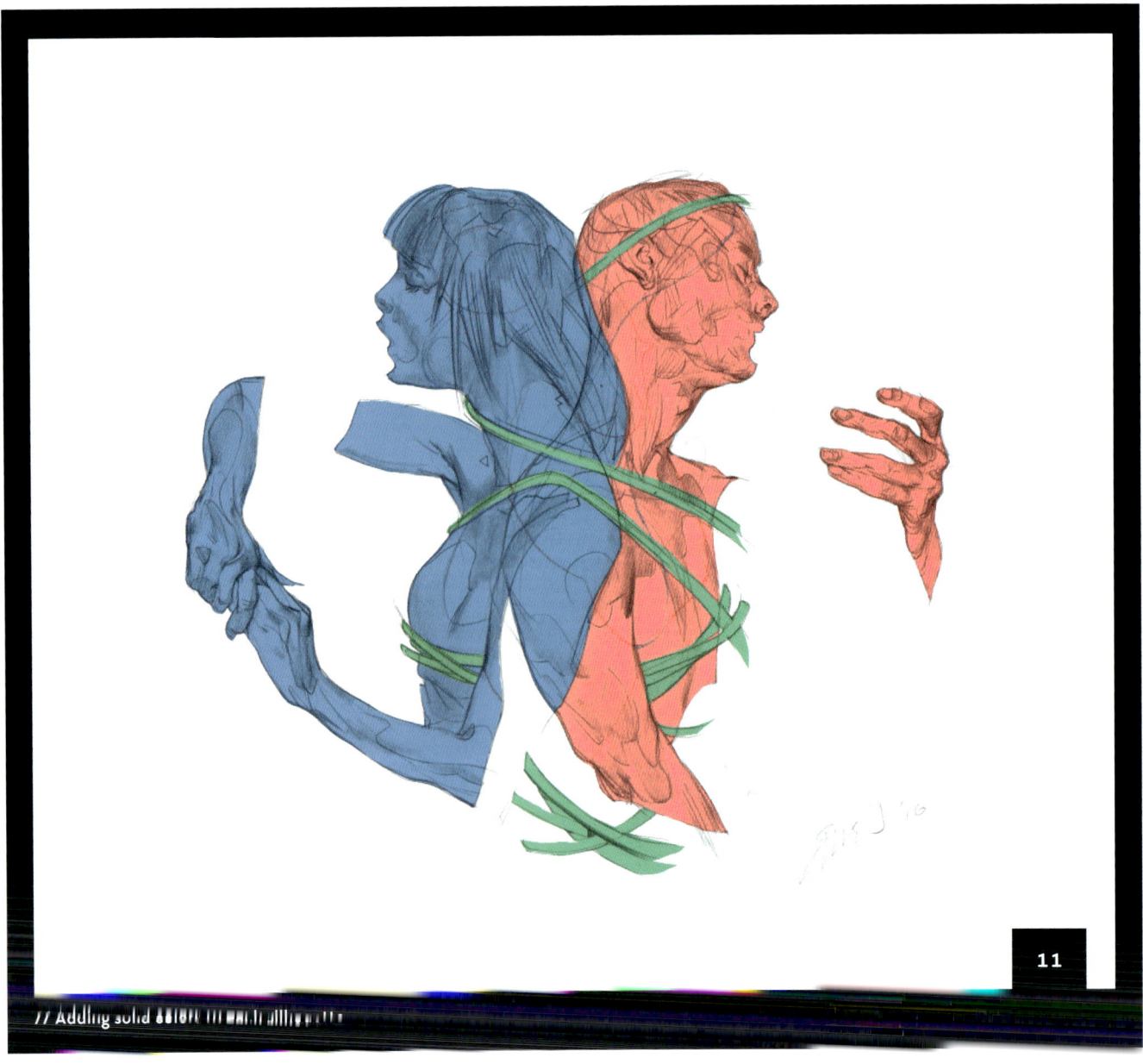

// Adding solid color in each silhouette

11

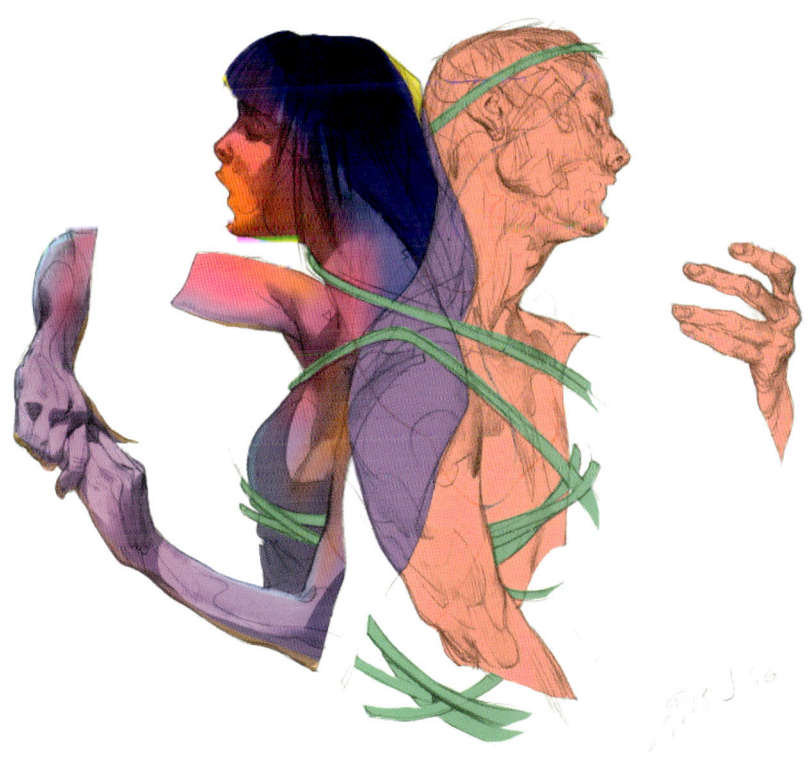

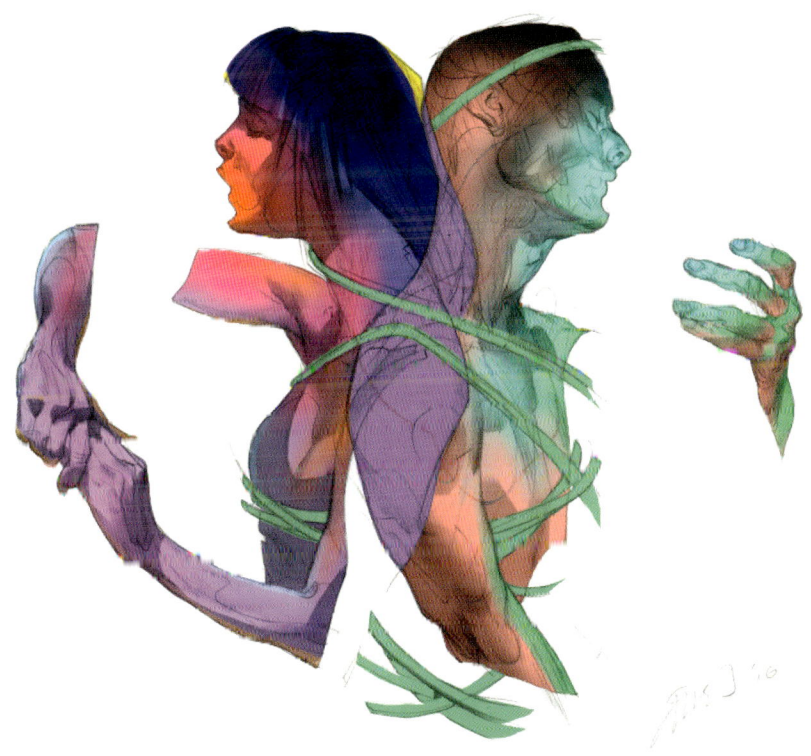

// Playing around with the color palette

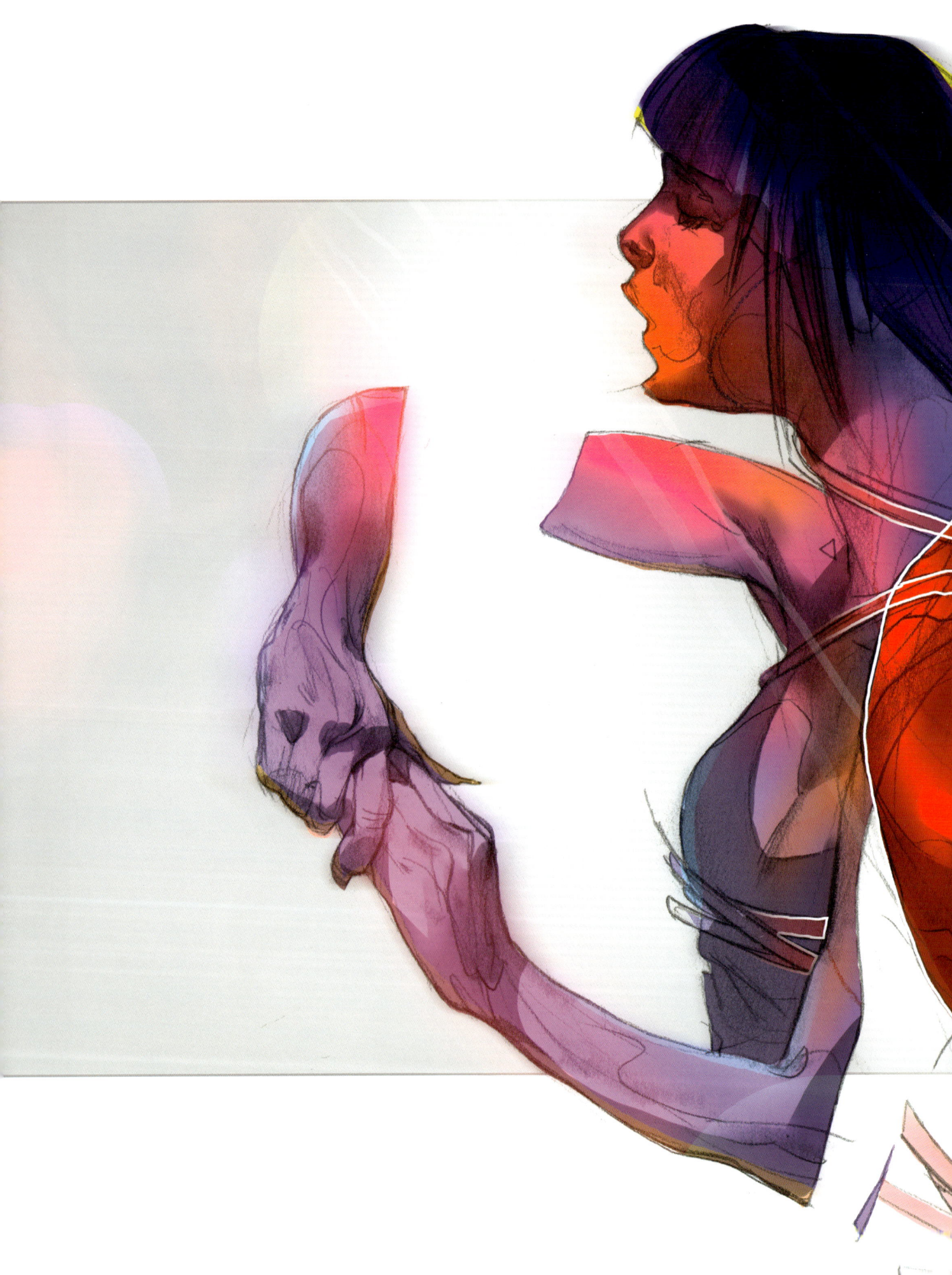

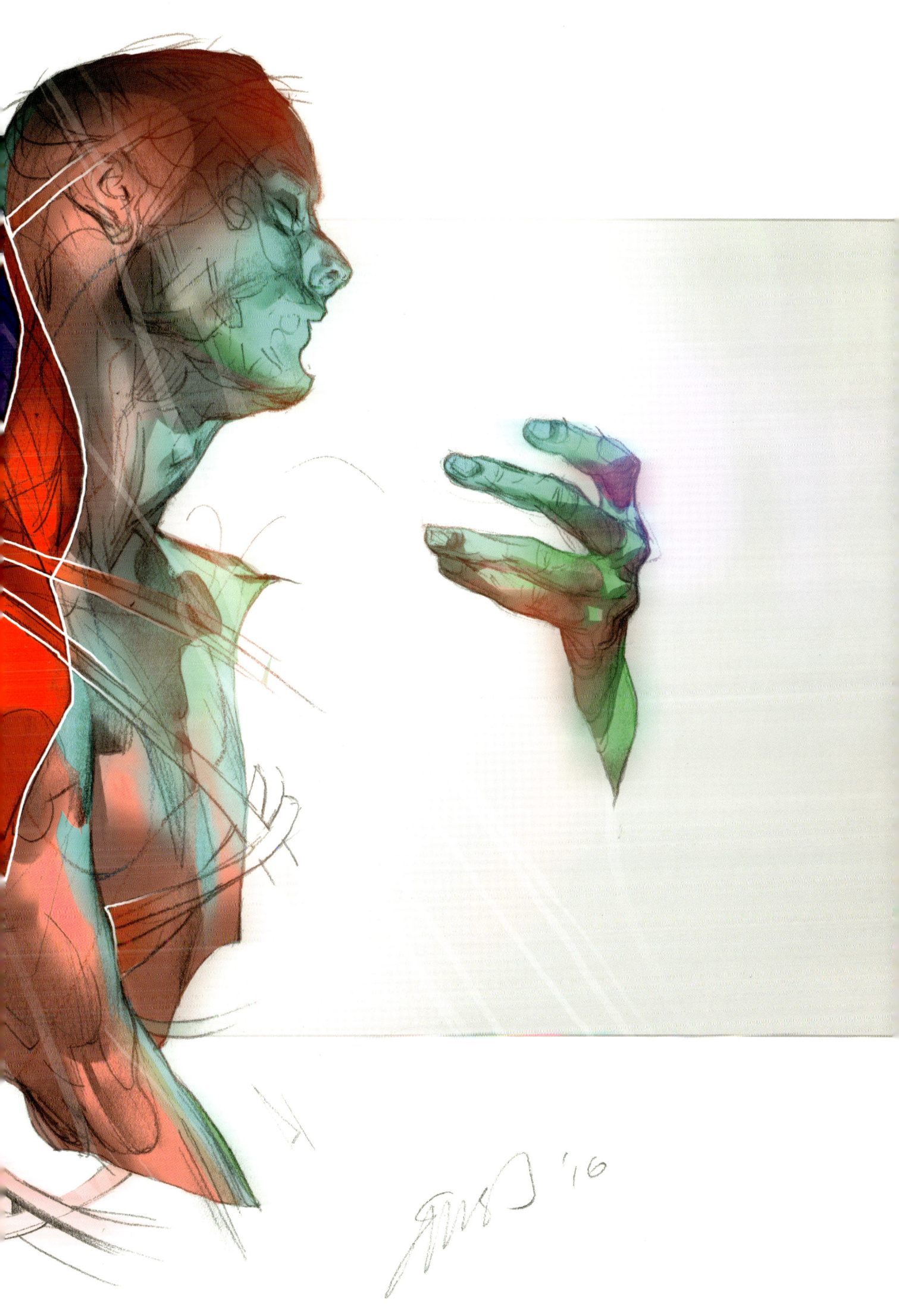

Emi Chen | www.emichenart.com

Mystery

In this tutorial I will show my process for creating a fully rendered illustration. I will focus on topics including idea generation, creating mood and atmosphere, and symbolism. In addition, I will go over some formal aspects of illustration such as composition, design, value, and anatomy.

In this image the theme is "mystery," and a lot of the decisions I make are based on trying to portray a mysterious feeling; I need to create an image that has an enigmatic sense to it. There are many aspects of this illustration that work towards trying to achieve that theme, and I will go through all of them step by step. By the end of this tutorial you will have the tool set to create your own illustration with a mysterious theme.

>01 Mind map
A mind map is a graphical diagram of related thoughts and words about a subject. It includes a branching-out of ideas from a central starting point. In this case, I want the illustration to revolve around the concept of "mystery," so I create a mind map with the focus on this word and what comes to mind. From there, I keep exploring various themes and subjects that relate to the word. I

try to exhaust all possibilities, exploring everything that I can until I am sure there are absolutely no more related ideas left.

>02 Thumbnails
Once I have a good understanding of the concept through words, I start creating thumbnails. This is when I begin to think about composition and what would look aesthetically pleasing. I also consider narrative. I typically limit myself to only three values for thumbnails. This helps me break down the shape design more easily, and allows me to organize the image into manageable parts. Typically, I make about twenty

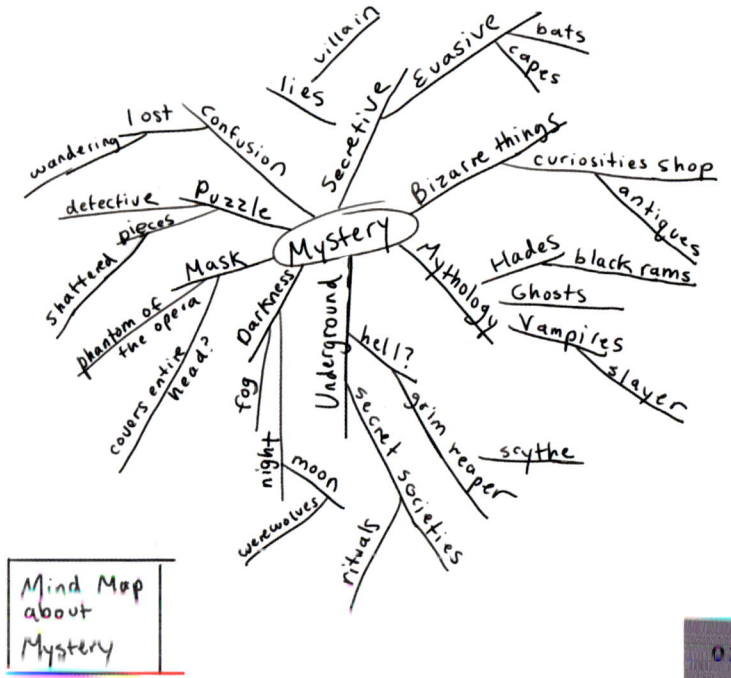

// The mind map I use for this illustration. Don't be afraid to really explore at this stage!

thumbnails for an illustration, but sometimes I make more depending on how many ideas I come up with that day.

>03 Sketches

Next, I choose three of the thumbnails that I think work best both narratively and compositionally, and start to flesh out these ideas further. I begin to paint in the anatomical gesture, and hint at material texture. I try to avoid over-rendering and detailing at this stage, since I know that I will eventually be throwing two of the sketches away. At this point, it is still only about the story and design. If adding something contributes significantly to either of those two aspects, I add it. If not, I leave it out for now.

I choose the first sketch in image 03 to take to the next step because it has the clearest flow and contrast, and the smoky, ethereal background fits the concept of "mystery."

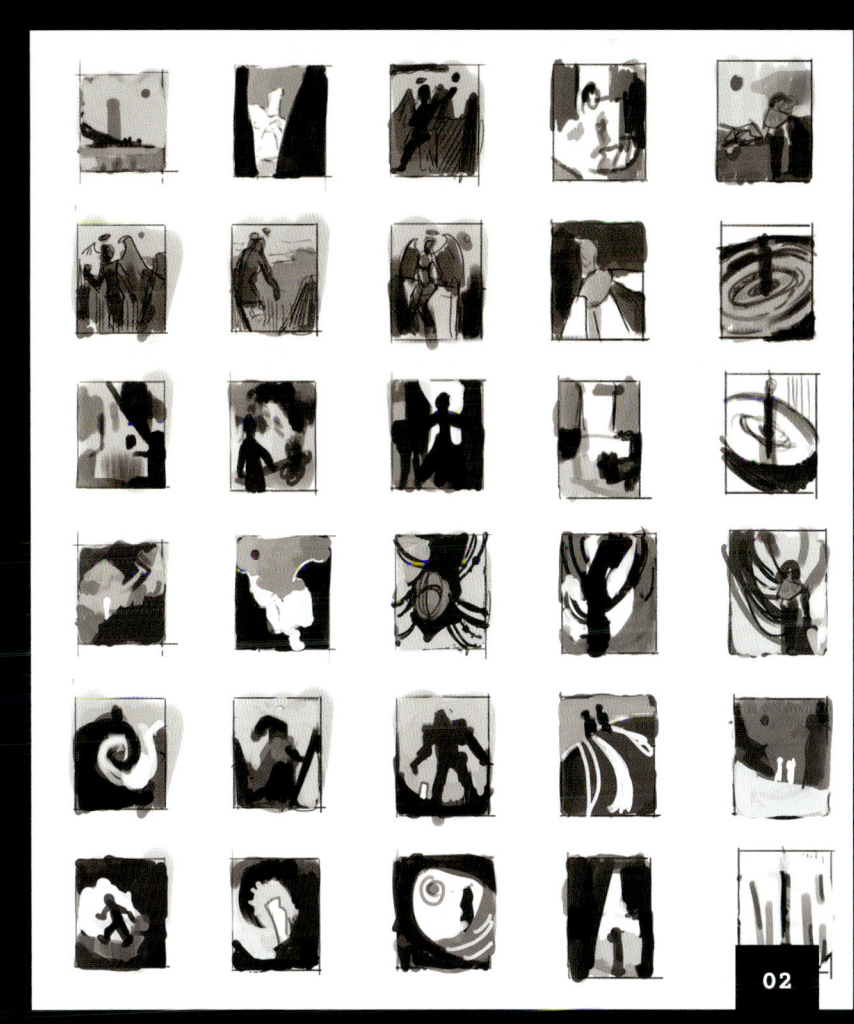

02

// Notice how small and rough these thumbnails are, just focusing on shape and design

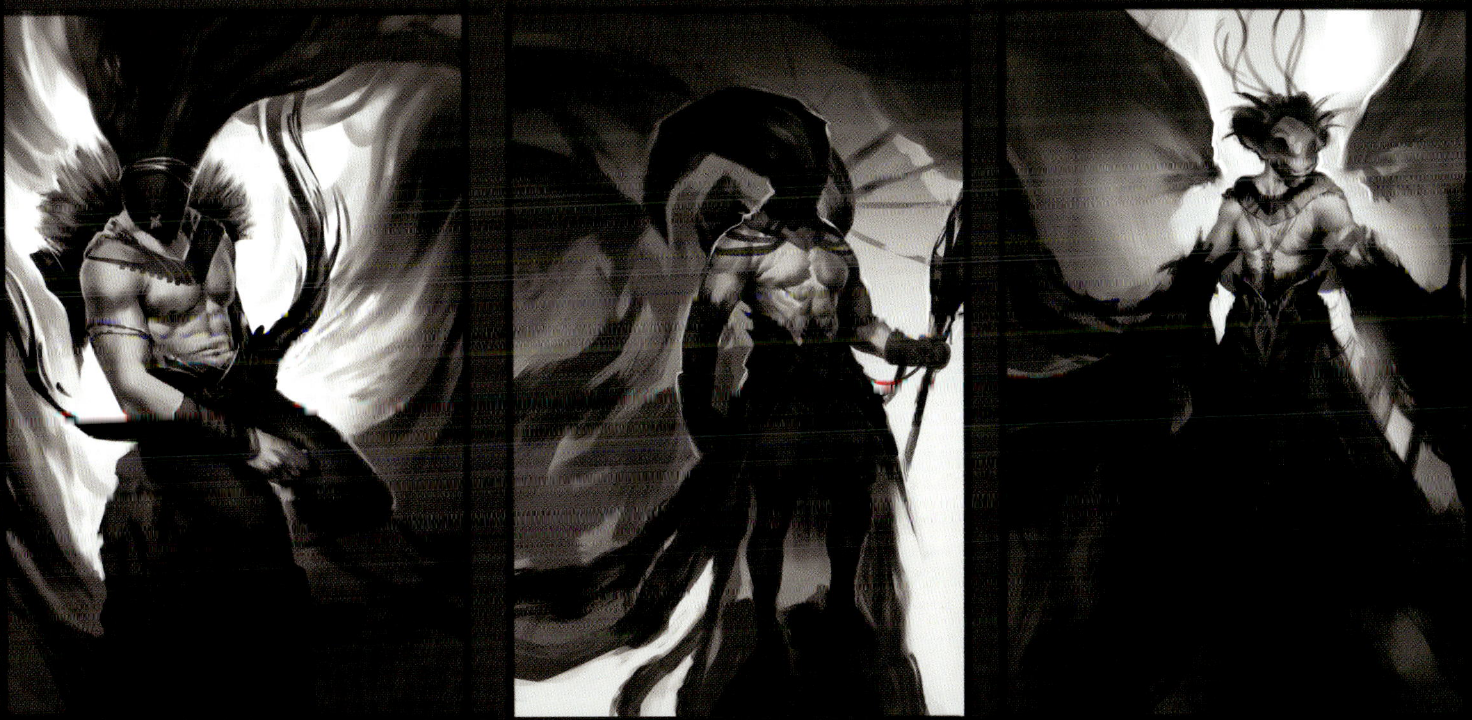

03

// Three compositions chosen from the thumbnails. The ideas that show potential are explored further in this sketch stage

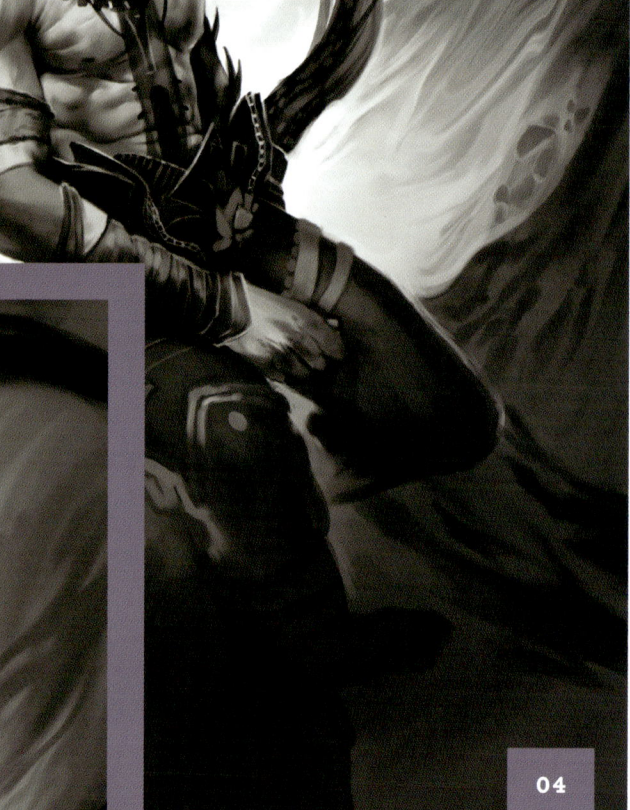

>04 Designing the character

Now that I have chosen the sketch I will take to completion, it is time to add specificity. Because this is a character illustration, the figure is the focus of the image. I therefore need to make sure that it is well designed and interesting to look at. I decide

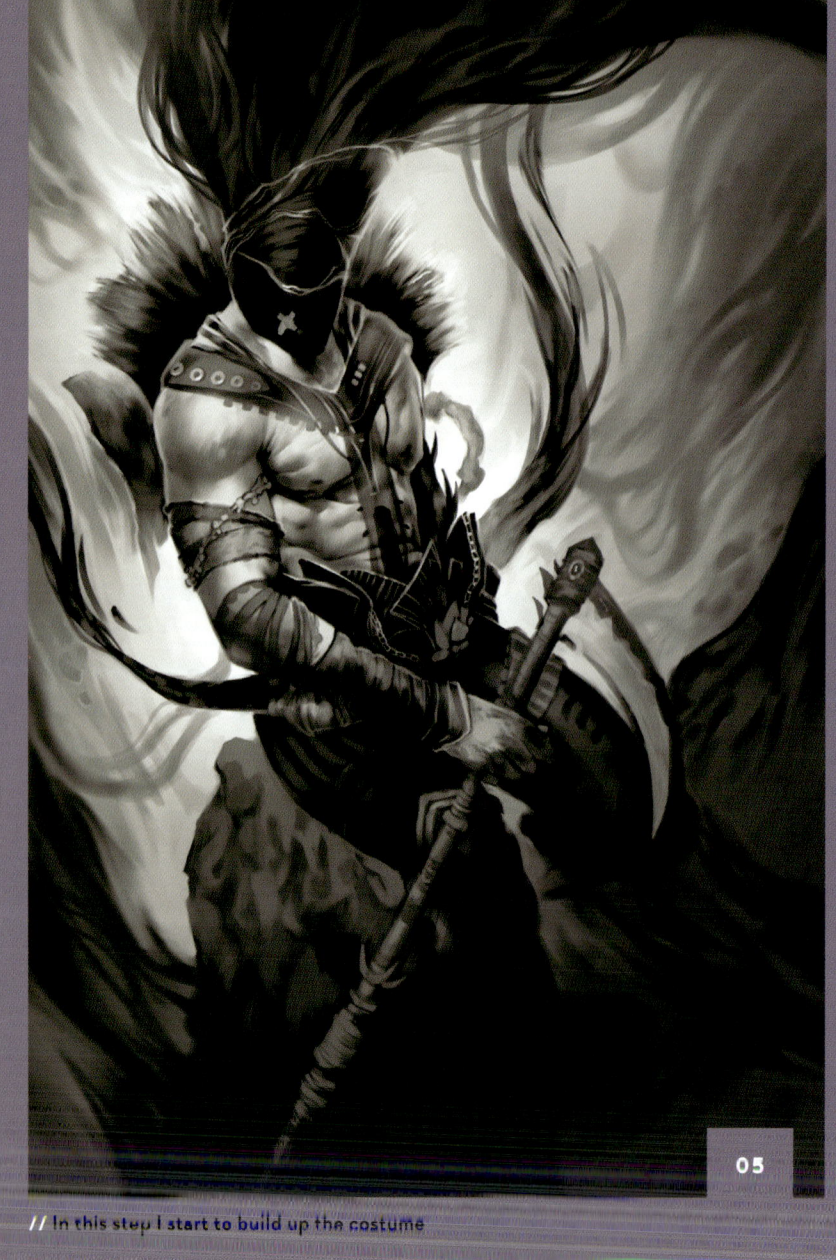

05

// In this step I start to build up the costume

04

// I focus on the character design here

to turn towards Greek mythology for inspiration; I've always found that the idea of an afterlife is shrouded in mystery, as is the character Hades. I look at classical sculpture as well as ancient Greek clothing design when designing the costume.

>05 Adding details and symbolism

Now that I have the basic character design laid out, I can start to add detail and render the costume. At this stage, I pay more attention to making sure all the materials are readable. For example, fur needs to look fluffy and metal needs to look reflective. I work on refining my brushwork so that it looks neat and clean. During this stage, I realize that it would be conceptually strong to add a scythe to the image because it evokes themes of death and the Grim Reaper, a well-known figure who is also conjures up mystery

>06 Levels adjustments

I realize that the image no longer reads as well as the smaller sketch did because there is too much midtone and darkness in it. In order to correct this, I add more contrast, making the overall image brighter and darkening the darker values.

Using Levels in Adobe Photoshop is a great way to add contrast, but it usually leaves the image looking a bit messy, often changing certain areas in a way that I did not intend. I therefore always end up painting over the adjustment or erasing portions of it.

>07 More symbolism

In order to really push the symbolism and story in this image, I decide to add some rams. Traditionally, herding sheep is known to be an action associated with heavenly or angelical themes. I want to use this symbolism to my advantage; not only is the character inspired by Hades, but the black ram is an animal known to symbolize Hades himself. I decide to show him herding sheep, but with a darker twist. Instead of holding a shepherd's staff, he is controlling the sheep using the Grim Reaper's scythe. This presents something of intrigue to the audience, adding to the feeling of mystery.

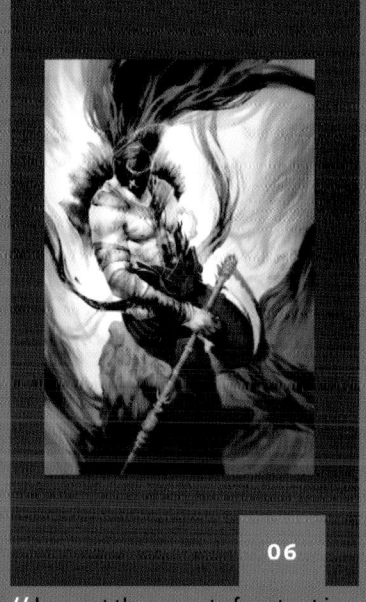

06

// I correct the amount of contrast in the image to improve its readability

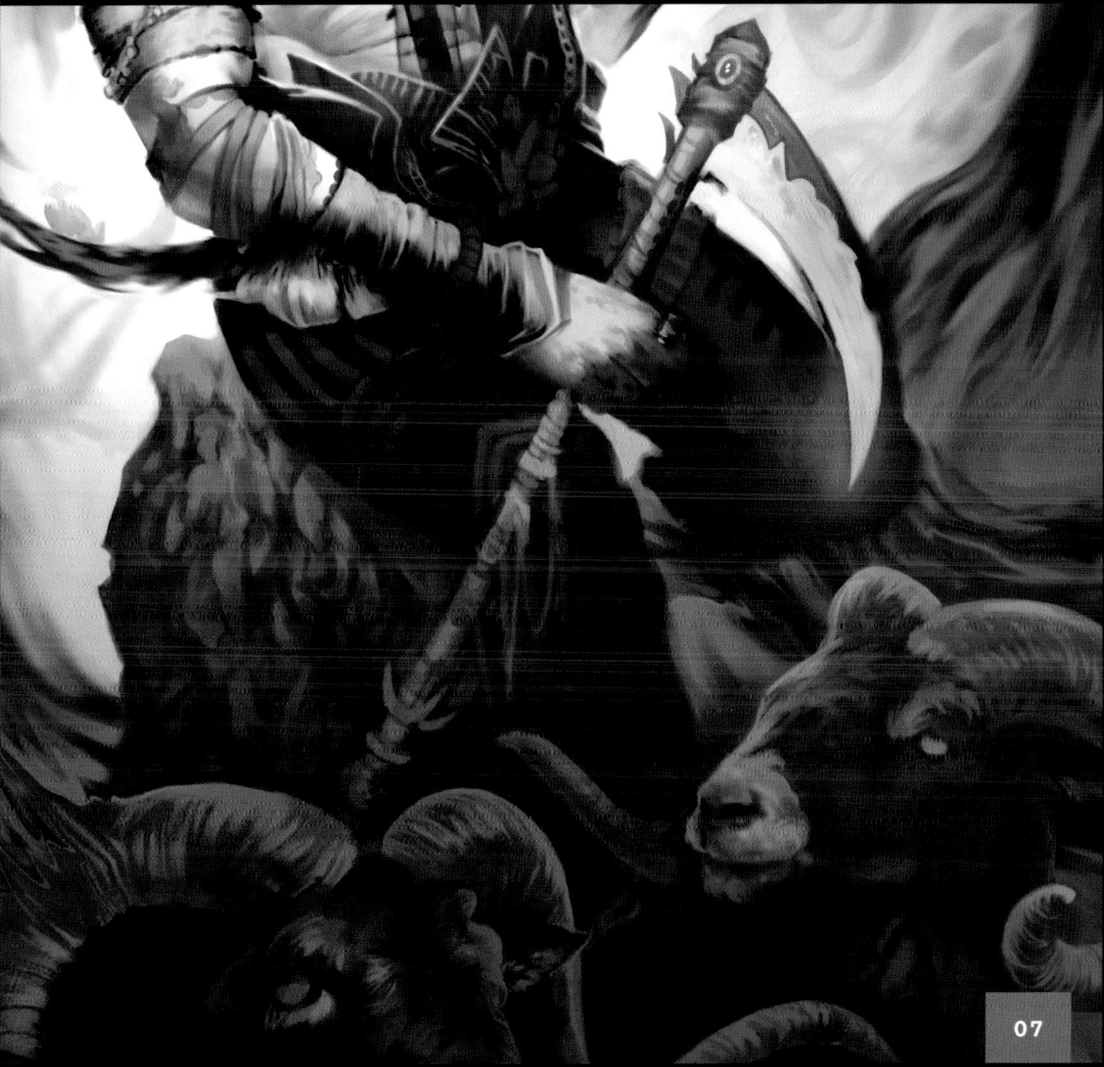

"I decide to turn towards Greek mythology for inspiration; I've always found that the idea of an afterlife is shrouded in mystery"

07

>08 Checking anatomy

In order to make sure the proportions and anatomy are correct, I produce a quick overlay drawing where I only look at the placements of the major bones. From here I can spot anatomical issues and make adjustments accordingly; I suggest referencing Leonardo da Vinci's Vitruvian Man. His calculations base everything around using the head as a reference measurement, a method which improves accuracy and helps to simplify everything. Other things you can do to improve anatomy are attending live figure drawing sessions and memorizing muscle shapes. After I know what needs to be adjusted, I can start working to make those changes.

>09 Adding anatomical details

I want the character to have a more worn-down, old look, as if he has been through some hard battles. This will add to the narrative behind the image and invite the viewer to wonder where he has come from. I add some textures and battle scars to his skin, making his exterior slightly tighter to imply that he's not a young hero. Although details like this are small, they really do help a lot with the storytelling, and with creating a convincing image.

>10 Improving flow and composition

In order to improve flow, I add a bright triangle near the top of the figure's head. This helps direct the viewer's attention to the focal point. I've found that triangle shapes are great to work with compositionally because they can act as arrows that point the viewer in the right direction. Other parts of the image that help improve flow are the lines in the background, which all lead to the figure. In my opinion, being able to move through the image with ease is one of the most important elements in establishing gracefulness in design.

// PRO TIP

Attend local figure drawing sessions

If you have figure drawing sessions available in your area, you should take advantage of them! Figure drawing teaches gesture, and allows you to practice working under a time limit. The presence of a live model is also great for gaining a sense of light and form that cannot be seen in a photo. Because the poses are usually very quick, it pushes the artist to capture only what is necessary. Even the longer poses are often limited to twenty minutes, so I have found that figure drawing sessions have taught me how to pace myself when drawing

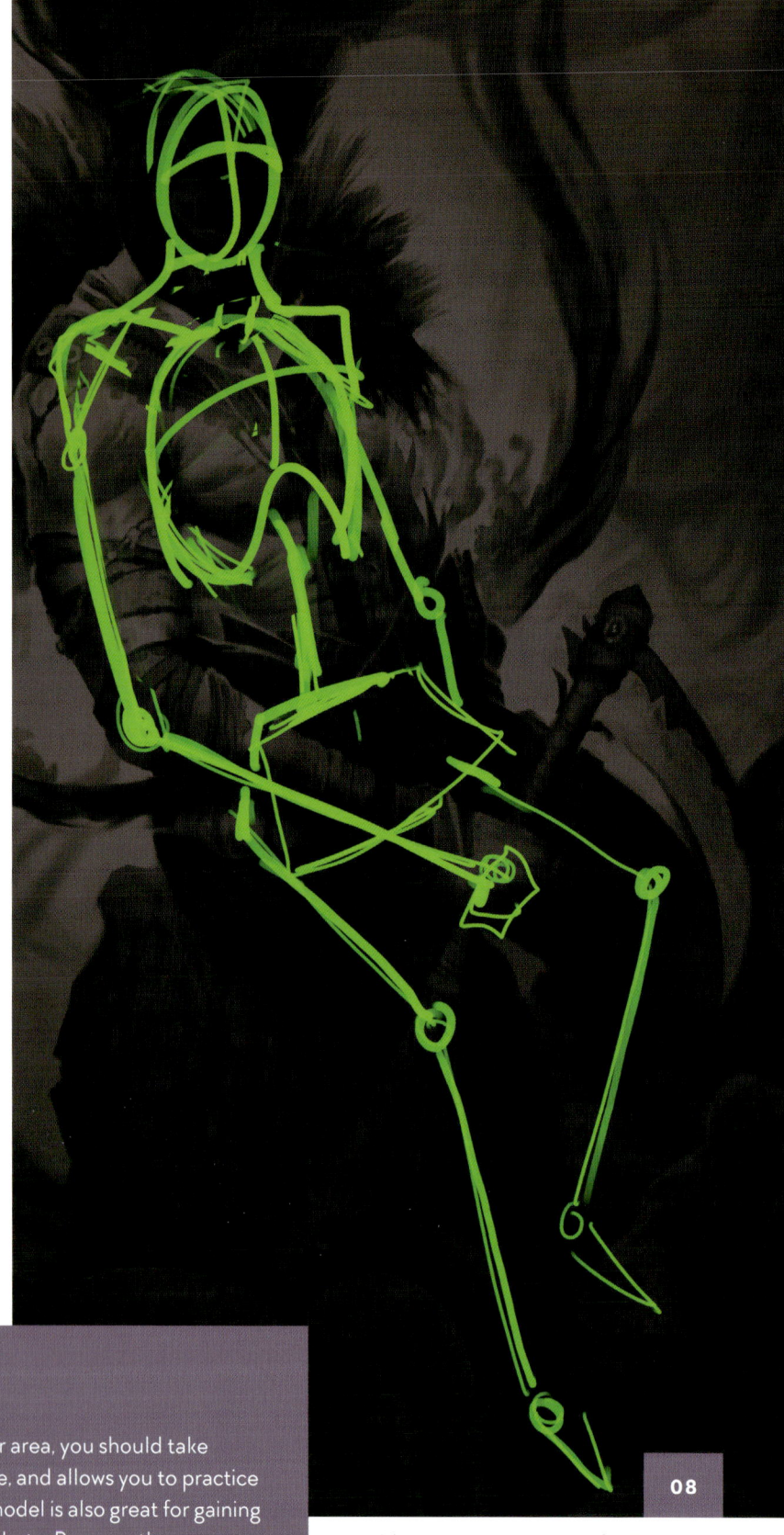

08

// A quick overlay drawing of a skeleton on top of the painting to help me correct the anatomy

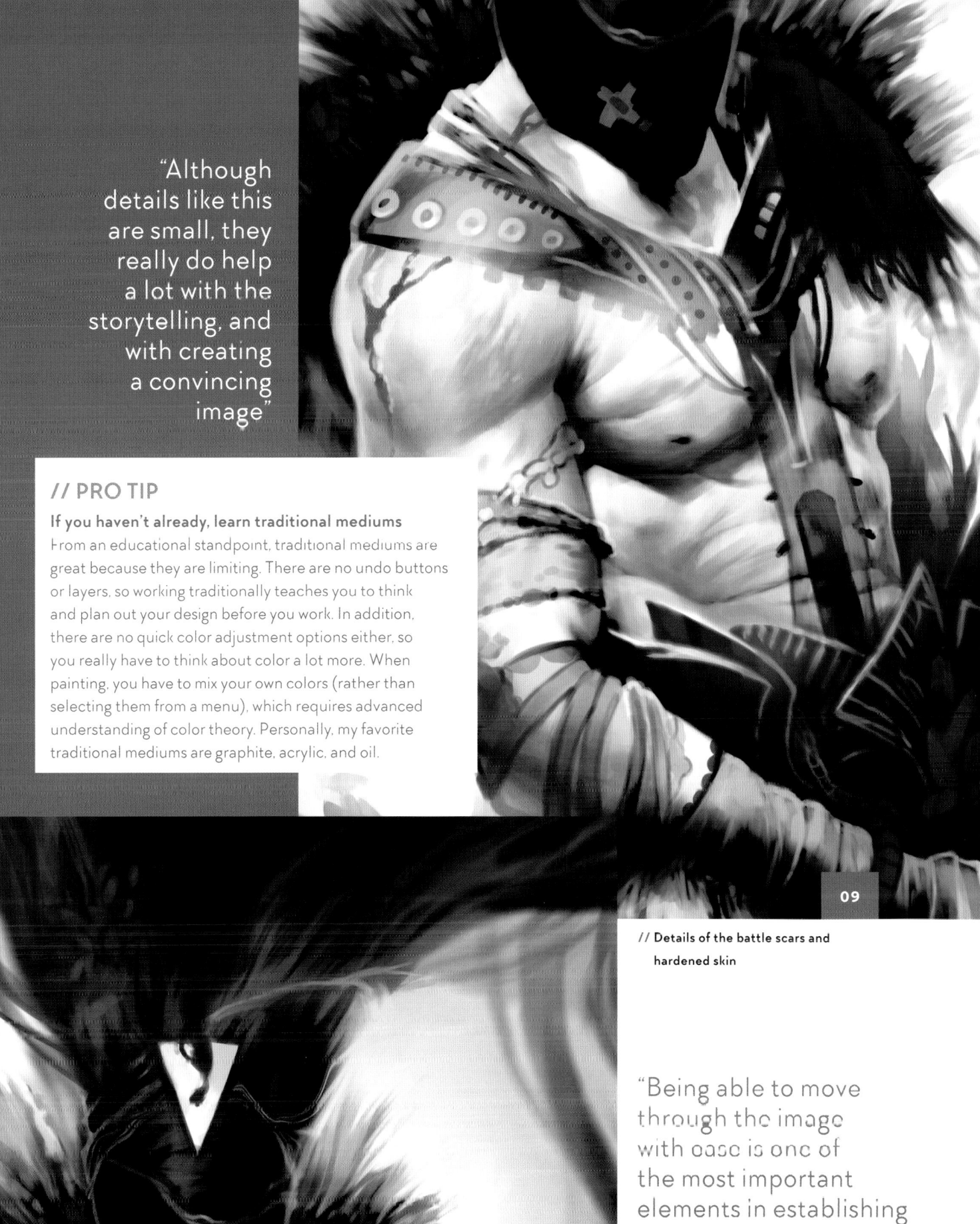

"Although details like this are small, they really do help a lot with the storytelling, and with creating a convincing image"

// PRO TIP

If you haven't already, learn traditional mediums
From an educational standpoint, traditional mediums are great because they are limiting. There are no undo buttons or layers, so working traditionally teaches you to think and plan out your design before you work. In addition, there are no quick color adjustment options either, so you really have to think about color a lot more. When painting, you have to mix your own colors (rather than selecting them from a menu), which requires advanced understanding of color theory. Personally, my favorite traditional mediums are graphite, acrylic, and oil.

09

// Details of the battle scars and hardened skin

"Being able to move through the image with ease is one of the most important elements in establishing gracefulness in design"

10

// The bright triangle on the figure's head is one of the elements I add to improve the image's flow

>11 Abstract details

This image in particular has a lot of abstract qualities to it (which are necessary for the theme of "mystery"). A great way to get quick abstract amorphous shapes is to use the Forward Warp tool in the Liquify filter in Photoshop. It creates an almost water-like texture which fits very well into the overall image. However, it's important not to go overboard. I make sure I only choose a few places to use this technique in as the image can quickly look garish if it is applied too much. Look at references of smoke and water if you are painting this effect traditionally.

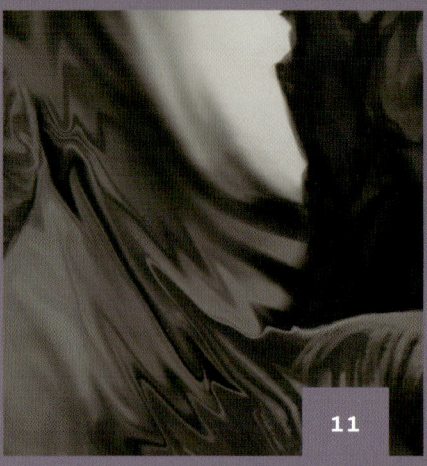

// I add some interesting water-like abstract details to the painting

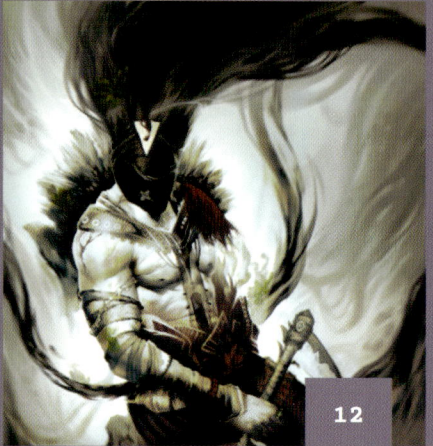

// I add subtle color into the black and white image

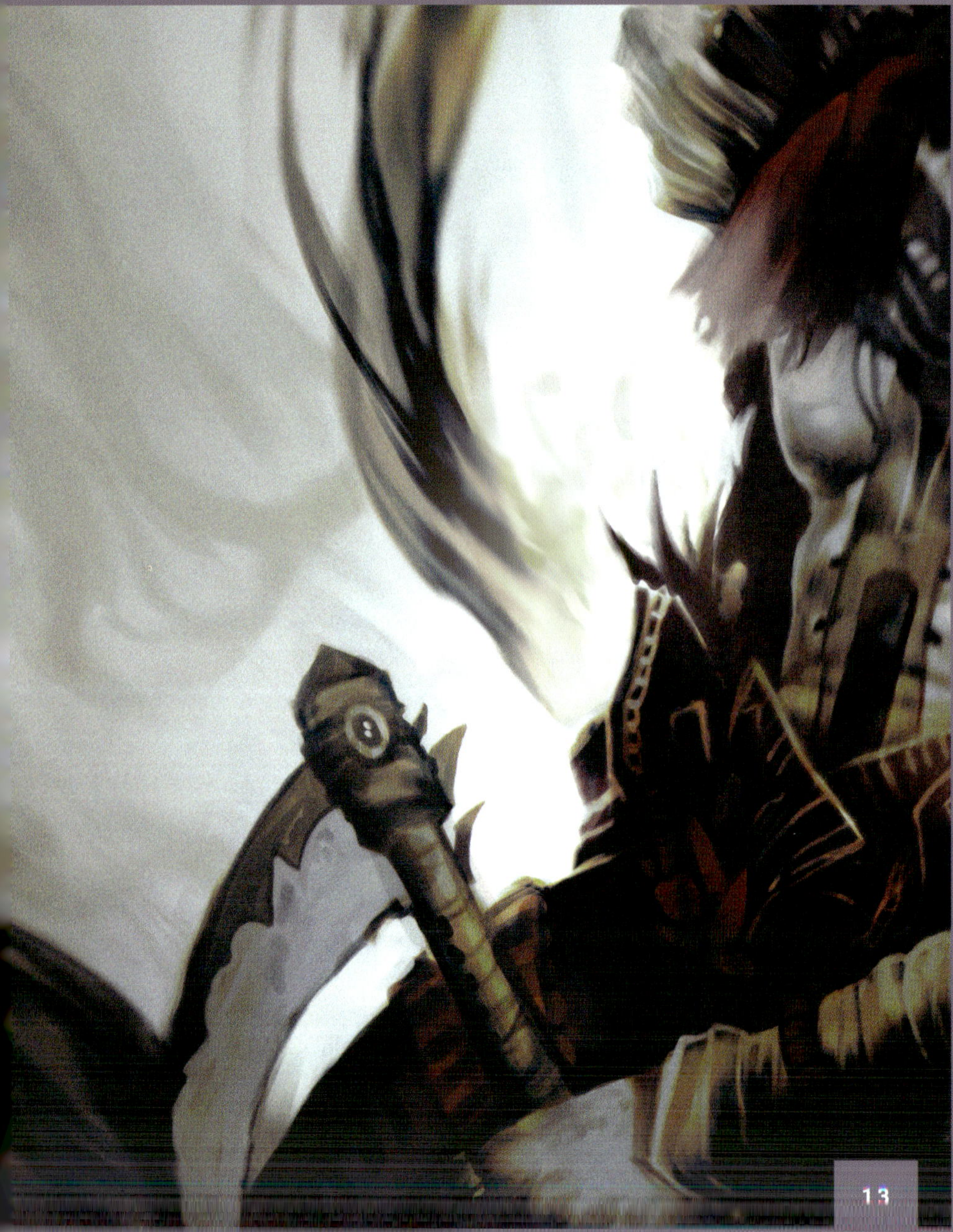

>12 Adding muted color

Now I start to add a hint of color. I don't want this image to be too saturated, because that would take away from its enigmatic quality. I opt for a limited palette with red as the accent color. In order to quickly add color to a black and white image, I use Photoshop's Color Balance feature. This allows me to control the hue of the highlights, midtones, and shadows separately. In addition, it makes very subtle changes to the values, which are usually pleasing.

>13 Darkening the image

After looking at the image for a long time, I realize that the lighting would make more sense if the figure was backlit, putting him in silhouette. Having a silhouetted character will help my goal of creating mystery because the character will be darkened and thus appear more obscured. This step also helps to simplify the composition, making the image easier to read visually. I tend to flip the image horizontally a lot during these final stages to make sure there are no small errors or mistakes in the image.

>14 Last tweaks

I now refine the tiny details and render things out. This is the step when I can relax and not really focus on making any major changes. All the hard work is done. I can just focus on getting all the final details right to enhance the feeling of mystery in the illustration.

// Flipping the image to check for errors

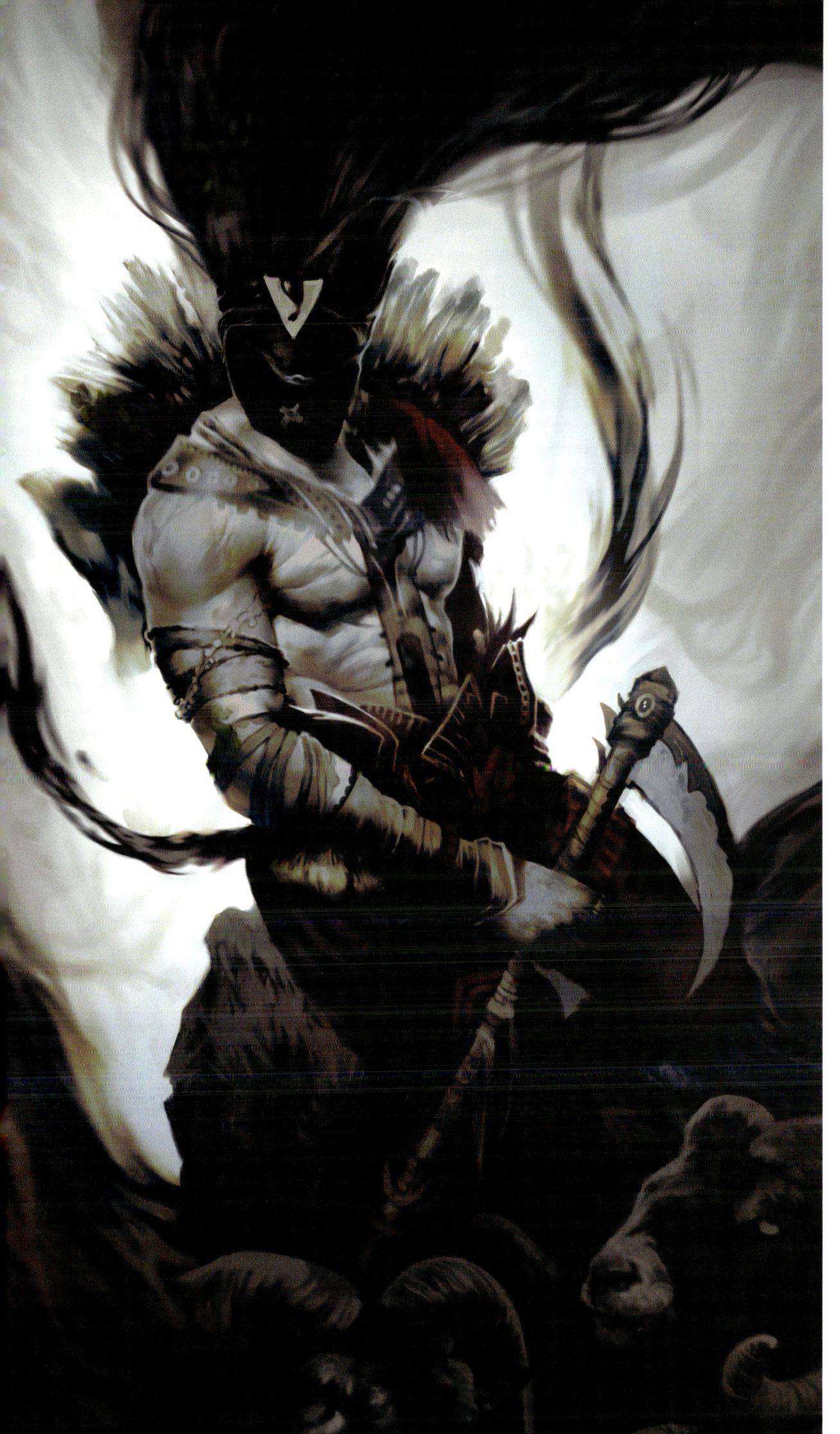

Kevin Hong | www.kevinhong.com

Nostalgia

Nostalgia is something that describes a "gentle sadness" or longing for the past. It's something that has strong personal associations, and is linked with an awareness of the impermanence and transience of life. It's this sensibility and awareness that has helped shape many influential works of art in film, video games, animation, and more.

For this tutorial, I will create an illustration based on this theme. In the following steps, I will try to elaborate on how I tackle conveying a sentiment that is universally shared but which is unique to each individual. I'll also show how I present narratives that can be readily understood and explain why and how I blend both traditional and digital media in my work, and how these contrasting elements inform the image and image-making process.

>01 Word salad
Whenever I begin an illustration, whether it be for a client or for personal work, I almost always start it out in writing. I've found that writing down different ideas and thoughts works better for me than jumping straight into thumbnails. It's usually this part of the process where I pick apart ideas and splice them together. Sometimes ideas or phrases seemingly unrelated to the project can find their way onto the page. This "word salad" can give rise to unconventional solutions.

>02 Collecting references
After generating some initial ideas, I create an image folder where I collect and store any and all references that I may find useful for the project and generating ideas. These range from photos and movie stills to paintings and animation cels. I generally try to find images that relate in some way to the given theme; in this case, images that evoke nostalgia or feelings of wistfulness. When I begin to finalize a sketch, I also

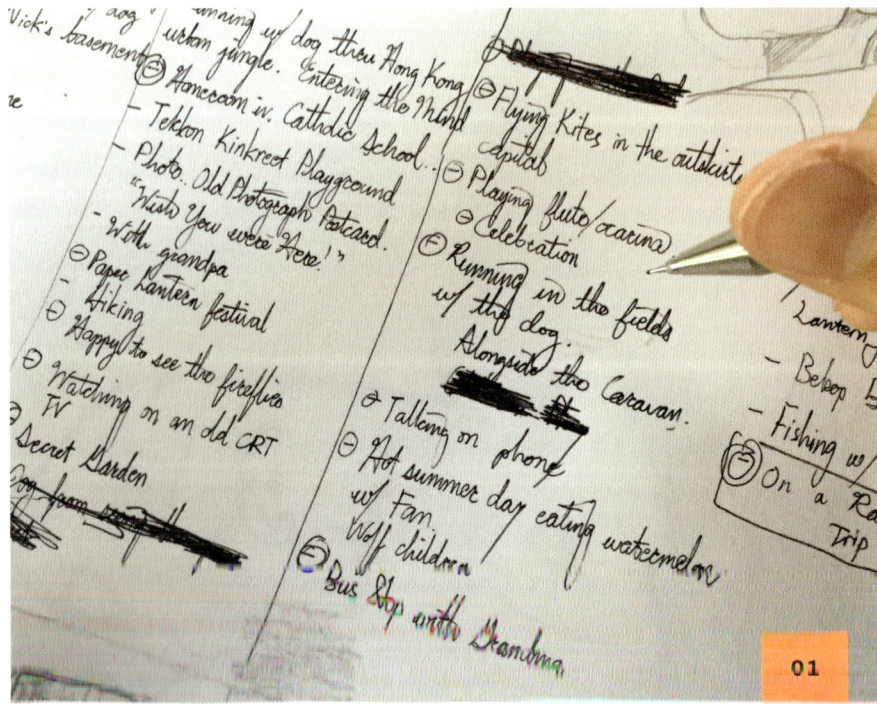

// My sketchbook is more words than drawings. I like to brainstorm by writing down all my ideas

add reference images that will aid me in designing the characters, props, and environments in my illustrated scenes.

>03 Initial sketches

Nostalgia is a very sentimental and wistful feeling linked with personal experiences, and although it's a universally shared emotion, what triggers it can be very different for each person.

That said, there are certain narratives that I think everyone can relate to. Moments of idling, waiting, or of childhood especially. With this in mind, I create several digital sketches trying to illustrate these moments.

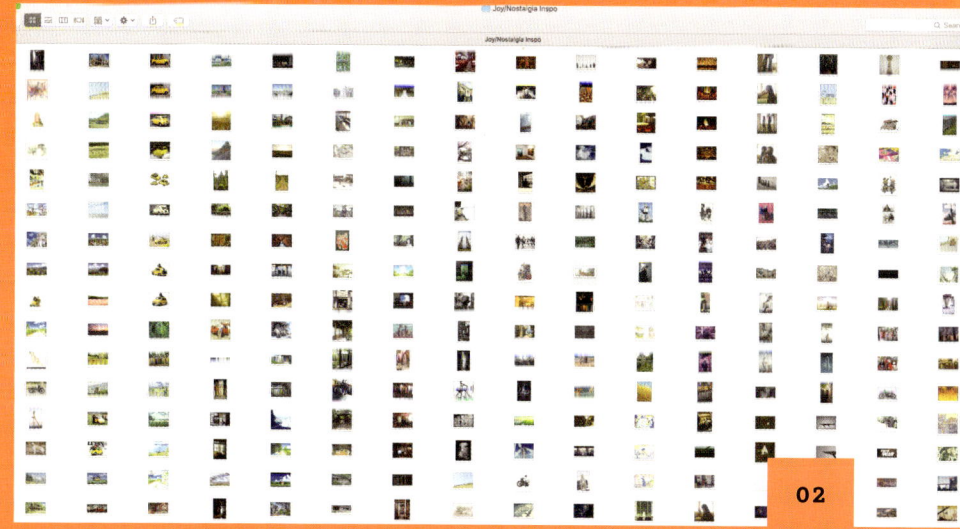

02

// I create a folder dedicated to the project where I store all the files that I may find useful

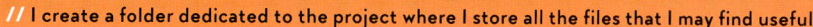

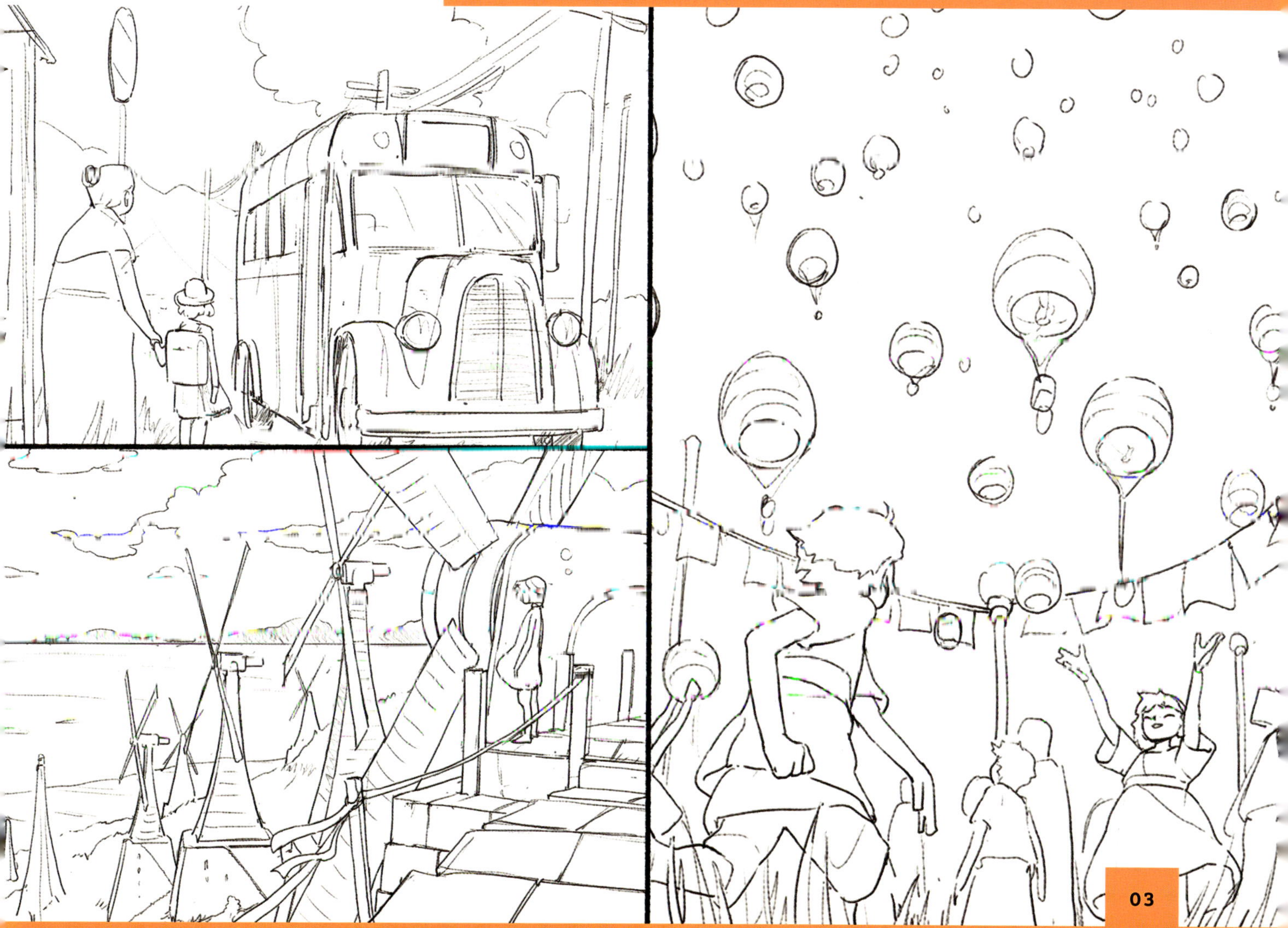

03

// Several sketches with different approaches. I try to focus in on a narrative that illustrates or evokes longing

>04 Further sketches

The sketch that I go with is one inspired by my memories of cross-country road trips as a kid. At the time, I found those trips to be very long and boring, but they are memories I now cherish. There were many long hours spent staring out of the window, lost in thought. Long journeys can be very meditative, and I think these experiences stay with you. When traveling, you become keenly aware of life's fleeting moments. It's those kinds of moments that I want to transmit in the sketch.

>05 Graphite

Once the sketch is approved, I enlarge it in Adobe Photoshop and print it out in segments. I stitch these segments together with tape, and use a lightbox to draw a larger, refined version on a 14 × 19" sheet of Arches hot-pressed watercolor paper. Using ArtGraf watercolor graphite and various pencils, I render a grayscale illustration that I will later convert into color digitally. While Photoshop allows

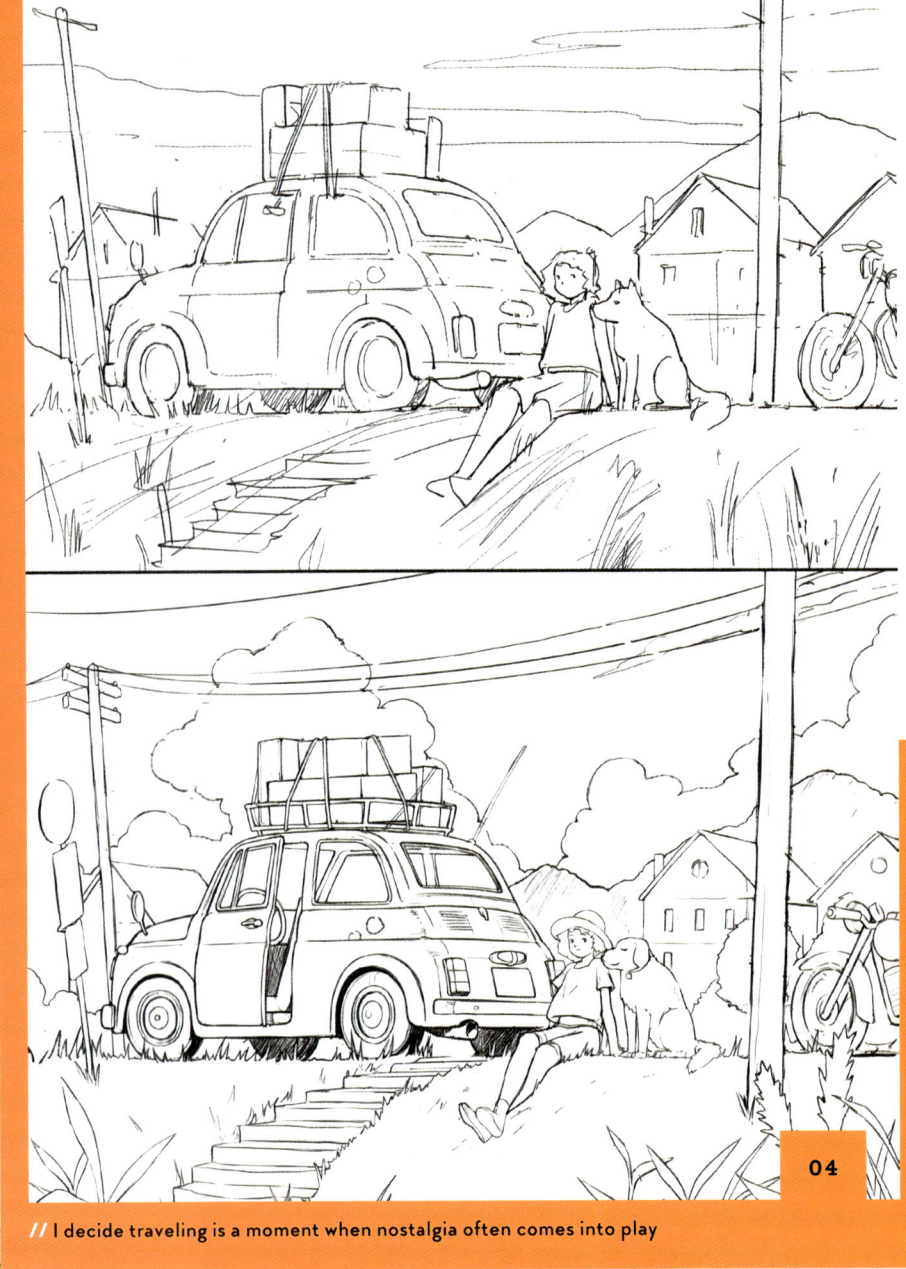

04

// I decide traveling is a moment when nostalgia often comes into play

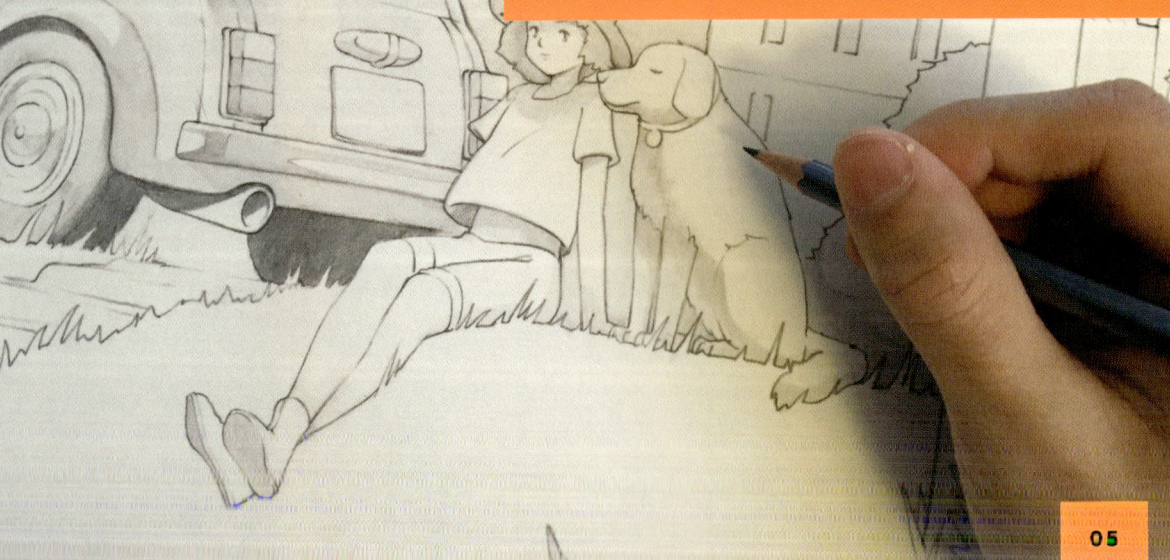

05

// Using pencils and watercolor graphite, I draft out the image on a large sheet of paper

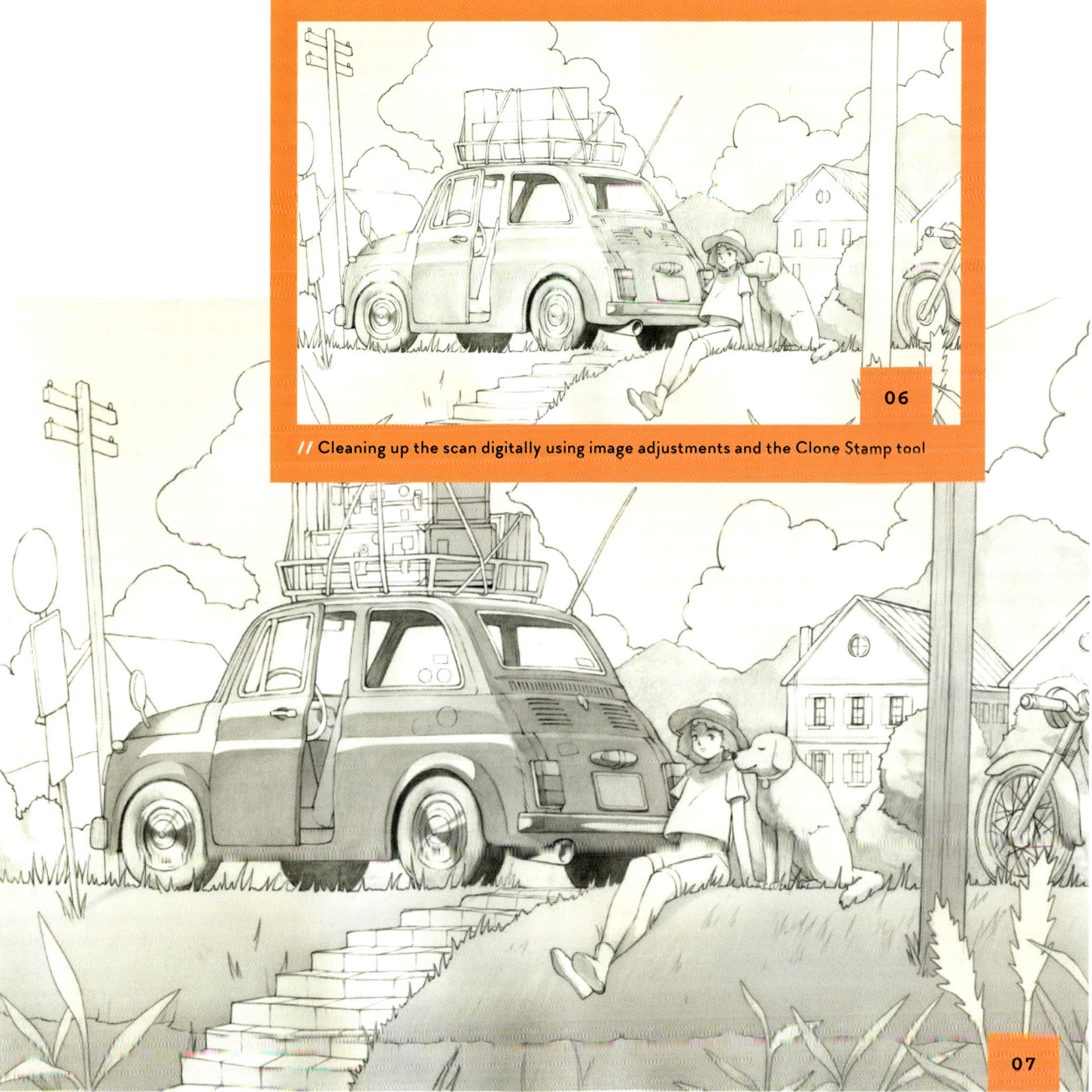

// **Cleaning up the scan digitally using image adjustments and the Clone Stamp tool**

// **I add gray tones to large areas, and add or edit minor details**

me to manipulate a piece in an almost infinite number of ways, I like to blend elements of traditional media with my work, which is why I begin most of my pieces traditionally. I believe traditional media evokes a certain kind of response in the viewer, and that there's an intrinsic charm in being able to see the physicality of a work.

>06 Scanning
After completing the drawing, I scan it in pieces and stitch these back together using Photoshop's Photomerge function. I then darken the values

using Curves and Levels adjustments, and clean the scan up using the Clone Stamp tool. I also lighten some tones by working with the Exposure tool set to Highlights. While making these edits, I try to maintain the texture of the original paper, since I will be setting the drawing as a Multiply layer over digital colors later. Having the texture helps maintain the "handmade" look that I am aiming for, so it's essential that I keep it intact.

>07 Shading and additional details
To flesh out the drawing, I create a new layer and use custom brushes and

scanned paper textures to fill out areas. I fill in larger areas like the grass and car digitally, so as to have clean and uniform tones. Since the car is metallic, I want to keep it looking relatively smooth.

I also complete areas that were left unfinished in the original drawing, such as the stone steps, the details on the luggage, the sign, the houses, and some of the minor details on the car and creek. In this step, I make sure I define the overall lighting and mood so that I will keep this in mind during the rest of the coloring process.

>08 Extra grain

To give the picture a more rustic look, I add a reddish grain texture and rebalance the values of the image with a Curves adjustment layer. This keeps the grain intact, making the image look more like a print. I like adding artificial grain to my images to make them look a little aged. I think these texture effects incidentally evoke a certain nostalgia for old printed materials like comic books.

>09 Sepia tone

The final adjustment I make to the grayscale image is to convert it into sepia, another hint towards nostalgia. I create a Gradient Map adjustment layer and set it to a red-orange tint. All of these layers are then placed into a layer group called "Lineart," with the group's blending mode set to Multiply. The sepia tone lends the image a warm aesthetic, but moreover, it will help blend the tones with the digital colors I add underneath.

Colors underneath a grayscale image may come out looking dull and muddied, but gradient mapping allows for more lush and vivid color palettes.

>10 Color flats

I start to block in flat color as follows: once I have the "Lineart" group, I create a "Colors" group underneath. I then create a "Flats" layer, and begin isolating and filling areas using the Lasso and Pen tools. When using these tools, I make sure I keep

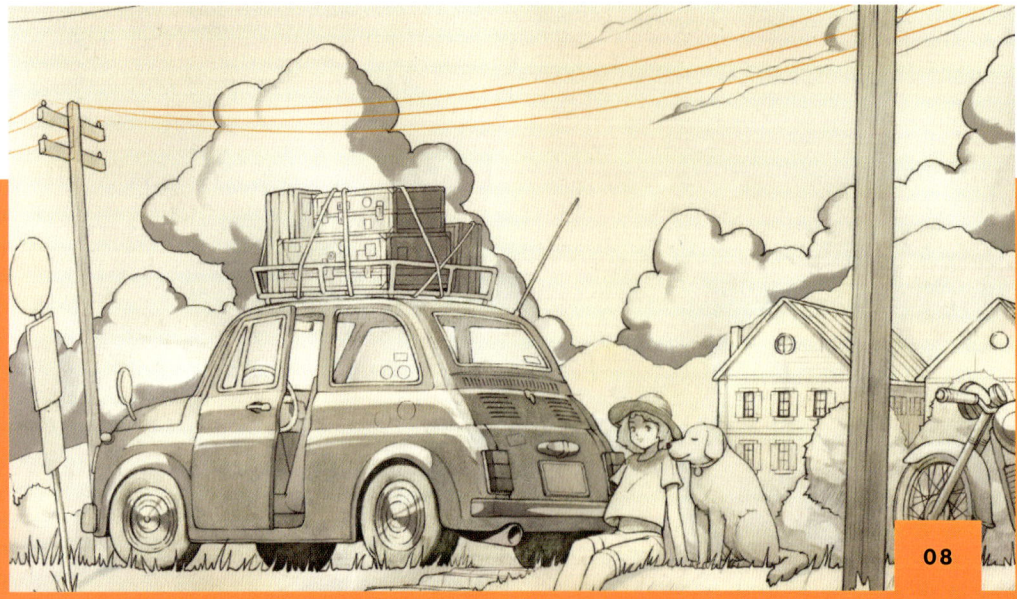

08

// I add a grainy paper texture to achieve an old printed look

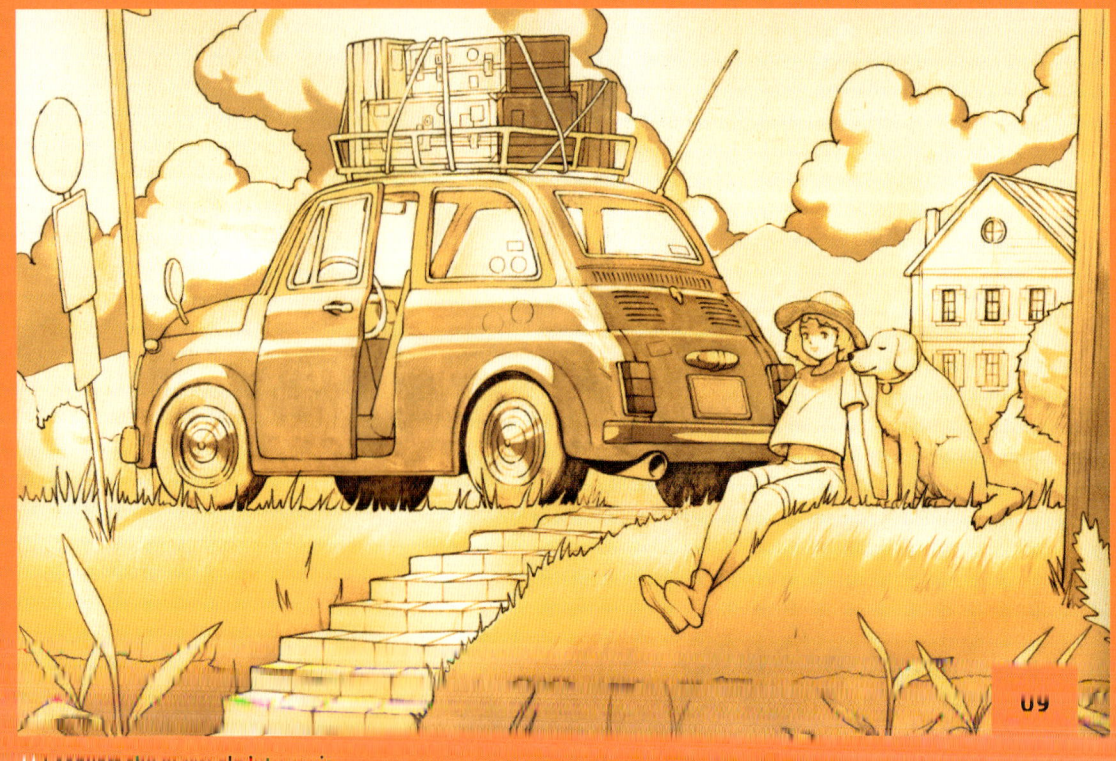

09

// I convert the grayscale into sepia

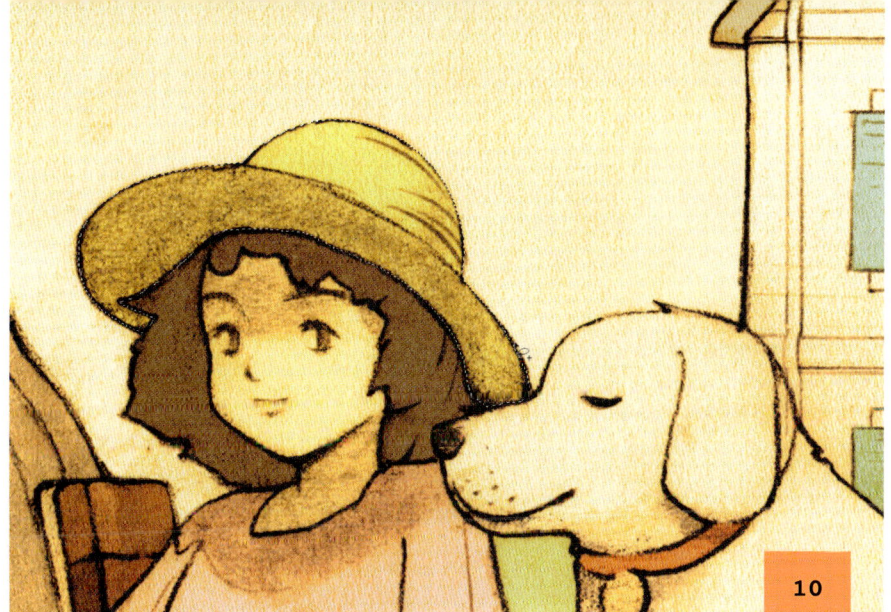

10

// I isolate and fill areas for quick and easy color editing

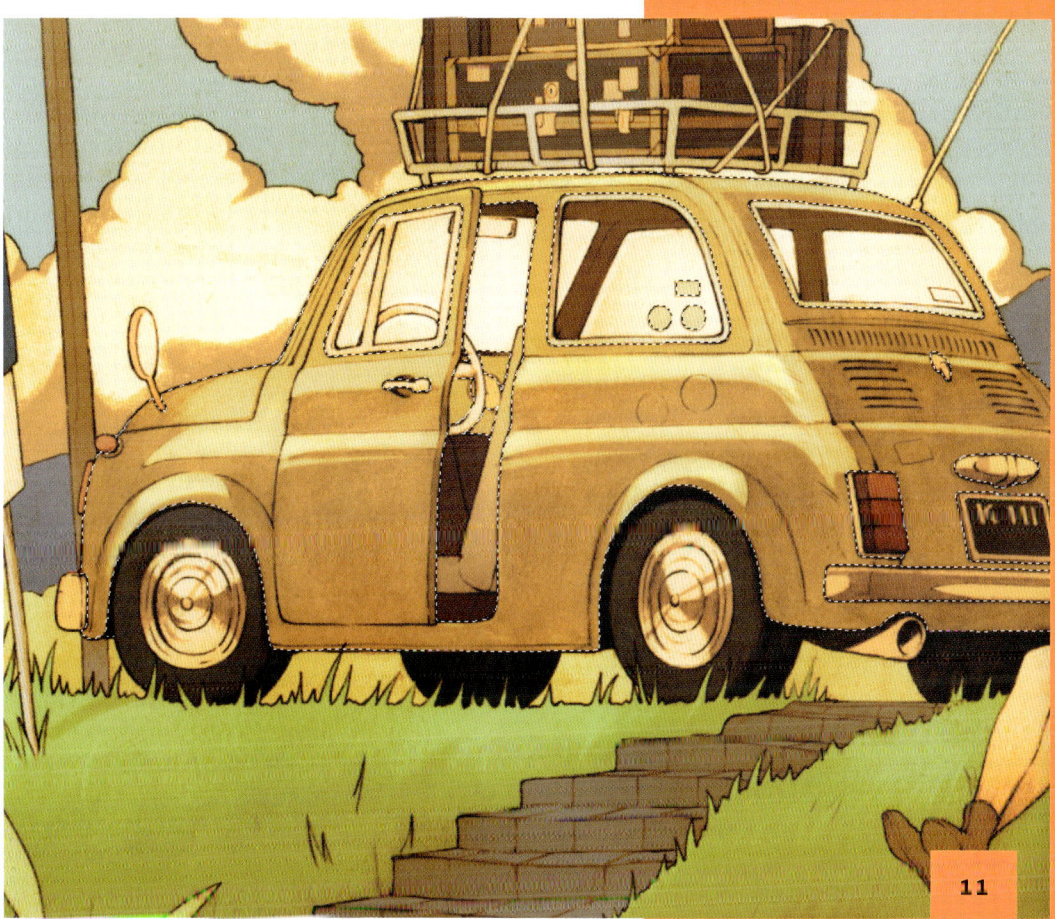

11

// Defining a color palette

"anti-aliasing" off. This is to ensure clean selections later on, as anti-aliasing would blur the edges and leave artifacts when adjusting hues. I also make sure that no two areas that touch have the same color so that the separate elements are distinct.

>11 Color palette
After the flat colors are finished, I begin to adjust the colors using the Hue/ Saturation menu to better unify the palette. I want the scene to be a warm

summer's day with an airy atmosphere, so I choose mostly vivid colors. Since the mountains are in the distance, I choose a muted blue to push them back. The sepia tone I added via the gradient map still makes some areas such as the clouds look unnatural, so I will adjust those in the next step.

>12 Unifying the colors
I make further adjustments to the palette by adding gradient maps

"I think these texture effects incidentally evoke a certain nostalgia for old printed materials like comic books"

masked to certain sections of the image. In particular, this desaturates the clouds, making them look less popcorn-like. I make overall hue adjustments. This stage is the final major adjustment to the colors, and helps to unify the overall palette.

"Softening helps to push the clouds and mountains further back in space, giving a more atmospheric feel"

>13 Painting shadows

Now I create a "Shadows" layer above the "Flats" layer and begin to paint in with a simple brush. I paint into all the major elements, adding values to the houses in the background, the grass, the girl and her dog, as well as the electric poles and signpost. I also add a yellowish tint for the grass to give it some luster, and add a subtle gradient to the sky. I paint the mountains with low contrast to account for atmospheric perspective.

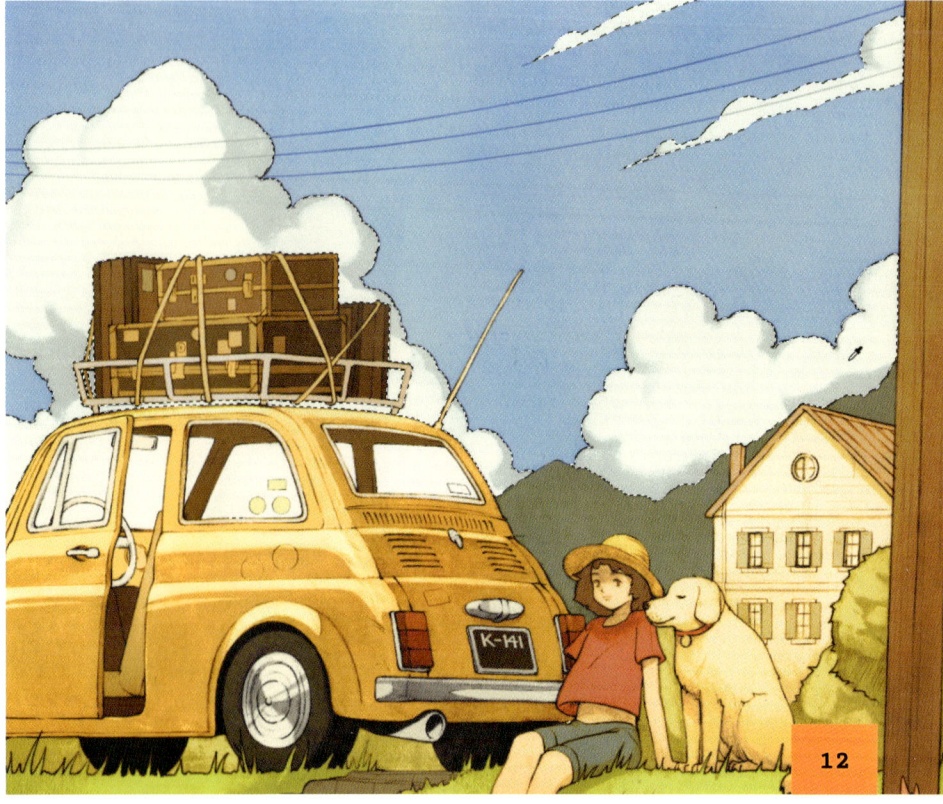

// I further unify the colors

>14 Softening the line art

Some of the line art, especially for the clouds and mountains, may look a little too harsh, so I soften some of the lines. Softening helps to push the clouds and mountains further back in space, giving a more atmospheric feel. This helps to refocus the foreground elements and characters, and creates a better spatial hierarchy. You can see the difference in image 14, along with a close-up of the texture I used earlier.

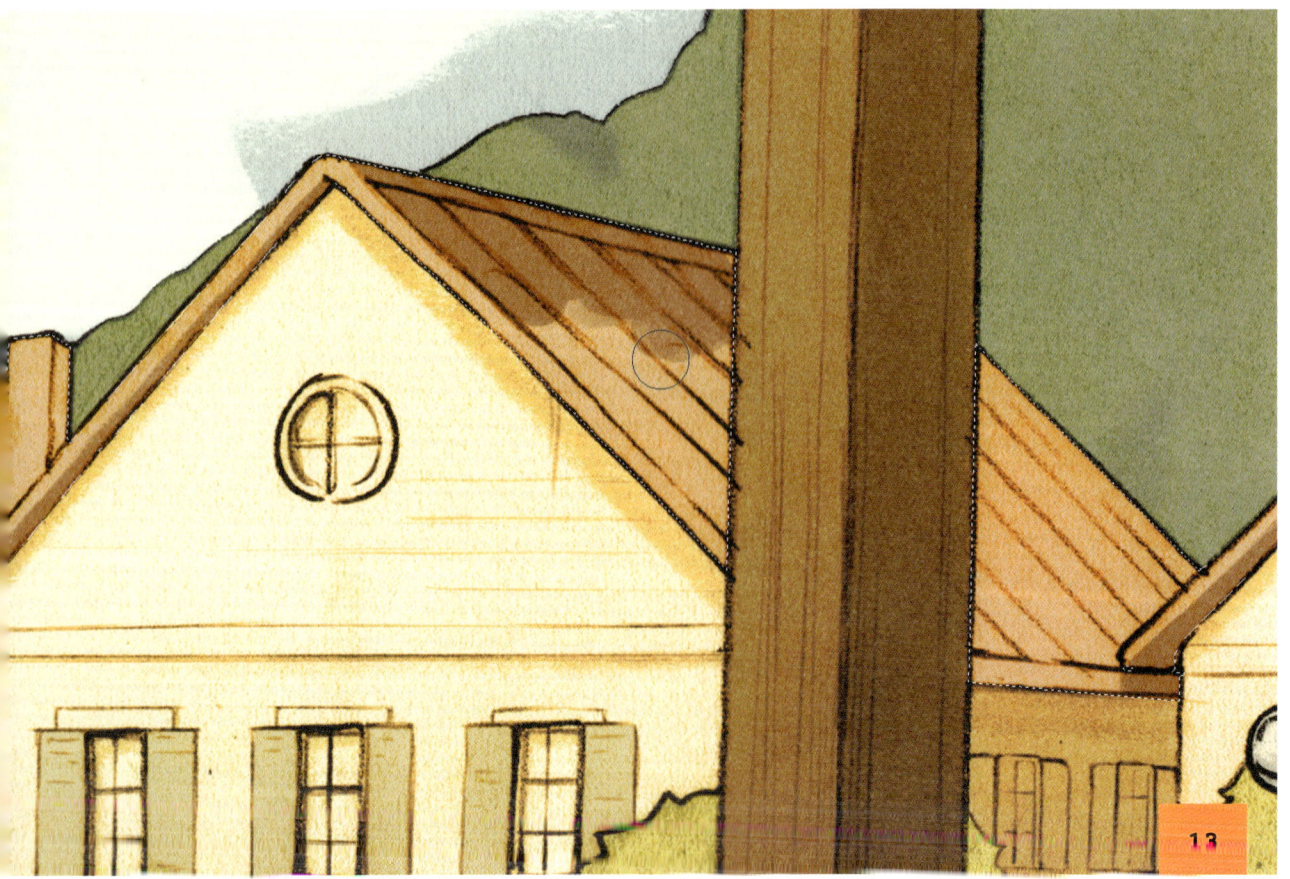

// I add in shadows, painting in with a simple brush

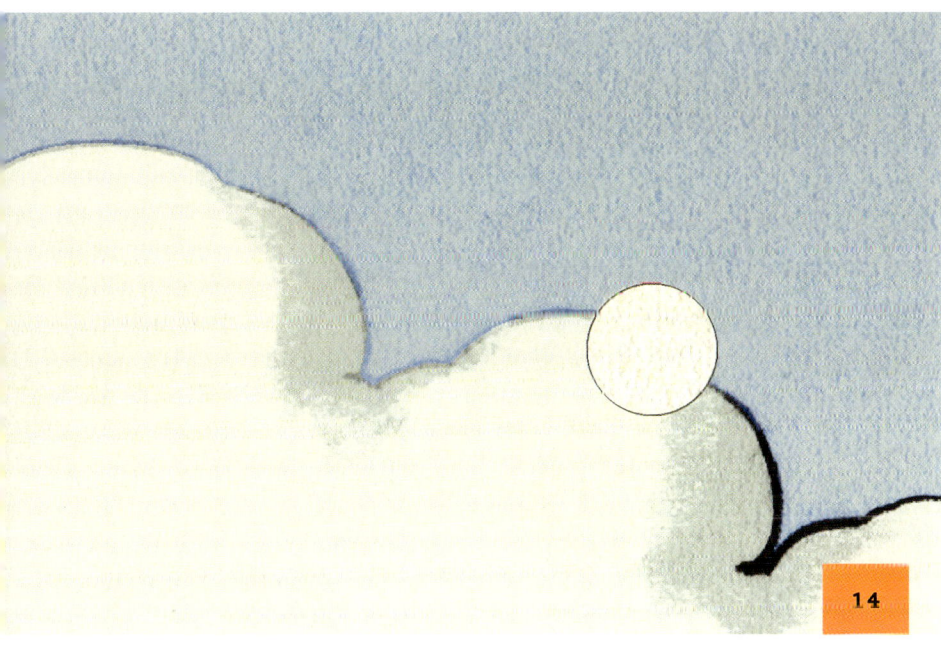

// I soften the outlines of background elements to bring back focus to the foreground and characters

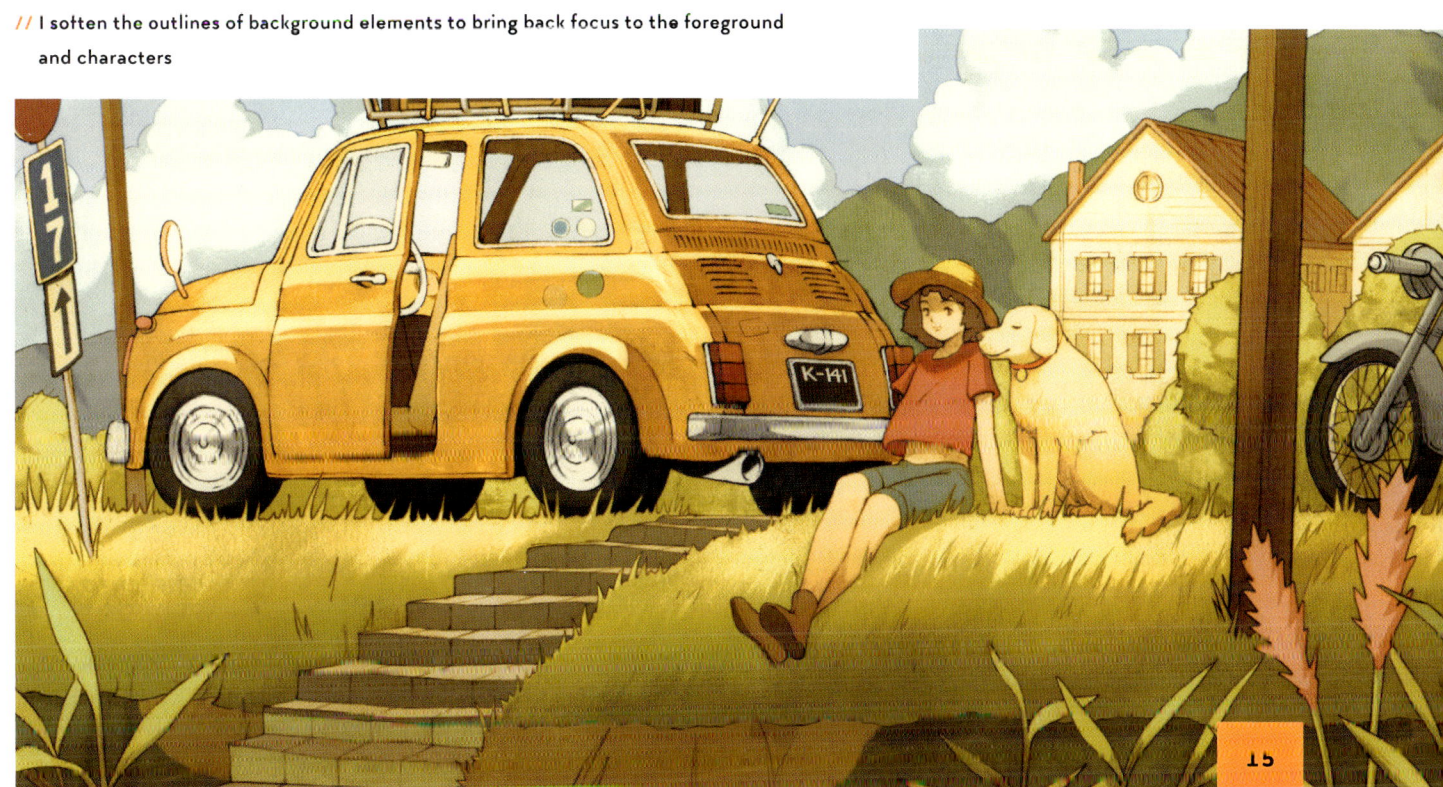

// I paint in the creek at the bottom of the image to finalize the scene and round out the composition

>15 Finalizing

The final element that I paint in is the creek that flows beneath the characters. The creek helps to establish a relaxed and meditative mood to the scene, and also helps to activate some of the negative space on the bottom half of the image. I use a muted blue and paint it in its own layer. I then add in the reflection of the car, and the illustration is complete.

>16 Final advice: how to be interesting

The key to making interesting work is to make art that you find interesting. Indulge in what you enjoy creating, and try not to sabotage that by making work that "conforms" to an industry or a field. If you make work that you really enjoy and work hard at perfecting your craft, then you will find clients who will commission you for being you.

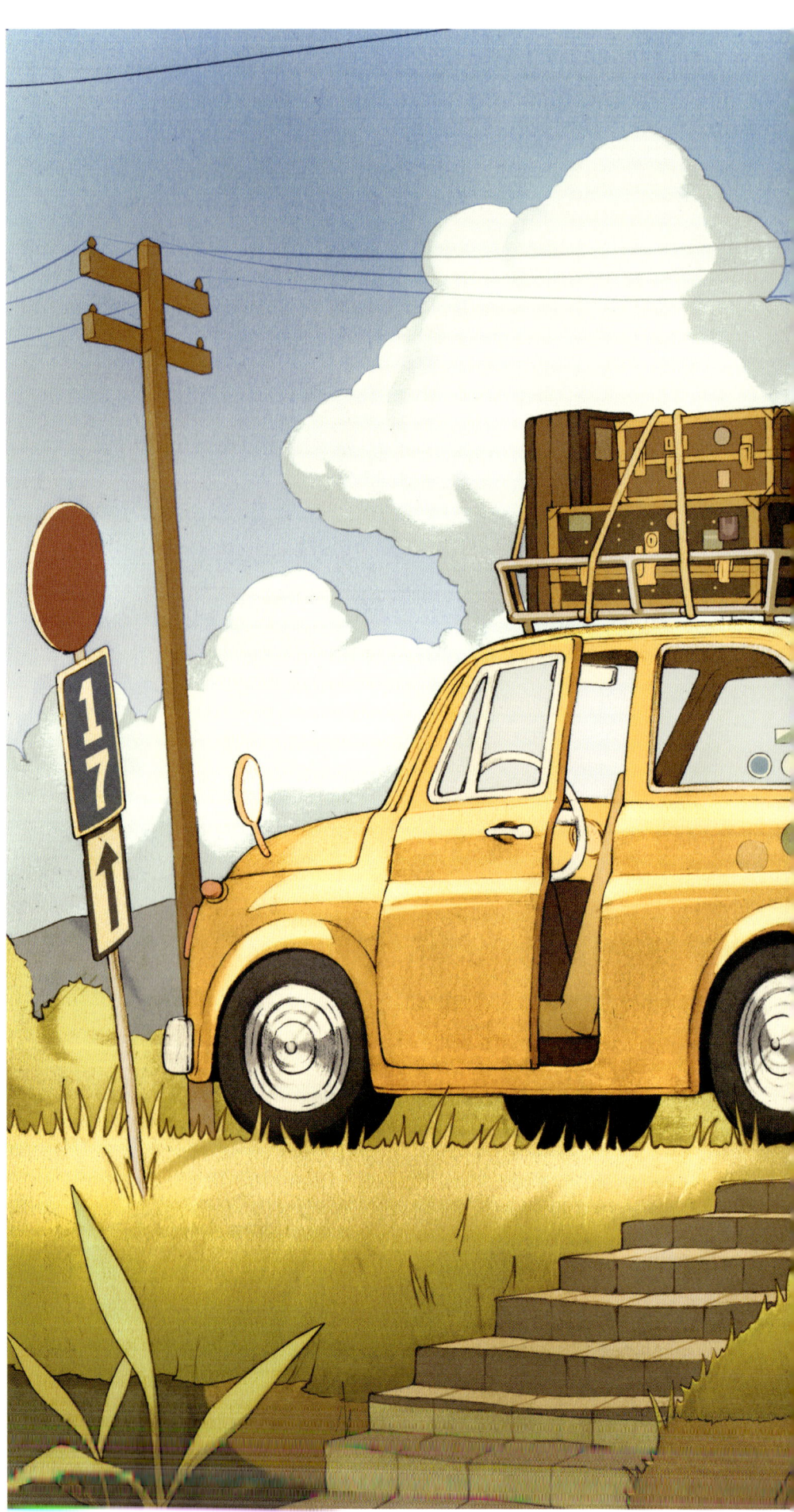

// PRO TIP

Experimentation
I developed my hybrid traditional/digital process over several years, and through constant experimentation. I still regularly read and watch tutorials, and always find new ways to enhance my work. With every piece, I try something new to spice things up. A dialog between yourself and your medium is a great one to have, and you should always try to keep that conversation entertaining.

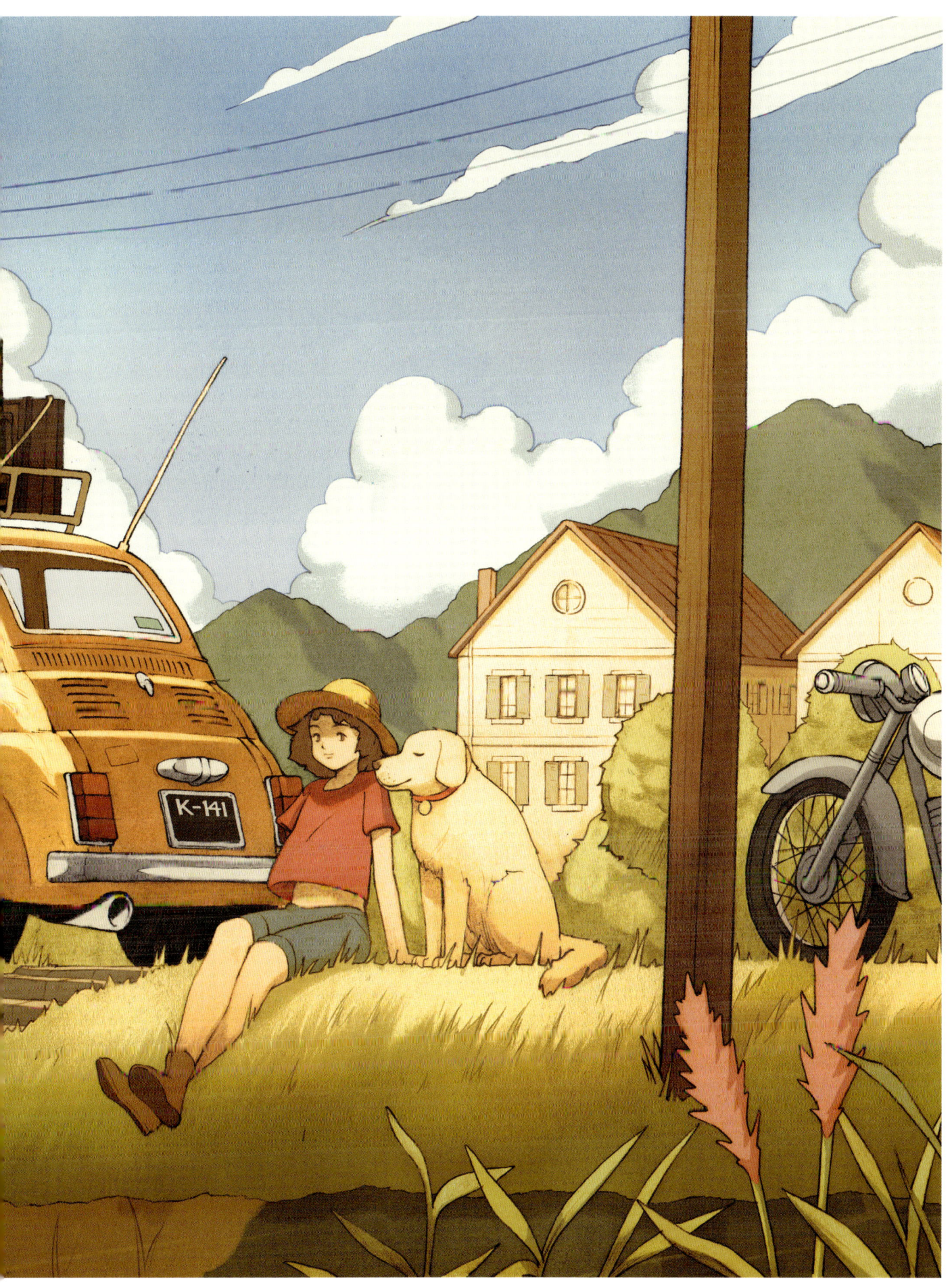

Kamil Murzyn | www.kamilmurzynarts.pl

Suspense

This tutorial will not so much show a linear progression of my workflow, but rather will talk through and analyze the different areas I consider in my painting so that you will be able to apply these thought processes to your own work. I'll cover several aspects of art, including narrative, storytelling, and more technical aspects such as framing and lighting.

I'll be telling a story about two ladies at a dance, who have come out onto the terrace to get some fresh air and gossip a little, but there is a huge creature waiting there, lurking above them in the shadows. This scene has plenty of opportunities to exploit to create a mood of suspense and danger. I suggest playing the soundtrack from *Jaws* before proceeding!

>01 Creature design
To boost the feeling of danger, I'll create a really horrible creature, partially hidden in shadows. I would like to create the design for this prior to sketching my compositions. My idea for a beast is something with six or more legs, something spider-like and able to easily climb walls and ambush his victims from above.

Starting with the design is thinking ahead. This scene will have a complicated pose drawn from a low angle, so knowing the anatomy of the creature will be helpful; I want to avoid inventing the design at the same time as putting it in a difficult pose.

What makes a creature design more terrifying is smuggling real anatomy into it, so I design a creature with a human muscle structure but slightly twisted limbs. This design choice is to make it more unnatural and scary. My quick drawing includes multiple strong arms and legs, large jaws, and unevenly distributed eyes, which should be enough to scare some ladies. Once this is complete, I move on to sketching the composition.

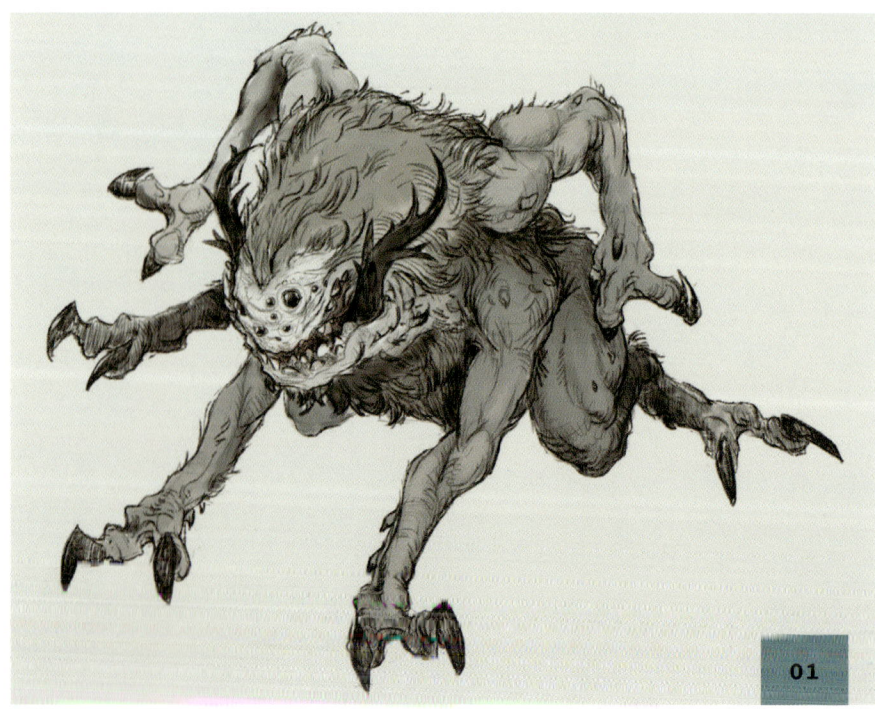

01

// Designing the creature beforehand is a sensible idea in this case

>02 Storytelling through composition

Now that I've picked the story, I have to figure out how to tell it using rules of composition and scene layout. In image 02 you can see my final sketch for this illustration, with some colored lines on it. The red lines create a frame, making an "image inside an image" that will help to visually isolate the most important part of the illustration. The blue lines are a "rule of thirds" guide; I try to place important things on these lines or, even better, where the lines intersect.

The yellow triangle indicates where the story is taking place and where all the characters are interacting. These yellow lines are also the path that the viewer's eye follows; it should be a closed shape, making the story circulate.

I try to position elements so that they provide a direction for the eye to move to next. In this example, the beast is looking towards the ladies, and drops of saliva lead towards the first lady. Her hands lead towards the second lady, the unaware character, who is holding a fan that brings the eye back up towards the beast's arm and back to the beginning. Creating these visual cues is a way to tell the story that I want. They might be abstract shapes, natural lines, or a character pointing or looking at something.

To add more suspense and a feeling of danger, I'm presenting a moment of the story right before something bad happens. As this is a narrative-driven image, I have to imagine all the characters in that particular moment, and pick an angle to paint them from so that they form a natural composition together. It's commonly understood that a very high or very low angle makes a scene more dramatic; I've chosen to draw the beast hanging above the ladies, so a lower angle is a suitable choice. I'm careful not to overdo it, though – the beast would look good sitting on the ceiling, but the other characters would be difficult to pose legibly and would suffer from a very low angle.

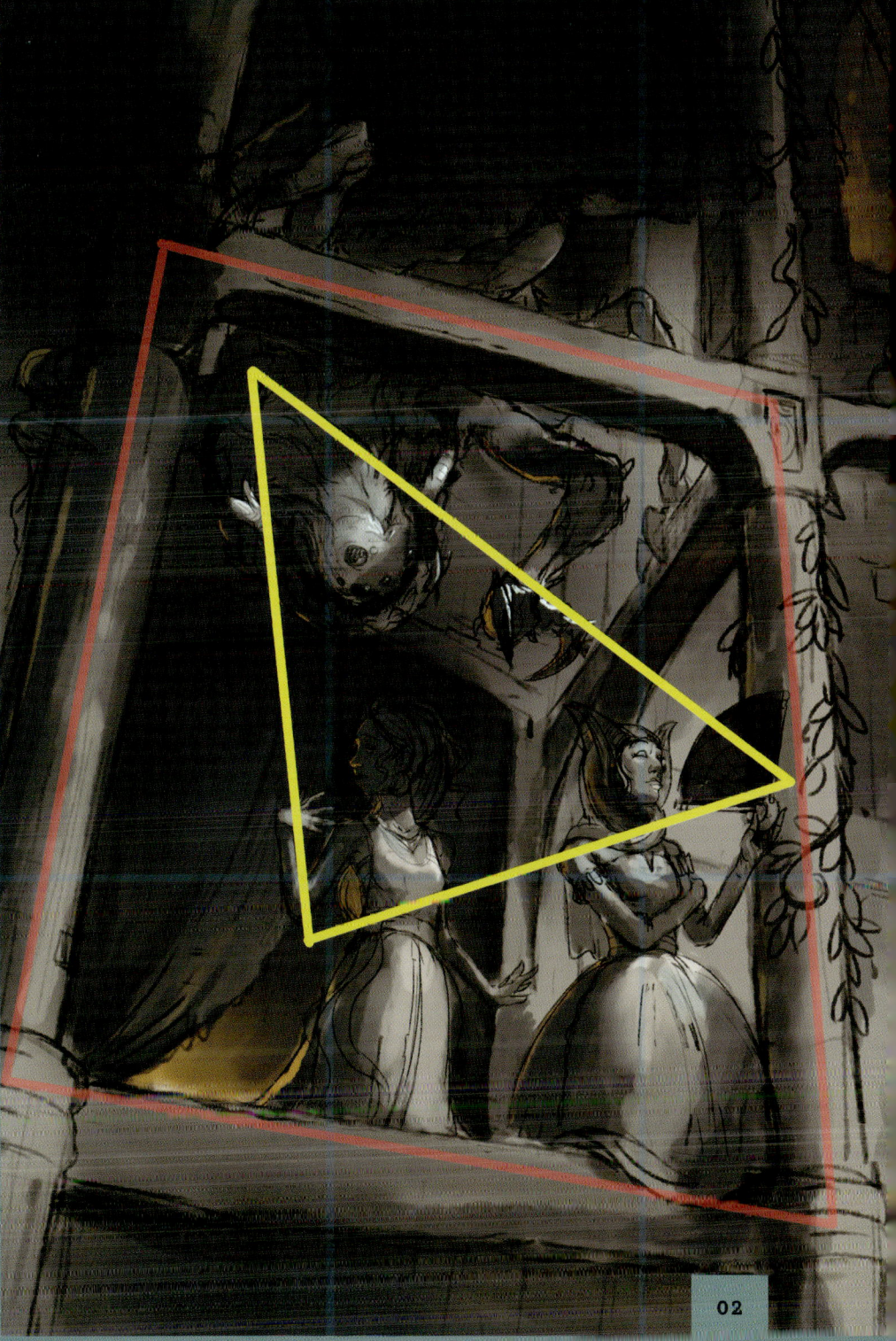

02

How to achieve a pleasing composition and guide the eye through the illustration

"Creating these visual cues is a way to tell the story that I want. They might be abstract shapes, natural lines, or a character pointing or looking at something"

"Hidden places, covered in shadows, naturally produce a darker, dramatic mood"

>03 Selecting focal points

In composition, a "focal point" is a place that is created to naturally draw the eye towards it, often using contrast, composition, saturation, or brightness to do so. Here I would like to draw focus to the characters, bringing them forward using more detail, saturated color, and lighting.

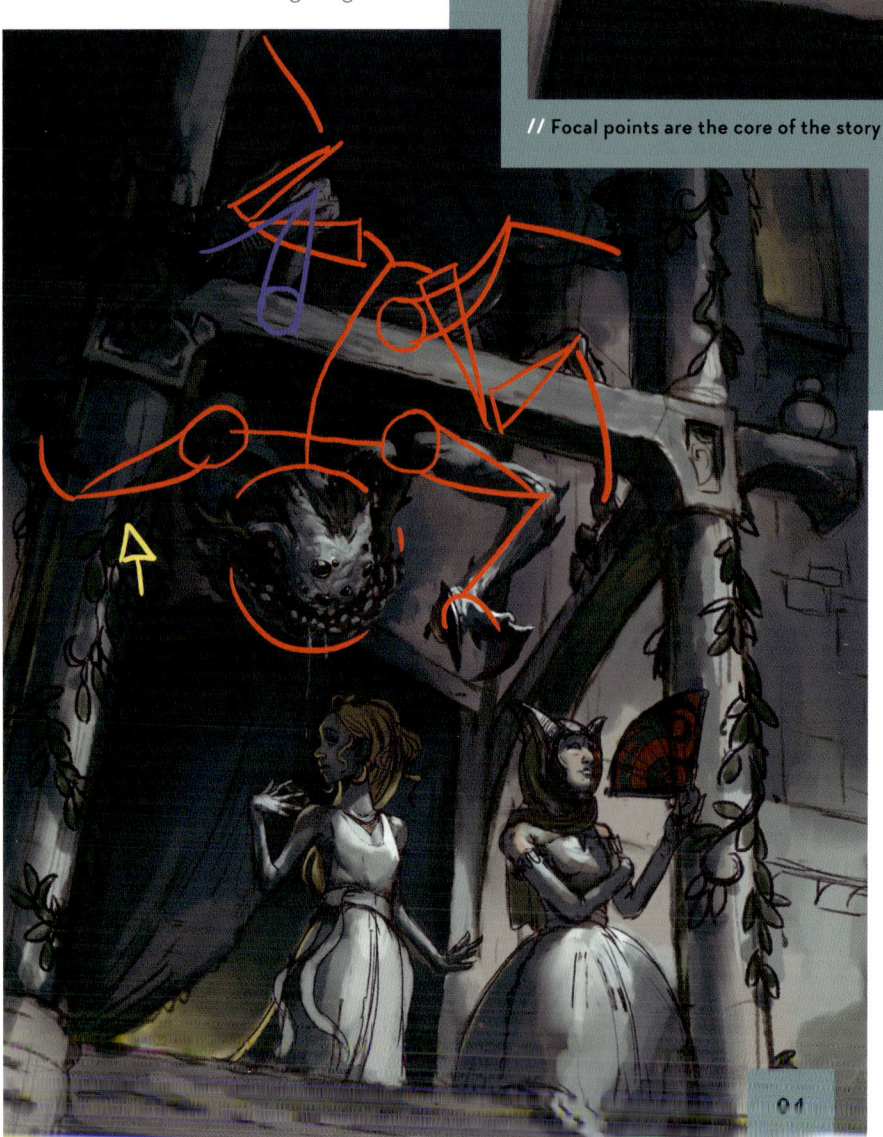

// Focal points are the core of the story

>04 Posing the creature

With so many limbs, it's quite tricky to place the creature in the environment I've prepared. It's helpful to quickly check anatomy on another layer or with tracing paper using a simple stick-figure drawing, but you don't have to be a hundred percent precise every time. Notice the limb indicated by a yellow arrow in image 04: it's slightly too long, but it helps very much to place the character in the correct pose; hiding it behind a pillar makes it less noticeable.

>05 Architecture and perspective

Next I work on the building elements of the scene. When I paint an illustration that contains some sort architecture, I don't rush into it. A good drawing with the

// It can be tricky to pose characters well while maintaining good composition

158

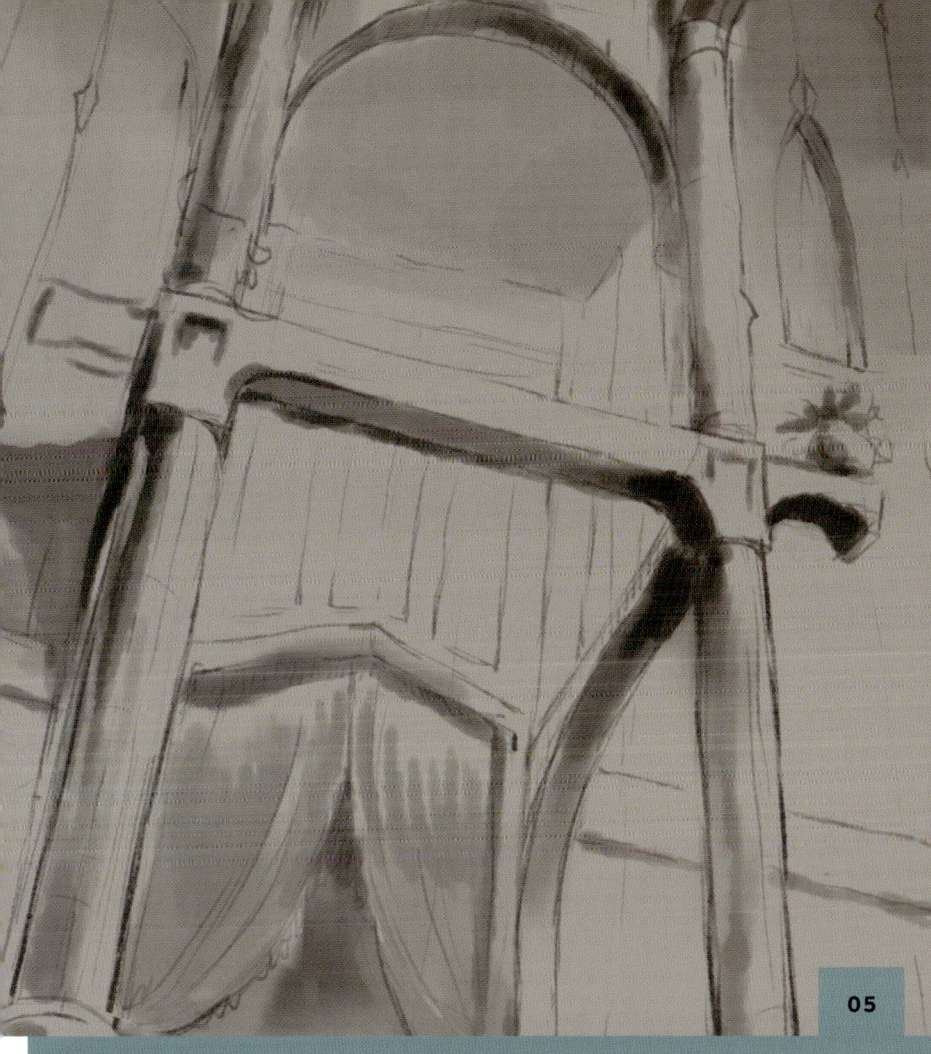

05

// I spend some additional time drawing all the architecture

right perspective is key, and helps you avoid later tweaking which, when it comes to perspective issues, can hurt a lot!

>06 Light and shadow

Image 06a shows a version of the scene with dramatically increased contrast, demonstrating how the contrast between light and shadow is used to form lines that create focal points and narrative flow. Hidden places, covered in shadows, naturally produce a darker, dramatic mood; I like to push it even further and combine these dark areas with very well lit "safe" places. Image 06b shows the painting so far.

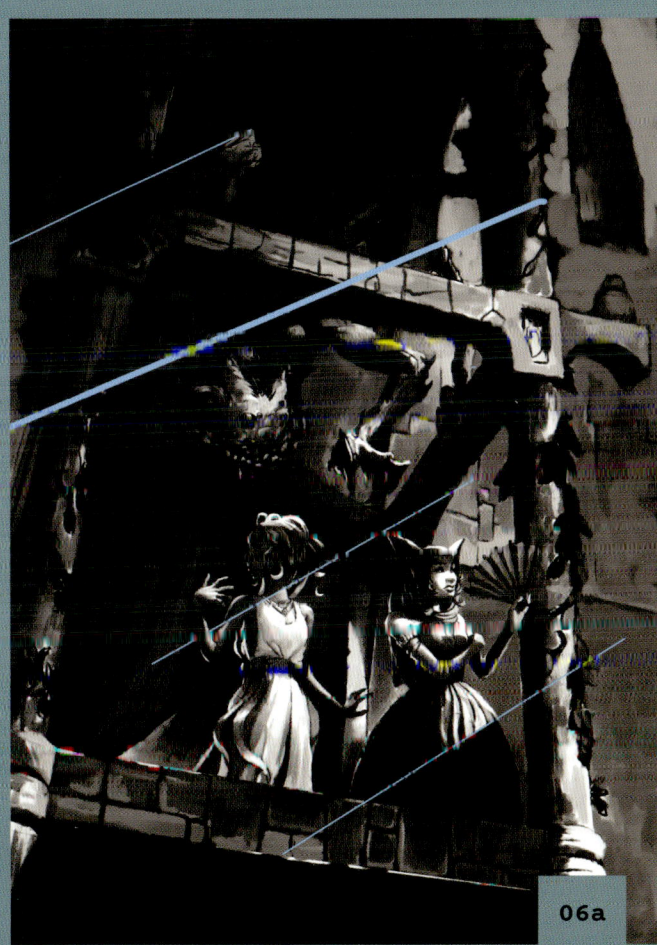

06a

// Light and dark areas are great compositional tools

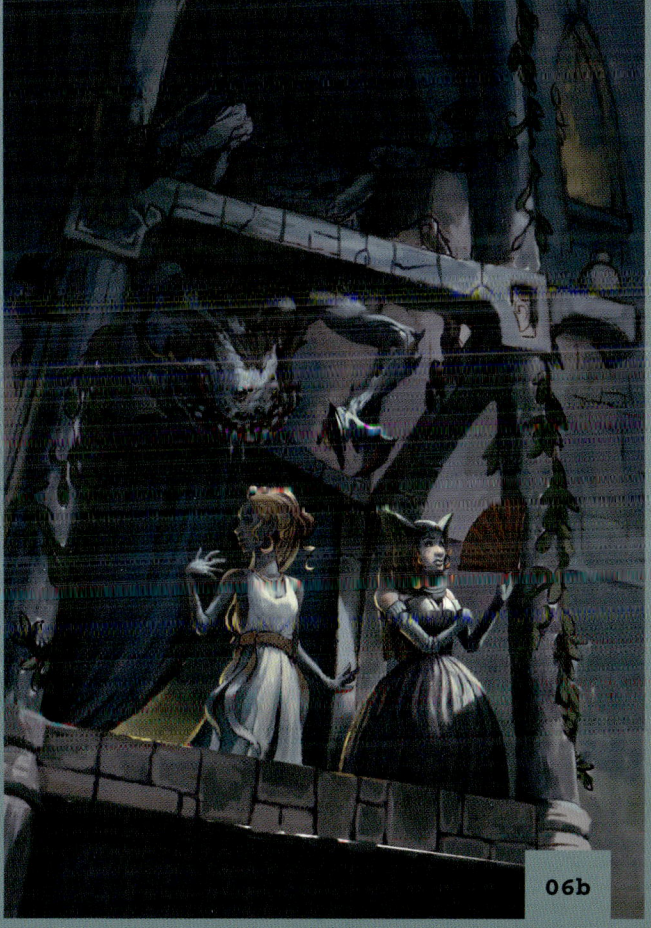

06b

// Building up the painting and mood

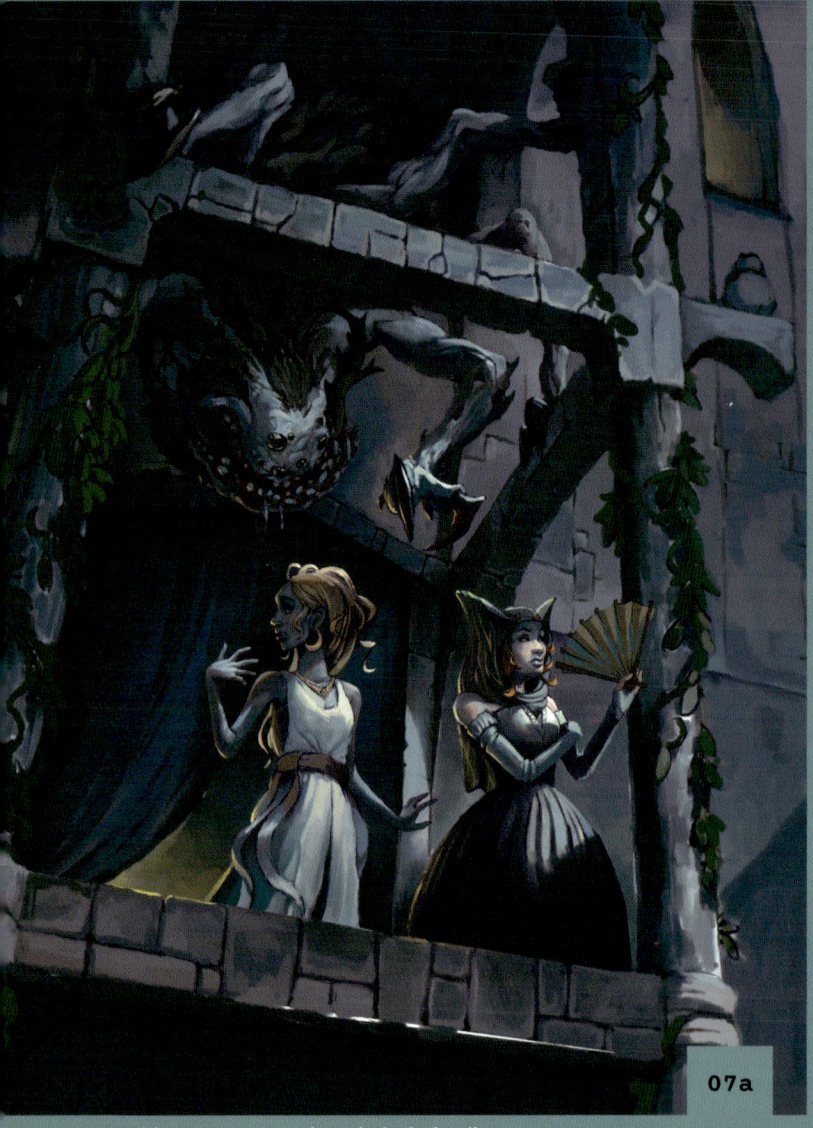

07a

// More progress on the painting's details

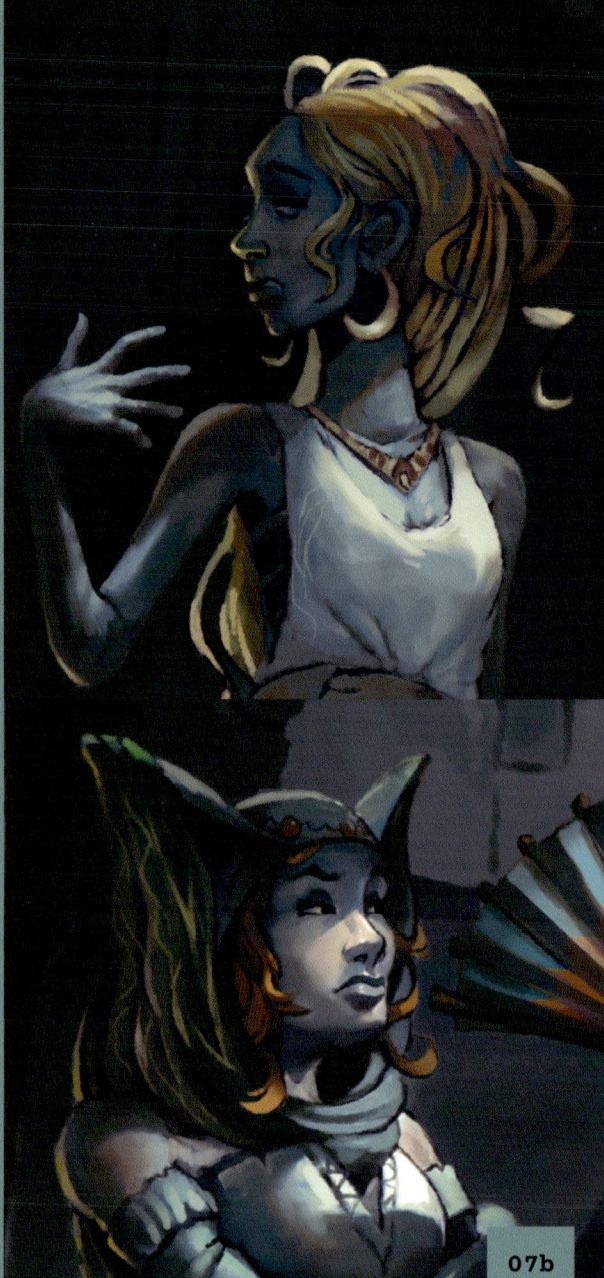

07b

// Gestures and expressions are a superior way of storytelling

>07 Gestures

The painting is becoming more developed now (image 07a), and I focus more on the character details. You can tell a lot of story with gestures and facial expressions. In this illustration, I've decided that drops of saliva are falling on the lady's arm and she is just realizing it with a little grimace on her face. This suggests that a second later, she will look up to see what is going on. The second lady is bored, not happy, and unaware of what is happening. I put extra effort into capturing the right gestures and facial expressions for the characters in order to give my illustration an additional narrative boost (image 07b).

>08 Mood and lighting

Lighting is a very important factor in creating any mood and directing a

story. I usually select a natural lighting condition which has some general rules, such as daylight, overcast light, or sunset; I then shift them to better fit the story and feeling I want to create.

For a suspense-themed illustration, it's a natural choice to pick lighting conditions that allow for high contrasts, so I choose a simple night sky with strong moonlight. Night and gloom always create a feeling of danger and horror.

At this point I realize that there is too much free room in the image, and decide to crop the scene and zoom a little closer towards the characters. I decide to cast a strong rim light from inside the building, which helps to cut out the ladies' silhouettes from the background,

and adds the flavor of a happy party story to the whole illustration.

>09 Gamut

To maintain the mood during the whole process of painting. I restrict my color palette to a gamut. When I pick a few colors that suit the feeling I want to create (in this case blue, violet, and green), it creates a shape on the color wheel: my color gamut. In the center of this is the color that becomes my "new" neutral gray, and represents what the general hue of my image is. I try to be consistent and only use colors from inside my gamut. This way, the whole picture will have one uniform tone.

>10 Color accents

I like to experiment a little with colors, using Photoshop's Color Balance tool

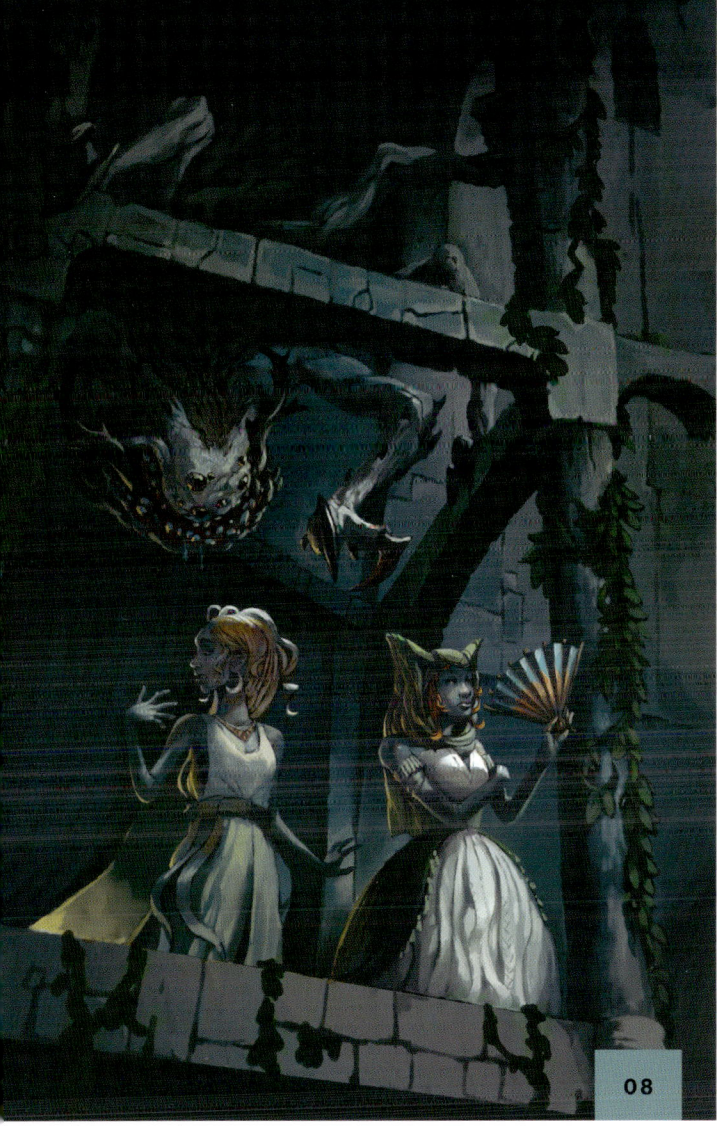

// I crop the image at this stage to improve the focus

// Controlling the colors helps me to create the right mood

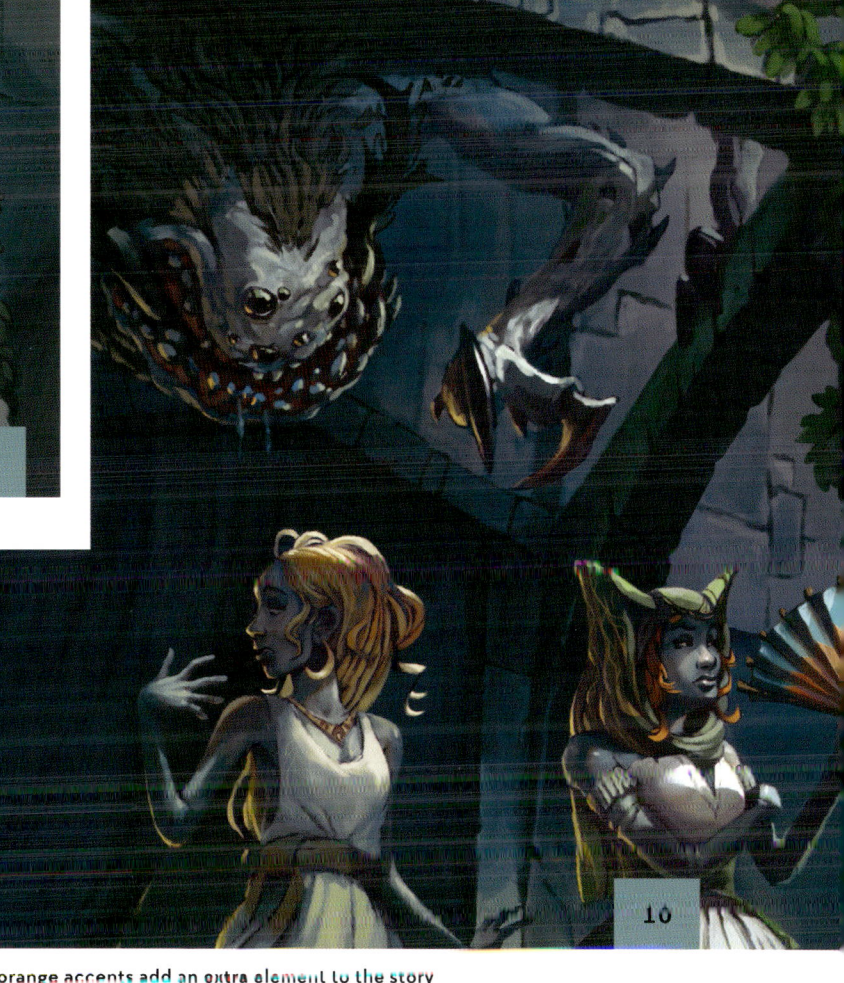

10

// Red and orange accents add an extra element to the story

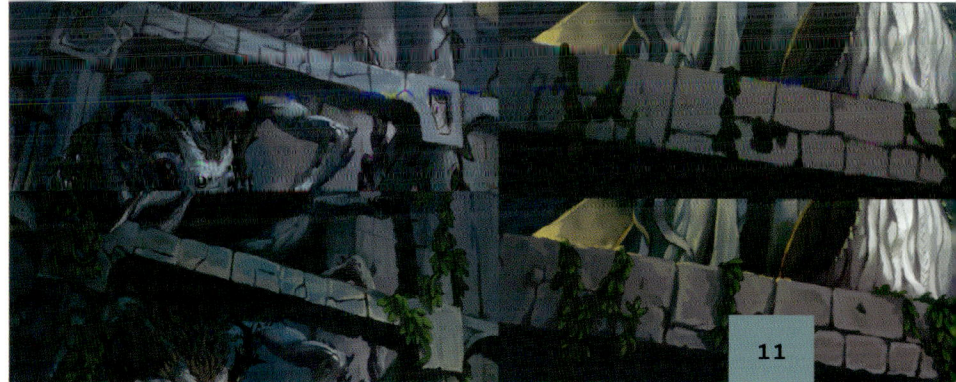

11

// Painting stone walls – a skill that every fantasy artist should have!

08

in this case. I don't want to change the colors globally, so instead I look for places around my focal points where a sudden shift from my color gamut to a new color might help to attract the eye. I have used a strong red for the beast's mouth and orange for the ladies' hair and fan. A little drop of color like this can help if an image is looking too monochromatic. Red and orange accents are associated with blood and fire, and suggest action. Putting them in an overall cool composition is a great visual move that smartens the story a lot.

>11 Painting stone walls
Even though they are not focal points, other features in the scene need to look believable. My method for easily painting stone walls is as follows: I start with simple lines to indicate cracks and breaks between the bricks, then I add lighting to the edges, and some value variations to quickly and easily create the illusion of form.

>12 Painting foliage

One of my general hints for painting foliage is to be precise. You don't have to render every leaf separately – it's fine for it to look very rough and flat – but it should never look random. I start with a middle value and block out most of the shapes for the hanging vines. Then I carefully add a lighter value and darker value, then little variations and shadows on the wall. Don't overdo areas – stay loose but be consistent.

>13 Enhancing occlusion shadows

Adding contact shadows is one of the best ways to create the illusion of form. To add more form to my painting, I therefore softly paint all the contact shadows in the scene. Occlusion shadows are usually the darkest shadows, and occur softly wherever shapes and planes are close to each other, like in corners, gaps, and slots.

Here I paint a very large but soft and subtle shadow on the ceiling, cast by the

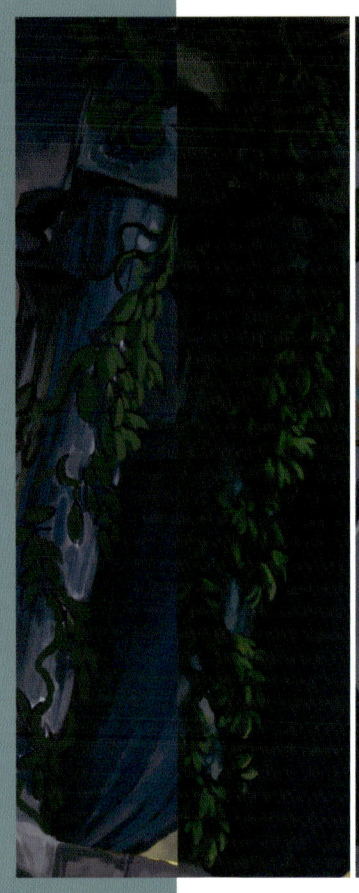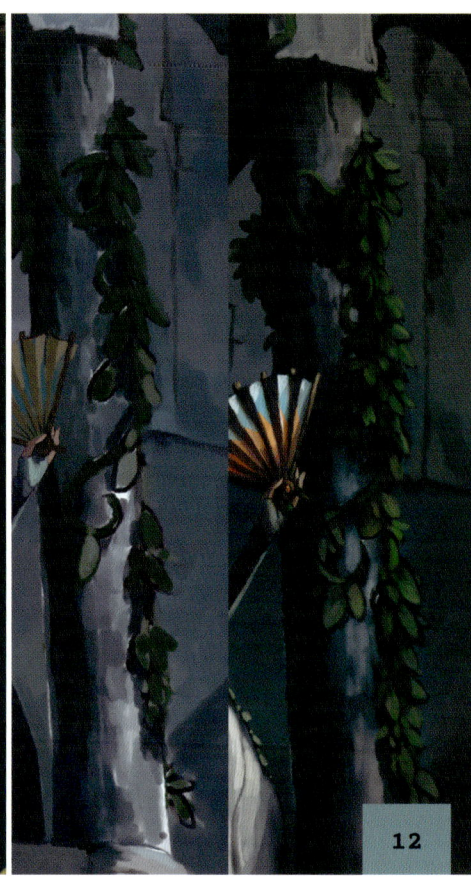

12

// My key to painting foliage is to be patient and precise

creature, that really helps to create the feeling that it's hiding there. Occlusion shadows between walls and vines are also important, so I spend additional time on these.

>14 Clean-up

In this stage, I start to finalize the illustration. I zoom in a little more and try to check the whole canvas for little mistakes, unnecessary lines, and bad-looking brushstrokes. This stage is not about polished rendering, but working on a consistent look. You can visually divide whole pictures into three parts: focal areas, which should be the most detailed and polished; the frame area I mentioned before, which may have more loose, blurry strokes; and the rest of the image, which may remain undefined and flat. This division is one of the major factors to consider when creating focal points.

For the finishing touches, I like to drop in a texture that simulates some kind of paper or real canvas, and make this very subtle, just to break up the flat areas a little. To make the scene more dramatic and to enhance the suspense, I add a soft vignette effect. A slight vignette can seem invisible at first, but can have a great visual effect on the viewer's brain and drive their eye towards the center. Use it wisely. Take a look at the final image on the next page.

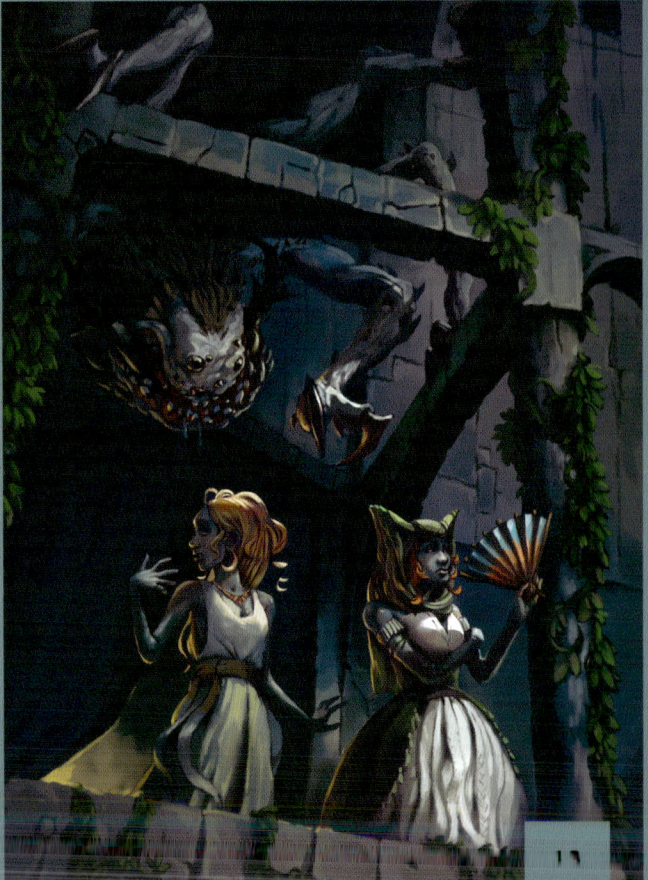

// Adding contact shadows is a great way to create form

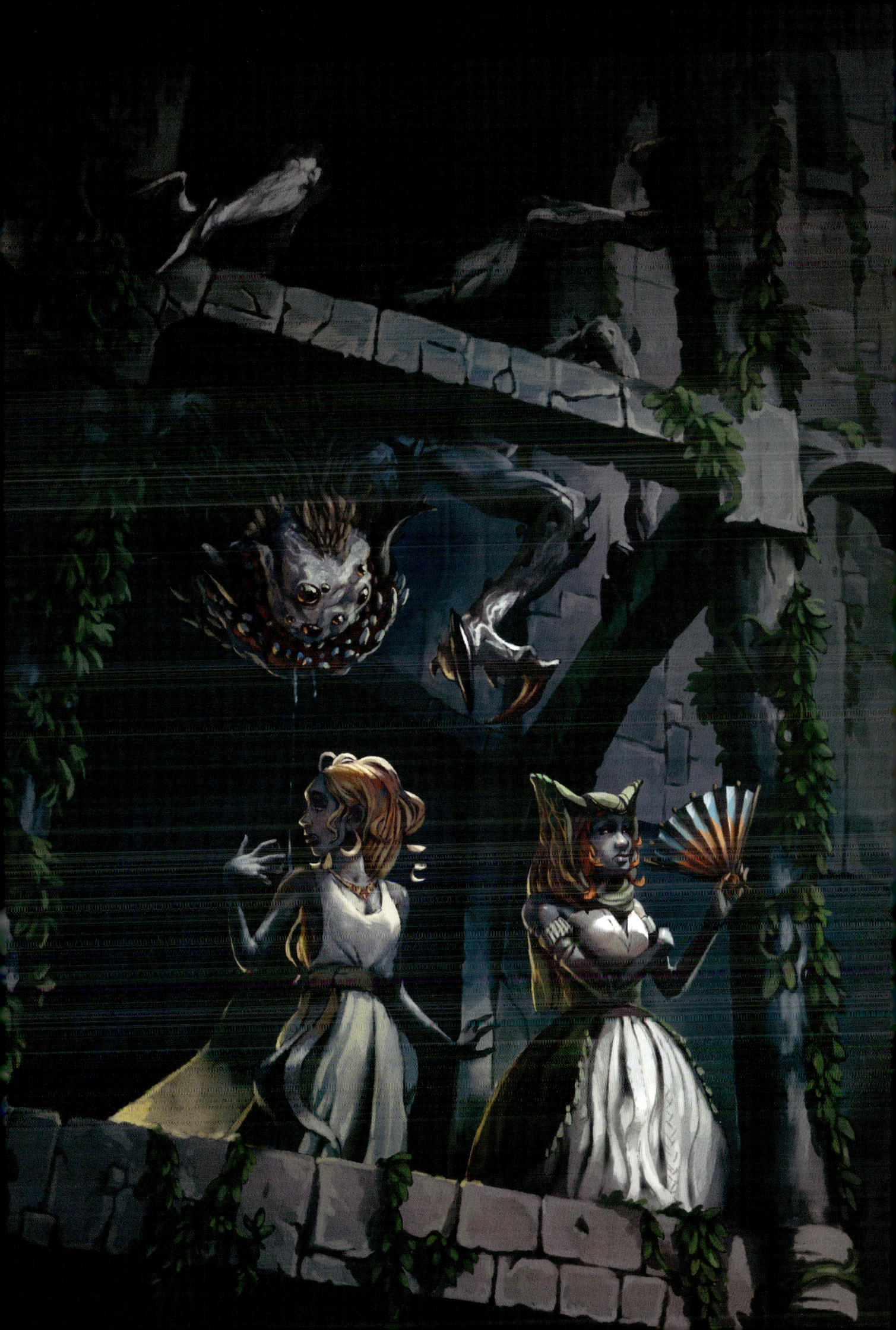

Andy Walsh | www.stayinwonderland.com

Tranquility

When I started contemplating making a tranquil image, I was thinking loosely of some natural foliage, a landscape, a sunset, some calm water, and so on. But it soon occurred to me that these common components of a tranquil scene are somewhat obvious, and that maybe I should consider a narrative-style illustration that highlights the emotion of tranquility and sets it against

something for emphasis; a kind of juxtaposition. I must admit that I spent a while trying to figure this one out, and it didn't come to me immediately!

I went through all my folders of art inspiration, setting aside images which conveyed tranquility as well as images which conveyed the right visual style. I came across some artwork of a turtle

standing in a kitchen, opening a fridge door, and I thought, "What if that was a penguin and he was using the fridge to keep cool? Also, what if there's a fun play on the light of the fridge, whereby it's kind of like sunlight and he's 'sun'-bathing but to keep cold?" If it were warm and sunny outside, it would further emphasize the message, and that could be my juxtaposition.

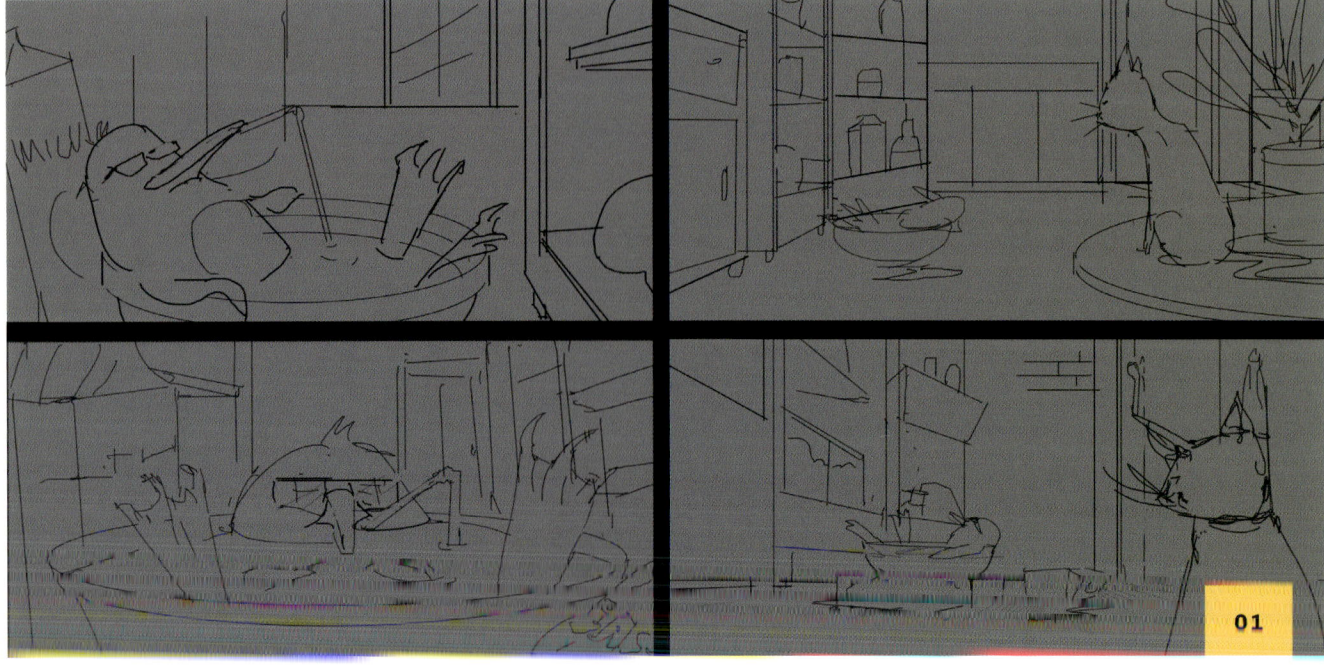

// The initial thumbnails don't need to look like works of art

Checking my inspiration folders helps to kick-start my ideas and ensure I don't end up creating something that's already been produced lots of times before. I usually divide my ideas folder into different aspects of inspiration: style of rendering, shapes, lighting, or ideas for specific characters. For this image, I'd like to recall the cartoon style of animated movies such as *Madagascar* and *Over the Hedge*.

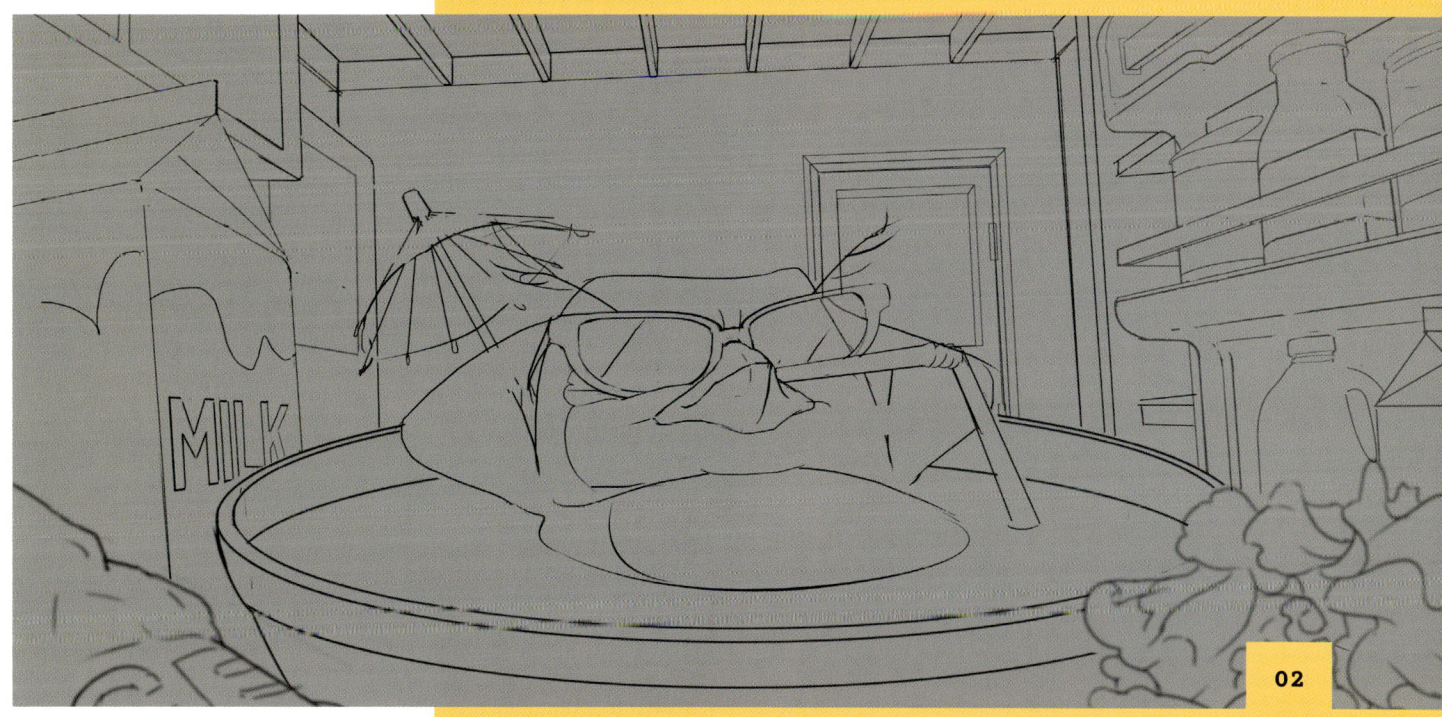

02

// **After selecting the right thumbnail, it's time to make it look pretty**

>01 Ideas and thumbnails

I've recently taken to doing very rough line drawings instead of full-blown painterly thumbnails. It's a lot easier to use lines rather than shape-masses in certain types of scenes because you're not "filling in" – it's just "bam," there's four walls, and you're done!

I explore the penguin idea I mentioned earlier. I think about having a cat looming nearby to contrast with the tranquility, as an alternative to showing the sunny and warm exterior. I'm just throwing down ideas at this stage; it's not intended for beauty.

>02 Final line drawing

I will be working digitally, so I now take my chosen thumbnail and resize it to full resolution. I choose this thumbnail because I feel it shows the penguin more prominently; plus, while drawing it, I found myself chuckling a little, which is a good sign. I like the idea that he could be drinking from the cold milk that he's bathing in.

For the final drawing, I lower the transparency of the rough lines and start drawing the detailed version on a new layer over the top. If you are working using traditional media you can mimic this step by simply drawing your initial sketch lightly and working on top of it or by tracing it onto what will be your final piece. There are still one or two elements of this final drawing that are a little rough, but they'll be cleaned up even more when it comes to the painting phase.

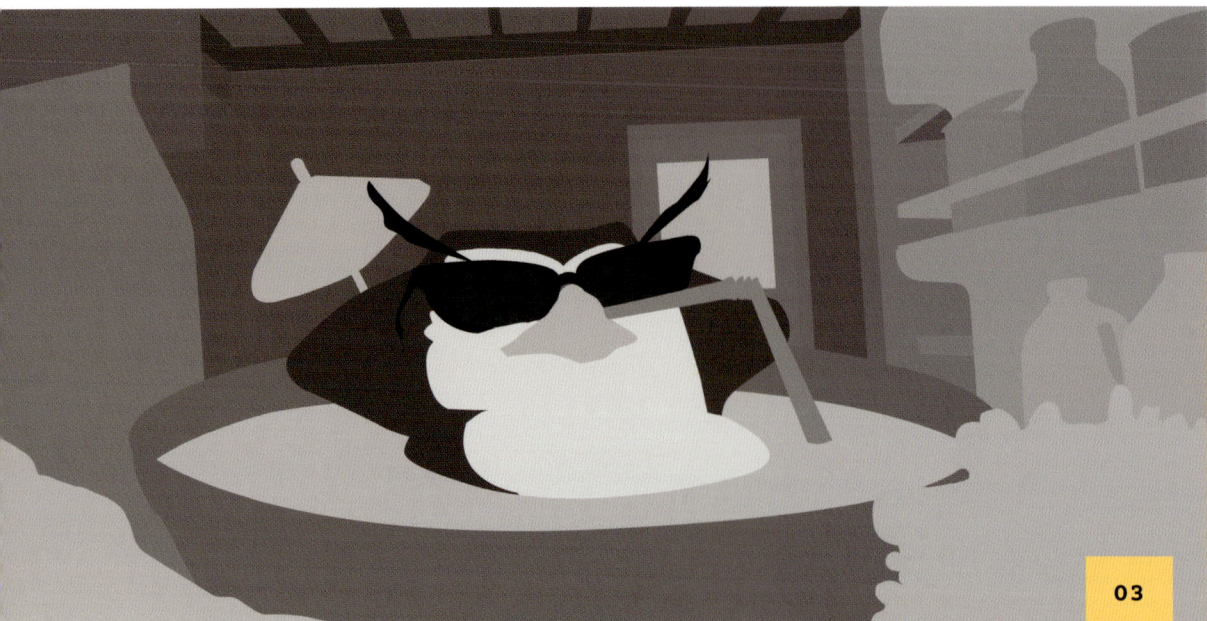

// I need to get a quick grasp on shapes and values

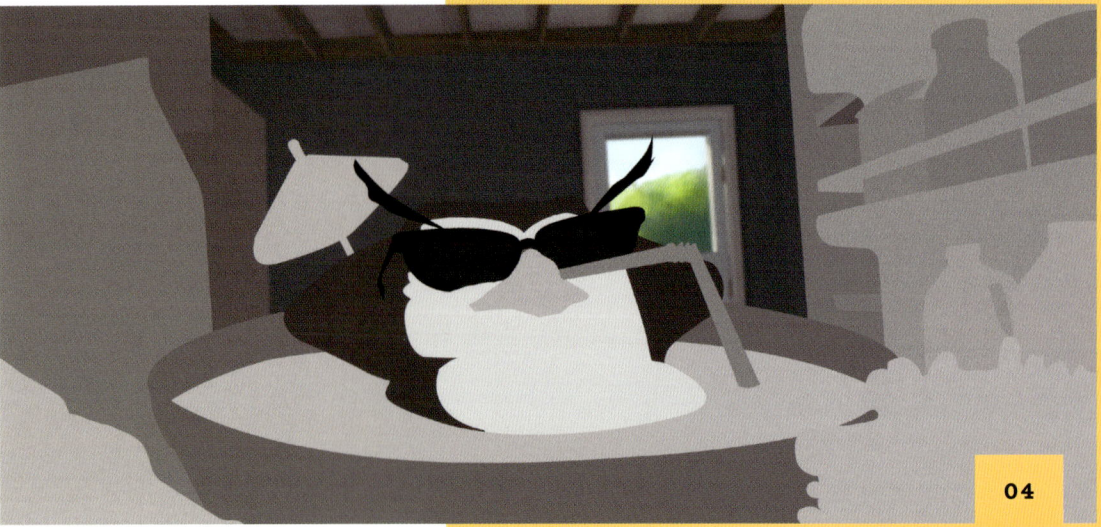

// Next I want to establish the lighting tone

>03 Basic shape block-in

At this stage I'm keen to see how it all comes together in some kind of value structure by blocking in the basic shapes. This stage brings the line drawing to life a little, so we can begin to visualize how it might be rendered. As I'm working digitally, I place everything on its own layer as the different elements will eventually be used as clipping masks and further separated into layer folders for better organization. If you are working traditionally, layers and clipping masks are of course not an option, but you can still spend this early part of the process defining the silhouette of the major elements in your scene. This isn't the only or necessarily the best way to proceed after the rough drawing; you could also create color thumbnails if you wanted to experiment with palette first.

>04 Setting the initial tone

Seeing as I'm starting from pure lines and shapes, I need to establish a light source or initial starting tone to then act as

"I decided early on that this piece would have a strong depth of field effect, as such a scene would if shot with a real camera"

a reference for the rest of the scene – not just in terms of light, but also in rendering style. This is how I tend to work: nail down one area, then step back and imagine that finish applied to the rest of the drawing, like a sort of testing ground. In this case I set the secondary, ambient light source from the exterior, which will inform the rest of the scene.

>05 Initial application of the tone

I go from background to foreground to see how the lighting from the first light source will affect objects in the room. As a general rule I keep the background unobtrusive, so that I don't lose focus on the penguin. I decided early on that this piece would have a strong depth of field effect, as such a scene would if shot with a real camera; we're very close to our subject and so this would create a small area of tight focus, and any objects behind or in front would be blurry. It's quick and kind of "Photoshoppy," but very effective at making things look real.

>06 Quick dip back into research

Usually I'd gather all my research from the internet and put it in a folder at the beginning, but this was quite different because there are no photos from inside a fridge! However, everyone has a fridge, so off I go to mine to take a few photos from inside. For this scene, I also grab one or two household items rather than using the internet. The bowl is one example – I just hold it and check out how the reflections and highlights work.

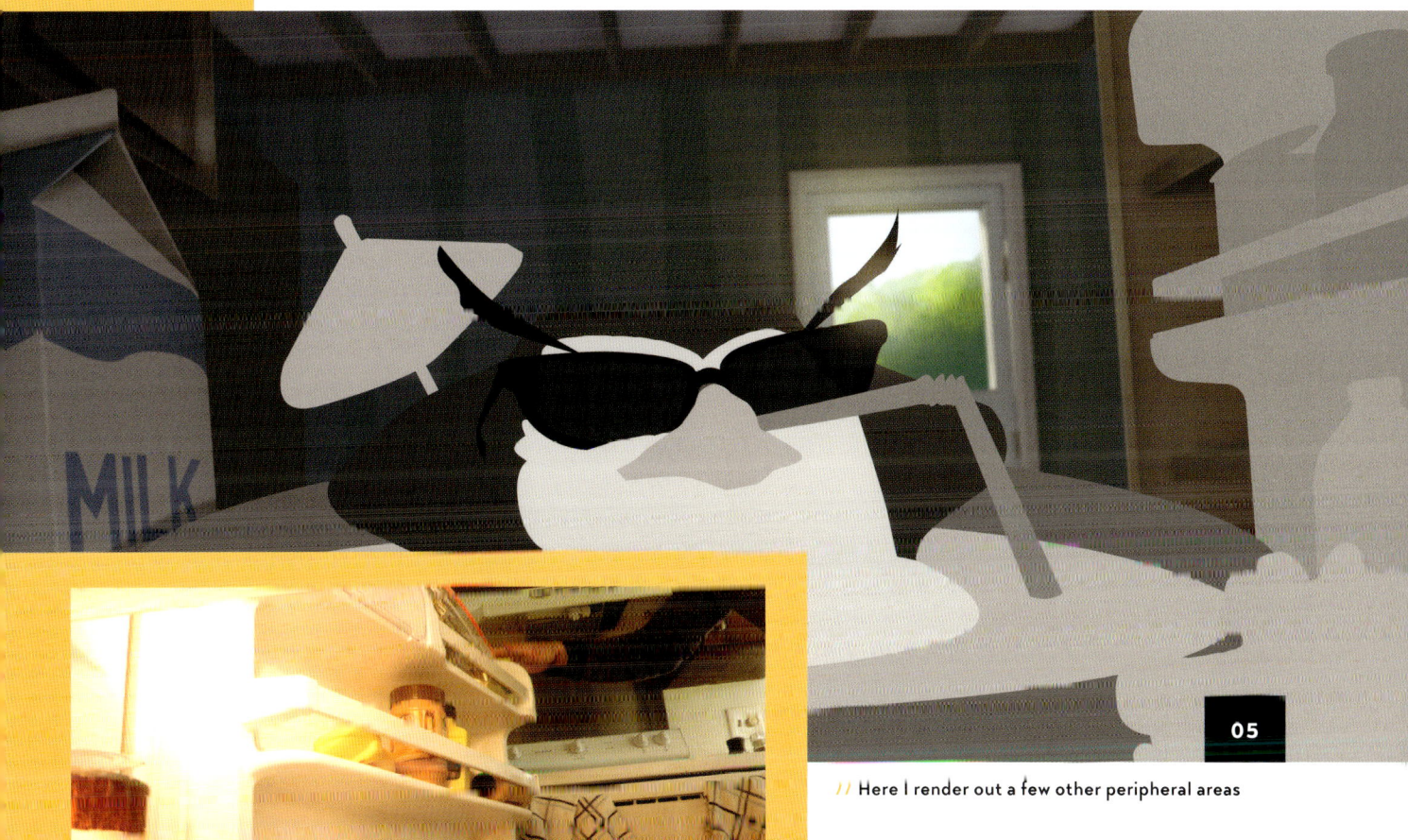

// Here I render out a few other peripheral areas

// So, I had to put my camera in the fridge for this shot...

// PRO TIP

Workflow is key

There have been times when I have an idea, maybe even a thumbnail, but absolutely no idea how to physically create the scene. Should I start by painting large shapes? Should I keep it all on one layer? Should I use a hundred layers? Should I work from background to foreground? It can be overwhelming. I class this is a technique-related area of art, not so much a fundamental, and techniques are almost always looked down upon as a focus compared to fundamentals. But you might have a great understanding of light and not know how to translate that into an image efficiently. I suggest you watch as many painting tutorials as you can and pay attention to the order in which the artists paint their scene. Try out a few things and see if you can borrow, in full or in part, someone else's workflow to then create your own. If you don't have an efficient workflow, you can feel stumped before you've even started!

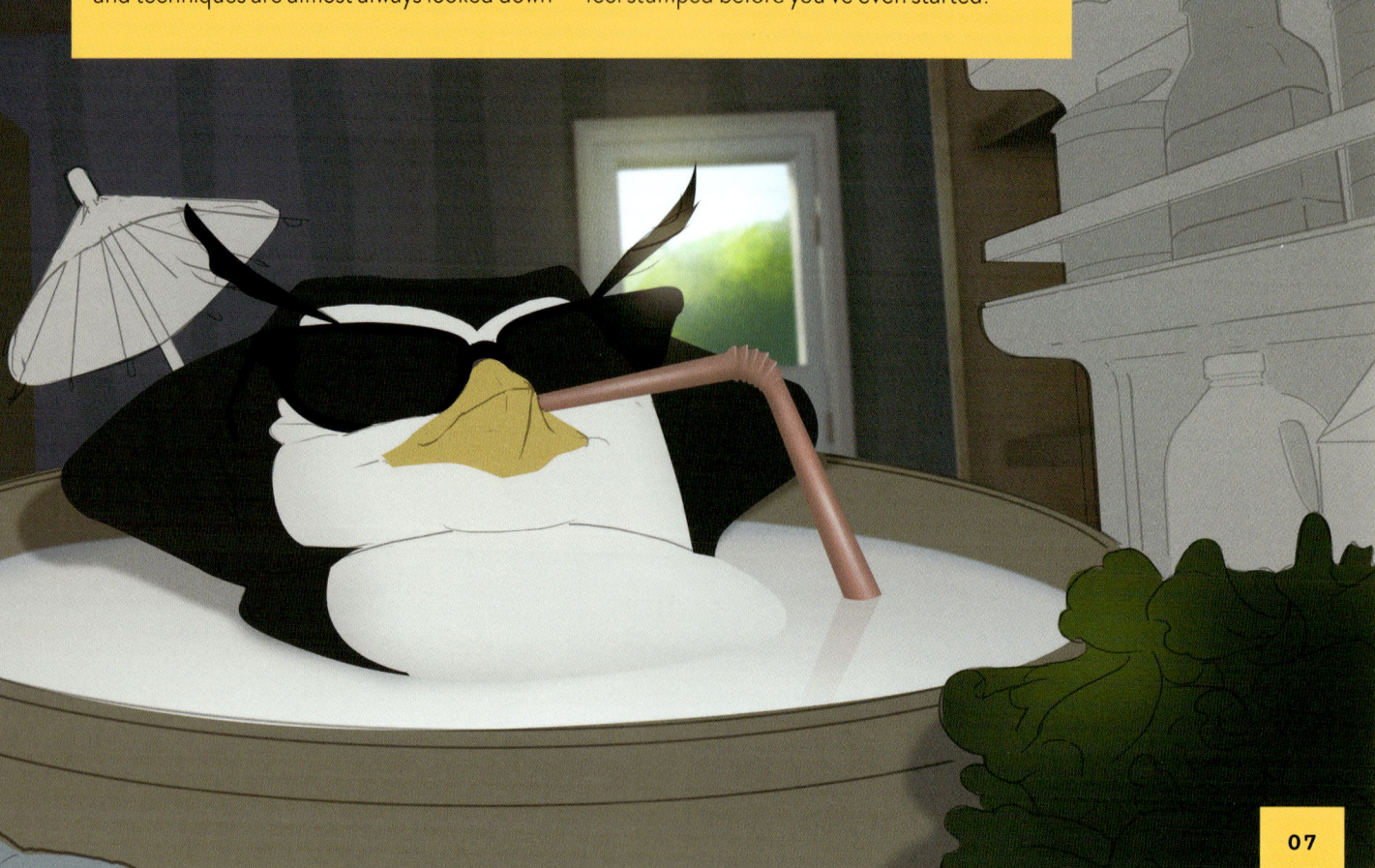

07

// Let's take a minute to reflect on rendering style

>07 A word on style

So far I've almost fully established my "style," but not quite. I have style in terms of overall shape and simplification of design, but now I'm getting into surfaces in the actual rendering. My goal is to make things look almost like a 3D animated movie, so that means that the lighting and surfaces need to look as real as I'm able to get them. This is why the previous step was so important in terms of seeing how objects look in real life. I'm about to move on to the fridge, and the prospect is a little daunting – but armed with my reference photos, I get to work.

>08 Initial lighting pass for the fridge

The lighting needs to be considered carefully in order to make sure it conveys the temperature and tranquility I am aiming for. In Photoshop, I switch on my lines for the fridge and its contents, and discern between bottom-facing planes and side-facing places. We won't see any top-facing planes, as they're above the angle of view in this scene. I have a

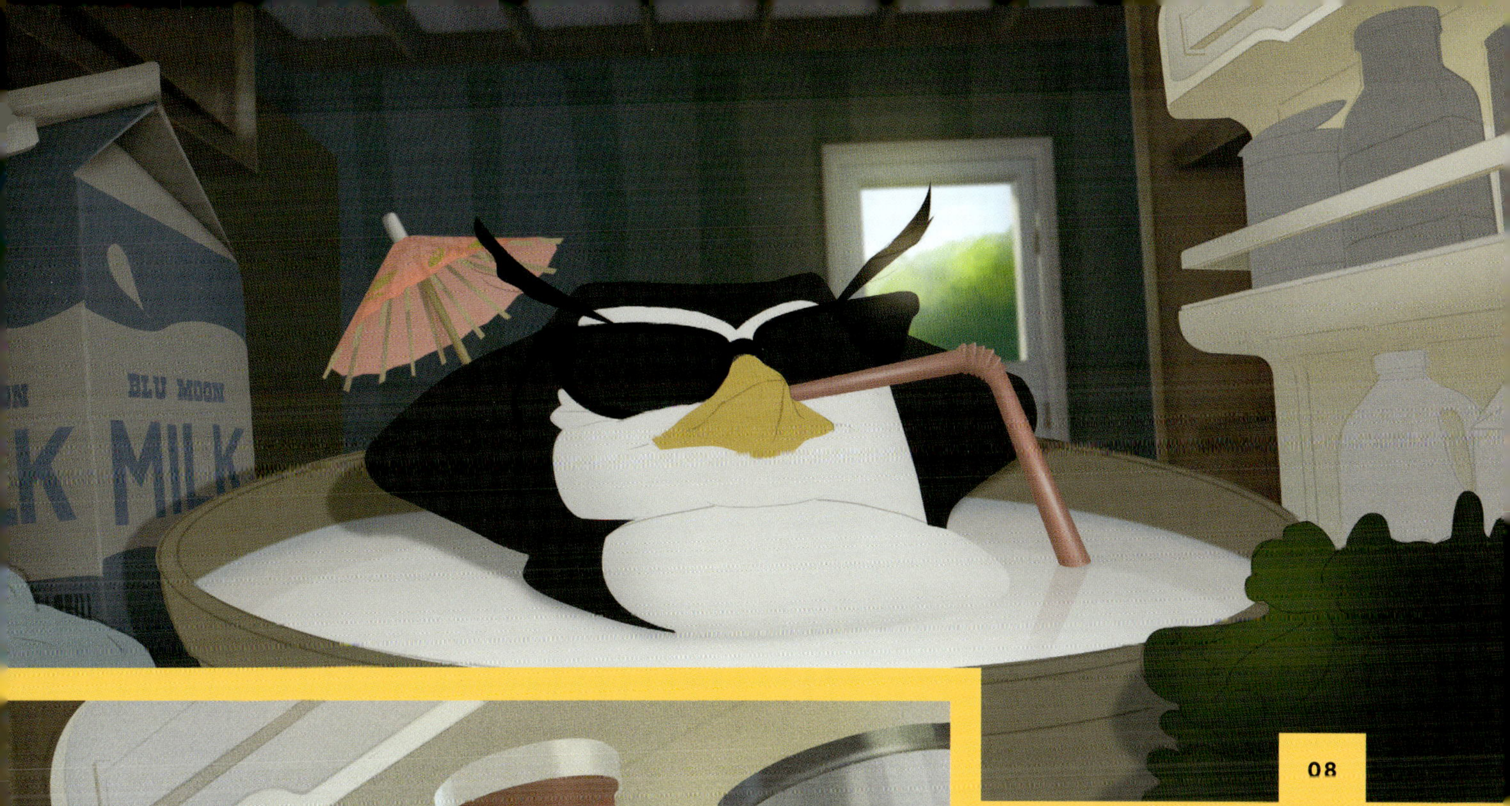

// I begin with a simple lighting block-in

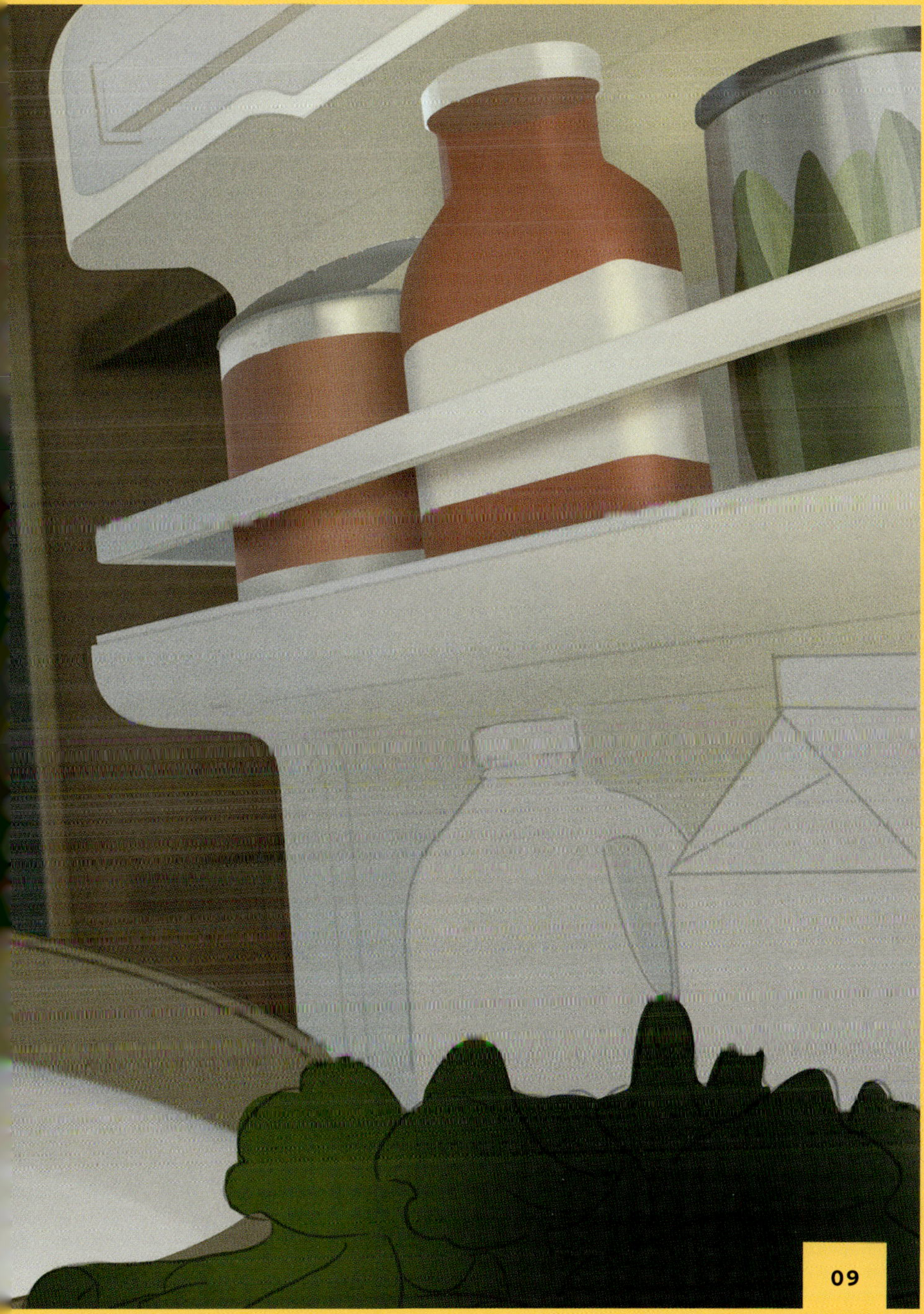

09

// Rendering objects helps to sell realism

light source that's strong but has a fairly sharp fall-off, so the lighting will be bright and warm at one end and get cooler as the fridge door moves away from the light source and towards the ambient bluish cool of the rest of the room. This interplay of warms and cools has been on my mind since the initial conception of the idea, and I'll be balancing these two elements throughout to emphasize the "warm" light playing on the penguin, albeit cold in temperature!

>09 Fridge objects

I turn to the internet for some reference here. The objects in the fridge are quite common, so easy to find. Once I've drawn them behind that little plastic bar and added some shadows, reflection, and surface quality, I further set in place the rendering style and see the image come to life. Remembering what I learned about glossy surfaces, I make sure I roughly imagine that each shiny object would reflect the orange glow of the open fridge door. There needs to be a contrasting, cooler light coming from the opposite angle. Once I combine these two lighting elements on reflective objects, they really start to pop.

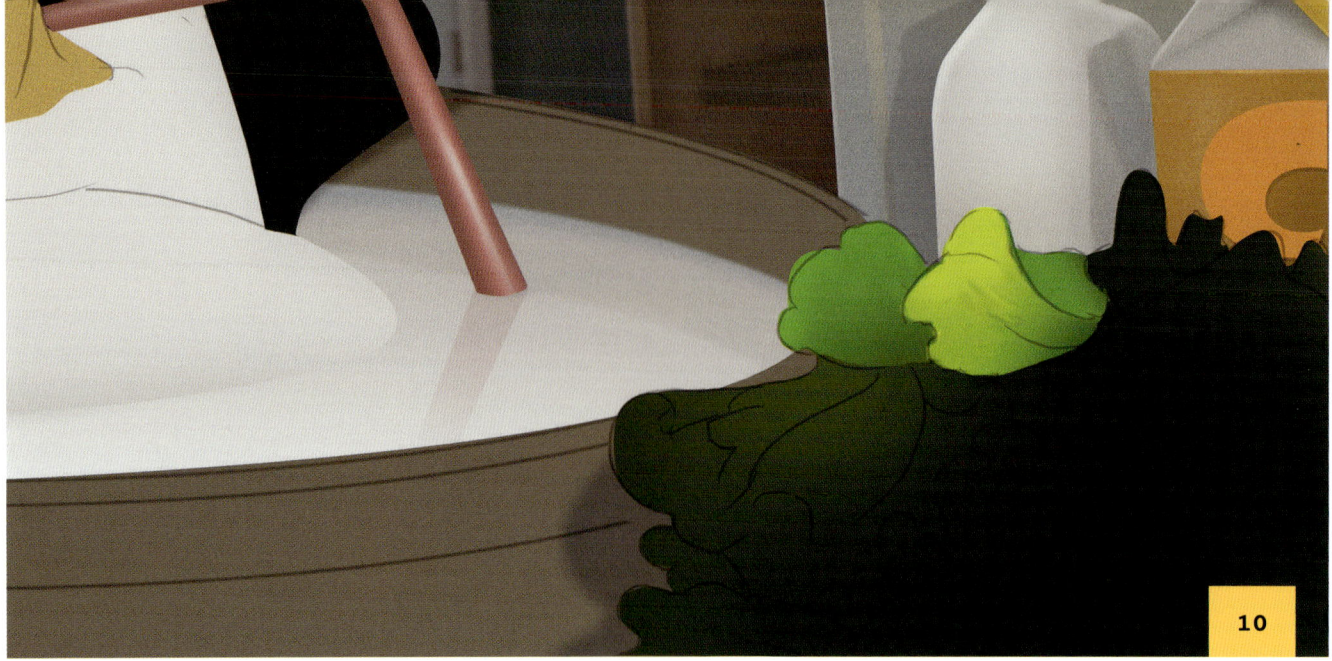

// Sometimes you have to know when to quit!

>10 Abandoning the lettuce

After finishing up the fridge, I move on to the foreground elements, namely the lettuce. I always knew that this would give me some problems, as it's a very detailed and organic object. Once upon a time, I'd have forced myself through the painting of the whole lettuce before realizing it wasn't working, but from experience I know there's a strong chance of it looking less than great after attempting just a small area of it. So here's where we weigh things up. Do we really want to take risks with something that's so close to the camera? If so much as one leaf is out of place, the illustration will be ruined. I therefore decide that it's time for a change of plan.

>11 Triumph of the watermelon

After the addition of the cocktail umbrella, perhaps subconsciously, I decide to change the lettuce to something more tropical-looking: a watermelon. I start off with the basic shape and, when adding the markings, am careful to observe its three-dimensionality. A bit of shadow is added, and then some surface depressions so it's not just purely smooth. Next I add a bit of bumpy texture, and finally, perhaps the trickiest stage, I add some reflective highlights both for the fridge's reflection and the cool light reflection from the opposite side. Success!

>12 Everything but the penguin

After the watermelon comes the ice, the bowl, and the milk. I want to save the penguin for last, as I know he'll be the main focus and biggest challenge. As I mentioned before, the bowl is based on an actual bowl I own, which is useful in figuring out how light interacts with it. Now, in terms of story and narrative, it's worth mentioning the details: I create my own basic milk brand for the carton, and also decide to add some cereal in the milk. All these little elements bring the piece to life and add extra dimensions to it.

>13 First penguin pass

It is very hard to make clearly readable forms on pure white and pure black local colors. A lot of the penguin's clarity is going to come from his beak and sunglasses. I'm very pleased once I have

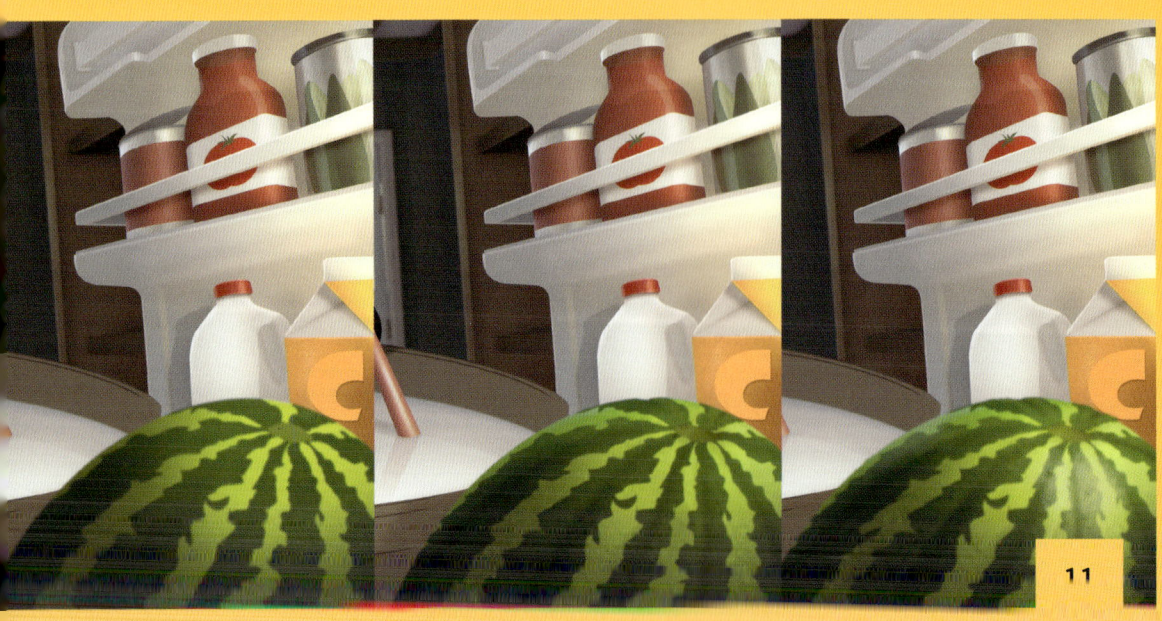

// Here's a step-by-step process for a typical object

"All these little elements bring the piece to life and add extra dimensions to it"

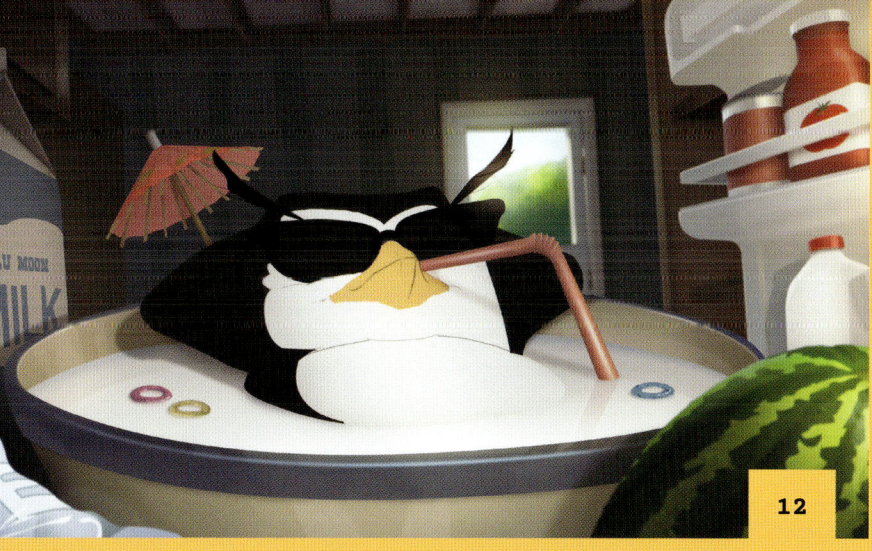

12

// Now almost all the peripheral elements are taken care of

shaded his beak in, as it really brings him to life. I like the very slight smile he's wearing. Again, I use some subtle secondary blue light to define his silhouette. Technically there is not an obvious source for this, but we can get away with some artistic license here as it's implied throughout the scene.

>14 Finishing up
I finish up the final background objects, which I keep discreet so they don't jar with our character (because there is some overlap). I also finish up Mr. Penguin, which is quite tricky; penguins appear to have fur rather than feathers, so I play up the furry element rather than trying to make his coat look like real feathers. The sunglasses give just the right amount of reflection to show the fridge interior. (I do try giving them a brighter reflection, for emphasis, but it just looks fake, as though they themselves are a light source.) Finally, I add an extra pop of cool blue to the upper left and warm orange to the bottom right, and there we have it – one tranquil penguin!

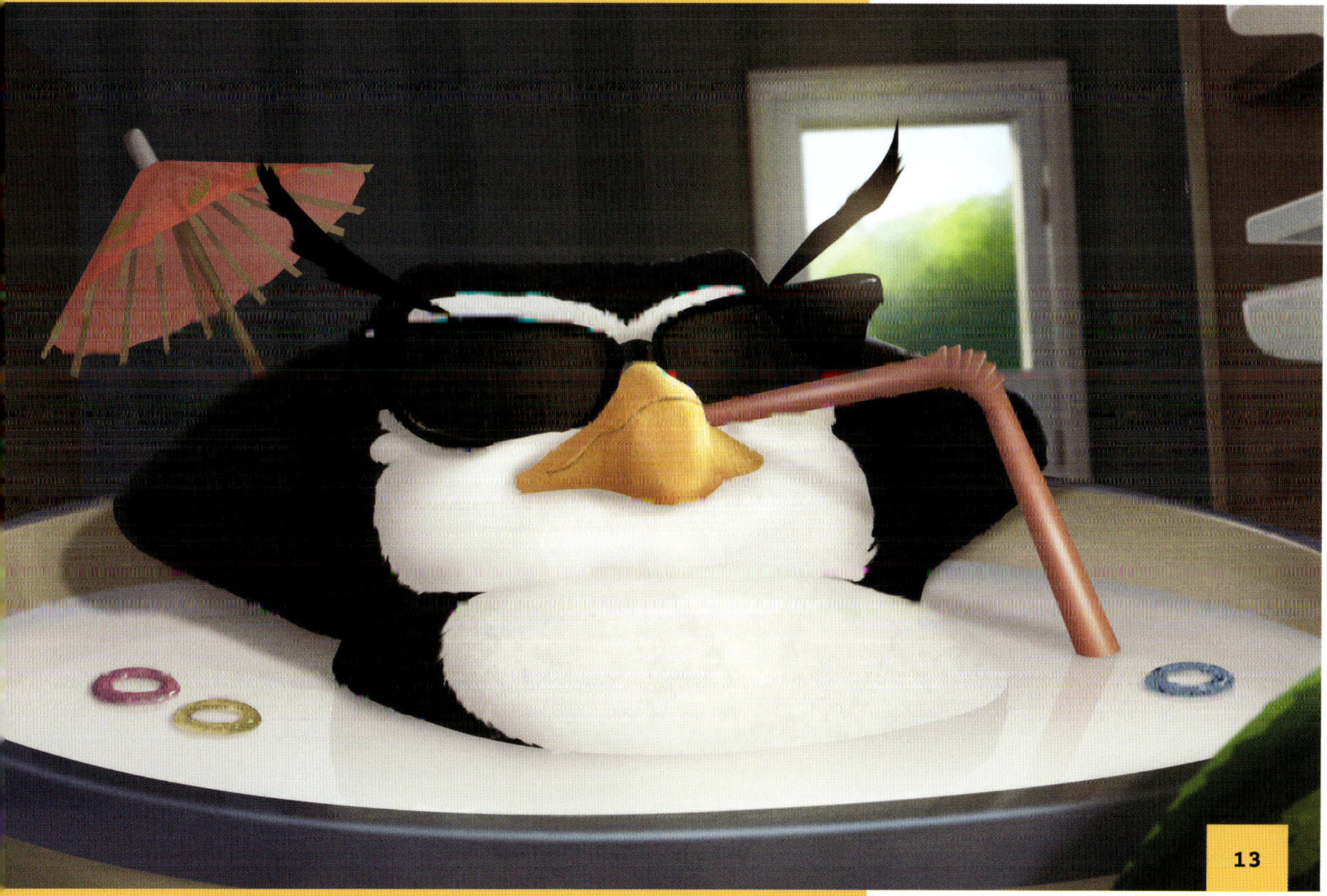

13

// Time to get stuck into the main focal area

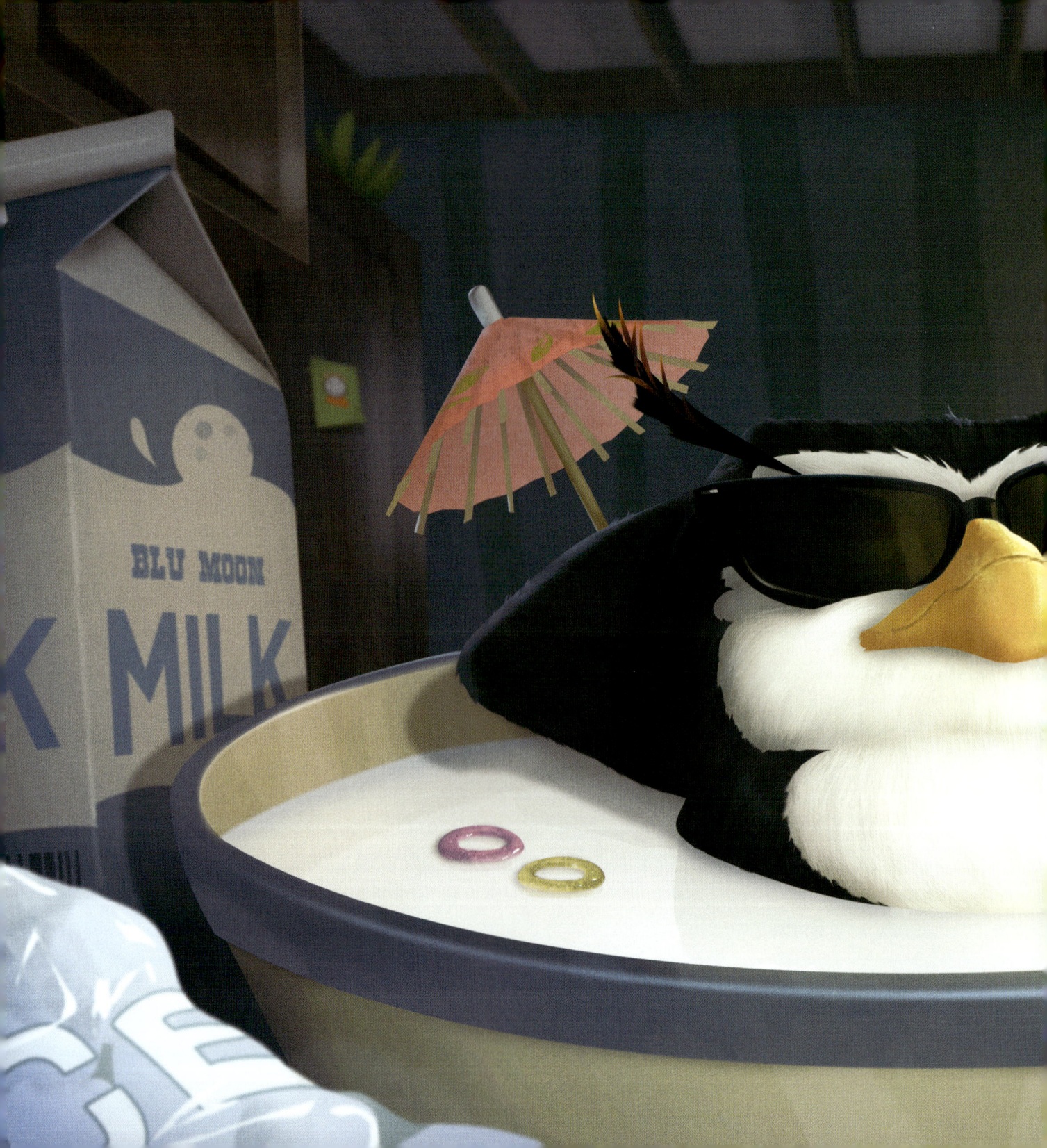

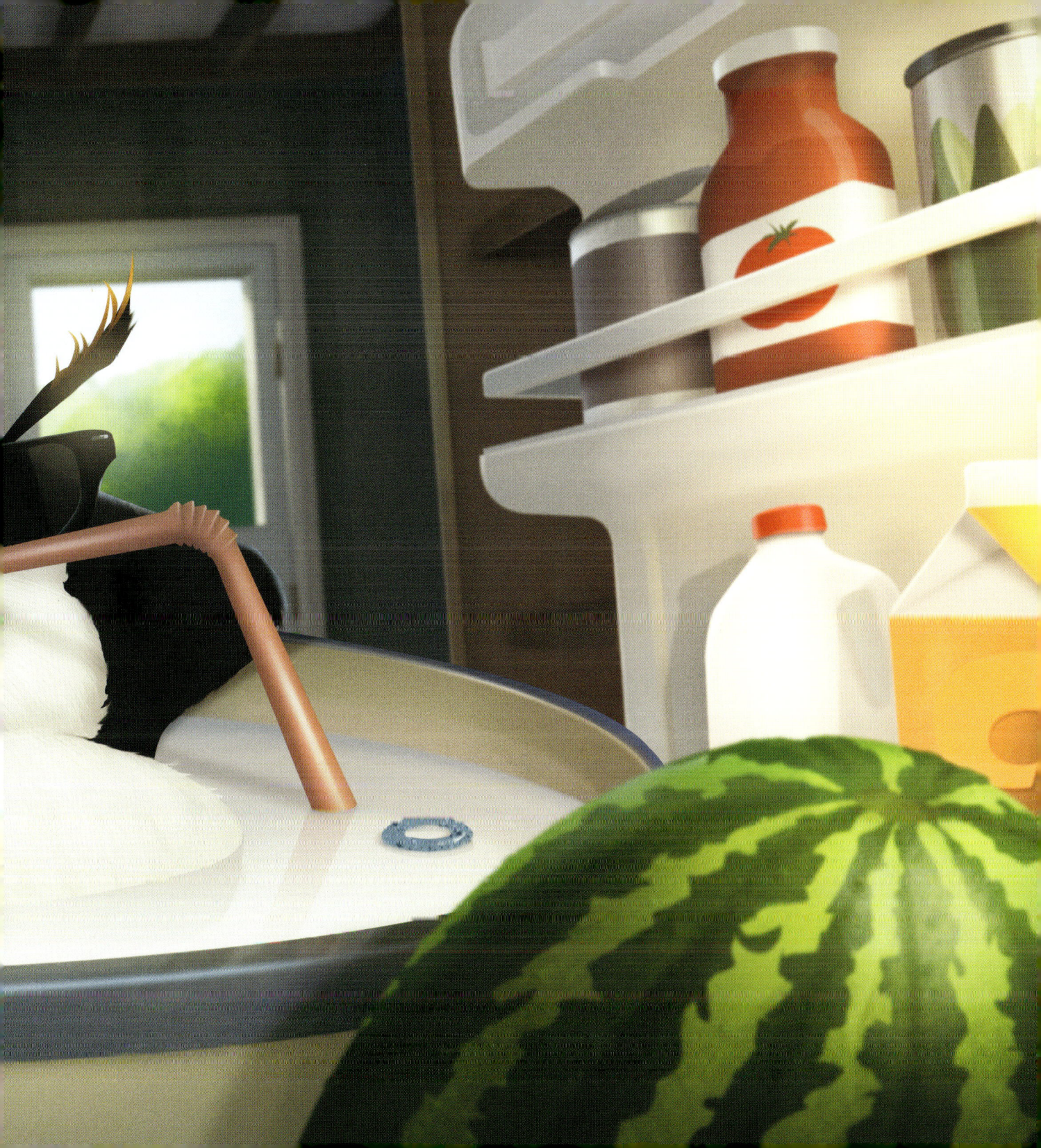

Brun Croes | www.bruncroes.com

Triumph

In this tutorial I will focus on developing an idea based around the theme of "triumph." This is a very broad subject which can be interpreted in several different ways. We will take a look at how elements such as lighting, color, composition, and symbolism can help us tell a story and achieve an interesting image. Through the course of the following steps I will show you how to go from an initial sketch to a final rendered illustration.

>01 Thumbnails

Before I begin my illustration, I need some inspiration. At this point I pick up my sketchbook and take a good look at the briefing. In this case, I am looking for a feeling of triumph or victory: perhaps someone finally finding that one object he desires so much, or a brave warrior finally defeating a troublesome enemy.

I always try to keep my thumbnails as loose as possible so that I can produce a lot of them in a small amount of time. They don't need to look good, but they should successfully translate my ideas onto paper quickly.

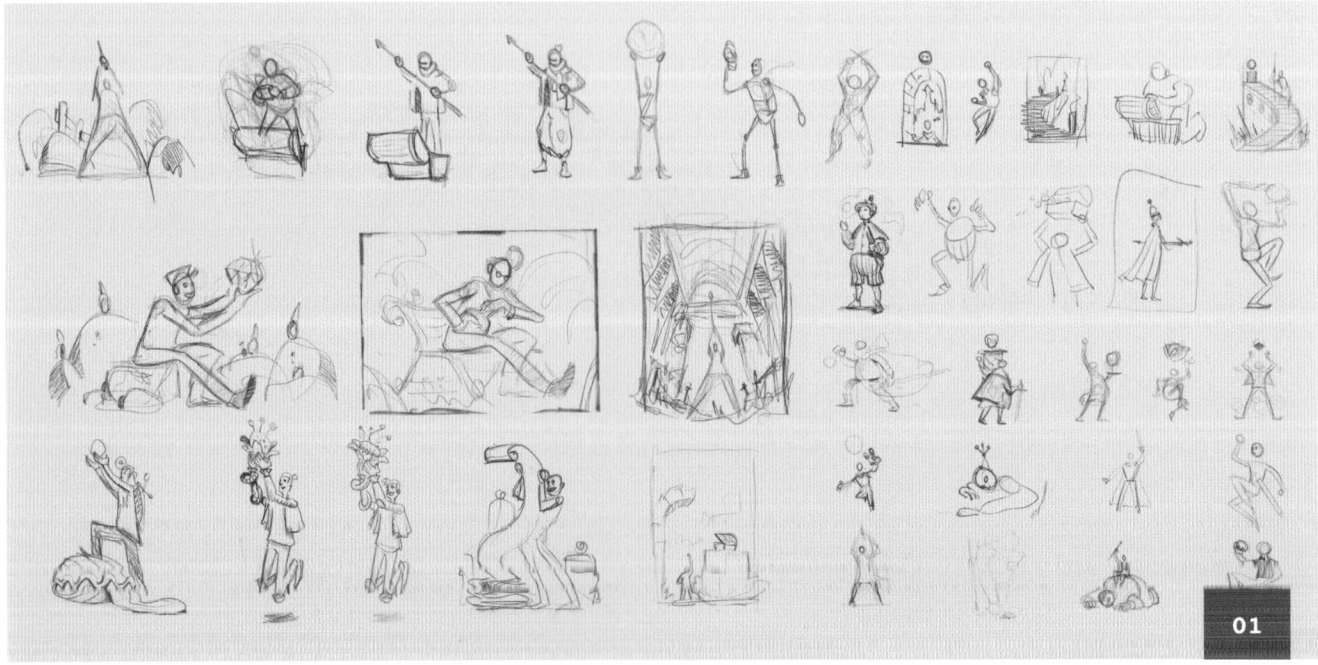

01

// An overview of all the thumbnails sketched before starting the final piece

"I always try to keep my thumbnails as loose as possible so that I can produce a lot of them in a small amount of time"

>02 Blocking in the shapes

I decide on one of the thumbnails: a man sitting on some stones, holding a gem or a piece of gold in his hands (image 02a). For this step I make some quick shapes based on the lines from the chosen thumbnail. I create shapes for the stones, ground, and character (image 02b). It's really helpful to see the general silhouette of the painting at this stage in order to check how the image will read; the silhouette already helps to tell a story. We can clearly see a figure sitting on some rocks, holding something raised above his head, as if to illustrate that he has finally achieved his goal.

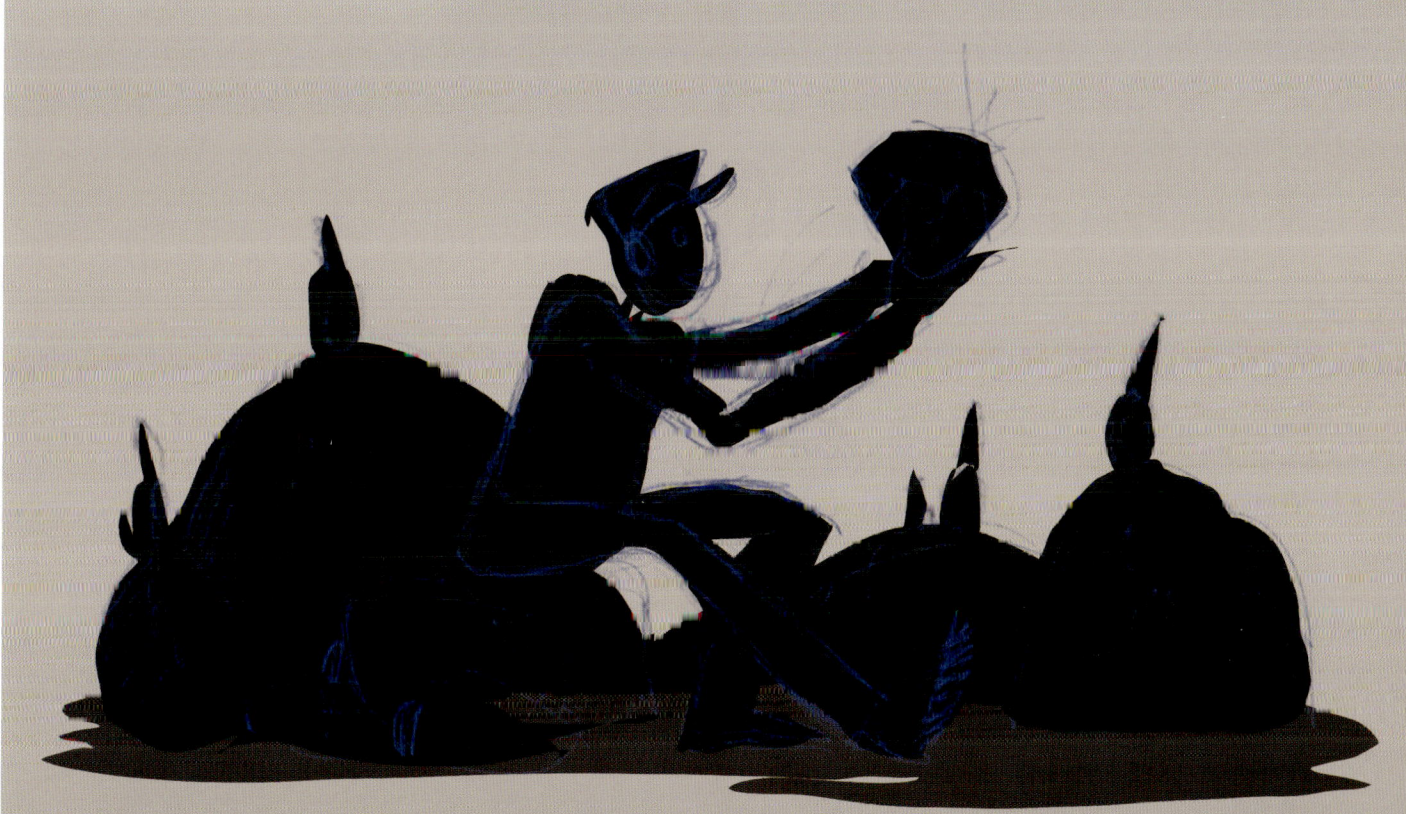

02a

// The expanded thumbnail sketch without blocking in

02b

// Blocking in shapes will help define the silhouette, and a good silhouette will help to sell the story behind the image

>03 Photobashing and smudging

I like using tricks to quickly generate ideas. Now that the silhouette and shapes are roughly in place, I fill them with blown-up pieces of photographs. You can use websites such as **www.textures.com** or the "usage rights" options on Google Image Search to find royalty-free images to use.

As I am working in Adobe Photoshop, I transform and stretch the photos within the silhouette shapes using clipping masks until I find something pleasing to my eye. Then, much like gazing at the clouds and finding images hidden in their shapes, I use the chaos of the textures to my advantage. I use a smudge tool to define some of the forms created by the photographs, and to make some unexpected new ones as well.

In addition to further defining the shapes, I create a new clipping mask layer, set its blending mode to Color Dodge, and use a soft round brush to bring in some light. To help illustrate the idea of someone holding up an object of value, I add extra light over the desirable object.

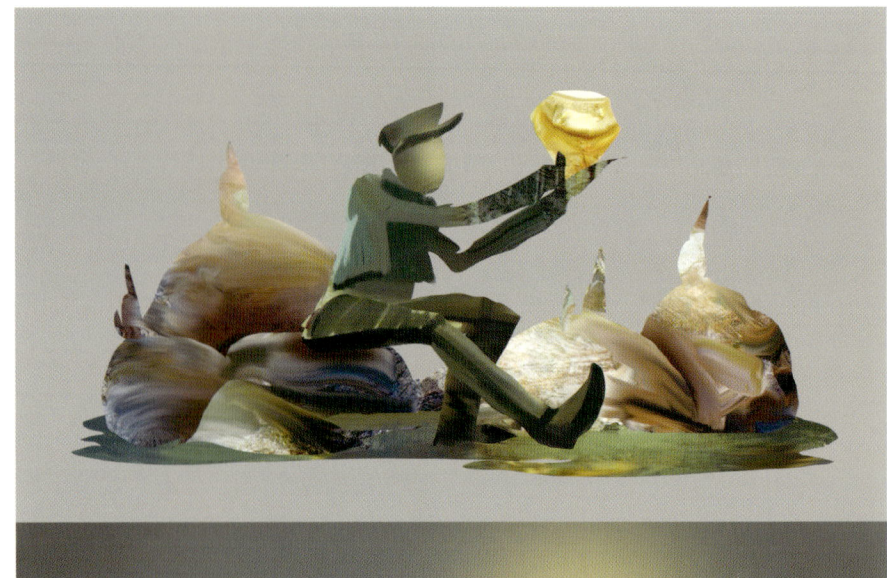

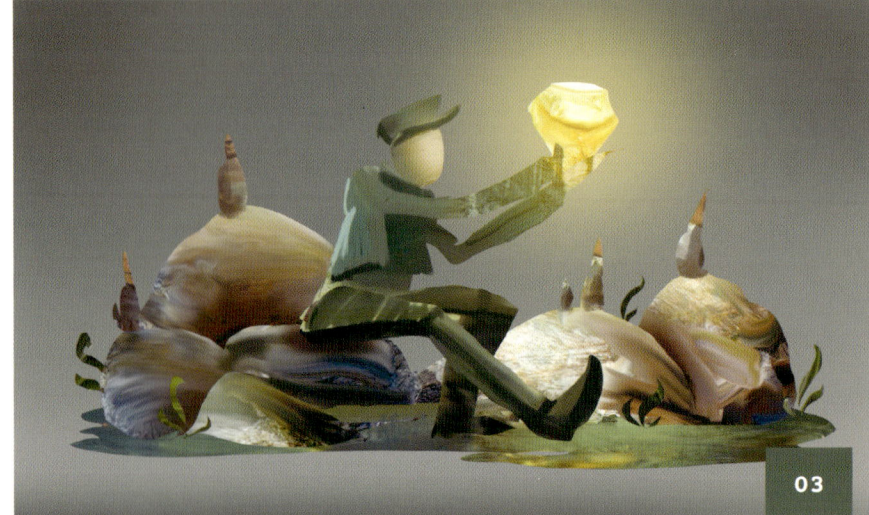

// By integrating photos within the previously created shapes, I can generate ideas quickly

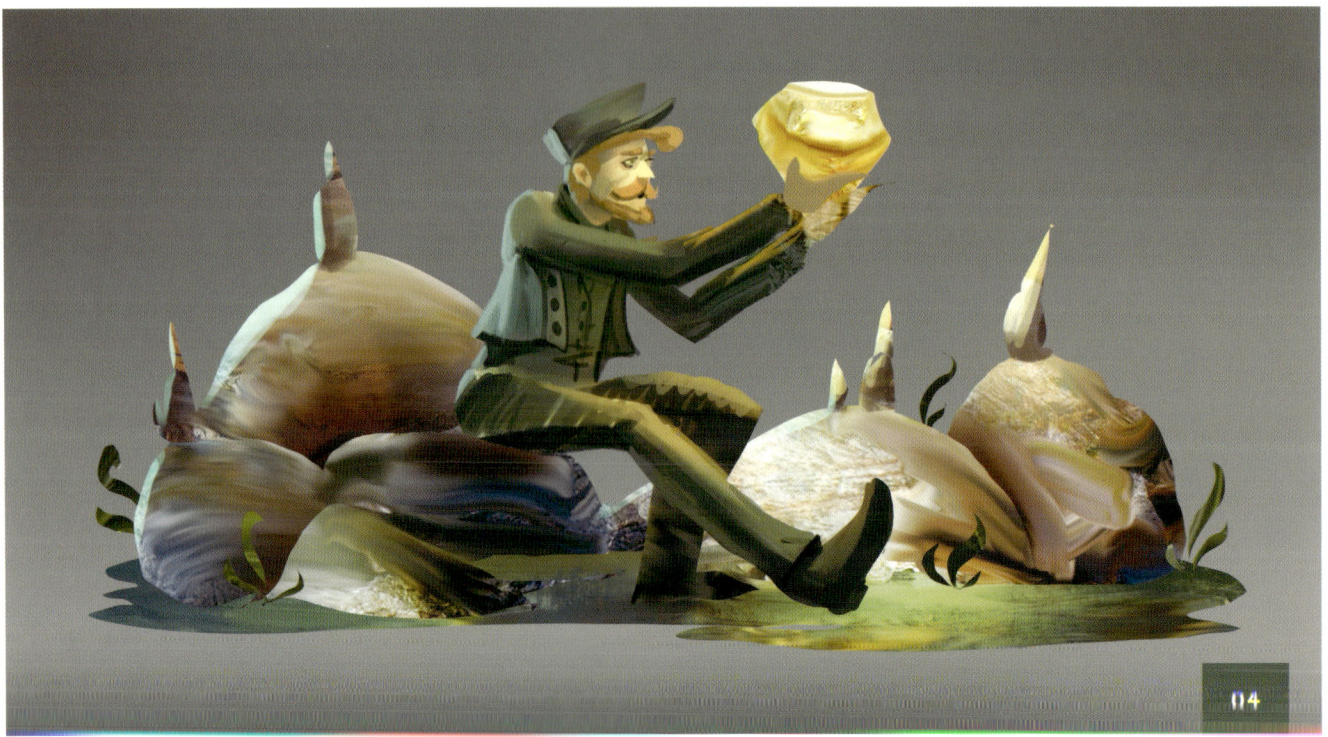

// Developing the character and scene

>04 Sketching

I start to sketch rough details for the character's face, posture, and clothes, and think about who he is. In my mind he starts to become a mine worker looking for gold or diamonds, and he's finally found his biggest treasure yet. The small spiked shapes on top of the stones could be small dwarves or birds looking on with awe. I feel like adding a rim light, too early to refine, but just as an idea to help me sell the atmosphere, and to give me an feel for where I'm going with the setting. I use a bright, cold greenish-blue to contrast with the warmth of the object in his hands, making the icon of triumph more distinct in the illustration

"The character and his discovery are now both clearly the main focus of the illustration"

>05 More light and shadow

Even though the design of the illustration needs a lot of work, I tend to get into lighting at an early stage. I use a slightly flattened round brush and a soft round brush to block in some more light using a warm color (from the precious stone); I use a colder color for the shadows. While doing this, I try to think about how to best place my brushstrokes: they can still be rough at this point, but their direction will help to guide the flow of the eye throughout this painting, and to define the forms of the objects in the scene.

To start tightening up the painting, I use a smudge tool to soften some of the brushstrokes already in place. I start cleaning up the rocks by painting over them with a slightly textured brush. To enhance the feeling of light radiating from the desirable object I make the background a bit darker, especially behind the character and his hands. This will help push the character to the foreground and demand attention from the eye. The character and his discovery are now both clearly the main focus of the illustration.

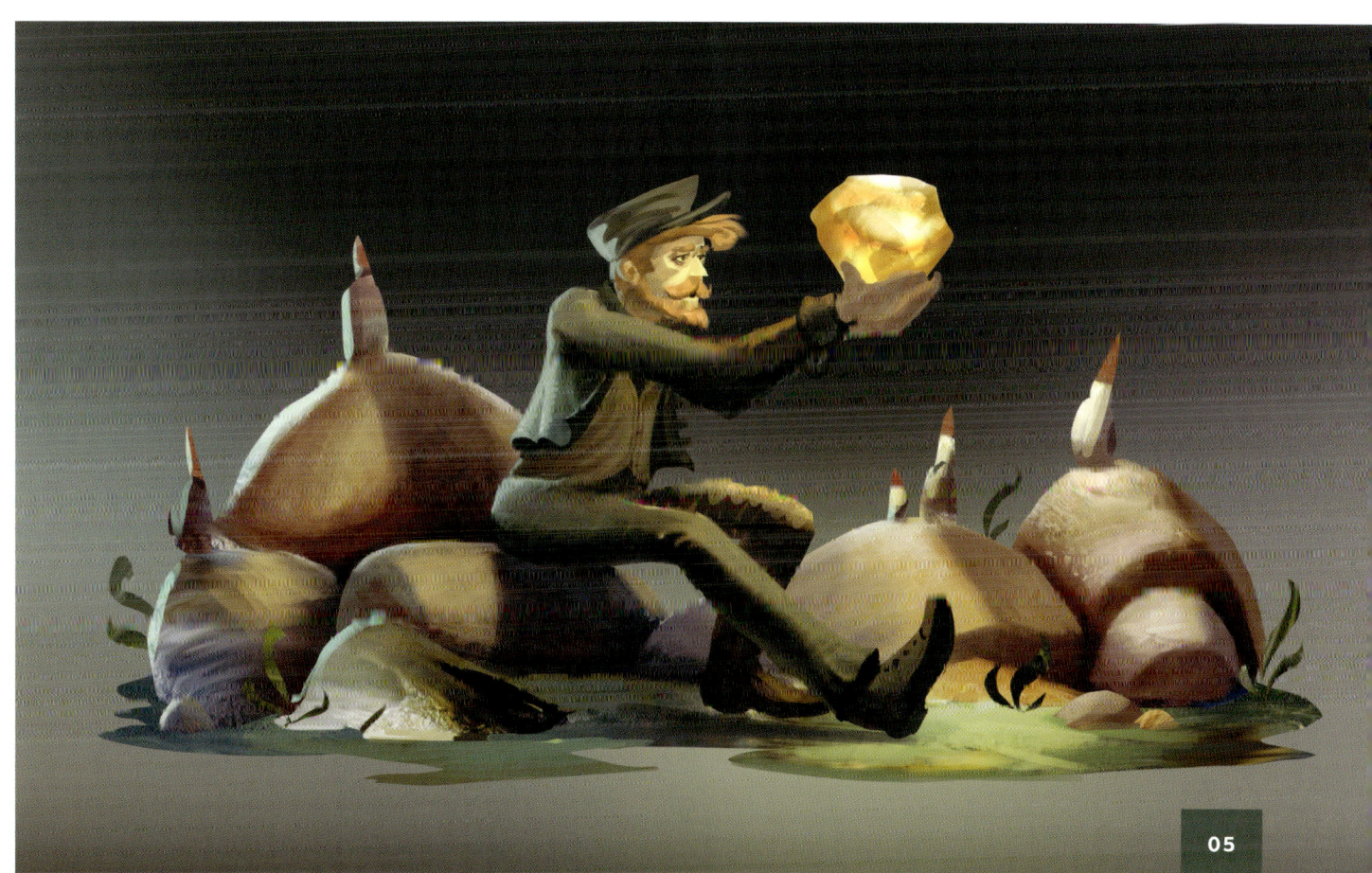

// Adding more atmosphere to the image

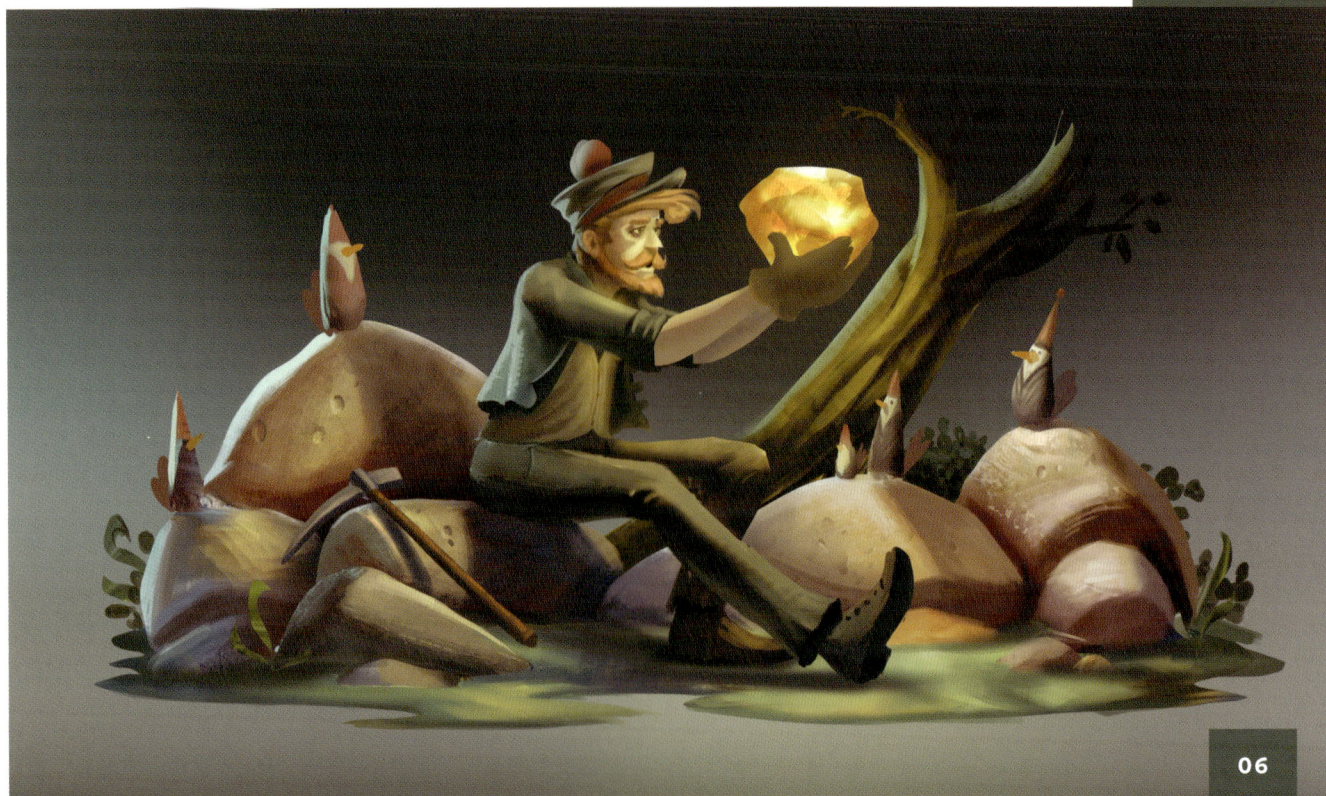

06

// Creating extra background objects

>06 Adding some life

I feel like the image is missing something, so I decide to give the surrounding a bit more life by adding a dead tree and some bushes. I'm careful not to overdo it, as I like how the emptiness of the environment helps to reflect the loneliness of the character and setting, which will heighten the significance of his achievement. I do this using the same techniques as before: making a shape for the tree, filling in with some textures, and using a smudge tool to define some shapes. The tree will also help to put the precious stone into a frame, as it is captured between the tree and the main figure.

To enhance the character's story, I give him a pickaxe that will help to sell his purpose, and also give his hat a bit more design, as if it belongs to some sort of work outfit. I adjust his posture to make his expression come alive more. I also start to give the birds on the stones a bit more life; I want them to be observing the scene mysteriously without distracting the viewer, so I make an effort to keep the detail on them as low as possible.

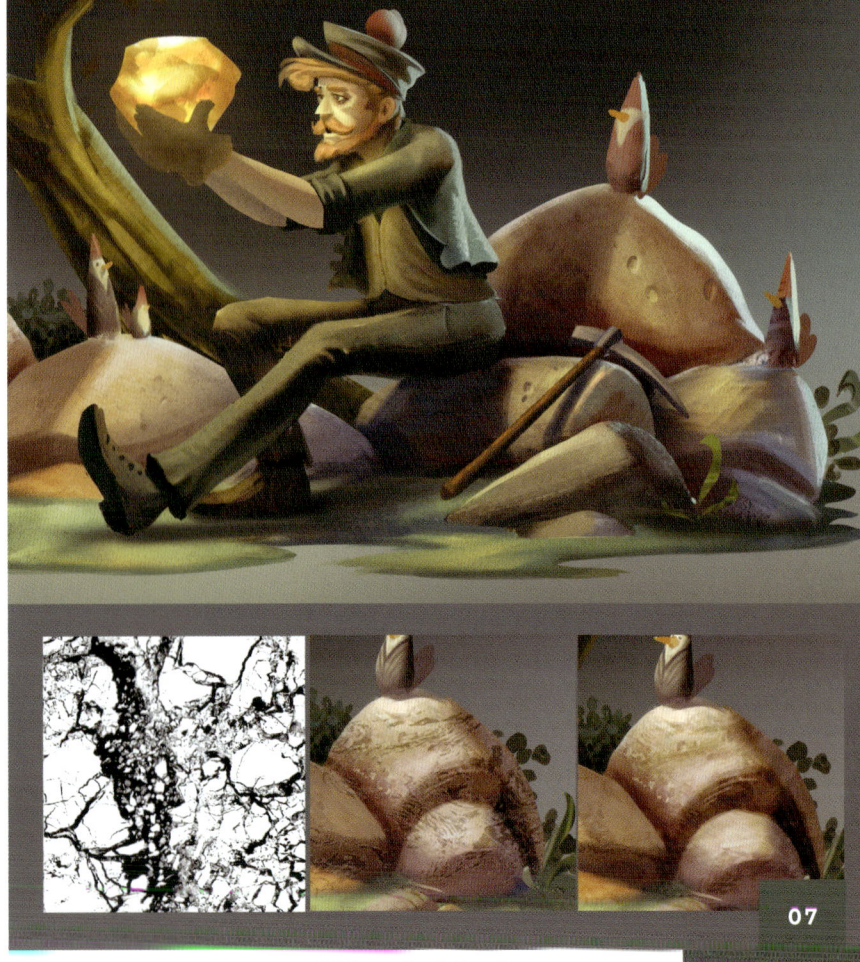

07

// Using textures to add more detail. Photo © mishan / Adobe Stock

>07 Bringing in more texture

I feel like I became a bit sidetracked by cleaning things up, so now I want to bring some texture back into the painting. It would be fitting if the stones have some sort of gold veins running through them. To achieve this effect, I find a heavily veined marble texture and introduce its vein elements into the environment shapes, filling the texture with a warm yellow color. I experiment with blending this until I find a satisfying outcome.

>08 Diamonds are forever

It's time to focus a bit more on the desirable object. What exactly is it going to be? I can't decide between a diamond or a piece of gold. Ultimately it doesn't really matter to the story, and we can leave it open to the viewer's opinion, but giving the object more definition is a good idea. I detail the rocks in the background with smaller versions of the precious stone: not only is this pleasing to the eye, it also helps to enhance the story of my character and his valuable discovery.

>09 The devil is in the details

Now it's time to add in some finer details: the "one-pixel brush details," as a friend of mine calls them. I take a very small brush, turn off the pressure sensitivity, and use it to add extra detail to elements such as the bobble on his hat and the fabric of his clothes. I add small stray hairs to their silhouettes to help sell their texture.

I add definition to the foliage between and behind the stones, as well as the ground, in a similar way. I like how this illustration is surrounded by a big gray emptiness, as if this piece of scenery was dropped somewhere. To help enhance this, I make some of the foreground come up a bit, like a carpet that hasn't been stretched completely. These little elements are a nice touch and give the eye some interesting details to search for when going over the whole image.

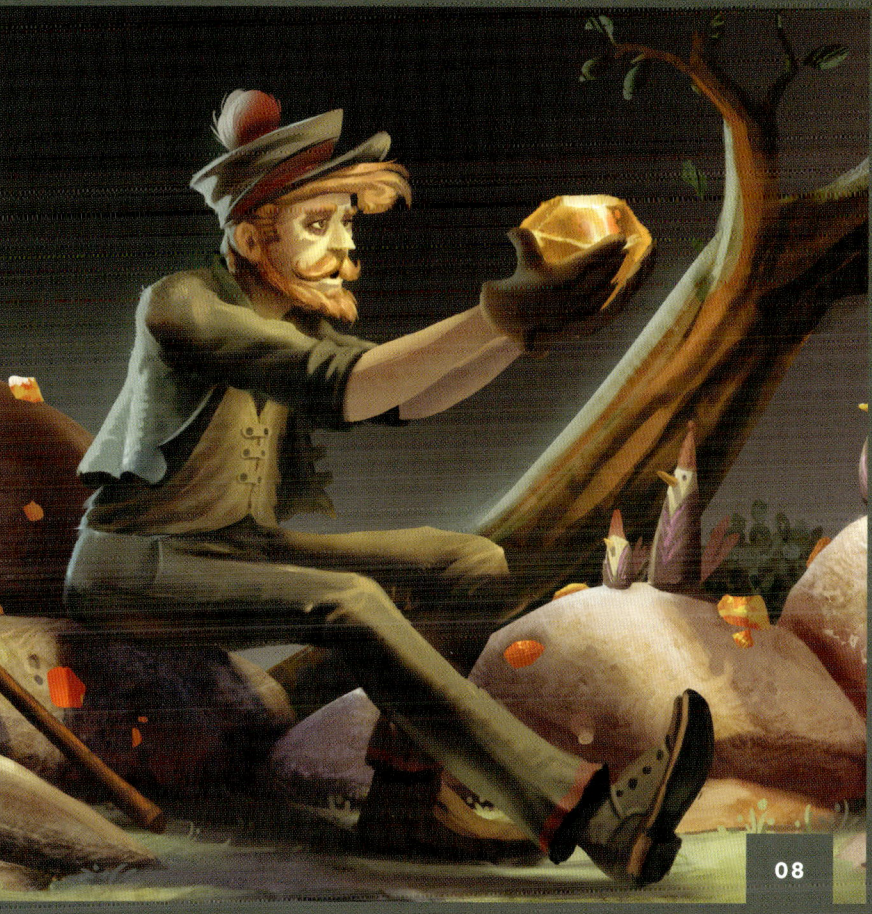

// The precious gems and minerals add interest and story

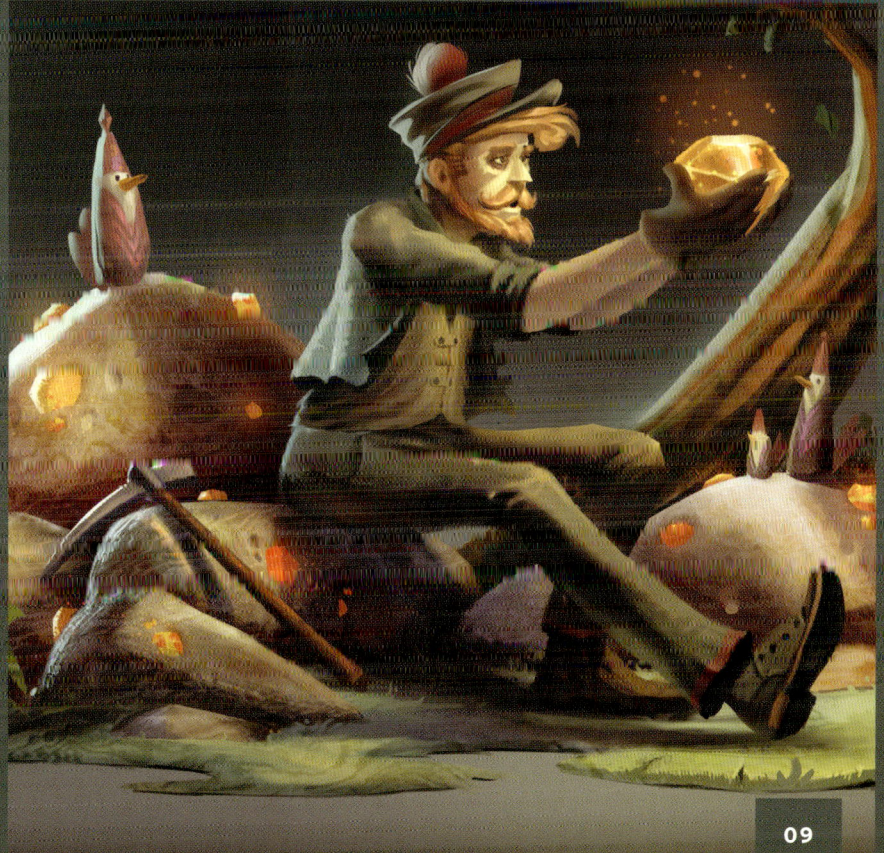

// Tiny details bring the environment and character to life

>10 Checking values with grayscale

I start adding more and more light into the scene to help me balance the image. I turn the painting into a grayscale image to check how the values are developing; this helps me to focus on light and dark spots and to keep an eye on the balance between them. It's a delicate process. I keep in mind where the focus should be in the image and try to set up the surrounding lights to reflect this. I want my character to pop out the most, so that's where I will place the most contrast.

>11 Costume design

I want to keep the design of the character's clothes as simple as possible; at best it serves as a basic uniform that gives a slight idea of a time period. I do however feel that it could use a bit more work. To maintain the simplicity I try to do this by altering its colors slightly. I use the red from his hat to create a rhythm of color throughout his clothes. The red is a nice contrast to his green uniform; it also helps to give the feeling of a different material on the inside of his jacket.

>12 Folds

The cloth on the character's arms is bothering me a bit; it doesn't feel natural, mainly because of how I have represented the folds in the cloth. I'm not someone who strives for realism, but I do like things to feel natural, so I look for a balance between something believable and a combination of brushstrokes that help direct the light over the folds. I do this by filling in some light and shadow parts while looking at references to guide me along the way. I also take the time to add more definition to other parts of his clothes, such as the inside of his jacket, which now has a more textured feel to it to help sell the material.

>13 Growing trees

After mirroring the image to see if there is anything that stands out as odd, I notice how the tree feels a bit out of place because I have left it untouched for a while. It's time to fix this. I use the bark of the tree to direct the eye

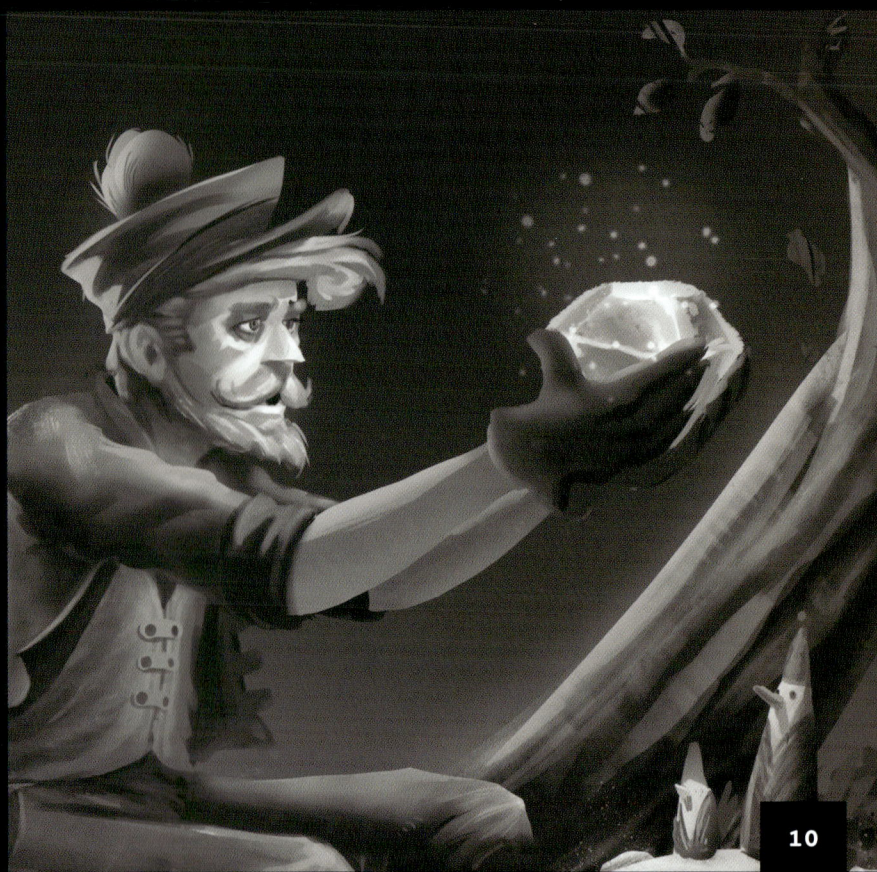

// Checking the image's values in grayscale

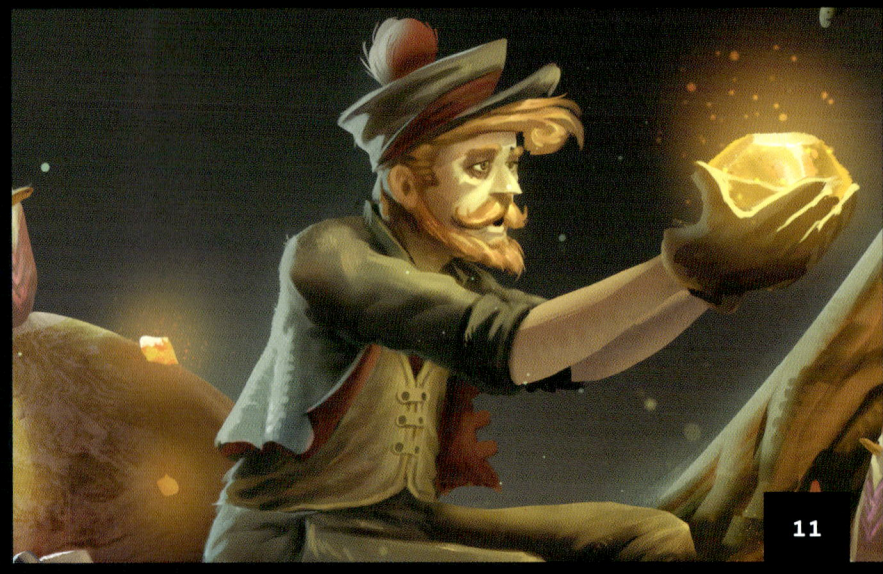

// Developing the miner's clothes further

more towards the character, which works well, especially in combination with the rim light. I make the tree's silhouette more interesting by giving it some dents and making it twist more around itself. I've also made its color less green, to distinguish itself more from the character and so not to detract attention from the focal area. Instead

I've made it a bit warmer, as if it picks up more of the light cast by the minerals.

>14 Face

I like where the character's face is going – he has a clear expression that floats between awe and fatigue, though I feel like he should be a bit older. I start adding in some more

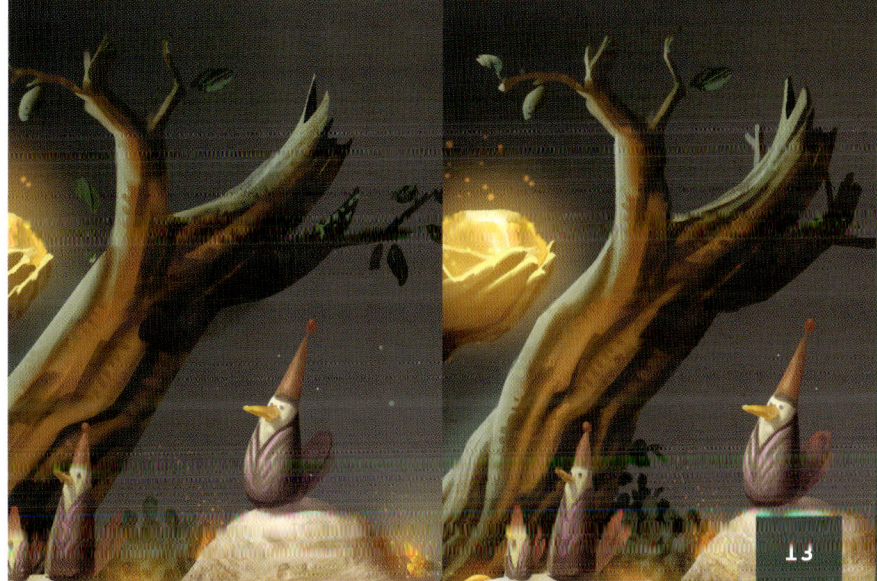

12

// It's not too late to tweak things that bother you

shadows, especially around his eyes and cheekbones, to enhance his slim face and age a bit. This helps to sell the fatigue in his face, heightening the drama and sense of achievement in the scene. I also add some extra detail and highlights into his hair at this point.

>15 Particles and bloom

I strengthen the image's final atmosphere in several ways. I start by adding some particles to the surroundings, mainly around the diamond/gold pieces sticking out of the stones, as if they have a magical radiance being emitted from them. I also add some general dust particles to the beam of cold light coming in from the left, which provides more depth. I also start adding some "bloom" lighting to the scene by creating a Screen layer behind all the shapes and adding in the cold rim light with a soft round brush to enhance their silhouettes. I also accentuate the gems with a warmer light.

Before calling the piece finished, I like to make a few final tweaks to my images. First I add some character to the piece by applying a texture above the painting. This mimics an effect that is more likely to be present in traditional art due to the surface that is worked on and the density of traditional tools. Then I check the balance of my colors and contrast, and adjust them if necessary. If you take a look at the final image on the next page you will see the miner bathed in the light of his triumphant discovery.

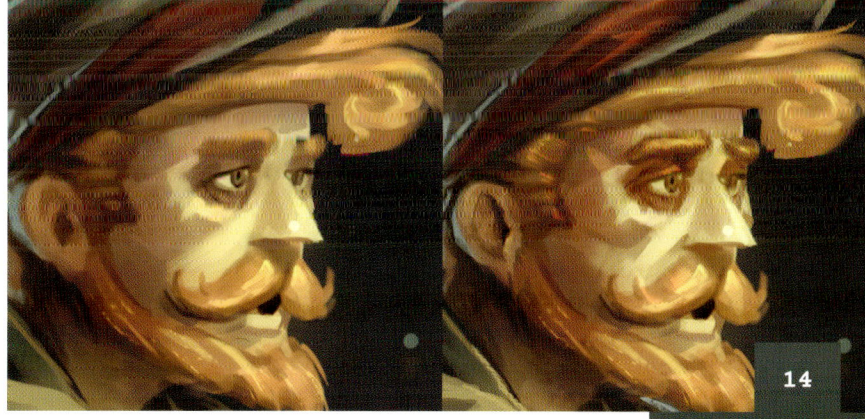

13

// Refining the tree to fit the rest of the image

14

// Developing the character through his age and expression

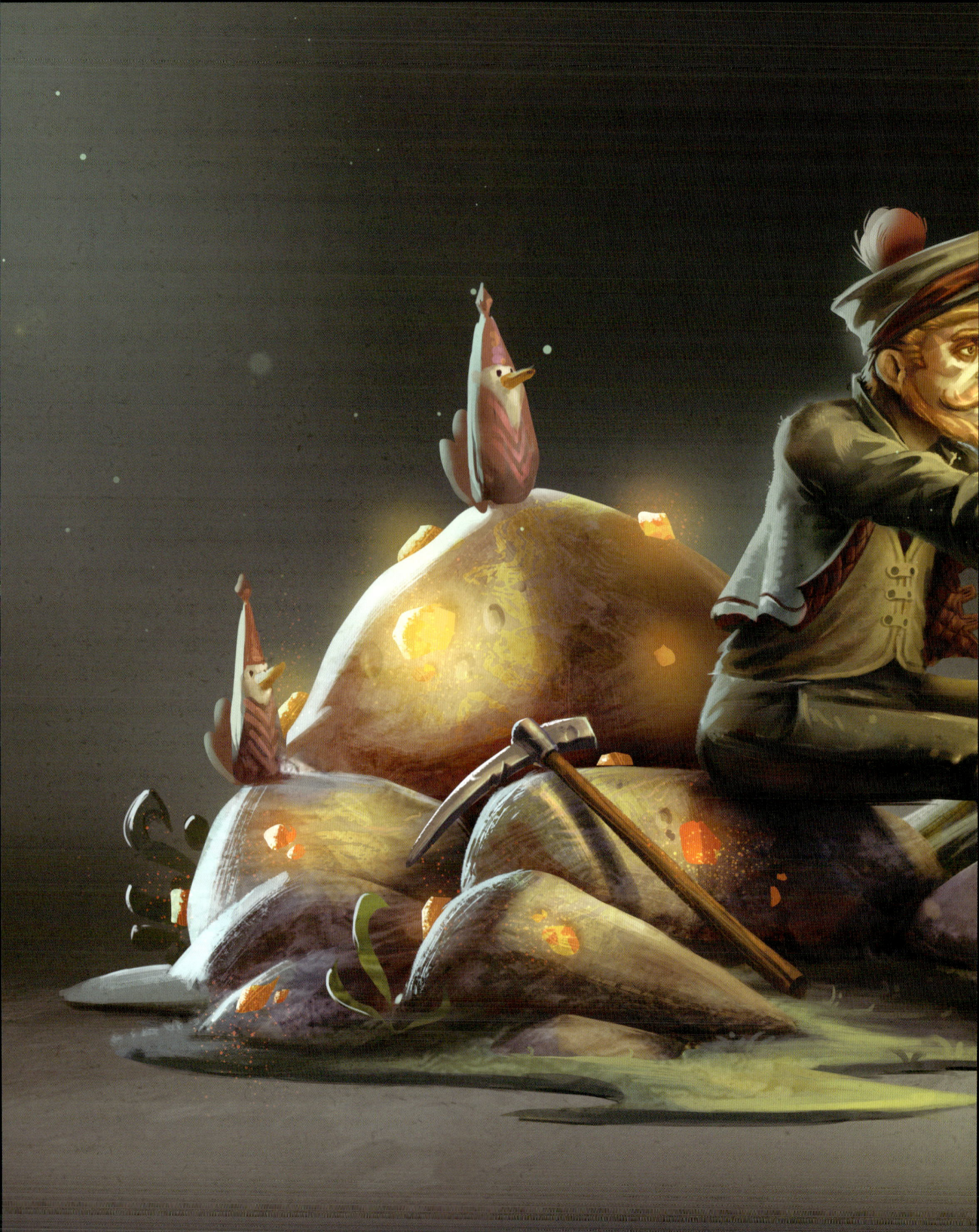

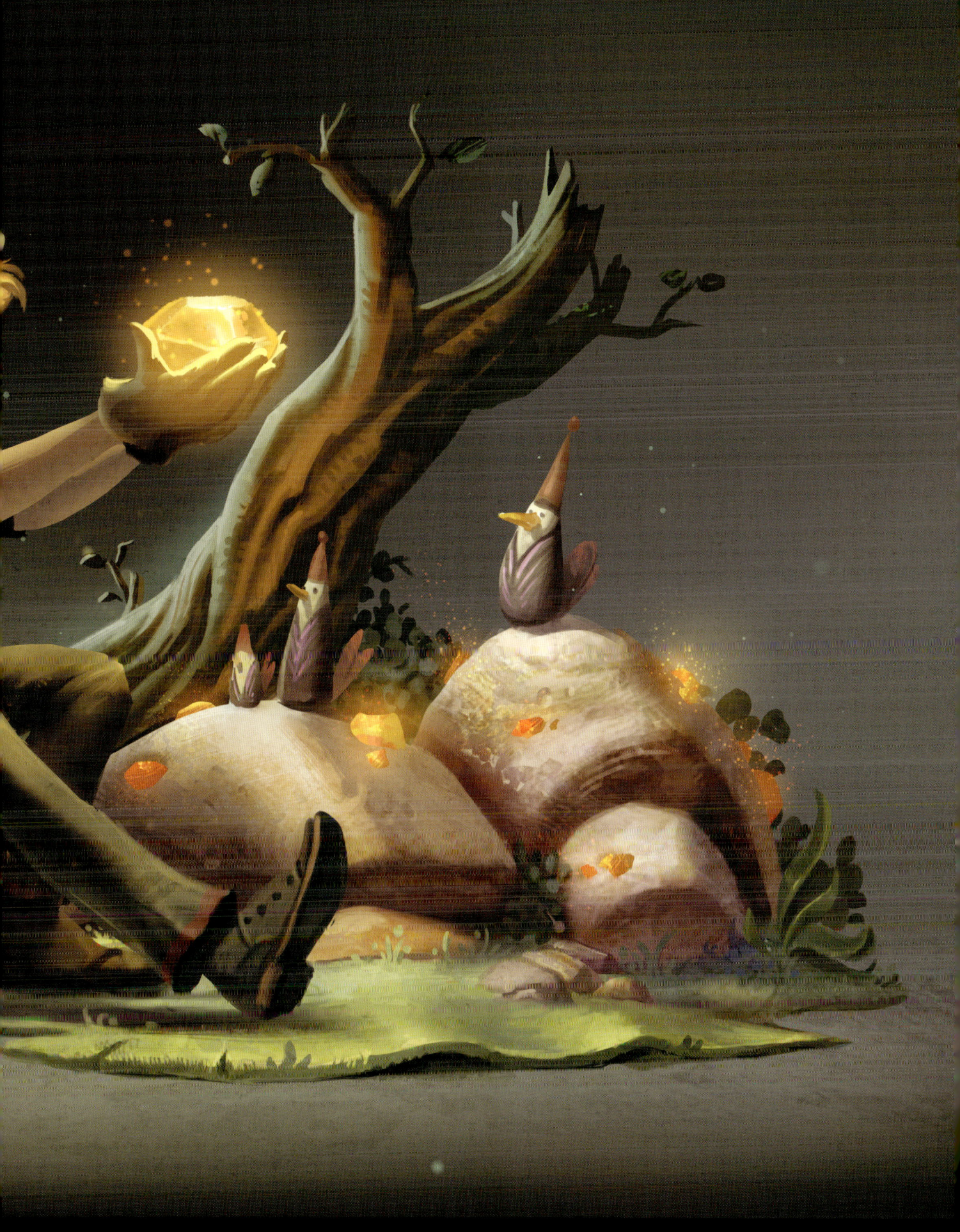

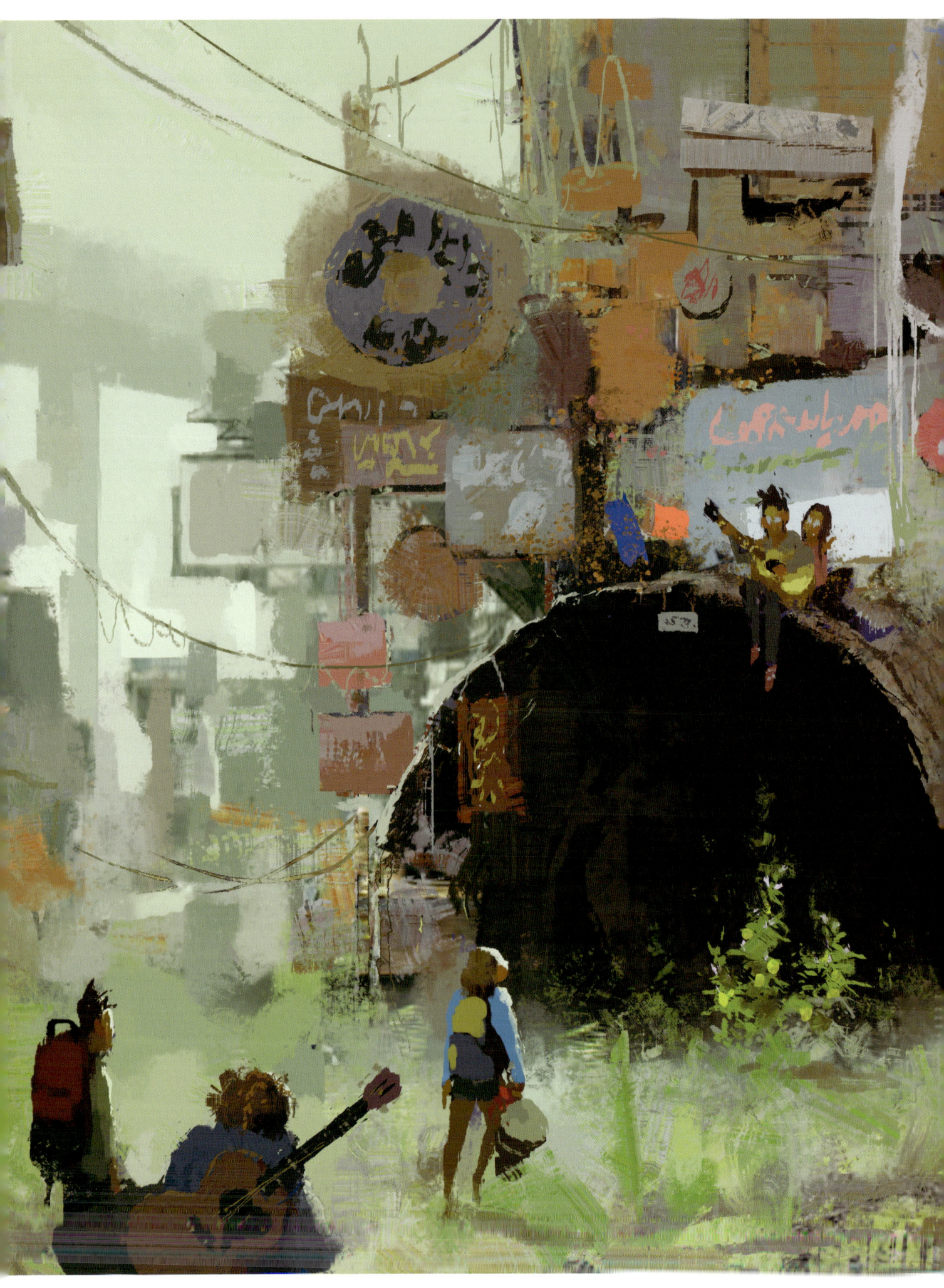

Cooperative project

Improvement can be difficult to achieve in isolation, and it's important to connect with other artists, share your work, and ask for feedback. In this special section of the book, you will see the same scene and theme interpreted by not one but two artists. They will offer each other feedback and encouragement throughout the process, helping one another to make the best images they can.

A cooperative project with Julia Blattman and Zac Retz

Discovery

Brief

The theme of this project is "discovery." In a post-apocalyptic world where people scavenge for supplies, using tunnels and train lines to find their way, two groups of people discover a mystical-looking plant growing. There is an element of the unknown, of strangers meeting, but discovering the plant should fill both groups with awe.

Outline

In this chapter each artist will work on their own version of the scene, starting with a sketch, then a progress image, followed by the final illustration; meanwhile the other artist will offer feedback and constructive suggestions during the process. Each artist will also share a paintover they produced in response to the other artist's progress image with the intention of offering a more visual form of feedback.

Over the course of the two pieces of work you will be able to observe not only how a concept can be improved upon, but also how artists can work collaboratively to produce something truly impressive while developing their own skills and thought processes.

Julia

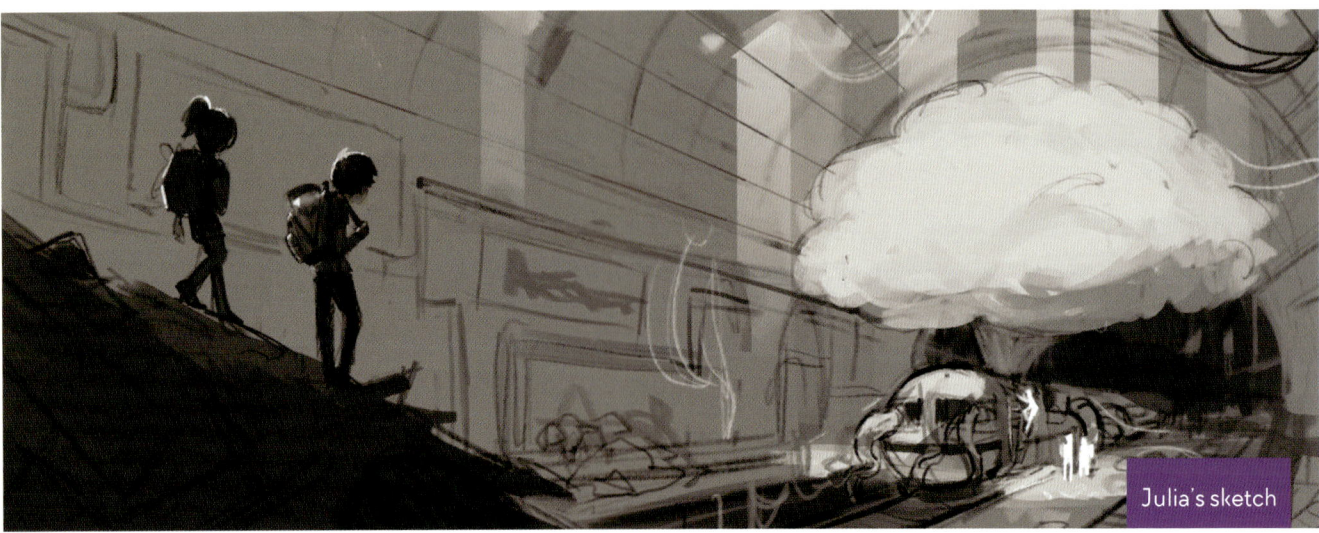

Julia's sketch

>01 Julia's sketch

Zac's comments: "Amazing storytelling and great design of the kids and their silhouettes. It's really creative to have a tree growing out of the train – this will be some great imagery!"

"Try to avoid splitting the composition in half: one solution is to have the junk pile more integrated throughout the foreground of the scene. Use some junk objects in the foreground to lead the eye, like a pipe, wires, or some garbage. Maybe some of the tree branches grew out of the windows of the train, then merged together. Try separating out the foreground and background with value. This scene may benefit by pushing a lot of atmosphere."

"Pick out some of the cool shadows in the background cast by the people, under the train, and from the tree. This will help push that feeling of light"

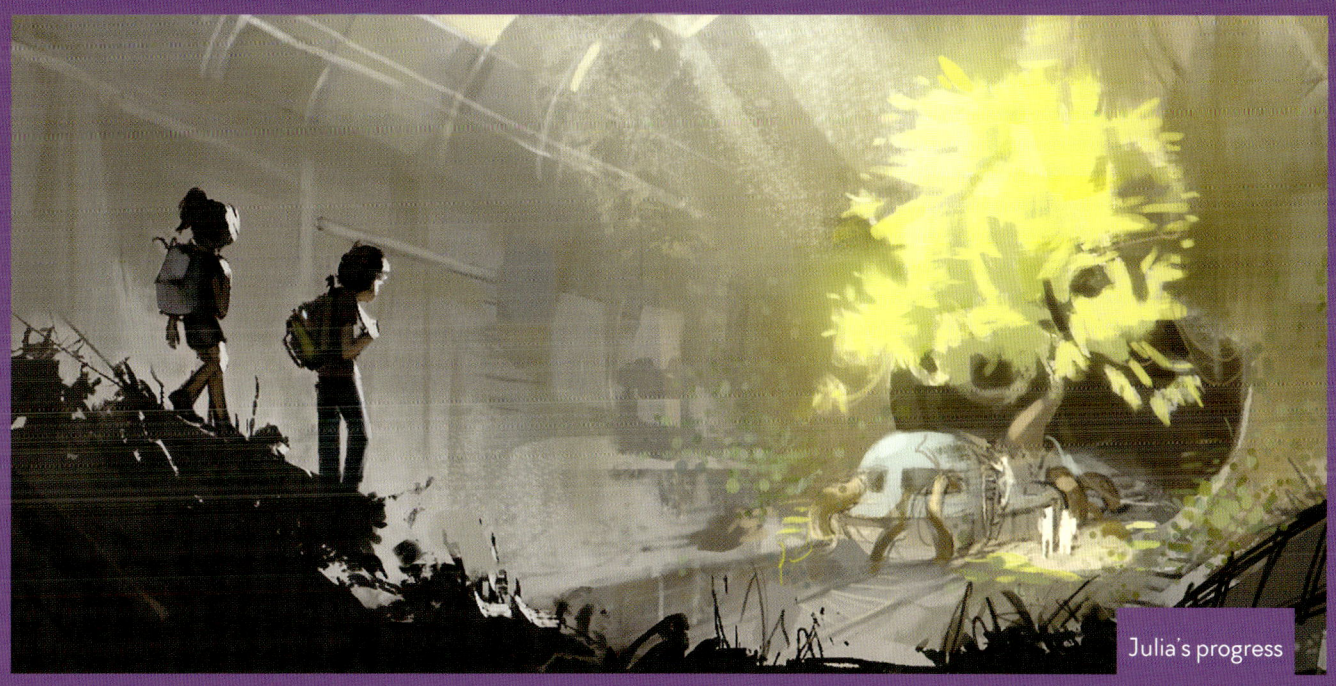

Julia's progress

>02 Julia's progress

Zac's comments: "You did a great job of keeping true to your original value structure from your sketch. There's so much depth and atmosphere. I think pushing some of the warms and cools will add a lot – maybe some purples in the shadows. If you put some deep, warm tones in the junk in the foreground, they will pull the foreground closer and help to show more space. Pick out some of the cool shadows in the background cast by the people, under the train, and from the tree. This will help push that feeling of light."

"In my paintover I've made the brights a little less bright and added some more junk leading towards the train."

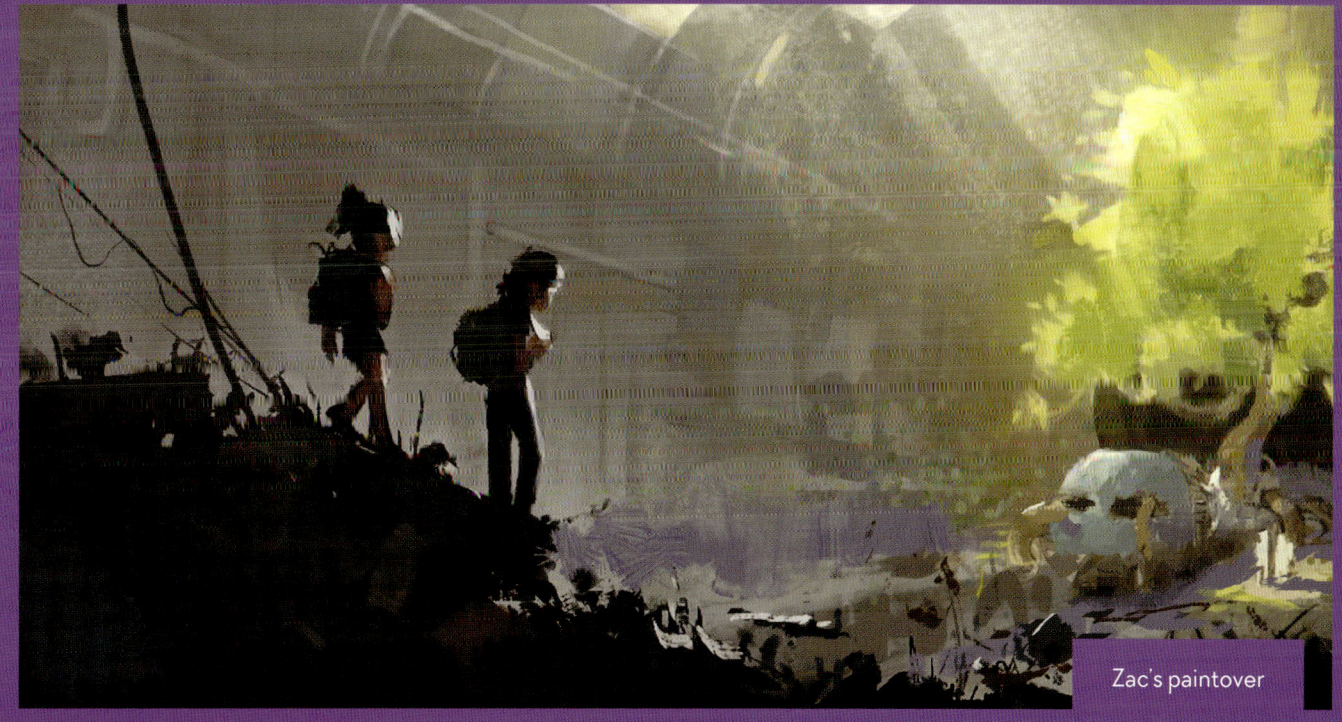

Zac's paintover

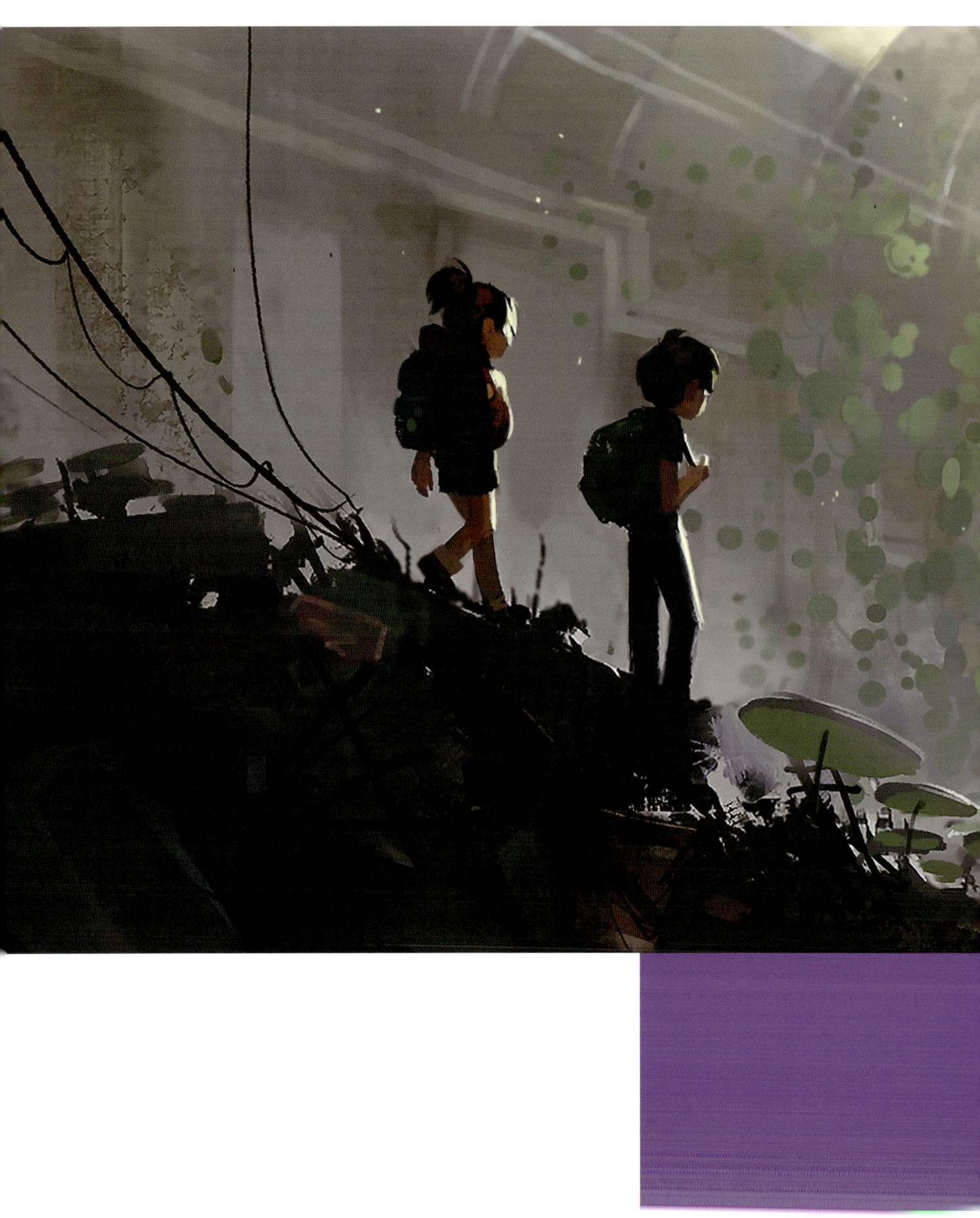

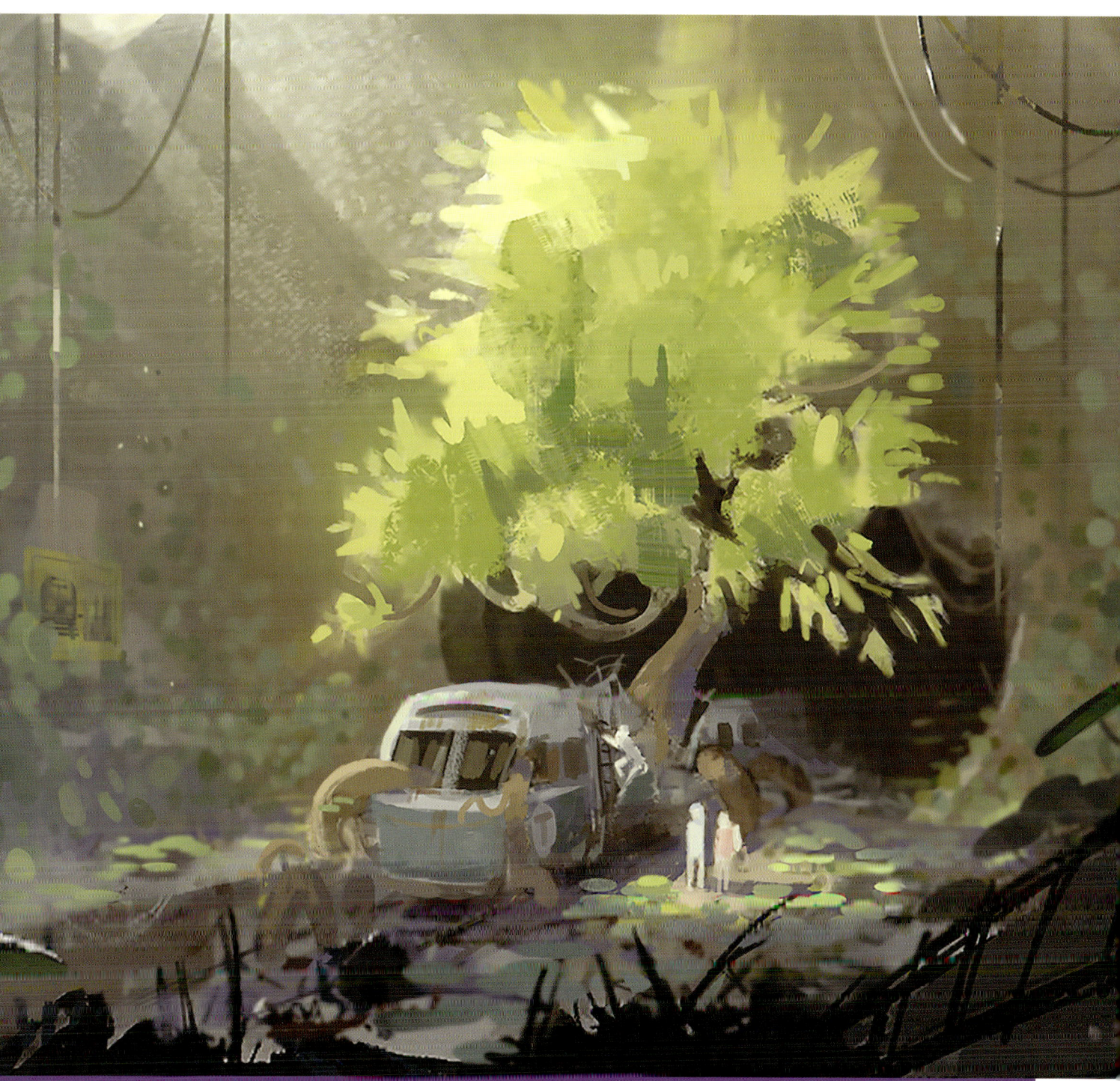

>03 Julia's final image

Zac's comments: "I really like the green plants that are growing along the walls and the mushrooms in the foreground. They're a really great touch. I like how the tree is almost glowing – it looks like it's very important. My suggestions would be to lose some of the edges in the foreground, just painting into it a bit more, keeping in mind that you want the viewer to look at the characters first. The rim light on the foreground characters could be more yellow, which would help to show that the yellow light from the windows above are affecting the characters. This would also help to further tie the image together. You could add floating particles in the air – bits of dust or dandelions, maybe with some in the foreground and out of focus. Little things like this will help push the feeling and mood of the image."

"Really great job, this looks like a video game I would like to play!"

Zac

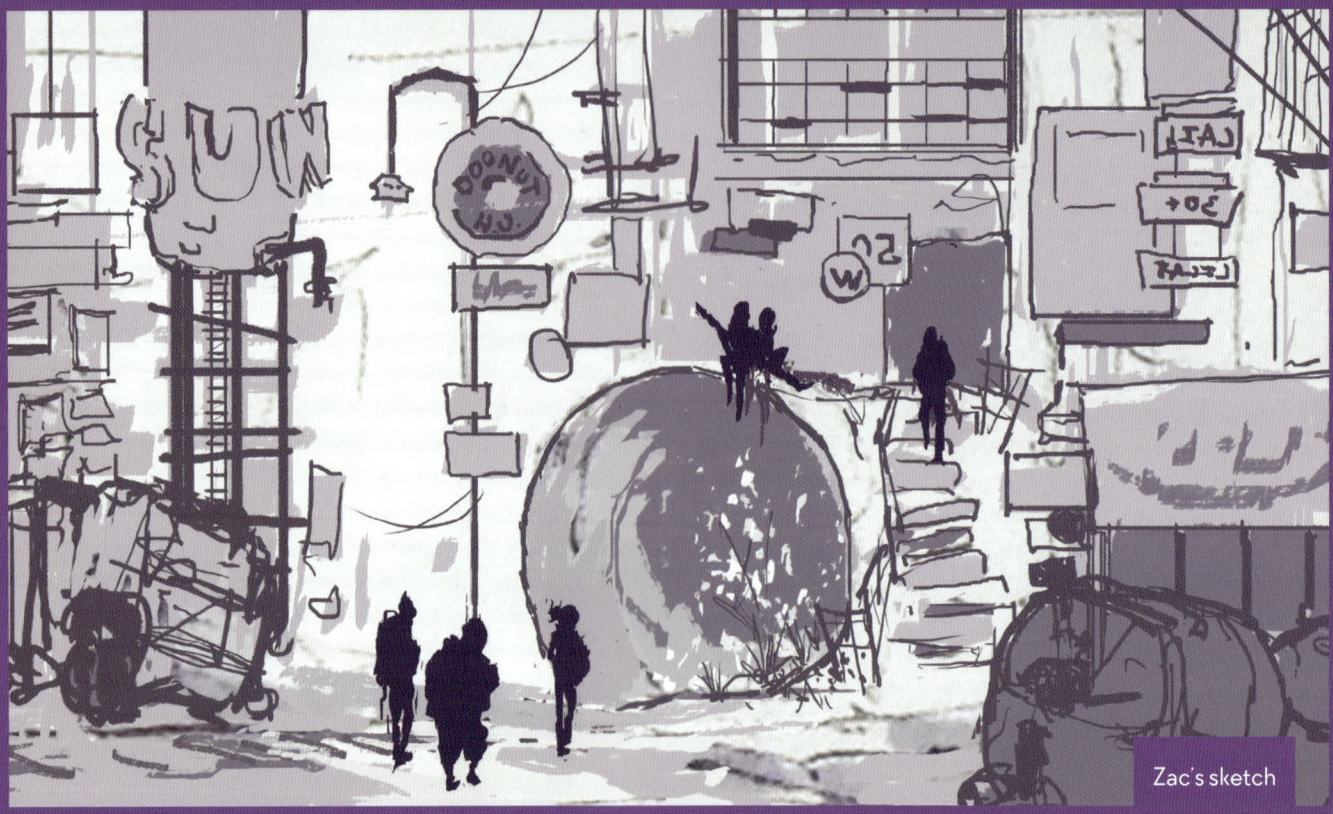

Zac's sketch

>01 Zac's sketch

Julia's comments: "This is looking amazing! I think it will make for a really fantastic painting. The subject matter is definitely right up your alley. You have a nice variety of big and small shapes here, making for interesting eye flow. I think you've captured the world these characters live in nicely; I love the clusters of signs and abandoned vehicles. I would suggest maybe extending the canvas a bit wider – I think it could make this look even more cinematic."

"I'm curious to see the lighting and time of day you choose, and to see how the characters develop. Right now it seems as if the characters sitting on top of the tunnel have been there for some time, and the group walking towards it have just discovered it. Great storytelling there! Looking forward to seeing what the mystical plant will look like in the tunnel."

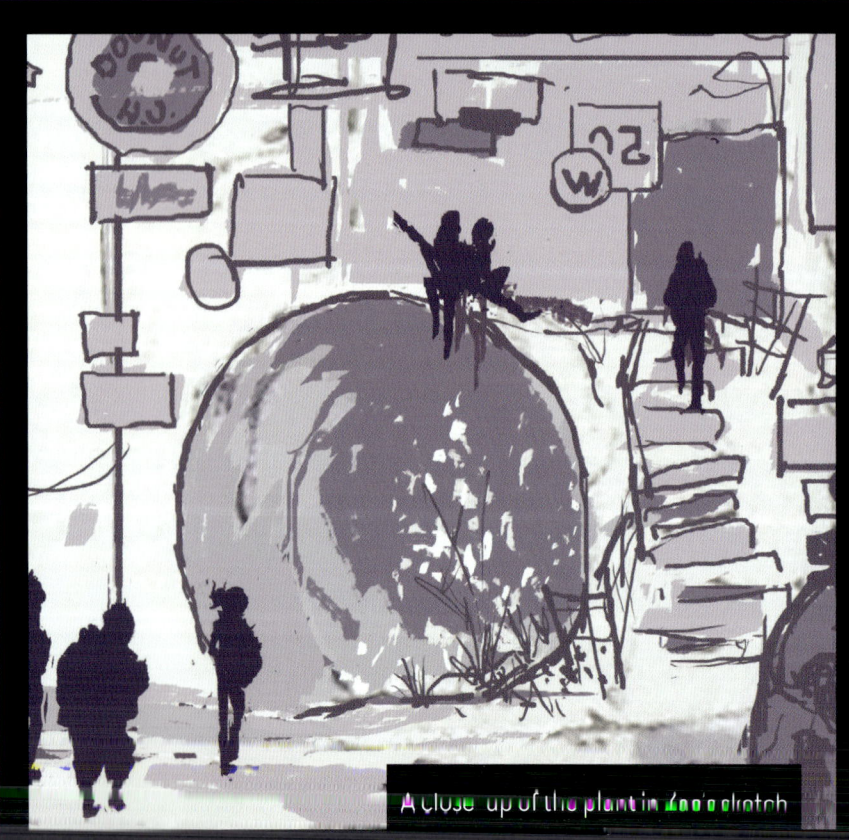

A close-up of the plant in Zac's sketch

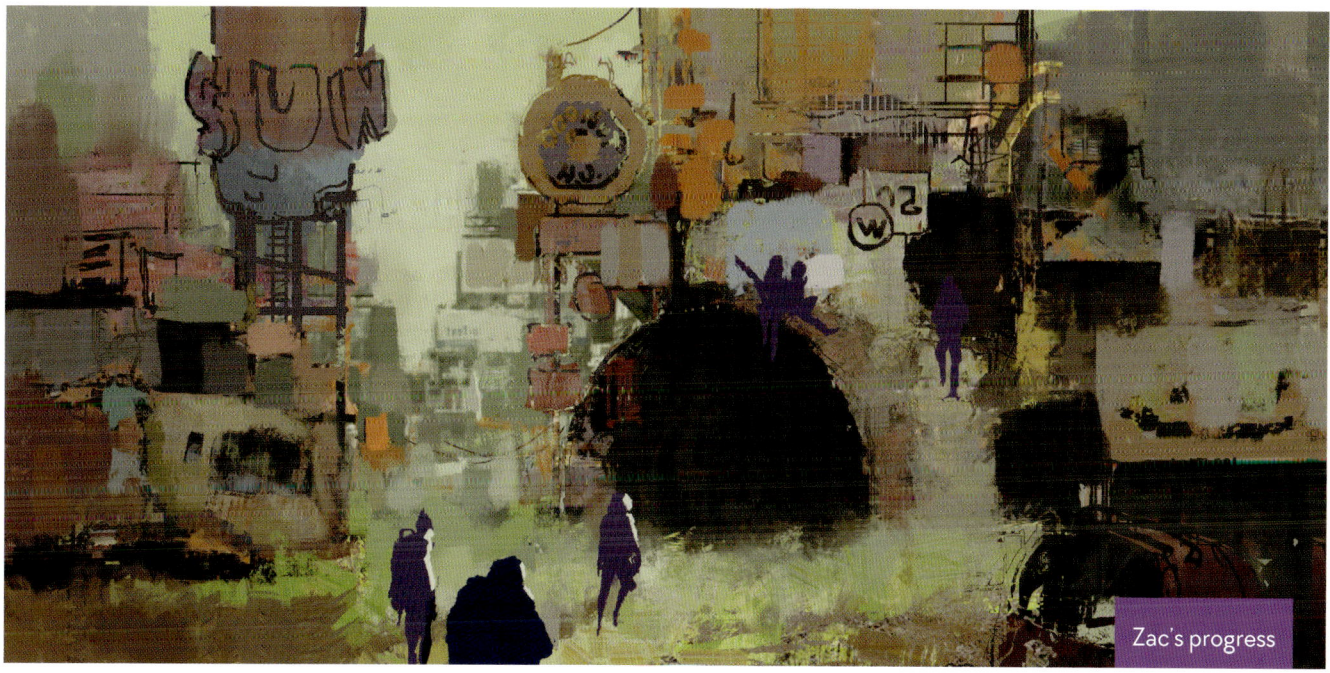

Zac's progress

>02 Zac's progress

Julia's comments: "I love the mood that the overcast greenish lighting gives the painting. I like how you placed the most saturated city signs around the characters sitting on top of the tunnel – smart choice. Your value grouping is working really well too! I would suggest having more directional lines towards the tunnel and characters, maybe with power lines, or even a distant bridge in the background. You could try making the sky a bit brighter, since right now it's similar in color and value to the ground."

"Other than that, I don't have much to say besides to just keep going! I'm curious as to what you will do with the plant growing in the tunnel, and if that will be the focal point. Some references that might inspire you are the detailed city backgrounds of the movie *Tekkonkinkreet*, and Jeremy Mann's foggy city landscapes, though I'm sure you're already familiar with these!"

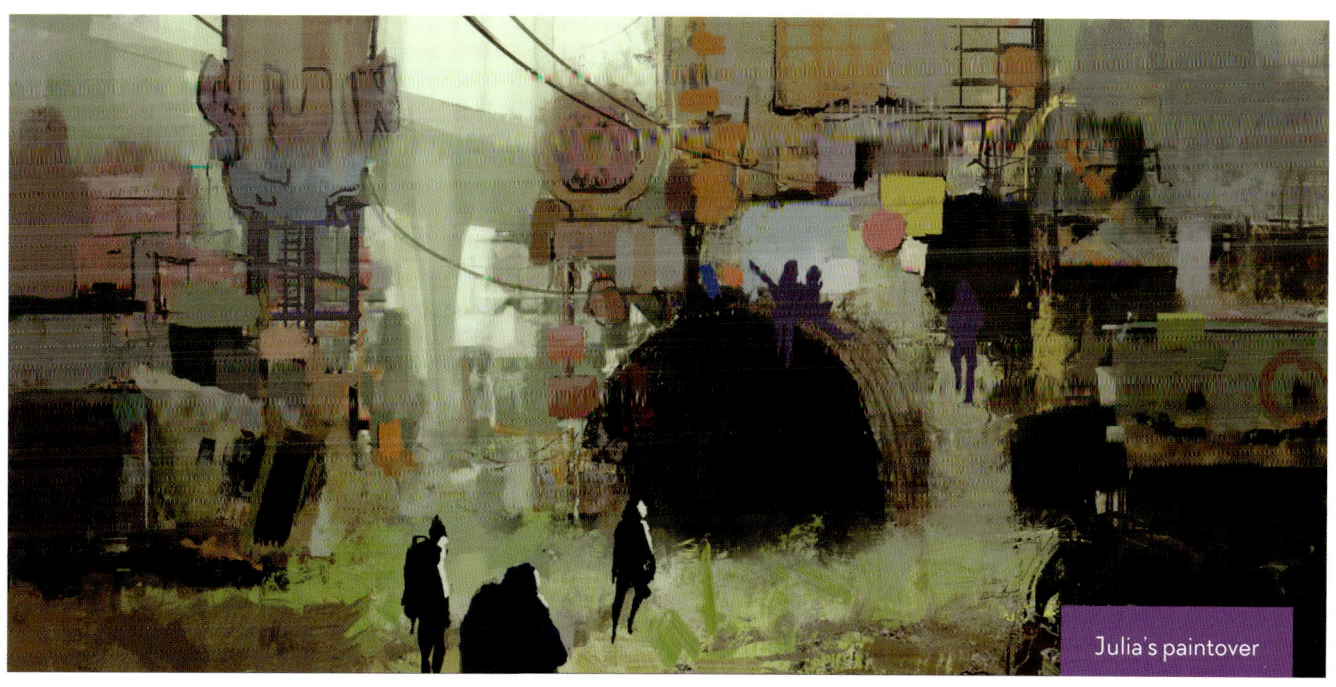

Julia's paintover

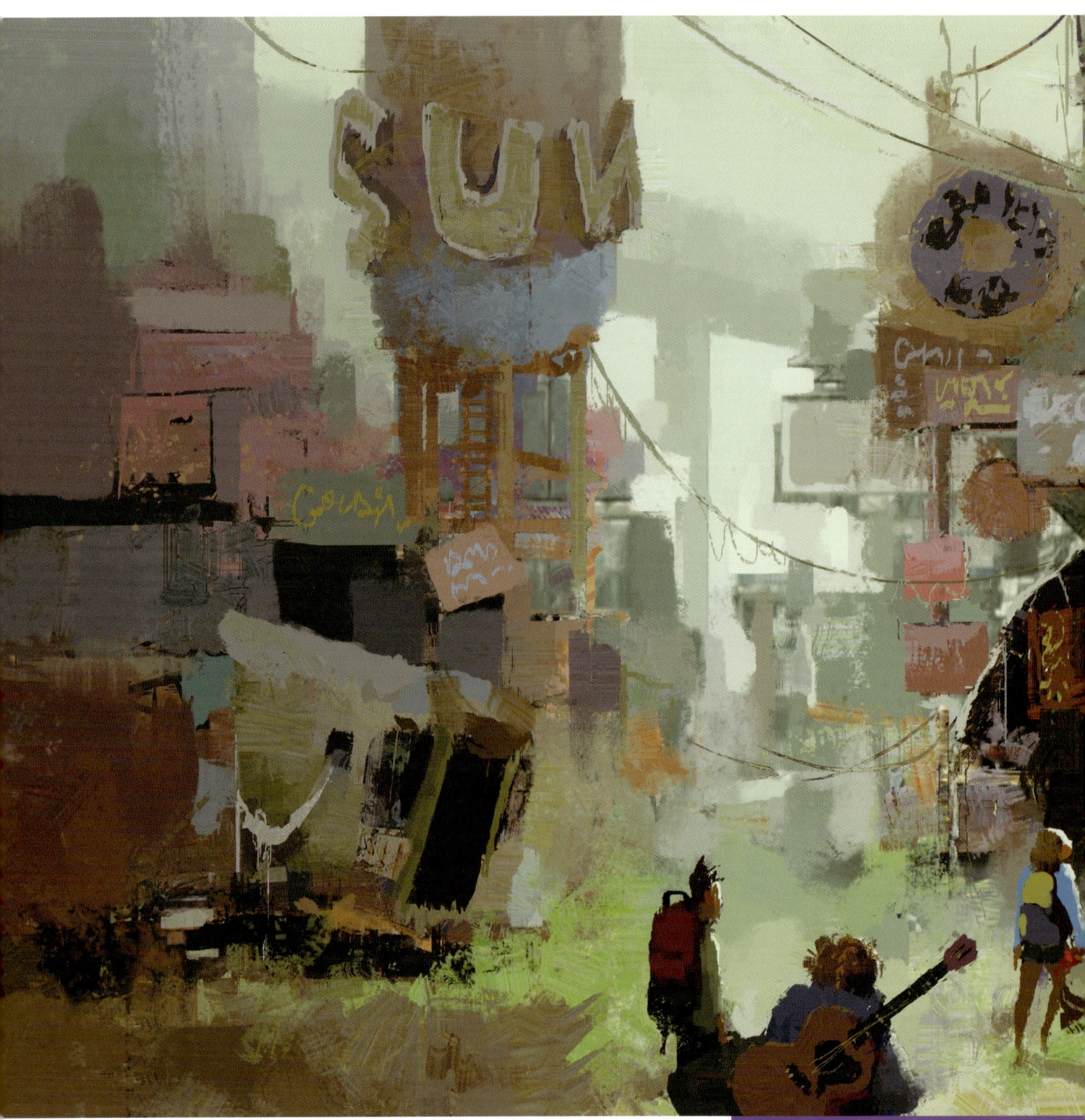

>03 Zac's final image
Julia's comments: "I think this turned out fantastically! I really love how you pushed the atmosphere in the piece; it gives a mysterious vibe to the world the characters are in. I think the way you lightened the sky in the background is effective, and the contrast really helps the illustration pop!"

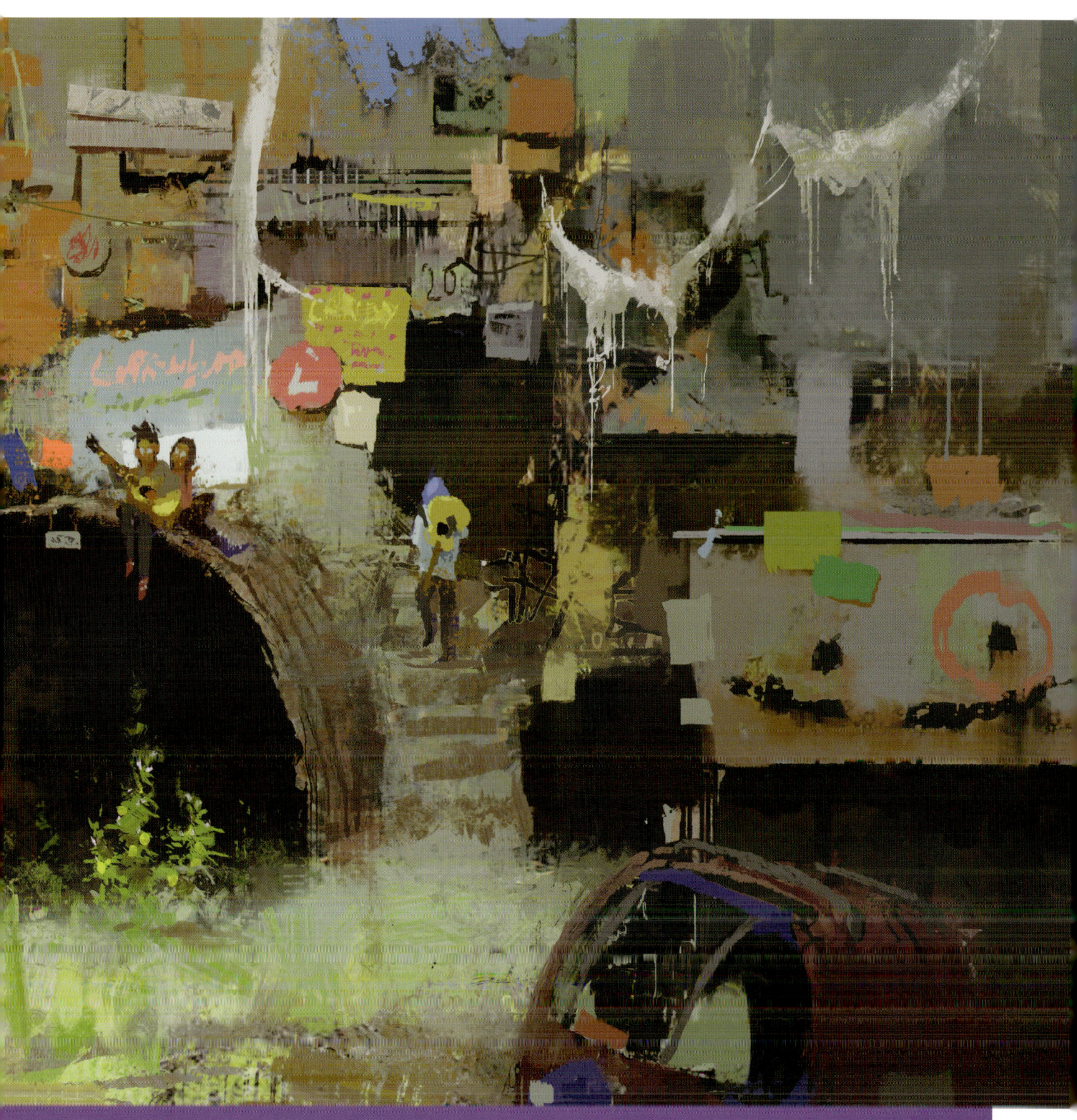

"I think you successfully portrayed the mood and storytelling of this piece. It makes me want to venture into that tunnel and see what's in there, or see what the characters do next (a potential jam session?). The way you've brought attention to certain areas by refinement is a smart way to tactfully lead the viewer's eye to certain areas. I love the lost edges that are happening in this!

However, if I were to add anything to it, I would maybe just define a few things further. I'm wondering if the object on the left side of the composition is an abandoned run-down truck or mobile home. I'm also curious as to what the white objects are that are hanging around the composition – I couldn't quite tell if you were going for

cobwebs or possibly hanging fabric. Maybe replacing those with just white tangled wires would be less distracting and tie in more with the environment. Overall it's a really strong piece! I think it ties in very well with the worlds you create."

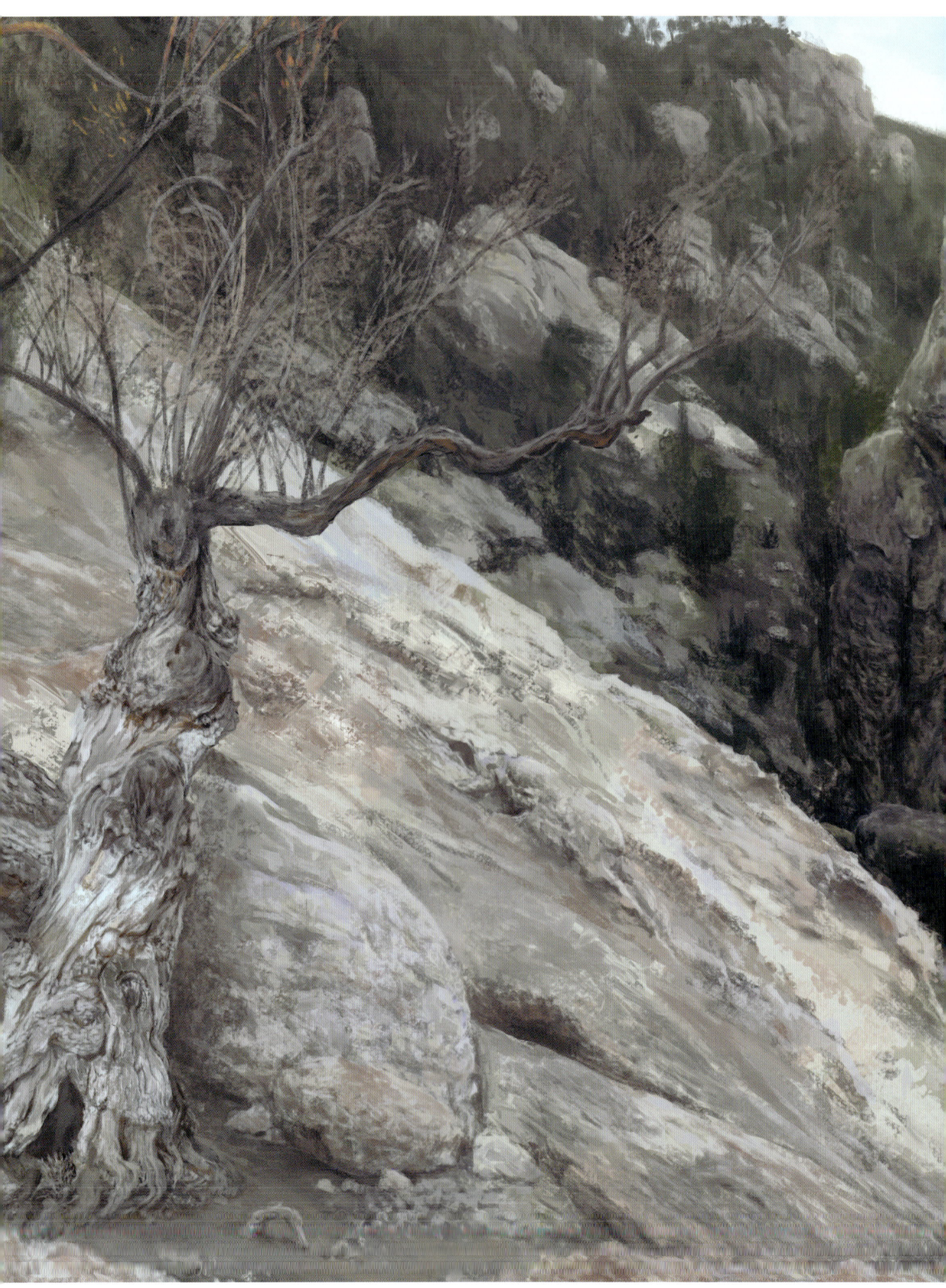

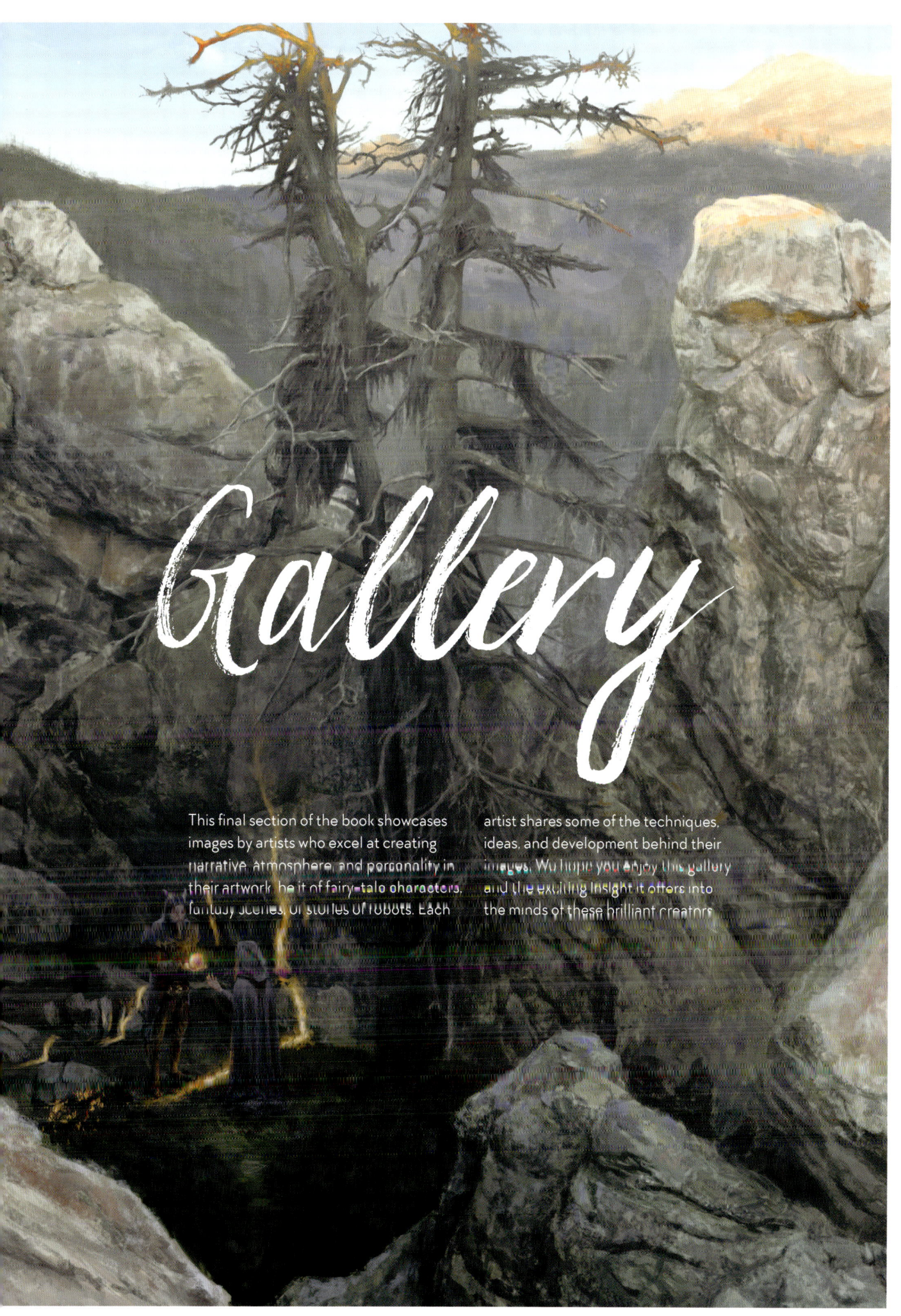

Gallery

This final section of the book showcases images by artists who excel at creating narrative, atmosphere, and personality in their artwork, be it of fairy-tale characters, fantasy scenes, or stories of robots. Each artist shares some of the techniques, ideas, and development behind their images. We hope you enjoy this gallery and the exciting insight it offers into the minds of these brilliant creators.

The Sister

Elisabeth Alba | www.albaillustration.com

I participated in the Month of Fear Halloween challenge (**www.monthoffearart.com**) and one of the prompts was "Sabbath: Witches and Devils." For this challenge, I wanted to create a creepy, moody portrait that would remind the viewer of old daguerreotype photographs. For that reason, I decided to keep the color simple; the simplicity also keeps the viewer focused. I took photographs of myself posing as the woman with directional lighting for reference, in order to truly capture the gesture and expression. I wanted her to look lost in another world and for her to hands to be very delicate.

There are a lot of creepy portraits in the world, so you have to think about how to push an image to make it more than just a creepy portrait. I wanted it to inspire the viewer's imagination as well, by adding elements that make the viewer pause and that allow a story to unfold. The woman's shadow shows horns and demon wings. Her eyes are glazed white with an unhealthy, pink sheen. The doll stares directly at the viewer with one visible eye, her mouth covered. The title, *The Sister*, is also simple, but allows the viewer to question "is she *the sister*, or is the doll *the sister*?" Isn't it creepy to think that the person who may be closest to you could be harboring a dark, terrifying secret?

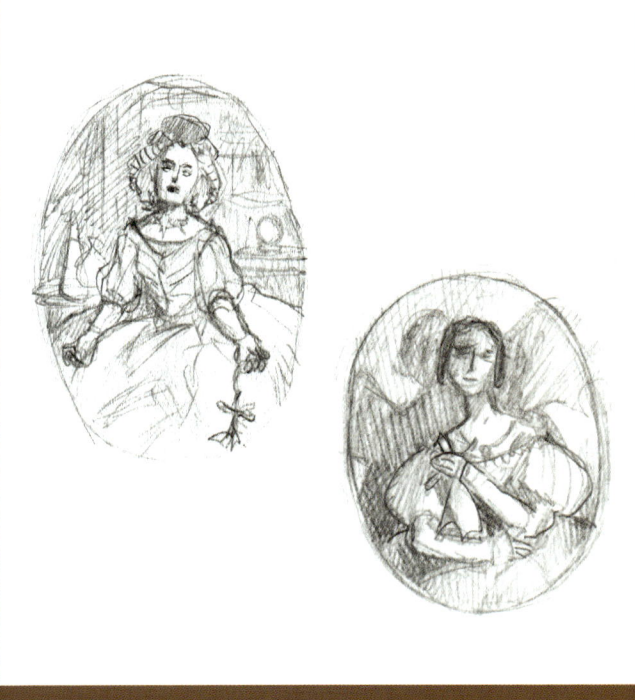

// I began with rough, small thumbnail sketches to work out the general idea and composition

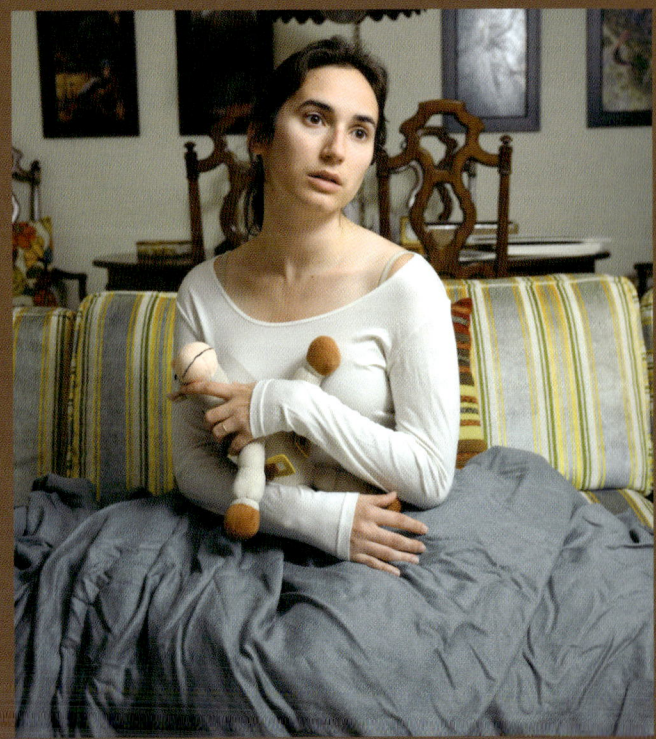

// I wanted to get the expression and gesture just right, so this is one of many photographs of myself posing as the character for reference

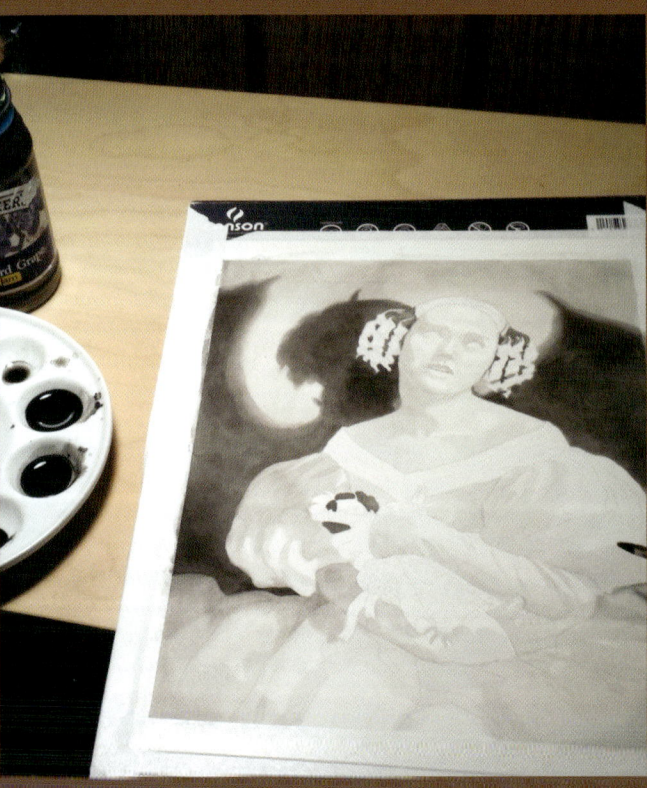

// In the midst of painting – building up ink washes

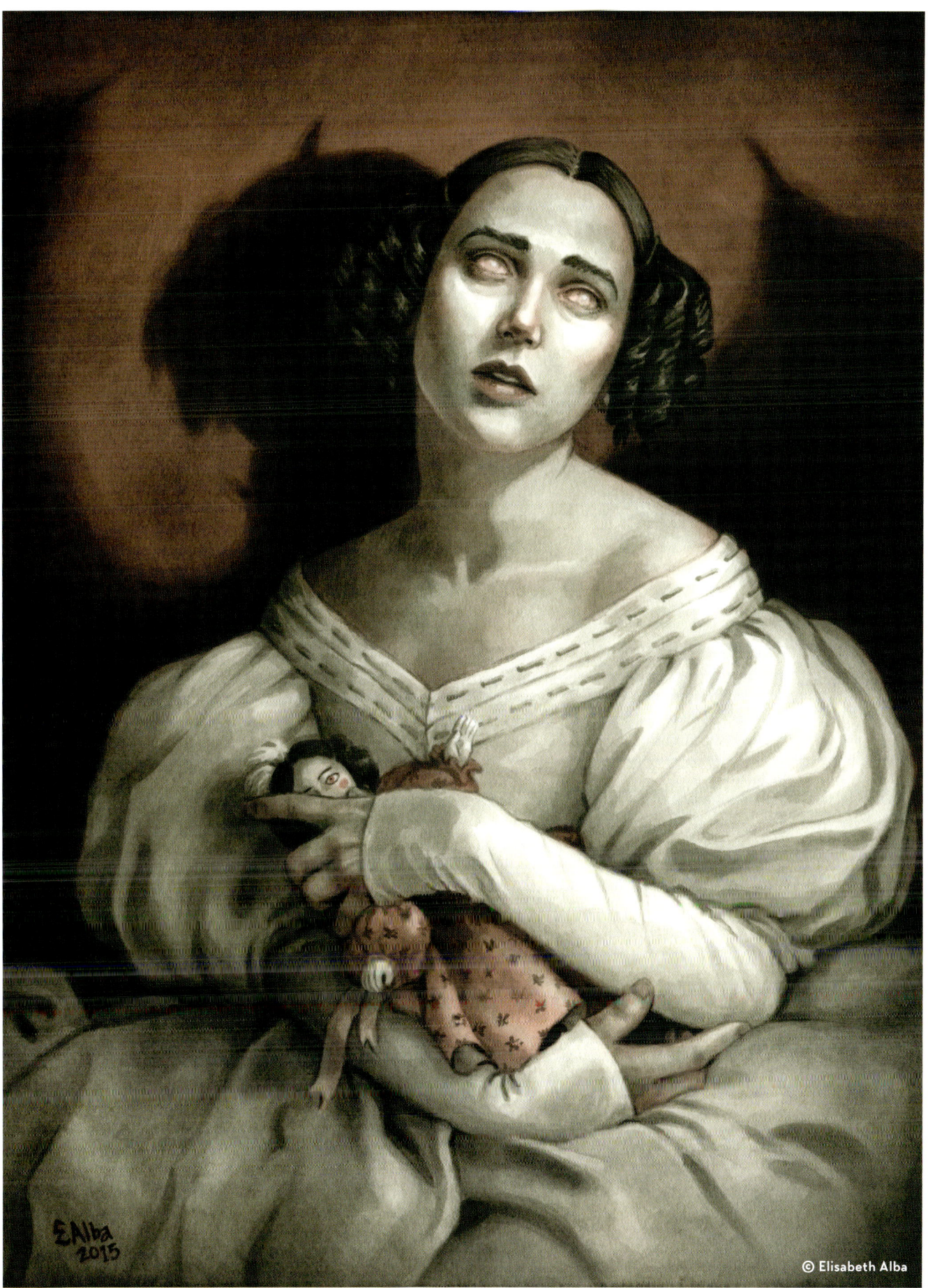

// The final painting, completed with Dr. Ph. Martin's Black Star matte ink and red watercolor, white charcoal, and Krylon Kamar spray varnish

Hjafa the Warlock

Alex Brock | www.alexbrockart.com

This was a school project which was part of a series I did for my thesis. I got the idea for this painting after taking a photo up on Mount Lemmon, and used the photo heavily for reference. In this scene, the sorceress Livorem ("whip" or "bruising" in Latin) is tasked with reviving the crippled Bat Lord Oeg

'Um to his former power by going on various quests and retrieving trinkets. Here she is bartering with Hjafa the Warlock to get a powerful crystal ball in the secluded shadows of his mountain dwelling. This was largely a photo study that I interpreted and enhanced to create a narrative

scene. I exaggerated the colors, set up a composition with characters, and moved or added features such as trees and rocks. This was also one of the most tedious and time-consuming things I have ever worked on and took over fifty hours. Almost all of that time was spent rendering and texturing.

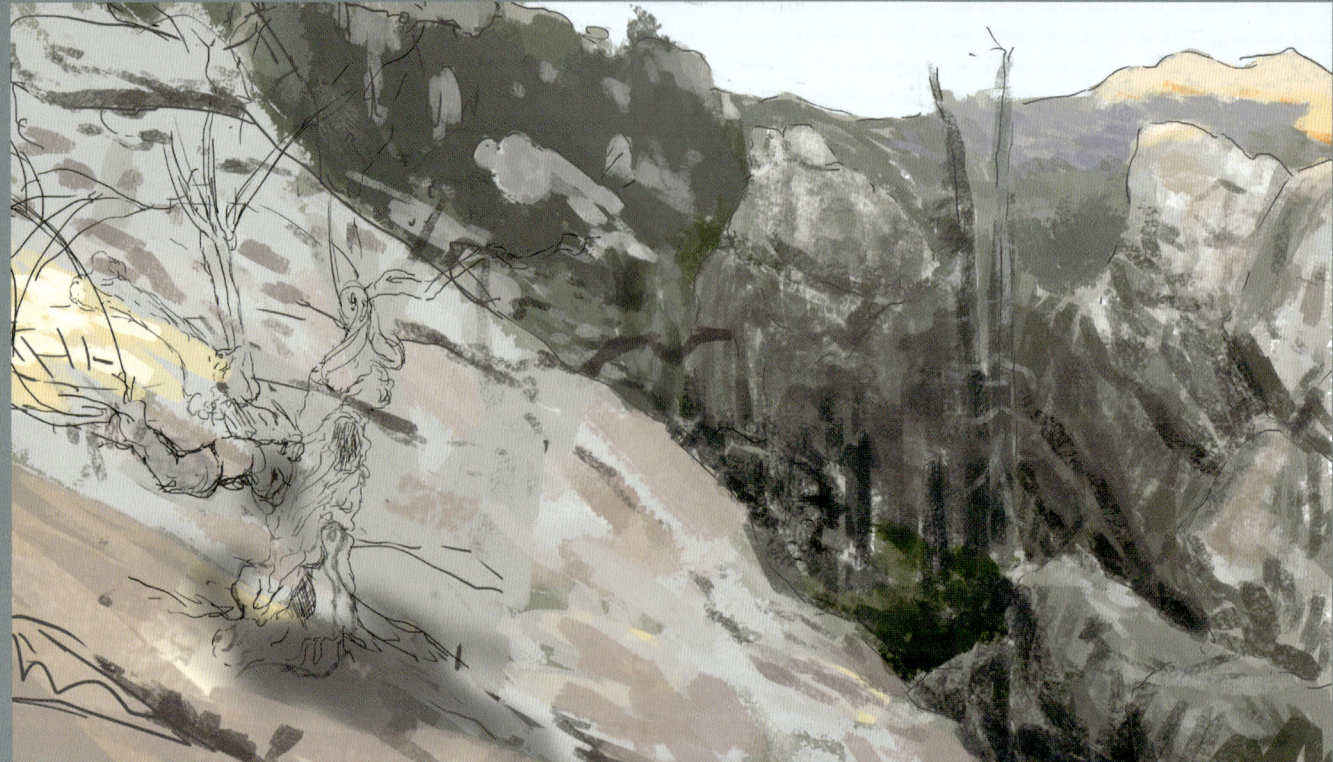

// Arranging the composition, placing everything where I think it fits best, and trying to get the colors and values accurate without going into detail

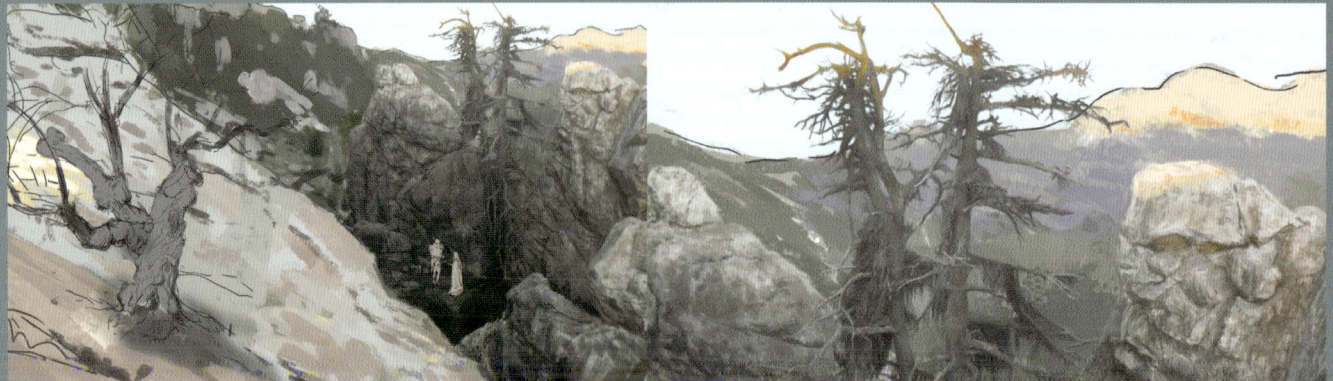

// I began rendering from the top of the left middle-ground rock and worked in a clockwise pattern throughout the piece. I followed the reference closely but added things such as sunlight kissing the tips of the trees

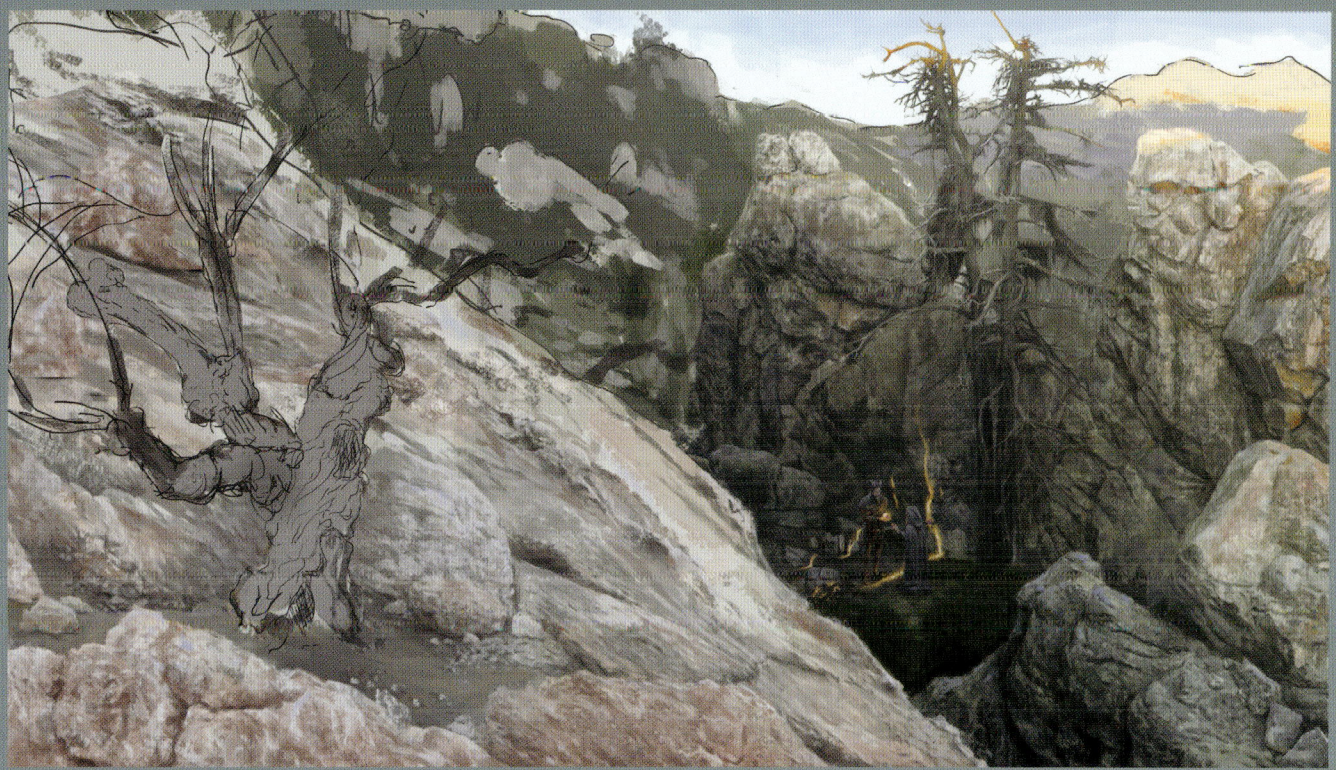

// More rendering, accentuating the colors to really drive home a sunset evening mood by adding hints of the cool reflected sky on the rocks

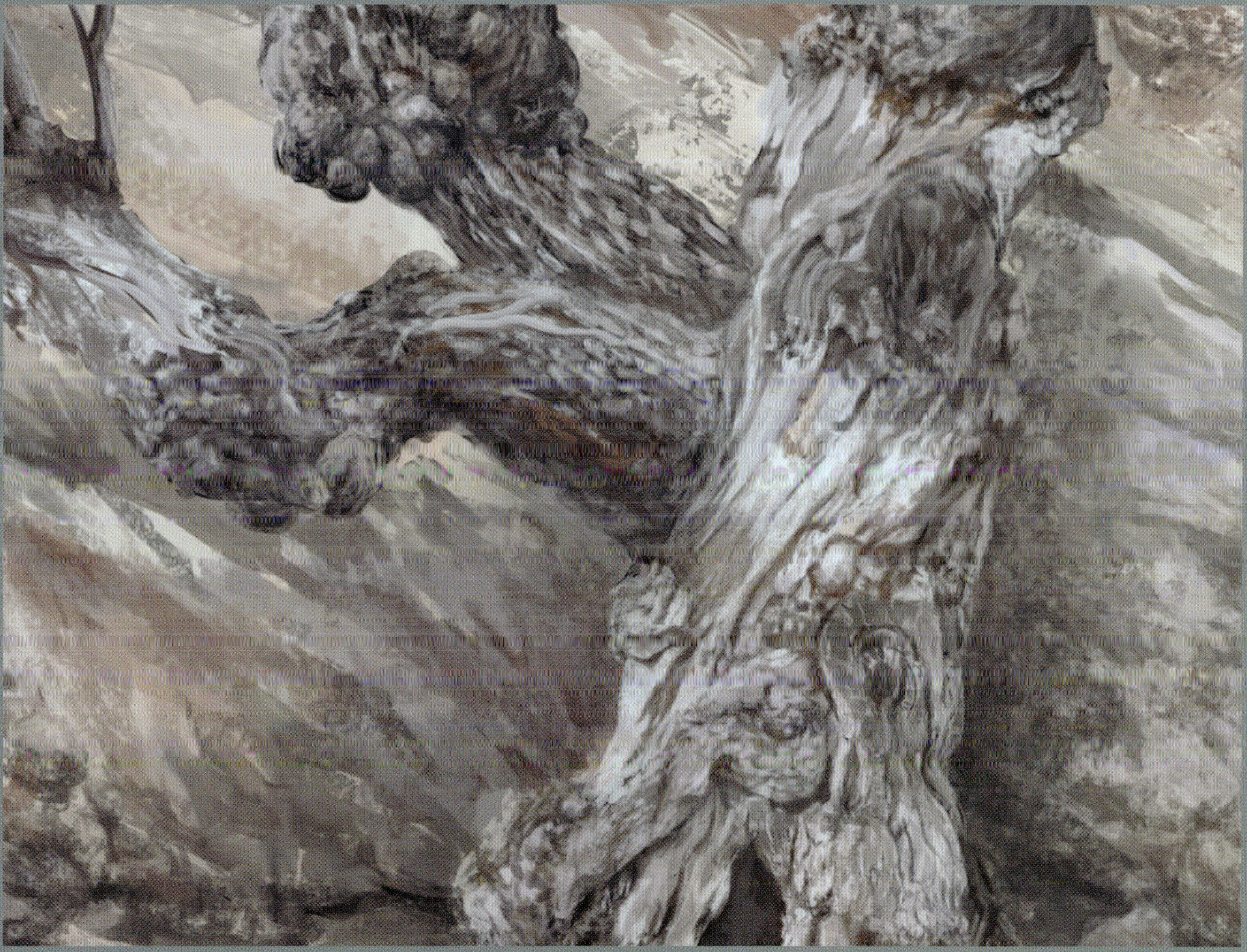

// A close-up detail of the tree's rendering

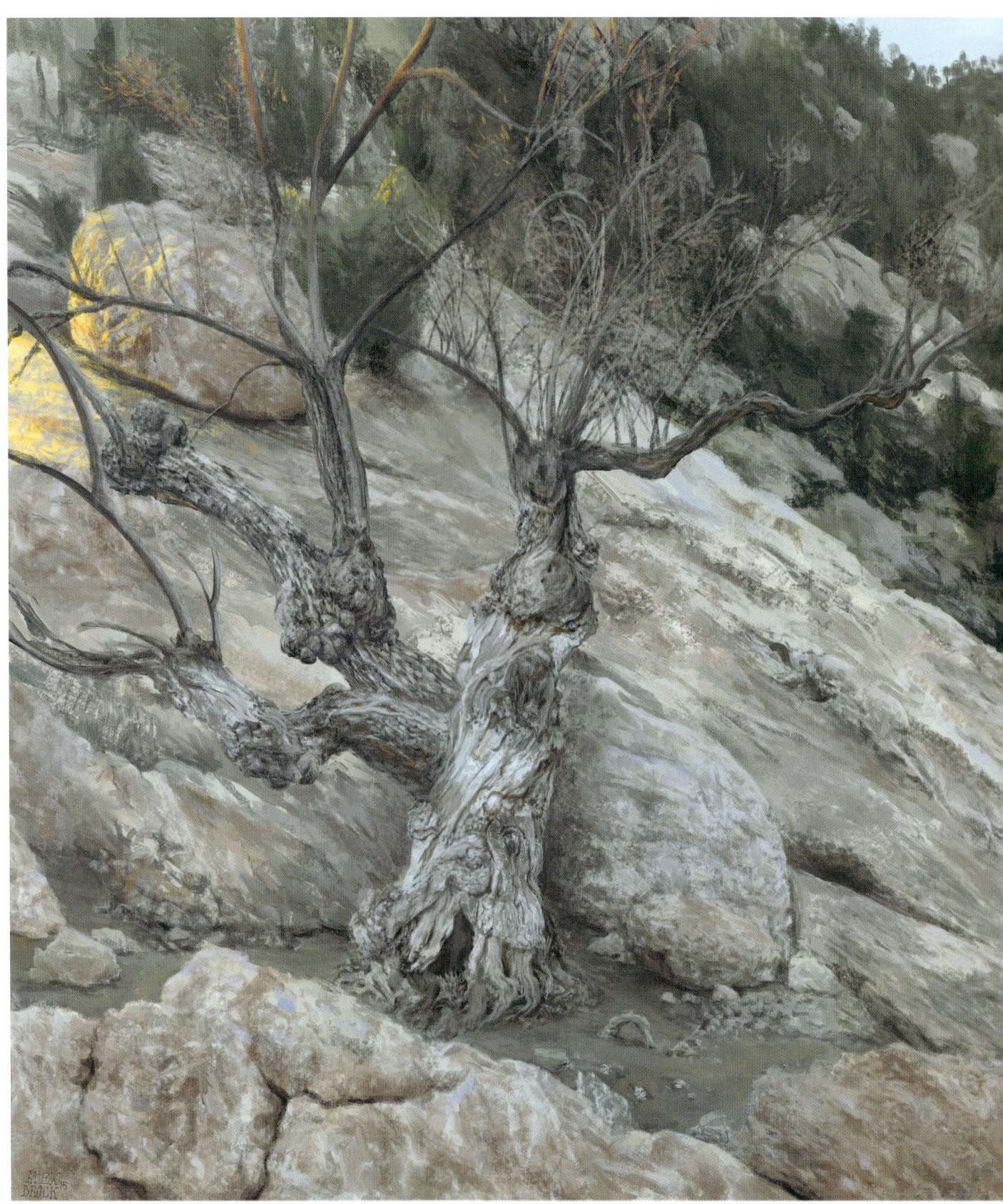

// I accentuated the colors even more for the final image, increasing contrast and adjusting hues

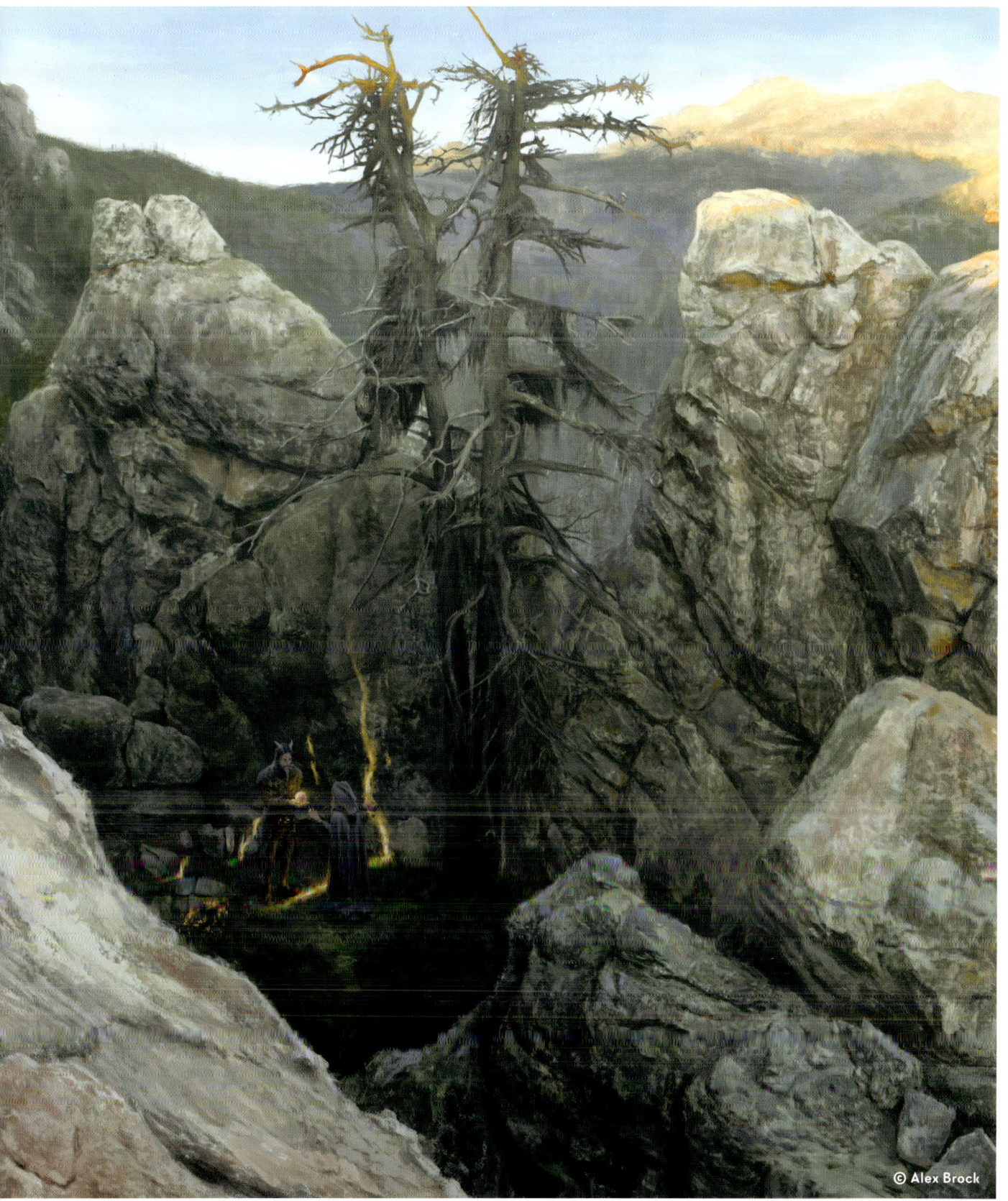

The Return

Lee Kent (Giang Nguyen Truong) | www.leekent.deviantart.com

I have a special interest in the cultures of Europe and North America, especially imagery of knights, war horses, and angels; this painting reflects that interest of mine. Three days were spent on finishing this painting, and during those days I found limitless inspiration and fun. Breaking the old rules I had set myself, I tried to embed more of a sense of traditional art, with the strokes and color tone of Renaissance art – the feeling of an oil painting! While we always want our paintings to convey a feeling to the audience, we should make sure that the painting pleases ourselves first. The painting is a story of a knight trying to come back and save his homeland from a war. What I was trying to create is the feeling of loneliness that knight feels, to make my story harrowing and heroic.

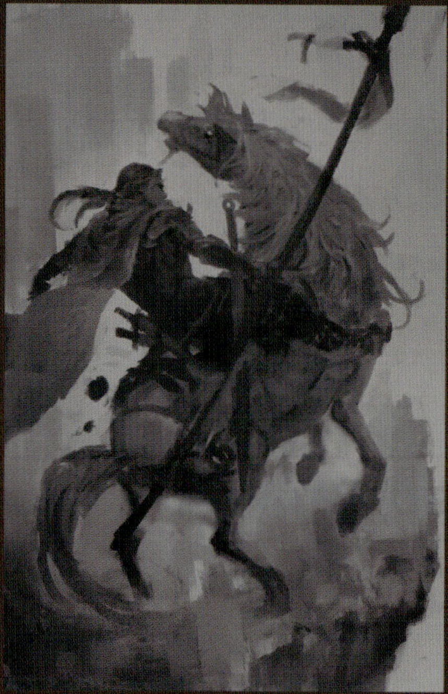

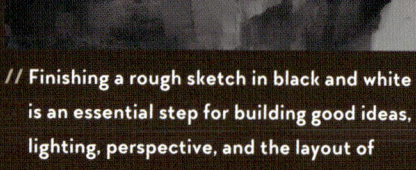

// Finishing a rough sketch in black and white is an essential step for building good ideas, lighting, perspective, and the layout of the painting

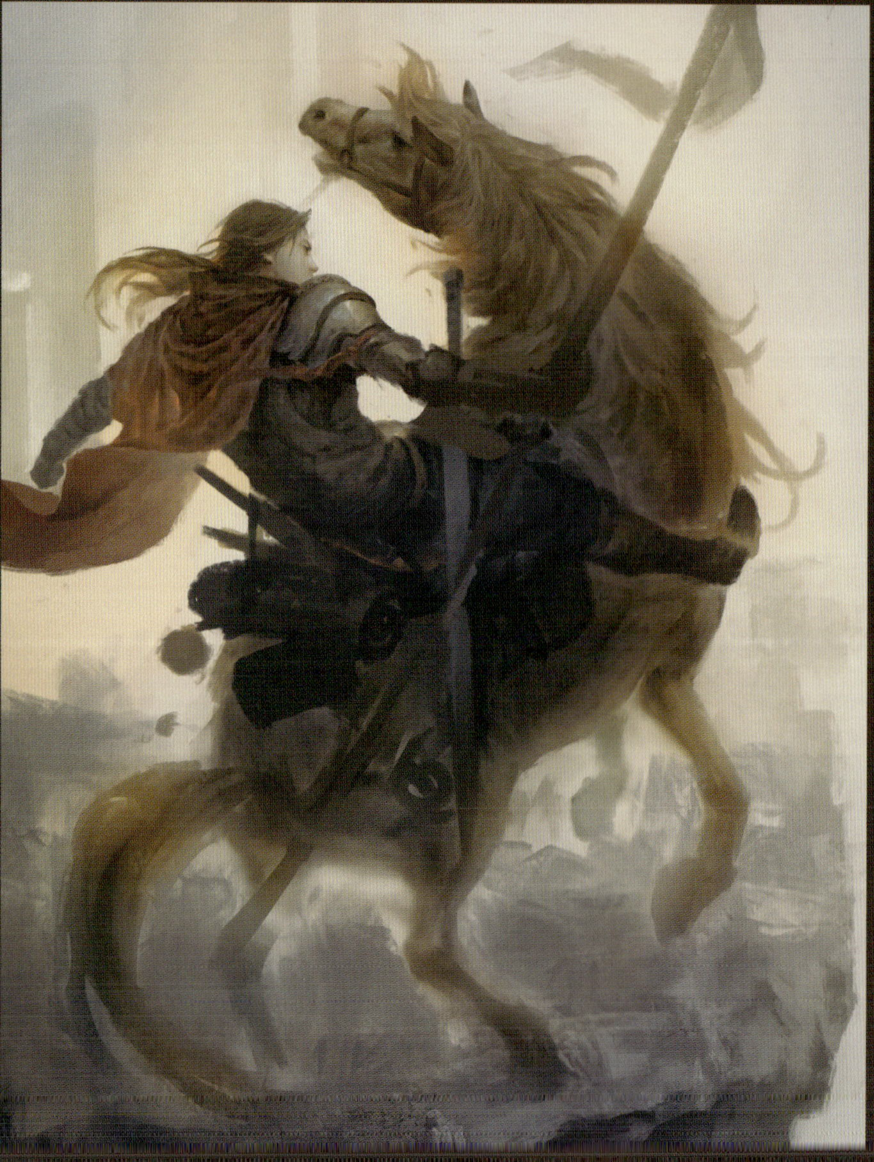

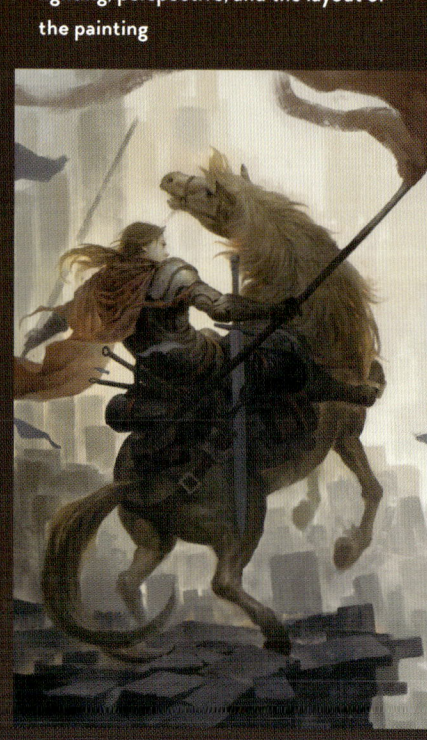

// I tried to add in more material to refine the painting, and to establish the final visual effects

// I used layer blending modes in Adobe Photoshop to add a base color. Since I created a grayscale sketch with specific and clear values, this stage was much easier

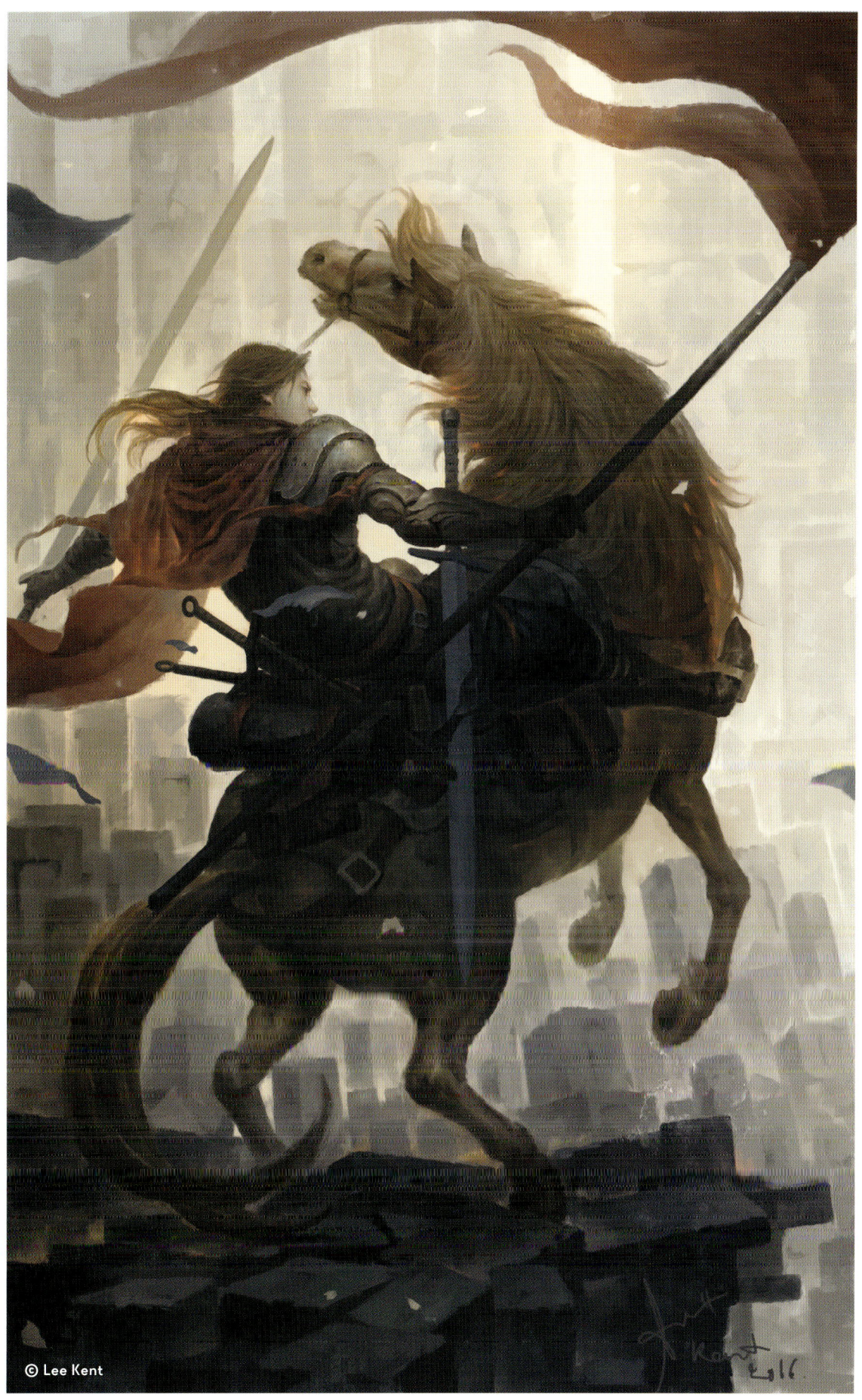

// The completed image, with lighting, colors, and effects

Le Retour

Florent Llamas | www.florentllamas.tumblr.com

When I started this picture, I had just returned from a trip to Vienna and had the desire to create a fantastic landscape with a castle inspired by the architecture of Wiener Rathaus, the city hall. I wanted a special atmosphere, quite misty and magical. The rider is going home, the sun drawing his silhouette as he approaches the imposing, majestic castle emerging out of the fog. The idea is that the rider is rediscovering this castle, perhaps at the end of a long journey.

I started drawing by laying down my sketch quite simply. Then I added details to the original sketch, combining painting, photos, and textures. Finishing touches were carried out to help create an effective atmosphere, adding lights, shadows, and birds, allowing the viewer to immerse themselves in the image.

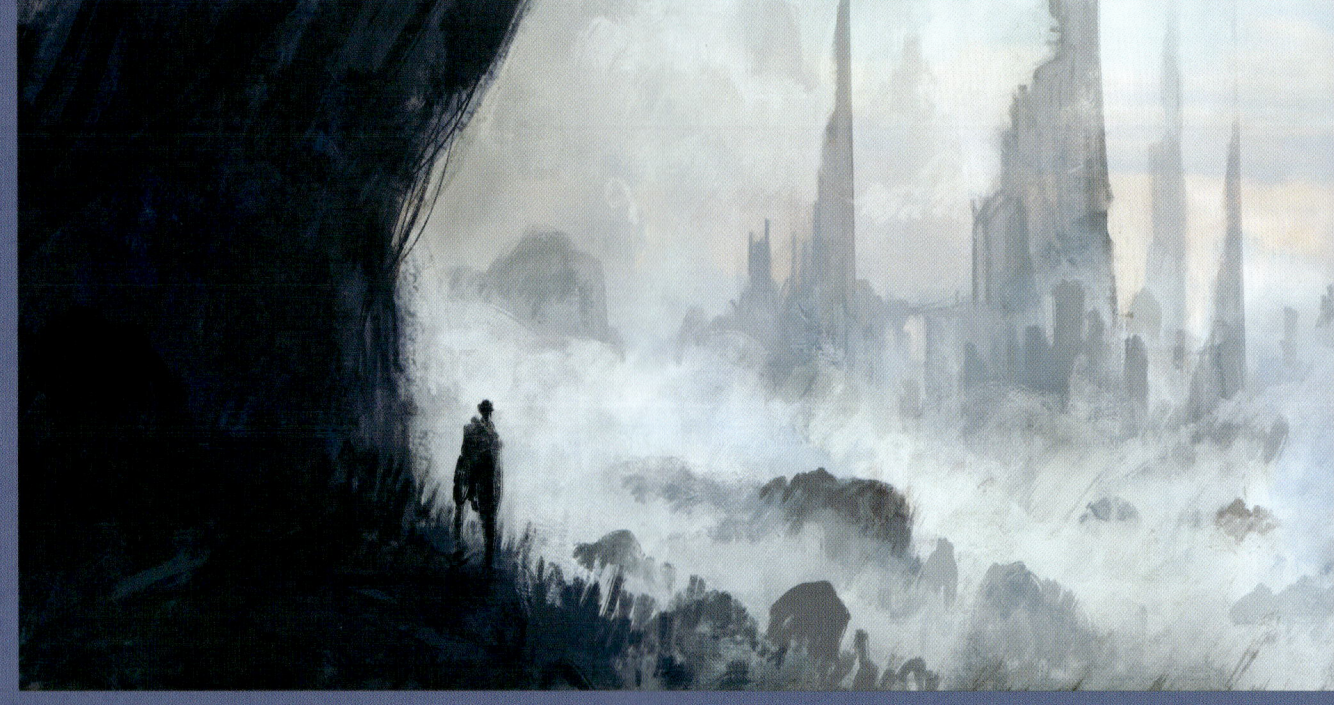

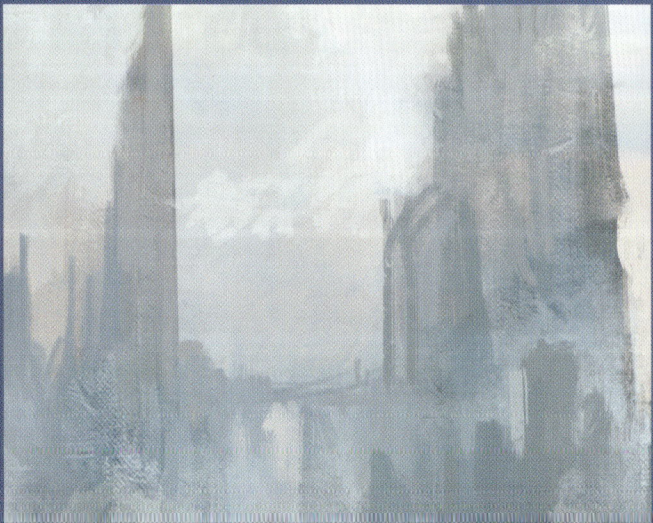

// I painted the initial idea quite simply, without thinking about the details, focusing more on the composition and important forms of image

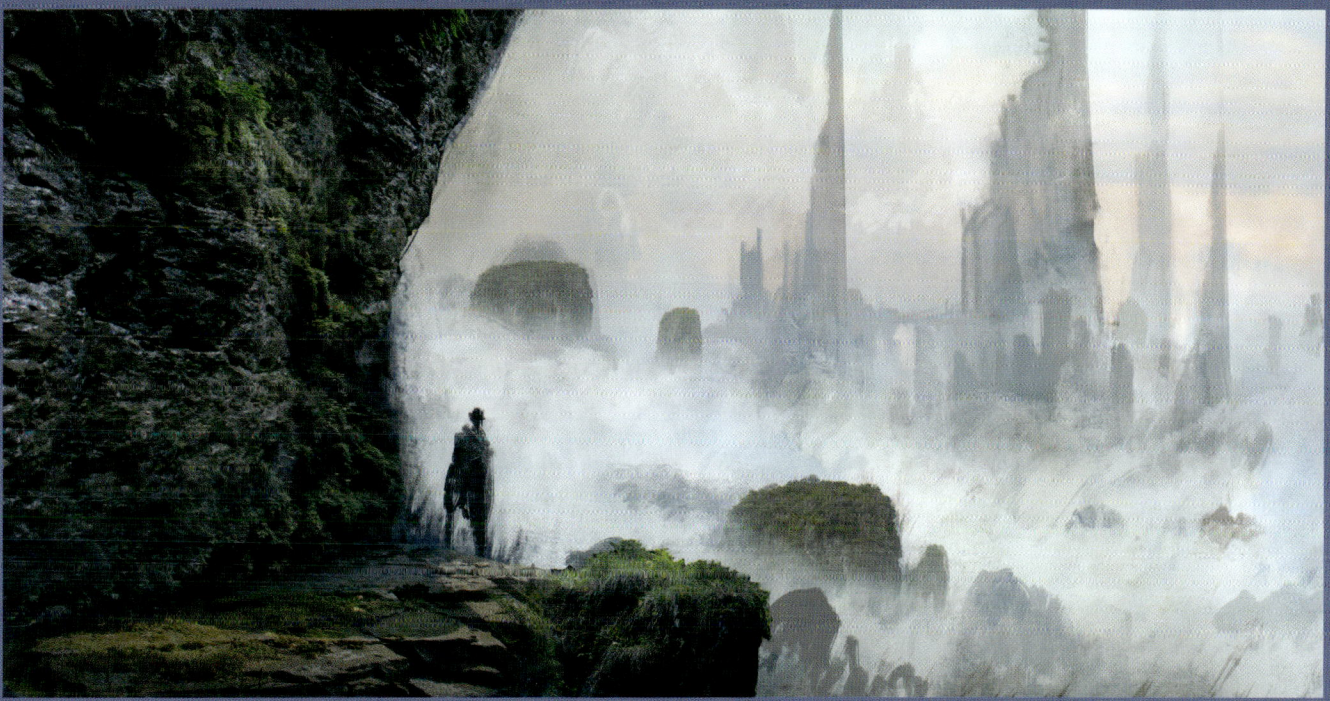

// Here I started adding detail and texture to the image

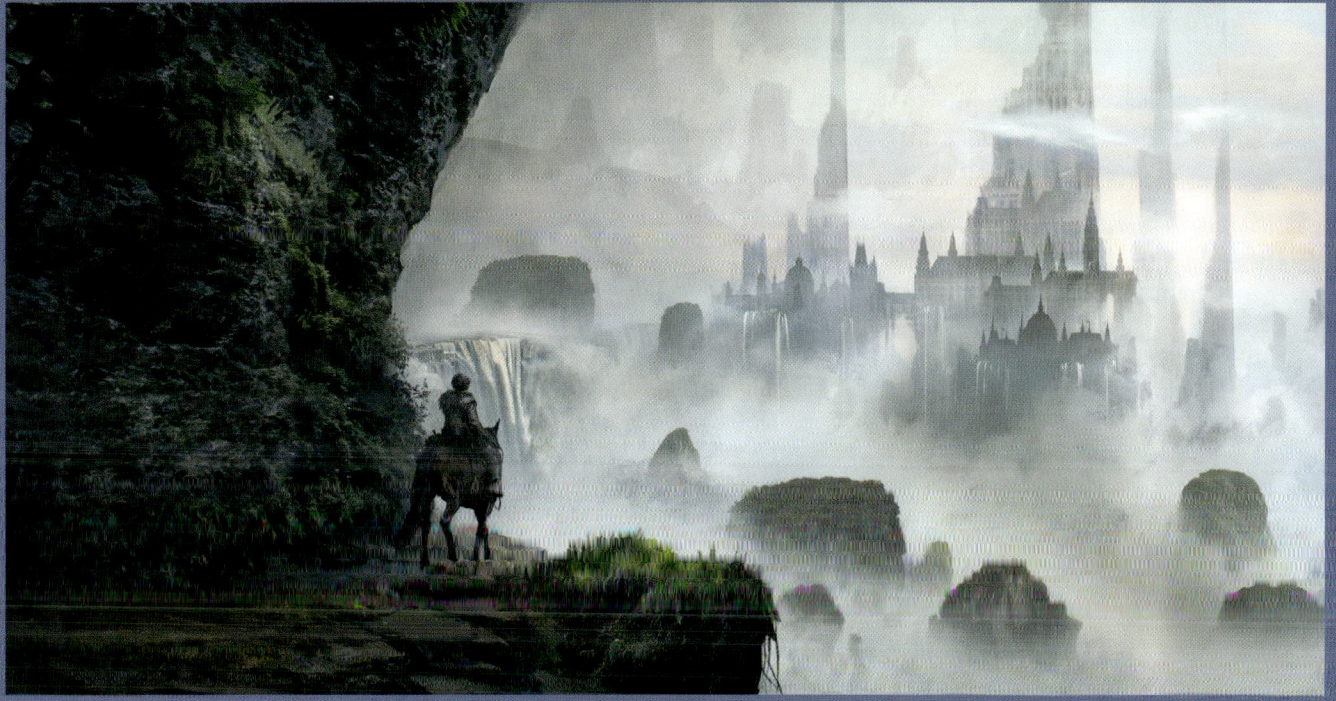

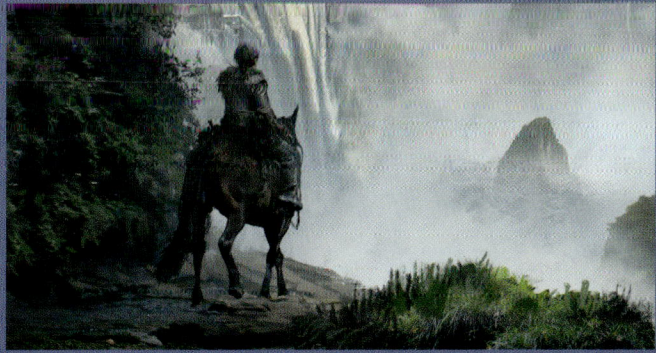

// I continued adding details and painting everywhere, refining the castle, towers, waterfalls, and clouds. I also added the knight

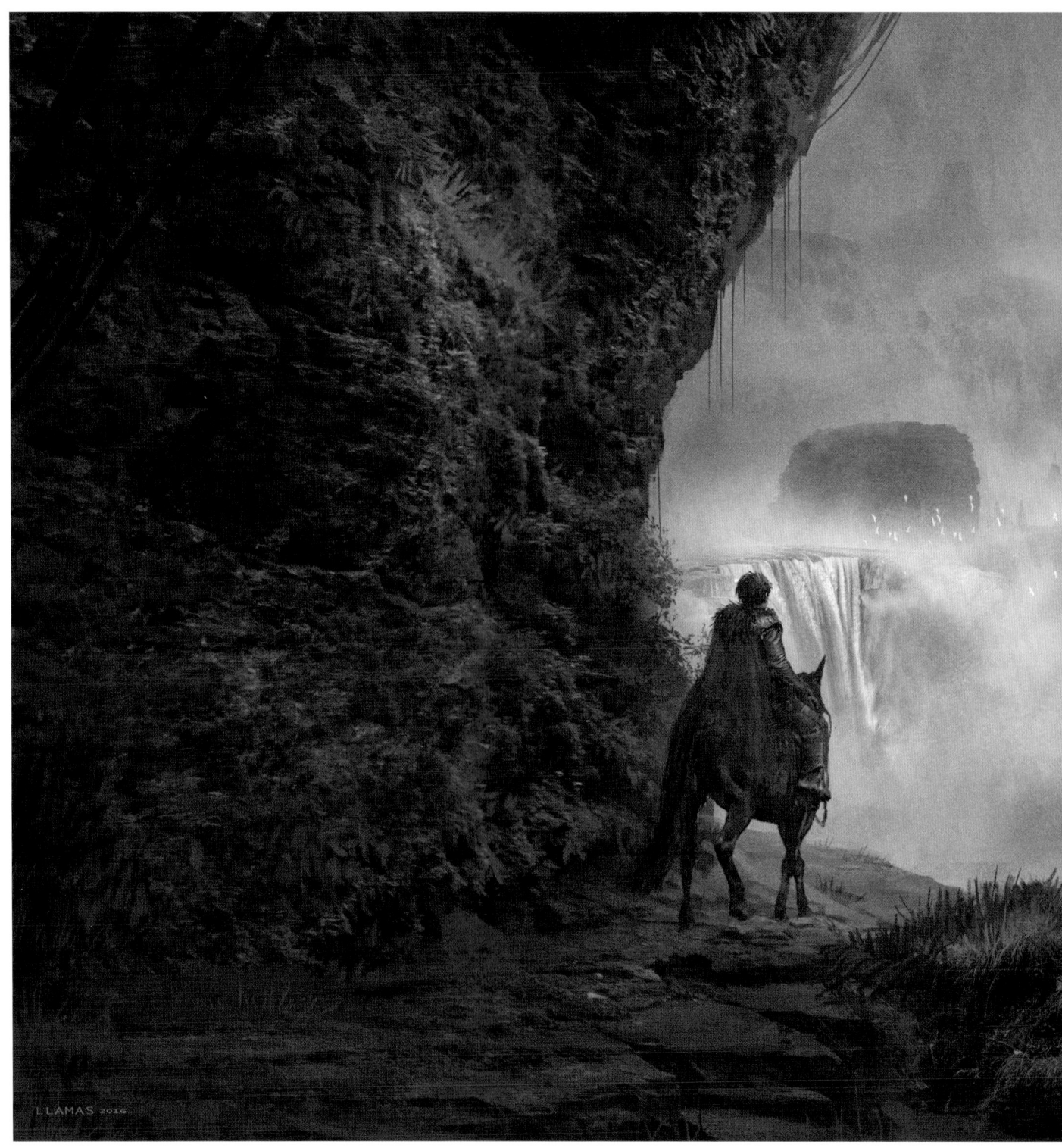

// Finishing touches and atmospheric effects such as the lighting, shadows, and birds make the image more immersive

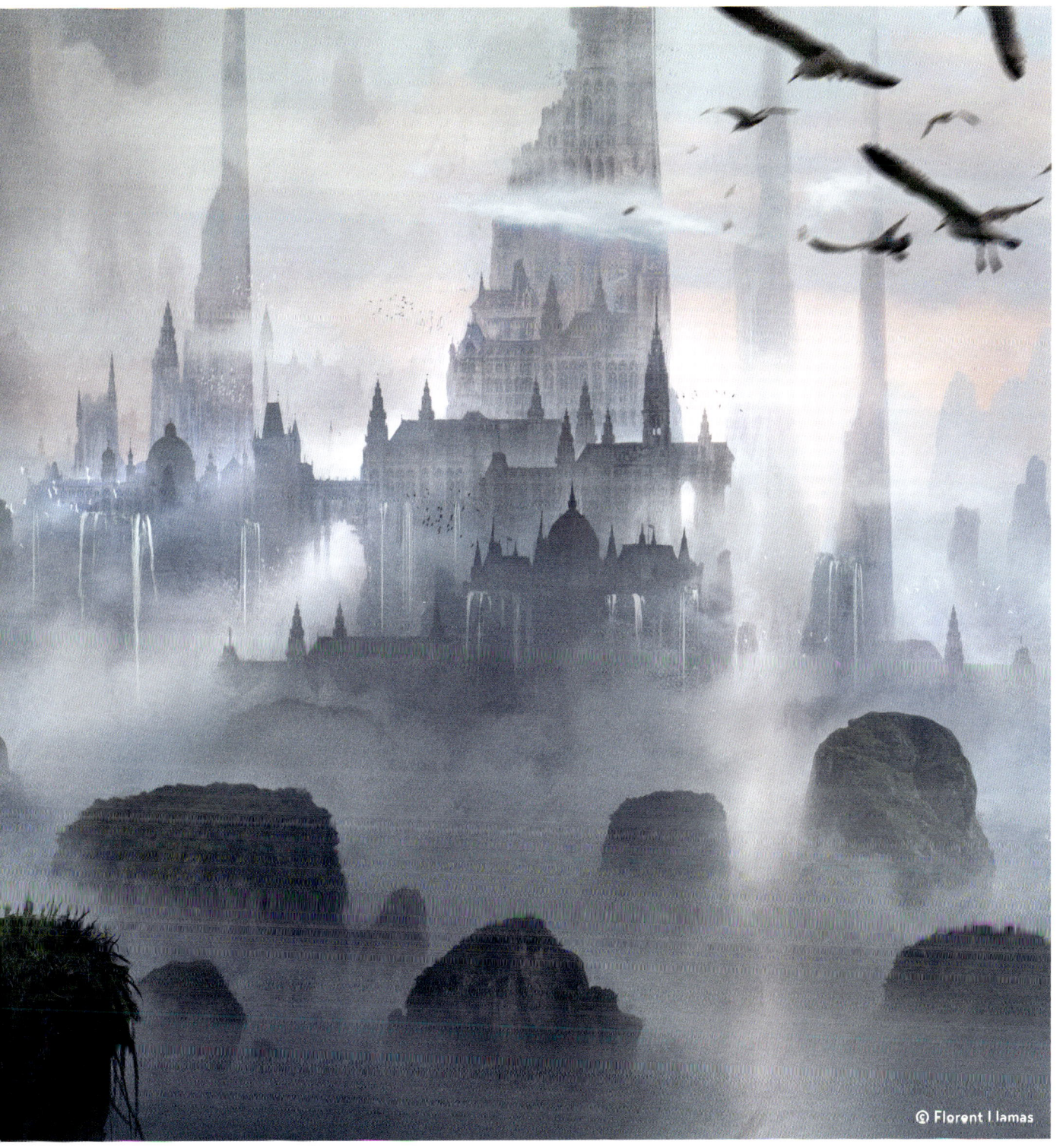

© Florent Llamas

The Birth of a Chef

Jonathan "Jenolab" Hamers | www.artstation.com/artist/jenolab

The idea in *The Birth of a Chef* is to imagine the precise moment in your life when you realize what you are really made for. This is maybe the story of my life: I want to tell stories, and draw them. In this scene, we have a robot carrying out his job with his co-workers. Then a moment of realization occurs – you don't know how or why, but it does. I have chosen robots and blue tones to illustrate the artificial routine of one's life. I used a red fruit and hot light to make a classic cold/warm contrast. I realize now that there are two ways to read this image. Some may think that the apple and light symbolize knowledge or spiritual meaning; others would consider that in cooking, a simple raw fruit is authentic and feels "good," in contrast with its surroundings. I always try to make narrative choices regarding my colors and designs.

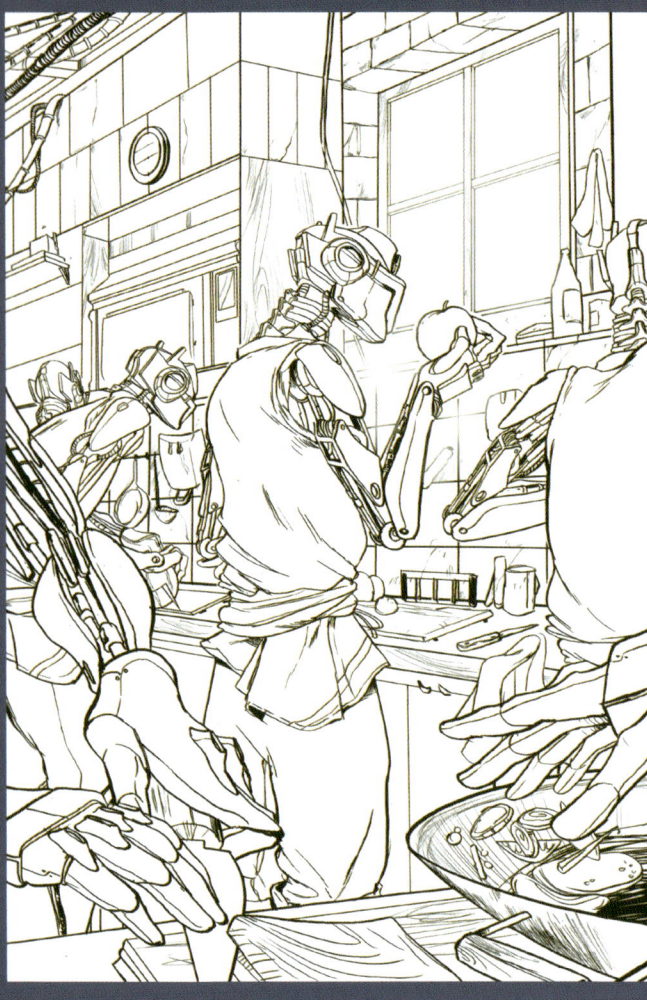

// The line work: the frame, composition, and story are defined. I used thin lines to make a natural, subtle base drawing

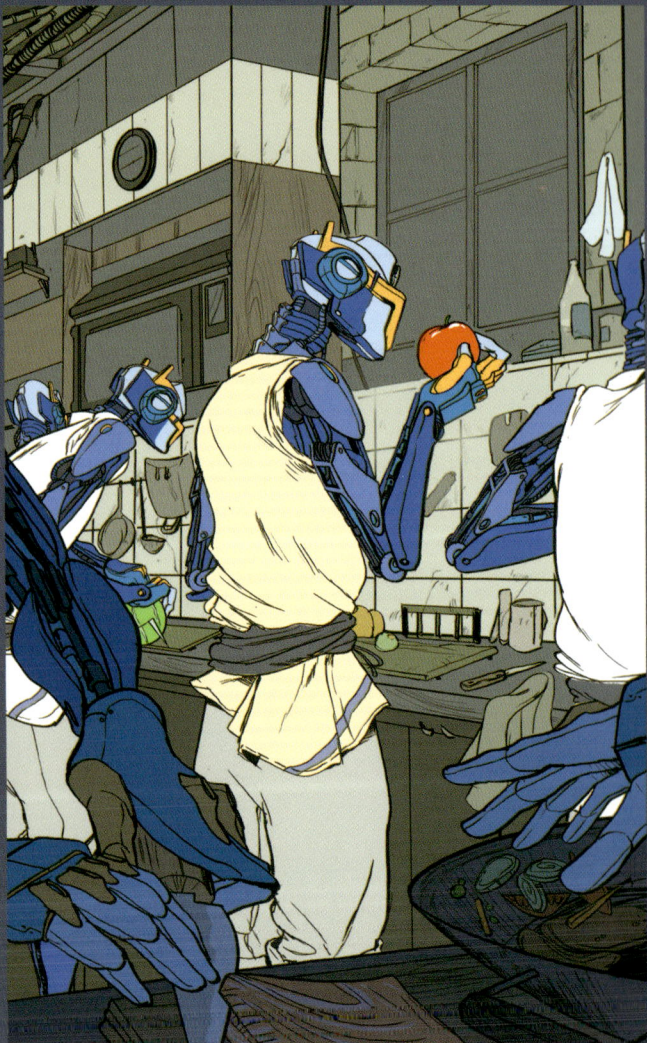

// The flat color: I painted each element individually so that if I needed to change their values it would be easier

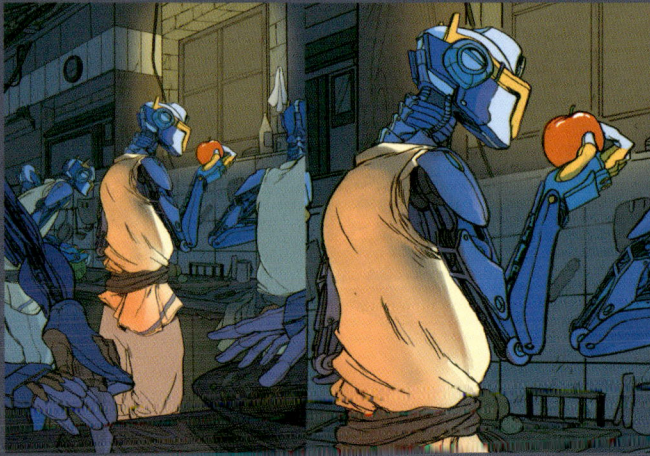

// Shadow and values: the picture is very close to being finished. I add layers and adjust the values in order to create the main atmosphere

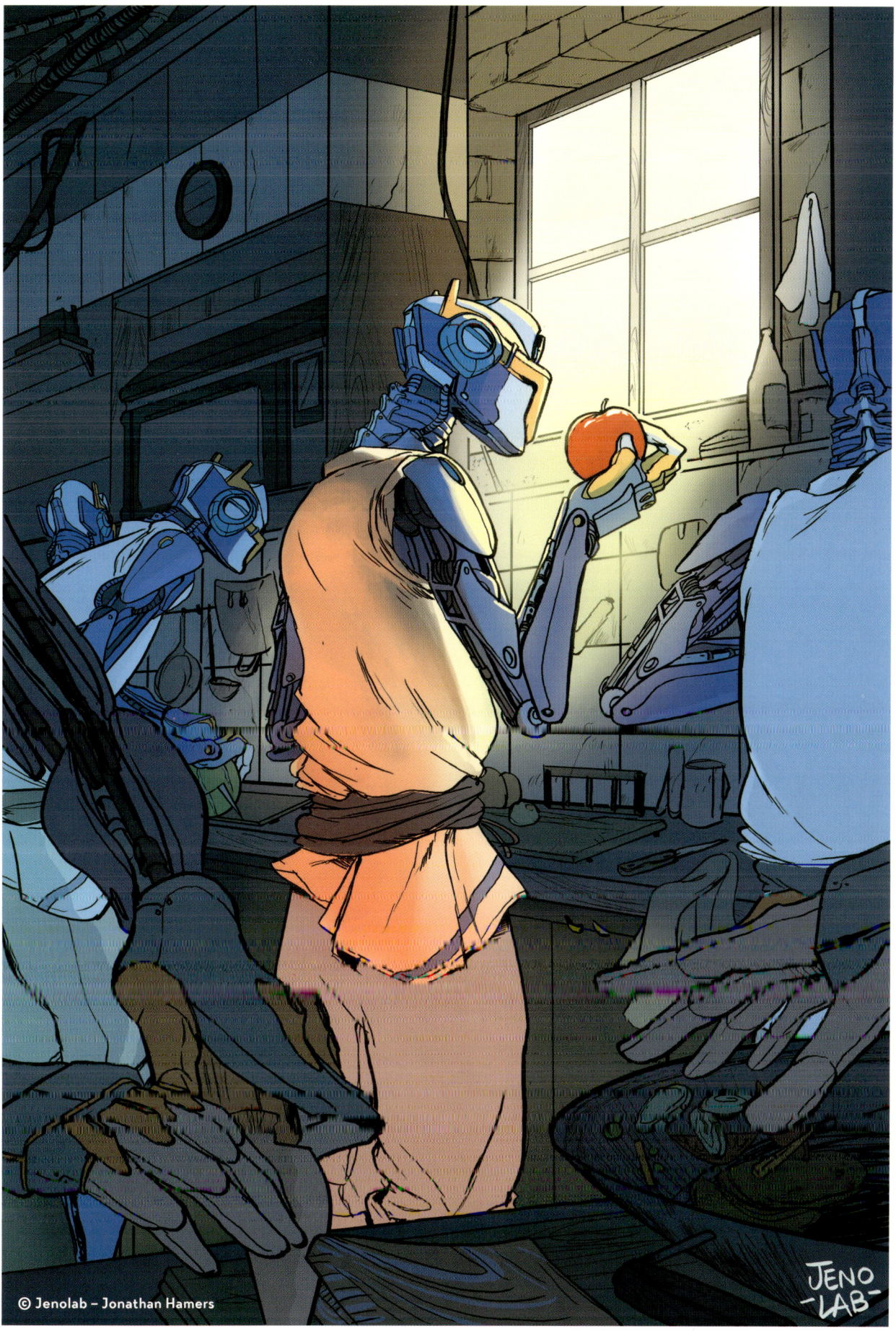

// Lights: I add lights to highlight the prominent elements of the picture. Now the image has meaning

Kaguul

Alex Brock | www.alexbrockart.com

This was for a school project where we had to design our own characters with a story surrounding them. Kaguul is an exiled demon banished to the mortal plane and forced to face the shortcomings and consequences of his new standing. He is just emerging from the doorway to Hell and setting out with an ego, ready to be shown humility. In this plane of existence he is much weaker and gaunt, having been stripped of his status, horns, wings, and most of his powers. He is about to learn that he might actually need some help. In order to return to his former glory, he will need to overcome a cabal of his old masters in a metal ballad/RPG-style epic. I was mostly inspired by a piece by Yu Dehong which had a lot of matte surfaces that looked awesome to my eye, and I wanted to try replicating some of those effects.

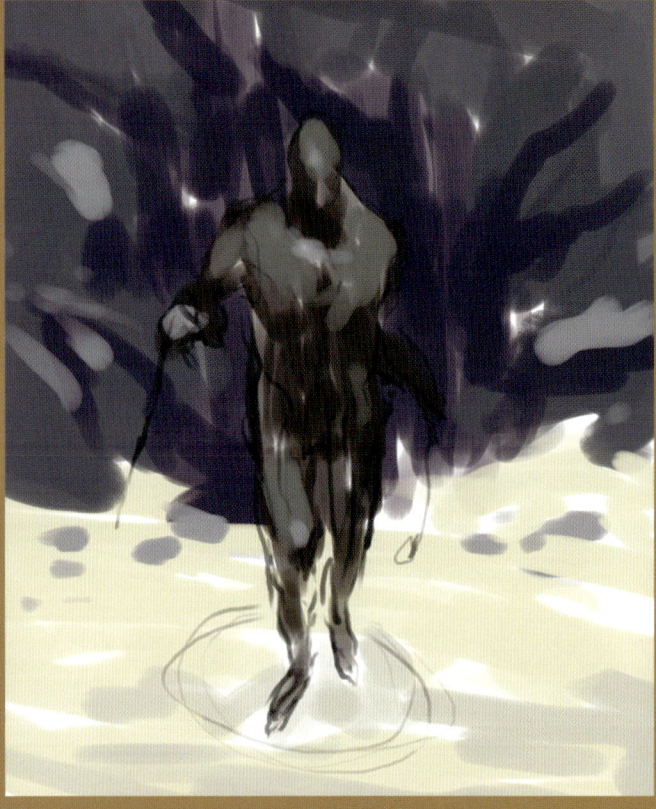

// I started with a rough gesture and composition, mainly focusing on color and value

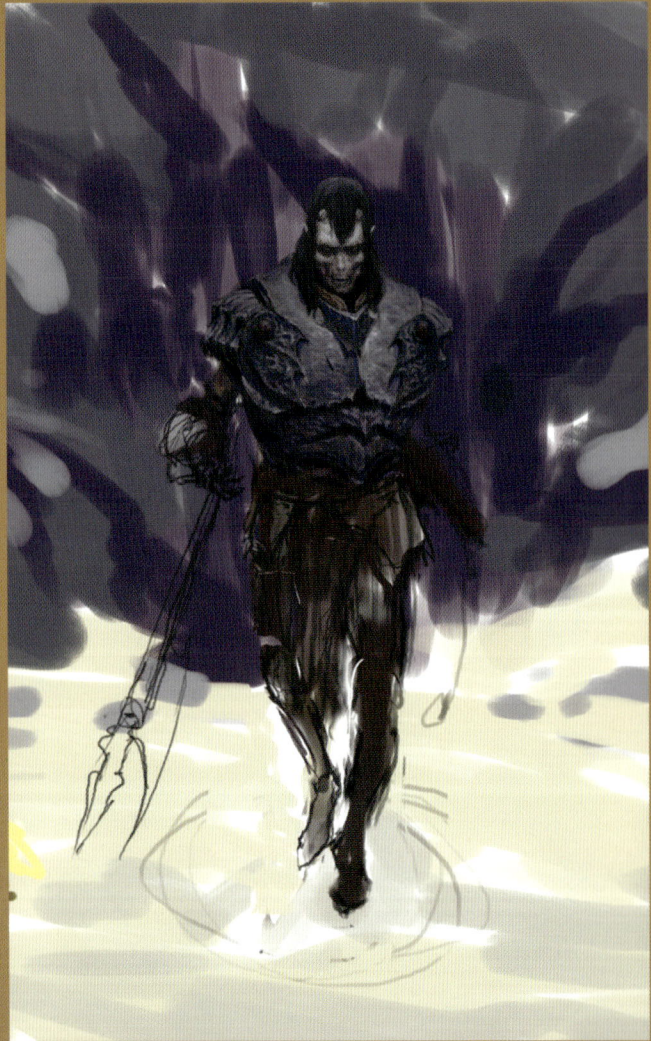

// I made a full pass of lines to flesh out the character details and began rendering from top to bottom, focusing on one part at a time

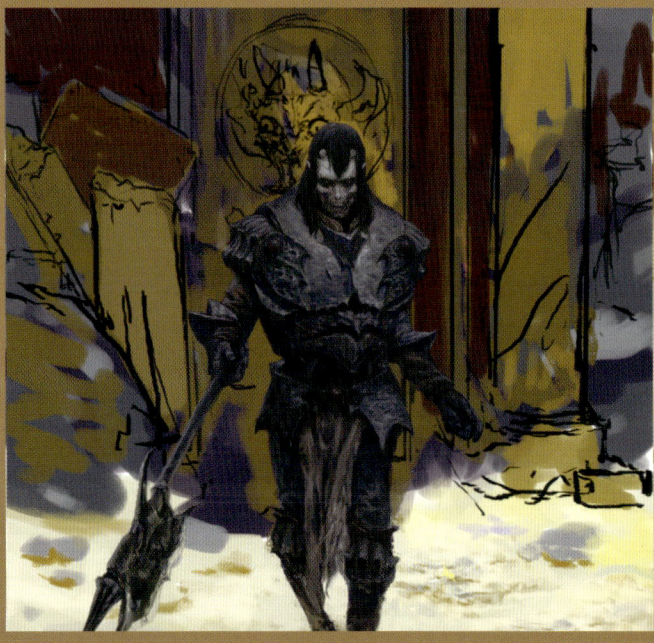

// After completing the character, I set up a new background with lines and the general color and value of the objects

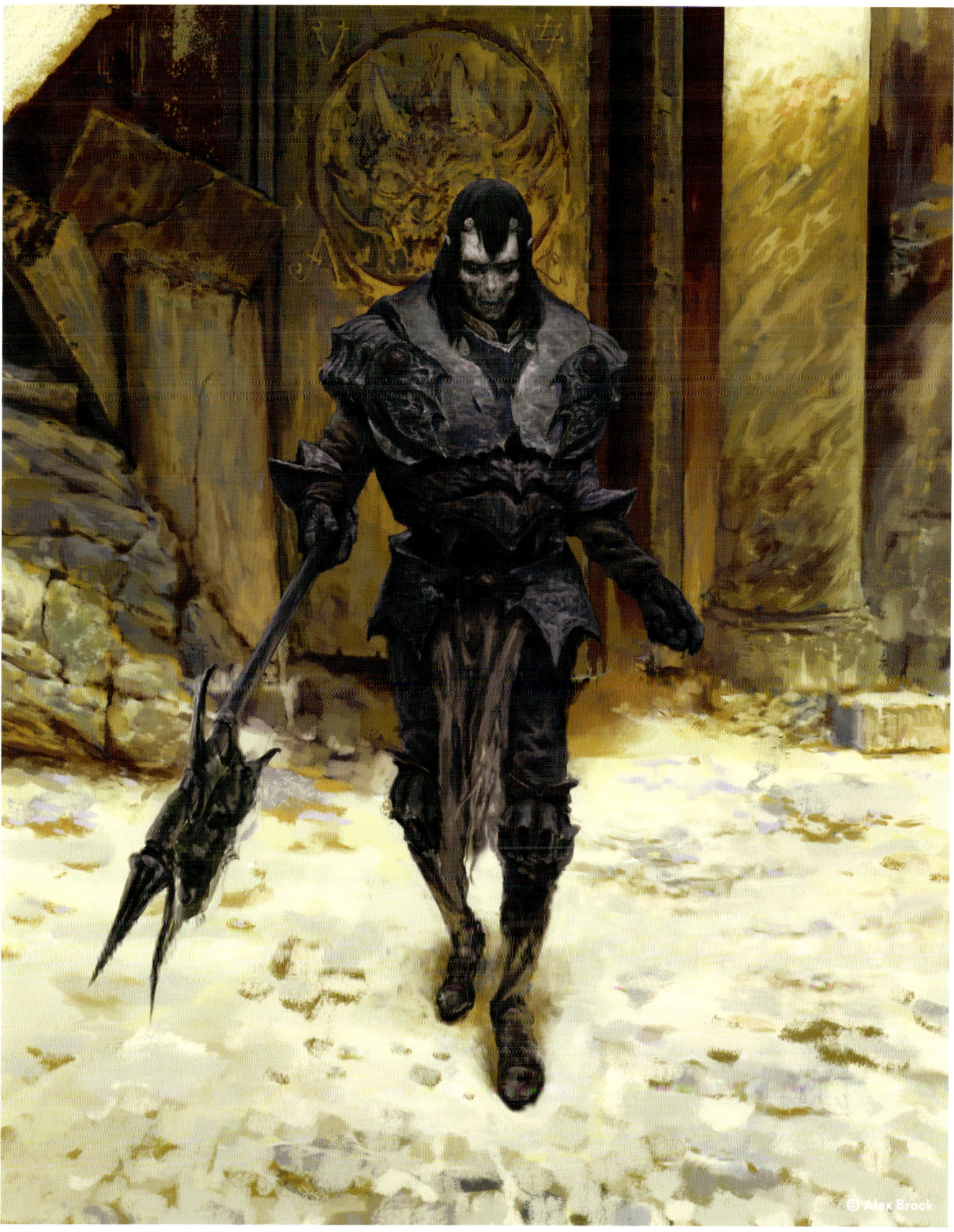

Here I tried to predict ambient bounce lighting in shadow. The background was heavily inspired by places like Petra

Out of Sight

Sebastian Gromann | www.sebastiangromann.com ——————————————

> "I love to grab ingredients of things that make me excited and curiously throw them in a mixer. That's the common recipe I use"

Creating personal work is great. It provides you with creative freedom in every decision and offers you the opportunity to experiment or implement newly gained knowledge for the first time.

In *Out of Sight* I wanted to exercise my compositional and environmental storytelling. I had just read a couple books on cinematography (*The Filmmaker's Eye* and the *Master Shots* series), which made me want to focus on the viewer's expectation when looking at a certain scene. I wanted to evoke a feeling of exciting tension, so I decided to only tease the viewer and let their imagination forecast what might be revealed in the subsequent scene.

Most of the time the story in my personal paintings is shaped by what has inspired me recently. I love to grab ingredients of things that make me excited and curiously throw them in a mixer. That's

the common recipe I use to produce a suspenseful and attractive outcome. This time my main ingredients were the visual language of the famous television series *Game of Thrones* and the video game *The Witcher 3: Wild Hunt*.

Combining my general idea and story recipe, I decided to portray a lone wolf character and showcase him in an ominous European forest. He is freezing and tired, the environmental conditions are rough, and he is just about to explore the next important landmark or stumble into a narrative event.

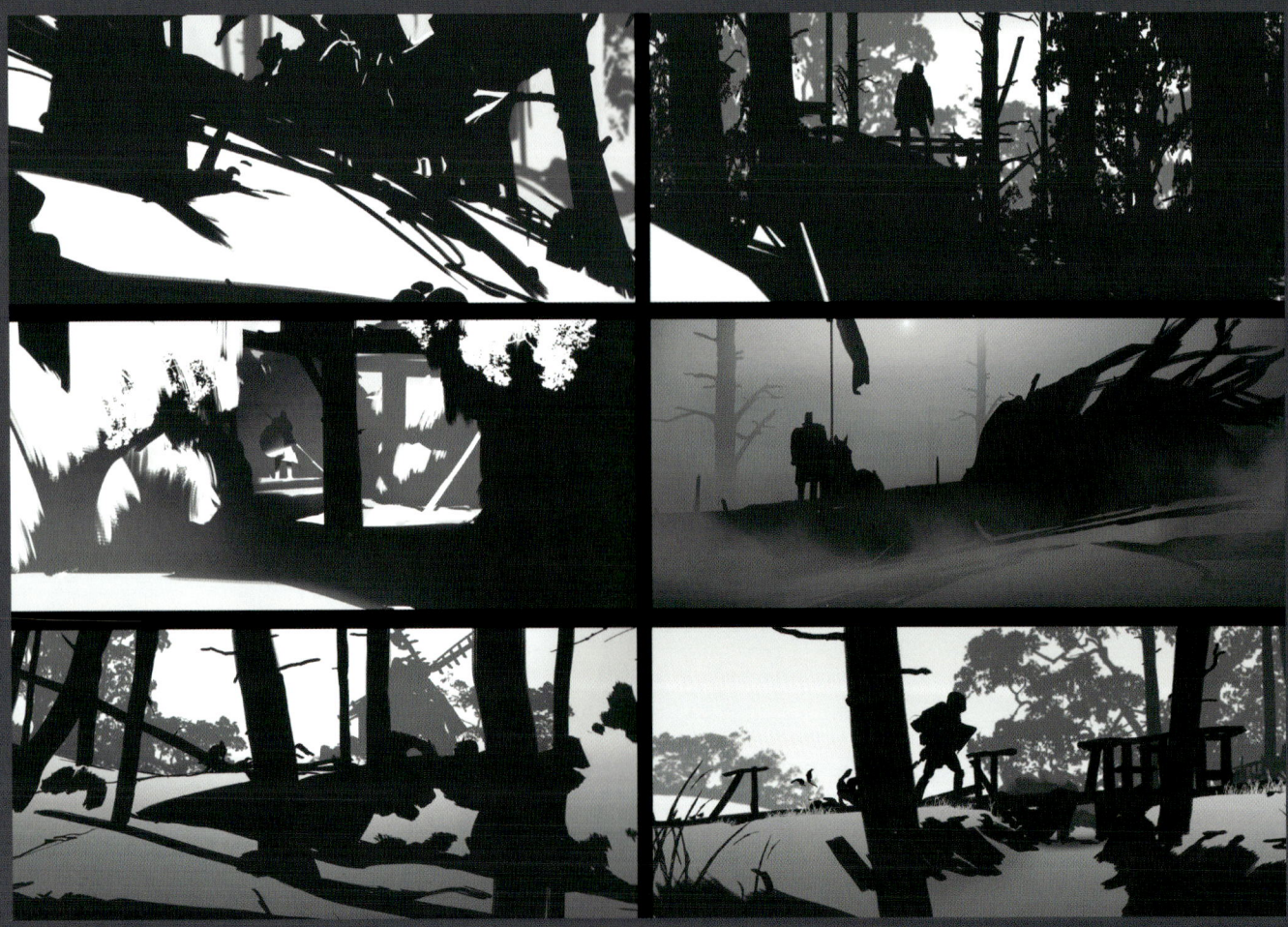

// After collecting numerous reference images (such as for the lighting scenario and vegetation) and knowing my plan of action, I started generating grayscale thumbnails

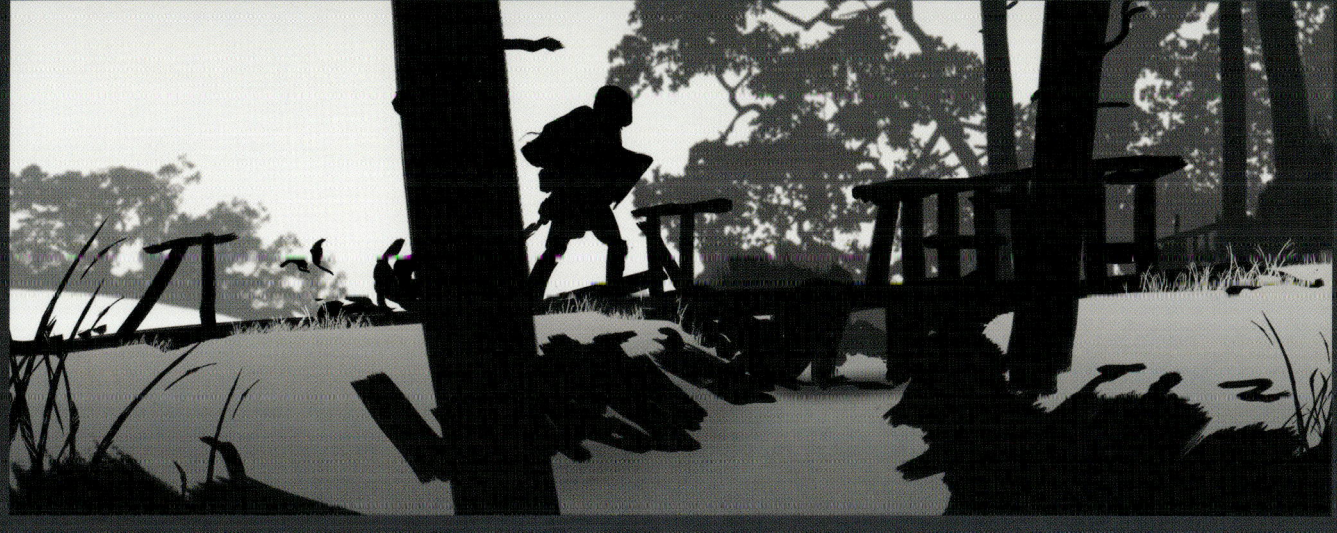

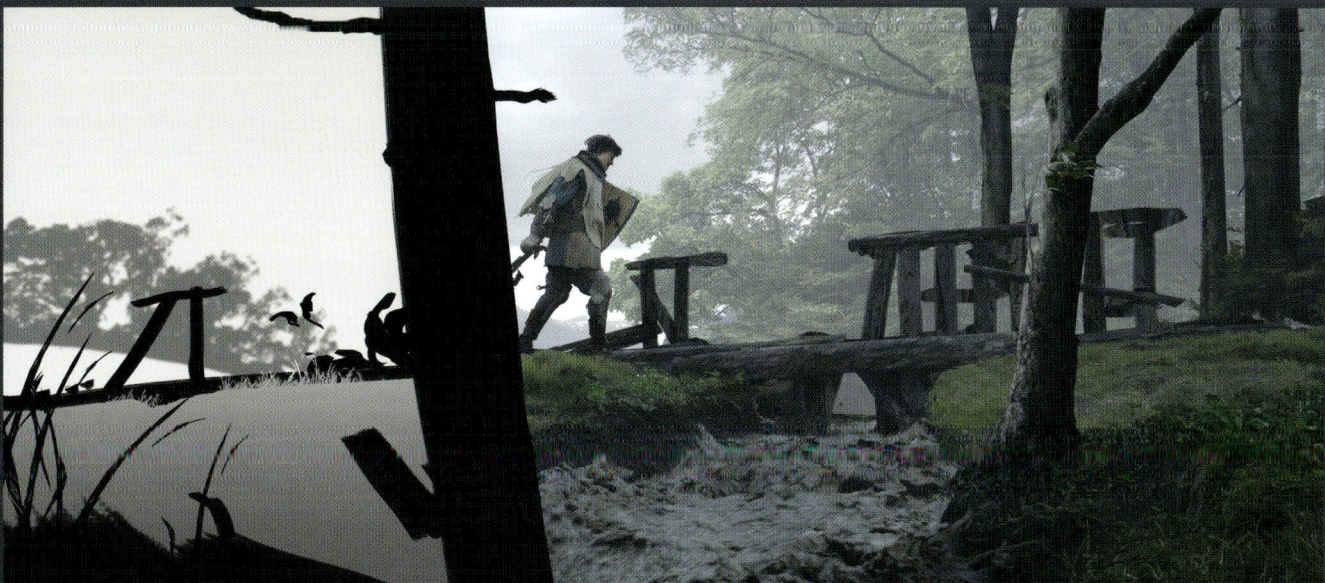

// The sixth thumbnail seemed closest to my original idea. I divided this grayscale image into different sections and started replacing the masses with suitable textures

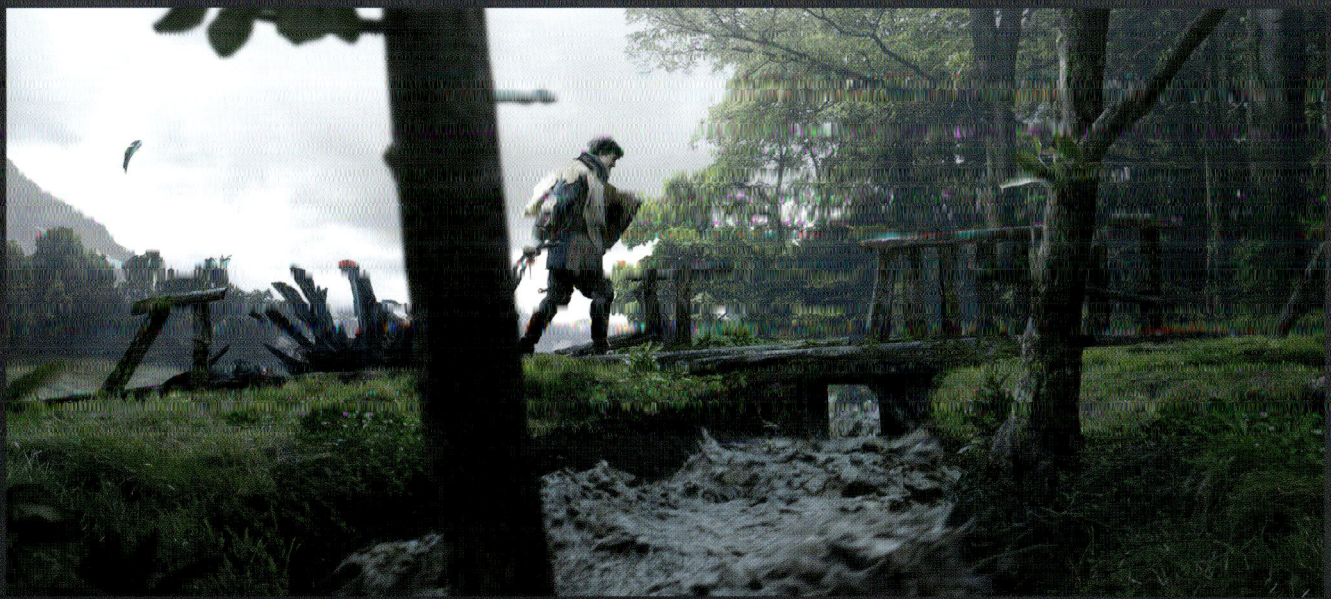

// I usually work my way from background to foreground and make sure the values roughly match my reference and thumbnail

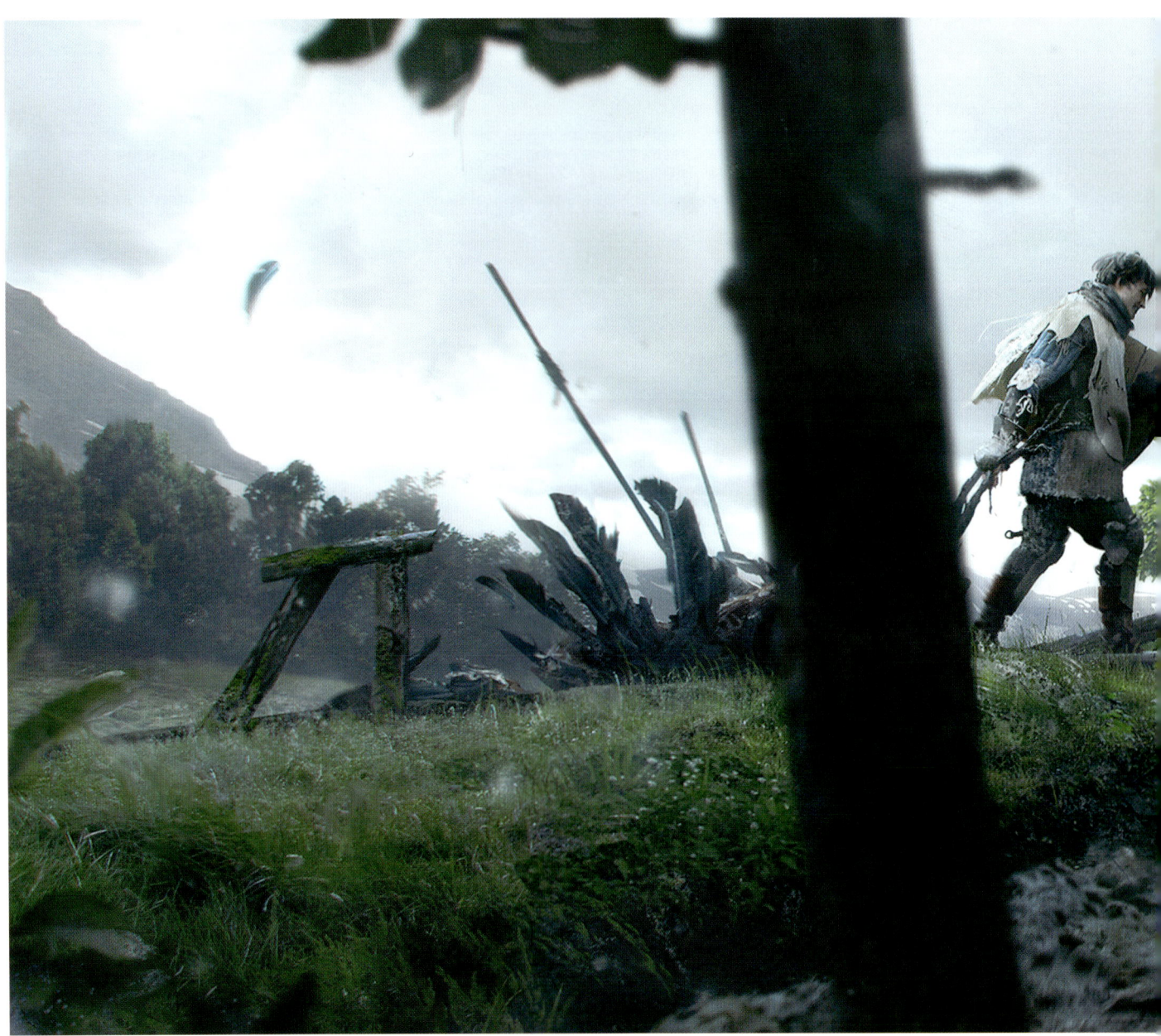

// The last ten percent of an image often takes the longest, but it's worth it. Here I placed little ice particles on top of the grass and on the character's clothing to reinforce the cold and therefore the aggravating time he is experiencing

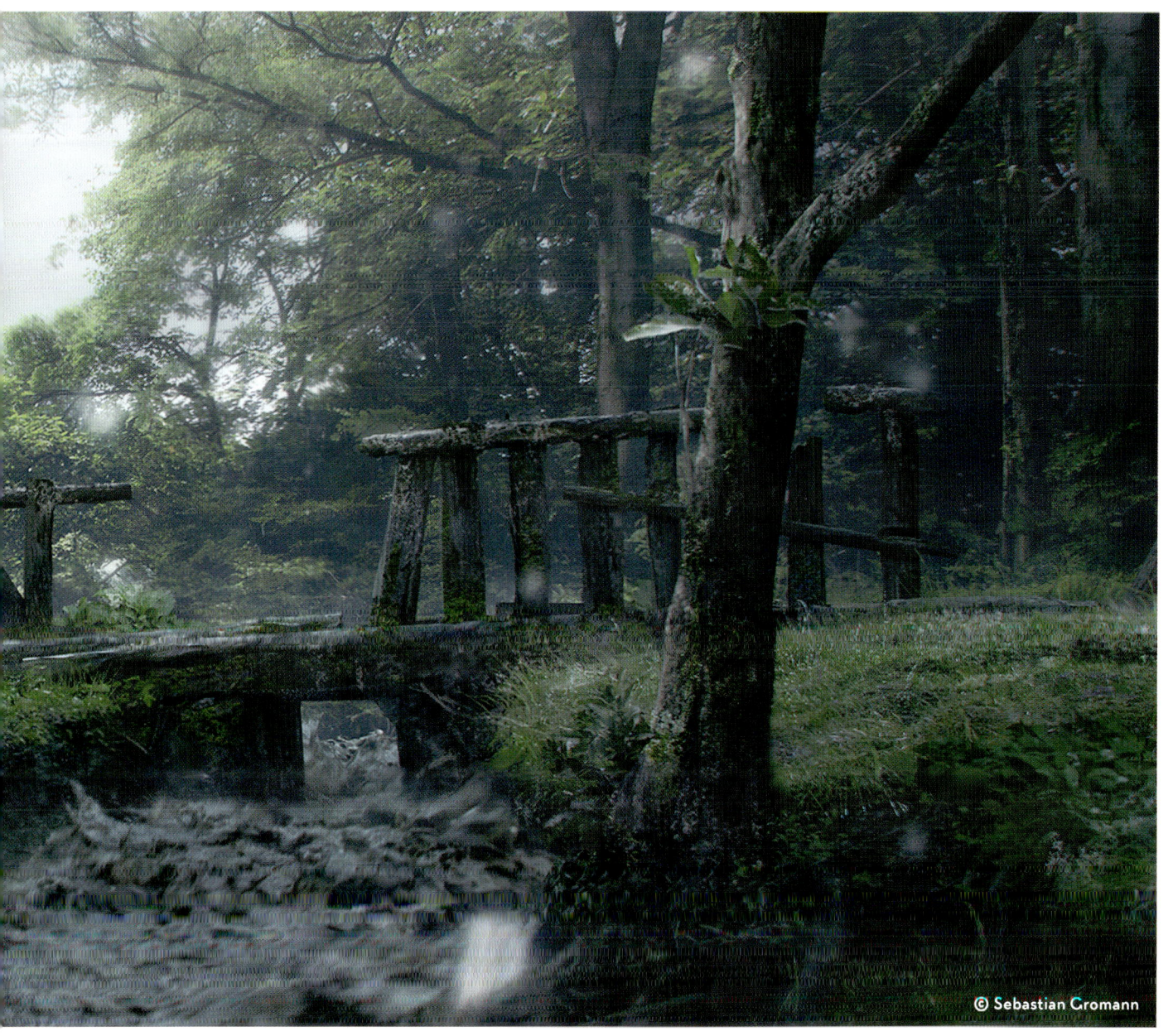

© Sebastian Gromann

Poison Apple

Elisabeth Alba | www.albaillustration.com

This illustration was created for the topic "Weapons: Love is war, choose your weapon" from the Month of Love challenge (**www.monthofloveart.com**). I had a lot of ideas and researched various love stories, including fairy tales. I recalled how Snow White was poisoned, and realized the poisoned apple given to her by the Queen could be considered a weapon of love. The Queen loves herself so much she would kill. Almost everyone knows the story, and many renditions have been created of the characters in it. I illustrate fairy tales often, and to me it's important to put my own spin on them. I used rich colors and gold paint (which look much brighter in the flesh!) to enhance the royal, opulent atmosphere.

I used photographic reference of myself posing to figure out different hand positions and facial expressions. I wanted her to be powerful, beautiful, and a little bit crazy. The design on the wall was inspired by patterning in a Gustav Klimt painting, and the odd pattern on her dress may remind the viewer of sharp bird beaks. I also made the dress fade into flat darkness. I didn't want the mirror behind her to show a magical figure, as I thought that would be too distracting, so instead I created a swirling void.

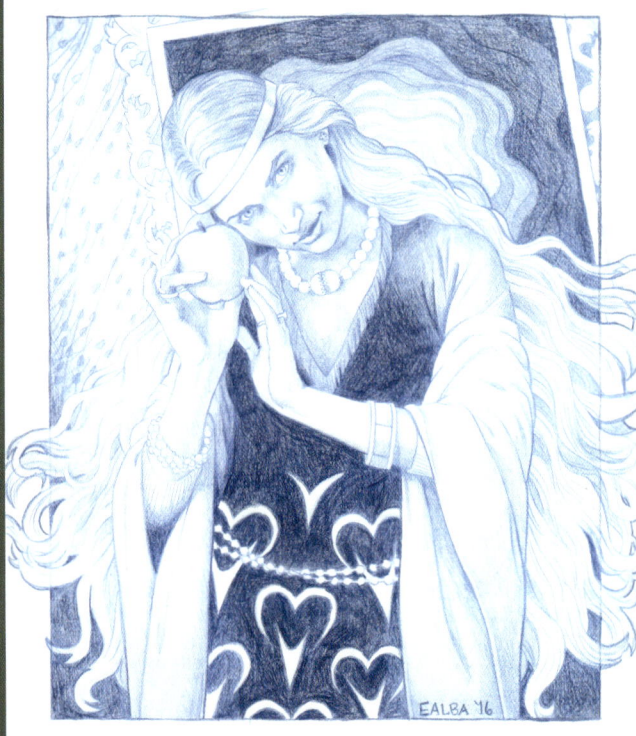

// I wanted a nice drawing to have along with the painting. I created it with blue lead, with which I enjoy sketching and drawing

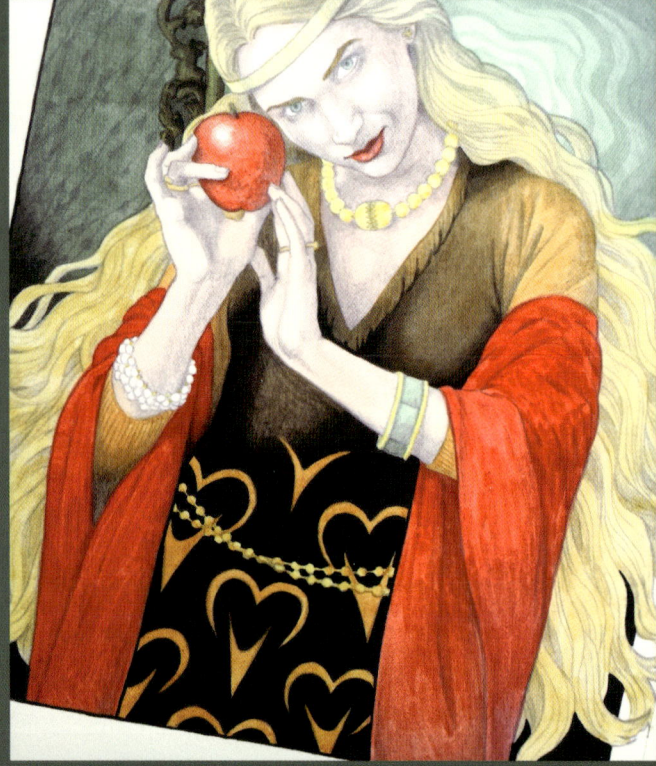

// I scanned the drawing and made a nearly-finished digital version before painting traditionally, in order to figure out all the colors in advance

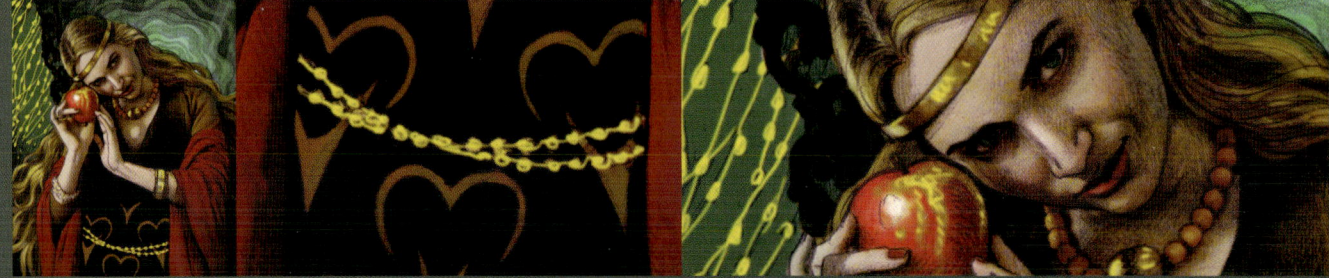

// Painting the base layer of color on top of my drawing printed on watercolor paper

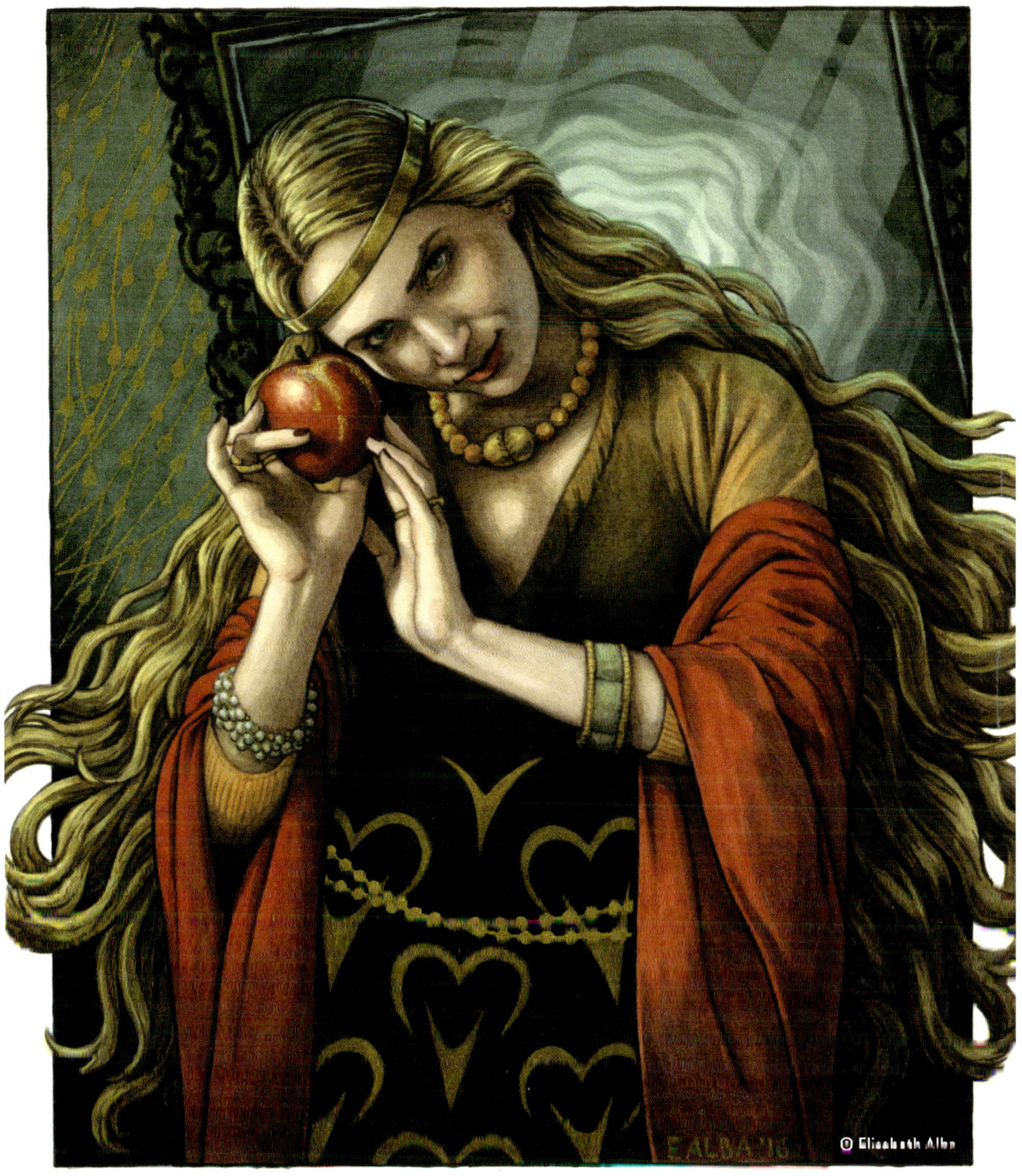

// Final painting. I used Dr. Ph. Martin's Black Star matte ink, Dr. Ph. Martin's Hydrus watercolors, Finetec gold watercolor, and Krylon Kamar spray varnish

Meet the Artists

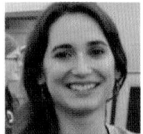

Elisabeth Alba
Freelance illustrator of fantasy, New Age, and children's publications
www.albaillustration.com

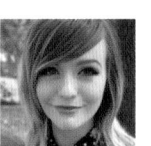

Julia Blattman
Illustrator and concept artist intern at Disney Interactive
www.juliablattman.com

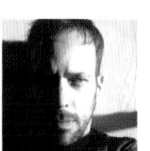

Alex Brock
Digital artist and illustrator with a special interest in dark fantasy art
www.alexbrockart.com

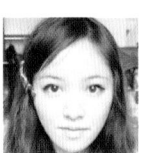

Emi Chen
Illustrator and concept artist intern at Blizzard Entertainment
www.emichenart.com

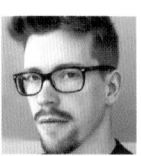

Brun Croes
Freelance illustrator, concept artist, and visual development artist
www.bruncroes.com

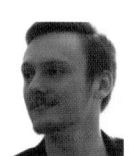

Sebastian Gromann
Concept designer working in video games and film
www.sebastiangromann.com

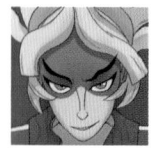

Jonathan "Jenolab" Hamers
Freelance illustrator and comic writer, inspired by the eighties, sci-fi, and fantasy
www.artstation.com/artist/jenolab

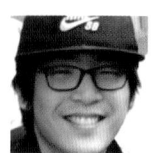

Kevin Hong
Freelance illustrator and graduate from the School of Visual Arts
www.kevinhong.com

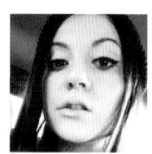

Eliza Ivanova
Animator at Pixar Animation Studios, born and raised in Sofia, Bulgaria
www.elizaivanova.com

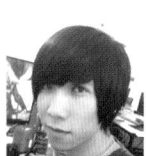

Lee Kent
Freelance concept artist and illustrator as well as a lecturer at Kart-Studio
www.leekent.deviantart.com

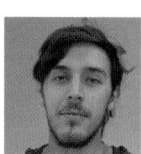

Sebastian Kowoll
Freelance concept artist working full time for the entertainment industry
www.skalienart.com

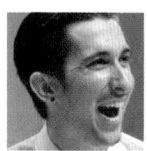

Florent Llamas
Freelance concept artist and illustrator based in France
www.artstation.com/artist/llamas

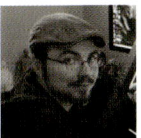

Damien Mammoliti
Ilustrator and concept artist for clients
including SEGA Europe and CD Projekt RED
www.boneandbrush.com

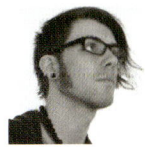

Zac Retz
Illustrator and visual development
artist at Reel FX
www.zacretz.blogspot.com

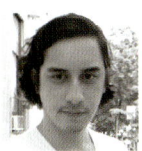

Zachary Montoya
Illustrator for video games,
comics, editorials, and books
www.zachmontoya.com

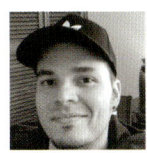

Juan Pablo Roldan
Freelance concept artist with a
passion for visual development
www.artstation.com/artist/roldan

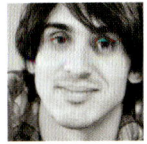

Kamil Murzyn
Illustrator living in Warsaw, Poland, who
enjoys making fantasy art and comics
www.kamilmurzynarts.pl

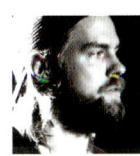

Ørjan Ruttenborg Svendsen
Freelance concept artist who enjoys fantasy
art, games, music, snowboarding, and cats
www.svendsenart.com

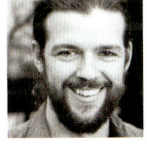

Scott Murphy
Artist for games and publishing,
interested in sci-fi and fantasy genres
www.murphyillustration.com

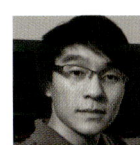

Ky Tran
Fantasy artist with a focus on creating worlds
and engaging stories through illustration
www.kytranart.com

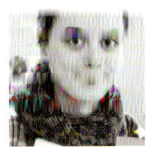

Maria Poliakova
Digital artist from Kiev, Ukraine, who
loves to explore color in her images
www.artstation.com/artist/tubikraski

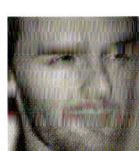

Andy Walsh
Freelance concept artist and illustrator with
an interest in atmospheric environments
www.stayinwonderland.com

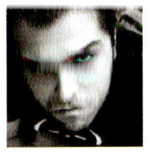

Ahmed Rawi
Concept artist and illustrator
for films and games
www.artstation.com/artist/rawi

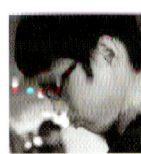

Tan Zhi Hui
Concept artist and illustrator currently
working at Passion Republic
www.artstation.com/artist/kudaman

Index

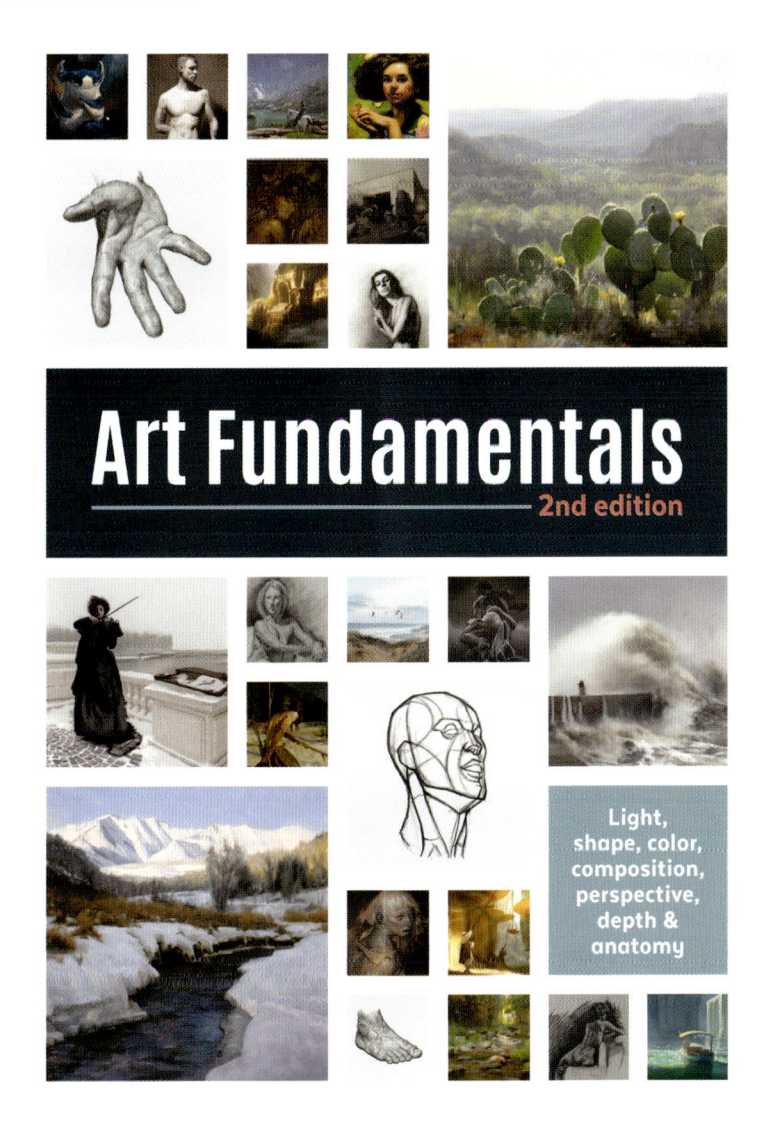

3dtotalPublishing

3dtotal Publishing is a trailblazing, creative publisher specializing in inspirational and educational resources for artists.

Our titles feature top industry professionals from around the globe who share their experience in skillfully written step-by-step tutorials and fascinating, detailed guides. Illustrated throughout with stunning artwork, these best-selling publications offer creative insight, expert advice, and essential motivation. Fans of digital art will enjoy our comprehensive volumes covering Adobe Photoshop, Procreate, and Blender, as well as our superb titles based around character design, including *Fundamentals of Character Design* and *Creating Characters for the Entertainment Industry*. The dedicated, high-quality blend of instruction and inspiration also extends to traditional art. Titles covering a range of techniques, genres, and abilities allow your creativity to flourish while building essential skills.

Well-established within the industry, we now offer over 100 titles and counting, many of which have been translated into multiple languages around the world. With something for every artist, we are proud to say that our books offer the 3dtotal package:

LEARN · CREATE · SHARE

Visit us at store.3dtotal.com

3dtotal Publishing is part of 3dtotal.com, a leading website for CG artists founded by Tom Greenway in 1999.